YEAR	L.C.S.	GR.

YEAR	L.C.S.	GR.

YEAR	L.C.S.	GR.

Parenting

Rewards & Responsibilities

First Canadian Edition

Canadian Authors

Jane Witte
Independent,
Educational Consultant
Innerkip, Ontario

Nancy J. FitzPatrick
Program Facilitator
Durham District
School Board
Whitby, Ontario

Glencoe Author

Verna Hildebrand, Ph.D.
Former Professor of Family
and Child Ecology
Michigan State University

McGraw-Hill Ryerson

Toronto   Montréal   Boston   Burr Ridge, IL   Dubuque, IA   Madison, WI   New York   San Francisco
St. Louis   Bangkok   Bogotá   Caracas   Kuala Lumpur   Lisbon   London   Madrid   Mexico City
Milan   New Delhi   Santiago   Seoul   Singapore   Sydney   Taipei

McGraw-Hill Ryerson

***Parenting
Rewards & Responsibilities
First Canadian Edition***

ISBN: 0-07-095066-0

http://www.mcgrawhill.ca

1 2 3 4 5 6 7 8 9 10   TCP   0 9 8 7 6 5

Printed and bound in Canada

National Library of Canada Cataloguing in Publication

Witte, Jane
      Parenting : rewards and responsibilities / Jane Witte, Nancy FitzPatrick. –
1st Canadian ed.

Includes index.
ISBN 0-07-095066-0

      1. Parenting. 2. Parent and child. J. FitzPatrick, Nancy, 1960– II. Title.

HQ755.8.W57 2004   306.874   C2004-902748-4

PUBLISHER: Patty Pappas
SPONSORING EDITOR: Debbie Davidson
MANAGER, EDITORIAL SERVICES: Linda Allison
PROJECT MANAGER: Jocelyn Wilson
DEVELOPMENT TEAM: Peter Traskey/Words & Numbers
SUPERVISING EDITOR: Anne Nellis
EDITORIAL ASSISTANT: Erin Hartley
MANAGER, PRODUCTION SERVICES: Yolanda Pigden
PRODUCTION CO-ORDINATOR: Mary Pepe
ELECTRONIC PAGE-MAKEUP: Cindy Deckert/Monotype

Acknowledgments

Canadian Consultants

Student Success
David Chambers
School-to-Work/Successful
    Pathways Co-ordinator
The Durham Catholic District
    School Board

Literacy
Cathy Costello
Curriculum Co-ordinator,
    Literacy
York Region District School
    Board

Family Studies
Annabelle Dryden, Ph.D.
Associate Professor, Family
    Studies Education
The University of Western
    Ontario

Equity
Donna Guerra
Instructional Leader, Equity
Toronto District School Board

Character Education
Marc Keirstead
Secondary Consultant
York Region Catholic District
    School Board

Child Care
Maggie Lance
Community Mental Health
    Counsellor
Child and Youth Wellness Centre

Career Education
Judi Misener
Principal, Sir William Osler High
    School
Toronto District School Board

Assessment and Evaluation
Garfield Newman
Curriculum Consultant
York Region District School
    Board

Literacy
Tamar Stein
Curriculum Consultant for
    Adolescent Literacy
York Region District School
    Board

Canadian Reviewers

Patricia Andres
Family Studies Department Head
Niagara District School Board

Terry Brennan
Social Studies/Family Studies
    Subject Council Chair
Catholic District School Board
    of Eastern Ontario

Patricia Cibinel
Chair of Social Sciences
Lakehead Public Schools

Susan M. Davies
Curriculum Co-ordinator for the
    Arts and Social Sciences
Hastings and Prince Edward
    District School Board

Janet Dickson
Head of Family Studies
York Region District School
    Board

Shawn Dodge
Family Studies Teacher
Lambton-Kent District School
    Board

Deborrah Estabrooks
Family Studies Teacher
Algonquin and Lakeshore
    Catholic District School Board

Wendy Fresque
Family Studies Teacher
Algoma District School Board

Nicole Gagnon
Family Studies Teacher
Greater Essex Catholic District
    School Board

Urmil Gupta
Family Studies Teacher
Toronto District School Board

Irene Grobin
Family Studies Teacher
Toronto Catholic District School
    Board

Muriel Jackson
Teacher
Toronto District School Board

Rupa Jolly
Teacher
Ottawa-Carleton District School
    Board

Christine Langlois
Family Editor
Canadian Living Magazine

M. Ruth Marshall
Family Studies Teacher
Toronto District School Board

Carol Ann McCaig
Teacher
Grand Erie District School
    Board

Ann McClure
Curriculum Consultant
Simcoe County District School
    Board

Randy Niedzwiecki
Teacher
Toronto District School Board

Lynda Parmiter
Teacher
Banting Memorial High School

Gail Robertson-Whitworth
Assistant Curriculum Leader
    of Social Sciences and
    Humanities
Toronto District School Board

Laurie Spittles
Family Studies Teacher
Peel District School Board

Linda Triantafillou
Consultant, K–12, Religion and
    Family Life
Halton Catholic District School
    Board

Glencoe Teacher Reviewers

Pamela M. Baggett, CFCS
Family and Consumer Sciences,
  Lead Teacher
Middleburg High School, Clay
  County Schools
Middleburg, Florida

**Rebecca Davis Bridges, M.S.,
CFCS**
Parenting Program
  Coordinator/Teacher
Scottsboro City Schools
Scottsboro, Alabama

Becky Burgue, M.Ed.
Family and Consumer Sciences
  Instructor
Gaither High School
Tampa, Florida

Jeanne A. Charlesworth, M.Ed.
Family and Consumer Sciences
  Teacher
Hatboro-Horsham High School
Horsham, Pennsylvania

Phil Goerner
Consumer and Family Studies
  Teacher
Skyline High School, St. Vrain
  Valley Schools
Longmont, Colorado

Jeri A. Gooding, M.A.E.
Former Family and Consumer
  Sciences Teacher
New Castle, Indiana

Joyce Hancock
Early Childhood Teacher
Dripping Springs High School
Dripping Springs, Texas

Marjorie S. Patton, M.S.
Family and Consumer Sciences
  Department Chair
Ben Davis High School, MSD
  Wayne Township
Indianapolis, Indiana

**Cynthia Rossi Sovich, M.Ed.,
CFCS**
Family and Consumer Sciences
  Teacher
Wake County Public Schools
Raleigh, North Carolina

**Azzie Brokenberry Williams,
M.A.**
Former Family and Consumer
  Sciences Teacher
Grand Cane, Louisiana

Glencoe Technical Reviewers

Karen B. DeBord, Ph.D.
Associate Professor, Child
  Development Specialist
North Carolina Cooperative
  Extension Service
North Carolina State University
Raleigh, North Carolina

Anne Hansen, Ph.D.
Former Head Start Director
Educational Consultant
Walla Walla, Washington

**Frances R. Murphy-Widmer,
R.N.**
OB-GYN Associates of Neenah
Neenah, Wisconsin

Sanit S. Shay, M.D., F.A.C.O.G.
Clinical Assistant Professor
University of Illinois School of
  Medicine
Peoria, Illinois

Contents

Unit 1: Preparation for Parenthood

Unit 2: Pregnancy and Birth

Unit 3: Infant Care

Unit 4: Child Development

Unit 5: Challenges for Families

Unit 6: Topics in Parenting

Special Text Features

Building Parenting Skills

Raising Children With Character

CAREER PROFILES

Spotlight On

Cross-Curricular CONNECTIONS

Parenting Q & A

Health & Safety

Highlighted Topics

CHARTS & DIAGRAMS

UNIT 1

Preparation for Parenthood

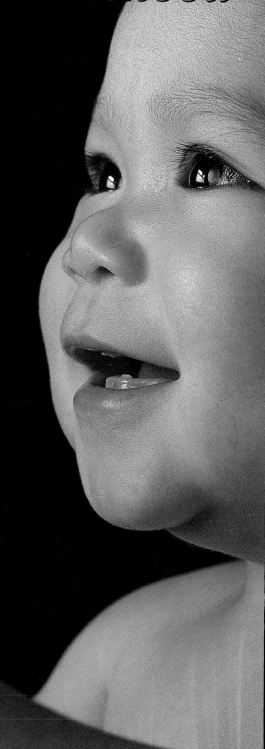

A Parent's Perspective

from Alexander

"When my father first saw my new son, he just stared at him for a while.

I wondered why he didn't say anything. 'What do you think, Dad?' Finally Dad said, 'He looks just like you did when you were born. It's like suddenly going back all those years.' He paused and went quiet for a while. 'What are you thinking, Dad?' He rubbed his chin and said, 'Well, I was just thinking of all the things I thought about when you were this new. My mind was full of all the wonderful things we'd do together, what a wonderful man you'd turn out to be.' He chuckled. 'You've turned out to be a fine young man, all right. Sometimes I wish we'd done more together, that I'd given you a bit more time....' I smiled and put my hand on his shoulder. 'You don't have to worry about that. I learned more from you just by seeing how you coped with things. I hope I do as well for Tommy here. But you know what?' Dad looked at me. 'It's great to know you felt the same things about me that I feel about Tommy.'"

Unit Expectations

While reading this unit, you will:

❖ Demonstrate an understanding of the need for preparation to become a parent.

❖ Demonstrate an understanding of the responsibility parents have for ensuring quality communication in their family.

❖ Describe the nature of and the responsibilities involved in parenting.

❖ Identify social and cultural variations in family forms and parenting approaches.

❖ Identify and evaluate various child-rearing practices and beliefs, and parenting techniques.

❖ Use appropriate social science research methods in the investigation of a wide range of issues that concern parents of young children.

CHAPTER 1

Parenting: A Lifelong Commitment

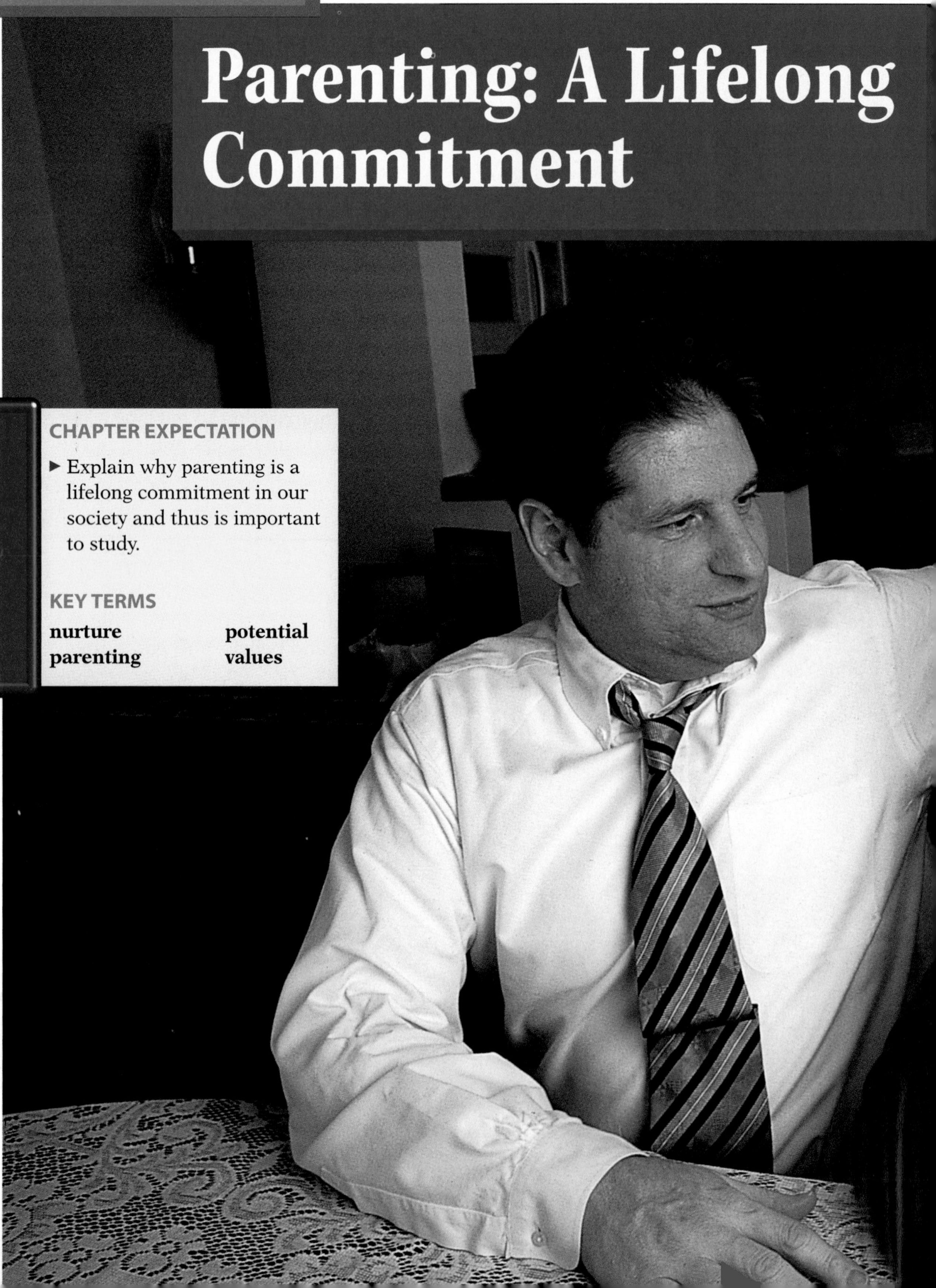

CHAPTER EXPECTATION

- Explain why parenting is a lifelong commitment in our society and thus is important to study.

KEY TERMS

nurture
parenting
potential
values

Mr. Klein repeated his son's question. "If I had it to do over again, would I have children? Why do you ask?"

Ryan explained, "In the parenting course I'm taking, we were talking about some of the big problems families face today, like drugs and violence. Some of us wondered why people even have children when so much can go wrong."

His father chuckled. "What's the alternative?" he asked. "Someone once said: 'A child is the belief that the world should go on.' I think people have children because they have hope. They believe they can be good parents and avoid the worst problems. They believe their children will make the world a better place."

Ryan looked doubtful. "Do *you* believe that?"

"I do," Mr. Klein said emphatically. "The fact that you're taking a course on parenting proves my point. You know that parenting is a serious job, and you want to do it well if you have children of your own someday. You're concerned about the future for all children. I'd call that a step toward making a better world, wouldn't you?"

"Yes, I guess I would," Ryan responded.

Mr. Klein smiled and placed his hand on Ryan's shoulder. "And getting back to your question, yes, I would have children again–and you're one of the reasons why."

◆

What do you think? What does "a child is the belief that the world should go on" mean to you?

In the past, families often had older family members nearby to help in raising children. Today, many extended families live far apart.
◆ **In what other ways is parenting different, and sometimes more difficult, today?**

Is Parenting Instinctive?

Who would have thought that someday people would be reading books and taking courses to learn about parenting? Your great-grandparents might have thought that was a strange idea. Even people from more recent generations might agree.

You can almost hear them protesting, "People have been raising children for years without training. Parenting is instinctive. It just comes naturally." But does it?

Check for youself. If you were a parent, would you know what to do if your infant cried constantly? What if your young child was afraid to go to bed at night? Parents deal with similar situations all the time. Can you instinctively think of reasonable solutions? If not, you're like most people who don't come equipped with all the answers.

If parenting skills were ever automatic, those days have surely disappeared. People who plan to "trust their instincts" find that intuition isn't always best.

The Reasons for Parenting Education

Many people can become parents, but being a good parent is a challenge. When you study **parenting**, you learn how to provide the care and guidance that can lead to a child's healthy development. This aim is one reason why parenting has become an important topic for study today.

If someone asks you why people need parenting education, you'll soon be able to give them even more reasons—like all the ones described in this chapter.

TO INCREASE KNOWLEDGE AND RESOURCES

Years ago more families lived near each other or in the same home. Older family members could easily advise the younger parents. If the baby bumped his head, Grandma could take a look and suggest what to do.

Building Parenting Skills

PARENTING WITH KNOWLEDGE

Knowledge is as essential to parenting as it is to any activity. Parenting knowledge comes from many sources. Some knowledge is based on scientific research, but some comes simply from other parents who have had a similar experience. By grasping every opportunity to gain knowledge, the future parent prepares for making good decisions and doing the right thing when caring for a child. As the single parent of two-year-old Dawn, Zach showed a knowledgeable approach when he:

▶ Talked with his sister about how to promote his daughter's development.

▶ Used information from a reputable parenting book to decide how to handle Dawn's tantrums.

▶ Asked questions that would help him decide whether the doctor Dawn was seeing was right for them.

▶ Used first aid practices to care for a cut on Dawn's hand.

▶ Recognized that the birthday toy his daughter received wasn't safe for play.

▶ Chose nutritious foods for Dawn's diet.

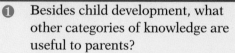

◆ ◆ Your Thoughts ◆ ◆

❶ Besides child development, what other categories of knowledge are useful to parents?

❷ Why does knowing a child as an individual, as well as knowing about children in general, help a parent?

❸ Some parents feel more comfortable handling a second child because they learned from their mistakes with the first. How can mistakes be avoided the first time?

Living far apart, the way many people do today, makes it harder for family members to help each other. One mother explained how she felt after leaving her hometown: "I used to see my parents every week. They answered many of my questions about raising Shawn. Now I miss the family support. We talk on the phone, but it's not the same as having my folks close by."

Whether or not families live far apart, many parents need other ways to learn parenting skills. Your parenting course will help you become knowledgeable. Just think what you'll need to know to raise a healthy, well-adjusted child. You'll need information about child development, physical care, safety, helping children learn, guiding behaviour, and much more.

Part of being knowledgeable is knowing how to find information. Can you recognize reliable sources of information and find answers to your questions? You'll need that ability if you become a parent.

TO COPE IN A CHANGING WORLD

People study parenting because the world is different today. Changes happen daily, so keeping up isn't easy.

More Options for Children

The typical child today has many more experiences and opportunities than your parents had when they were growing up.

TECHNOLOGY. With technology alone, the changes have been remarkable. While computers, the Internet, e-mail, and DVD players may seem commonplace to you and your friends, they weren't part of life for families just a few years ago. Technology teaches and entertains children. Parents must make sure children use technology safely and appropriately.

TOYS AND ACTIVITIES. Children also have toys, games, and equipment that adults never would have imagined during their own childhood. School activities, sports, and special-interest classes of all kinds are plentiful in most areas. Some parents struggle to include a child's activities as they balance busy work and personal schedules.

Parents who didn't grow up with computers and electronic devices may be unsure about how children should use them. ◆ **What types of technology do you accept and understand more easily than your parents?**

DECISIONS FOR PARENTS. New opportunities for children can be exciting. They help children develop skills in art, music, sports, and many other areas. The more options children have, however, the more decisions parents have to make. Should a six-year-old have special classes and practices several days a week? If you become a parent someday, you'll need information to help you decide such questions. Through parenting education, you can find ideas.

Influences on Children

Today's parents have to guide children through one challenging situation after another. Without guidance themselves, parents may not know what to do.

During a meeting at one school, parents talked about their concerns. Several were worried about the influence of gangs and drug use by young people. Parents voiced concerns about children who were home alone after school and about those who came to school hungry. They wondered what they could do for troubled children.

All families have problems. Many of the same problems have been around for a long time. As some have increased, however, more parents worry about protecting children. Where do they find solutions? Parenting education teaches people how to get through difficult times and possibly avoid some tough situations altogether.

TO BUILD A STRONG SOCIETY

Parenting education helps both parents and children, but it also does something on a larger scale. Learning to be an effective parent can make a difference to Canadian society as a whole.

Cross-Curricular **History CONNECTIONS**

Changes in Parenting

❖ In the 1600s, children were viewed as imperfect creatures who needed the strictest discipline. They customarily went to work for other families as servants, farmhands, or apprentices long before they were 15. The oldest son, who would inherit his father's property, stayed behind to work at home. Households often included lodgers or workers living in close quarters with the family.

❖ Family life was often harsh and practical rather than loving. Many children died long before they could reach adulthood. Few adults could expect to live long past their forties, and those who did eventually had to be looked after by their surviving children. A short life span meant many men and women remarrying after the death of a spouse, with the resulting mix of step-parents and step-brothers and sisters.

❖ The value placed today on close, nurturing families is in part a product of lives that are healthier, longer, more prosperous, and—for many—with enough free time to enjoy people and activities.

What are three advantages most children today have that children in the 1600s did not?

Families First

What happens if you construct a house with a weak foundation? It will eventually fall. Families are the basic building blocks of society. Without healthy families, what will happen to society? A national concern about families has been growing because people want their communities and country to stand strong for the future.

SCHOOL COUNCIL
MEETING
Tuesday, 7:30 P.M.
Room

Involved parents know what's going on in their children's lives. They look for ways to make life better within their own family and within the community.
◆ **Why is this important?**

If families have problems, that can spell trouble for other families. For example, if crime and violence take hold in a neighbourhood, what might happen? The crime and violence will continue to increase. Good citizens become victims. Fear increases. People move away and the neighbourhood deteriorates further. Our society has to spend time, energy, and money trying to fix the situation instead of using its resources in unproductive ways.

Crime and violence aren't the only problems that can threaten a community. Once a problem takes hold, it often leads to others. The problems caused by a few can spread until the entire community is affected.

Looking for Solutions

What does it take to prevent harm to society? Elected officials work on family-related laws aimed at improving life for families. Programs in many communities offer classes, information, and resources for families.

Many solutions have been offered, but perhaps the best ones begin at home. Parents who are skilled and knowledgeable have a better chance of raising children who will build communities, not tear them down. When parents form healthy families, their children are more likely to raise well-adjusted families too, and that's good for society.

If society wants healthy families, steps need to be taken to produce them. Parenting education increases the skills that parents have, giving another good reason to make the study of parenting part of a well-rounded education.

TO GAIN THE REWARDS OF PARENTING

Although parents don't win trophies or receive plaques for what they do, their job does come with rewards. A job well done can bring lasting pleasures.

Learning to parent well is worthwhile. If you became a parent, wouldn't you want your child to become the best that he or she can be? People want to experience the rewards of parenting, but that doesn't happen without effort. By becoming a skilled parent, the rewards can last a lifetime.

Internet Connects

http://www.mcgrawhill.ca/links/parenting
To learn more about families in Canada, go to the Web site above for *Parenting: Rewards and Responsibilities, First Canadian Edition,* to see where to go next.

Simple pleasures, like blowing bubbles, are as much fun for parents as for children. ◆ **What other rewards of parenting do people enjoy?**

A Youthful Perspective

With their humour and liveliness, children have a way of keeping parents youthful and reminding adults of simple pleasures. For example, when a child first sees an airplane flying overhead or a bee gathering nectar, the moment is special. Parents can forget about everyday concerns and relive the excitement of childhood.

A parent who has forgotten how rain forms or what thunder is may sense a new need to understand the world. The child's desire to know leads to the parent's desire to teach.

All children deserve a home where they can thrive and learn. The parent who learns how to create such an environment is often rewarded with the joy of sharing a child's wonder and excitement.

Emotional Fulfillment

Sensing the love of a child warms the heart. Parents know that feeling when an infant smiles back or a toddler gives a hug. They know it the first time a child says "mama" or "dada." They feel it when a child is excited to see them.

Even through the child's teen years and into adulthood, emotional fulfillment can continue as long as the bond stays strong. Eventually, many years later, a son or daughter who has known a parent's devotion may return that devotion by giving caring attention to the aging parent.

The love and respect of a child is something parents want to cherish throughout life. How sad it is when events interfere with the bond between parent and child. When parents learn how to preserve that bond, their life with the child is much more satisfying.

Family Continuation

Raising children gives the feeling that a family will last. Many people want to build a family for this reason. They like the realization that their family and traditions will continue to exist through their children and grandchildren.

Parents hope to raise children who eventually have happy, healthy families of their own. If you raise a strong family, your children have a better chance of doing the same. You can learn how to preserve this positive cycle as you study parenting.

Personal Growth

People who learn good parenting skills and put them to work are rewarded with their own personal growth. They develop skills, strengths, and understandings they might not gain in other ways.

Putting a child first teaches self-sacrifice. A parent who feels responsible for someone else learns to focus on what's really important in life.

Parents can learn more about themselves and their own thinking through their children. Each child is a separate individual, often with different ideas. A teen's budding awareness of social issues, for instance, can renew a parent's own sense of idealism.

Internet Connects

http://www.mcgrawhill.ca/links/parenting
To learn more about parenting from A to Z, go to the Web site above for *Parenting: Rewards and Responsibilities, First Canadian Edition,* to see where to go next.

Children are proud to master new skills. Parents are proud to teach a skill and watch a child succeed. ◆ **As a parent, what skills would you teach to your children?**

Sharing activities, such as bicycling, also provides opportunities to communicate in a relaxed atmosphere of pride and success.
◆ **What activities did you share with your parents?**

Parents are often surprised when their child shows an independent spirit. "How do I help my daughter become the person she wants to be and instill the principles that are important to me at the same time?" one father wondered. Parents often find answers as they learn skills for guiding children.

A Sense of Pride

Children are often a source of pride for their parents—from something as simple as tying a shoelace for the first time to a milestone as special as graduating. Not only do parents feel pride in their children, but they are also justified in feeling proud of themselves.

As they grow, children learn new lessons daily. One parenting challenge is learning how to help a child have successes. A parent begins with a helpless infant and works to produce a young man or woman who is independent and caring. Most parents would say there is no greater accomplishment in life.

TO MEET PARENTING RESPONSIBILITIES

"I just want to be a good parent," a new mother or father says fervently. That wish is the top reason why many people want to learn more about parenting. They want to do the job well, and they're looking for help.

Children have the right to be nurtured, protected, taught, and guided. Meeting these responsibilities as a parent is what this course is all about. By fulfilling these aims, you have a better chance of someday gaining the full rewards that parenting has to offer.

Nurturing Children

What if you planted a garden and then ignored it? You seldom watered it and you didn't pull the weeds or fertilize the plants. Without nurturing your garden, it probably wouldn't become what you had hoped.

To **nurture** is to encourage growth and development. Just as nurturing a garden makes it become the best that it can be, the same is true of children.

Every child is born with potential. **Potential** is what a person is capable of becoming. What each child becomes, however, hinges heavily on the care received.

When you nurture a child, you pay attention to everything the child needs for optimal growth and development. You provide good care and try to make sure the child is content and secure. You teach the child about the world and how to get along in it. You give love, and the child thrives. Without nurturing, it is very difficult for children to reach toward their full potential.

Protecting Children

If you think that protecting a child is easy, think again. Protection can be complicated.

Infants and toddlers need constant supervision. The growing child sees life as an adventure and doesn't always recognize dangers. Parents must pay attention all the time. Would you know what to do if a child swallowed an adult's medication? Would you know how to prevent that from happening in the first place? Learning safety principles and putting them into action is a parent's obligation.

As children become more independent, parents become a little less protective, allowing their independence to develop. That basic parental instinct to protect, however, continues even as children become adults.

Teaching Children

Successful adults think creatively. They know how to evaluate information and apply what they know to their lives. They also know how to use reasoning to solve problems. With parental help, children can become adults who have these skills.

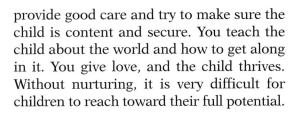

Protecting children is a moment-by-moment responsibility. Some hazards are less obvious than others.
◆ **What other kinds of protection do children need besides wearing life jackets around water?**

You will read more later about how the brain develops most rapidly in the early years of life. How well it develops depends on the close attention parents and other caring adults pay to children right from birth. Nurturing a child is critical to brain development; so is making sure a child has opportunities to learn.

Effective parenting means looking for opportunities to teach a child. The knowing parent turns over a rock in the dirt to show a child what's underneath. The parent points to sights outside the bus or car window and talks about them. Skilled parents find many everyday ways to teach children and make those moments fun.

Guiding Children

Guidance shapes behaviour and attitudes. With proper guidance, a child can become the kind of person others like to be around. Parents want their children to earn respect, and get along well with others. To accomplish these goals, a parent teaches a child to live by certain rules and be a good person.

Parents use their own **values** to guide children. Values are ideas about what is important. They are recognized when you hear someone say, "You ought to . . ." Since young children naturally imitate others, parents are constantly setting an example for children to follow.

Parents can learn many useful guidance skills. By learning to communicate well with children and how to direct behaviour effectively, parents guide children more easily.

Internet Connects

http://www.mcgrawhill.ca/links/parenting
To learn more about children in Canada, go to the Web site above for *Parenting: Rewards and Responsibilities, First Canadian Edition,* to see where to go next.

Time for Education

Preparing to do a job makes good sense. In medical school a doctor learns how to treat patients. In technical school a mechanic learns to make engine repairs. You can train for almost any job. Doesn't it make sense to prepare for parenting too?

One mother explained her thoughts about parenting education this way: "I never really knew what parenting was all about with my first child. I wish I'd known more when Samantha was little. Knowing how to handle behaviour wasn't easy. Sammie got control of things too often, and I've struggled to undo the mistakes I made.

Children long for guidance, but it takes strong communication skills to lead them well. Parenting education helps you build these skills.

Using Parenting Skills

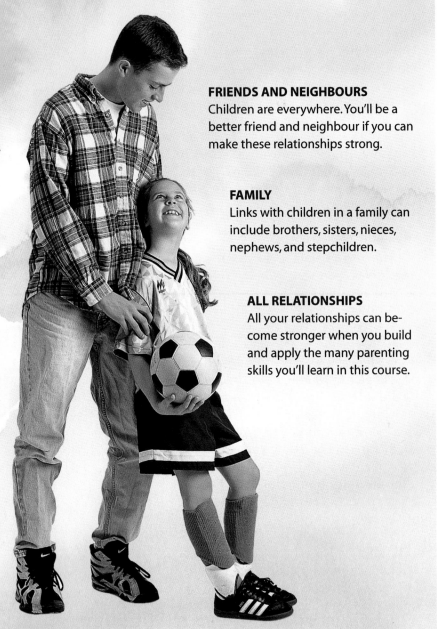

BABYSITTING
As a babysitter, you need the ability to handle routine care as well as emergencies.

CAREERS THAT INVOLVE CHILDREN
Whether you become a teacher or a bus driver, you can put your parenting skills to work.

VOLUNTEERISM
People volunteer to help in crisis nurseries and in park district summer programs. What else might involve children?

FRIENDS AND NEIGHBOURS
Children are everywhere. You'll be a better friend and neighbour if you can make these relationships strong.

FAMILY
Links with children in a family can include brothers, sisters, nieces, nephews, and stepchildren.

ALL RELATIONSHIPS
All your relationships can become stronger when you build and apply the many parenting skills you'll learn in this course.

Not everyone will become a parent. Does that mean this course is a waste of time? Not in the least. Even if you don't have children of your own, they may still be part of your life. The skills you learn in a parenting class can be put into practice in many ways. ◆ **Which of these might be part of your life now and in the future?**

"It's different with Jeremy. When he was a baby, I took a parenting class, and now I subscribe to a magazine for parents. What I've learned has made a difference. I'm more confident about what I'm doing these days, and I'm raising a happier, healthier child because of that. I feel better about myself too."

FOCUSING ON SKILLS

To be a confident parent like Samantha's mother, you'll need certain skills. Even if you don't become a parent, you can still use what you learn, as the illustration on page 14 shows.

You can develop parenting skills in two ways—through information and practice. Both of these are part of the course you're now taking. There's plenty of information ahead. You'll read what authorities have to say on many topics. You'll also learn how to make decisions concerning you and your future family. Most of all, you will learn what children are like and what they need from you in order to thrive.

To become truly skilled, however, you need practice. Throughout this course, you will be asked to try your skills and to develop them. How would you help two children settle a disagreement? You might try out ideas with friends. What would you say to a child who is not co-operating? You might test your approach with a young family member. By practising skills on your own whenever you can, you polish those skills for what's ahead.

PART OF THE SOLUTION

Someone once said, "If you're not part of the solution, then you're part of the problem." Combined with other families someday, your family will be part of the whole that makes up society. If you can tackle the job of parenting with skill, you are likely to build healthy families.

Since the condition of the whole depends on the condition of all the parts, parenting with success will be good for your community. Just as important, it will be good for you and good for your future family. Isn't that reason enough to take full advantage of the opportunity you have right now to learn all you can about becoming a skilled parent?

Pilots learn many of the skills they need with equipment that simulates flying. ◆ **How could you use the same principle to build parenting skills?**

Looking Back

- ♥ A number of reasons support the need for parenting education.

- ♥ Today's changing world makes learning about parenting more important than ever.

- ♥ Society can benefit from positive parenting skills and suffer from poor ones.

- ♥ Parenting can offer great satisfaction to those who strive to do the job well.

- ♥ Parents are responsible for the well-being of their children. Necessary skills and knowledge can be learned.

- ♥ Learning parenting skills can benefit anyone who deals with children.

Knowledge and Understanding

1. Like many others of their generation, Ashley and her husband left their rural community for city job opportunities. How might that distance from family affect them when they become parents?
2. How have changes in the world affected the need to learn more about parenting?
3. Why are families important to society?
4. What are five possible rewards that parenting can offer?
5. Rank the five basic rewards of parenting in order of importance to you. Briefly explain your choices.
6. How can becoming a parent affect a man's or woman's personal growth?
7. What are four basic responsibilities of parents?
8. Why is it so important to nurture a child?
9. How do parents guide children?
10. Why might this course be useful to people who never become parents?

Review

Thinking and Inquiry

11. Do you think some people have better instincts for parenting? Why or why not?
12. Paula and Rick want to have children because all their friends are having them. What problems do you foresee for them?
13. Your parents may say that parenting offered more challenges for them than it did for their parents. Explain how you see your future challenges as a parent.
14. Think of four or five issues or questions that you have that you hope this parenting course can answer. Write them on a separate sheet of paper at the front of your notebook. Refer to them from time to time to see if you have addressed them.

Communication

15. Your friend is teasing you about taking a parenting course. Write a note to your friend explaining the benefits of taking this course, your views on parenting, and how this course can affect your future with children.
16. You have just read an article in the local newspaper stating that we should be educating future parents. Write a letter to the editor explaining how this is being accomplished already through the parenting course that you are currently taking.
17. Create a poster that shows what future parents can learn from a parenting course.

Application

18. Survey five parents to find out what formal preparation they took before becoming parents. Write a paragraph that summarizes your findings.
19. "Parenting is a lifelong commitment, worth preparing for." Develop a one-page handout to explain this statement to future students in this course.

Maggie Lance, Community Mental Health Counsellor

What volunteer activities did you do as a teenager that led you to choose a career that involved working with children/people?

▶ Reading for the Love of It (a program with the Board of Education).
▶ Volunteering to do art for a pamphlet about a children's program.
▶ Volunteering at a home for the aged.
▶ Volunteering as a Sunday school teacher.
▶ Volunteering to assist with a park recreation program.
▶ Volunteering to coach baseball.

*Please describe your **specific education pathway.***

▶ Graduated from the University of Guelph, College of Social Sciences, in 1985.
▶ Majored in Sociology with a minor in Early Childhood Education.
▶ My electives were in Psychology, Art, Criminology, Nutrition, Physiology, Geriatrics, and Statistics.

Have you completed any further study to enhance your professional development?

▶ Courses on child protection issues.
▶ Suicide intervention training.
▶ Trauma-assessment training.
▶ Specific trauma therapy training.
▶ Training to perform psychometric assessments.
▶ Training to be a behaviour consultant.
▶ Training to facilitate child abuse interviews.
▶ Eye Movement Desensitization Reprocessing (EMDR) trauma therapy training.
▶ Dual diagnosis training.

*Please describe your **career pathway.***

Family and Children's Services of Leeds and Grenville, Brockville, Ontario
Date:　　August 1994–December 1998
Position:　Social Worker, Family Service Unit
Responsibilities:

▶ Working with children and their families on protection issues.
▶ Working with children in the care of Family and Children's Services.
▶ Partnering with community resources.
▶ Involvement with prevention and support to better the lives of children.

▶ Working closely with the court system. (Completed affidavits, made court appearances, served individuals with court materials, was a witness in court, and prepared children for the court process.)
▶ Working as a team player with inter-agency resources (Resource Department, Intake Department, the lawyer, etc.).
▶ Training for Core Protection, Attachment Disorder, interviewing children.
▶ Completing presentations for community agencies and resources.

S.D.G. Developmental Services Centre, Child & Adolescent Services, Cornwall, Ontario
Dates:　　November 1990–August 1994
Positions:　Full-time *Case Co-ordinator*
　　　　　　Psychometrist/Consultant on a six-month contract
Responsibilities:

▶ As a Case Co-ordinator, working with clients who were developmentally handicapped from newborn to 18 years of age.
▶ As a Psychometrist/Consultant, working with developmentally handicapped clients of all ages.
▶ Offering developmental programming, case co-ordination, and support to children and their families.
▶ In addition, performing psychological assessments, as well as behaviour consultations to the clients, families, and agencies involved with the client.

Children's Aid Society, Cornwall, Ontario
Dates:　　August 1990–1991 (casual)
Position:　Case Aid
Responsibilities:

▶ Working with children in foster homes regarding their access to their biological parents, or in the court system.

Sir James Whitney School for the Deaf, Belleville, Ontario
Dates: February 1990–August 1990
Position: Parent Advisor
Responsibilities:
- Working on an individual basis with a child with a hearing deficiency and developmental delays, to assist overall communication.

Renfrew County and District Health Unit, Renfrew, Ontario
Dates: March 1989–January 1990
Position: Infant Stimulation Worker
Responsibilities:
- Working on an individual basis to promote the development of infants and toddlers who were at risk of delays.

During my teenage years I fulfilled the following positions:
- Babysitting and summer activities with children
- Summer program with Leeds and Grenville Board of Education
- Summer employment with St. Lawrence Lodge for the Aged
- Summer employment with the Brockville Jail
- Summer employment with Leeds and Grenville Interval House (home for abused women and their children)

Did you switch jobs along the way? If so, please provide reason(s) for the change in job.

I began working with children with special needs, then I moved into the area of children in need of protection, and now I assist children with mental health issues.

Please describe your current position.

Child and Youth Wellness Centre, Brockville, Ontario
Member of Children's Mental Health Ontario
Dates: December 1998–Present
Position: Community Mental Health Counsellor
Responsibilities:
- Counselling families and children from the ages of six to 18 years of age.
- Counselling children and families dealing with mental health issues.
- Individual counselling.
- Family and parenting support and assistance.
- Active involvement with community resources involved with our clients.
- Facilitating and co-facilitating groups for our clients.
- Strong working relationship with inter-agency resources (In-Home Program, MST Program, psychiatrist, psychologist, etc.).
- Regular training.
- Presenting on various topics to organizations in Leeds and Grenville.

*What are the **rewards** of your current position?*

Each day brings new challenges and expands my knowledge of struggles that children and youth need to deal with on a daily basis. Each day brings endless rewards—for example, a suicidal teenager who attends a session and leaves with a new perspective; a child who has not attended school in months leaves a session willing to meet with the school; when a child in need of protection has the courage to inform the authorities of his mistreatment.

*What are the **challenges** of your current position?*

Some of the challenges of my position are advocating and communicating the needs of children to professionals who may have different views. Another is assisting high-needs families solve small issues so that they can begin to tackle larger issues.

A large challenge in my position of working with children and families is meeting all the direct needs and the administrative responsibilities. An example of this would be heading to the office to spend the day completing necessary paperwork and entering the office to have a suicidal client in crisis waiting for me.

Looking back over your education and career pathways, as a young person in high school, did you ever believe you would follow the pathways you have?

I always thought that I would work with children. My dream was to be a teacher with special needs children. I did not end up being a teacher in a classroom, but I have spent much time during my career teaching parents and children many skills.

Do you have any comments for young people who might be considering their own educational/career pathway?

Follow your heart and dreams. Anything that you feel is important is worth pursuing. Once you begin your educational and career path, be open to new opportunities that may be presented to you.

What other careers are related to your career?
- Child and Youth Worker
- Social Worker
- Psychologist
- Psychiatrist
- Teacher
- Guidance Counsellor

Developing Parenting Skills

CHAPTER EXPECTATIONS

While reading this chapter, you will:

▶ Explain why parenting is a life-long commitment in our society.

▶ Determine the personal qualities, skills, and experiences that are necessary for parenting.

▶ Demonstrate an understanding of how to interact with and observe children.

▶ Effectively identify methods for collecting information from a variety of sources.

KEY TERMS

caregiver   resources

objective   role model

Frank eyed the blanketed bundle that his older brother Rick extended toward him. "Put one hand under her body," Rick explained, "and use the other one to support her head." Frank positioned his hands as Rick had instructed and held his infant niece.

"She's so little!" he said softly. "And so light. You hardly know there's a baby in there." Frank gazed at the tiny, sleeping face and curled fists. He still couldn't believe Rick was a father. He thought of some of the images the word held for him: memories of their own father, especially when they were growing up; thoughts of his friends' fathers, and how each one was different; even the way television dads were shown. Somehow he still didn't have a complete picture of what it really meant to be a father.

"You've got it now," Rick said. "You're a natural."

Frank carefully handed the infant back. "I think there's more to being a dad than learning how to hold a baby." Watching Rick gently rocking his baby daughter, he wondered: Do I have what it takes to raise a child? What does it take, anyway?

◆

What do you think? How do you think a parenting course would benefit Frank?

A patient parent makes time for children—time to listen without interrupting and time to show genuine interest. ◆ **How do you feel when people show these courtesies to you?**

Exploring Parenting Skills

Can you imagine anyone saying, "Well, I became a skilled parent today"? Probably not, since learning to parent doesn't happen overnight. Instead, parenting ability grows slowly.

Parents aren't the only ones who take care of children. A **caregiver** may be a grandparent, aunt or uncle, older sibling, child-care worker, or foster parent. The caregiver's role is to love, care for, and guide a child.

Not everyone has all the qualities and skills needed to care for a child effectively, but they can develop them. Some very important skills and qualities are described in this chapter. Make these your strengths and you'll have a head start when it comes to parenting.

Patience in parenting means that eleven-month-old Joey's mother overlooked the mess he made while happily feeding himself. Patience means that four-year-old Amber's father listened to her description of a trip to the zoo, although she interrupted the hockey game he was watching.

The "sweet fruit" of patience is what results. Joey made progress in learning a new skill. Amber could tell that her father cared about her. The bonds of love grew. These results are better than any short-term satisfaction each parent might have gained from being less patient.

All parents are impatient occasionally, but routine impatience tells children, "You're not worth my time." Few qualities are appreciated as much by children as patience. Childhood is all about developing and learning. Children need parents who are patient enough to let them explore and make mistakes.

Developing Patience

How do you make yourself more patient? The first step is deciding how patient you are now. If you're not sure, ask others who know you well. Do you focus on what's really important in life? Are you even-tempered over minor distractions? Do you value your relationships enough to do what others want and need some of the time?

Paying attention to your actions is a way to look at patience. Do you get upset when things aren't done right away or not done your way? Then stop, count to ten, and make a fresh start. You may see a different approach that works better. You may feel better inside when you stop pushing yourself and others needlessly.

Busy parents adapt their parenting skills every day. They have to be flexible to do well as a parent.

CONFIDENCE

To keep a family on course, parents must believe in themselves. When parents have faith in their abilities, they have the courage to act. Not acting means that events happen without control or guidance.

Clarissa avoided confronting her five-year-old son when he didn't pick up his toys the way he was supposed to. She felt guilty for upsetting him if she reminded him about the toys. Clarissa's insecurity may lead to problems as Troy discovers that he can break rules, do what he wants, and control the situation.

People who lack confidence are often afraid to make decisions. They may be unable to set rules and stick by them. Not doing these things, however, is hard on children. Sensing that no one is really in charge can make children feel insecure. Some children try to take charge themselves, which can lead to struggles and confusion over leadership in the family.

Building Confidence

You may have heard that "it takes money to make money." The same is true of confidence. You gain confidence from success, but it takes confidence to risk trying something that might result in failure. To build confidence that may help you as a parent someday, use these ideas:

- ♥ *Realize that you will never be successful unless you try.* "Try and try again" has been the rule of thumb leading many people to success.

- ♥ *Identify your strengths and past successes.* Let them inspire you to seek new challenges.

- ♥ *Talk with friends and relatives about any self-doubts and setbacks you might have.* They can help you build confidence.

- ♥ *Increase your knowledge.* Knowledgeable people often react with greater confidence because they have information to guide them. Knowledge arms you to make decisions more easily and quickly.

- ♥ *Help build the confidence of others.* What you do for them will be returned to you.

Internet Connects

http://www.mcgrawhill.ca/links/parenting
To learn more about family well-being, go to the Web site above for *Parenting: Rewards and Responsibilities, First Canadian Edition,* to see where to go next.

The confident parent isn't afraid to take charge. Whether teaching a child gardening skills or making sure homework gets done, the parent knows what needs to be done and does it.

TAKING A REALISTIC APPROACH

Which of these two statements is true: "Parenting is an unending joy" or "Parenting is a life of sacrifice"? If you think realistically, you'll see that neither one is quite accurate. Both statements describe extremes. The truth is in between. Reality is rooted in facts and truth. People who parent realistically:

♥ *Have reasonable expectations for their children*. Wanting a three-year-old to behave like his five-year-old sister isn't realistic. Neither is expecting a child to read at an unusually early age. Realistic parents encourage children without frustrating or pressuring them.

♥ *Have reasonable expectations for themselves*. Reasonable parents set challenging goals, but they don't try to be perfect. They focus on the important things in life and make those a priority.

♥ *Live by their own standards rather than those of others*. To be realistic, parents need to do what works best for them and their children.

♥ *Accept truths about children*. When parents understand children, raising them is easier. Knowing that children often get messy, for example, helps parents be more tolerant of children who love to play in the mud and roll in the grass. They react with less anger and more constructive ways of guiding children.

Aiming for a Realistic Attitude

How do people learn to think realistically? Developing a few useful thinking habits is a place to start. Try to look for the facts and then act accordingly.

You've probably heard someone say, "You can't believe everything you hear." How true that statement is. Many people speak without authority. Besides that, they may remember facts incorrectly.

Children can easily be upset by events that don't seem significant to the adult. Sometimes the adult isn't even sure what may be wrong. ◆ **How would a realistic parent respond to a troubled child?**

As you gather information, you must be the judge. Is the person who is talking—or writing—in a position to know the truth? Ask questions if you need to and do some checking, especially when it's important to have reliable information. Just because a source *seems* knowledgeable doesn't necessarily make the person right.

RESOURCEFULNESS

When it was too cold for her child to go outdoors and play, one mother brought in a pan of snow for her young son to play with. The indoor snow thrilled him. Resourceful parents recognize what is useful to them. Then they put those things to work.

Resources can be ideas, time, money, skills, possessions, and other people. Making good use of all of these is helpful to everyone. You may need to conserve resources to make them last, or you can stretch resources by combining or trading them with other people.

Becoming Resourceful

How does your resourcefulness rate? Can you locate needed information? Are you creative in substituting what you have for what you lack? Have you gotten to know people whose skills and knowledge can help you?

Learning to recognize your resources and how you can use them is a first step to becoming resourceful. Too many people say "I can't" because they fail to recognize what will help them be able to say "I can."

A SENSE OF HUMOUR

Seeing the lighter side of life is a must for parenting. Both parents and children benefit.

Resourceful parents know how to find information.
◆ **What kinds of answers might parents find on the Internet?**

For one thing, humour can ease a tense situation. Any close relationship can lead to conflict at times. When a child and parent reach the boiling point, humour helps let off steam.

Children need to feel free to express themselves and to risk making mistakes. A light-hearted atmosphere makes that easier for them. They know that a parent is likely to respond good-naturedly and not always in anger.

Parents who model humour help children gain a healthy, balanced, and positive perspective on life. Research shows that laughter is good for health. When children enjoy laughter and learn to see the bright side, emotional well-being grows.

Developing Your Sense of Humour

Most people have a sense of humour. How they handle it is the real question.

One night a tired father snapped repeatedly at his five-year-old twins during dinner. Sensing their hurt feelings, he got the dog biscuits and put one biscuit on his plate. "I've been barking like Duke all night," he explained, "so I may as well eat like him too!"

This example illustrates the first rule of humour. You can make fun of yourself or a situation, but never of another person, especially not a child. A child's self-image rests heavily on a parent's approval. Children are deeply hurt when someone laughs *at* them. Parents must use humour carefully.

Think about how your own sense of humour works for you. Do you laugh at jokes that make fun of other people? Do you become a comedian at others' expense? Anyone who uses these approaches to humour hurts others. When people disregard the feelings of others, they lose respect themselves. Wise parents make sure that their sense of humour doesn't hurt their children.

Parenting Q & A

Sorting Through Advice

Q "As a new mother, I really appreciate the voice of experience. But what should I do when one person gives me seemingly good advice and someone else tells me just the opposite?" *Lynn*

A As you're seeing, parenting advice can be contradictory. To help you sift through well-meaning advice, try these ideas. First, ask yourself if the advice makes sense. If what you're hearing contradicts all current beliefs, you should probably ignore it. Try to determine how current the advice is. Some ideas about child care have changed as the understanding of children has grown. Also, judge the reliability of sources. What experience or education does the person have? Are the comments swayed by emotion? Finally, think about motive. Is the person trying to help, or will he or she gain something by promoting the idea?

SENSITIVITY

If you were trying to raise your mark in math, you probably wouldn't appreciate a friend who begged you to go to a movie on the night before the math exam. You'd want your friend to be understanding and perhaps even help you review for the exam. All people, children included, want others to realize how they feel. That shows sensitivity.

Sensitive parents try to see through a child's eyes before they react. Suppose four-year-old Kiley cried when her stuffed bear lost a leg. Her stepmother didn't become angry about the crying. She also didn't tell Kiley she was having a tantrum over "nothing." Instead, Kiley's stepmother realized how important the bear was to Kiley. She comforted her and took the bear on a pretend trip to the doctor to repair the leg.

Sensitive parents know how their own actions affect a child's feelings. They guide with a firm hand yet preserve the child's sense of self-worth. Considering the situation and the child's age, personality, needs, and abilities helps parents react sensitively.

Developing Sensitivity

One idea that can help you become a more sensitive person is this: always try to put yourself in the other person's place. The following practices can help:

♥ *Listen to what you say and how*. How might someone interpret your words? A sensitive choice of words is unlikely to offend people.

♥ *Think about why a person is saying or doing something*. The reasons behind someone's actions can provide clues to what is really going on.

♥ *Develop caring mannerisms*. Try listening before you speak. When listening to people, look them in the eye. You might put a hand on their shoulder. What other ways come to mind?

Internet Connects

http://www.mcgrawhill.ca/links/parenting
To learn more about ideas and issues on the well-being of Ontario's young people, go to the Web site above for *Parenting: Rewards and Responsibilities, First Canadian Edition*, to see where to go next.

When parents live in the same household, parenting as a team helps them handle daily routines.
◆ **When parents live in separate households, can they still operate as a team? How?**

WORKING AS A TEAM

No matter what you do in life, learning to work with others is a skill you will need. That's true in parenting too. Parenting is a team effort that begins with the family and extends to those who provide support. For example, one mother worked closely with her child's speech therapist to improve a speech impairment. One father stayed in close touch with his child-care provider to make sure that everything was going smoothly for his young son.

Becoming a Team Player

As part of a team, parents must find ways to work well together and also with others. How would you rate yourself as a team member? Do you listen to others' points of view and take them seriously when appropriate? Do you try to get your point across without threats, anger, and accusations? Do you treat others the same way you would want to be treated?

Raising Children With Character

This Year's Crop

Quinn stared out the window at the pouring rain. "Stop," he whispered fiercely. *"Stop now."* Even at age seven, he knew what the non-stop rain meant to his family.

A hand touched his shoulder. Quinn's father said quietly, "It doesn't look very good out there, does it, son?" Looking up, he found his father gazing intently across the fields. Quinn shook his head without expression.

Bill looked down at Quinn's sombre face. His own weathered features softened into a smile. Kneeling beside his son, he gave Quinn's shoulder a gentle squeeze. "This reminds me of the spring you were born," he said. "We had rains a lot worse than this. The fields flooded. We lost half the crop."

Quinn looked worried. "What did you do?"

Bill shrugged. "Replanted. We can do it again if we have to. It means more work, but that's nothing new to us, is it?" He grinned and tousled his son's hair.

Quinn started to smile, then grew solemn once again. "Dad, I can help. I can do something."

Bill couldn't reply at first. Something in Quinn's earnest expression struck him. When did he start calling me Dad instead of Daddy? Was this the first time? thought Bill.

◆◆◆◆◆ Thinking It Over ◆◆◆◆◆

1. Why do you think Quinn calls his father Dad at this moment?
2. How is Bill modelling these qualities of character for Quinn: courage; optimism; willingness to work hard; and perseverance?

Parents who model teamwork allow their children to participate in activities even though their skills may not be fully developed.

Building the skills of a good team player takes effort. You can practise with any groups you belong to, including your family. Learning teamwork can help prepare you to work well with everyone who may support and advise you as a parent.

Ways to Learn Skills

Parenting skills don't stop with the ones you've just read about. To prepare yourself for parenting, you can learn more about the skills you need in several ways. The rest of this chapter has suggestions.

LEARNING FROM OTHERS

Can you imagine learning to tie your shoes from instructions in a book? Some skills are better learned by example. Many people learn to parent by example. Most of the time, that's positive, but not always.

Many people learn parenting skills from their own parents. They may adopt a parent's way of disciplining or style of relating to children. The parent becomes a **role model**, a person whose behaviour and attitudes are imitated by others.

Many significant adults in a person's life—a favourite aunt or uncle, a grandparent, or a good friend's parents—can be models for parenting. Many positive parenting skills can be learned from these role models.

Using Good Judgment

When watching others, however, you may see actions you prefer to avoid. As one person said, "If I ever have children, I'm going to do things differently." Actions that are harmful to children must always be avoided in parenting. An adult whose behaviour is inappropriate doesn't make a good role model.

As you notice how people parent, be careful about your judgments. Not all people parent the same way, and that doesn't necessarily make one way right and another wrong.

Until you walk in the shoes of a parent, you may not realize how difficult the job can be. Mistakes are easily made. You can strive to do a good job without losing respect for those who are not perfect but who do their best.

Parenting Publications

To get expert advice on parenting, people turn to recognized authorities on raising children. Books and magazines on the subject have become increasingly popular.

Since authorities don't always agree, you must learn to evaluate sources and opinions. You will want to know the expert's education, experience, and reputation. Comparing different voices on parenting can help shape your own views.

LEARNING THROUGH EXPERIENCE

After helping with his four-year-old half-sister's birthday party, 16-year-old Cyril was tired. "I got used to the running and screaming," he said. "They were just having fun. But here's what I don't get. Don't they know you have to eat ice cream fast, before it melts all over? And why can't four-year-olds drink juice without spilling? Until I started giving them half-cups, I kept having to wipe up the floor."

Cyril's observations show how a person can learn from experience. Every experience you have with children helps prepare you for parenting. The more you learn ahead of time, the easier it will be to make decisions with any children you may have.

What experiences could teach you about children? You could help friends, neighbours, or family members with their children. Volunteering is another idea.

LEARNING IN THE CLASSROOM

As the need to know more about parenting grows, the number of parenting courses is increasing. Courses are found in schools all across the country and are also provided by community colleges, universities, and social agencies. Classroom learning is for anyone these days. Perhaps it should be mandatory for everyone.

LEARNING BY OBSERVATION

If "a picture is worth a thousand words," what is a real-life experience worth? The most detailed, descriptive text can still be

Spending time with children, whether neighbours or family members, can teach you so much about parenting. ◆ **If you don't have children nearby, what could you do?**

improved by observation. By watching adults interact with children, you see both positive and negative examples of parenting in action. Informally, you might watch teachers, coaches, neighbourhood children, and relatives. If you do volunteer work with children, you might make observations while you are working.

You can also do more formal observations. If you ask permission, you might be able to observe children and teachers at a child-care centre, preschool, or elementary school.

Why Observe Children

Children tell a great deal about themselves without even realizing it. What you learn through observation will help you understand them better.

From the words and actions of children, the experienced observer can learn: how children grow and accomplish developmental tasks; whether a child's development is advanced or delayed in some area; what activities might be appropriate for a child or group of children; how a child feels about himself or herself; and when a child is in distress.

How to Observe Children

Children tend to perform when they know someone is watching, which defeats the purpose of observing them. To make formal observations of children, choose a time when you can stay in the background, rather than participate. You'll be able to view the details of the action this way.

Observations are more useful when you watch children in typical settings and activities. As you observe, focus on only one or two children. Record what you see as soon as possible, including all details.

Formal observation techniques help you gain knowledge about children. Some secondary schools have child-care programs where you might be allowed to observe. ◆ **What could you learn?**

Observations should be written in **objective** language. That means recording exactly what you saw. Leave out judgmental observations and interpretations.

Compare the following descriptions of a preschool scene:

♥ Four-year-old Ben was pushing a truck along the floor. Melissa, age three, took the truck away from him and began to play whith it. Ben watched for a minute and then said, "I had it first. Give it back."

♥ Ben was happily playing with the truck when Melissa rudely wrenched it away. Ben didn't cry or get angry. You could tell he was older and more mature because he simply demanded the truck back.

Which is the more valuable observation? The first one is actually better. It provides a clearer description of what happened. Words like "happily" and "rudely" are judgmental. "You could tell he was..." is an interpretation. Formal observations should record the facts, not analyze behaviours.

Remember that all your observations must be kept confidential.

What to Look For

As a beginning observer, you may not be able to analyze what you see as insightfully as a professional would.

Internet Connects

http://www.mcgrawhill.ca/links/parenting
To learn more about the development of children and school readiness, go to the Web site above for Parenting*Parenting: Rewards and Responsibilities, First Canadian Edition,* to see where to go next.

When you observe children, you should describe what you see in objective language.
◆ **How would you describe what is going on between these two children?**

However, you can identify: repeated behaviour and the surrounding circumstances; efforts a child makes to accomplish a task and the success of these efforts; and conversations among children.

A Candidate for Parenting

Suppose you were writing a classified ad that began: "Wanted: Parents. Qualified applicants only. Requirements include . . ." How would you complete the ad?

Parenting is a demanding position. Your "Help Wanted" ad might be long. Could you find a candidate who has the skills for the position? More to the point, would *you* be a good candidate for the job?

Review

Looking Back

♥ Parenting skills, such as patience and resourcefulness, can be learned and improved.

♥ Confident parents help make a family run smoothly.

♥ Parents need to have realistic expectations for their children and themselves.

♥ Resourceful parents recognize what is useful to them.

♥ Family living is enjoyable when a sense of humour and sensitivity are displayed.

♥ Being a team player makes a parent's job easier.

♥ People can learn parenting skills in several different ways.

Knowledge and Understanding

1. Who, besides parents, might be the caregiver of a child? How is their role the same as a parent's?

2. Why can patience be both "bitter" and "sweet" at the same time?

3. What problems can a family encounter when the parents are not confident?

4. What is the risk of having unrealistic expectations for children? How can parents avoid this pitfall?

5. Which resources are typically limited for most families? What is an example of a resource that could be traded?

6. Why should you pay attention to how your sense of humour affects others?

7. When five-year-old Meg came home from kindergarten, she wasn't as spirited as usual. How might a sensitive parent react?

8. When would teamwork skills be necessary for a parent?

9. Drake's three-year-old refused to pick up the blocks she was playing with. Which of the parenting skills would he find most useful at this time and why?

10. What is a role model?

11. What are three possible ways to learn more about children?

12. What are three things you might be able to learn by observing a child in a play setting?

Review

Thinking and Inquiry

13. Which parenting skills described in this chapter do you think contribute the most to raising a well-adjusted child? Explain your answer in a paragraph.
14. Think about the qualities of parents described in this chapter. Choose the three qualities that you possess that would make you a good parent and explain why.
15. Think about two things you would have to work on before you became a parent. How would you go about making changes?

Communication

16. Create a pamphlet to give to new parents on parenting. Include:
    ♥ Skills needed
    ♥ Characteristics of good parents
    ♥ Factors to consider when raising a child
    ♥ Key concepts to remember
17. Choose four parenting skills from this chapter, then find a synonym and antonym for each one. Write a one-page description of the difficulties a child would face if his or her parents practised the opposite of two of the good skills.

Application

18. A parent who is a joker teases his six-year-old on a regular basis about body size, food habits, interests, and friends. How can this affect the child? How would this make the child feel? What advice would you give to this parent?

Approaches to Parenting

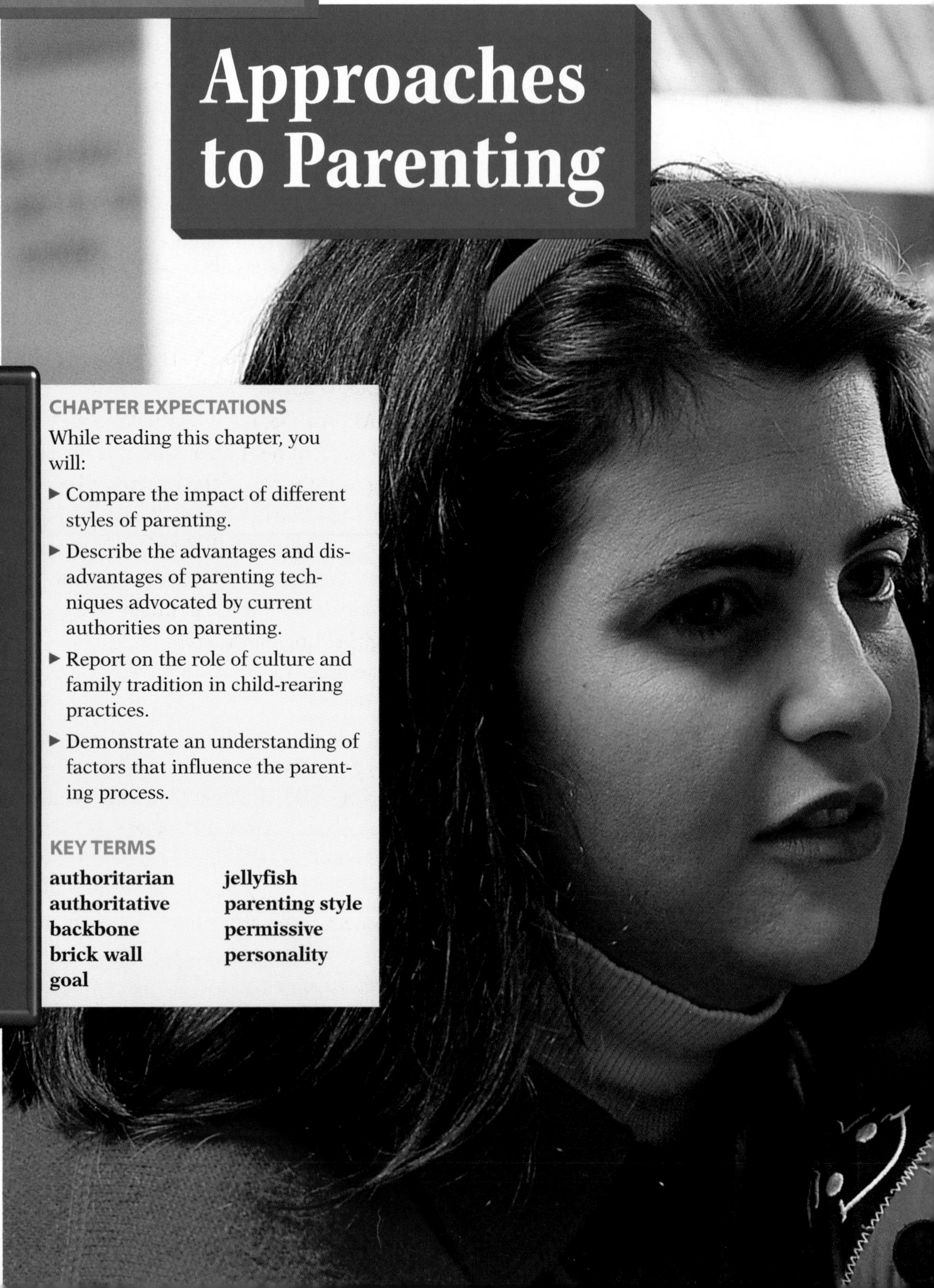

CHAPTER EXPECTATIONS

While reading this chapter, you will:

▶ Compare the impact of different styles of parenting.

▶ Describe the advantages and disadvantages of parenting techniques advocated by current authorities on parenting.

▶ Report on the role of culture and family tradition in child-rearing practices.

▶ Demonstrate an understanding of factors that influence the parenting process.

KEY TERMS

authoritarian	jellyfish
authoritative	parenting style
backbone	permissive
brick wall	personality
goal	

Waiting as the receptionist scheduled her son's next checkup at the clinic, Jennifer heard a commotion behind her. Two children, about three years old, were pushing toy trucks roughly across the waiting room floor, complete with sound effects.

"Sean," one mother said firmly, "please put down the truck and come over here with me. I want you to see the pictures in this book." The little boy glumly obeyed.

Meanwhile, the other child looked uncertainly at her father, who was watching over the top of the magazine he was reading. "Carrie, I think that game is over," he said quietly, holding her gaze for a long moment. The child set the truck aside, looked about, and smiled at a girl sitting on the sofa.

Jennifer reflected on the scene as she settled her own infant in his carrier. As she left, she noticed Sean engrossed in the picture book, and the girls quietly sorting a set of blocks. Jennifer was impressed. Each parent had handled his or her child's behaviour in a different way, yet both seemed equally effective. Cameron, she promised her son silently, someday I'm going to do just as well with you.

——————— ◆ ———————

What do you think? How would you have reacted if you were the parent of one of the preschoolers in the waiting room?

A fun-loving person will be a fun-loving parent. ◆ **How is a child affected by this kind of spirit?**

What Influences Parenting?

If you have children someday, will you parent the same way your friends do? How will their approaches to parenting compare to yours? Because you're all different, the way you handle parenting will be too.

The kind of person you are and the experiences you have will help shape the parent you become. How much control, then, do you have over your approach to parenting? As you will see, the answer is, "Plenty!"

PERSONAL INFLUENCES ON PARENTING

When you parent, your actions will be affected by qualities and attitudes within you. These personal characteristics are still developing.

Personality

When you wait in line, do you observe people around you or strike up a conversation? Are you impatient to get through the line, or do you wait calmly? Actions like these reveal your **personality**, your special blend of intellectual, emotional, and social traits.

A parent's personality has a strong impact on children. If a parent is happy and optimistic, for example, the child is more likely to be the same. Unfortunately, negative as well as positive traits can be passed along to children.

Certain personality traits in a parent can hurt children. The bad temper of a mother can scare them. If a father who is cold and distant withholds affection, the child may feel unloved. Parents need to examine their own personalities.

As you grow, you gain greater control over how your personality develops. You can take a close look at yourself and ask others you trust for suggestions. The person with a temper can learn to manage emotions. The person who doesn't show affection can work on being more expressive. Such improvements can benefit the entire family.

Internet Connects

http://www.mcgrawhill.ca/links/parenting
To learn more about ideas and issues on the well-being of Ontario's young people, go to the Web site above for *Parenting Rewards & Responsibilities, First Canadian Edition,* to see where to go next.

Feelings About Children

People who don't like children aren't good prospects for parents. Those who do like children have a built-in incentive to be good parents. Feelings about children, however, go beyond liking or disliking.

Beliefs about children and childhood influence the environment you create. Such beliefs include ideas about how children spend their early years. They include opinions about what children learn, and when, and what behaviour is reasonable. Your own memories of growing up will help you decide these and similar issues.

Parenting Values

What's important for good parenting? Would financial security be high on the list? Is spending time with children more important than making money? Is a good education needed for parenting? Answers to questions like these reveal your parenting values, or what you think is most important for parenting.

Raising Children With Character

A Change in Plans

Nisha peered out the screen door. Five-year-old Safa sat hunched on the steps outside, the backpack with her overnight clothes beside her. Nisha glanced at the clock. He was over a half hour late, and still Safa sat there waiting. Maybe he won't show up at all, Nisha thought, with a twinge of anger. It wouldn't be the first time.

Then she pulled a fruit juice bar from the freezer. Slipping up behind Safa, she thrust it before her. "Surprise!"

Safa took the treat with a half-hearted smile and began to pick at the paper. "I don't think Daddy's coming," she said forlornly.

Nisha was tired of making excuses, but she did her best to comfort her daughter. "Something must have happened," she said. "I think he'd be here if he could. Why don't we play a game while you wait? And if Daddy doesn't make it today, you can go with Raj and me on the hay wagon ride tonight. Raj is bringing Preeti. I'll bet she'd like some company."

Safa brightened, just briefly. "What if Daddy comes while we're gone?"

Nisha thought a moment. "We'll leave him a note," she said. "That way he'll know where to find you. Either way, we'll have a good time tonight."

◆◆◆◆◆ **Thinking It Over** ◆◆◆◆◆

1. What is Safa's father teaching her about trusting others?
2. Can Safa's mother build trust in the child despite what has happened? How?

Parenting Goals

A **goal** is a conscious target that requires planning and effort to reach. When Rosaline became a mother, she set a very clear goal. No one in her family had ever gone to college, and she wanted that opportunity for her daughter. Rosaline didn't wait to take action. She put a little money away in an education fund each month, and she also made sure that Sophie's schoolwork came before other activities.

As you can see, a parenting goal affects the way you parent. Having clear goals helps keep a person on track. They force you to think about where you're headed and what steps are needed to get there.

OUTSIDE INFLUENCES ON PARENTING

The shaping of a parent comes from outside forces as well as personal ones. All the experiences you are having now as you move toward adulthood are contributing to what you will be like if you parent.

Families and Culture

Everything about the way people live makes up their culture. Culture is linked to locations, religions, and ethnic heritage. The foods you eat, the language you speak, and the customs you follow are all part of your cultural background. The actions of a parent are deeply rooted in cultural experience.

Values and beliefs are also part of culture. Within a culture, each

As a parent, you inherit some traditions and create others. Either way, traditions help tie your family together. ◆ **What traditions besides Kwanza do parents use to teach their values and culture?**

generation teaches the next about educating and guiding children. Different cultures may follow different values. In some societies a preteen might have to care for the family's younger children, while in others a young person isn't given that responsibility. Many customs arise from needs and circumstances. Thus, one cultural approach differs but is not better than another.

Parents with different cultural backgrounds may have different approaches to discipline and to setting rules. For example, Old Order Mennonites feel that technology can distract individuals from their cultural beliefs. Children raised in this culture may be restricted from watching television. Cultural values also affect social behaviours towards children, such as touching, hugging, or kissing.

Economic Conditions

Economic conditions affect parenting on two levels—individual as well as social. People have some control over the first and less over the second.

Raising a child today is expensive. The strain of making financial ends meet can be hard on a parent. Some need to work two jobs, taking away time from the family. Two employed parents may have trouble getting everything done at home. No matter what their income level, parents can become discouraged or worried about bills.

Money is not the key to happiness, but it does offer security and opportunity. People who get a good job and learn how to manage their money well are less likely to have financial problems. Without serious financial worries, positive parenting is easier.

In society, economic changes can affect a family's finances. A healthy economy means people can buy more with their money. If that changes, consumers have to be more cautious. Those who barely get by may have problems. When companies close or downsize their workforce, incomes are lost. The impact can be serious.

People can try to be prepared for what may happen. Some want to have children when they are financially prepared. To get through emergencies, people can build a nest egg by regularly saving money. Families who live on less than their income may survive better if their income drops. Improving job skills gives people the chance to find a better job. A smart approach to financial matters helps parents meet their responsibilities as well as keep an upbeat attitude.

Financial circumstances affect parenting. While one parent might have the resources to provide ballet lessons for a child, another might encourage a child to join a school sports team. ◆ **What contributes to effective parenting in both situations?**

Social Policies

If a few students break the rules on the school grounds at lunch time, what might happen? The whole student body might be restricted to the building at noon. In society, there are examples that show how a few people can ruin things for the rest. The same principle applies to parenting.

Protective laws are enacted to ensure that parents live up to their responsibilities. Family-related laws cover such areas as domestic relations and violence, divorce, and child care. Although the laws aim to protect, people interpret the impacts differently. When this happens, controversy can arise.

The law prohibits excessive use of force on a child. This has led to controversy over the use of corporal punishment or spanking.

Parental Roles

Social change affects ideas about parenting. When Doug's grandparents were young, parenting duties were clearly divided by gender. Mothers provided daily child care, and fathers earned the family's income.

Doug saw the pattern change while he was in middle school. When his mother started working at a hospital, his parents began to share responsibilities. Doug's views on parenting were influenced by both the model he saw at home and the changing cultural trends and values. As a result, Doug and his wife share work and child-care responsibilities. Can you predict how Doug's involvement will someday affect his child's ideas on parenting?

Building Parenting Skills

PARENTING — A LEARNING PROCESS

When you consider parenting a learning process, you are open to other points of view. As a parent, you are flexible enough to explore new ideas and accept useful advice. You give children freedom and responsibility when the time is right. As the parent of two young children, Lee showed that he was open to learning when he:

▶ Attended a talk by a child-care expert whose methods seemed worth exploring.

▶ Listened to his friends' ideas on parenting, looking for tips that would help him.

▶ Agreed to take a family camping trip even though he had never camped before.

▶ Previewed a new television show before deciding whether it was suitable for his daughter.

▶ Let his son try out for youth basketball even though he thought the boy might be too short to compete.

◆ ◆ Your Thoughts ◆ ◆

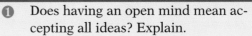

❶ Does having an open mind mean accepting all ideas? Explain.

❷ What would you do if your six-year-old wanted to take a gymnastics class, but you preferred a dance class?

❸ What would you do if your mother disagreed with some interesting advice you found in a reputable parenting book?

Theories

Three-year-old Omar was a challenge to his father. Omar took a long time to eat, get dressed, and put away toys, but he cried and fought if Jamal tried to help. Jamal read in a parenting magazine that a three-year-old needs a sense of accomplishment. Jamal then understood that Omar wanted to do things himself.

After that, Jamal allowed extra time for Omar to eat and get dressed, and he began to look for ways to make his son feel capable. Jamal pointed out success by saying things like, "You put on your own shirt! Way to go, son!" Gradually, Omar's behaviour and attitude began to improve.

This example shows how parenting is shaped by theory. What Jamal learned helped him understand his child better, and his approach to parenting changed.

THEORISTS. The chart on pages 44 and 45 surveys influential theorists in child development. Some of them lived years ago, when studying and promoting child development was just beginning as an organized field.

Each theory has its own unique beliefs and concepts. Sometimes theories are grouped together by similarities. Erikson and Piaget, for example, both developed theories based on the stages people go through as they develop. Erikson focused on the development of personality, while Piaget focused on the development of intellect.

As research continues, new theories are introduced. No one theory fully accounts for all behaviour. Instead, child development authorities use a combination of several theories—to explain children's behaviour.

AGES AND STAGES. To use theories, you must understand their terminology. Child development theories distinguish between *ages*, the length of a child's life at a given point in time, and *stages*, the periods of development that children go through as they mature. In this text, the age categories are:

- ♥ *Infant*. Birth to the first birthday.
- ♥ *Toddler*. Age one to the third birthday.
- ♥ *Preschooler*. Age three to the fifth birthday.
- ♥ *School-Age*. Age five to puberty.
- ♥ *Adolescent*. Puberty to adulthood.

Internet Connects

http://www.mcgrawhill.ca/links/parenting
To learn more about individual and family well-being, go to the Web site above for *Parenting Rewards & Responsibilities, First Canadian Edition*, to see where to go next.

Depending on their style, parents handle situations differently. ◆ **How might a parent react if a child wasn't doing as well as he should in school?**

Influential Theorists in Child Development

Erik Erikson (1902-1994)
Personality

Erikson was a German psychologist and lecturer at Harvard and Yale Universities. He refined Freud's ideas on personality development, and said human development unfolds naturally in eight stages, each with an emotional task to be mastered. A person who masters each stage and moves on to the next develops well emotionally. His approach offered a new view of development by looking at a wide range of influences on children's behaviour, including culture. His theory was weak in explaining how children moved from stage to stage.

Jean Piaget (1896-1980)
Intellect

A Swiss psychologist and educator, Piaget was interested in intellectual growth. He noticed how children first learn by using their five senses. Later, he saw how they use increasingly complex thought processes. Piaget described in detail the intellectual stages that children go through as their minds develop. His theory neglected the effects of emotions and culture on development, but his observations of children's behaviours were the basis of later research and discussion.

Urie Bronfenbrenner (1917-)
Human Development

Bronfenbrenner is an American psychologist and lecturer who believes that human development is strongly affected by the surrounding environment (e.g., school, home) as well as by settings that indirectly influence a person's life (e.g., the parents' workplace). Social interactions and cultural beliefs are important, and less attention is given to biology. Bronfenbrenner is concerned about the changes going on in the lives of children and families today and the effects.

Lev Vygotsky (1896-1934)
Social Learning

Vygotsky, a Russian psychologist and lecturer, stressed the role of social interaction in learning. To teach effectively, he believed, you must understand the child's social situation, as well as child development. Children learn when pushed to the level of learning that is one step beyond their current level. As language and thinking skills strengthen each other, they emerge together. His emphasis on social processes in development left only a minimal role for biological mechanisms such as genetics.

Lawrence Kohlberg (1927-1987)
Moral Reasoning

This American philosopher and educator studied moral development in children. He held that moral growth occurs in stages, as a child develops intellectually and socially. With more advanced thinking skills, children are better able to understand increasingly complex questions of right and wrong. Partly because Kohlberg's research didn't include females, experts are seeking more information about moral development.

Sigmund Freud (1856-1939)
Psychiatry

The founder of modern psychiatry, this Austrian physician theorized that childhood experiences, even when forgotten, affect a person's actions and personality as an adult. He also believed that the positive and negative sensory experiences infants associate with feeding and toilet-training affect personality.

Maria Montessori (1870-1952)
Education

Montessori, an Italian physician and educator, based her teaching methods on many of Piaget's theories. She stressed that practising motor skills helps children interact with their environment. Montessori believed that teachers must provide the right materials when children are ready to master particular skills. As self-motivated learners, children complete activities on their own. Montessori was one of the first educators to see the value of play in child development.

Robert Coles (1929-)
Moral Development

A professor of literature and social ethics at Harvard University, this American psychiatrist believes that the actions of parents shape moral character in children from birth. He also believes that moral development suffers if parents protect a child's self-esteem so much that they fail to teach clear principles of right and wrong.

B.F. Skinner (1904-1990)
Behaviour

An American psychologist and educator, Skinner supported the theory that development results from learned responses, and the environment is the chief influence on behaviour. Adults and children repeat behaviour that is rewarded and avoid behaviour that brings punishment or no reward. These principles have been used effectively by parents and teachers to address problem behaviours. In this approach, children have a passive role in their own development.

Albert Bandura (1925-)
Social Learning

This Canadian psychologist and educator believes that environment shapes behaviour and vice versa. As a social learning theorist, Bandura says children learn by observing and modelling others. Rewards don't produce learning but do cause children to show their learning. An important contribution is the idea that seeing others rewarded is as effective as being rewarded oneself. However, this approach does not specify how children's thinking changes over time.

T. Berry Brazelton (1918-)
Infant Development

This American physician and child psychiatrist created an assessment scale for newborns, which measures a baby's ability to respond to sounds, lights, and touch. Brazelton feels it is important to help parents better understand and interact with their children within their families. He stressed the value of focusing on an individual's strengths rather than on what they've done wrong.

J. Fraser Mustard (1927-)
Brain Development

Born in Toronto, this physician and founder of the Canadian Institute for Advanced Research co-authored a large study on the early development of young children. The study drew attention to important changes in brain development, learning, and behaviour in children under six. Mustard believes that community support for early childhood development has important benefits for society. His approach has been criticized for its emphasis on community resources without suggesting ways to improve parenting.

Developing a Parenting Style

Have you ever noticed how two parents may handle the same situation with children in different ways? You were noticing **parenting style**, the way a parent consistently interacts with children. A parenting style results from everything that influences a person's ideas about raising children.

Parenting style shows over time and includes all parent-child interaction. What does the parent expect of the child? What rules does the parent set and enforce? How does the parent respond to the child? These are a few of the elements that come together to make up parenting style.

DIFFERENT PARENTING STYLES

For the most part, parenting styles fall into three broad categories: authoritative, authoritarian, and permissive. As you read about these types, remember that most parents combine elements of each one, but a parent's overall style tends to be one of the three types.

Authoritative parenting is characterized by warmth, support, acceptance, and indirect positive control and guidance of children's behaviour. Guidelines are in place to help children learn to live in society. Guidelines are flexible to adapt to different situations. Authoritative parents whose child's bedtime guideline was 8 p.m. would allow their child to stay up later on special occasions.

Children raised with this style of parenting tend to be better adjusted socially and emotionally, and have a better self-concept.

Authoritarian parenting is characterized by strict discipline, more control by parents, and controlled emotions. Children's behaviour is managed through reward and punishment. Rules are much more rigid, and children are expected to follow them closely. Authoritarian parents whose child's bedtime rule was 8 p.m. would very rarely change the rule.

Children raised with this style of parenting may feel rejected by their parents. Often they have problems both socially and emotionally due to the lack of flexibility in their upbringing. When physical punishment turns to abuse, children suffer emotional consequences.

Permissive parenting is characterized by few rules and little parental control or guidance of children's behaviour. Children may control the family. Permissive parents often overindulge their children. Guidelines or rules seldom exist. Permissive parents would

When a parent uses the democratic style of parenting, the child has an opportunity to express ideas. ◆ **In what situations might a parent choose the democratic style?**

not have a set bedtime for their child; the child would go to bed on his or her own timeline.

Children raised with this style of parenting tend to be impulsive, irresponsible, and immature in their behaviour. They have not been taught to consider how their actions affect others.

Optimum parenting provides a balance between over-control and permissiveness. Children's behaviour needs to be guided, not stifled.

Barbara Coloroso's Parenting Styles

Barbara Coloroso is a renowned speaker and writer about parenting and raising children. Her lectures are filled with funny anecdotes that demonstrate important points about how to raise children. She is famous for her three styles of parenting and how they affect children. The following are her version of the styles and characteristics of each.

Brick Wall
- ♥ Hierarchy of control
- ♥ Litany of rigid rules, thou shalt nots, and don't you dares
- ♥ Rigid enforcement of rules
- ♥ Punishment imposed by adults
- ♥ Rigid rituals, rote learning
- ♥ Use of sarcasm, ridicule, and embarrassment to manipulate and control behaviour
- ♥ Threats and bribes are used extensively
- ♥ Relies on heavy competition
- ♥ Learning takes place in an atmosphere of fear
- ♥ Children learn love is highly conditional
- ♥ Children learn what to think and are easily manipulated

- ♥ High-risk group for sexual promiscuity, drug abuse, and suicide

Jellyfish
- ♥ Anarchy
- ♥ No recognizable structure, rules, or guidelines
- ♥ Punishment and rewards are arbitrary and inconsistent
- ♥ Mini-lectures and put-downs are typical tools
- ♥ Second chances are given often
- ♥ Threats and bribes are commonplace
- ♥ Learning takes place in an environment of chaos
- ♥ Emotions rule behaviour of parents and children
- ♥ Children learn love is highly conditional
- ♥ Children are easily led by peer influence
- ♥ High-risk group for sexual promiscuity, drug abuse, and suicide

Backbone
- ♥ Network of support is developed
- ♥ Democracy is learned through experience

- ♥ Provides an environment that is flexible and conducive to creative, constructive, and responsible activity
- ♥ Rules are simple and clearly stated
- ♥ Consequences are logical, realistic, and palatable
- ♥ Discipline with authority gives life to learning
- ♥ Motivates children to be all they can be
- ♥ Lots of smiles, hugs, and humour
- ♥ Provides second opportunities
- ♥ Learning takes place in an atmosphere of acceptance and high expectation
- ♥ Children learn to accept their own feelings and control their own behaviour
- ♥ Encourages competency and co-operativeness
- ♥ Love is unconditional
- ♥ Teaches children how to think
- ♥ Buffers students from sexual promiscuity, drug abuse, and suicide by reinforcing the messages "I like myself," "I can think for myself," and "There is no problem so great it can't be solved."

Source: Coloroso, B. (1989). *Winning at Parenting—without beating your kids.* Littleton, Colorado: Kids are worth it!

IDENTIFYING PARENTING STYLES

A comparison will show you how each parenting style works. Eight-year-old Claire received some money as a gift and wanted to spend it. The toy she had in mind seemed like a waste of money to her mother. Depending on her parenting style, Claire's mother might choose one of the responses below. Which style does each response most reflect?

- ♥ "I know that toy seemed fun at Nickie's house, but it doesn't look very sturdy. We'll go to the store so you can see other toys you'll like just as much. I think we can agree on something that makes good use of Grandma's money."

- ♥ "No, that's not a good way to use your money. I want you to save half of what Grandma gave you. You may spend the rest on something else."

♥ "You may buy what you like with your money. It's up to you."

The first response shows the authoritative style. Claire's mother considered the child's wishes but made it clear that the final decision would be made with parental input. The second response is an example of authoritarian style. The mother made the decision. The last example depicts the permissive style. Claire's mother left the decision to her.

MAKING PARENTING STYLES WORK

As a parent, which of the three styles do you think would suit you? Certain principles can help you make a style work:

♥ *Choose a style that feels right for you*. You will be more effective doing what makes you comfortable.

♥ *Consider the child's personality*. A child who has a high degree of self-control might be a good candidate for permissive parenting. A shy child who is frightened by a strongly authoritarian parent may gain confidence from the limited freedom of the authoritative style.

♥ *Use each style in moderation*. The authoritarian parent, for example, doesn't need to make every decision for a child. How will children learn to think and act on their own if not given chances to do so? Eventually, they may rebel. Children raised too permissively, on the other hand, can easily get into situations they are not ready to handle.

♥ *Identify areas where two parents' styles conflict*. If parents have different styles, they still need areas of agreement. Young children, especially, may be confused if parents react differently in the same situation.

Blending Styles

By blending styles, parents adapt their actions to the situation. When dealing with children of different ages, parents may need to change styles. Josie and Frank tucked their six-year-old in bed promptly at eight o'clock, as they did every night. Later they asked their 12-year-old for ideas on how to spend a family vacation. Which two styles do their actions reflect?

Any parenting style a person uses works best when combined with positive parenting skills. You'll read about many of these in the "Building Parenting Skills" feature throughout this text. ◆ **What positive qualities do you think this father combines with his style of parenting?**

Parents may use different styles with the same child. For example, a parent might allow a child to make food choices at home, when only healthful foods are available. At a fast-food restaurant, however, where some choices are less nutritious, the parent might expect the child to pick from only certain items.

Being Predictable

Blending parenting styles is a useful technique, as long as a parent doesn't change styles suddenly and without thinking. When feeling stressed, one parent became very authoritarian and controlling. Another was uncharacteristically permissive after a good day at work.

Children need to know what to expect from parents. Otherwise, they feel uncertain about what may happen. They lose confidence in the parent, as well as respect. Children may learn to take advantage of situations.

Forming a Parenting Philosophy

"If you don't know where you're going, you might wind up someplace else." This saying is worth remembering as you study parenting.

Everything you learn about parenting will help shape your thinking. As your ideas come together, you will form a "parenting philosophy," a set of beliefs that describe your approach to raising children. Your philosophy might be expressed in a statement that begins, "I believe that a parent should..." or "To me, parenting means..." This philosophy will guide you. Being true to these beliefs and values will help you wind up where you want to be as a parent, and not "someplace else."

Internet Connects

http://www.mcgrawhill.ca/links/parenting
To learn more about parenting from A to Z, go to the Web site above for *Parenting Rewards & Responsibilities, First Canadian Edition,* to see where to go next.

Some people put their parenting philosophy into action— even though they've never put it into words. ◆ **Is part of this father's philosophy showing? How? What are the advantages to writing a philosophy of parenting?**

Review

Looking Back

♥ Both personal and outside factors affect a person's approach to parenting.

♥ Many theories exist to explain how children develop in different areas. They influence how children are raised.

♥ Three basic parenting styles are usually used by parents.

♥ Parenting styles can be blended, but should be used in ways that don't confuse children.

♥ Your approach to parenting is your parenting philosophy.

Knowledge and Understanding

1. What personal influences are likely to affect the way a person parents?
2. Why is setting goals an important part of parenting?
3. What are five outside factors that influence a person's parenting style?
4. Why does society make laws that affect families?
5. Is a three-year-old considered a toddler or a preschooler?
6. How does personality—the parent's and the child's—play a role in choosing which parenting style to use?
7. Can a parent be too permissive or too authoritarian? What could happen?
8. Why is being predictable an important trait for parents?

Review

Thinking and Inquiry

9. What personality traits do you think might interfere with effective parenting? How difficult would it be to change these traits?

10. Do you think having an adequate income makes the job of parenting easier? Why or why not?

11. Based on your own observations, do you feel that males and females parent in a different manner? Explain your answer.

12. Find a book or Web site that offers advice on parenting. Read the advice given. Which style of parenting is being suggested? Explain your answer.

13. Compare the theories of three of the different authorities on parenting discussed in the chapter. Discuss the strengths and weaknesses of each one.

Communication

14. Write a scenario where a child misbehaves. Then write three different solutions to the scenario, one showing the authoritative style of parenting, one showing the authoritarian style of parenting, and one showing the permissive style of parenting.

15. Describe your personal parenting philosophy. Write a 100-word essay explaining how you would approach parenting in your future.

16. Which parenting style do you think you would use? Explain why.

Application

17. With a group of classmates, compare how parents might apply the three parenting styles in the following situations: (a) a three-year-old refuses to eat peas; (b) a six-year-old wants to ride the new two-wheeled bike around the block, out of the parents' sight; (c) a thirteen-year-old wants to go to a party with some older teens.

18. List each parenting style. Suggest personality traits in a parent and child that suit each style. Explain your reasoning.

19. Suppose you have a six-year-old who announces at the supper table: "Jaime's whole family is flying on a plane to Mexico this summer. They just got to go to Florida too. It's not fair. Why don't we ever get to go anywhere?" Your four-year-old pipes up with the same question. Money is much tighter in your family than in Jaime's. How would you respond? Which parenting style does your response most resemble?

Changing Roles of Parents

CHAPTER EXPECTATIONS

While reading this chapter, you will:

▶ Identify what parents bring to their role from their own family background and past experiences.

▶ Identify and describe the responsibilities parents have for children of different ages.

▶ Summarize the lifestyle and relationship changes that parents experience when raising children.

▶ Compare the changing roles of parents and children as both grow older.

▶ Determine the personal qualities, skills, and experience you perceive as necessary for parenting.

KEY TERMS

adoptive family	nuclear family
blended family	role
diplomacy	single-parent
extended family	family
foster family	stepparent

"**D**ad," Luke asked his father as they made dinner, "when you marry Lisa, will she be my real mom?"

Mark had been wondering when he would have to answer that question. Luke barely knew his mother. Mark had had sole custody of Luke for most of his seven years. "What do you think, Luke? What does a real mom do?"

Luke looked thoughtful. "Well... she takes you to school... and makes you clean up... and goes camping with you... and to the store. Kip's mom plays ball with him sometimes."

"Lisa does some of those things with us already," Mark pointed out, "and Grandma used to do them with me when I was little. So it sounds like Lisa is kind of a mom already. And I know she loves you; she told me so. That's what moms do most of all."

Luke fell silent, and Mark wondered if he understood. Finally Luke asked, "Should I call her mom?"

"Do you want to?" Mark asked. Seeing Luke's thoughtful frown, he said, "I know—that's a hard question. It can wait. I don't think Lisa cares what you call her. She just wants us to be a family, and I do too."

———————◆———————

What do you think? How has Luke determined what a mother's role should be?

Children need parents who are good role models. That means wearing many different hats within the family. This father is acting as a teacher. ◆ **What other roles does he have while raising his son?**

A Parent's Role

As a student, what do people expect of you? To come to class? To complete assignments and contribute to discussions? Those duties are part of a student's **role**, the behaviours expected in a certain social relationship. For every role you have, whether a son or daughter, sister or brother, volunteer, or team member, you have responsibilities to fulfill.

The same is true of parenting. Society counts on parents to do what they are supposed to do. They must guide, manage, and provide loving care for their family.

Guiding a Family

Thanks to the work of good leaders, society operates as it should. Leaders guide groups, keeping their purpose in mind and directing the group toward goals. They look out for the group's best interests. The most important decisions are often made by leaders.

Leadership is as important to a family as to a nation or corporation. Parents show family leadership by making decisions based on their values, even when children may not agree. Parents who provide good guidance have clear rules, procedures, and structures for their children. They provide explanations to their children, so they understand the reasoning behind the rules. At times, parenting means consulting all members in the family to reach decisions and guide children.

Good parents know that you can't do everything alone. For advice and support, many parents turn to their **extended family**, all their immediate relatives, including grandparents, aunts, uncles, and cousins. Extended family members can offer the insights of several generations and a wide range of life experience and learning.

PARENTING IN DIFFERENT FAMILY TYPES

The parenting styles you read about in the last chapter affect the way parents lead. An authoritarian parent, for example, leads more forcefully than a permissive parent does. The form of a family also influences how a parent parents. Families are different—in size and in how people and relationships combine. Depending on the form, parenting may be handled by one or more people and responsibilities may be divided differently.

Nuclear Families

A family with a husband, wife, and one or more biological or adopted children is called a **nuclear family**. Believing that "two heads are better than one," many couples today prefer to handle most parenting tasks together. Discussing a situation allows them to examine an issue from several angles before reaching agreement.

In some households, however, one parent makes most major decisions alone. In still other families, each parent takes responsibility for certain areas, usually depending on skills or preferences. For example, since Danielle is a good money manager, she handles the finances. Her husband, Carl, likes to cook, so he does all the grocery shopping.

Parenting Q & A

Finding Role Models

Q "Ever since my wife died, I've worried about my daughter not having a female role model. I'm not ready to remarry, but doesn't she need to be around a woman she can identify with?" *Tristan*

A Finding positive role models is a concern for all parents, but especially for those without partners. Girls *and* boys need to see how adults interact on a regular basis. You're right that they need role models of their own gender to learn behaviours and attitudes that become part of their identity. Other family members may already be filling this need for your daughter, especially those who spend a lot of time with her. If parents don't provide models, children may find negative ones on their own. Neighbours, family friends, coaches, caregivers, and other reliable people in child-related fields are possible role models.

Building Parenting Skills

PARENTING WITH CO-OPERATION

Co-operation is doing your part to reach a common goal and working with others to make the job easier for everyone. Parents need to co-operate with spouses, teachers, and others who help them care for and nurture their children. As a divorced mother of two, Miranda showed a co-operative spirit when she:

- Worked with her former husband to set up a time when their children could go on a short trip with him.

- Agreed to watch her brother and sister-in-law's children in exchange for watching hers.

- Took turns driving in her son's carpool with the parents of his three teammates.

- Followed the doctor's directions carefully when giving her son prescription medicine.

- Tried out several suggestions from her daughter's teacher for sparking an interest in reading.

Your Thoughts

❶ Why is co-operation between parents especially important?

❷ How can co-operation help parents who are divorcing and working out the custody arrangements for a four-year-old?

Single-Parent Families

When one or more children live in a household headed by one parent, a **single-parent family** exists. These families may result from divorce. Never-married people may become parents through birth or adoption. Other parents are left single by the desertion or death of a spouse.

Parenting in the single-parent family is usually handled by one person. Some responsibilities may be shared with a parent who doesn't live in the household. For instance, one divorced father, though he lives apart from his children, helps his teen son study for algebra tests and drives his daughter to her weekly piano lesson.

Blended Families

The household of a **blended family** contains a couple and one or more children from a previous relationship. If not biologically related to a child in the family, the parent is called a **stepparent**. A parent may have other children who live elsewhere, often with the other parent.

Parenting in a blended family can be handled as it is in a nuclear family. In a blended family, however, those parents outside the home typically also have input, especially when children spend time in both parents' households.

There are special challenges faced by parents in blended families to ensure the well-being of all children. Good communication is needed by all parents involved, both stepparents and biological parents.

Foster Families

Children who cannot live with their parents may live in a **foster family**. Parents in a foster family household care for children on a temporary basis, from a few hours up to several years. They provide a stable home environment to support the child's development. Family members work as a team with government agencies to meet the needs of the foster child.

Adoptive Families

The household of an **adoptive family** includes children who have become a permanent part of the family through legal processes. Adoptions may be arranged through government, private, or international agencies. Adoptions of relatives may be arranged through the courts. Parents in adoptive families may face unique challenges when children are older, from other countries, or have special needs.

Internet Connects

http://www.mcgrawhill.ca/links/parenting
To learn more about individual and family well-being, go to the Web site above for *Parenting Rewards & Responsibilities, First Canadian Edition,* to see where to go next.

BUILDING PARENTING SKILLS

Imagine you and two friends want to rent a video. One friend likes action adventure movies, the other enjoys romances, and you're in the mood for a classic comedy. Your friends ask you to "get something we like." How long do you think it will take to find a movie that pleases everyone?

Parents face similar situations. They have to consider the interests and opinions of each member, but they still have to take action. To balance authority with involving others, parents build and use helpful skills. Three important skills are described here.

Using Effective Communication

Good communication goes hand-in-hand with good parenting. Parents provide avenues for communication. Will family members leave notes on a bulletin board? Can someone be reached by phone or e-mail at work? Would family meetings be useful? A strong parent makes sure that everyone has the means to communicate when necessary.

Parents should also aim for clear understanding. Suppose your spouse announced one morning before work, "Callie's cold has gotten a lot worse." Does that statement mean *"One of us* has to stay home with her today" or *"You* need to stay home with her today"? What might happen if you misinterpret the message?

Part of building a strong family is making sure that family life is rich with joy and good feelings. ◆ **How can parents find simple everyday ways like the one shown here to fulfill that need?**

Effective parents follow the principle, "say what you mean, and mean what you say." They state facts clearly and express feelings honestly. They also practice other good communication skills, such as making eye contact and staying calm during a disagreement.

Using Diplomacy

Good parenting is more than giving directions to others. How you put words together makes a difference.

Successful parents use **diplomacy** (duh-PLOH-muh-see), tact, and skill in dealing with others. They practise diplomacy by showing respect. They listen and think before speaking. In addition, they choose words that won't be offensive.

For example, how diplomatic is Andre if he makes this comment to five-year-old William: "You always want to wear that ugly shirt. It doesn't even match. Don't you have any sense?" Using diplomacy, Andre might say, "Your green shirt would look great with those brown pants. I'll bet Grandpa would like to see you in that outfit."

Making Decisions

Making decisions just for yourself is one thing, but making them for an entire family is quite another. Family decisions seem endless. "Where can I get the best price on baby food?" "How do I get my four-year-old to stop drawing on the walls?" "How do I convince my spouse to control anger?"

Parents can't turn away from decison making, although sometimes they wish they could. Families need parents who settle issues with skill and confidence. They recognize the best options, so they aren't afraid to take action.

Making decisions in the family setting is easier if you have first practised making them for yourself. Chapter 5 explains a useful decision-making process. You can use it now to prepare for a role in parenting.

Internet Connects

http://www.mcgrawhill.ca/links/parenting
To learn more about parenting from A to Z, go to the Web site above for *Parenting Rewards & Responsibilities, First Canadian Edition,* to see where to go next.

Parents can't lead without making decisions. Sometimes they take charge and make decisions alone. At other times, they allow children to have a say in what will happen. ◆ **Which type of situation is this?**

THROUGH THE FAMILY LIFE CYCLE

Does a parent ever "retire" from the job? Unlike an elected official, a parent's "term of office" lasts indefinitely. The duties change, however, as the family moves through the family life cycle. This cycle describes a basic pattern of stages typically followed by a family with children. Each stage has different parenting challenges.

Beginning Stage

Two people marry and learn to live together as a couple during the beginning stage of the family life cycle. They strengthen their relationship as they make decisions together about education, careers, the home, and about having children. Since these decisions will affect any children in their future, they are already acting as future parents.

Raising Children With

Character

A Matter of Values

Paul was looking over the selection at the video rental store when his son Riley hurried up to him. "This is the one," he said excitedly, holding out the video in his hand. "I want to see this one."

Paul looked at the title in dismay. The movie had been a big hit. From the publicity and from talking with other parents, however, Paul had decided that it was not for his family.

"I'm sorry, Riley. This is a very violent movie. You know how your mom and I feel about that. We don't watch that stuff, and we don't want you to either."

"But, Dad," Riley pleaded, "all the kids at school have seen it."

Paul shook his head. "Sorry, fella. I've made up my mind. Let's find something else."

Riley scowled. "I don't *want* something else," he muttered.

Paul shrugged good-naturedly. "Well, you don't *have* to get a video. Maybe tonight would be a good time to start on that book you got at the library."

◆◆◆◆◆ **Thinking It Over** ◆◆◆◆◆

1. What pressures did Paul feel to give in to his son's wishes?
2. Why did Paul act on his beliefs?
3. Why do some parents decide to watch questionable videos with their child?

Parenting Stage

In this lengthy stage, the couple have children and help them grow to independence. Strong parenting skills are critical as children move from infancy, to childhood, and to adolescence.

The demands on parents change as a child grows. They are totally responsible for an infant and continue to make most decisions for a very young child. Gradually, parents let children assume more personal responsibility and make simple decisions themselves.

Throughout adolescence, teens are given more freedom as they move closer to adulthood. Parents still need to be there to provide guidance and support for their children in the many challenges they face at this point in their lives.

No matter what age the child is, parenting is very demanding. Childhood is a time of rapid growth and influential events. A parent's guidance is critical. The more they learn about parenting, the more skilled they become. Most parents do their best to be wise and responsible.

Midlife

Sometime during middle age, parents may have to adjust to a home without children. The "empty nest" used to be a common stage in the middle-age period of adult life, beginning as young as the early forties. Now, as couples fulfill educational and career goals before having children, this stage can range from early forties to mid- to late fifties. Children now often leave home and then return to the parents' home for support for short periods of time. Such children are sometimes called "boomerang" children.

After the children have been raised and are independent, couples may have more time and energy for their relationship, careers, and community involvement. Parenting doesn't end, but it may become easier.

Parents are frequently asked for advice and support as their children start careers, marry, and renew the family life cycle. Grandparenting becomes a joy of many.

As the population lives longer, many people find extra years added to midlife. The image of grandparents is changing to one of vital, active adults.

Retirement

By the time parents reach retirement age, their children usually have less need for their

Middle age can be a wonderful time for a couple. If child responsibilities are behind them, they can turn their energy and finances in other directions. ◆ **How do middle-age couples you know handle life? Are some still linked to child raising? Why?**

guidance. Even so, their role as parent does not end. Years of experience have given them something valuable that others can use—wisdom. Now, instead of making the decisions, they advise and counsel.

Leaving a career behind, parents may enjoy more leisure time. They may be able to help with grandchildren, becoming role models and leaders for a new generation.

Variations of the Life Cycle

The family life cycle describes a basic pattern of how families grow and recreate themselves. Fewer families today, however, follow the stages straight through from beginning to end. You've probably seen many exceptions to the rule: couples who never have children; adult children who return to live at home; grandparents who raise grandchildren. What other variations can you think of?

MORAL GUIDANCE

Parents, with the help of schools and religious organizations, are raising the employees, business owners, politicians, professionals, and parents of the future. Most children grow to be honest, helpful, and productive citizens. Unfortunately, however, incidents of vandalism, hatred, and crime are all evidence of moral problems in society. Younger and younger children are increasingly involved in problem behaviour.

Even though parents are not always to blame when a child "goes bad," a growing number of citizens want parents to be accountable for the actions of their children. That sends a strong message to those who plan to parent. If you're going to have children, you need to raise them to be

As you see here, moral guidance shows in obvious ways in some family activities. Sometimes, however, it's more subtle. ◆ **What are some subtle ways that parents teach moral principles?**

responsible people. Otherwise, society may someday ask you, as a parent, to pay a price. What responsibilities do parents have for their children's actions?

What Can Parents Do?

Parents can promote morality first through role modelling. Parents can't expect children to be different from the examples they see around them. Suppose Glen becomes angry when his daughter lies about breaking a lamp, but then he talks about cheating on his income tax. What message does that send to his daughter?

A child can be influenced by many things in life, but parents are the strongest influence overall. Children develop a sense of right and wrong when they see these principles at work in their parents' lives.

Managing Family Life

Besides leaders, many successful companies have managers who organize and oversee tasks so that work gets done. In the family, parents are both leaders *and* managers.

Effective parenting is impossible without good management skills. Sandeep and Darshan, the employed parents of a five-year-old, have learned to manage despite Darshan's sales job that takes him out of town several days at a time. When he is gone, Sandeep has full responsibility for Anis. When he is home, Darshan takes care of her.

Likewise, where parents live will have an impact on managing family life. For example, John is a single parent of eight-year-old Brianna. His ex-wife, Martha, lives an hour away. The distance prevents Martha from seeing Brianna daily.

Successful family management is more than child care, however. Parent-managers attend to the physical and emotional health of family members. They set up a budget to make sure expenses can be met. They co-ordinate the schedules of all family members. They set goals and help settle conflicts.

As you can see, family management is a complex business. Chapter 25 has more on this topic. There you'll read about how parents can identify resources and use the management process. You'll look at ways that parents balance work and family life. They can put you on the road to becoming a skillful family manager someday.

Internet Connects

http://www.mcgrawhill.ca/links/parenting
To learn more about National Child Benefit, child care and families, and inter-country adoption services, go to the Web site above for *Parenting Rewards & Responsibilities, First Canadian Edition*, to see where to go next.

Can you parent well without knowing management skills? Not likely. ◆ **Why will management skills be especially important for this mother?**

Providing for a Family

What comes to mind when you hear a parent described as "a good provider"? A person who works hard to pay for things the family needs and wants? Someone who plans and invests for the future?

Financial stability is only part of providing for a family. As a parent, you must also take care of your child's emotional and intellectual needs in order to raise a healthy, well-adjusted person.

MASLOW'S THEORY ON NEEDS

Psychologist Abraham Maslow developed a theory that shows the importance of meeting children's needs. Maslow's Hierarchy of Human Needs is illustrated by the pyramid below.

Maslow believed that people must meet basic physical needs before they can deal with other needs. To understand his theory, begin at the base of the pyramid and move upward. Suppose a young child is often hungry and doesn't feel safe. The child will probably have trouble relating well to others. If social needs are not met, the child may not develop a good sense of self-worth. Certainly, reaching potential isn't likely.

With parental help, children can become adults who feel successful, content, optimistic, and enthusiastic. By helping children in the many ways described throughout this course, parents hope to give children the best possible chance for reaching the highest level of the pyramid.

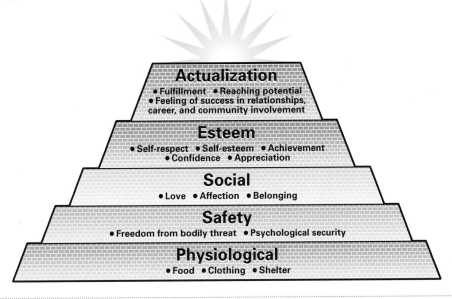

Maslow's Hierarchy of Human Needs

Actualization
- Fulfillment • Reaching potential
- Feeling of success in relationships, career, and community involvement

Esteem
- Self-respect • Self-esteem • Achievement
- Confidence • Appreciation

Social
- Love • Affection • Belonging

Safety
- Freedom from bodily threat • Psychological security

Physiological
- Food • Clothing • Shelter

Each level in Maslow's pyramid indicates needs that people have. Beginning at the bottom, the needs at each level must be met before those on the next higher level can be realized. ◆ **What can parents do to meet a child's needs at each level of the pyramid?**

Electronic Babies

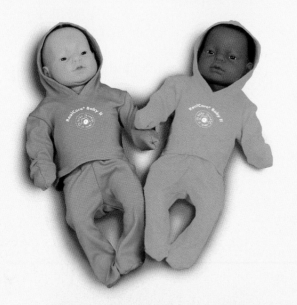

RealCare Babies from the "Baby Think It Over" program are computerized dolls that can be used to simulate a real baby. Each doll weighs close to 3.1 kg (7 lbs), about what an average newborn weighs. It measures about 53 cm (21 in.) long. These dolls come in different skin tones, and look and feel very realistic. On first glance, they might even be mistaken for an actual baby.

The doll is programmed to fuss, cry, and make cooing sounds. A teen looking after this "baby" must provide constant care for a period of time set by the teacher. Like a real baby, the doll requires feeding, burping, diapering, and rocking. The assigned "parent" wears a wristband with an electronic sensor that is detected by the doll. A control unit records how well the student is caring for the simulated baby. Teens may also keep a journal and discuss their experiences with their class.

The computerized doll helps teens find out what it's like to look after a real baby. Teens discover what effect an infant has on their daily routines and how their social life changes. In a study at the University of Windsor, researchers found that, after caring for simulated infants, teenaged girls had a better understanding of the changes in thinking and emotions that go along with becoming a parent.

"Just be there for me." If a child had any message for a parent, this might be at the top of the list. Parents who make time for their children are performing a critical role of parenting.

More Than Economics

You've already read about the high expense of raising a child. Even parents with a comfortable income may think of what more money could provide for their children. As Maslow's pyramid confirms, however, providing what a child needs cannot be supplied with money alone.

Look again at the pyramid. How many of the levels rely on money? Certainly the lower-level needs do—food, clothing, housing, and other essentials. On every higher level, though, money is less critical. In fact, it can actually interfere with meeting a need. Parents who rely too heavily on money often overlook the fact that some needs are better met in other ways.

When Needs Conflict

When the needs of a parent and child conflict, what should a parent do? Remember that happy, fulfilled parents are more likely to raise happy, well-adjusted children. Parents who put every need of the child before their own may eventually wear down. By paying attention to their own needs and interests, parents help children see that others have rights too. That's a good message to send to children.

On the other hand, parents are responsible for the children they bring into the world. A parent's right to a personal life is never an excuse to neglect a child's needs. Rather, parents need to find a balance that allows them to consider what is important to each family member.

Rights and Responsibilities

In a sense, parenting is like a contract. When you become a parent, you agree to lead, manage, and provide for your family. By committing to raise a healthy family, you help strengthen society.

If parents live up to the responsibilities of their "contract," what can they expect in return? For the sake of families, many parents today are speaking out for certain parental rights. They want safe schools, family-friendly employment policies, and legislation that improves the quality of family life. How can parents draw attention to their concerns? Here are some ideas:

♥ Ask for flexibility on the job to meet children's needs and be a more effective employee.

♥ Stay informed about laws and regulations that affect families. Write letters to newspapers and politicians, attend public meetings, and join supportive groups.

♥ Vote for candidates who will work to protect the needs of families.

More than ever before, people are realizing that family life suffers without societal support. Parents are discovering common concerns. With the power of their combined voices, parents can make a difference in the condition of families.

When you have a child, make a commitment to parenting. Earning the love and admiration of your child can make you proud to be a parent.

Review

Looking Back

♥ The most important role of a parent is to lead the family.

♥ There are different forms of families: nuclear, single-parent, blended, foster, and adoptive.

♥ Effective communication, diplomacy, and decision-making skills are necessary components of being a good parent.

♥ The family life cycle describes the basic stages that many families go through, although the stages can vary for individual families.

♥ Parents are role models for their children's moral development.

♥ Using management skills can help a family run smoothly.

♥ Maslow's Hierarchy of Human Needs maintains that basic needs have to be met before higher-level needs can be reached.

♥ Many parents believe that fulfilling their responsibilities earns them certain rights.

Knowledge and Understanding

1. What is Billy's family form called if he lives with his mother, stepfather, and stepbrother?
2. How does parenting in a family differ between a nuclear family and a single-parent family?
3. Describe three important skills needed when parenting.
4. Create your own example of a parent using diplomacy with a child.
5. Which stage of the family life cycle generally lasts the longest? Which stage do you think is the most demanding and why?
6. Mike and Elsa's first child was born on their twelfth wedding anniversary. How is their life likely to be different from the model of the family life cycle?
7. Why is setting a good example such an important part of parenting?
8. What management tasks does a parent need to accomplish?
9. If you become a parent someday, how would you go about addressing each of the needs in Maslow's theory?
10. Why should parents avoid focusing only on their children?

Review CHAPTER **4**

Thinking and Inquiry

11. What might make parenting especially challenging in a blended family? How can the challenge be managed?

12. Single-parent families are sometimes called "broken homes." Is this term accurate? What does it imply? What term would you find more appropriate? Why?

13. Mrs. Krusinski makes her belief known that women should stay home to raise their children. Her volunteer commitments require her to have a babysitter almost every day. Comment on the relationship between her belief and her behaviour.

14. Make a list of "parents' rights." Compare your list to those of your classmates.

15. How is the role of a parent like that of a leader and a manager? Use examples to support your answer.

16. Describe three ways in which new parents can build their parenting skills.

Communication

17. Starting next month, suppose your spouse must work one night a week. Your spouse's community group meeting is already a weekly commitment, as is hockey on Wednesday evenings. You view this amount of time away from family as a problem. How would you express your concern diplomatically? Write a dialogue to show how you would handle this situation.

18. Write a Want Ad for a parent, including a description of the characteristics they bring to parenting, the different roles parents play, responsibilities they have, and rewards of the job.

19. Create a poster to represent the life cycle of a parent, noting the different demands, roles, and responsibilities at various stages of the life cycle.

Application

20. Suppose your ten-year-old is in trouble with the law for destroying property on the school grounds. The authorities are acting as though you are at fault. How does this make you feel and what will you do? Write a one-page discussion of your feelings.

21. Choose one of these family issues and tell how you would promote it in society: a children's hour on network television; making it harder for children to rent an R-rated movie; priority seating on buses for pregnant women and parents with small children; pre-marital counselling for all couples; higher salaries for child-care professionals.

22. Write a skit showing two different ways that parents act as role models for their children. One should be a positive behaviour, while the other should be a negative behaviour. Perform the skit for your classmates.

Chapter 4 Changing Roles of Parents   **69**

CHAPTER 5

Personal Readiness

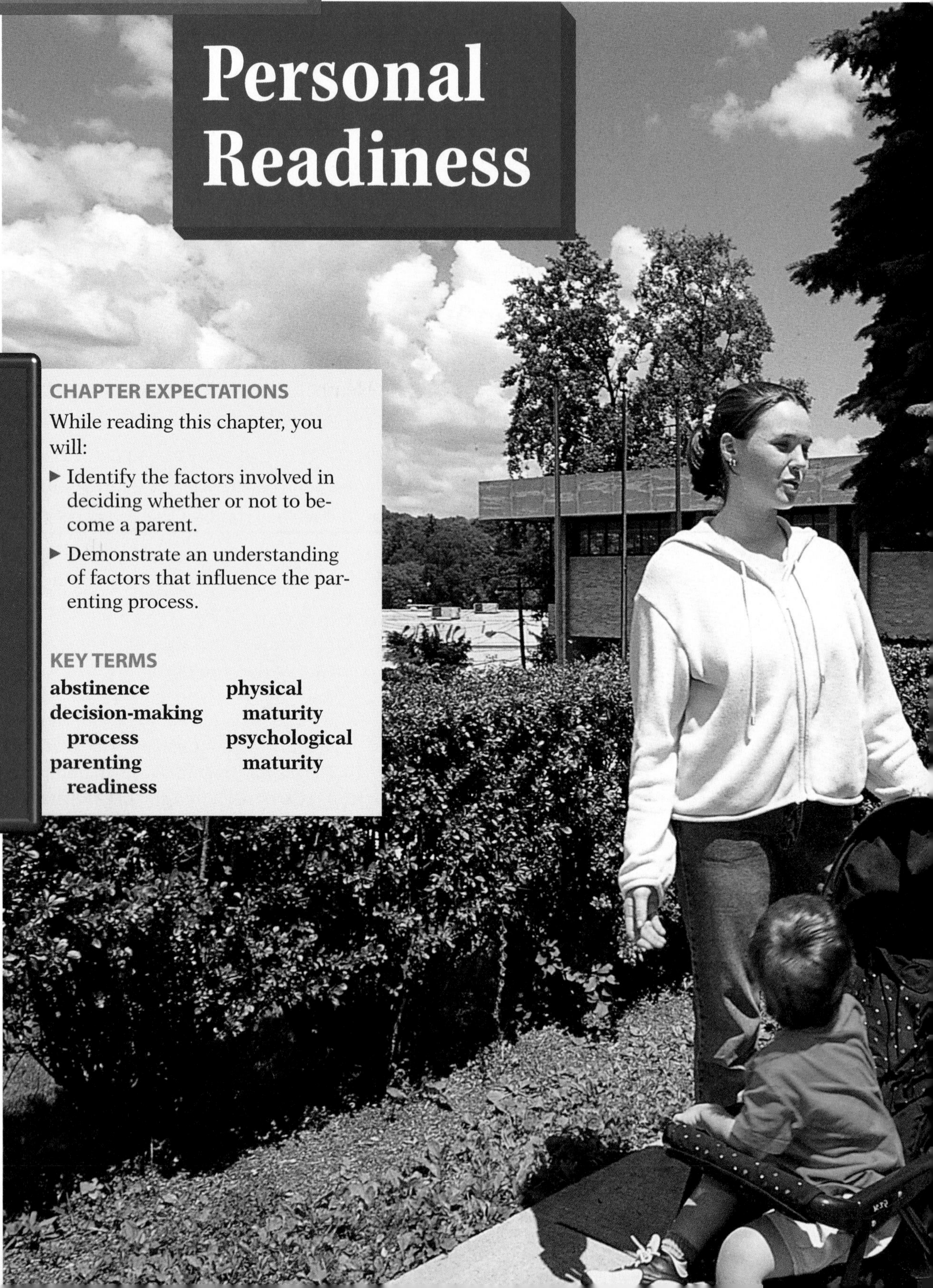

CHAPTER EXPECTATIONS

While reading this chapter, you will:

- Identify the factors involved in deciding whether or not to become a parent.
- Demonstrate an understanding of factors that influence the parenting process.

KEY TERMS

abstinence
decision-making process
parenting readiness
physical maturity
psychological maturity

"Could that be Heather?" Julia thought, her eyes on the young woman pushing a baby stroller toward her. "Julia, hi!" Heather called out in recognition. "How are you? It's been so long."

"Over three years since graduation," Julia replied. "Your little boy's not a baby anymore."

"That's for sure," Heather responded. "And he's a handful."

"Are you still in school?" Julia asked.

Heather looked down. "No, I . . . uh . . . dropped out during my second year at university. We just couldn't afford it. David's still taking classes—as much as he can. He has to put in so many hours at work, and he's not happy with his job. We don't see him much, but if he can finish school and get something different, it'll be worth it. Then we'll be able to afford a bigger apartment."

"But you were really interested in graphic arts, Heather. And you have so much talent. Couldn't you . . . ?"

"Not now," Heather interrupted. "Working part-time at Canadian Tire is all I can handle. Maybe someday, but nothing's as simple as it used to be. Things change, you know."

Things do change, Julia thought as they parted a few minutes later, but at least I have some control over that. I know I do.

◆

What do you think? Often people learn lessons from the experiences of others. What has Julia learned from Heather?

Many people eagerly look forward to becoming grandparents after their own children are grown. ◇ **What should a couple say if their parents urge them to have a child before they are ready?**

Choosing to Parent

Few decisions affect a person's life more than deciding whether and when to become a parent. That's why this decision deserves careful thought.

THE WRONG REASONS

People have children for many reasons, but not all of them make good sense. Some are based on myths, misinformation, and faulty logic, as you can see here:

♥ **To prove adulthood.** Once they reach puberty, most people are physically capable of having a child. There is nothing adult, however, about becoming a parent before you can take on the personal and financial responsibilities of adulthood.

♥ **To please someone else.** Chandra's mother and stepfather couldn't wait to become grandparents. Jenny's boyfriend insisted that a baby would be a symbol of their love for each other. Fortunately, neither Chandra nor Jenny was convinced that the time was right for motherhood. People must live life their own way and at a pace comfortable for them.

♥ **For emotional benefits.** Having someone to love and to love you back might sound appealing, but it should never be the motivation for having a child.

♥ **For respect and status.** "People pay attention to mothers and fathers. If I become a parent, I'll be treated with respect, not like some kid," Corey thought. People with such ideas learn quickly that respect has to be earned.

The right time to have a child is a personal decision. ◆ **Why is having a child because your friends do a risky idea?**

♥ *To escape a situation.* Veronica wanted to change her life and move out of her alcoholic parents' home. Jill felt tied down by spending 40 hours a week at a job she didn't like. Obviously, having a baby would be a drastic "solution" for either young woman.

♥ *Because society expects it.* "It's instinctive to want children," Diana thought. "So why don't I feel that way?" Not all people want to parent. They find other ways to feel fulfilled. Some couples are physically unable to have children, but many other satisfied people are childless by choice.

♥ *To improve a floundering relationship.* Studies have indicated over and over that bringing a child into a troubled marriage is more likely to put additional strain on the relationship rather than improve it.

♥ *To be like "everyone else."* Having friends who are parents doesn't make it the right time for you. Many couples are choosing to delay parenthood until they are older and better established. In 2001, one-third of women giving birth to their first child were 30 years or older. Ten years before, only one-fifth of first births were to women in this age group.

Having children for reasons like these isn't fair—to the parent, to the child, or to society. Each suffers when parenthood happens for the wrong reasons. Becoming a parent because you truly want to raise a child is a sound reason. Even that, however, is not enough if you aren't ready for the responsibility.

Readiness Matters

When asked why they want to have children, many people say they want to be parents because they love children. Love is a powerful motivation for good parenting. Love is essential, but is it enough? Actually, much more is involved.

The ability to raise a child properly takes **parenting readiness**. If you are ready, you have certain personal qualities that will help you be a successful parent. In addition, circumstances in your life will enable you to raise a child properly.

You've probably seen what can happen when people aren't ready to be parents. Financial problems, an unhappy home life, lost goals—these can all occur when people have children before they are ready. Having a child is a life-altering event that should be approached with careful thought and decision-making skills.

Of course, parenting readiness is no guarantee against problems. Some couples have successfully raised children by learning as they go. The odds for success are better, however, when you are truly ready for the responsibilities of caring for a child. The job will be less frustrating and much more rewarding.

CHOOSING ABSTINENCE

Unplanned pregnancy and the dangers of sexually transmitted diseases are not a worry for teens who practise abstinence. **Abstinence** (AB-stuh-nuns), refraining from sexual intercourse, has other rewards as well. By abstaining from sex, you can feel good about yourself. Your actions show you respect yourself and others. People who let values guide their actions control the direction of their lives.

Abstinence doesn't mean that you can't show affection. Actually, many non-sexual actions express caring. Some couples show love and affection through letters and being thoughtful. Help with an unpleasant task says, "I care about you." Just sharing the day's events or discussing dreams and plans builds closeness. All of these are genuine acts of love and respect.

Many family counsellors report their teen clients want to learn how to say no to sex without hurting their partner's feelings.

These suggestions can help you practise abstinence:

♥ Avoid situations that could lead to sexual intimacy. Plan activities to include other people and public places.

♥ Discuss feelings with a partner before an intimate situation happens. Make sure each understands and respects the other's view.

♥ Practise ways to say no. Focus on the value of the relationship. Use reason. Try different messages to suit the partner and the situation.

♥ When difficult situations arise, ask yourself: Will I be proud to recall this moment in a few hours, months, or a year? In five years? Will I be able to tell my parents what happened?

♥ Say no firmly and convincingly. Don't wait to be asked.

♥ Find other teens who have chosen abstinence. Knowing that others share your views can give you confidence.

Examining Readiness

If you have a drivers' licence, you had to pass a test. Many careers that you might choose also require testing. Just think how many workers today have to prove their abilities before they take on a job. Teachers, nurses, cosmetologists, and electricians are just a few careers that involve qualifying steps.

Although parenting is one of the most important jobs a person can have, no licence and no testing are required. When

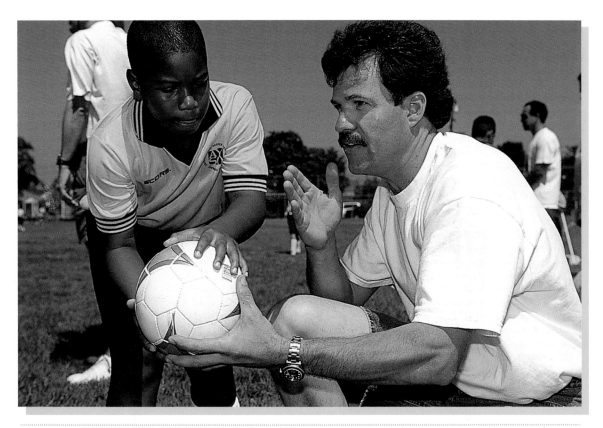

Volunteer work with children helps you explore feelings about having your own children someday. ◆
What could you learn from working with children?

the time comes, people have to judge their own readiness to parent. Fortunately, you can take a look at several basic indicators to help you decide whether you are prepared to raise a child. The first indicator to consider is maturity level.

MEASURING MATURITY

As a person grows from childhood through adolescence and on to adulthood, higher levels of maturity are typically reached. Physically, the body of a fully grown person emerges. Psychologically, the mind and emotions develop. This development occurs gradually and continues throughout life. Those who have gone beyond adolescence have had more time and experience to help them reach the maturity level needed for parenting.

Psychological Maturity

As the mind and emotions develop, a person moves to higher levels of **psychological maturity**. How can you tell if someone is psychologically mature? You notice by their behaviour and attitudes. Answering questions like the ones below gives clues to your own level of maturity:

♥ Do you accept responsibility without being reminded or pressured?

Psychological maturity means living for tomorrow as well as today. Small steps lead toward large goals, such as a home and a good job. ◆ **Why do some people fail to think about tomorrow?**

♥ Do you perform a job well because of a sense of pride and respect for work?

♥ Can you give up short-term comfort for long-term gain?

♥ Can you set aside your own needs when someone else's needs are more important?

♥ Do you make and keep commitments?

♥ Are you confident about your ability to handle whatever comes your way?

♥ Are you controlling the direction your life is taking?

♥ Do you set your own goals and are you self-motivated to reach them?

♥ Can you make decisions based on reason rather than emotions?

♥ Can you solve problems skillfully?

♥ Could you live on your own and take care of yourself?

♥ Do you have a strong and positive sense of self?

♥ Are you even-tempered and peaceful?

♥ Do you have a positive outlook on life?

A person who can truthfully answer yes to most of these questions is likely to have a high level of psychological maturity. This quality may be the single most important requirement for parenting. Do you see why?

Internet Connects

http://www.mcgrawhill.ca/links/parenting
To learn more about Canadian family issues, go to the Web site above for *Parenting Rewards & Responsibilities, First Canadian Edition,* to see where to go next.

When people still have much growing up to do, they aren't prepared to raise a child. Most people don't reach a high level of psychological maturity until they are adults. Some people never get there.

Physical Maturity

The birth of a healthy baby depends in part on the mother's level of **physical maturity**. She won't be able to handle a pregnancy well unless her body has reached the proper stage of physical growth and development.

Although the physical ability to bear children begins at puberty, a female's reproductive system doesn't reach its mature growth until several years after that. Full growth and development increase the chances for a safe and healthy pregnancy. In addition, the mature female's skeletal structure has room for the developing child.

THINKING ABOUT HEALTH

Health is something else to think about when planning to have a child. Both parents should be in good physical health. Before deciding to become a parent, people should ask themselves these health-related questions:

♥ Are a nutritious diet, enough sleep, and regular medical checkups part of your lifestyle?

♥ Do any medical conditions exist that could affect, or be affected by, pregnancy? Some examples are eating disorders, diabetes, kidney disease, and sexually transmitted disease.

♥ Would the baby be at risk for any inherited disorder?

♥ Are the mother's immunizations and vaccinations up to date?

Parenting Q & A

Putting the Past in Its Place

Q "My childhood wasn't very happy. Can I be a good parent despite that?"
Mariel

A You'll be glad to know that the answer is yes. Even those who grow up in a negative environment can still become good parents. It's up to you to break any cycle of harmful behaviour. When you learn from experience, you can take steps to make things better in the family you raise yourself. Observe people and families you admire to see how they operate. A professional counsellor can help you overcome problems that might interfere with positive parenting. Measuring readiness for parenting is especially critical. You may want to delay parenthood in order to examine your life and personality more closely. Turning to resources can be helpful. Parenting courses and books show how to improve and develop the right skills.

♥ Does the mother need extensive dental work?

♥ Would a baby be at risk from parents or other family members who abuse alcohol or drugs, or who smoke?

If the answer to any question indicates health concerns, parents should talk to a physician before planning a pregnancy.

CONDITION OF THE RELATIONSHIP

Parenthood should be the outcome of a solid relationship, not the test of an unsteady one. Unfortunately, not all couples follow this principle when they think about having a child.

Tara, for example, was certain that a baby would help her troubled relationship with Evan. She figured Evan would be thrilled to learn that he was going to be a father. When he saw what a good mother she was, surely he would be impressed. Raising a child would bring them together and make them a team—or so she thought. Tara was bitterly disappointed when nothing worked out as she had hoped.

Before having children, couples need to be sure that their commitment to each other is firm. Their love should form a strong foundation for building a family. Day by day, they learn how to withstand the disappointments and difficulties life can bring. A marriage stands a better chance of surviving if it is firmly established in a strong relationship well before children arrive. Children, in turn, benefit from the stability of a good marriage.

A woman who takes good care of herself has a better chance of having a safe pregnancy. ◆ **What types of exercise do you prefer to keep yourself fit?**

Questions About the Relationship

Had Tara thought about questions like the ones that follow, she might have planned differently. Answering yes to all of the questions signals a strong relationship. A couple needs to ask:

♥ Is the relationship satisfying? Do you each feel that you get as much from the relationship as you give to it?

♥ Is the relationship comfortable and respectful? Are you both generally happy with each other's actions and respectful of each other's ideas?

♥ Is the relationship stable? Has it lasted long enough to be sure that infatuation hasn't been mistaken for love?

♥ Do you both work to settle disagreements, or do they remain unresolved? Do disagreements centre around reasonable issues?

♥ Do you share a common philosophy about having and raising children? That is, do you agree on issues such as these: how many children to have; how to divide responsibilities; and attitudes about discipline, education, and religion?

By talking openly and honestly, couples make discoveries about their relationship. ◆ **What might happen if one person isn't willing to communicate?**

LIFESTYLE CONSIDERATIONS

There's no doubt about it. Having a baby changes the way you live, and some people are not ready to face the changes. Real-life experiences teach this principle best, as you can see from the following comments:

♥ **Beth.** "John and I love our daughter very much, but I think having her has been hard, for him especially. He wasn't really ready to be tied down. John still likes to spend a lot of time out with his friends.

That leaves me alone taking care of Emmy. I keep wondering when John is going to start acting more like a husband and father."

♥ **Ben.** "Before the baby came along, Katie and I spent a lot of time with our friends. We took weekend bike trips, played tennis, went out to movies—you name it. We've had to cut way back on all that, and I miss it."

Sarina. "I guess I wasn't really prepared for how different things would be with a baby around. I don't feel like I ever have time for me anymore. I even get lonely. With feeding, changing diapers, laundry, and everything else, it seems like every waking hour of the day is filled."

Exploring Life First

Being a parent takes time, more time than the inexperienced person realizes. Just ask a parent to estimate how many hours are spent each day *with* the children. Then have them add the time they spend doing things *for* the children. Chances are, the parent has had to set aside personal interests. That isn't always pleasant to do.

Some people like to travel. Many enjoy active social lives. Most have a hobby or a sports interest. Sacrificing these before you are ready can lead to disappointment and resentment. When one parent is unwilling to limit personal interests after a baby arrives, the child may not get needed attention and the other parent must carry most of the workload.

Many people allow themselves a few years to explore their interests before they begin to raise a family. As one parent said, "I saw so much of the country in the years before I married and

had a child. Those were great experiences. By the time I settled down into a family lifestyle, I was ready for it."

People who realistically examine their readiness for having a child think seriously about how their lifestyle will change. They ask themselves what interests and activities they are willing to limit or put off in order to concentrate on raising a child. If the sacrifices seem too great, they may decide to allow themselves some time for personal growth before having children. That can still leave many years ahead for raising a family.

Internet Connects

http://www.mcgrawhill.ca/links/parenting
To learn more about families in Canada, go to the Web site above for *Parenting Rewards & Responsibilities, First Canadian Edition,* to see where to go next.

Many parents establish a career before taking time out for motherhood. ◆ **What challenges face the parent who decides to combine a career with parenthood?**

Building Parenting Skills

PARENTING WITH CONFIDENCE

Confidence is a belief in yourself that allows you to take action. Just as being well prepared for a test gives you more confidence, preparation for parenting can help make you a more confident parent. Confidence often grows with experience. When you handle situations with confidence, your child feels more secure. The child realizes that you are in charge and you know what you're doing. Before he became a parent, Warren showed his confidence when he:

▶ Told his curious parents that he and Tammy would make a decision about having a child when the time was right for them.

▶ Asked Tammy to look at their financial situation with him before planning a pregnancy.

After becoming a parent, Warren showed his confidence when he:

▶ Established rules for his six-year-old son, Mitch, and expected them to be followed.

▶ Went to Mitch's teacher to ask for assistance with a problem Mitch was having.

▶ Spoke calmly to the parent of Mitch's playmate about some bullying behaviour.

◆ ◆ Your Thoughts ◆ ◆

❶ Give examples that show how confidence and arrogance differ.

❷ Children can be very demanding if given the chance. What effect might this have on a parent who lacks confidence?

❸ How could a person increase feelings of confidence about parenting?

❹ Bart told his son not to go sledding on the hill because he felt it was dangerous. When Bart learned that his son's friends were going, he had to decide what to do. How might confidence help Bart?

CONSIDERING GOALS

When Aaron was 20, he had dreams for his future. He wanted to be an architect. He married while still in college and, soon after, their first child came along, then a second. Making a steady living had to become Aaron's highest priority. His dreams were put on hold. In fact, they were never achieved.

A child can change a person's life—just as it did for Aaron. Once a child is born, you can't resign from the responsibilities. Children are lifelong, life-altering responsibilities. Frequently, original goals take second place. They are often lost forever.

Future goals should influence a decision about when to have children. These questions need to be asked:

♥ Will plans for education have to be sacrificed?

♥ Will career goals have to be changed?

♥ Will such goals as buying a car, living independently, or building a savings account have to be put off?

Without thinking, people often let life run its own course. It doesn't have to be that way. People can make sure that life's events occur in the best sequence for them. Meeting certain goals before having a child has positive long-range benefits. Job satisfaction and financial security, for example, often hinge on education. These can be significant to a family's lifetime well-being.

FINANCIAL CONSIDERATIONS

Most parents agree that children are priceless. Practically speaking, they are also very expensive, as you can see in the chart below. People who don't think about the costs involved may be in for some surprises.

While Canada's universal health care pays for hospital stays and visits to the doctor, having a baby involves other costs. A pregnant woman needs new clothes for her expanding body. She may also need a healthier diet. Ongoing costs are listed below. Other costs are less obvious. The family may need a larger car, for example, or more insurance.

The Cost of Raising a Child: 2003*		
Expense	Cost of Raising a Boy to Age 18**	Cost of Raising a Girl to Age 18**
Food	$ 28 132	$ 24 584
Clothing	$ 14 622	$ 16 336
Health Care	$ 4 620	$ 4 620
Personal Care	$ 2 676	$ 3 492
Recreation, Reading, Gifts, School Needs	$ 16 855	$ 16 855
Transportation	$ 3 907	$ 3 907
Child Care	$ 54 397	$ 54 397
Shelter, Furnishings, Household Operation	$ 39 274	$ 39 274
TOTAL	$164 483	$163 464

*Manitoba Agriculture and Food
**These projections are based on Budget Guides 2003 data and do not include inflation.

In this chart you can see what it might typically cost to raise an only child to age 18. Imagine how the costs would increase when parents save for their child's post-secondary expenses. ◆ **What would be the average cost per year to raise a child?**

While having a baby causes expenses to go up, the couple's income may go down. If one parent stops working, even temporarily, because of pregnancy or to care for the child, the household income will be affected.

Asking Financial Questions

Financial problems are a leading cause of marital troubles. The wise couple takes a careful look at finances before deciding to have a child. They can use the following questions to help determine financial readiness:

♥ Is there a steady source of income? Does it meet expenses? How much income goes into savings? What other expenses are there?

♥ What costs will result from pregnancy, birth, and providing for a child?

♥ Do you have extended health care coverage? It pays for expenses above and beyond provincial health care benefits, such as semi-private rooms in a hospital.

♥ Who will take care of the baby? If it is one of the parents, will one income be enough? If paid child care is needed, how much will it cost?

♥ Will larger living quarters be needed immediately? In six months? In a year? Will income cover a move and higher rent or mortgage payments?

The Decision-Making Process

No matter how much thinking people do about their readiness for parenting, their ideas are only helpful if they lead to a sound decision. That's where the **decision-**

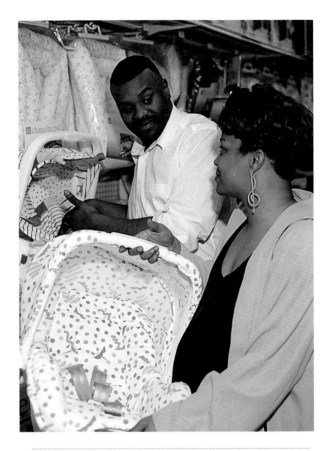

Looking at price tags can be a shock for first-time parents. Those who are financially prepared can enjoy a shopping trip together.

Internet Connects

http://www.mcgrawhill.ca/links/parenting
To learn more about statistics on Canadian families, go to the Web site above for *Parenting Rewards & Responsibilities, First Canadian Edition,* to see where to go next.

making process comes in. With this step-by-step system, people evaluate information in order to reach a reasonable conclusion. On pages 106-107, you can read how one couple used the decision-making process to reach their own answer.

The method is useful when making any decision, not just those about parenting readiness. In fact, if you become a parent, you can use the decision-making process in many situations involving your children.

Making Decisions

A Process That Works

These six steps will help you make important decisions in life. Here Isabel and Victor used them to decide whether the time was right to have a child.

1 Identify the exact decision to be made.

After a year of marriage, Isabel began to wish for a child. For Isabel and Victor, the decision to be made was clear: "Should we have a child now?"

2 List all the options.

Victor and Isabel identified two options, either to have a child or not. Other decisions, of course, have many possibilities.

3 Weigh the pros and cons of each option.

Knowing their decision would have long-lasting consequences, Victor and Isabel thought carefully. They were anxious to start a family, and Isabel's parents wanted a grandchild. On the other hand, Isabel and Victor needed time together as a couple. Moreover, Isabel was taking classes that would prepare her for a career and a better income.

4 Consider values.

Victor and Isabel asked themselves: "What's important to us and to our future family?" By examining their priorities, they could see what meant the most to them.

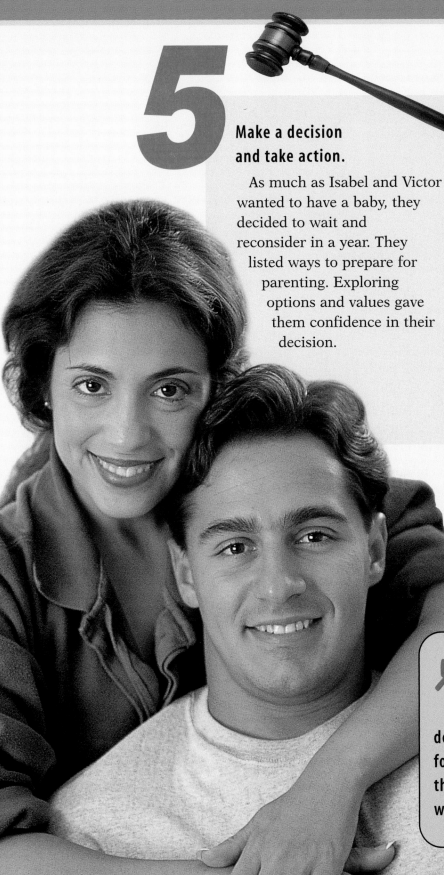

5 Make a decision and take action.

As much as Isabel and Victor wanted to have a baby, they decided to wait and reconsider in a year. They listed ways to prepare for parenting. Exploring options and values gave them confidence in their decision.

6 Evaluate the results and take responsibility for the consequences.

A year later, Isabel and Victor reviewed their list and progress. Their financial situation was better, and Isabel was only a few months from graduation. For them, the decision-making process was beginning again.

YOUR TURN

Think about an important decision that is coming up for you. Apply the six steps of the process in order to decide what you should do.

Review

Looking Back

- ♥ Having a child for selfish reasons hurts the child, the parents, and society.

- ♥ Abstinence has its rewards.

- ♥ Couples with parenting readiness have a clear advantage when raising children.

- ♥ Being able to accept responsibility and to make sacrifices for someone else's well-being are part of psychological maturity.

- ♥ The parents' health and the mother's physical maturity are important factors in making a decision to have a child.

- ♥ A stable relationship where parents respect one another is an important foundation on which to build a family.

- ♥ Couples who delay having children until they've achieved certain important goals are more likely to be content parents.

- ♥ Prospective parents need to anticipate the future income needed by the family.

- ♥ The six steps of the decision-making process can be used for determining parenting readiness, as well as for making other decisions.

Knowledge and Understanding

1. What are eight poor reasons for having a child?
2. How is parenting readiness an advantage to couples and their children?
3. From the signs of psychological maturity, which five do you think would have the greatest impact on parenting?
4. What medical conditions might affect, or be affected by, pregnancy?
5. Describe the kind of relationship that indicates readiness for a couple to become parents.
6. How does the birth of a child affect the parents' lifestyle and goals?
7. What can happen when people get "tied down" to a family before they have had a chance to explore life?
8. What "hidden" costs should couples take into account when assessing their financial readiness?
9. What are the six steps of the decision-making process?

Review

Thinking and Inquiry

10. What qualities or conditions do you think most signal that a person is not yet ready for parenting? Why?
11. When two people are not ready for parenthood, what might happen to their family? What might happen if one partner agrees to quit school to take care of their child while the other goes to school?
12. Why do older individuals have a better chance of being ready for parenthood? When might this not be the case?
13. Study the chart on page 104, showing the cost of raising a child. Which costs surprise you the most? Which expenses might vary greatly, depending on the family's lifestyle?
14. What are the benefits and drawbacks of delaying parenthood?

Communication

15. Suppose that your friend is eager to become a mother. She has a good part-time job after school and on weekends. "Wouldn't it be great to come home to a darling baby? I'd be a better mom than my mother's ever been," she has remarked to you. Write a dialogue you would have with your friend.
16. You and your spouse are discussing the right time to have a child. You feel you are both ready in every way, but your spouse wants to wait until your financial situation is more stable. You'll need a new car soon, and your spouse is paying off a school loan. You argue that if you put off having children until you're completely secure financially, you will never have them. Your spouse is unconvinced. How do you settle the disagreement?

Application

17. Fill in one week of a weekly planner. Include work, school, social activities, and other appointments. Fill in a second week as it might appear if you were a teen parent. Compare the two. What can you conclude about the impact of parenting on a teen's lifestyle?
18. Write two case studies, one describing a couple who is ready to have children and one describing a couple who is not ready.
19. Explain how you will know when you are ready to have children. What do you plan to accomplish first?

CHAPTER 6

Teens and Parenting

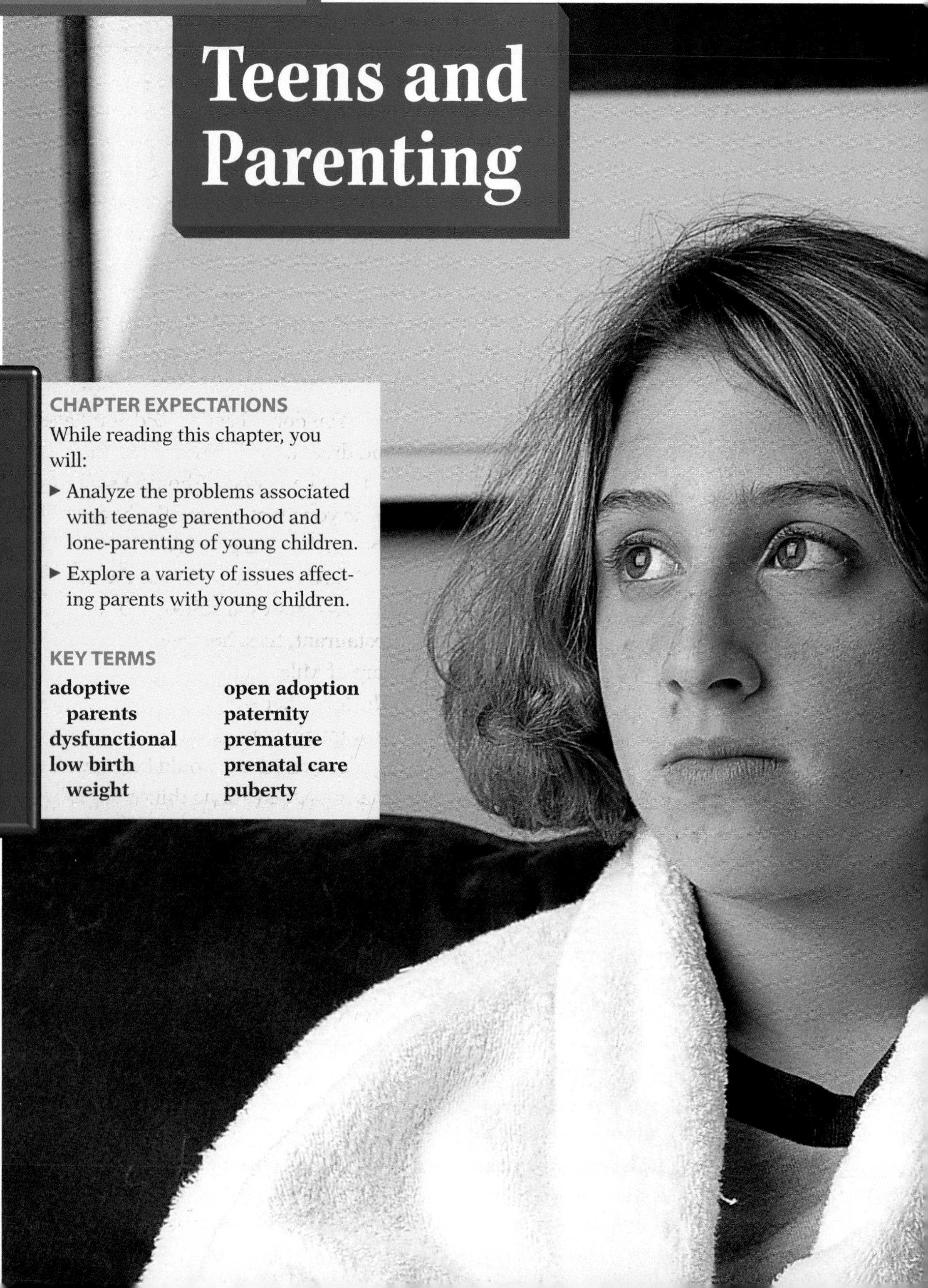

CHAPTER EXPECTATIONS

While reading this chapter, you will:

- Analyze the problems associated with teenage parenthood and lone-parenting of young children.
- Explore a variety of issues affecting parents with young children.

KEY TERMS

adoptive parents
dysfunctional
low birth weight
open adoption
paternity
premature
prenatal care
puberty

Courtney woke from her dream and reached for the lamp. She'd been trying on a blue prom dress. At first it looked great on her. Then it got tighter and tighter until she couldn't breathe. The dream puzzled her. She'd never owned a blue prom dress—she'd never gone to the prom.

In the soft light Courtney stumbled to the crib and picked up the squalling infant. She hoped his crying hadn't awakened her parents. "What's wrong, Miles? You can't be hungry. I fed you an hour ago. You don't feel wet. Did you have a bad dream, too?" She rocked the baby, but still he fussed. "Should I sing to you, or do you want to hear the history speech I'm giving today?"

Courtney thought about the day ahead—classes at school, working in the restaurant, then homework and taking care of Miles in the evening. She sighed. She loved her son, but if she'd known how much work he'd be, how much harder everything would be . . . well . . . she would have done things differently.

She stopped herself. That was past. She and Miles would have a future—somehow. Courtney was determined to finish her high school classes and graduate. That wasn't turning out to be easy. As Miles finally settled down, Courtney fell back into her bed. She had a couple hours before the alarm would ring its wakeup call.

———— ◆ ————

What do you think? How would you interpret Courtney's dream? What's ahead for her? For Miles?

89

Having a child is exciting, but the feelings seldom replace what teen parents miss out on in life. ◆ **What do you think a teen misses by becoming a parent too soon?**

Parents Too Soon

Each year, tens of thousands of teens have babies. Because these parents have not yet matured themselves, this situation is often referred to as "children having children."

People are concerned about these statistics—with good reason. Although many teens manage their lives responsibly, few are ready for the physical, emotional, and financial demands of parenting. Daily life for most teens is full of new feelings and experiences. The teen years are a time to explore life's possibilities and prepare to meet its challenges. Most teens still need time to develop the skills and qualities they will need to be capable, caring parents.

Roots of Teen Pregnancy

After reading Chapter 5, you know what parenting readiness means. A stable relationship, physical and psychological maturity, and financial security are part of readiness. Since few teens have these, can they be ready for parenting?

Most teens don't want to become parents too soon. As one teen put it: "I have trouble giving up a weekend night for a babysitting job. How could I give up entire years of my life right now to care for a child?" Too often, however, some teens act against their better judgment and give in to the pressures that can lead to teen pregnancy.

INTERNAL INFLUENCES

The pressure to become sexually active can be very strong. Some of the pressure comes from within. Understanding what goes on inside the mind and body can help teens be prepared to cope with the pressures.

Sexual Feelings

As **puberty** is reached, young people enter the stage of development when they are physically capable of reproduction. Puberty typically begins between ages ten and fourteen, but may begin as early as age eight, especially for females.

Internet Connects

http://www.mcgrawhill.ca/links/parenting
To learn more about statistics on Canadian families, go to the Web site above for *Parenting Rewards & Responsibilities, First Canadian Edition*, to see where to go next.

Puberty is marked by deep, sometimes unpredictable feelings that include sexual desire. Often teens are not prepared for these new emotions. They may have urges to become sexually active, but they haven't yet learned how to recognize and manage the feelings. How should they react? How can they control their behaviour? What are the consequences if they aren't in control? When psychological maturity lags behind physical maturity, teens may not even think about how to answer questions like these.

Reluctance to Talk

Because they are still growing emotionally, many teens have trouble talking about serious subjects. Some are uncomfortable talking with adults about sexuality. Even teens who want to explain their thoughts, feelings, and values to a partner may feel embarrassed to do so.

Rather than admit their own lack of knowledge, teens may listen to myths and half-truths. Unfortunately, lacking information about sex and acting on misinformation can result in teen pregnancy.

Being unable to talk to others and act on concerns about pregnancy are warning signs. These signals indicate that neither the teen nor the relationship is mature enough for successful parenting.

Desire for Love and Attention

More than 85 percent of births to never-married teens result from unintended pregnancies. Some teens, however, intentionally become pregnant in order to satisfy needs for love and attention.

As 16-year-old Hardeep said, "I saw all the attention mothers and babies get. They have baby showers, and all their friends come around. I wanted a baby to love me.

Some females have children at a very young age.
◆ **How prepared are they to handle the responsibilities of parenting?**

Now I know that my daughter is the one who needs love. My friends were excited about her for a few weeks, but they lost interest. I don't hear from them much anymore. I know I'd probably feel the same if I were them, but I'm still lonely. The baby's father and my friends walked away from this. I can't."

EXTERNAL INFLUENCES

Outside forces also play a part in teen pregnancy. These influences come from several directions.

People who pressure others for sex are thinking only of themselves.
◆ **How would low self-esteem be a problem in these situations?**

Societal Pressures

Teens live in a society that often seems to promote sexual activity. You've seen the images in the media, from popular songs to advertisements. These repeatedly remind people that they are sexual beings. Sex is associated with pleasure, prestige, and romance, but rarely with responsibility and the long-term commitment of marriage.

The aim of advertising messages is to sell products, not to educate about real life. Ads, movies, and television shows seldom link sexual activity to its frequent consequences—pregnancy and sexually transmitted diseases. Teens who are good at thinking and analyzing, however, are able to question what they see and hear. Those who understand what can happen to them don't fall for the messages.

Pressure from Peers

Many teens feel pressured by their peers to have sex. Both males and females may be influenced.

Some young men talk as though having sex makes them men. In truth, maturity makes the man, and maturity means acting responsibly. Responsible people care about what happens to others. They don't want to have children they can't support, and they don't want to ruin the lives of others. A mature male teen doesn't allow these things to happen.

The attitude of female teens can be affected by peers. A young woman whose friends are teen mothers may begin to think that early motherhood is a typical way of life. Fortunately, many recognize that delaying parenthood can result in a more fulfilling life for a mother and her future children.

Raising Children With Character

A Plan for Tomorrow

As Charlene taped the picture of a lovely garden scene over the kitchen window, seven-year-old Tory watched, bewildered. "Why are you covering the window, Mommy?" the child asked.

"Because I want us to see something different. This is your future, Tory, not what we've been looking at out there. Look at those flowers and trees," Charlene sighed. "Aren't they beautiful? Here now, sit with me and we'll look at our library books. This is a girl just like you, but she's already grown up. She got good grades, went to college, and now she has an important job."

The two continued reading together, one of their favourite pastimes. Tory was learning about a world that wasn't part of her life yet, but that Charlene was determined would exist for Tory someday. Gradually Charlene's dreams were becoming Tory's too.

"Uh-oh," Charlene said. "Mr. Riley wants me at work early tonight. You won't get to college if I don't get to work. Now, you scoot on down to Ms. Wilson's apartment—and take her some of those tomatoes. And take your math flash cards, too. Ms. Wilson said she'd practise with you." Charlene gave Tory a hug before the little girl skipped down the hall.

◆◆◆◆ **Thinking It Over** ◆◆◆◆

1. What concerns does Charlene have about the present and the future?
2. What does Charlene value?
3. How is Charlene promoting these qualities in Tory: optimism, faith, and a work ethic?

Pressure from Partners

Pressure to be sexually active also comes from partners. One argument, that "everyone is doing it," has two flaws. First, regardless of what "everyone" is doing, the individual must deal with whatever happens. More important, the argument is false—not "everyone" is doing it. Canadian statistics show that sexually active teens are not the majority. Abstinence is a choice that offers many rewards.

The pressures to "give in" come in many forms. The tactic may be to imply that the person is acting childish by abstaining from sex. Often such comments are made to teen females by males who are several years older, which adds to the pressure. In fact, it is the person who is exerting the pressure who is immature.

Another argument that a partner may use is: "You would if you loved me." Anyone who demands sex as proof of love is showing a lack of love and respect for the other person.

Males as well as females may apply pressure, so all teens need to think ahead about how to say no effectively.

Effects of Teen Pregnancy

"We'd heard about the consequences of getting pregnant, but I guess we just didn't pay attention. I never thought it would happen to us." With these words, one teen summed up what many experience. Often teens don't take the possibility of pregnancy seriously. Later, the teen parents—and others—realize the effects.

EFFECTS ON TEEN PARENTS

Pregnancy, of course, affects the teen parents themselves in many ways. Some experiences are similar for males and females, but some are not.

Medical Problems

Since teen females give birth, they experience the physical effects. Medical complications are a serious risk because young females are not physically mature.

Because they are such a high-risk group, teens need more prenatal care than adult women. **Prenatal care** is the medical attention required throughout pregnancy. Unfortunately, teens are also less likely to seek it. Regular medical care improves the chances that both mother and child will come through pregnancy and childbirth safe and healthy.

Health & Safety

TEEN PREGNANCY

Pregnancy carries certain medical risks at any age, but teens encounter added hazards. Here are some of them:

- If a female's skeletal structure is not fully developed, she can experience problems with her spine and pelvic bones during pregnancy and birth.
- Teens whose bodies are still developing may have difficulty delivering a full-term baby.

- If a teen has poor eating habits, her body competes with the fetus for what limited nutrients are available. An inadequate diet increases the risk of low birth weight. Pregnancy worsens the impact of a poor diet on a teen's developing body.
- A teen is more likely to experience premature labour than a woman just a few years older.

- Teens are at risk for such health problems as pregnancy-induced hypertension (high blood pressure with other complications), a potentially life-threatening condition.
- Rates of miscarriage and stillbirth are higher for teens than for adults.
- The death rate from complications of pregnancy is much higher for teens under age 15 than for adult women.

Financial Responsibility

Both teen parents are legally responsible for providing financial support until the child is 18. Although some teens get financial help from their families, not all families are willing or able to provide money.

Teen mothers usually have limited financial resources and many quickly fall into poverty. Government assistance doesn't allow the kind of lifestyle that some teens imagine. Most parents want to raise a child under better circumstances than the financial situation of a teen mother typically allows.

Teen fathers are seldom prepared to support a child financially either. A teen father is legally responsible, however, whether he marries the mother or never sees her again. Even if the father marries someone else and has other children, he is still responsible. A male who refuses to acknowledge **paternity**—biological fatherhood— can be forced to take a blood test or genetic test to determine whether the child is his.

The courts take a strong stand regarding financial responsibility. Child support payments may be automatically deducted from paycheques, employment insurance benefits, and tax refunds. Provincial authorities may also enforce support payments by taking over bank accounts and assets including property, inheritances, or lottery winnings.

Teen fathers who accept their responsibilities show that they care about the life they have created. Teen fathers who don't care often have regrets as they grow older.

Cross-Curricular Mathematics CONNECTIONS

Comparing Earnings

When teens become parents, their education almost always suffers. Supporting a child can be difficult.

To appreciate how serious the effects might be, look at these numbers. Suppose a typical high school dropout in early 2004 was earning minimum wage, $7.15 an hour at the time. With a high school diploma, that person's pay would have likely been closer to $9 an hour. With a college diploma, typical earnings would have been over $11 an hour. As a new university graduate, the person would have likely earned over $16 an hour. **During a 40-hour week, what would the person earn at each level of education?**

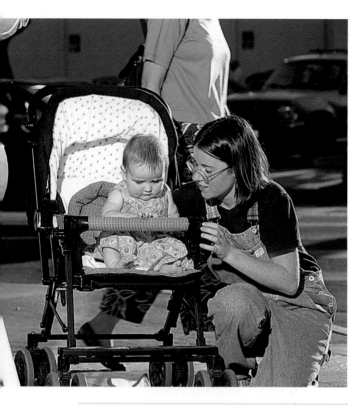

At first an infant may seem like a toy doll to a teen mother. ◆ **What might make her emotions change from enchantment to frustration?**

Education and Job Concerns

Pregnancy can seriously hinder education for both parents. Many teen females drop out of school when they become pregnant, and almost half never earn a secondary school diploma or equivalency. Many need at least a part-time job after the baby is born but soon discover that their earnings don't go far in paying for expenses, including child care.

For males, finishing high school can be a problem too. Some fathers go to work full-time in order to help support the child. Other teen fathers manage to work part-time and continue with school.

With a secondary school education or less, teen parents have little hope of getting a satisfying job that pays well. They may not be able to have the things they want in life, such as nice clothes, a car, and a home. They discover how important education and training are for a future, but the challenge to get these becomes much more difficult.

Emotional Problems

Parenting takes an emotional toll on both teen parents. Adolescence can be an anxious, confusing time made more difficult when pregnancy occurs. Pregnancy increases concerns about the future, forcing teens into decisions they aren't ready to make.

Teen mothers tend to feel isolated. Caring for a child adds stress and loneliness to their lives. They worry about what's ahead for themselves and their child. Over the years, a typical pattern has left teen mothers caring for their child without the father's support. Abandoned mothers feel hurt and upset when males don't care about them and their innocent sons and daughters.

Teen fathers often react to a partner's pregnancy with feelings of shock, anger, or guilt. They may feel anxious about what to do and have the urge to run from responsibility. Many make the mistake of doing that. Sadly, some lack the maturity and conscience to do what is right.

If a teen male doesn't feel comfortable as a nurturer and caregiver, that's no excuse for ignoring responsibility. If he hasn't been close to his own father or hasn't had a role model to show what a caring male parent is like, he can learn. If frustration and resentment could potentially result in abusive behaviour toward the mother and child, he needs to seek help from a counsellor.

Some teen fathers are setting a better example. They want to be important to their child. Since they don't want their child to have a troubled life, they provide support and become involved in raising the child.

EFFECTS ON THE CHILDREN

Many children of teens face a discouraging future. Babies are more likely to be **premature**, that is, born before development is complete. Because their internal organs are underdeveloped, they often have difficulty breathing and regulating body temperature. They may not be able to fight off infections. They may also have physical and mental disabilities, including blindness, epilepsy, and learning difficulties.

Most premature infants also suffer from **low birth weight**, defined as a weight of less than 2500 grams ($5\frac{1}{2}$ pounds) at birth. Such babies are 40 times more likely to die in their first year of life than infants of normal weight. The number of low birth-weight babies is 50 percent higher for teens than for 20-year-olds. You will read more about premature infants and their families in Chapter 11.

Since teen parents often lack the emotional maturity to deal with the stress of parenting, their children are more likely to be neglected, abandoned, or abused. Those born with mental or physical disabilities may have learning and behavioural problems in school. Sons of teen parents are more likely to spend time in prison. Children of teens tend to become sexually active at a young age themselves, and the cycle of teen pregnancy continues.

Internet Connects

http://www.mcgrawhill.ca/links/parenting
To learn more about ideas and issues on the well-being of Ontario's young people, go to the Web site above for *Parenting Rewards & Responsibilities, First Canadian Edition,* to see where to go next.

The infant of a teen mother is more likely to have problems. Prematurity is one of the risks.

EFFECTS ON THE FAMILIES

Teen pregnancy affects more than the teen mother, father, and child. Their extended families are also involved.

Because teens are seldom ready to parent, someone else may have to make sure the child has proper care. That means providing the right food, health care, clothing, a home, stimulation, protection, and guidance. Often the grandparents or other relatives of the child feel the need to step in.

When Points of View Differ

In many instances, a teen mother and her child live with the teen's family. When responsibility for a child overlaps between teen and parent, confusion and conflict are

Internet Connects

http://www.mcgrawhill.ca/links/parenting
To learn more about Canadian family issues, go to the Web site above for *Parenting Rewards & Responsibilities, First Canadian Edition,* to see where to go next.

common. How might a teen's parent feel? The parent might feel angry about the pregnancy, yet concerned about the teen's and the baby's future. Pressures to give financial and physical support may cause stress and fatigue. The adult may be confused about how to parent a teen who is also a parent.

Both teen parents may experience hostility from their partner's family. A male who fails to support the child sets himself up for such feelings.

When the relationship between parenting teens and their parents is strained, they may need to talk to a professional counsellor. A teen who lives up to his or her responsibilities is more likely to gain parental support and keep peace in the family.

IMPACT ON SOCIETY

Teen pregnancy takes an enormous toll on society. First is the money spent by all levels of government and private organizations. Millions of dollars are spent on programs that benefit teen parents and their children. Among other things, this money allows community groups to offer food, education, day care, and other social support. The money also funds services for children in the early years under age six, children with developmental delays, and children who are neglected or abused.

Many teens trade their future for a lifetime of difficulties when they become parents before they are ready.
◆ **Why is society concerned about what happens to them?**

Building Parenting Skills

PARENTING WITH COMMITMENT

The word commit can mean to reserve something for a specific use. Parents commit their time, money, and energy to raising their children. Commit can also mean to pledge or dedicate yourself to something. This certainly applies to parenting. Parenting is a daily, long-lasting responsibility that takes commitment. For teen parents, commitment presents an extra challenge. As teen parents, Emma and Mark showed commitment when they:

▶ Made sure that each of them was involved in their infant son's daily life in a positive way.

▶ Enrolled in a program aimed at teaching parenting skills to teens.

▶ Gave up activities that conflicted with their new family responsibilities.

▶ Gratefully accepted their parents' help, but vowed not to take advantage of them.

▶ Started planning how they could build a bright future for themselves and their son.

◆ ◆ Your Thoughts ◆ ◆

❶ Can a parent commit to a child and leave out any of these three: time, money, or energy? Explain your reasoning.

❷ Why might it be harder for a teen to commit to parenting than for someone who is older?

❸ What sacrifices do parents often make in order to fulfill their commitment to raising healthy, well-adjusted children?

Lost Potential

Lost potential is also a great cost to society. Although a few teen parents are able to build an independent life for themselves and their children, many are not. Putting an end to a young person's dreams means that goals, ambitions, and desires are left behind. Instead, those who begin parenting too soon may spend years struggling just to raise their children and support themselves. Many feel a loss of hope and control. Many never regain the opportunity to develop their minds and skills in ways that would have been good for them and society.

Just think how conditions like these shape communities. Families headed by teens risk becoming **dysfunctional** (dis-FUNK-shuh-nul). In such families, the parents don't fulfill their responsibilities as parents, causing problems for themselves and their children. What do you suppose might happen to a society when many citizens find themselves in this situation?

Options for Teen Parents

When 17-year-old Derek's girlfriend became pregnant, he recalled: "At first I didn't want to deal with it. I stopped seeing Renee and didn't tell anyone. Then Renee and the school counsellor met me after class one day. The counsellor said that we had to make some decisions because the situation wasn't going to go away. Once we started talking, I felt better. The counsellor made us see that our lives weren't over. We had options, but we had to face them."

As Derek discovered, teen parents-to-be are wise to find help and advice early. They are more likely to reach a decision they won't regret and that will make the best of a tough situation. Teens need time to think about all their options, including the ones explained here, and plan what to do.

SINGLE PARENTHOOD

Remaining single is an option that some teen parents choose. Many teen females, however, don't even have a choice if the fathers do not want to be involved.

Single parenthood is often hard on both parent and child. A source of money is a major concern. Many teen parents end up on some form of social assistance. There is support for teen parents from national, provincial, and local levels of government. The type of support available has to do with where you live and your access to different services. Different levels of government have responsibilities for different things. Health Care and Education are the responsibilities of the provincial government, and thus policies are different in each province. Some examples of support include: subsidized housing; grants/loans for post-secondary education; subsidized child care; and parent-support groups/services such as Early Years Centres in Ontario. These are just a few examples of support systems in place. Teens may also look to their families for support. The support of families can come in the form of time and/or money. Both types are usually needed and appreciated.

A single parent should make every effort to continue education at least through secondary school. Schools must offer the opportunity to earn a diploma to pregnant and parenting teens. They may attend additional classes focusing on prenatal care and parenting.

Teens who marry quickly after having a child may not be able to make the marriage work over time. Marriage for the wrong reasons is seldom successful.

MARRIAGE

Marriage may seem like a solution to teen pregnancy, but it rarely improves the situation. A successful marriage is based on friendship, respect, and love. Staying together and working out problems takes commitment. Few teen relationships are that solid. It takes a great deal of maturity to do this.

Teens who marry tend to have less education and lower incomes than older couples. Since they no longer share many of their peers' interests or concerns, they often feel isolated from friends. They don't fit into the adult world either. Pressures like these contribute to a teen divorce rate that is two to three times higher than for more mature couples.

ADOPTION

Placing a baby for adoption is another option when teen pregnancy occurs. The **adoptive parents** legally acquire the rights and responsibilities of parenthood for a child who is not biologically their own. Adoption gives the child a chance to be raised in a stable home. The adoptive parents are grateful to have a child to love and raise. In addition, the teen parents gain a fresh start.

These three benefits are strong reasons for choosing adoption. The decision, however, can be a difficult one. For some, adoption is a sacrifice. In a traditional adoption, the teen parents give up all legal right to have a role and a say in the child's future.

The pros and cons of adoption must be given serious thought. Looking past the immediate attraction of a lovable infant is necessary. Those involved need to think about the future of the child as well as the teen parents as they try to reach the right decision.

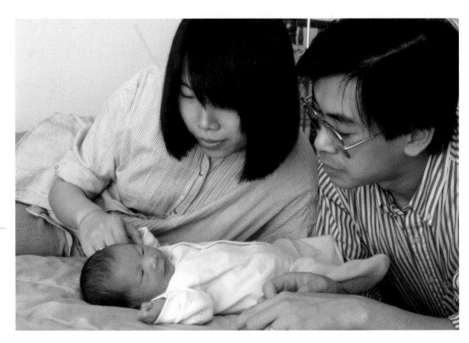

No perfect solution exists for the pregnant teen. Choosing adoption is a possibility for those who can't provide what the baby needs.

Open Adoption

Recent trends have made it easier for some teens to choose adoption. **Open adoption**, in which birth and adoptive parents share information about themselves and the child, has become more common. In privately arranged adoptions, the birth and adoptive parents may meet several times before the child is born and continue as the child grows.

Another alternative is adoption by the baby's grandparents. Grandparents may also work with the province's Children's Aid Society to become the child's foster parents. If a teen becomes a fit parent in the eyes of a CAS worker, custody may be given back.

SOURCES OF SUPPORT

"The only thing worse than being 15 and pregnant," said one teen, "is being 15 and pregnant and thinking you're alone. I know. I've been there." Her words ring true for many teens who face an unplanned pregnancy. They are a reminder that no one needs to face a problem alone. Seeking help is not a sign of weakness. Teens who face pregnancy have several sources of advice and support:

♥ **Parents and family.** Many teens are understandably reluctant to tell their parents about a pregnancy. They feel they have disappointed their family and betrayed their trust. Many parents do react with shock and often some anger. Later, however, many offer love and support. Siblings and other family members can also give comfort. Sometimes they are a "buffer" with parents when emotions run high.

♥ **School guidance counsellors.** Guidance counsellors can help in a variety of ways.

A pregnant teen must have health care—as soon as possible. Look under "physicians" in the Yellow Pages of the phone book.

They can help teens access community resources, such as subsidized housing, counselling services, and prenatal classes.

♥ **Health-care professionals.** Every pregnant female must include health-care professionals in her support system. A doctor or specially trained nurse can confirm pregnancy and track the teen's condition with tests and examinations. Regular visits help ensure both the mother's and baby's health. Proper health care is critical to the health of both the mother and her developing child. If a teen is uncomfortable seeing the family's doctor, then she should access health care through a walk-in clinic or emergency department at the local hospital. A health card is all that is needed to obtain health care in Canada.

♥ **Religious leaders.** Like others in the support network, members of the clergy help teens think through their situation and options.

♥ **Social service organizations.** Help is available from publicly and privately funded groups. Public health departments, through public health nutritionists and nurses, offer information on nutrition and health care during pregnancy. Apprenticeship programs offer job training for young adults. There are systems of grants and loans available to support post-secondary education. Family resource centres and charitable agencies offer used baby clothing. Some organizations advise on prenatal care and offer adoption counselling. Others help teens discuss the pregnancy with their parents. Social service professionals can recommend support groups when appropriate.

Teens need to feel they can discuss sexual pressures with their parents.

♥ **Media attention.** Newspapers, magazines, and television are among the media focusing attention on the serious problem of teen pregnancy and the need for action.

♥ **Educational programs.** Community and school programs are providing teens with information about what it's really like to support and raise a child.

Working together as a community, our society can help teens to face the realities of parenting. Understanding the lifelong consequences for themselves and their future children is an important first step. "It won't happen to me" is a belief that society needs to help dispel in the teenage population.

If teens do become parents, they need a support system to help them learn to be good ones.

Looking for Solutions

Teen pregnancy is a continuing crisis that many communities view as one of their top health problems. As babies continue to be born to young parents who can't take proper care of them, frustration grows in society. People are looking for ways to bring about change. No single solution, however, can solve the problem. Instead, efforts are mounting from many directions:

♥ **Guidance from parents.** Parents need to help children form and act on strong values.

Looking Back

♥ Very few teens are physically, emotionally, or financially prepared to become parents.

♥ Teens who want to become parents often have an unrealistic view of how a baby will change their lives.

♥ Abstinence is the one certain way to avoid pregnancy and ensure educational and career opportunities.

♥ Teen mothers and their babies face serious health risks and other problems.

♥ Teen parenting has serious negative consequences for the teens, their children, and society.

♥ Teens who have a child have options that include raising the child alone, marrying their partner, or placing the child for adoption.

♥ Teen parents have several possible sources of advice and support before and after a baby is born.

Knowledge and Understanding

1. Why are the teen years a poor time to become a parent?

2. Why do some teens want to become parents? Why are these poor reasons?

3. How does the media influence teen pregnancy?

4. What problems do teen mothers face?

5. How does fatherhood affect a teen?

6. How can the lives of children be affected by having a teen parent?

7. Why might a teen's parent react negatively if the teen becomes pregnant or is responsible for a pregnancy?

8. Why is the failure rate for teen marriages so high?

9. What are the advantages of adoption when teens become pregnant?

10. What are five possible sources of help for teen parents?

Thinking and Inquiry

11. Why is teen pregnancy everybody's problem?

12. Do you think that offering support to teen parents shows approval of their actions? How can family, friends, and society help without encouraging teen parents to repeat their actions?

13. Copy the following chart into your notebook and complete it.

Options for Pregnant Teens	Advantages	Disadvantages
Keeping the baby		
Traditional adoption		
Open adoption		

Communication

14. Suppose you are the parent of a teen. Like most parents, you have hopes for his or her future. One evening, your teen nervously breaks the news that you are going to be a grandparent. Write a short skit to show how you would handle the situation.

15. Your friend is 17 years old. Obviously upset, he confides that his girlfriend is pregnant. Her parents are pushing for a marriage, but his family wants him to have as little to do with the young woman as possible. Your friend feels a strong sense of responsibility. He cares for his girlfriend, but the strained relationship with his parents is hurting him. What could you say that might help him find a solution?

16. How should teens respond to a partner who pressures them to have sex? Write a dialogue.

17. Illustrate the realities of teen parenting with a poster called "Parents Too Soon." Use the information in the chapter as a basis for the poster.

Application

18. Ask several older adults about attitudes toward teen pregnancy and parenting when they were your age. How has this view changed over time?

19. Find out what resources are available to help support pregnant teens and teen parents in your community and province.

20. Copy the following chart into your notebook and complete it.

Group/Level of Support	Type of Support
Community support – public	
Community support – non-profit organizations	
Provincial support – public	
Provincial support – non-profit organizations	

21. Complete the following calculations to determine the difference in earning power you would have if you had to quit school to find a job due to teen pregnancy, and if you completed post-secondary schooling before having a child.
    a) Find out the minimum wage and calculate it by 40 hours per week and 52 weeks per year to come up with a yearly income.
    b) Choose a career that you would like to pursue and find out what the starting salary is for that career.
    c) Calculate the difference between the two incomes.
    d) Write a summary paragraph of what you have learned.

CHAPTER 7

Planning a Family

CHAPTER EXPECTATIONS

While reading this chapter, you will:

▶ Outline the stages in the biological process of conception.

▶ Demonstrate an understanding of how new parents can become capable and confident in making choices that are in the best interests of their children before birth.

▶ Evaluate prenatal care/support programs available for parents in the community.

KEY TERMS

biological parents	infertility
chromosomes	ovaries
conception	sperm
gene	testes
heredity	uterus

Seven-year-old Malik spotted an unfamiliar container as he helped his neighbour, Eldon, sort items for recycling. "What's this?" he asked.

Eldon smiled. "That's a special drink for Jennifer." Jennifer was Eldon's daughter. "She can't drink milk like most people. She has a condition called PKU, which means her body can't handle certain foods."

"How did she get it?" Malik asked.

"She was born with it. We knew she might have it before she was born, because of a test that was done. Since we found out right away, we were able to give her the right kinds of foods from the start."

Malik and Eldon wheeled the containers to the curb for pickup. "What else can't Jennifer eat?" Malik asked.

"Oh, there are quite a few foods."

Malik looked thoughtful. "I'm having a birthday party pretty soon," he explained. "I want Jennifer to come, but I don't want to give her something that makes her sick."

Eldon smiled. "That's very kind of you, Malik. Jennifer is lucky to have you for a friend. We'll talk to your parents and see what we can work out."

━━━━━━ ◆ ━━━━━━

What do you think? How did technology benefit Jennifer and her parents?

━━━━━━━━━━━━━━━

107

When you choose a marriage partner for yourself, you choose a parent for your future children. ◆ **What qualities would you look for?**

Forming a Plan

Every day you see people plan for positive results, whether completing a homework assignment, searching for a job, or planning an event. When it comes to creating a family, however, many people give little thought to planning. The family you have will likely be a central part of your entire life. Shouldn't that family be formed with careful thought?

DECISIONS TO MAKE

Many decisions are made when planning a family. One of the first is partner selection. Choosing someone who will make a good parent for any children you have is an important consideration. As a couple, you can then decide when you are ready to become parents. By starting a family after you are prepared for the responsibilities, many problems can be avoided.

In developing a family plan, you make decisions about having children. How many do you want and how soon? How far apart in age will children be spaced? Are there any genetic factors to think about before having children? By talking about what's most important to them, couples move toward agreement. Knowledge about reproduction, heredity, and genetics helps them make sound decisions as their vision of family becomes reality.

Understanding Human Reproduction

When you understand how human reproduction works, some decisions about having children are easier to make. By knowing terminology, you'll be able to talk more intelligently with the professionals who give you advice and assistance.

Human reproduction is a function of the male and female reproductive systems. These systems produce tiny cells that have the amazing ability to form a new life.

The Process of Conception

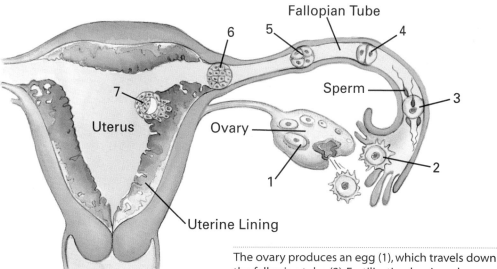

The ovary produces an egg (1), which travels down the fallopian tube (2). Fertilization begins when a single sperm cell unites with an egg (3). The fertilized cell begins to divide into two cells, then four, then eight, and so on (4 and 5). The clump of cells travels down the fallopian tube toward the uterus (6). Two weeks after conception the cells that will eventually form the baby are firmly planted in the uterine wall (7).

FEMALE REPRODUCTIVE SYSTEM

A female is born with thousands of partially formed reproductive cells called ova, or eggs. Ova are stored in **ovaries** (OH-vuh-reez), the female reproductive glands. When a female reaches puberty, her ova start to grow. Picture a tiny speck of dust to realize the small size of one mature ovum.

Beginning at puberty and continuing throughout the reproductive years, an ovum matures in one ovary about once a month. The mature ovum is released by the ovary and travels down one of the two fallopian tubes (fuh-LOH-pee-uhn) to the uterus. The **uterus** (YOO-teh-russ), or womb, is the pear-shaped organ where a child develops before birth.

Inside the uterus a lining of blood vessels and other tissue forms each month. During menstruation, the lining sheds, taking the released ovum with it. This cycle repeats about every 28 days throughout a woman's reproductive lifetime, or about 40 years.

MALE REPRODUCTIVE SYSTEM

Sperm are the male reproductive cells. Males begin producing these microscopic cells at puberty. A healthy male may produce sperm for the rest of his life.

Sperm originate in the two **testes** (TES-teez), the male reproductive glands. When sperm are expelled, they travel through small tubes until they reach the urethra (yu-REE-thruh), a narrow tube through the penis. Four to five hundred million sperm, surrounded by a protective, milky fluid called semen, may be released at one time.

Internet Connects

http://www.mcgrawhill.ca/links/parenting
To learn more about health promotion approaches in Canada, go to the Web site above for *Parenting Rewards & Responsibilities, First Canadian Edition,* to see where to go next.

CONCEPTION

Conception, also called fertilization, occurs when male and female reproductive cells unite after sexual intercourse. During intercourse, sperm are deposited near the lower end of the female uterus. The sperm that enter the uterus quickly swim into the fallopian tubes. If an ovum is present, the sperm swarm the ovum and try to break through the surface. Only one sperm is successful. At this moment of fertilization, the surface of the ovum seals out the remaining sperm, which eventually die.

Once the ovum has been fertilized, it attaches to the wall of the uterus. There, the lining of blood vessels and other tissue remain to nourish the developing child until birth. For almost all women, menstruation stops until the pregnancy is over.

When Can Conception Occur?

Certain myths give false ideas about conception. An understanding of the reproductive process helps you see the truth in each of these situations:

♥ *Can pregnancy occur before a female has had her first menstrual period?* Yes. An ovum can be released before the very first menstrual period begins.

♥ *Can pregnancy occur the first time a female has intercourse?* Yes. As long as an ovum and sperm are present and unite, it makes no difference whether it's the first time.

♥ *Can pregnancy occur during the menstrual period?* Yes. The ovum may be alive and present at this time.

♥ *Can pregnancy occur even if intercourse is incomplete?* Yes. A few sperm may be released, and only one is needed.

Conception can occur only when a living ovum and sperm are in the same place at the same time. When can that happen? Deposited sperm can live for four or five days in the human body. An ovum might typically survive for about 24 to 48 hours in the female's fallopian tubes. Pregnancy, then, can occur if intercourse takes place during the four or five days before the ovum is released and for about two days afterwards.

This time period, however, is difficult to pinpoint. Females usually don't know exactly when an ovum will be released, especially if the menstrual cycle is inconsistent. If something affects the cycle, the ovum may be released at an unexpected time, often without the woman realizing. Stress and illness, for example, can cause the cycle to change.

Planning Pregnancy

Pam and Larry's first child was born the first week of June. For two teachers, the pregnancy couldn't have been timed better. They were able to spend the summer getting to know their new son. The couple planned to have another June baby in two years, but their second son was born on the first day of the following school year, just 15 months after his older brother.

While plans work well for some families, others face challenges and sometimes disappointment. A family plan is only a guide.

Ellen and Vic's plans for two children resulted in a boy and a girl. ◆ **What kinds of reactions do people have when they want a boy or girl and they have the opposite? What causes these reactions?**

CONTRACEPTION

Couples often try to time a pregnancy around other life events. That may mean trying to postpone pregnancy for a while. They can do so in different ways.

Contraception is the use of drugs, devices, or techniques to prevent pregnancy. Each method, as shown in the chart on page 112, has characteristics that need to be understood and evaluated by a couple. Information about contraception needs to come from reliable sources and be based on the facts about reproduction.

Decisions about contraception are extremely personal. A couple should discuss how they feel and consult a health care professional. Personal values, religious beliefs, age, health, and economic situation enter into a decision. When a couple decide to use contraception, both partners must be comfortable with their choice and committed to its proper use.

Methods of Contraception

Method	Function	Disadvantages	Effectiveness
Abstinence	No sexual intercourse.	None.	100%
Oral Contraceptive: Hormone pill taken daily.	Prevents monthly release of ovum.	Prescription needed. Can cause weight gain, headaches, mood changes. Health risks for women who are over 35, smoke, or have family history of certain diseases.	94-97%
Male Condom: Latex sheath that fits over penis.	Traps semen. Reduces risk of sexually transmitted diseases.	Can break or slip off. Can only be used once. Damaged by hot or cold and petroleum products.	86-90%
Female Condom: Polyurethane pouch inserted into vagina.	Prevents sperm from reaching womb.	One-time use only. Can break. Incorrect use decreases rate of effectiveness.	79-95%
Diaphragm: Dome-shaped latex cup stretched over a flexible ring; inserted into vagina.	Blocks entrance to uterus. Used with spermicide.	Must be fitted by health professional. Must remain in place for at least 6 hours. Increases risk of bladder/urinary infections.	84%
Cervical cap: Small latex or plastic thimble; inserted over cervix (narrow opening of uterus).	Provides barrier by fitting snugly over cervix and blocking entrance to uterus. Used with spermicide.	Must be fittted by health professional. Difficult to insert. Must remain in place for at least 8 hours.	82%
Spermicide: Foams, creams, gels, and vaginal inserts.	Sperm-killing chemical. Used with condom, diaphragm, cervical cap.	Not very effective when used alone. May cause allergic reaction.	74%
IUD (Intrauterine device): Small plastic or metal device inserted into uterus.	Prevents pregnancy by interfering with implantation of fertilized ovum.	Doctor must insert. Increases risk of pelvic infection. May increase menstrual flow and cramping.	94%
Hormone implant: Capsules inserted beneath skin in upper arm.	Prevents monthly release of ovum for up to 5 years.	Doctor must insert. May cause irregular bleeding, missed menstrual periods, weight gain, headaches, mood changes. Visible under the skin.	99%
Hormone injection: Injection given once every 3 months.	Prevents monthly release of ovum for 3 months.	Doctor or nurse must inject. May cause weight gain, headaches, abdominal pain, irregular periods.	99%
Sterilization: Surgical procedures (tubal ligation for female, vasectomy for male).	Clamps or seals fallopian tubes; cuts or ties tubes carrying sperm to penis.	Minor surgery with some risk of infection. Requires surgery to reverse. Vasectomy reversal is expensive and outcome uncertain. Tubal ligation reversal requires major surgery with 70% success rate.	99%
Natural family planning: System determines when ovum is likely to be released.	Prevents pregnancy by avoiding intercourse during fertile period.	Requires accurate record keeping. Illness or irregular menstrual cycle can throw off calculations. Errors easily made.	80-90%

FERTILITY PROBLEMS

While some couples carefully plan to postpone pregnancy, others face the opposite situation. **Infertility**, the inability to conceive a child, can be heartbreaking to those who want to have a family. Couples who have tried to conceive a child for over a year without success are said to be infertile.

The cause of infertility varies. Most often the physical structure or health of the body is the cause, but stress and emotions can play a role.

Many couples who have trouble conceiving a child consult a medical specialist. This professional can conduct tests to determine if there is a problem and to learn how to treat it.

Today's technology offers couples the option to have a medically assisted pregnancy. Fertility drugs and other techniques are available for couples who want this type of help. This can be an expensive process since it is not covered by provincial health plans.

If a woman has problems with pregnancy or infertility, her mother may have useful information about the family history. This knowledge can help doctors treat the woman.

Understanding Heredity

"He has his mother's nose." "She must have gotten her musical talent from her grandfather." Comments like these are observations on **heredity**, the transfer of traits from parent to child. Most children have apparent traits from both of their parents and their respective families.

How does heredity take place? An ovum and a sperm each contain 23 **chromosomes**, long, thread-like particles in the cell nucleus. When a sperm and ovum unite, they create a single cell with 23 pairs of chromosomes, or 46 in all. As this cell divides and reproduces, every resulting cell will contain copies of those 46 chromosomes.

On each chromosome are thousands of genes. A **gene** is a hereditary unit that determines a particular physical or mental trait. An individual's genes are randomly acquired from parents, grandparents, and earlier ancestors. Because genes come together in random combinations, every person is unique.

The number of possible combinations of genes is staggering. According to one scientific estimate, as many as 64 trillion different genetic combinations are possible. This arrangement of genes, or genetic makeup, is the blueprint for a human being. The blueprint determines a person's height, hair colour, and personality, plus thousands of other traits. Every cell in a person's body carries the same genetic blueprint for that person.

DOMINANT AND RECESSIVE GENES

Sperm and ova are different from the rest of the cells in the body. Since these cells must unite to form a new person, they cannot have 46 chromosomes each. Through a special type of cell division, sperm and ova form with only 23 chromosomes in each one.

When reproductive cells form, genes are distributed randomly. For example, one ovum might carry a gene for brown eyes, while another ovum carries the gene for blue eyes. The same is true of sperm. If an ovum and sperm that each have the gene for brown eyes happen to unite, the child will have brown eyes.

What happens when an ovum with the gene for brown eyes unites with a sperm that has the gene for blue eyes? The stronger, or dominant, gene is expressed. In other words, that trait shows in the child. Since the gene for brown eyes is dominant, the child will have brown eyes.

A trait that is weaker, such as the one for blue eyes, is said to be recessive. A brown-eyed child who also has the gene for blue eyes is called a carrier. That means the child has a recessive gene for a trait that is not expressed. To be expressed, a recessive trait must be inherited from both the mother and father.

Could parents who both have brown eyes produce a blue-eyed baby? Yes, if each parent is a carrier of the gene for blue eyes, and an ovum with this gene unites with a sperm that has it too.

Heredity determines what a person looks like. ◆ **Why would some siblings in a family look more alike than others?**

GENDER DETERMINATION

Will the baby be a boy or girl? The answer is settled at the moment a sperm fertilizes an ovum.

To understand what happens, first think of the cells that make up a person. Of the 46 chromosomes in each cell, two are specialized chromosomes that determine gender. In a female these are alike (XX). In a male, they are different (XY).

Remember that when cells divide to form reproductive cells, the resulting cells contain half the original number of chromosomes. Thus, each reproductive cell receives only one gender chromosome, either an X or Y. Since females have two X chromosomes, all ova will have an X. Since males have an X and a Y, sperm can contain either one of these.

At fertilization, a sperm unites with an ovum. If a sperm carrying an X chromosome fertilizes the ovum, the chromosome pair will be XX and the baby will be female. If the sperm carries a Y chromosome, the resulting pair will be XY and the baby will be male. As you can see, the father determines the child's gender.

Knowing whether a child is male or female before birth is an option that most parents have today. Some like to be prepared ahead of time. Others prefer a surprise at the time of birth.

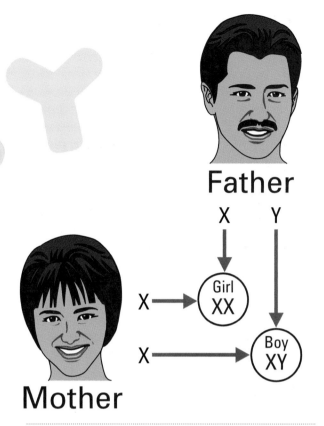

The father determines the gender of a child. ◆ **Can you explain why?**

MULTIPLE BIRTHS

One mother chuckled when people marvelled at her triplets. "We knew we wanted three children," she quipped, "so to save time, we had them all at once."

Anyone who keeps an eye on the news is aware that the number of surviving babies born at one time has increased beyond what was ever thought possible. Twins are born about once in every 89 births, and triplets occur once in approximately 7900 births. One mother in about 705 000 has quadruplets. Amazingly, five, six, and even seven babies are now part of the multiple-birth phenomenon. Most of these occur after medical fertility treatments.

Having more than one child at a time can be exciting, but there is also a serious side. The health of the mother and babies is at greater risk with multiple births.

Fraternal or Identical

Multiple births arise from two unusual happenings at conception. Either fraternal or identical siblings result.

FRATERNAL. With fraternal siblings, a woman produces two or more ova during the same menstrual cycle. If all are fertilized by sperm, she will have a multiple birth. Children conceived from separate ova and sperm are called fraternal.

Although fraternal siblings are born at the same time, they each have a different genetic makeup. Multiple-birth children who are fraternal are no more likely to resemble each other than are siblings born at different times.

IDENTICAL. Multiple births also result if a single fertilized cell divides and separates. Each separate cell then goes on to develop into a baby. Twins born from the splitting of a single cell are called identical. Identical twins look alike because they share the same arrangement of genes. The same is true for identical triplets and other identical multiple births.

Understanding Genetics

The genetic blueprint that determines what a person will be like is both mysterious and exciting. It can also be a worry for parents.

Unfortunately, some genes are abnormal, causing disease and disability. Many people know that they might be carriers of an abnormal gene because they know of family members who have a certain condition. When a recessive trait is passed through generations, however, a couple may not know they are carriers until their child is born with an impairment.

Some parents are excited by the idea of raising twins or other multiples, but some find it challenging.
◆ **Why do you think there's a difference?**

GENETIC DISEASES

You might be surprised to learn that everyone has defective genes. In most people, however, the resulting traits are not noticeable. In other individuals, genetic defects create disabling conditions.

Over 200 genetic disorders have been identified. A few common ones are:

♥ *Down syndrome.* Down syndrome can be detected with genetic testing, which is recommended for older parents, especially women over age 35. A child with the disorder has an extra chromosome on the twenty-first pair, called trisomy-21. People with Down syndrome have moderate to severe mental impairment, heart defects, and sometimes physical challenges. Special education and physical therapy enable many to lead productive, happy lives in spite of their challenges.

♥ *Cystic fibrosis.* Cystic fibrosis affects the lungs and digestive tract. Children with this disease have frequent lung infections due to a buildup of mucus. They also have trouble gaining weight because mucus blocks the duct that normally carries digestive enzymes to the intestines. The lack of enzymes results in incomplete digestion of food. Children with this disease benefit from lung exercises and special diets.

♥ *Muscular dystrophy.* This disorder can be inherited from one or both parents. The skeletal muscles of children with any form of mus-

Children with Down syndrome are typically very loving. Many families find special joys in sharing life with these children.

cular dystrophy gradually weaken and cause permanent disability. Signs of some forms of muscular dystrophy appear as early as birth; other forms appear in later childhood, adolescence, or early adulthood. Intense physical therapy gives many people with muscular dystrophy varying degrees of independence; however, no cure is known.

Internet Connects

http://www.mcgrawhill.ca/links/parenting
To learn more about parenting from A to Z, go to the Web site above for *Parenting Rewards & Responsibilities, First Canadian Edition,* to see where to go next.

Building Parenting Skills

PARENTING WITH REALISM

Realistic parents face the facts—before they have a family and after. Children can be cute, lovable, and lots of fun. The realistic person, however, takes the work, expense, and challenges into account when planning a family. While parenting, realistic actions make life safer and easier. For example, since you can't expect a small child to sit still for a long car trip, you plan frequent stops and take along toys and games for amusement. Before and after his baby was born, Graeme showed a realistic attitude when he:

▶ Researched and talked to a counsellor about a genetic disease that his mother said his great-grandfather might have had.

▶ Decided that he could be happy with a son *or* a daughter before their baby was born.

▶ Went to bed earlier after the baby was born in order to have plenty of energy for a full day of work and child care.

▶ Made sure the family had basic first aid supplies on hand.

▶ Suggested to his wife that they postpone having another child until they could afford the down payment on a house in the community where they would like to raise their children.

◆ ◆ Your Thoughts ◆ ◆

❶ Why is a realistic outlook important when deciding whether to have a child?

❷ For each example about Graeme, what might happen if he were to take an unrealistic approach?

❸ Suppose your eight-month-old daughter tears up a magazine. What would be a realistic view of her actions?

❹ While Alex watched a football game on television, his sons, ages three and seven, played alone outside. What was unrealistic about Alex's actions?

♥ *Sickle-cell anemia.* This blood disorder most commonly affects people of African or Middle Eastern descent. With sickle-cell anemia, malformed blood cells interfere with circulation enough to leave major body organs starved for oxygen. The lack of oxygen causes pain, fatigue, swelling in the joints, and often early death. Medication can relieve the symptoms, but no cure has been found.

♥ *Tay-Sachs disease.* This disease typically strikes people descended from Jewish communities in Eastern and Central Europe. Children with the disease lack a blood enzyme that breaks down fats. Fats accumulate, particularly in the brain and nervous system, causing the cells to rupture. The ruptured cells lead to increasing blindness, deafness, loss of motor skills, and mental impairment. Death usually occurs before the child's fourth birthday. Tay-Sachs disease is presently incurable.

♥ *PKU.* Phenylketonuria (fe-nul-KEE-tun-UR-ree-uh) is the body's inability to break down phenylalanine (fe-nul-A-luh-neen)—one of the amino acids necessary to change proteins into a form the body can use. Left untreated, the buildup of this amino acid causes gradual mental impairment. Fortunately, newborns are now routinely tested for PKU. A carefully controlled diet can prevent or control the disease's effects.

GENETIC COUNSELLING

Genetic counselling can help parents who have concerns about diseases and disorders that might be passed to their offspring. Genetic counselling offers expert information about heredity, especially inherited disorders.

Why might parents seek genetic counselling? Those who know that a genetically passed disease is part of their family history can benefit from such counselling. A couple whose ethnic background puts them at risk for a specific disorder may also want information. Parents who have a child born with a genetic disease or disorder usually seek counselling before having more children.

Genetic counsellors are specialists trained in diagnosing genetic conditions. Counsellors begin by taking a detailed medical history of the families of both partners. In some cases counsellors use tests to detect defective genes. After analyzing the data they collect, the counsellors talk to prospective parents about their risk of having a child with a particular disease or disability. Counsellors also explain how the disorder may affect the child and the family.

Parenting Q & A

Just Your Size

Q "My fiancé and I have been talking about having children, but we don't agree on how many we want. How can we decide?" *Tamika*

A The number of children a couple has is a personal matter, but that doesn't mean that any choice is as good as another. Responsible people go beyond simply "wanting." They think realistically. Ask yourselves: What are the financial costs? Can we manage these costs without risking our family's health and security? Do we have the energy to raise the number of children we want? Are we emotionally equipped for that number? How should we space births? Thinking far into the future can help you reach a decision. Talk about what might affect your plans, such as a job loss or promotion. How would you manage pressures from family and friends who disagree with you? Whatever your decision, you should both support it.

Genetic counselling cannot prevent birth defects, nor can counsellors tell a couple whether to have children. The information genetic counselling provides, however, helps couples make knowledgeable decisions as they consider parenthood.

Roads to Parenthood

When a male and female conceive and have a child, they are known as the **biological parents**, or birth parents, of that child. In planning for a family, however, some people choose alternative ways to become parents.

CHOOSING ADOPTION

People adopt for many reasons. A couple may have infertility problems. Health problems might make pregnancy difficult or dangerous for some women. Those who have inherited disorders may not want to risk passing a defect on to their children. Some people simply want to give a loving home to a child who needs one.

Children become available for adoption when biological parents give up their role as parents. Some are emotionally unprepared to raise a child. Others are unable to provide what the child needs. Sometimes birth parents who are neglectful or abusive have their legal rights terminated by the province, making their children available for adoption. If biological parents die, relatives or others might adopt the children.

People who want to become parents through adoption may have to wait a long time for an infant. Their wait may be shorter if they are willing to take an older child or a child with a disability.

People who want to adopt often work with a public agency, which will investigate the prospective parents and counsel birth parents. Private arrangements are often faster and may give birth parents more input in choosing a family for their child. The lack of provincial involvement, however, may increase the risk of something going wrong.

LEGAL GUARDIANS

When a parent dies or is unable to care for a child, a relative or family friend may be named as legal guardian. This adult, appointed by the courts, takes legal responsibility for a minor. This legal relationship ends when the child reaches legal age, either 18 or 21. Parents can set up guardianship for their children in their will, although it is always the court's decision as to who will be the legal guardian.

BECOMING A FOSTER PARENT

When Emily was four years old, her mother had some problems that left her unable to care for the child. The provincial Children's Aid Society placed Emily with a foster family until she could return home.

Foster parents are adults who have temporary custody of children. They must be approved and licensed by the Children's Aid Society, and they receive a small payment to offset the child's expenses.

Internet Connects

http://www.mcgrawhill.ca/links/parenting
To learn more about individual and family well-being, go to the Web site above for *Parenting Rewards & Responsibilities, First Canadian Edition*, to see where to go next.

Parents may ask a close friend or relative to be named as legal guardian of their child in the event of their death. An attorney takes care of the legal paperwork.

Foster parents take in children who have been removed from their homes while their parents learn parenting skills or receive treatment for a problem. These children may return to their homes if and when the parents are able to provide a caring, stable environment. Some children are in foster care while they await adoption.

Many people who care about children fulfill their need to parent through foster care. By opening their home to children who need them, foster parents offer the warmth and nurturing of a loving family.

Looking Back

♥ A family plan involves making decisions about having children.

♥ Conception occurs when reproductive cells unite.

♥ Couples have options for timing pregnancy when planning a family.

♥ Genes, located on the chromosomes of each reproductive cell, determine inherited traits. Genes may be dominant or recessive.

♥ Multiple births are now more common than they were in the past.

♥ Defective genes can cause seriously disabling and sometimes life-threatening conditions.

♥ Genetic counselling informs couples about their risk of passing genetic disorders to their offspring.

♥ The possibility of becoming a parent is not reserved for biological parents.

Knowledge and Understanding

1. Why might a couple want to plan their family?
2. Why is it difficult to pinpoint the time when fertilization can occur?
3. Briefly explain how conception occurs.
4. What are three options a couple might have if they wish to delay pregnancy?
5. When is a couple said to be infertile? What other options do they have?
6. How does an individual acquire his or her genetic makeup?
7. How does a dominant trait appear in a person? A recessive trait?
8. How is gender determined?
9. The youngest Wyman children are twins, John and Stephanie. What type of twins are they?
10. What part does genetic counselling play in planning for a family?
11. Why are newborn babies tested for PKU?
12. What is another name for biological parents?
13. The Children's Aid Society sent Nathan to live with the Browns while his mother was unable to care for him. What are Mr. and Mrs. Brown to Nathan?

Thinking and Inquiry

14. Just because you plan a family doesn't mean you will have exactly the family you plan. Does that mean you shouldn't plan? Explain your reasoning.

15. Mark is thrilled to have a baby daughter. He has been telling people that her gender was no surprise since his wife comes from a family of six girls. What is incorrect about his theory?

16. Lennie doesn't believe he is the father of his estranged wife's baby. "That baby has blue eyes," he says, "and Tanya and I both have brown eyes." What would you say? How could they obtain proof?

Communication

17. Suppose you and your spouse were planning to start a family soon. Your spouse's sister has recently given birth to a child with a serious birth defect. Now you are both concerned about planning a pregnancy. What might you do? Write a dialogue you would have with your spouse and your doctor.

18. Camille is thinking about using a fertility drug to become pregnant. The drug is known to frequently cause multiple births, and Camille and Bart already have two children. Describe what you would do if you were Camille or Bart.

19. April, a teen mother, says, "How can I plan my family? It's too late for that." Write your response to her.

Application

20. As a class, debate this statement: "The effort and expense of achieving a medically assisted pregnancy would be better spent on raising an adopted child."

21. Use the Internet to look for any recent findings or developments concerning a genetic disease. Share your findings with the class.

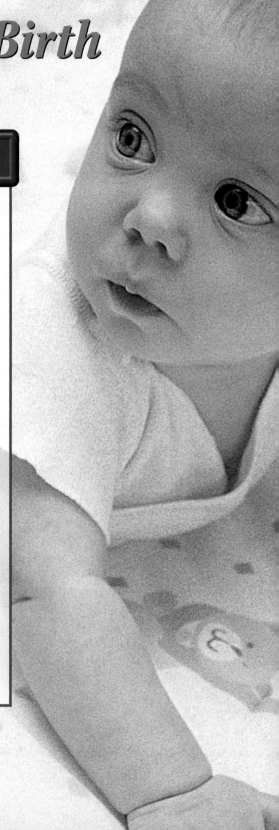

UNIT **2**

Pregnancy and Birth

A Parent's Perspective

from Amanda

"When you've never given birth before, you keep wondering what it will be like. At first, I didn't even believe I was pregnant. How could something as awesome as a new life be starting inside me when I couldn't even feel it? Well, that really changed as I got bigger. My whole body seemed out of control. I'll have to admit that every time I looked in the mirror during my ninth month, the word 'elephant' came to mind. And then there was the fear. Could I actually do this, I wondered? Could I handle labour and delivery? Would the baby be okay? So what if a zillion other women have had babies. This was me. And then I had her. Giving birth was probably the most difficult thing I've ever done. If I could share one piece of advice with other women, I'd encourage them to take a childbirth preparation class. I did, and it made all the difference in the world."

While reading this unit, you will:

❖ Describe factors that contribute to the healthy development of children before and during birth, and in the first few months after birth.

❖ Explain patterns in the social, emotional, intellectual, moral, and physical development of children.

❖ Evaluate your own practical experiences involving children.

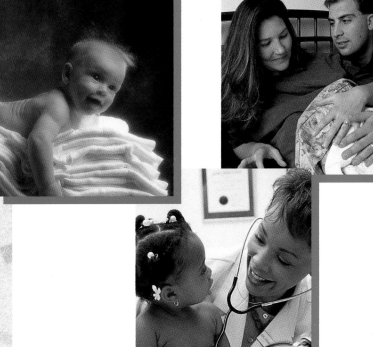

Pregnancy

CHAPTER EXPECTATIONS

While reading this chapter, you will:

▶ Outline the stages in the biological process of conception, pregnancy, and birth.

▶ Demonstrate an understanding of how new parents can become capable and confident in making choices that are in the best interests of their children before and during birth, and in the first few months after birth.

KEY TERMS

amniocentesis	placenta
amniotic sac	registered
anemia	midwife
chorionic villus	Rh factor
sampling	trimesters
(CVS)	ultrasound
embryo	umbilical cord
fetus	zygote
obstetrician	

Deanne eased herself into the chair in her doctor's office. "Is it just me, or has this chair gotten smaller?" she asked.

Dr. Luring looked over Deanne's chart. "It's not the chair," she said with a smile. "You've gained 2 kilograms since last month, 8 kilograms altogether. That's good for your stage of pregnancy."

"It feels more like 20 kilograms." Deanne laughed. "I have to put my feet up every day after work. I'm not used to pampering myself so much."

Dr. Luring chuckled and said, "I'm glad you're taking good care of yourself—and keeping your spirits up too." She went on to ask Deanne some questions and check her condition. Then she asked, "Now, is there anything you want to know? Anything you'd like to talk about?"

"No," Deanne began. "Well . . . actually . . ." she sighed. "I guess I'd just like to know that everything's going to be all right."

The doctor nodded sympathetically. "You're not the first one with that request. I'll tell you this: you're doing everything you should be doing to have a healthy baby. As for your other concern," she added with a grin, "I'm getting a bigger chair."

◆

What do you think? How would you describe the relationship Deanne has with her doctor? How might that help her during her pregnancy?

127

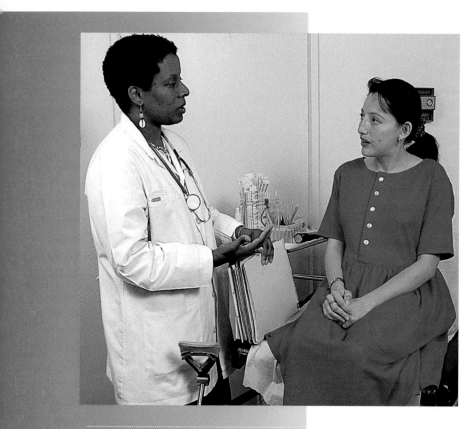

Once a woman realizes that she may be pregnant, she needs to see a health-care provider so that prenatal care can begin. Even if she has concerns about costs or anything else, the provider can help her make sound decisions.

MISSING A MENSTRUAL PERIOD

Typically, Janelle could glance at her calendar and know when to expect her next period. When it was only two days late, she was convinced that she was pregnant. She was right. A year earlier her sister-in-law hadn't even suspected that she was pregnant at such an early stage. Because of irregular menstrual periods, her pregnancy wasn't confirmed until she was more than two months pregnant.

In early pregnancy, some women have a slight staining of menstrual blood during the usual time for their period. They may feel mild menstrual cramps when their period is due, causing confusion about pregnancy.

OTHER INDICATIONS OF PREGNANCY

You may have heard or read about women who gave birth after being unaware that they were even pregnant. Very few women could realistically have such an experience. Besides missing menstrual periods, several other signs tell a woman that she might be pregnant.

Fatigue, enlarged and tender breasts, nausea, bloating, and food cravings can be

Early Signs of Pregnancy

When two people are ready and eager to be parents, the confirmation of pregnancy is an exciting moment to share. A woman doesn't actually know right after conception that she is pregnant. Within a few weeks, however, her body gives several signs that might make her wonder. The most common is the absence of menstruation.

signs. The enlarged uterus can be felt by a doctor during an exam. After six weeks, pregnant women usually report an increased need to urinate.

PREGNANCY TESTS

Has your mother or another relative told stories about waiting anxiously for a week or more to hear if she was pregnant? Today's tests offer results in just minutes. Women can confirm pregnancy with a home pregnancy test or a laboratory test done by a health-care provider. Both work by detecting a hormone that is present only in pregnant women.

Internet Connects

http://www.mcgrawhill.ca/links/parenting
To learn more about conception, pregnancy, and parenthood, go to the Web site above for *Parenting Rewards & Responsibilities, First Canadian Edition,* to see where to go next.

Selecting Medical Care

For some pregnant women, making a choice isn't necessary when it comes to health care professionals. Where they live often determines who will provide prenatal care and deliver their babies. In some areas, such as rural or northern Canada, there may be a limited number of health-care professionals qualified to deliver babies.

A pregnant woman needs to decide whether she wishes to be cared for by a doctor or a midwife. Midwifery care is not publicly funded in some provinces. Pregnant women may visit more than one health-care professional with a list of questons before they decide on their primary caregiver.

MEDICAL SPECIALISTS

Obstetricians (OB-stuh-TRISH-uns), doctors who specialize in delivering babies,

deliver the majority of babies born in Canada. Doctors who are gynecologists but do not practise obstetrics do not deliver babies.

Many family practice physicians, trained to care for the entire family, also deliver babies. If problems arise, they consult with obstetricians.

A **registered midwife** is trained to care for women with low-risk pregnancies and to deliver their babies. If necessary, registered midwives will consult with an obstetrician or pediatrician. Registered midwives are preferred by some women because of the personal attention they give.

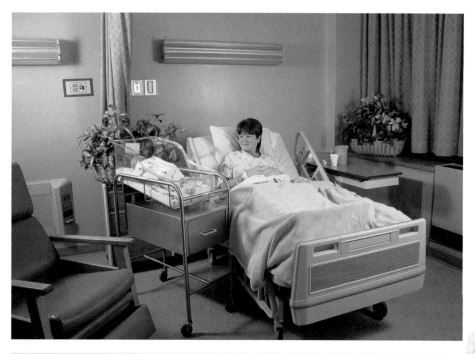

All pregnant women with a valid health card are entitled to hospital care. Some have extra health insurance through their place of work. ◆ **What might these benefits pay for?**

THE COSTS OF HAVING A BABY

Having a baby is expensive. The services of a medical professional, medical tests, and a hospital stay are usually covered by provincial health-care plans. However, depending on where the baby is born, additional costs may be the responsibility of the parent. For example, the cost of a private or semi-private room for the mother's hospital stay, and the cost of ambulance service may be extra. Some parents have medical insurance through their employers that will cover these costs.

Other out-of-pocket costs are not covered by workplace health insurance. Circumcision is not covered by most provincial health-care plans. Publicly funded midwifery care is available only in some provinces. In other provinces, parents who wish to be cared for by a midwife must pay for these services.

Although Becky and Justin did not have to worry about the cost of health care, there were other costs to think about. In the baby's first year, parents need to buy formula, baby food, clothing, and diapers. Some babies require prescription medication. If parents do not have medical insurance through their workplace or a provincial drug care plan, they must pay for medication. Parents who return to work may need to pay for childcare. According to Manitoba Agriculture and Food, in 2003 the cost to raise a baby from birth to age 1 was about $10 000. Of this amount $4500 was budgeted for the cost of childcare, $1700 was for clothing, and $1450 was for food.

THE FIRST EXAM

Choosing a doctor must not be delayed, because the first visit should occur early in pregnancy. Typically, the first appointment is the longest one.

Tiffany's initial visit began with her obstetrician asking for a complete medical history of both her and her husband. Dr. Stein assured her that all information was confidential. There were questions about her menstrual history, other pregnancies, and diseases or genetic problems. Tiffany was also asked if either of them smoked, drank, or had a sexually transmitted disease.

The nurse weighed Tiffany after she changed into a hospital gown. After taking her blood pressure, the nurse drew blood from her arm. One purpose of the blood test is to detect **anemia**, a low blood count, or too few red blood cells.

After requesting a urine specimen, the nurse asked Tiffany to bring one to every future appointment. Urine tests can determine infection, diabetes, and hypertension.

Dr. Stein returned to perform both an external exam and an internal, or pelvic, exam. This allowed the doctor to determine the size and position of her uterus.

The doctor performed a Pap smear by scraping cells from her cervix, the narrow lower end of the uterus. This routine test checks for cancer or precancer of the cervix. The internal exam was a little uncomfortable, but not painful.

Health & Safety

THE Rh FACTOR

Routine prenatal care includes testing blood for the **Rh factor** (Rhesus). If this protein is present in a pregnant woman's blood, she is termed Rh-positive; if not, she is Rh-negative. Since Rh-positive people account for about 85 percent of the population, the factor is usually of no concern.

Serious problems can arise, however, if an Rh-negative woman carries a baby who has inherited Rh-positive blood from the father. This is called *Rh incompatibility*. As the baby passes through the birth canal—whether live, miscarried, or aborted— some of its blood enters the mother's circulatory system. Her immune system regards this foreign blood type as a threat and begins producing antibodies against it. While that child may not be harmed, future pregnancies could result in brain deformities, jaundice, or miscarriage as the antibodies attack the baby's red blood cells.

Women who test Rh-negative are vaccinated with a blood protein called RhoGAM, which prevents the body from producing antibodies. An immature fetus may be given a blood transfusion, allowing development in the uterus until survival is likely at delivery.

Available treatments have made infant death or defect due to Rh incompatibility completely avoidable. A woman should remind her doctor if she is Rh-negative, especially if she is receiving care from several doctors in a group practice or a public clinic.

Regular Visits

Health-care providers schedule monthly appointments for maternity patients. During the seventh month, visits usually increase to every two weeks. Weekly visits are standard during the ninth month. Doctors and midwives welcome fathers-to-be at checkups. By attending, fathers can feel more involved in the pregnancy.

Some women jot down questions and concerns between visits so they don't forget to ask. Phoning the office is also acceptable.

Spotlight On
The Due Date

A due date is only an estimate. Some studies indicate only about 5 percent of all babies are born on their due date. Most are born within two weeks after or before that day. The due date is determined by adding seven days to the date of the woman's last menstrual period and then counting back three months. For instance, if a patient's last period began on March 5, the resulting due date would be December 12. Other methods are used to determine dates for women with irregular menstrual cycles.

Internet Connects

http://www.mcgrawhill.ca/links/parenting
To learn more about the health and welfare of children, go to the Web site above for *Parenting Rewards & Responsibilities, First Canadian Edition*, to see where to go next.

Prenatal Development

Prenatal development begins at the moment of conception and ends at birth. Development progresses through three stages: zygote, embryo, and fetus. The illustrations beginning on page 158 show the changes that occur during these stages.

Changes in the expectant mother's body result from the fast-paced development occurring in her uterus. An expanding abdomen is the most obvious characteristic of pregnancy, but certainly it isn't the only one.

Pregnancy is divided into **trimesters**, three segments, each three months long. While no two pregnancies are the same, certain physical and emotional changes are typical of each trimester.

THE FIRST TRIMESTER

Surabhi was surprised that she could wear her regular clothes during her first trimester. She hadn't realized that weight gain is usually minimal, only three or four pounds, during the first three months. Like most pregnant women, Surabhi noticed an increase in the size of her breasts and her abdomen. Pressure on her bladder from the enlarging uterus caused a need to urinate more frequently. Her main complaints were not getting enough sleep and feeling irritable.

Surabhi's physician explained that changing hormones were responsible for the changes she experienced, including her fatigue. Surabhi was thankful that she had no morning sickness to report.

Growth of the Fetus

Month	Length	Weight
Third Month	2.5–8 cm (1–3 in.)	28–56 g (1–2 oz.)
Fourth Month	8–15 cm (3–6 in.)	56–140 g (2–5 oz.)
Fifth Month	15–20 cm (6–8 in.)	140–340 g (5–12 oz.)
Sixth Month	20–25 cm (8–10 in.)	340–900 g (12 oz.–2 lbs.)
Seventh Month	25–36 cm (10–14 in.)	900 g–1.4 kg (2–3 lbs.)
Eighth Month	36–43 cm (14–17 in.)	1.4–2.3 kg (3–5 lbs.)
Ninth Month	43–53 cm (17–21 in.)	2.3–4.6 kg (5–10 lbs.)

These length and weight ranges are approximate. They show what the fetus might measure and weigh during the course of each month. The fetus gains most of its weight during the last 13 weeks of development. Although a birth weight of 3.4 kg (7½ lbs.) is typical, weights do vary considerably. ◆ **What might explain the variations in length and weight?**

THE SECOND TRIMESTER

Feeling the baby move, called *quickening*, is a highlight of the second trimester. Health-care providers are interested in when their patients first feel movement. Quickening usually occurs during the fourth month and helps confirm the due date.

Women begin to wear larger clothes or maternity clothes as their weight gain accelerates. Eating correctly is important, and expectant mothers must keep in mind that pregnancy is *not* a time to diet.

"I feel great. The morning sickness is over and food tastes good to me again," Susan told her midwife. "It's funny, though. Larry has been teasing me because I'm so clumsy. I drop things all the time. And I can never find my keys."

Susan's midwife explained the reason for the clumsiness: Susan's centre of gravity was changing. Her ligaments were stretching to prepare for the birth, making her limbs more "loose." As for her absent-mindedness, she could blame hormones.

Other possible discomforts of the second trimester include backaches, constipation, heartburn, bleeding gums, and leg cramps. Dizziness is fairly common but should be reported promptly to the doctor. Mood swings are not as likely by the sixth month. For some women, morning sickness continues into the second trimester and beyond. At least 80 percent of morning sickness sufferers, however, report relief after the first trimester.

The Months Before Birth

The miracle of birth is preceded by a nine-month developmental process. The growth and changes that take place are amazing.

WHAT HAPPENS IN THE FIRST STAGE?

The Stage of the Zygote (Two Weeks).
After the sperm unites with the ovum, the new cell is called a **zygote** (ZY-goht). The zygote divides into two cells, then four, then eight, and so on. Within five days, the zygote contains about 500 cells. Within a few more days, the zygote travels down the fallopian tube and attaches to the wall of the uterus. The zygote is changing into a ball of cells with a hollow centre. On about the fourteenth day, the zygote implants in the lining of the uterus.

WHAT HAPPENS IN THE SECOND STAGE?

The Stage of the Embryo (Six Weeks).
Once implanted in the uterine wall, the zygote is called an **embryo** (EM-bree-oh). The **umbilical cord** (uhm-BILL-ih-kuhl) extends from the embryo at the navel and connects to the **placenta** (pluh-SENT-uh), tissue attached to the uterine wall. The embryo is cushioned inside a fluid-filled pouch called the **amniotic sac** (am-nee-OTT-ik). Nutrients and oxygen from the mother's bloodstream pass to the embryo through the placenta and umbilical cord. Waste products return to the woman in the same way and are discharged through her body.

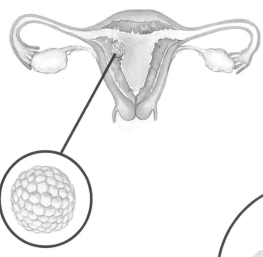

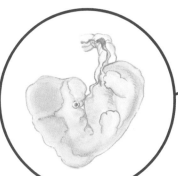

During this stage, all major body systems begin to develop. The central nervous system, blood vessels, stomach, and heart are beginning to form, as are the eyes, lungs, arms, legs, hands, and feet. The brain grows at a rapid pace. By the eighth week, the embryo is no more than 2.5 cm (1 in.) long but is starting to resemble a human being.

WHAT HAPPENS IN THE THIRD STAGE?

The Stage of the Fetus (Seven Months).
At the end of the second month, the embryo passes into the third and final stage of prenatal development. The unborn child is then called a **fetus** (FEE-tus). From a small embryo about the size of a walnut, the fetus will increase 50 times in size. During this time, fetal development is a process of growth and maturation. The body, head, arms, and legs grow rapidly. Organs develop for blood circulation, breathing, and digestion. Nerves and muscles also develop. The heart pumps blood through a long network of veins and arteries. The brain, the most intricate part of the body, develops rapidly.

Third Month

➤ Nostrils, mouth, lips, teeth buds, and eyelids form.

➤ Fingers and toes are almost complete.

➤ Gender is evident.

➤ Heartbeat can be heard with a stethoscope.

➤ All organs are present though immature.

Fourth Month

➤ Skin is less transparent than before.

➤ Fine hair covers the entire body.

➤ The fetus can suck its thumb, swallow, hiccup, and move around.

➤ Facial features become clearer.

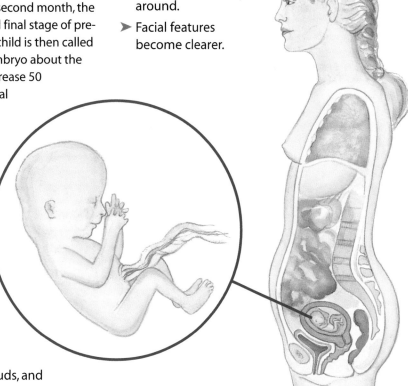

The Months Before Birth continued

Fifth Month

➤ Hair, eyelashes, and eyebrows appear.

➤ Teeth continue to develop.

➤ Organs are maturing.

➤ Hands are able to grip.

➤ The fetus becomes more active.

Sixth Month

➤ Eyes open and close.

➤ Muscles in the arms and legs strengthen.

➤ Fat deposits begin to appear beneath wrinkly skin.

➤ Breathing movements begin.

Seventh Month

➤ A thick white protective coating called vernix covers the fetus.

➤ Nervous, circulatory, and other systems mature.

➤ Periods of fetal activity are followed by periods of rest and quiet.

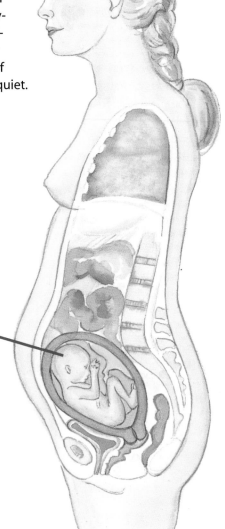

Eighth Month

➤ The fetus hears sounds and may be startled by sudden noises.

➤ The fetus usually moves into a head-down position.

Ninth Month

➤ Increased fat under the skin makes the fetus look less wrinkled.

➤ Fetal movement decreases with less room to move.

➤ The fetus gains disease-fighting antibodies from the mother's blood.

➤ The fetus descends into the pelvis, ready for birth.

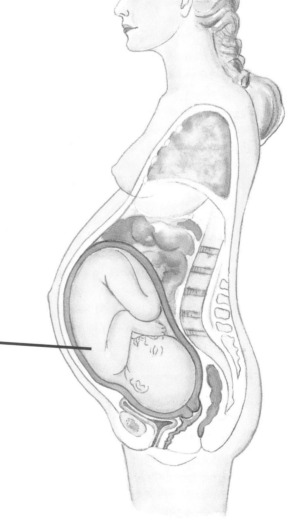

Spotlight On
Morning Sickness

About half of all pregnant women experience morning sickness in the early weeks of pregnancy. Nausea, and sometimes vomiting, can occur in the morning or at any time of day. Fortunately, there are ways to deal with morning sickness. What works for one woman may make another mother-to-be feel worse. These tips are worth trying:

✔ Get up slowly in the morning.

✔ Nibble on crackers.

✔ Eat frequent, small meals to avoid an empty stomach.

✔ Drink liquids between, instead of with, meals. Eat ice chips if necessary.

✔ Try chewing gum or sucking on hard candy.

✔ Avoid caffeine.

✔ Avoid strong smells, including tobacco smoke.

✔ Limit stress. Allow people to help you.

THE THIRD TRIMESTER

What does it feel like to be eight or nine months pregnant? Some women are quite comfortable. Others are not. One reason is the added weight they carry, especially in the final three months of pregnancy.

Physical discomforts that were possible in the second trimester can show up at this later stage. Hemorrhoids, varicose veins, and swollen ankles and feet are also common, but doctors and nurses can give tips to minimize the problems.

During the eighth month, the mother may experience shortness of breath because the top of the uterus is pushing against the woman's diaphragm. As time for delivery approaches, most women experience *lightening*. The fetus drops lower in the abdomen. As the fetus settles, breathing becomes somewhat easier, but pressure on the bladder increases.

Emotions can range from apprehension to anxiousness. "I worry about the baby being healthy," said Anna. "Then sometimes I feel like I just want to get this over with. I feel like I've been pregnant forever."

Fathers-to-be are often anxious too. Concerns might range from facing the realities of fatherhood, to what kind of father they will be, to a fear of the additional responsibilities.

WARNING SIGNS

Some discomfort is typical of most pregnancies, but certain symptoms need to be reported immediately. These are:

♥ Vaginal bleeding.

♥ Extreme puffiness in hands and/or face.

♥ Severe or persistent abdominal pain.

♥ Severe headache.

♥ Dizziness.

♥ Blurred vision.

♥ Sudden weight gain of more than a kilogram (two pounds).

♥ Sudden increase in thirst followed by little urination.

♥ Painful or burning urination.

♥ Chills and fever over 38°C (100°F).

♥ Feeling no movement for 24 hours (after 20 weeks of pregnancy).

♥ Feeling little movement (after 28 weeks of pregnancy).

Prenatal Tests

The health of every expectant mother should be monitored closely during pregnancy. Today's technology makes it possible to check on the condition of the fetus too. Tests can help determine if the baby needs special medical treatment before or after birth.

Some parents prefer not to have any testing done. Others use the test results to help them make decisions about the pregnancy and about future pregnancies. When a test is recommended, the parents should discuss the advantages and the risks with the doctor.

ULTRASOUND

The most common procedure during pregnancy is **ultrasound**. As a wand is rubbed across the mother's abdomen, a video image is produced by sound waves bouncing off her internal structures. Mothers may receive a two-dimensional picture of the fetus, called a sonogram, as a result of an ultrasound.

Often done in the doctor's office, ultrasound is considered safe. During a typical pregnancy, a health-care provider may order one or two ultrasounds. Ultrasound can detect more than one fetus, defects in the fetal organs, the position before delivery, and the baby's gender. The procedure also helps determine due date.

Dizziness is a warning sign that should be reported immediately.

AMNIOCENTESIS

Drawing fluid from the amniotic sac by inserting a fine needle into the mother's abdomen is called **amniocentesis** (am-nee-oh-sen-TEE-sis). The test is done between the fifteenth and eighteenth weeks of pregnancy. Mothers over the age of 35 are most likely to be tested since they have a higher incidence of babies born with Down syndrome. Besides Down syndrome, an "amnio" tests for hundreds of other genetic and chromosomal disorders.

Amniocentesis carries a very slight risk of infection that could lead to miscarriage. Ultrasound is performed during the procedure so the doctor can see where the fetus is when inserting the needle. Parents with a family history of certain diseases are advised to consider amniocentesis as a diagnostic tool.

MULTIPLE MARKER SCREENING TESTS

Sophisticated tests performed on a sample of blood between the fifteenth and eighteenth weeks of pregnancy are able to screen for certain birth defects. The test does not *prove* that a fetus has a disorder. Based on substances in the mother's blood, the degree of likelihood that there could be a problem is given.

♥ *hCG.* A high level of a substance called hCG (human chorionic gonadotropin) can indicate a greater likelihood of having a baby with Down syndrome. A doctor is likely to follow up with amniocentesis.

♥ *MSAFP.* Another substance measured by the second-trimester blood test is maternal-serum alpha-fetoprotein or MSAFP. AFP is a protein produced by the liver of the fetus and detected in the mother's blood. A low level of AFP may indicate Down syndrome. A high reading might indicate another defect. Based on the readings alone, a physician wouldn't conclude that there was a problem. Another blood test and possibly different procedures, such as ultrasound and amniocentesis, would be recommended.

Sonograms give the future parent a view of how the fetus is developing. ◆ **Why do you think such images are exciting for a parent-to-be?**

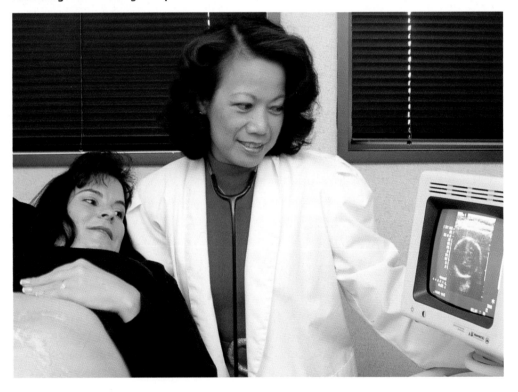

Jill and her husband were alarmed when the obstetrician asked to repeat her MSAFP test. They were relieved to learn that less than 5 percent of the women with high readings from the first test are subsequently found to be carrying a baby with problems.

CHORIONIC VILLUS SAMPLING

Chorionic villus sampling (kor-ee-AHN-ik) (CVS) is the first test for birth defects that may be performed during pregnancy. During the tenth or eleventh week, fragments of the placenta are removed from the uterus through a tube. The tube is inserted through the abdomen or the vagina. As with amniocentesis, the procedure is done at a medical centre. Ultrasound is used at the same time to guide the physician.

CVS can detect certain disorders, such as cystic fibrosis and Down syndrome. In the future CVS may be able to detect thousands of disorders. It carries a slightly higher risk of miscarriage than amniocentesis. There have been some reports of babies born with a deformed limb after CVS has been performed.

Parenting Q & A

Technology and Decisions

Q "My wife's sister has had some prenatal tests we've never heard of. How do you know what to do when medical technology comes with questions people never used to face?" *Rob*

A Technological advances offer solutions to long-standing problems. At the same time, of course, they challenge you to learn more and make decisions, sometimes difficult ones. Prenatal technology is no different. For example, amniocentesis can detect many birth defects. What does a couple do if it shows a deformity? Should life-saving prenatal surgery be performed if the child is still left seriously disabled? In the case of abortion and medically assisted pregnancy, the procedures themselves are controversial, regardless of the circumstances. Other questions arise: Should a procedure be available to all who seek it? Only to those who can afford it? Who should decide these matters? Prospective parents like you and your wife can prepare for tough decisions by developing clear values, good communication skills with each other, and good decision-making skills.

When a Pregnancy Ends

Some pregnancies end spontaneously, usually during the first trimester. A defect in the fertilized ovum or a woman's physical problems may be the reason. A pregnancy can also be terminated by medical procedures.

MISCARRIAGES

According to a Canadian survey, at least one in six pregnancies ends in a miscarriage, the spontaneous expulsion of the fetus from the uterus. Most occur during the first 12 weeks of pregnancy. Some researchers believe that more than 20 percent of all pregnancies end in miscarriage before women ever realize they are pregnant.

Possible signs of miscarriage include cramps in the centre of the abdomen and bleeding. Women who suspect a miscarriage should put their feet up or lie down and call their doctor for instructions.

Many myths persist about miscarriage. Physical activity, stress, and minor falls are *not* believed to cause them.

For most expectant parents, miscarriage is a sorrowful event. "I was devastated when I miscarried after ten weeks," Emily recalled. "What I really hated was when people said I was young and could have more children. They just didn't have a clue about what we were feeling."

A pregnant woman should report any warning signs to her health-care provider. Many problems can be corrected if treated promptly.

Pregnancy—A Natural Process

Maintaining a positive attitude is indispensable for pregnant women. Remembering that their condition is a natural one and learning as much as possible about pregnancy can help mothers-to-be have a healthy and happy nine months. Unlike patients in the waiting rooms of many medical offices, most expectant mothers aren't suffering from an "illness." They are experiencing a natural process.

Internet Connects

http://www.mcgrawhill.ca/links/parenting
To learn more about family issues, parenting, child development, and how-to advice, go to the Web site above for *Parenting Rewards & Responsibilities, First Canadian Edition,* to see where to go next.

Pregnancy comes with emotional changes for the mother and father. Supportive people who share their thoughts and feelings can help each other adjust.

CHAPTER 8

Review

Looking Back

- ♥ Missing a menstrual period is the usual indicator of pregnancy.

- ♥ Many women have a choice in health-care providers. The exams and the timing of visits are fairly standard, no matter which type you see.

- ♥ Prenatal development consists of the zygote stage, embryo stage, and fetus stage.

- ♥ Each trimester of pregnancy has unique characteristics, ranging from fatigue to clumsiness. All vary with the individual, however.

- ♥ Bleeding and pain are serious warning signs that require calling the doctor or midwife.

- ♥ Prenatal tests are now available to identify possible problems with a fetus.

- ♥ Miscarriages are physical occurrences with great emotional impact.

Knowledge and Understanding

1. What are three possible indications of pregnancy?
2. What is the difference between an obstetrician, family practice physician, and a registered midwife?
3. What typically happens at a woman's first prenatal appointment?
4. Which stage in the months before birth do you think is the most amazing? Why?
5. What is the fluid-filled pouch that encloses the embryo and fetus called? What is its purpose?
6. What are three possible ways of dealing with morning sickness?
7. Why do expectant mothers sometimes become clumsy?
8. What are five signs that something could be wrong during pregnancy?
9. How does an ultrasound differ from amniocentesis? Which is more common?
10. When do most miscarriages occur? Is it possible to miscarry and not know it?

Review

Thinking and Inquiry

11. What are the advantages of pregnancy tests done by a laboratory? Of home pregnancy tests?
12. What is the difference between the discomforts of pregnancy and warning signs that something could be wrong? Name several discomforts of pregnancy and compare them to warning signs in pregnancy.
13. Why do women visit their health-care providers more often as their pregnancy progresses?
14. Why is a pap smear a test that every woman (pregnant or not) should have?

Communication

15. The ultrasound technician says that he can tell you your baby's gender. Would you want to know ahead of time? Why or why not? What would be your thoughts if you were having twins? Write a letter to your unborn baby explaining your reasoning.
16. Design a flyer for the public health department outlining the possible warning signs of trouble during pregnancy.

Application

17. If a pregnant woman's last menstrual period began on March 20, what would be her due date? What is the likely range of time when the baby would be born?
18. Suppose that a close friend has confided only in you that she may be pregnant. She has not purchased a pregnancy test or called a doctor. You want to encourage her to see a doctor right away. What advice would you give your friend?
19. Visit your provincial health care plan Web site to find out what is paid for by your provincial health care plan. What services are not covered?

Prenatal Care

CHAPTER EXPECTATIONS

While reading this chapter, you will:

▶ Outline the stages in the biological process of conception, pregnancy, and birth.

▶ Demonstrate an understanding of how new parents can become capable and confident in making choices that are in the best interests of their children before and during birth, and in the first few months after birth.

KEY TERMS

Canada's Food Guide to Healthy Eating
fetal alcohol syndrome (FAS)
gestational diabetes
nutrient density

preeclampsia
rubella
sexually transmitted diseases (STDs)
stress
teratogens
toxoplasmosis

It was 3 a.m. Robin sat up in bed and placed a hand over her abdomen. She could feel the baby kicking.

"What's wrong?" Steve asked, sleepily awakening to his wife's motions.

"I'm starving," Robin replied. "I really, really want some of that chocolate mint ice cream we bought today."

Steve glanced at the clock. "At 3 a.m.?" he asked. "Is this another one of your cravings? Wasn't it horseradish sauce last month?" Steve wearily pulled himself up to a sitting position.

"Well, yes," Robin said, "but I think I'm over that. Right now all I can think about is a dish of ice cream, especially chocolate mint. Do you want some?"

By this time Steve was awake. "No, but I'll pamper you tonight. I'll get some for you." Steve patted Robin's hand, lifted himself slowly from the bed, and shuffled toward the doorway.

"Oh, Steve," Robin smiled impishly, "Would you top the ice cream with a little horseradish sauce, please?"

———— ◆ ————

What do you think? In what ways do you think a sense of humour can help a couple through pregnancy and childbirth?

All parents want to have a healthy baby. ◆ **How can they make that dream a reality?**

"Now I can eat whatever I want. No more counting calories and fat grams!" Holly exclaimed. "And after work, don't look for me in my jogging clothes. I'll be on the couch in front of the TV."

Her friend just laughed. She knew Holly was joking about her pregnancy. As nurses, both women knew the importance of exercise and eating right during pregnancy.

A BALANCED DIET

Pregnancy is definitely not a time to skip meals or diet to lose weight. It *is* a time to avoid junk food and eat food that is healthy. Not only will nutritious foods help the baby, but they can also relieve some common discomforts of pregnancy. For instance, drinking plenty of water and eating foods high in fibre help prevent constipation and hemorrhoids. Avoiding greasy or spicy foods can prevent heartburn.

Changing Habits

Women who are healthy and well nourished when they become pregnant have a head start, but when that's not the case, helpful new eating habits can be developed quickly. A first step is learning about nutritious foods and stocking the kitchen with them. Changing habits might also be necessary. For example, taking a nutritious lunch to work instead of eating at fast food restaurants is a good idea.

Nutrient density is the relationship between the amount and types of nutrients a food has and the number of calories it

Eating Right

How many times have you heard the expression "You are what you eat"? The statement takes on special meaning for pregnant women. The food they consume has to keep their own body strong while building another tiny person.

contains. Contrast a lunch of a cheese-burger, fries, and a soft drink with a meal of a turkey sandwich on whole grain bread, fresh fruit, and low-fat milk. You can guess that the sandwich, fruit, and milk have a much better and higher nutrient density, making that meal a better choice.

Pregnant women need to consume 300 to 500 more calories than they normally do each day for appropriate weight. Most of these extra calories should come from essential nutrients found in foods that appear on the lower portion of the *Canada's Food Guide to Healthy Eating*. The Rainbow on page 150 is a guide to how many servings from the food groups people should eat each day. The nutrients found in the food groups include protein, carbohydrates, fats, vitamins, minerals, and water.

Protein

Protein is especially important for a growing fetus. The amino acids in protein help build the brain, muscles, hair, skin, nails, and immune system. Meat, poultry, fish, eggs, beans, and milk contain protein. High-protein supplements should *not* be used.

Carbohydrates

More than half of an expectant mother's daily calories should come from carbohydrates. A variety of foods with complex carbohydrates is the most desirable. They are foods that originate from plants: grains, cereals, pasta, peas, beans, nuts, and seeds. Foods like whole-grain bread, rice, potatoes, and corn are good choices.

Carbohydrates are also found in foods with low nutrient density, such as candy, soft drinks, and desserts. They should not be eaten in place of foods that supply necessary nutrients.

Studies have shown that the health of a newborn is directly linked to a pregnant woman's diet. ◆ **Why are fresh fruits and vegetables a much better choice than typical fast foods?**

Fats

Some people go to great lengths to avoid fats. In truth, they are vital for good health and energy, and to allow the body to use vitamins A, D, E, and K. Fats, however, should account for no more than 30 percent of a woman's calories, pregnant or not. Calories from fat can add up quickly, so it's wise to limit fried foods. Broiled, steamed, roasted, and baked foods are better choices.

Canada's Food Guide to Healthy Eating

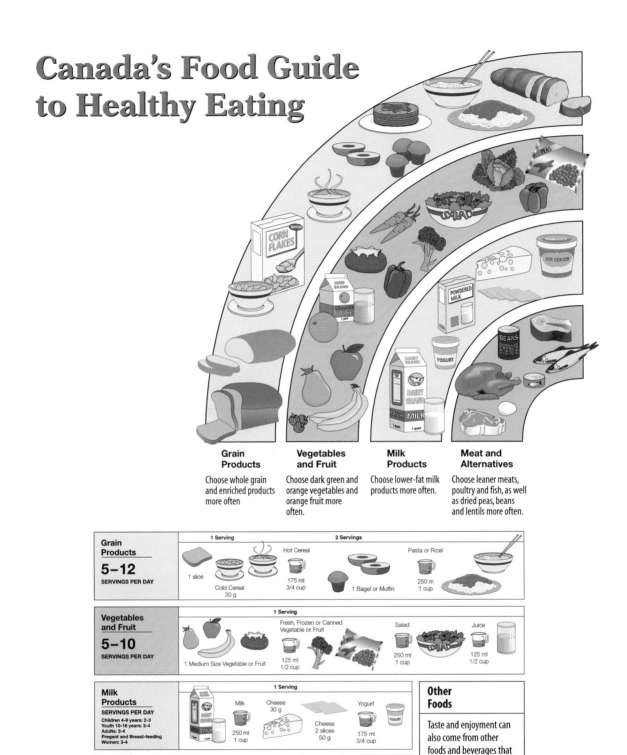

Grain Products

Choose whole grain and enriched products more often

Vegetables and Fruit

Choose dark green and orange vegetables and orange fruit more often.

Milk Products

Choose lower-fat milk products more often.

Meat and Alternatives

Choose leaner meats, poultry and fish, as well as dried peas, beans and lentils more often.

Grain Products

5–12 SERVINGS PER DAY

1 Serving			2 Servings		
1 slice	Cold Cereal 30 g	Hot Cereal 175 ml 3/4 cup	1 Bagel or Muffin	Pasta or Rice! 250 m 1 cup	

Vegetables and Fruit

5–10 SERVINGS PER DAY

1 Serving				
1 Medium Size Vegetable or Fruit	Fresh, Frozen or Canned Vegetable or Fruit 125 ml 1/2 cup	Salad 250 ml 1 cup	Juice 125 ml 1/2 cup	

Milk Products

SERVINGS PER DAY

Children 4-9 years: 2-3
Youth 10-16 years: 3-4
Adults: 2-4
Pregant and Breast-feeding Women: 3-4

1 Serving			
Milk 250 ml 1 cup	Cheese 30 g	Cheese 2 slices 50 g	Yogurt 175 ml 3/4 cup

Other Foods

Taste and enjoyment can also come from other foods and beverages that are not part of the four food groups. Some of these foods are higher in fat or calories, so use these foods in moderation.

Meat and Alternatives

2–3 SERVINGS PER DAY

1 Serving				
Meat, Poultry or Fish 50–100 g	1/3–1/2 Can 50–100 g	1–2 Eggs	Beans 125–250 ml 100 g 1/3 cup	Peanut Butter 30 ml 2 tbsp

Vitamins

Erika knew her eating habits weren't good, so she counted on getting what she needed from potent vitamin tablets. What she didn't know was that too many vitamins could be very harmful to her and her baby. Erika's physician did prescribe a vitamin-mineral supplement but also stressed the importance of a healthy diet. A growing number of doctors prescribe only an iron supplement and insist that patients get the necessary vitamins from nutritious foods. Some of the most important vitamins during pregnancy are:

♥ *Folic acid.* Also known as folate, folic acid helps produce extra blood. Especially important during the first trimester, .4 mg of folic acid is recommended daily to prevent birth defects of the nervous system. Broccoli, green leafy vegetables, and orange juice are rich in folate. Breads, pasta, and grain products are now fortified with folate.

♥ *B vitamins.* In addition to folic acid, other B vitamins are important for nerve cells and the formation of red blood cells. Many are found in meats, grains, and milk products.

♥ *Vitamin A.* Vitamin A is vital for developing cells, bones, and vision, but too much can cause birth defects. Milk products, as well as fruits and vegetables that are orange, dark green, and deep yellow, contain vitamin A.

♥ *Vitamin C.* Vitamin C helps produce collagen, which gives structure to bones, muscles, and blood vessels. It also helps the body absorb iron. Besides orange juice, good sources are melon, tomatoes, and green peppers.

♥ *Vitamin D.* Development of bones and tissue are aided by Vitamin D. Milk, egg yolks, and sunlight are sources.

Internet Connects

http://www.mcgrawhill.ca/links/parenting
To learn more about parenting from A to Z, go to the Web site above for *Parenting Rewards & Responsibilities, First Canadian Edition,* to see where to go next.

If a mother-to-be doesn't consume enough calcium-rich foods, the fetus will rob calcium from her bones. Later in life she could develop osteoporosis, a disease that produces fragile bones.

Minerals

Many valuable minerals are found in foods. Calcium and iron are two of the most important minerals for expectant mothers and their babies.

CALCIUM. You have probably heard that calcium builds strong bones and teeth. The fetus draws calcium from the mother's body if she doesn't consume enough for both of them. Milk, yogurt, and broccoli are sources of calcium.

IRON. Pregnant women need twice the iron that other adults require. Iron is used to create the blood supply of the fetus. It bolsters the mother's red blood cells, which supply oxygen to the fetus. Dried fruits and organ meats are good sources of iron, but taking a supplement is still advisable.

Water

Drinking at least eight glasses of water, juice, and other liquids each day is essential to good health for the mother and the developing fetus. More is recommended if the weather is hot or the woman is retaining water.

WEIGHT GAIN

Most doctors now recommend that a woman gain 10–15 kg (25 to 35 lbs.) during pregnancy, depending on the size of her frame. This may sound extreme to weight-conscious women, but it is important to the health of the baby.

Parenting Q & A

Changing Tastes?

Q "I'm not usually a chocolate fanatic, but now that I'm pregnant, I want a chocolate bar every day. We used to eat eggs and bacon, but now I can't stand the taste or smell. Is my body telling me that eggs and bacon aren't good for me, but chocolate is?" *Linda*

A Many pregnant women develop food cravings and dislikes. Changing hormones are partially responsible. Sometimes a pregnant woman craves a food her body needs, but your craving for chocolate is different. You can give in occasionally, but a chocolate bar has extra calories and no nutritional value. Try a cup of yogurt or granola bar instead. Your reaction to eggs and bacon fits with a pregnant woman's aversion to some smells. Because of bacon's high fat content, you can skip it. Try a scrambled or poached egg since extra cholesterol is okay during pregnancy. Have you ever heard of an expectant mother craving non-food substances, such as clay, ashes, or laundry starch? This condition, called pica, may signal a serious lack of iron. Of course, you should tell your doctor about this or any craving.

With a prenatal weight gain of less than 10 kg (20 lbs.), babies often have a low birth weight. When a mother gains too little weight, the fetus must live off her fat stores, resulting in calories but no nutrients.

The baby accounts for only part of the weight gain. The placenta, additional blood, and expanded tissues weigh about twice what the fetus does. The chart below shows a breakdown of weight gained during a typical pregnancy.

Weight is seldom gained at a steady pace, but women should avoid sudden jumps or drops in weight. An average or ideal weight gain is 1–2 kg (3–4 lbs.) during the first trimester, about 6–8 kg (12–14 lbs.) the second trimester, and then 4–5 kg (8–10 lbs.) during the final three months. About a kilogram (pound) a week is typical during the second trimester, but gaining 1 kg (1½ lbs.) one week and .5 kg (½ lb.) the next isn't a problem. A sudden big gain may indicate water retention, which can be extremely serious.

Adequate Activity and Rest

Most healthy women are able to continue their normal activities for most of the pregnancy. Working women often continue their jobs until their due date. Others decide to quit or begin a maternity leave earlier.

Getting plenty of sleep is important. Ten hours a night is not uncommon. Fatigue is most likely during the first trimester and then again during late pregnancy, but can occur anytime. A pregnant woman should make time for a nap or a warm (not hot) bath, or to put her feet up. Three out of four expectant mothers experience swollen ankles and feet. Elevating the legs can help relieve swelling.

EXERCISE

Exercise is also important during pregnancy. Physically fit expectant mothers not only feel better, but they are also in top shape for labour and delivery. What can a woman do if she gets plenty of sleep and is still tired? Exercise may be the answer. Rather than making her more tired, experts find exercise can help energize an expectant mother.

Physical discomforts, such as backache, constipation, heartburn, and swollen ankles, can be minimized by exercise. Are there times when exercise could do more harm than good? Definitely. Women should discuss any athletic activities with their health-care providers. They may be asked to modify an activity somewhat but will be encouraged unless the activity is a contact sport or could result in a fall.

Typical Weight Gain	
Baby	3.5 kg (7.5 lbs.)
Placenta	.5 kg (1.5 lbs.)
Amniotic Fluid	1 kg (2 lbs.)
Uterine Enlargement	1 kg (2 lbs.)
Breast Growth	1 kg (2 lbs.)
Fluids and Blood	4 kg (8 lbs.)
Fat and Nutrient Stores . . .	3 kg (7 lbs.)
Average Gain	**15 kg (30 lbs.)**

Health & Safety

Exercise is good for expectant mothers, but some sensible guidelines need to be followed. If a pregnant woman was jogging, swimming, or cross-country skiing before she became pregnant, health-care providers usually give the green light to continue. Generally, doctors also approve of riding a stationary bike and exercise classes for pregnant women.

Women in strenuous or contact sports need to consult their doctor or midwife, however. Racket sports, gymnastics, volleyball, and basketball can be risky. The doctor should also be asked about sports that could result in a fall, such as downhill skiing and horseback riding.

Some general rules for exercise during pregnancy include:

▶ Don't exercise on your back (after the fourth month).
▶ Never exercise so long that you become exhausted.
▶ Don't exercise on an empty stomach.
▶ Stop immediately if you have pain or bleeding or become dizzy.
▶ Cut back by the ninth month.
▶ Drink plenty of fluids.
▶ Avoid becoming overheated. Don't exercise in hot or humid conditions. Stay away from hot tubs and saunas.
▶ Don't dive (platform, deep sea, or sky).
▶ Don't surf or water ski.

Clothing Choices

One variable expense of pregnancy is for clothing. Some women spend hundreds of dollars, while others are able to get by on a very small budget.

By the fourth month, most expectant mothers are uncomfortable in their regular wardrobe. They can shop for maternity clothes at department or discount stores, maternity shops, and second-hand stores, or order from catalogues. Others select patterns for maternity clothes and sew a few outfits.

Experts recommend choosing comfortable, easy-care fabrics. They advise against shopping sprees in early pregnancy. By the ninth month, some of the garments that seemed roomy may not fit.

Borrowing from friends and relatives is a welcome option for some. "My cousin offered me two bags full of maternity clothes. I had a better wardrobe while I was pregnant than I usually do," said Parmajit, who invested only in maternity underwear and a pair of flat shoes one size larger than usual. "Two of my jumpers were loose enough to keep wearing to work. My husband's shirts and sweats were great for around the apartment."

Understanding Emotions

Pregnancy is an emotional time. Mood shifts and irritability are common. Hormones play a role, and so does the worry that life will never be the same again.

A mother-to-be has many options in maternity clothes these days. Some maternity stores even have try-on pregnancy pillows that show how a garment might fit in several months. ◆ **Would that guarantee a good fit for every woman?**

"I can't remember the last time I cried before I got pregnant," Jamie told the midwife at her four-month check-up. "Now I cry at movies, in the car, listening to the radio...wherever. Sometimes it just happens out of the blue. Other times, I'm on top of the world and I feel thrilled at the idea of becoming a mother."

COMMON WORRIES

As pregnancy progresses, women are commonly concerned about the health of their baby. Many report feeling more dependent on their partners. Both parents need to feel comfortable communicating their feelings to one another. The father-to-be may also be apprehensive about adjusting to parenthood. Being able to gain strength from each other is ideal during pregnancy.

A mother-to-be wants someone to listen to her. She needs a partner, friend, relative, or professional counsellor to whom she can speak freely. Many women choose a midwife because they feel comfortable sharing their feelings.

REDUCING STRESS

Mood swings during pregnancy can be worse when the mother-to-be is under stress. **Stress** is physical and emotional tension caused by pressures, change, and important events. Some stress is part of daily life for most people. When it results in headaches, poor appetite, or sleep problems, stress becomes a problem for expectant mothers. Some studies have shown a link between stress during pregnancy and premature births.

A woman can have mood swings during pregnancy, and so can the father-to-be. Interestingly, studies show that couples tend to have their low points at different times. ◆ **How can this timing difference be helpful to them?**

Identifying the stressors in her life is the first step to reducing a pregnant woman's stress level. Then she can look for ways to avoid or cut back on those things. Asking "How important is it?" can help weed out unnecessary responsibilities. The therapeutic effects of a warm bath, nap, listening to music, or writing in a journal can be well worth the time.

Dangers to the Fetus

Substances and exposures that can cause birth defects are called **teratogens** (tuh-RAT-uh-juhns). They include substances like alcohol and drugs, as well as other things the mother might be exposed to, such as infection and harmful fumes.

All women who could become pregnant should be aware that a fetus is like a sponge. Every substance a pregnant woman is exposed to is transmitted to the developing fetus. Unfortunately, irreversible damage can result from a woman's behaviour early in pregnancy before she realizes she is expecting. To avoid such a tragedy, women who might become pregnant should practise a lifestyle that would give a baby the best possible start.

ALCOHOL

No amount of alcohol is considered safe for a fetus. Brain damage and miscarriage can occur even if the expectant mother occasionally drinks a small quantity.

Is every baby born to a mother who drank during pregnancy going to have problems? No, but sharing wine, beer, or hard liquor with an unborn baby is a game of chance that no one should play. Women with drinking problems should speak frankly with their health-care provider about getting help immediately.

Health & Safety

Exposure to certain chemicals can be dangerous during pregnancy. Women who have contact with chemicals or do strenuous work should discuss their work environment with their health-care provider. Cutting back on hours or asking for a different job temporarily might be necessary. Some other products to avoid are:

▶ **Hair-care products.** No solid evidence proves that the chemicals could damage the fetus, but nonetheless, permanents and hairdyes are not recommended during pregnancy.

▶ **Household cleaners.** Expectant mothers can clean, but with a few precautions. Strong-smelling household cleaners should be avoided. Chlorine-based products should never be mixed with ammonia. Products with a pump spray can be substituted for aerosol sprays. Rubber gloves should be worn.

▶ **Paint products.** The expectant mother shouldn't paint the nursery. She should stay away from paint, especially paint removers.

▶ **Lead.** Everyone should avoid exposure to lead, especially pregnant women.

Fetal Alcohol Syndrome

Women who have four or more drinks a day run a high risk of having a baby with **fetal alcohol syndrome** (FAS), a condition that is the leading cause of mental challenges. In Canada, one child a day is born with FAS, often resulting in some facial disfigurement. Clumsiness, behavioural and social problems, and stunted growth are other characteristics noted in children with FAS.

Fetal alcohol effects (FAE) is more subtle than FAS. Its victims are often labelled mildly mentally challenged because of their short attention span and poor memories and judgment. No cure exists for FAS or FAE. Both go undiagnosed frequently.

SMOKING

Premature births and low birth weight are linked to smoking by the mother. Smoking reduces the amount of oxygen the fetus receives. Research shows that second-hand smoke can also be damaging.

Smoking is believed to cause complications in pregnancy as well. If a smoker hasn't quit before becoming pregnant, she should do so right away.

ILLEGAL DRUGS

Tremendous harm can come to a baby whose mother has used crack, cocaine, heroin, LSD, or other drugs during pregnancy. The newborn may be addicted at birth and is at risk for a stroke, brain

A pregnant woman can't rely on labels to tell her whether a medication is safe to take. She must talk to her health care provider before taking anything and then follow instructions if a medication is prescribed.

damage, and even death. Low birth weight and premature birth are likely. Many of these children face a lifetime of learning and behavioural problems.

Like other teratogens, marijuana crosses the placenta and can put the fetus at risk. There have been some reports of children born with characteristics that are similar to FAS. If an expectant mother has used drugs during pregnancy, she must be honest with her physician. The stakes are too high to hide such information.

Caffeine

Caffeine is plentiful in soft drinks, coffee, and tea, but pregnant women are wise to avoid it. Although not considered to be a teratogen, high caffeine intake has been linked to an increased risk of miscarriage and low birth weight.

Other adverse effects for pregnant women are possible. Caffeine draws fluids and calcium needed by the mother and fetus out of her body. It interferes with iron absorption, can prevent needed rest, and make mood swings more severe.

MEDICATIONS

A drug does not have to be illegal to harm a fetus. That's why a health care provider wants to be informed of any prescription drugs a patient is taking. If the drug is unsafe during pregnancy, the doctor may be able to prescribe a substitute.

Expectant mothers should consult the doctor or midwife before taking any over-the-counter medications. Products as common as aspirin and antacids can even be

harmful. Patients who take vitamin supplements should take them exactly as the physician prescribes.

AVOIDING INFECTIONS

Pregnant women should avoid people who have colds, flu, and other contagious illnesses, if possible. Washing hands after being in public places is always a good idea. Having a cold during pregnancy won't hurt the fetus, but not being able to take cold medicine can be uncomfortable.

Internet Connects

http://www.mcgrawhill.ca/links/parenting
To learn more about individual and family well-being, go to the Web site above for *Parenting Rewards & Responsibilities, First Canadian Edition,* to see where to go next.

Health & Safety

Often called STDs, **sexually transmitted diseases** affect millions of people. The term refers to diseases that are usually spread through sexual contact with a partner who already has the disease. Many women are unaware that they have an STD, and their partner may also not realize that he is infected. If a woman thinks she might have an STD, she should tell her health care provider in order to prevent these effects on the fetus:

▶ Genital herpes (HER-peez) may cause brain damage or mental challenges.

▶ Syphilis (SIF-uh-luhs) can cause severe damage to the fetus, or stillbirth.

▶ Gonorrhea (gahn-uh-REE-uh) can cause blindness.

▶ Chlamydia (kluh-MID-ee-uh) may result in eye infections that can turn into more serious infections.

▶ HIV, the virus that leads to AIDS, can be transmitted to the fetus by HIV-positive mothers.

Several common diseases aren't particularly harmful to adults but can seriously affect a fetus:

♥ *Rubella.* German measles, or **rubella** (roo-BELL-uh), is a relatively mild illness that can severely damage the brain, heart, eyes, and ears of a fetus. The risk is greatest during the first trimester. One in seven women has had rubella and has no need to worry. Most physicians test for rubella immunity at the first prenatal visit. For peace of mind, women can ask to be checked with a blood test before becoming pregnant. If they haven't had the disease, an immunization can be given at that time.

♥ *Chicken pox.* As many as 95 percent of women of childbearing age have already had chicken pox. Chicken pox can be dangerous to the fetus during the first half of pregnancy. As time for delivery approaches, it is a risk again. A pregnant woman who suspects she has chicken pox should call her health-care provider immediately.

♥ *Toxoplasmosis.* The eyes and brain of a fetus can be damaged by a disease that may be contracted from eating undercooked meat or from contact with cat feces. A blood test may be able to show if a woman has ever had **toxoplasmosis** (tocks-oh-plaz-MOH-sis). Expectant mothers should ask someone else to clean the cat's litter box and shouldn't garden where cats may have gone to the bathroom. Meat and poultry should be cooked thoroughly. Utensils used for raw meats should be washed well before touching other foods.

Internet Connects

http://www.mcgrawhill.ca/links/parenting
To learn more about innovative health promotion approaches, go to the Web site above for *Parenting Rewards & Responsibilities, First Canadian Edition,* to see where to go next.

Most women go through pregnancy without complications. Any concerns a couple may have can be discussed with a health-care provider.

X-RAYS

Pregnant women need to avoid radiation. X-rays should be delayed until after the baby is born, unless they are necessary for the mother's health. When technicians are informed of a patient's pregnancy, they can take precautions so the fetus is not affected.

PREGNANCY COMPLICATIONS

Maternity patients are monitored at every visit for **preeclampsia** (PREE-ah-CLAMP-see-ah), a type of high blood pressure. Also called toxemia or pregnancy-induced hypertension (PIH), the condition occurs in 5 to 10 percent of all pregnancies, most often in first-time mothers.

Preeclampsia is the reason pregnant women must immediately report sudden weight gain, puffiness in their hands and face, blurred vision, and severe headache. Left untreated, the condition turns into eclampsia. Convulsions, coma, and permanent damage to the mother can result. Being deprived of oxygen puts the fetus at risk.

Another possible complication in pregnancy is called **gestational diabetes** (jess-TAY-shun-ull dy-ah-BEET-is). This type of diabetes almost always disappears after delivery. Diagnosed by a routine glucose screening test during the sixth or seventh month of pregnancy, gestational diabetes affects about three percent of expectant mothers. Most can be treated with a special diet and exercise plan.

Delivery Countdown

Every pregnancy is different, but one thing is definite. No one is pregnant forever. After nine months or so, the time for delivery arrives. Women who have been careful about diet, exercise, and rest; have followed their health-care professional's orders; and have avoided risky behaviour can feel confident that they have done their part to give their babies the best possible start in life. Can you think of any better investment?

The fat stores in a woman's body provide calories but no nutrients to a developing fetus. ◆ **What might happen to a fetus if a woman tries to diet during her pregnancy?**

Review

Looking Back

♥ Women should seek a balanced diet, choosing many foods on the basis of nutrient density.

♥ Mothers-to-be should gain 10–15 kg (25–35 lbs.) at a fairly steady pace during pregnancy. Weight gain picks up around the fourth month, about the same time most women need maternity clothes.

♥ Exercise is encouraged during pregnancy, but health-care providers should approve the exercise or sport first.

♥ Mood swings are typical during pregnancy. Every expectant mother needs someone to listen to her feelings and concerns.

♥ Pregnant women must be aware of the risk that certain chemicals, infections, and environmental hazards pose to their unborn babies.

♥ Expectant mothers can help ensure having a healthy baby by avoiding risky behaviour, eating right, exercising, getting adequate rest, and following doctor's orders.

Knowledge and Understanding

1. How much more food does an expectant mother need to consume daily than a woman who is not pregnant?
2. What is nutrient density?
3. Why is it important for pregnant women to consume folic acid?
4. Why is dieting a very dangerous practice during pregnancy?
5. Why is exercise beneficial for pregnant women?
6. What are at least three possible ways to manage stress during pregnancy?
7. If you were an obstetrician, what five substances would you warn your patients about and why?
8. In what specific ways can STDs affect a fetus?
9. What are three infections that can harm a fetus?
10. Why is it so important for pregnant women to guard against preeclampsia?

Thinking and Inquiry

11. Why do you think some of the ideas about unsafe practices during pregnancy have changed over the years?
12. Cynthia is pregnant. Her job often gets so busy that it is very difficult to stop for lunch or even for a break. She cares about the customers and wants to keep doing her best. What do you suggest to her?
13. Suppose a pregnant woman is embarrassed or afraid to tell her obstetrician about a drug problem or a sexually transmitted disease. What could happen to her baby if she withholds this information from her doctor?
14. "Exercise is harmful to a pregnant woman." Do you agree or disagree with this statement? Give reasons for your opinion.

Communication

15. Compose a written script for a radio or television commercial stating the perils of Fetal Alcohol Syndrome.
16. Design a one-page fact sheet for teenagers, outlining a specific STD.
17. You have been asked to give a presentation on healthy eating habits and nutrition to a prenatal class. Develop the agenda for the presentation, including point-form notes on your content.

Application

18. Choose five nutrients or minerals. For each one, look for food sources that may provide these nutrients. Suggest several food choices for a pregnant mother.
19. Plan a menu for a pregnant woman for three consecutive days. Include three meals and two snacks each day. Be sure to follow *Canada's Food Guide to Healthy Eating.*
20. Make a list of five to six items that may cause stress in a pregnant woman. Exchange lists with a partner and suggest one way to help relieve stress for each item on your partner's list. After you have finished, discuss your responses together.

Preparing for Birth

CHAPTER EXPECTATIONS

While reading this chapter, you will:

▶ Outline the stages in the biological process of conception, pregnancy, and birth.

▶ Demonstrate an understanding of how new parents can become capable and confident in making choices that are in the best interests of their children before and during birth, and in the first few months.

▶ Evaluate prenatal and postnatal care/support programs available for parents in the community.

KEY TERMS

birthing room	parental leave
delivery	pediatrician
formula	prepared
labour	childbirth
layette	sibling

"What did you say Mrs. Darrow called that thing?" Pauline asked her daughter Tanya as she folded a tiny undershirt. Tanya and Barry's first child was due in a few months, and Pauline was helping sort through some used baby items given by a neighbour.

"An empathy belly," Tanya repeated. "It weighs about 12 kilograms and has straps that fasten over the shoulders to hold it in place. All the fathers at childbirth class had to try it on. Barry looked about eight months pregnant."

"I'll bet he loved that," Pauline laughed.

"He did—at first. You know him. At first he was clowning around, acting like he couldn't walk, lurching from side to side. Then Mrs. Darrow had him try to tie his shoes, and carry a couple bags of groceries, and… well, I think it opened Barry's eyes. He does all the vacuuming now, and the laundry, so I don't have to haul those loads up and down stairs. And I think he really understands now when I say I'm tired and need to rest."

"You mean," Pauline grinned and raised her brows, "he's been more *empathetic* since he tried on the empathy belly?"

◆

What do you think? What are some other ways that empathy might help as Barry and Tanya experience the birth of their child?

A mother-to-be often wonders what's ahead. She may have certain fears.
◆ **Why would planning and preparing be helpful?**

Planning for childbirth can dispel fears, since wise planning starts with getting information. New parents may be surprised to learn of all the decisions and preparations they need to make before the baby arrives. They should discuss options with their obstetrician. Health clinics, hospitals, public health offices, and the Internet are also good sources of information. Friends and relatives who have had babies can offer tips that worked well for them.

Pregnancy and childbirth are easier when expectant parents share in preparations. Talking about names, shopping, fixing space for the baby—all of these are more enjoyable for two. A father's involvment throughtout the pregnancy brings him closer to the mother and child at birth.

Preparation Pays Off

When people aren't prepared for an event, what happens? Aren't these possible: problems, anxiety, disappointment, confusion, and mistakes? No one wants these results when having a baby. Preparation can make the difference between an unpleasant experience and one that goes smoothly.

PREPARED CHILDBIRTH CLASSES

To feel truly "ready and able," many parents-to-be choose the prepared childbirth approach. In **prepared childbirth**, expectant parents understand and take an active role in the birth process. They are better able to recognize a healthy sign or a cause for concern and how to respond.

Studies show that women who have had childbirth education typically have shorter labours than those who have not.
◆ **Why would this be true?**

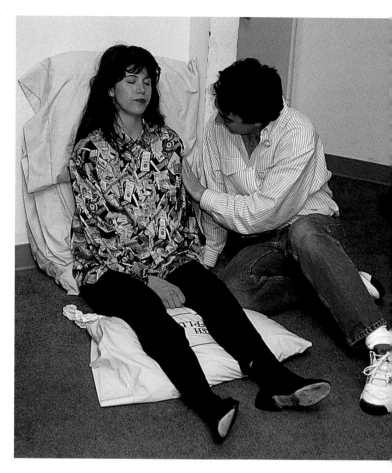

Typically, parents register for a prepared childbirth course in the woman's first trimester. They begin weekly classes around the sixth or seventh month of pregnancy. Courses are offered by hospitals, municipal public health units, and other health-care groups.

During these classes, obstetric specialists describe the stages of childbirth and tell parents what they can expect at each one. Videos of birth are presented, as is information about possible complications. Small class sizes, about eight to 12 couples, allows for questions and individual instruction.

Tours of birth locations are usually offered. Couples learn about each site's policies and admission procedures. They may be allowed to pre-register at that time.

Mutual support is another advantage of these classes. Expectant couples can swap stories, advice, and information. Some classes hold reunions after the children are born, when babies are brought for "show and tell."

Prepared Childbirth Methods

Most prepared childbirth classes teach the Lamaze method, the Bradley method, or techniques based on them. These methods share the philosophy that women should work *with* the birth process, rather than *against* it.

Both methods teach techniques that minimize discomfort and aid the birth process naturally. Included are taking a short walk or a warm shower, changing positions frequently, and getting a light massage. Rhythmic breathing and relaxation skills help the mother manage contractions and avoid pushing until the cervix has opened wide enough for birth. Using these techniques usually reduces the need for painkilling medication, allowing the mother to respond to her body's cues.

Childbirth Coaches

Both the Lamaze and Bradley methods stress the role of the coach, who helps the mother through the birth. The coach, who is usually the father, learns how to give his partner practical help. For example, he might give a gentle massage or back rub to relieve tension. He also gives emotional comfort by offering words of encouragement, describing soothing scenes, and just by listening. He helps the woman focus on breathing and relaxing.

After working together throughout the pregnancy, the mother-and-father team help bring their baby into the world. The experience brings many couples closer. Studies show that childbirth is less stressful for the mother who has constant support throughout labour and delivery.

If the father cannot attend childbirth classes, a woman may ask a close friend or relative to train as coach. She may hire a trained labour assistant, who will support her through the pregnancy and birth, and maybe even until the infant is home and thriving. Either way, the mother should make sure the birth facility she has chosen supports prepared childbirth and allows coaches to assist.

Parenting Q & A

Childbirth Choices

Q "This is my first baby. I'd like to have a natural childbirth, with no anesthetic. My mother says for a first baby, I really will need something. What should I do?" *Marie*

A Actually, you have many choices today for managing physical and emotional stress during childbirth. "Natural," drug-free techniques include heat therapy, massage, and even acupuncture. The mother participates fully in the birth, and the baby is not unintentionally medicated through the placenta. Some medications make infants less responsive in the first hours after birth, but don't worry. Only drugs proven to have no long-term effects are used. As you explore your options, find out what people you know have done, but be sure to listen to your doctor's recommendation. If you're going to experience the challenge of childbirth, you deserve a say in how to manage it. Requesting medication, as many women do, is no sign of weakness, if that's what will work best for you.

Selecting a Birth Location

A site for the birth should be chosen well before the expected birth date. Types of birth locations vary among communities but generally include a hospital delivery room, a birthing room, and the woman's home. If the couple has selected a specific doctor or midwife to attend the birth, the location is usually limited to where that person practices.

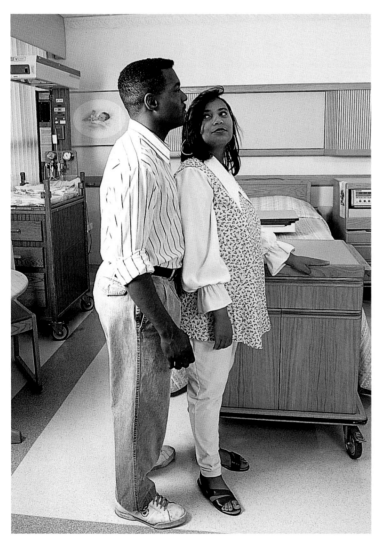

HOSPITAL DELIVERY ROOM

More than 98 percent of births in Canada take place in a hospital. A woman is usually admitted when she is in **labour**. This series of contractions of the uterine muscles gradually begin to push the baby out of the mother's body.

In the labour room, the mother is examined to check progress. Monitors may be used to track the baby's vital signs. Otherwise the mother is free to walk about the room. If she has been through childbirth preparation, she and her coach can do breathing and relaxation exercises.

Near the time of **delivery,** or birth of the baby, the woman is transferred to the delivery room. This is a sterile hospital area used only for this purpose. Equipped for surgery and emergency procedures, this area is recommended when the health of mother or child is at risk.

After delivery, the mother is moved to a recovery room, where she is watched for complications. In some hospitals, labour, delivery, and recovery all take place in the same room. After recovery, the mother goes to a regular hospital room.

Couples often visit the birth location ahead of time. ◆ **What questions might they want to ask?**

Most babies stay in the room with the mother. The baby may also stay in the nursery and be brought to the mother for feeding. Mother and child are released from the hospital one to three days later, depending on the health of the mother and baby.

BIRTHING ROOM

"When my baby was born," Sylvie recalled, "I wanted a place where I could feel comfortable and relaxed, and where my baby would feel welcomed. The delivery room seemed so sterile and impersonal for such an intimate event."

Parents who share Sylvie's feelings have an alternative to a delivery room. A **birthing room** is specifically designed for labour plus delivery. These rooms in either a hospital or a birth centre provide some of the "comforts of home." Features may include a king-size bed, easy chairs, music, television, a refrigerator, and a bathroom with an oversize tub. The room may have special equipment. A birthing bed splits apart for use during delivery. The woman can hold onto gravity bars to assume a squatting or sitting position when giving birth.

Spotlight On
—Birth Plans

After weighing their options, a couple can make a birth plan, a written description of their preferences for labour, delivery, and the infant's care. The plan can be a letter or a list of instructions. Some hospitals supply a questionnaire.

Parents should discuss their plan with the obstetrician or midwife during a prenatal visit to give the health-care provider a clearer idea of their expectations. The couple can learn whether their choices agree with the birth site policy. They may discover how medical conditions that might develop during pregnancy or delivery could affect their plans. Based on this information, the couple can present a finalized copy of their plan to the birth site staff.

The document details the couple's decisions about:

✔ *Medication.* Parents can list which medications will be used, if any, and under what conditions.

✔ *Prebirth procedures.* After consulting the obstetrician, the couple can decide which exams and monitoring are worthwhile.

✔ *Who can be present during labour and delivery.* Parents should specify if they want other children, in-laws, or friends to attend.

✔ *Treatment of complications.* These important decisions should be made before problems arise, based on medical advice and the couple's values.

✔ *Feeding the infant.* A breast-feeding mother should indicate when she wants to begin nursing and whether the baby may be given extra feedings.

✔ *Where the baby will stay.* The couple may want the child to remain with the mother if possible, rather than in the nursery.

During labour, a woman may bathe or sit and talk with family. Family members, sometimes even children, are encouraged to stay through some or all of the birth process. The mother and newborn stay in the room for six to 12 hours after delivery.

Birthing rooms in hospitals have access to the same health and safety features found in a delivery room. Those in birth centres are usually staffed by midwives and are equipped with units that supply oxygen, tubes for giving fluids, and an infant warmer. Centres usually accept only women who are at low risk for complications. Most centres are affiliated with a nearby hospital, where a woman is quickly transferred in an emergency.

Home Birth

A small number of couples prefer to give birth at home, usually attended by a midwife who may or may not have medical training. Because of the high medical risks involved, at-home births are not advised. Those who choose this option must include plans for quick medical assistance in case of emergency. In some provinces, at-home births attended only by midwives are not regulated.

Some births occur at home or elsewhere because the woman cannot reach the hospital or birth centre in time. Fortunately in most communities, dialing 911 or the local emergency number brings quick medical assistance. The woman is usually taken by ambulance to the nearest hospital.

Pediatricians understand the health needs of children. You can tell when they enjoy working with children.
◆ **How might the way a child feels about doctors be shaped by the pediatrician you choose?**

Finding a Pediatrician

Parents should choose a doctor for their infant before the due date. This way, the woman's obstetrician can share medical information with the baby's doctor immediately before and after the child is born. Many parents select a **pediatrician** (PEE-dee-uh-TRISH-un), a doctor who specializes in the treatment of infants, children, and adolescents. Others go to a family doctor or a clinic.

To choose their infant's doctor, some parents ask for recommendations from their obstetrician, the birth centre, or relatives and friends who have children. The provincial College of Physicians and Surgeons or a local hospital may be able to provide information about which doctors are accepting new patients. Before making a choice, parents might want to know:

♥ What are the doctor's office hours?

♥ Is someone on-call for emergencies or to answer questions?

♥ At what hospital does the doctor have privileges?

♥ What procedures will take place if a pregnancy becomes high risk?

An interview with the doctor may reveal something of the doctor's philosophy of child care and manner of dealing with parents. Does the doctor answer questions patiently and thoroughly? Is he or she friendly and easy to approach, or serious and distanced? Most importantly, does the doctor inspire confidence?

Choosing a Feeding Method

During pregnancy, parents should also decide whether to breast-feed or bottle-feed the baby. This subject can be discussed with the obstetrician or pediatrician. Childbirth classes usually offer information on feeding methods, and hospitals have breast-feeding classes.

Each feeding method has advantages. If the baby is thriving and the parents are comfortable with a method, they have made the right choice for them.

BREAST-FEEDING

In many cultures, breast-feeding has always been the only safe and practical way to feed infants. This was true of Western societies until the early 1900s. In recent decades, many women have rediscovered the advantages of breast-feeding:

Many health professionals recommend breast-feeding. This mother can cuddle the hungry baby in one arm and still have the other free for a big brother who needs attention.

♥ **Perfect food.** Breast milk is easier to digest than cow's milk. Breast-fed babies rarely suffer from constipation, unlike many bottle-fed infants. Because they nurse only until full, they are less likely to be overfed.

♥ **Antibodies.** Breast milk carries disease-fighting agents, called antibodies. Antibodies help protect the baby from illness during the first few months of life. Studies show that breast-fed babies generally have fewer illnesses than bottle-fed babies and develop fewer food allergies as they grow.

♥ **Convenience and economy.** A mother's milk is ready at all times, at the right temperature, and requires no preparation. Parents don't need to buy a large supply of bottles or formula. Breast-feeding need not be a problem for working mothers. They can nurse the baby at home and express, or pump out, the milk into bottles for a caregiver to feed later. If an employer offers on-site child care, the mother may be able to arrange her schedule to meet the child's. Sometimes a caregiver brings the infant to the workplace for feeding.

♥ **Physical benefit for mother.** Breast-feeding releases a hormone that stimulates the uterus to return to its usual condition.

♥ **Bonding.** Mothers who breast-feed often enjoy a special bond with their infant, which first-time mothers find especially encouraging. They feel more confident in their parenting skills, which increases an infant's sense of love and security.

BOTTLE-FEEDING

For women who cannot or do not wish to breast-feed, bottle-feeding is a healthy alternative with advantages of its own. Bottle-fed infants can be fed with just as much love and cuddling as those who are nursed. Bottle-feeding allows fathers, grandparents, and other relatives to share the work and rewards of feeding the baby. The mother also has a chance to rest. She can leave the infant for many hours at a time if necessary.

Bottle-feeding gives Dad a chance to do the feeding.
◆ **How can a father still participate in a baby's care if the mother is breast-feeding?**

Bottle-fed babies are given infant **formula**, a commercially prepared mixture of milk or milk substitute, water, and added nutrients, most notably iron. Formula is available ready to use. It may also be purchased as a concentrated liquid or a powder, which are both mixed with boiled water.

A pediatrician can recommend a formula. If the infant seems allergic to a cow's milk formula, the doctor may suggest soy milk. Children should not be given cow's milk until they are about one year old.

Supplying Infant Necessities

"I've been pricing some things we'll need for the baby," Tamara announced. "I can't believe how much it will cost! How does anyone afford it all?"

Since infants grow rapidly, wise parents buy only a few small-sized items. Some babies never need clothing in the newborn size and may wear a larger size than the label indicates. Parents need to think ahead about how the baby will grow. A snowsuit purchased for a baby born in late spring should be based on how big the baby will be in six months or so.

Purchased new, a **layette** (lay-ETT), a collection of infant clothing and equipment, can easily cost more than a thousand dollars. Buying some quality used items saves money for other essentials. Buying items several weeks before the due date lets parents relax before the upcoming birth and spend more time with the infant.

Baby clothes should be comfortable, washable, and slipped on and off easily. Dressy clothes are seldom needed before age one. One-piece sleepers are a good choice because they are washable and look good for outings. Shoes aren't needed until the child starts to walk.

To avoid irritating a newborn's tender skin, wash new clothes and blankets in a mild detergent before they are first used. If the family has a washing machine, parents can buy fewer clothes and launder them more often. When families use a laundromat, they can save money and time by having more clothing.

Basic garments for the "well-dressed" newborn include four to six undershirts, four to six gowns or one-piece sleeper suits, two sweater and cap sets, four to six pair of socks or booties, two to three dozen cloth diapers (if cloth diapers are used), and two to four waterproof pants (for use with cloth diapers).

For such a tiny person, an infant's equipment can really take up space. From bottles in the refrigerator to a crib in the bedroom, storing everything can test a parent's organization skills. Parents may need to get creative with space. In a small home,

Reusing another child's clothing saves money. This is especially true for infants, as they grow rapidly.

a curtain can close off part of a bedroom for the baby. Diapering supplies are more conveniently stored in the open.

DIAPERS

To a baby, happiness is a clean, dry diaper. This "simple" pleasure can be a challenge for parents, since a newborn goes through about 80 diapers a week. Parents have two basic choices for diapers: cloth and disposable.

Cloth Diapers

Cloth diapers are the more economical choice because they can be laundered and reused. However, infants who wear them also need plastic, waterproof pants and need more frequent changes. Parents who choose cloth diapers have two laundering options.

HOME LAUNDERING. This saves money but costs in time and effort. Diapers must be laundered frequently. With a supply of two dozen diapers, parents could be washing three times a week.

USING A DIAPER SERVICE. This service, available in some communities, delivers sterilized diapers and picks up soiled ones weekly. A special deodorized container is provided to keep dirty diapers between pick-ups. Parents pay for this convenience, but the diapers are less likely than home-laundered ones to cause rashes.

Disposable Diapers

Disposable diapers are noted for convenience and offer other advantages besides. They come with a waterproof liner. They are available in a variety of sizes and thicknesses, ranging from newborn to toddler.

One thing's for sure: babies need a seemingly endless supply of diapers. Is it any wonder that parents envision a "mountain" of diapers when they think of paying for them and doing the laundry?

They are comparable in cost to a diaper service fee. Disposables, however, can cause diaper rash. Since they cannot be reused, they contribute to the environmental problem of waste disposal.

To reduce the sizeable weekly expense of disposables, some parents use cloth diapers at home and disposables when travelling. Keeping a dozen cloth diapers on hand is a good idea, whatever option is chosen. They are useful as an emergency supply, or if the baby develops an allergy to other diapers. They can also be used as burping pads.

FURNITURE AND ACCESSORIES

Babies' furniture needs are as basic as their food and clothing demands. A newborn can even get by temporarily with a wicker basket or dresser drawer for a bed. Items that most parents find essential include:

♥ *A chest of drawers or open shelves to store clothing and other items.* Changing supplies are kept in easy reach on top.

♥ *A 137-cm (54-inch), approved-safe crib, which serves a child until age three.* A carriage or bassinet (small baby bed), with a firm mattress that is covered with a tight-fitting cribsheet or pillowcase, will do for a newborn.

♥ *Several fitted sheets and a waterproof pad or mattress to cover the crib.* Flannel-covered rubber or plastic sheets are available. A large towel can be placed between the sheet and mattress to absorb moisture.

♥ *A bumper pad tied in at least six places to prevent tiny arms and legs from poking through the bars.*

Notice that a pillow is not listed. Infants are not strong enough to move their head, so a pillow could accidentally cover the face and smother them. Blankets should be used with caution for the same reason.

Health & Safety

CRIB SAFETY

A crib can be a dangerous place. It contributes to more infant and toddler deaths than any other household item. For safety's sake, parents should make sure that:

► Bars are no more than 6 cm (2⅜ in.) apart. A larger gap could trap an infant's head.

► End panels are free of decorative cutouts, which can also cause strangulation.

► The mattress fits snugly in the crib. A baby can get wedged in just a two-finger space between the bars and mattress.

► A crib with drop sides has a childproof locking mechanism. This keeps the baby from accidentally dropping the sides and taking a tumble.

► Paints used on cribs are lead-free. Infants may chew on anything in reach, and lead-based paints are a chief source of lead poisoning in children.

► The top of the rail is at least 66 cm (26 in.) higher than the mattress when the mattress is at its lowest level. Older infants may climb out otherwise.

► Corner posts have no decorative knobs that can snag an infant's clothing.

► There are no rough edges or exposed bolts to cause cuts, scrapes, or welts. All bolts should stay securely tightened to avoid a choking hazard.

FEEDING EQUIPMENT

Breast-feeding requires few supplies: nursing bras, disposable nursing pads, and two or three bottles for extra feedings. A breast pump to express milk may also be needed.

For bottle-feeding, parents need six to eight bottles in 120 mL (4-oz.) and 240 mL (8-oz.) sizes. The smaller size is for newborns and for giving water. Other necessities include bottle caps, extra nipples, a sterilizer, and a bottle brush for scrubbing. An insulated bag keeps bottles of formula cold when travelling.

BATHING SUPPLIES

Special portable, plastic tubs are available for bathing. A large plastic dishpan set in a kitchen sink works just as well, however, and is at a comfortable height for the parent. Both tub and dishpan should be large enough for playful kicking.

Additional bathing supplies include several soft washcloths and bath towels; a mild, pure soap; and a gentle baby shampoo.

TRAVEL EQUIPMENT

All provinces require young children in automobiles to be buckled into a car seat that meets current provincial safety standards. This applies even to the newborn's ride home from the birth site. Installing the seat correctly is equally important for safety. Some hospitals rent out car seats and provide instruction on installation. An infant carrier or stroller and a large tote bag for the baby's supplies make outings more convenient and enjoyable.

Internet Connects

http://www.mcgrawhill.ca/links/parenting
To learn more about the health, well-being, and rights of all children, go to the Web site above for *Parenting Rewards & Responsibilities, First Canadian Edition,* to see where to go next.

Even in a low-impact crash, an adult will probably not be able to hang onto an infant. An infant car seat keeps the baby secure.
◆ **What direction will the baby face when placed in the seat?**

Making Work Arrangements

A woman must take some time off work to have a baby. That statement is one of the few facts that apply to all couples. How much time a mother and/or father take depends on their situation and resources. Some women must return to work as soon as possible; others never do.

PARENTAL LEAVE

Parental leave is paid or unpaid time off from work given to a parent after the birth or adoption of a child. This time is available to most parents who work for businesses that have employee benefits. Otherwise, they might take vacation or personal days.

Parents use these days to recover from the stress of childbirth and settle the infant into the home. They need to establish a new daily routine and adapt to the responsibilities of parenting. Equally important, they need this time to build emotional ties between parent and child.

New mothers use maternity leave to help them recover physically from giving birth. Most women begin maternity leave shortly before the baby is due. Some are able to take an extended leave of six months or even a year. Ontario's Parental Leave program allows for either parent to take a leave of one year for the purpose of parental care of their new infant. Some employers offer the mother the option of returning to work part-time.

While not yet as common as maternity leave, more fathers are taking paternity leave. Indeed, newer studies reaffirm the value of a father's active presence in the lives of his children, both male and female. By staying home to care for the newborn, a father begins this relationship from the very earliest possible time.

Internet Connects

http://www.mcgrawhill.ca/links/parenting
To learn more about choosing quality child care, go to the Web site above for *Parenting Rewards & Responsibilities, First Canadian Edition*, to see where to go next.

Many employers are discovering that fathers need and want time off from work when a baby is born. ◆ **How can having that time be helpful to mother, baby, father, and employer?**

FUTURE CHILD CARE ARRANGEMENTS

Many new parents are torn between the desire to work and the desire to stay with their baby. For others, the decision is easier. Every expectant parent, however, should think ahead about child care arrangements. A parent's choice in caregiver has a deep impact on a child's well-being. In later chapters you will read about the variety of child care options and the creative solutions some parents find.

Preparing Siblings for the Birth

Accepting a new baby is the ultimate act of sharing for **siblings,** brothers and sisters of the child. They are giving up the security of their familiar routine and their most prized possession—their parents—to the newcomer. Preparing children for the new arrival can help later when the baby is there, demanding attention.

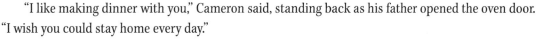

Raising Children With Character

First Things First

Six-year-old Cameron dropped a fistful of shredded cheese onto the pizza. His father, Derek, smoothed it evenly over the crust and other toppings. "Perfect," he pronounced. "I think this is our best pizza ever."

"I like making dinner with you," Cameron said, standing back as his father opened the oven door. "I wish you could stay home every day."

"I like it too," agreed Derek, easing the pizza onto the oven rack, "but you know parents have to work to take care of their family."

"Will you have to make up work when you get back," Cameron asked, "like when I stay home sick from school?"

"Probably," Derek said, "but right now, I have important work to do here."

"Like what?"

"Like finishing the nursery before the baby comes," Derek replied, "and taking care of Mom— and making pizza with you!"

"This isn't work," Cameron protested with a laugh. "This is fun!"

◆◆◆◆◆ **Thinking It Over** ◆◆◆◆◆

1. How would you describe Derek's priorities?
2. How does Derek help Cameron adjust to having a new sibling?

When careful preparations are made for birth, a mother-to-be has time to concentrate on her health. She needs to be rested and ready for the exciting event ahead.

PREPARING BEFORE BIRTH

When Kim and James were expecting their second child, they knew Kim's growing abdomen would trigger questions from three-year-old Mia. Showing their happiness and excitement, they told her that she would soon have a brother.

To prepare her for the event, Kim and James helped answer Mia's questions. Using children's books from the library, they explained pregnancy and birth in simple terms. They described some of the changes they would make after the baby arrived. At a class for siblings at the birth centre, Mia saw where her mother was going and what would happen. Visiting other families with babies gave her an idea of what to expect from her own new sibling.

Mia was also involved in preparations. Kim took her to look at cribs. Mia and James made lists of names. The family began using the name they chose, to help Mia think of the baby as a person.

As Kim's due date neared, James explained to Mia, "We don't know just when Mama will go to have baby Paul. You might be asleep or at preschool. Grandma Tracer will stay with you until I come home."

The parents knew, however, that Mia's biggest concern was one she could not put into words: Will you forget about me after the new baby comes? They told Mia that having another child did not change their love for her. They spent extra time bathing her, reading to her, and just cuddling. James and Kim watched and listened for signs of worry or anger. They urged Mia to express her feelings about the baby's arrival, accepting even negative ones.

PLANNING A WELCOMING

Parents should remember the older child after the excitement of the birth. Asking a sibling to help plan the baby's homecoming lets the child feel more involved and valued. One six-year-old, for instance, drew a new "family portrait" as a homemade birth announcement.

A sibling who is in child care might be invited to stay home for a few days after the birth. "Sibling leave" helps the child get to know the baby and feel less shut out. Some children, however, prefer to be with friends in a setting where the baby is not the focus of attention. Techniques like these, along with extra love and attention, help siblings begin a smooth transition.

Making Final Preparations

Ideally, the last weeks before delivery are days of rest and anticipation. If a couple hasn't visited the birth location with their childbirth class, they should arrange for a tour. Rushing to the hospital or birth centre in the excitement of labour is no time to discover they don't know which door to use.

This is also the time to pack a bag of clothing and personal care items for the mother, her coach, and the newborn. The chart below lists some useful articles.

Keeping Focused

"When I was pregnant," Jasmine recalls, "I heard so many stories of people whose plans for a perfect birth went completely off track but still came out all right. Those stories helped me stay calm when I went into labour at home while my husband was still at our daughter's basketball game. It went into overtime and he didn't want to miss the end!"

Jasmine's experience makes an important point. Preparation is invaluable but can't guarantee a perfect experience. Parents-to-be should focus on their most important goal: a safe and healthy delivery, the kind of reception every child deserves.

Three to Get Ready: Packing for the Big Day		
For the Mother	For the Coach	For the Newborn
✖ Toothbrush and toothpaste ✖ Comb and brush ✖ Soap ✖ Cosmetics ✖ Sanitary napkins ✖ Nursing bras and pads, if needed ✖ Bathrobe ✖ Slippers and socks ✖ Loose-fitting clothes to wear home	✖ Health card ✖ Employee Medical Plan Information (if applicable, for semi-private or private hospital room) ✖ Preregistration forms ✖ Camera (possibly video) ✖ "Comfort" aids, including music, lotion for massages, and reading material ✖ Phone numbers of relatives and friends ✖ Snacks	✖ Blankets ✖ Car seat ✖ Sleeper suit, undershirt, and booties ✖ Diapers ✖ Waterproof pants (for cloth diapers) ✖ Receiving blanket ✖ Heavy bunting or blanket if cold

Review

Looking Back

♥ Preparing for the baby's birth and home-coming helps an expectant couple appreciate these events more and worry about them less.

♥ In prepared childbirth classes, couples learn what happens during the birth process and how to take an active part in it.

♥ Delivery rooms and birthing rooms in a hospital or birth centre are preferred sites for having a child.

♥ Before the baby arrives, parents should choose a baby doctor who makes them feel comfortable.

♥ Couples should decide whether to breast-feed or bottle-feed their infant.

♥ Supplies for the infant should be gathered with an eye toward cost, safety, and convenience.

♥ Couples should learn about their options for parental leave from work and for future child care.

♥ Older children need to be prepared for the birth of a sibling.

Knowledge and Understanding

1. How can a prepared childbirth class reduce an expectant couple's anxiety?
2. Why do expectant mothers often want and need a coach?
3. Describe the differences between a delivery room and a birthing room.
4. What should parents look for in a pediatrician?
5. Describe some advantages of breast-feeding for an infant.
6. For what reasons might a parent choose to bottle-feed?
7. Give some guidelines for choosing baby clothes.
8. Which would you choose for diapering a baby, cloth or disposable diapers and why?
9. What items might you choose to help a baby sleep safely and comfortably?
10. What safety concerns are related to these crib parts: bars, mattress, drop side, and rail?
11. Why is parental leave so valuable to working parents?

Review

Thinking and Inquiry

12. Dara and Ramon, an expectant couple, are eager to take a childbirth class. They work different shifts, however, and can't schedule a class together. What other options do they have?

13. Geoff and Lanie plan to take their four-year-old son with them when Lanie goes to the hospital to deliver. Do you think this is a good idea? Why or why not?

14. To encourage his daughter to accept her new sibling, a father tells the child, "You're the big sister now. You must look out for the baby and help us take care of him." How do you think the child will receive this message?

Communication

15. Prepare one side of a debate that "All babies should be breast-fed." Choose a partner with the opposing view and listen to his or her view. Have you changed your mind? Explain.

16. Create a list of questions you would take to your first prenatal appointment with your doctor.

17. How would you explain to an older child that a new baby will soon be joining the family?

Application

18. Work with a partner to create a list of qualities an expectant parent should look for in a birth location, a childbirth coach, and a pediatrician.

19. If you are an older sibling, describe your reaction, as you recall it, to learning that your parents were going to have another child. Based on your experience, what tips would you offer parents for helping a child accept this news?

Heather Wood, Midwife

What volunteer activities did you do as a teenager that led you to choose a career that involved working with children/people?

I volunteered for UNICEF's International Year of the Child committee, promotion and communications activities for International Women's Day activities, and as a canvasser for one of the political parties in Saskatchewan. I have always enjoyed working with people, including paid work as a waitress and as a babysitter.

*Please describe your **specific education pathway**.*

After high school I took a degree in English and Political Studies at the University of Regina. Then, in 1997, I entered McMaster University's four-year Midwifery Education Program. When I entered the program, it was the only undergraduate midwifery degree program in Canada. I obtained a Bachelor of Science in Midwifery.

Have you completed any further study to enhance your professional development?

Midwives are continually upgrading their skills and knowledge. We attend medical and midwifery "rounds" several times a month. The Association of Ontario Midwives and the Canadian Association of Midwives have conferences that offer many practical workshops.

*Please describe your **career pathway**.*

My career pathway has had many forks and sideroads. I had several jobs when I was in high school and university, including waitress, cashier, travel counsellor, secretary, researcher and writer for a commissioned history book, typesetter, proofreader, and newspaper editor. I particularly enjoyed working with people and learning new skills.

After receiving my first degree, I worked as the editor of a monthly women's newspaper, and then as the managing editor and a volunteer board member for a literary book publishing company.

Did you switch jobs along the way? If so, why?

I had my first child in 1984 and this began my interest in midwifery. I continued to work in the editing and writing field, establishing my own company. I also began to help other women as a doula (labour supporter) when they had their babies, taught prenatal classes, and began learning about pregnancy, childbirth, babies, and midwifery. I also began to attend workshops about midwifery.

I established a business that offered midwifery services, doula services, prenatal classes, and workshops on becoming a midwife. I did a lot of volunteer activity to promote midwifery, including establishing a consumer group called "Friends of the Midwives," to support midwives, and working on a Government of Saskatchewan committee to implement midwifery in the province.

*Please describe your **current position**.*

I now work full time as a midwife with The Hamilton Midwives in Hamilton, Ontario. Our small group of midwives provides prenatal, labour, birth, and postpartum care to pregnant women and their babies. We have our own clinic where we see our clients. We deliver babies in two local hospitals and in women's homes. We see our clients at home after their babies are born, which means we are not always in the office.

*What are the **rewards** of your current position?*

I love my work. I meet many new people during a very exciting, sometimes stressful, time in their lives. I get to share my knowledge and skills about pregnancy, labour, and birth, and to learn from women and their families. We build a relationship that helps a woman give birth and begin parenting with confidence and support. I work with skilled health professionals to support women and their families as they bring a new baby into the world. I feel privileged to work with all women as they go through the joys, challenges, and sorrows that this time may bring.

*What are the **challenges** of your current position?*

Midwives in Ontario work on call. This means that we work when our clients need us, not on a known schedule or shift. Some weeks when many babies are born, we get very little sleep and our days are very full of births and visits. Legislated midwifery is still quite new in Ontario and in Canada, and it takes time to train new midwives.

Looking back over your education and career pathways, as a young person in high school did you ever believe you would follow the pathways you have?

In high school I wanted to be a writer and researcher. Because there was no university training for midwives in Canada when I was in high school, this career path did not open up to me until long after I finished high school.

Do you have any comments for young people who might be considering their own educational/career pathway?

As you determine what training you need, think about what you love to do. If you are passionate about learning and acquiring skills, you will bring this passion and enthusiasm to your work. I have always done work that I love, which makes it easy to get up each day to go to work.

What other careers are related to your career?

Midwifery is a helping profession in the health field. Training to become a midwife is specific to this profession. However, there are many related careers, including: nurse, doctor, massage therapist, nutritionist, and social worker, to name just a few.

The Birth Process

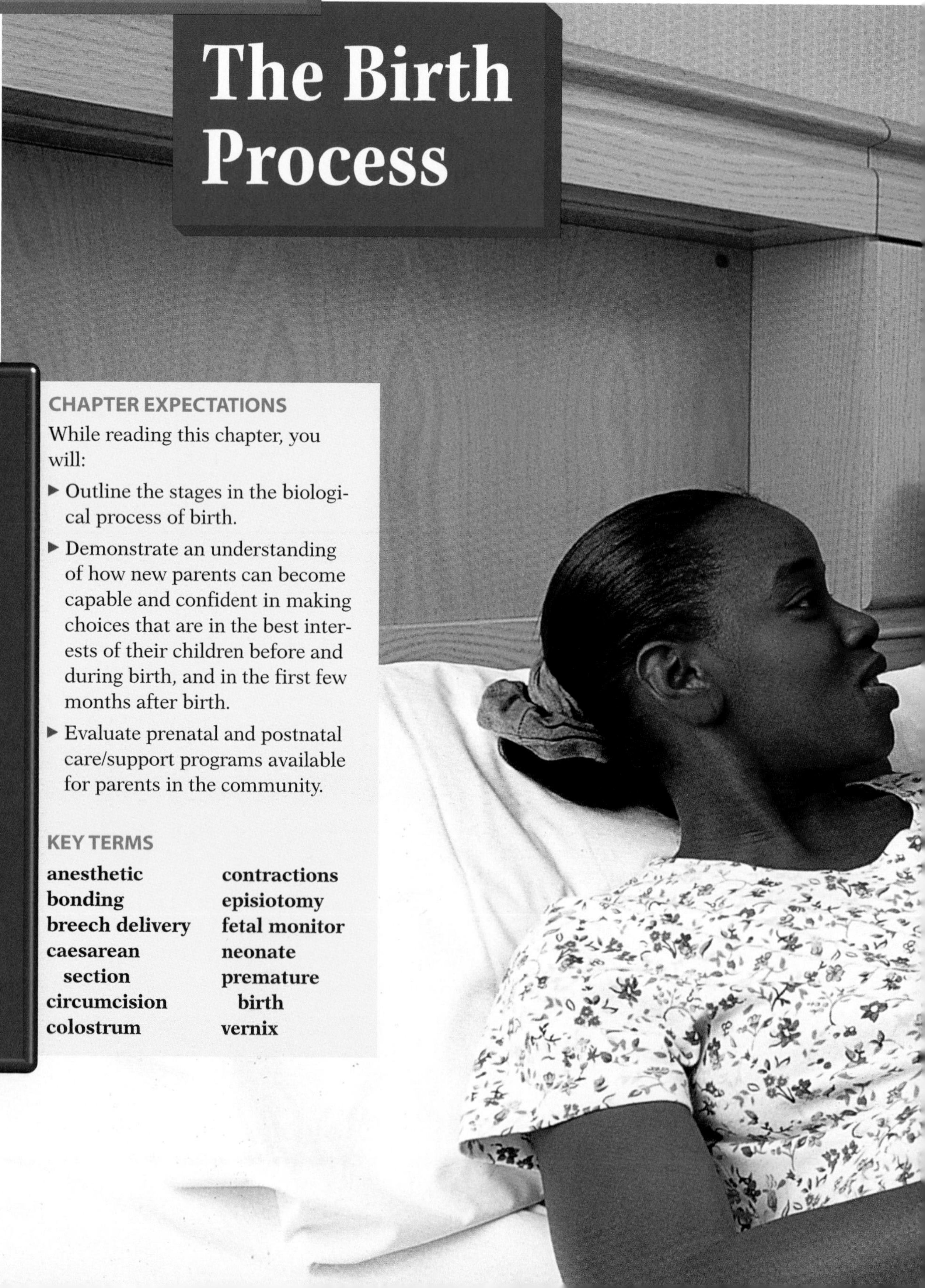

CHAPTER EXPECTATIONS

While reading this chapter, you will:

▶ Outline the stages in the biological process of birth.

▶ Demonstrate an understanding of how new parents can become capable and confident in making choices that are in the best interests of their children before and during birth, and in the first few months after birth.

▶ Evaluate prenatal and postnatal care/support programs available for parents in the community.

KEY TERMS

anesthetic
bonding
breech delivery
caesarean
  section
circumcision
colostrum

contractions
episiotomy
fetal monitor
neonate
premature
  birth
vernix

Laura drew a deep breath and gripped Matt's arm until the contraction passed. Matt checked his watch. "That was the longest one yet," he announced. "You're doing great. Do you want more ice?"

"No," murmured Laura, "but a cold cloth would feel good." She sighed, smiling weakly as her husband mopped her face. "Is it too late to change our minds?"

"Are you kidding?" Matt said. "After all you've been through the last nine months? This is the big payoff!"

Gradually, Laura's contractions became more frequent and intense. She no longer wanted to chat. While Laura closed her eyes to rest, Matt thought about the hours ahead. He was nervous about going into the delivery room. He remembered his brother's excitement after seeing his son born. But what if I get queasy? Matt wondered. After all, he thought, I could sit with that fellow I saw in the waiting area.

Two long hours later, the nurse checked Laura. "It's time," she said. "She's ready to push." The nurse left for a moment and returned, holding out a surgical gown, mask, and gloves. "You'll need these if you're going to be the first to hold your daughter," she said with a questioning look. Matt hesitated, then smiled and reached for the items. "I wouldn't miss this for anything," he said.

◆

What do you think? Why might a father be nervous about attending the birth of his child?

187

As her due date approaches, a mother-to-be eagerly anticipates the big event. She looks forward to trading the weight of a full-term pregnancy for a baby to hold in her arms. She wants to put a successful delivery behind her.

The End of the Beginning

"Hannah's birth wasn't difficult," Crystal recalled of her first child. "She just wanted to make a grand entrance. Twice I went to the hospital, but it was 'false labour.' When Hannah finally did arrive, you can bet we were thrilled to see her."

An anecdote like Crystal's illustrates the uncertainty surrounding the hours before birth. Once birth begins, however, the chain of events proceeds rapidly.

The three stages of childbirth—labour, pushing and delivery of the baby, and delivery of the placenta—are usually completed in less than 24 hours. A couple who have gone through childbirth preparation will be ready for the twists and turns of this journey. A woman won't be alarmed by the physical changes and emotional swings. Her partner will be a supportive, reassuring guide.

Stages of Childbirth

Crystal referred to false labour, the cramps and backache that may occur several days before labour starts. Two other signs are more reliable indicators that labour is near.

First, a pink spotting of blood, called *the show*, is discharged from the vagina as the mucous plug of the cervix loosens. Next, the woman's "water breaks." The amniotic sac surrounding the fetus ruptures, causing fluid to trickle or gush from the vagina. The loss of protective fluids increases the chance of infection. If a woman is not already at the birth site, she should go there right away. Labour has begun.

In contrast is the woman whose pregnancy lasts several weeks past her due date with no sign of labour. This delay could signal a complication. The child may be in distress or may be growing too big to deliver easily. When continuing a pregnancy poses health risks to the mother or child, labour may be *induced*, or caused to begin. The doctor injects a drug to begin contractions or causes the amniotic sac to rupture (or both).

FIRST STAGE: LABOUR

A woman in labour experiences **contractions**, a tightening and relaxing of the muscles of the uterus. Contractions help *dilate* (widen) the cervix and push the baby from the uterus through the vagina. Contractions may begin at the upper part of the uterus and move around to the back or begin in the lower back and move to the front.

In some women, contractions resemble menstrual cramps. Those felt in the lower back are called *back labour.* Contractions grow stronger, longer, and more frequent as labour progresses, whether a woman rests or tries to "walk them out."

Early Labour

In early labour, a woman may experience nausea, leg cramps, shakiness, or hiccups. Emotionally, she may feel relieved but excited. Although she may feel energetic, she needs to save her strength for later. She might sleep or distract herself with a quiet activity, such as rechecking the hospital bags. A light, nutritious snack helps keep up her energy. She should empty her bladder every hour or so during labour.

Early labour contractions are mild. They may come every 20 to 30 minutes and last 30 to 40 seconds, timed by the childbirth coach using a stopwatch. The coach can also double-check important details: Does the car have gas? Are there any delays or detours en route to the hospital?

Once labour begins, the parents-to-be know that the trip to the birth location is coming soon. Most expectant mothers have a bag packed and ready to go. As the time grows closer, they may double-check to be sure they have everything they'll need.

After several hours of early labour, the woman usually calls her doctor or midwife. Generally, she is told to go to the birth site when contractions are one minute in length and occur every five minutes or less.

Admission Procedures

After the expectant mother is admitted to the birth location, she changes into a hospital gown. At a birth centre, she may be able to keep her own clothes. An identification band is put on her wrist.

A nurse or doctor performs a pelvic examination, the first of several during labour, to check the degree of dilation and the position of the fetus. The mother's pulse and blood pressure are checked regularly throughout this stage. Her contractions and the baby's heartbeat are registered by a **fetal monitor**. This device resembles a wide belt that wraps around the mother's abdomen and connects with wires to a machine. The woman may get a sugar-water solution through the veins to maintain blood sugar and energy. For fluids, she is offered ice chips.

After this initial preparation, the woman is given a bed in the labour room or birthing room. If tests detect any problems, she may need to stay in bed for more monitoring. Otherwise she can move around the room. A nurse or midwife is available at all times.

Internet Connects

www.mcgrawhill.ca/links/parenting
To learn more about Parenting from A to Z, go to the Web site above for *Parenting Rewards & Responsibilities, First Canadian Edition,* to see where to go next.

As labour moves from early to active, a woman works with contractions by using the techniques she has learned in childbirth classes. ◆ **How can her coach support her?**

Active Labour

During active labour, contractions grow more intense. They come three to four minutes apart and last 40 to 60 seconds. This hard work gets results, dilating the cervix up to about 7 cm (2.8 in.).

Some women walk as much as possible, putting gravity to work for them. Sitting in a rocker or comfortable chair or lying on one side gives rest between contractions. Women who experience back labour may find relief by getting on hands and knees.

To release tension, a woman can talk, sing, shower, or have a massage. If her spirits or energy begins to fade, her coach offers encouragement, helps with breathing and relaxation exercises, or massages tightened muscles.

Transition

The transitional phase rapidly moves childbirth from labour to the stage of pushing and delivery. Transition commonly takes about 90 minutes, compared to 14 hours of early and active labour. Contractions, regular and extremely powerful, last from 60 to 90 seconds and come every two to three minutes. The cervix dilates fully to 10 cm (4 in.).

Spotlight On
Medication During Childbirth

Even if a couple has indicated a preference for a medication-free childbirth, a woman may be asked about medication when she is admitted to the birth facility. Some women accept a drug to help them relax without dulling the senses much, so they remain alert enough to participate.

Many women progress through the challenging periods of labour using breathing and relaxation techniques alone. Scientific studies show that constant support from partners and others reduces the need for medication.

No one would suggest, however, that a woman endure serious labour pain. An **anesthetic** (an-ehs-THET-ik) is medication that reduces or eliminates pain. Most hospitals require that a specialist trained to administer drugs be present in the delivery room as a precaution. Anesthetics are of four basic types:

✔ *Systemic.* This injection into a muscle or vein can relieve tension or nausea.

✔ *Local.* Used when an incision must be made, this injection numbs a small area.

✔ *Regional.* This injection numbs a larger area–in this case, the lower half of the body. A *spinal block* is injected into the spinal canal. An *epidural* is injected outside the spinal canal. It is possible to regulate the medication so the woman can feel the urge to push.

✔ *General.* This leaves the woman unconscious and is used mainly for surgical deliveries.

Transition is the most difficult part of labour. Medications are more likely to be given during transition than at any other time. A woman may feel nauseous, drowsy, or feverish, then chilled. She starts to feel like pushing as the baby's head presses on her lower back and pelvic area but is told to wait. Some women grow angry at those around them. Continuing may seem impossible. Women need to use techniques learned in childbirth classes.

Prepared partners, knowing what behaviour is possible, try to remain comforting and supportive. A coach can offer ice chips or mist the woman's face and arms with water. The birthing professionals encourage her progress.

Panting exercises learned in childbirth class help the woman avoid putting pressure on the cervix (pushing) before the cervix has fully opened. She can continue to walk or change positions for comfort.

SECOND STAGE: PUSHING AND DELIVERY

A woman "turns the corner" in the second stage of the birth process, which lasts about two hours for a first birth and one hour or less for subsequent births. With the cervix fully dilated, she is allowed to push down with her abdominal muscles. If she has not had any medication up to this point, she probably will not need it now.

Preparing for Delivery

In a hospital with separate rooms, the woman is moved from labour room to delivery room. At a birth centre, the room used for labour is readied for delivery. The woman's pelvic and vaginal area is scrubbed, then painted with an antiseptic

The second stage of labour ends with the delivery of the baby. The challenges of delivery are often quickly put behind when parents see their newborn for the first time.

solution. Her body is covered with a sterile cloth. On the delivery table, she may lie on her back or lean forward. Some birth facilities allow alternative positions: kneeling, squatting, or lying on one side with the upper leg supported.

The woman's coach, scrubbed and dressed in a sterile gown and mask, takes an active role as delivery nears. Looking into the woman's eyes, the coach helps her respond to her body's cues to breathe, bear down, and relax. Also assisting are the doctor or midwife, one or more nurses, and possibly an intern or medical student.

Delivery

Contractions are very strong during delivery, coming every minute or two and lasting almost as long. During a contraction, the woman takes a deep breath, pushes to the count of ten, then repeats. She may feel burning or stinging in the birth canal. Between contractions, she may relax enough to laugh and joke.

Aided by this forceful pushing, the baby travels down the birth canal, facing backwards, with the head down. The skull is made of flexibly joined plates of bone, allowing it to be temporarily moulded into an odd shape as it descends the narrow passageway. As the head begins to emerge, called *crowning*, the baby turns upward.

Spotlight On
The Newborn's Appearance

After floating in amniotic fluid for nine months, then squeezing through the birth canal, the newly born infant appears far different from the little bundle the parents take home a little later. Parents will note:

✔ **The skin.** The newborn's skin is covered with **vernix** (VUR-niks), flecks of blood and a greasy, white material that keeps it from getting waterlogged by amniotic fluid. Vernix also smoothes the passage through the birth canal. It is washed away by a birth attendant. The skin may appear greyish-blue, but that changes with the first cries and deep breaths. The skin may look transparent or slightly wrinkled, or be covered with fine hair, called *lanugo* (luh-NOO-goh). Newborn acne, if present, disappears within days. Birthmarks may or may not fade over the years.

✔ **The head.** The head is slightly pointed from its passage through the mother's pelvis. It takes a round shape within a few days. The journey down the birth canal can produce a lump on the head called a *caput* (KAY-put). A scalp monitor used during labour may leave a swollen red mark. Any hair present at birth may fall out, replaced by new hair in a few months.

✔ **The eyes.** Light-skinned babies almost always have slate blue eyes at birth. The eyes of darker-skinned infants are brown. Individual eye colour develops over several weeks or months. Eyes may at first appear crossed because the newborn is unable to focus on a single object. The drops given at birth to prevent infection sometimes cause swelling.

The Birth of a Baby

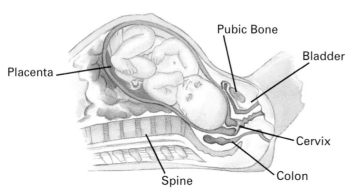

Placenta — Pubic Bone — Bladder — Cervix — Colon — Spine

 A As labour begins, the fetus is head down in the uterus and the cervix is still narrow.

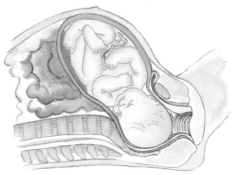

 B The cervix starts to dilate.

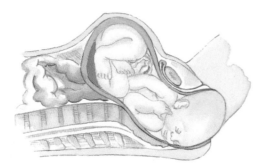

 C The muscles of the uterus begin to force the head through the birth canal.

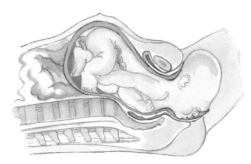

D The head emerges and turns upward.

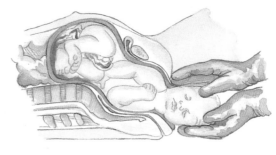

E The shoulders emerge, helped by turning the baby's head. The baby exits quickly after the shoulders are out.

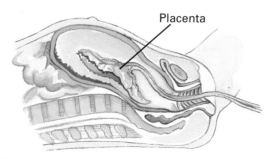

Placenta

 F Delivery of the placenta occurs soon after the baby is born.

At this point, the doctor may perform a common procedure called an **episiotomy** (ih-pee-zee-OTT-uh-mee). This is a small cut made at the vaginal opening to ease the passage of the baby's head. This cut, made under a local anesthetic, lessens the risk of tearing, which is harder to repair.

As the baby's head emerges, an attendant gently suctions mucus from the baby's mouth and nose. The head expands the birth canal so the rest of the body can pass through easily. The baby's body rotates to one side, gently guided by the doctor, enabling the shoulders to emerge one at a time. A few more contractions complete the baby's exit. The child has been born.

Sometimes the father helps receive the baby. The doctor holds the infant by the legs to let the mucus run from the mouth. The father or the attendant then clamps or ties the umbilical cord and cuts it. Neither the mother nor the baby feels the cut. Mother and child are wrapped in warm blankets.

Bonding

Routine procedures and tests on the baby are often delayed so the parents can hold their child immediately. Lying on the mother's stomach or in her arms, the newborn feels her skin and heartbeat. The father is close by. As the parents talk to and caress the baby, the infant sees their faces, hears their voices, and feels their warmth. This physical closeness begins the process of **bonding**, the creation of a loving link between a parent and child.

Sometimes health problems require that the infant be separated from the parents so medical procedures can be performed on the mother or baby. Bonding, however, occurs in the first days, weeks, and months of life together.

Complications

Unfortunately, not all births proceed normally. If a woman cannot push the baby out by herself, the doctor may use *forceps*, a pincer-like instrument, to reach into the birth canal and pull the baby out. A *vacuum extractor*, a metal or plastic cup that uses suction to pull the baby out of the birth canal, is another possibility.

In a **breech delivery**, a baby is born with feet or buttocks first. A surgical delivery, called a **caesarean section** (si-ZAIR-ee-uhn), may be needed. In this procedure, the child is delivered through an opening cut in the abdominal wall and uterus.

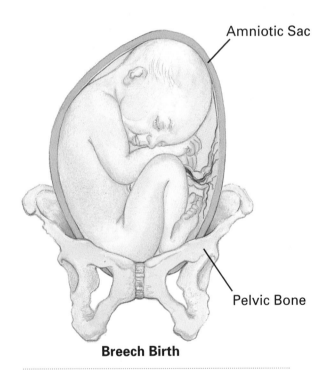

Amniotic Sac

Pelvic Bone

Breech Birth

Most babies are born head first, with the face toward the mother's back. A fetus positioned with the buttocks near the cervix is in breech position. Either the buttocks or the feet emerge first instead of the head. Breech deliveries are more common in premature infants. Many fetuses do not assume a head-down position until the last few weeks or even days of pregnancy.

The first thing new parents want to do after delivery is hold their newborn. In that moment their bond as a family is formed.

Caesarean delivery may be used in other complications, more specifically when:

♥ A long or difficult labour threatens to injure the mother or child.

♥ The fetal monitor shows the baby's heart rate dropping dangerously.

♥ A woman experiences *placenta previa*, where the placenta covers the opening of the uterus and prevents the baby from vaginal delivery.

♥ A woman's pelvis is too small or she has a multiple birth.

Like any major surgery, caesarean section carries certain risks for the mother. It requires a longer recovery period than a vaginal delivery. It should be performed only when the woman's or infant's health is in danger.

THIRD STAGE: DELIVERY OF THE PLACENTA

Occupied with her infant, a new mother may barely notice this final stage of birth. Mild contractions expel the placenta and other membranes through the birth canal. A nurse massages the abdomen to assist the process, which takes 10 to 30 minutes.

If an episiotomy was performed, it is now repaired. The stitching is done under local anesthetic. The stitches will be absorbed into the body and need not be removed.

After delivery, the uterus shrinks, accompanied by contractions and strong cramps. Bloody discharge may continue for several days to as much as six weeks.

Caring for the Mother After Delivery

The hours after delivery offer the mother a well-earned rest. She is kept under observation for at least an hour. Her pulse, breathing rate, and blood pressure are checked every 15 minutes. Significant changes in any of these signs could indicate a number of complications.

Having gone hours without food, a woman may be extremely thirsty and dehydrated. She is usually allowed a snack.

Later, a woman may feel some discomfort from an episiotomy. A nurse will show her how to keep the incision clean to avoid infection.

If a woman plans to breast-feed, the baby should nurse briefly and frequently to stimulate milk production. For a few days after delivery, the breasts produce **colostrum** (kuh-LAHS-trum), a yellow fluid rich in nutrients and antibodies, which help protect the newborn from infections.

Typically, a mother and child leave a birth centre in nine hours after delivery. The average hospital stay is one to two days following a vaginal delivery, four days for a caesarean section. Many hospitals have a rooming-in plan that allows the infant to stay in the mother's room, sometimes returning to the nursery at night. The father can visit anytime. A nurse is available to answer parents' questions and to demonstrate care of the baby.

Caring for the Newborn

The **neonate** (NEE-oh-nate), as a newborn baby in the first month of life is called, receives medical attention from birth. The doctor or registered midwife puts drops into the neonate's eyes to prevent possible infection from sexually transmitted diseases, and also gives a vitamin K injection. The baby is checked for proper development, then weighed, measured, and washed.

Before the baby leaves the delivery room, an identification band that matches the mother's is placed on the wrist or ankle. The infant's footprints are recorded for the hospital records. These procedures ensure that mother and child are correctly matched on leaving the hospital.

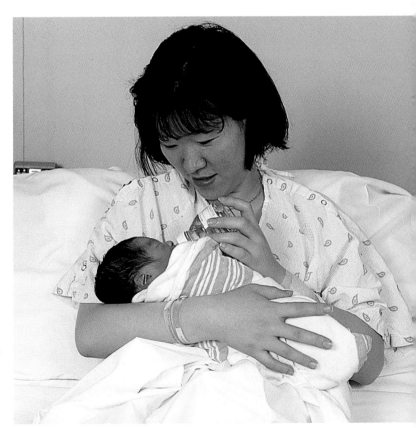

A new mother needs two important things: rest and time with her baby. In the past, many mothers spent several days in the hospital after delivery.
◆ **Why do you think that has changed?**

NEONATAL CHECKUP

Most babies are born healthy. Fewer than four percent of all infants are born with birth defects, many of which are minor and easily corrected.

Newborns are given a quick medical checkup to detect any problem that requires emergency treatment. The checkup includes simple tests for rating their physical condition.

The Apgar Scale

One test is the Apgar scale, named for Dr. Virginia Apgar, who invented the test in the 1950s. As shown in the chart on page 199, the infant receives points in each area.

Newborns who score seven points or more are in good to excellent condition, needing only routine care. Infants scoring between four and six points may need resuscitation. Those scoring less than four points are in poor condition and require dramatic life-saving measures.

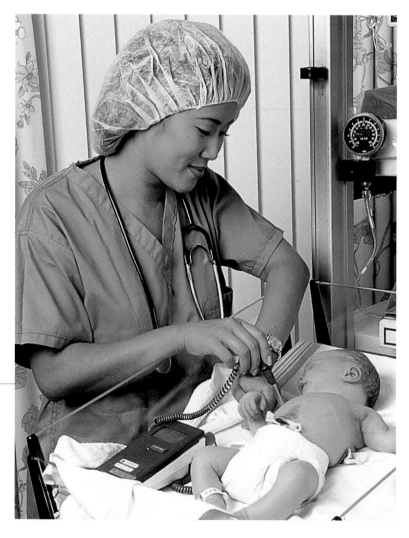

Some hospitals place all newborns in an intensive care unit (ICU) nursery, but some do not. Whatever the facility, the baby is monitored carefully before being dismissed to go home.

The NBAS

A second test, the Neonatal Behavioural Assessment Scale (NBAS), was developed by T. Berry Brazelton, a leading pediatrician in the United States. The NBAS is used in many hospitals worldwide and takes about 25 minutes to administer. The exam tests the baby's ability to maintain a deep sleep when disturbed by a light, rattle, and bell. The examiner records the following:

♥ Whether the baby's state changes during the exam. Does the baby stay asleep, become alert, or scream?

♥ How much and what kind of stimulation—noise, light, and movement—upsets the baby.

♥ Whether the baby quiets himself or herself when upset.

♥ Whether the baby can return to a sleep state despite the stimuli.

Other parts of the exam test motor skills and ways the baby reacts to people and stress.

PREMATURE INFANTS

About seven percent of all pregnancies in Canada result in **premature birth**, meaning the infants are born three or more weeks before their due date. Because they are born before prenatal development is complete, premature infants face numerous health problems.

Many premature infants have a low birth weight. A baby of 2.5 kg (5½ lbs.) or less is considered at risk, although infants weighing less than 1 kg (2 lbs.) at birth have survived.

Premature infants often have health problems, such as undeveloped lungs and infection. They need the care of specialists and special equipment. Many must be placed in an *isolette*, a transparent, box-like device that controls temperature, humidity, and oxygen level. Here, connected to feeding tubes and monitors, they finish prenatal growth outside the uterus. Premature infants may be hospitalized for days or months, in the

The Apgar Scale

	0 Points	1 Point	2 Points
Heart Rate	Absent	Under 100	Over 100
Breathing	Absent	Slow; irregular	Good; crying
Muscle Tone	Limp; no or weak activity	Some movement of limbs	Active motion
Responsiveness	No response to stimulation	Grimace	Cough or sneeze
Skin Colour: Dark	Greyish or pale	Strong body colour, but greyish limbs	Strong body colour; pink lips, palms, soles
Skin Colour: White	Blue or pale	Body limbs pink, not blue	Completely pink

care of specialists. Experts rate the baby's development by the due date rather than the actual date of birth.

CIRCUMCISION

One of the first procedures some newborn males undergo is **circumcision** (sur-kuhm-SIH-zhun). In this surgical procedure, part of the foreskin is cut away from the tip of the penis. Circumcision is usually done the second day after birth. Some doctors believe that delaying the procedure until the second week, however, reduces the risk of infection.

Circumcision is part of a religious rite in some faiths. Medical experts debate its health advantages. Some think circumcision makes the foreskin easier to clean, and, thus, helps prevent infection of the penis. The decision whether to circumcise an infant should be left to the parents.

BIRTH CERTIFICATE

It is the parents' responsibility to apply for a birth certificate, which indicates that the birth has been recorded. Hospitals provide a form for the parents to complete. Once the birth has been registered with the province's office of vital statistics, a birth certificate can be obtained.

Health & Safety

A DELICATE CONDITION

Imagine watching outside the neonatal intensive care unit where your child, born six weeks prematurely, lies on an electric blanket. The tiny body is hooked up to tubes, bottles, and monitors. Nourishment comes through a needle in the vein. One machine works the underdeveloped lungs; another cleanses the blood. The child is the centre of almost constant attention. Someone is either drawing blood, suctioning fluid from the lungs, or changing the bag that collects urine.

You think of the dangers your baby faces: lung infection, blindness, chemical imbalance, bleeding in the brain—and that's just in intensive care. You feel guilty and helpless: Was it something you did? What can you do now?

Parents who have been through this ordeal say that getting involved helps you cope. Learn the names of the staff members who care for your child. Spend time with the infant; however, think about your health and other family relationships. Personalize the baby's space as much as possible. A small stuffed toy and a baby blanket can both be sterilized and might not interfere with any tubes or patches. In short, make the fragile little stranger *your* child.

Parents may be able to contribute to the baby's health also. Some premature infants can be nursed for brief periods. In fact, studies suggest that the breast milk of a mother of a premature infant is especially nutritious. Infant massage, when permitted, has been linked to increased alertness, faster weight gain, and shorter hospital stays. Just holding or touching the baby for a little while can be beneficial.

Finally, remember that prematurity is usually not a parent's fault and that 90 percent of these babies survive. Staying positive and involved is the best thing for parent and child.

A birth certificate should be kept in a safe place with other important documents, for it is a child's proof of identity. A child cannot get a health card or social insurance number without a birth certificate and, thus, will not be able to obtain paid health care or some financial benefits. A birth certificate is also essential for proving:

♥ *Legal age.* In order to vote, serve in the military, get a driver's licence, get married, or sign a contract.

♥ *Citizenship.* In order to vote or obtain a passport.

♥ *Relationships.* In order to identify parents, guardians, and heirs.

Only the Beginning

Two-day-old Nathan slept, exhausted by preparations for going home from the hospital. "Look at him," his father Murray marvelled, "out like a light."

That raised a smile from Moira, the new mother. "Just wait half an hour, when he wants to be fed or have his diaper changed."

Murray chuckled. That fits us, too, he thought. Like Nathan, they were catching their breath before getting caught up in the whirlwind of activity that comes with parenting an infant. So much would be happening in the weeks and months to come. As Murray said to Moira, "This little guy is going to be calling the shots for a while. We'd better be up for the game."

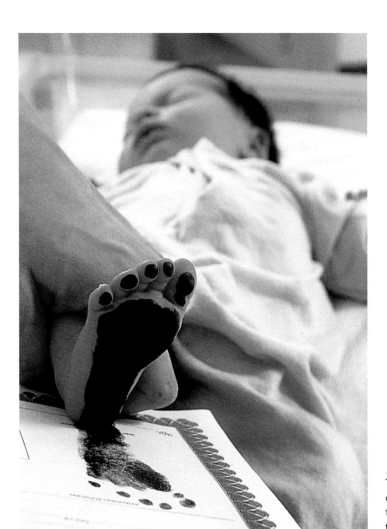

Taking a record of the baby's footprint on the birth certificate can establish the identity of the child. ◆ **Why is this a good idea?**

Looking Back

♥ The three stages of childbirth are labour; pushing and delivery of the baby; and delivery of the placenta.

♥ Women recognize certain signs that labour is beginning.

♥ In delivery, a woman works with uterine contractions to push the infant through the birth canal.

♥ Bonding between the parents and infant begins shortly after birth and continues in the days, weeks, and months ahead.

♥ Complications during delivery may require a caesarean section, where the baby is removed through an opening made in the abdominal wall and uterus.

♥ During the recovery period, the mother's vital signs are monitored for any signs of complications.

♥ Immediately after birth, newborns receive a medical checkup.

♥ Premature infants often have health problems that require special care and extended hospitalization.

Knowledge and Understanding

1. How can a woman determine whether she has begun labour?
2. What is the purpose of contractions?
3. What pattern do contractions follow, in length and strength, from early labour through delivery?
4. Describe ways that a coach can support a woman during various stages of childbirth.
5. Based on what is happening, how is a woman likely to feel through each stage of labour?
6. Why is it helpful for women to learn panting exercises in childbirth classes?
7. Why do doctors perform episiotomies?
8. In what situations might a caesarean section be used?
9. Describe the mother's care after childbirth.
10. What are the five signs rated by the Apgar scale?
11. What special care might premature infants need?

Review

Thinking and Inquiry

12. About one of every five deliveries in Canada is a caesarean. Many health experts question whether the procedure is medically necessary in all of these cases. Why would a doctor perform a caesarean if it were not needed? Why would a woman allow it?

13. What might a couple do if they do not receive a birth certificate for their infant? If they lose the birth certificate?

14. Some parents feel disappointed a few hours after their child is born. Why might they feel this way?

Communication

15. Design a poster showcasing the advantages and disadvantages of either cloth or disposable diapers.

16. Your friend Dianne is expecting her first child. She has heard many different versions of what childbirth is like from different people. Dianne confides in you that she is concerned about what it will be like for her. She wonders how she will feel and act. What can you say to help her?

17. Create a fact sheet for prospective parents, listing the major tasks, purchases, and the time lines to follow in preparation for the birth of their child.

Application

18. With a partner, write a dialogue between a woman in the transition phase of labour and her supportive childbirth coach.

19. It is 13 km (8 mi.) from your home to the birth centre. The speed limit along the route is 50 km (30 mi.) per hour. Assuming you drive the speed limit and there are no stops along the way, how long should it take you to get to the birth centre?

20. In a group, discuss the misinformation you have heard about labour and childbirth. Compare them to the facts that you have read in this and other chapters. Make a chart presenting the falsehoods and the truths.

Infant Care

A Parent's Perspective

from Kurt

"When I first laid eyes on Brian, I couldn't believe what I was seeing.

He was so small, and he looked so fragile. After Brian was born, they asked me if I wanted to hold my son. Can you believe it? I said no. Looking back, I know that I was just feeling afraid. I didn't want to drop him, or hurt him, or anything. What did I know about holding a newborn baby? I couldn't shake those feelings entirely, and Marnie noticed. One day she said to me, 'He won't break, you know. All you have to do is be careful to support his head and neck.' I'm much more confident now. I bathe Brian, and feed him, and everything. My brother-in-law even showed me a good way to carry Brian. He calls it the 'football hold.' I'm kind of partial to that one."

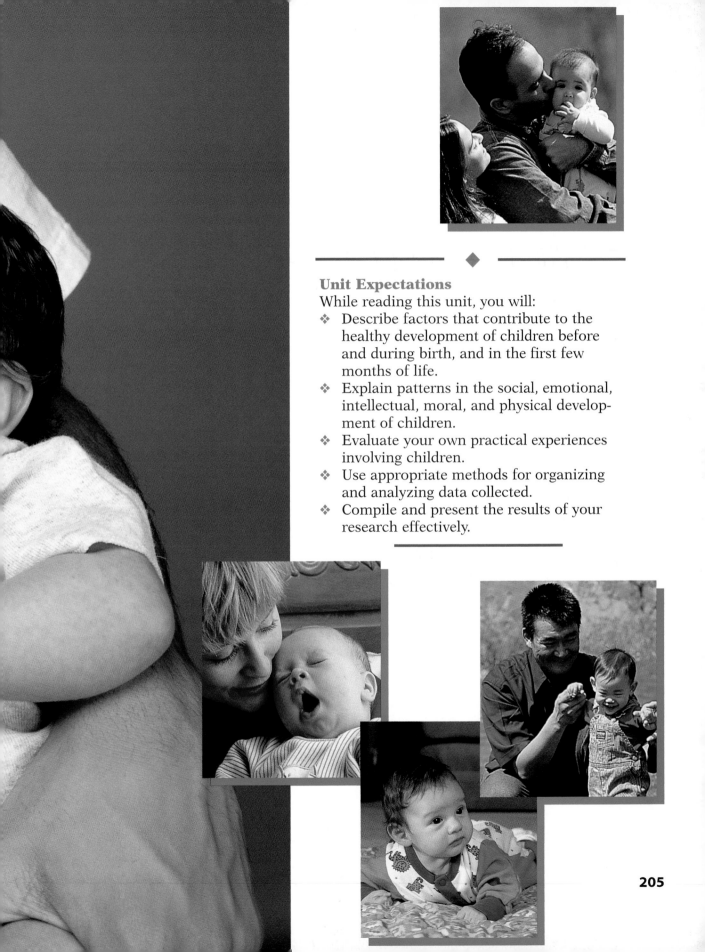

Unit Expectations

While reading this unit, you will:

- ❖ Describe factors that contribute to the healthy development of children before and during birth, and in the first few months of life.
- ❖ Explain patterns in the social, emotional, intellectual, moral, and physical development of children.
- ❖ Evaluate your own practical experiences involving children.
- ❖ Use appropriate methods for organizing and analyzing data collected.
- ❖ Compile and present the results of your research effectively.

Adjusting to Parenthood

NO SMOKING

CHAPTER EXPECTATIONS

While reading this chapter, you will:

▶ Demonstrate an understanding of how new parents can become capable and confident in making choices that are in the best interests of their children before and during birth, and in the first few months after birth.

▶ Explain how development from conception to three years of age affects and is crucial for development in later life.

▶ Analyze behaviours, conditions, and environments that influence positive or negative growth and development of the fetus, infant, and young child.

▶ Summarize the main points of information gathered from various reliable sources.

KEY TERMS

depression
lochia
postnatal
postpartum
depression

As Derek walked toward Suzanne's hospital room, he took a deep breath. In the 18 hours since his wife had given birth to their first child, he had gone back and forth between joy and anxiety. His thoughts kept returning to how life was about to change for them in so many ways.

Walking through the door, Derek saw Suzanne sitting in the rocking chair. Casey dozed peacefully against her shoulder. The afternoon sun slanting through the window was the only light in the room.

"Hey, we missed you!" Suzanne laughed softly as Derek sat on the bed beside her and gazed with pride at his precious new daughter. "I can't wait to show Casey the view from the kitchen window at home. We'll watch the robins making a nest outside, and listen to Mr. Calzoni singing opera next door, and smell hamburgers on the grill. I think I'll join the mother's group at church. I'm going to need their advice! Maybe we could take Casey to . . ." Suzanne stopped and smiled. "I know I'm getting carried away, but little things are so exciting now. Everything seems—possible. It's true, isn't it? Having a baby changes everything."

What do you think? Do you agree with Suzanne that "having a baby changes everything"? Why or why not?

Physical Adjustments

Because giving birth is an everyday occurrence, people sometimes forget how strenuous it is for a woman. Attending to a new baby only adds to the strain. Recovery after giving birth takes time, rest, and good care. Having a new baby in the house also takes its toll on the father. Both parents can make physical adjustments that help.

A MOTHER'S PHYSICAL ADJUSTMENT

Aside from tiredness, the first physical change a new mother might notice is a vaginal discharge, called **lochia** (LO-kee-a). Lochia is the normal discharge of blood, tissue, and mucus from the vagina, which occurs for several weeks after birth. Essentially, the uterus cleans itself out. If bleeding becomes excessive, the doctor should be called.

During the first few weeks after giving birth, the mother perspires more and goes to the bathroom frequently. Her body is getting rid of the excess fluid of pregnancy.

Although not noticeable on a daily basis, the uterus slowly shrinks to its previous size and position. Mothers may become aware of the contracting uterus, especially if they breast-feed. As the uterus shrinks, the mother's stomach does too. The places where the skin stretched during pregnancy may be left with stretch marks. These slightly darker areas tend to fade in time.

If a new mother breast-feeds, she may experience some physical discomfort at first, such as soreness around the nipple. The feeling usually disappears within a few weeks. Warm showers may help in the meantime.

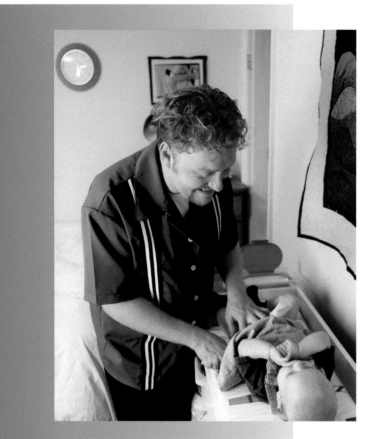

Parents want to raise happy, healthy children. That process gets off to a good start when new parents learn how to adapt well to life with an infant.

What's Ahead?

Birth signals the beginning of a new stage of family life. For first-time parents, the infancy stage in their child's life is full of surprises and learning experiences. Combined with the physical and emotional adjustments parents have to make, this period from birth to 12 months can be a joy and a challenge. Knowing what to expect helps parents adapt more easily.

Women who had an episiotomy during childbirth may experience some physical discomfort as they sit and stand for the first few weeks. The incision from a caesarean birth may also be sore. A woman's doctor can recommend measures to ease these discomforts.

Medical Checkup

About four to six weeks after birth, the mother has a **postnatal**, or after childbirth, physical examination. The obstetrician who counselled the mother during pregnancy and delivered the baby usually does the examination.

The doctor answers the parents' questions and gives advice about the baby's care and feeding. The doctor also makes sure that the mother's uterus is returning to normal and that no other complications are affecting her health. If necessary, the episiotomy or caesarean incision is checked for proper healing.

Even though medical checkups are scheduled following birth, a new mother should feel comfortable about calling the doctor's office whenever she has problems.

Rest and Sleep

Like a typical newborn, Maria's son slept through much of his first few weeks of life. Maria, on the other hand, was tired. She fed Owen every few hours around the clock. While Owen napped during the day, she tried to get things done. Exhausted, Maria wished for a night of uninterrupted sleep. What mistake do you think Maria made?

During the first six weeks following birth, Maria's body was gradually changing back to a pre-pregnant state. She needed proper

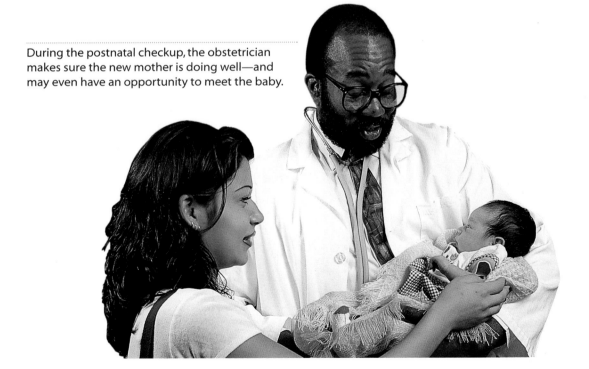

During the postnatal checkup, the obstetrician makes sure the new mother is doing well—and may even have an opportunity to meet the baby.

rest to help restore her good health. Without it, Maria started feeling worse instead of better. She finally followed a friend's advice: "When he takes a nap, you take one, too. The laundry and dishes can wait for a while."

The friend also suggested that Martina turn off the telephone and put a "Do Not Disturb" sign on the door. Other good ideas included asking relatives and friends not to visit during parent nap times; scheduling specific times for visits; and doing only essential household tasks for a few weeks.

Proper Nutrition

Good nutrition is as important for a new mother as it was during her pregnancy.

Eating well provides the energy a mother needs to care for the baby and helps her own body recover.

For good milk production, a breast-feeding mother's nutritional needs remain the same as they did when she was pregnant. You read about the number of servings that provide this need in Chapter 9. The recommended diet for a nursing mother is 500 calories more than she needed to maintain a healthful, prepregnancy weight, including 65 grams of protein.

FLUIDS. A mother who breast-feeds also needs plenty of fluids to help with milk production. Many breast-feeding mothers are naturally thirsty. Every day, she should drink at least three litres of liquids—12 cups or glasses. Water, milk, and juice are all good choices. Since caffeine can be passed to the baby through breast milk, caffeine drinks should be avoided.

WEIGHT LOSS. While many new mothers are anxious to lose weight, breast-feeding mothers shouldn't go on strict diets. During the early weeks of breast-feeding, dieting can decrease the milk supply and cause fatigue.

To lose weight, a new mother—whether nursing or not—should eat varied foods that provide important nutrients without extra fat and calories. These include fruits and vegetables; low-fat milk and yogurt; lean meats, poultry, and fish; and whole-grain breads and cereals. She should avoid foods high in calories and low in nutrients, such as french fries, chips, cakes, and candies.

The doctor can give advice on food choices and weight loss. As with anyone

As a new mother recovers from giving birth, her level of exercise can be slowly increased. Her degree of fitness before birth will likely affect how quickly she recovers.

who wants to lose weight, a gradual loss of about 500 g (1 lb) a week is safest and most likely to be maintained.

An Exercise Plan

Many a new mother has been surprised to discover that she still looks four or five months pregnant after giving birth. The additional weight gained during pregnancy may take several weeks or months to lose. Until the weight is lost, some non-maternity clothes may not fit.

With exercise a new mother can return to her previous weight and proportions. In addition, exercise helps tone muscles and improve her emotional outlook. As soon as the doctor approves, a new mother can begin some gentle postnatal exercises. Stretching and walking are a good way to start, with more strenuous activities added gradually.

A FATHER'S PHYSICAL ADJUSTMENT

When his child was born, Nick was up all night with his wife Ramona as she went through labour and delivery. After a few hours sleep, he went back to work for a while before returning to the hospital. Once Ramona and the baby came home, Nick was up part of every night to help with feedings. In the mornings he went to work as usual. After work, he did household jobs and helped care for the baby.

Like many fathers, Nick felt the physical strain of parenthood. Because he knew that Ramona had more to overcome physically, he felt guilty about his own feelings.

Fortunately for Nick and other fathers, such situations don't usually last long. Like the mother, they can temporarily put off some tasks and activities. If possible, taking a few days off from work is worthwhile.

Emotional Adjustments

When a new baby arrives on the family scene, is it love at first sight? Surprisingly, it might not be. Many parents expect to be overwhelmed by feelings of love as soon as they see their newborn. Actually, the lifelong bond between parent and child develops gradually.

New parents may also be surprised by conflicting emotions. They may be excited to have the baby, yet anxious about all the responsibilities. These mixed emotions are

Not everyone adjusts to parenthood in the same way. ◆ **How might understanding help two people who are reacting differently to the role of parenthood?**

Building Parenting Skills

PARENTING WITH OPTIMISM

Optimistic people look at the bright side of things. Because they tend to be happy and generate happiness in others, they are often nice to be around. Optimistic parents raise their children in an atmosphere of hope and confidence. They teach children to look for the best in people and situations. As a parent, Melanie showed optimism when she:

▶ Smiled and talked cheerfully to her new-born daughter.

▶ Decided that a warm bubble bath would help her get over a low feeling she had one evening when her baby was a few weeks old.

▶ Told eight-year-old Trevor that she liked the way he helped her take care of his new baby sister.

▶ Assured Trevor that he would enjoy third grade as much as second.

▶ Taught her son about world leaders who have helped bring about justice and peace.

▶ Took Trevor to a community clean-up and recycling program.

▶ Asked Trevor to tell her about his dreams of flying the space shuttle.

◆ ◆ Your Thoughts ◆ ◆

❶ In a difficult parenting situation, why is an optimistic response the most helpful one?

❷ How can parenting with optimism affect a child's self-esteem?

❸ How can a parent be optimistic and realistic at the same time?

❹ Describe how an optimistic parent might react when the teacher says a child is behind in math skills.

natural and understandable. If anything, they show that parents are well aware of both the joys and challenges of caring for a child.

Talking to others builds confidence. A parenting couple can share their thoughts. Friends and relatives who are already parents can give reassurances.

A MOTHER'S EMOTIONS

Sometimes a mother's emotions are un-steady following birth. As Helena recalled, "I was sitting there, rocking Lucas in my arms, and I just started crying. I had no idea why. I had a beautiful new son. My life was going well. I should have been happy, but all of a sudden I wasn't."

What Helena experienced isn't unusual. The feelings even have a name—**postpartum depression**. This depression is the moodi-ness, anxiety, and possibly anger some-times felt by a woman who has recently given birth. The feelings may surface as early as a few days after the baby is born or several weeks later. Such moods may come on without warning and for no apparent

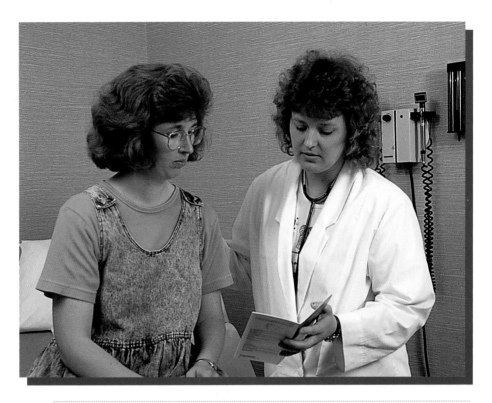

New mothers can talk to the doctor if they have mood swings after giving birth.
◆ **Who else might be a sympathetic listener?**

reason. The mood change can be puzzling to a new mother and frustrating to those around her.

With a closer look, this condition is not so mysterious. About 80 percent of all mothers experience at least some postpartum depression. The reasons are understandable. In Helena's case, she was still sore from delivery. She also had many new responsibilities. How could she care for her son, manage her home, and still work part-time, she wondered? Besides all this, Helena's hormone level had dropped, which is natural after a woman gives birth.

For most mothers, postpartum depression disappear within a few weeks without any treatment. Some don't even notice any effects. By getting proper rest and help, a new mother may avoid the depression.

Even just talking with her doctor or another understanding person can make her feel that all is well.

More Serious Problems

About 20 percent of new mothers have a more severe form of postpartum depression, which prevents them from giving their infants good care. In addition to the above symptoms, these mothers may feel guilt, despair, and detachment. Their self-esteem and self-confidence drop dramatically. They may even stop eating. These effects can last a month to a year or longer.

In this situation, comforting the mother does little good. The baby's father or a close relative who recognizes the symptoms should see that the woman gets prompt assistance from a mental health professional.

A FATHER'S EMOTIONS

Imagine what a father might feel at the birth of his child. Are his feelings the same as the mother's? A new father likely shares the mother's sense of pride and excitement. He may also share some doubts and have some of his own.

A father's concerns can range from how to physically handle the tiny baby to how to take care of financial responsibilities. He gains confidence in caregiving by getting "hands-on" experience. Worries about finances can be met with practical steps, such as working out a budget, setting spending goals, and investing money in a savings plan.

When family and friends focus their attention on the mother and child, a father may feel like an outsider. Becoming actively involved in caring for the child and moving on with the new routines of daily living can eliminate these feelings.

Managing New Roles

When "baby makes three," a couple begins to think and operate differently. Not only does their relationship change, but their life does too.

Brandon, a new father, recalled an eye-opening encounter: "Stacy and I were out shopping when a woman from the mother's club that Stacy belongs to came up and said, 'I remember you. You're Amber's mom.' I looked around to see whom she was talking to. Then it hit me. Stacy, my wife, was Amber's mom."

Brandon wasn't used to thinking of his wife as a mother. She had a new role, and so did he. He was already an electrician, a husband, a son, and a volunteer fire fighter. Now he was a father too. Juggling the duties of each role would be more complicated with another one added.

The greatest gift a father can give to a child is his time. ◆ **Why would this gift be so much better than simply buying the child toys?**

FATHERHOOD

In the past a father provided for the family but had little to do with household activity or the children. That picture is changing. Fathers today want to be involved with their children. As a result, researchers say, fathers have a happier life and tend to be more giving and caring as they grow older.

Families fare better with supportive fathers around. Mothers have a less stressful life when fathers share the work, child care, and household responsibility. In turn, that's good for dads and children.

Research clearly shows that children need involved fathers. With positive fathering, children tend to have a healthier self-esteem. They are more outgoing, flexible, and able to cope. They do better in school and have fewer problems with drugs, crime, violence, and teen pregnancy.

The lessons and skills learned from a father aren't the same as those learned from a mother. With their unique approach, dads encourage risk-taking, independence, and individuality.

Mothers used to nurture while fathers provided. Now those roles are blending, and the evidence points to real benefits for children.

SHARING RESPONSIBILITIES

Pressed for time and with less energy, couples sometimes disagree over duties and philosophies. Even couples who thought they agreed may find their ideas changing with actual practice. Questions about who should handle child-related responsibilities, household work, and income-producing work are typical role questions. What are a mother and father *supposed* to do? That's a good question for new parents to explore.

Many fathers enjoy a variety of activities with their children.

When dividing home and child care duties, think about what might work with each partner's schedule. Doing so can prevent resentments from building and help protect the relationship. That way neither parent is likely to feel overwhelmed.

The Role of Demographics

Where family members live has a huge impact on their roles. Parents who live in different cities or provinces share parenting responsibilities differently than parents who live together. Likewise, family members, siblings, and relatives have more opportunities to share in the responsibilities of a family if they live close by. Over time the demographics of families change. People age and take on more or less responsibility, as appropriate for that family structure.

When two people become parents, they are equally responsible for the child. They both help care for the child, even when that means inconvenience or making sacrifices.

became very careful with their spending. They simplified their life by buying only essential items. Since Carl often worked late, he missed spending time with their son. To help, Rita changed the baby's naptime so that he would be awake when Carl was home.

Arrangements like the one Carl and Rita chose work for some but not all. Only the parents can decide what is best for their family. As the child grows or if the work situation changes, parents might use different solutions. Depending on their financial situation, their values and career goals, and the needs of the infant, these options offer other possibilities:

♥ Working different shifts to eliminate the need for outside child care.

♥ Arranging with an employer to work at home, or starting a home-based business.

♥ Using in-home child care.

♥ Using an infant or child care centre.

MANAGING WORK AND CHILD CARE

How do you care for a child when you have to work? This question is a common one faced by parents today. For a couple, deciding whether one or both will work can be difficult.

When Carl's and Rita's son was born, Rita stopped working. Carl began putting in more hours on the job to help them get by on one income. To save money, the couple

MAKING TIME FOR EACH OTHER

Suppose you were so busy with school, work, and family commitments that you had no time for your best friend. You saw each other during lunch and spoke for a few minutes between classes, but nothing more.

That's how it is for many new parents. The demands of parenting are so heavy that couples can't find time for each other. Intimacy, the feeling of deep attachment between two people, can be lost if close contact and sharing are limited. Love can suffer if two people put their relationship on hold.

While children are a high priority, the couple's relationship is too. To find time for each other, a couple might:

♥ Hire a babysitter once in a while if possible.

♥ Accept invitations from friends and family members to watch the baby.

♥ Trade babysitting services with a neighbour.

♥ Enroll in a course or activity that includes child care. Many programs sponsored by churches, schools, and health clubs offer free or low-cost babysitting.

♥ Devote the baby's naptime or first hour of bedtime to each other.

COMMUNICATING

Finding time to spend together gives couples the chance to communicate. Without realizing, busy parents might forget to talk to each other. Couples need to be sure that communication doesn't suffer.

Since many new issues arrive with a baby, the couple has things to discuss. How will they handle baby expenses, medical care, and future plans? To make wise decisions and feel good about them, a couple must share ideas.

Good communication makes solving problems easier and even prevents them from happening. Can you predict what might happen with weak communication if one spouse feels that the other puts the baby first in his or her life? What if one spouse feels that the other prefers work to home life?

Because taking care of a new baby can be overwhelming, couples need to refresh themselves and their relationship.
◆ **What suggestions do you have for new parents who need a change of pace?**

Adjusting As a Single Parent

Not everyone has a partner in parenting. Singles face many of the same challenges that couples have. The difference is that singles have no partner to share the load.

Successful single parents don't try to do everything alone. Instead, they become skilled in finding the help they need. In a two-parent family, one partner could watch the baby while the other runs errands. The single parent might work out an arrangement with a friend or family member to stay with the child.

Time and energy are usually stretched thin for singles, who are often full-time workers as well as full-time parents. Survival with sanity means making very good use of the same management skills that help couples. Parents can combine tasks—for example, heating the soup while folding clothes and talking to the baby. They can make lists—of jobs that need doing, calls to make, groceries to buy. They can get organized—plan the order of errands to run on the way home and make a cleaning schedule. What other ideas would help single parents manage well?

Single parents often feel that they must be both mother and father to a child. ◆ **For what reasons do you agree or disagree with this idea?**

FEELING ISOLATED

At times a single parent may feel isolated. Loneliness and stress can be a problem. Physical health may be threatened if the single parent feels too busy to eat right and exercise. Single parents need to stay connected with others. Perhaps even more than couples, singles need a support network of family, friends, and relatives for social contact. Support groups can also provide companionship and practical assistance.

Adoptive Parents

Waiting to adopt a child can take years. Because they have no arrival date to rely on, adoptive parents may postpone buying supplies and equipment. The uncertainty can be frustrating. When a baby does arrive, the flurry of activity begins as last-minute preparations are made. Although not every adoption occurs just this way, the situation is still different from what birth parents experience.

EMOTIONAL ADJUSTMENTS

Adoptive parents feel emotions that birth parents do not. A typical worry is that the birth parents may try to regain custody. Because of going through so much to become parents, adoptive parents may feel guilty if they have moments of impatience or anger with the baby. Friends and relatives who treat an adopted child differently from birth children can be another challenge.

Such issues can be resolved. Over time parents sense the permanence of the adoption and feel more secure. Consulting with their legal advisors helps deal with any concerns. Time also helps adoptive parents bond with the child and realize that they have the same emotions that birth parents do. As parents show that the child is truly their own, friends and relatives usually follow their lead.

Adjustments for Family Members

New parents aren't the only ones who have to adjust to a new baby. Other family members do too. A brother or sister may need some guidance to feel comfortable with the baby.

Internet Connects

www.mcgrawhill.ca/links/parenting
To learn practical information on the formative years of a child's life, go to the Web site above for *Parenting Rewards & Responsibilities, First Canadian Edition,* to see where to go next.

Adoptive parents feel deep gratitude and joy, but they may have some insecure feelings too. ◆ **What might make adoptive parents feel insecure?**

Children who feel loved and appreciated are more likely to extend those same feelings to a new sibling. ◆ **How would you help prepare an older child for the arrival of a baby?**

SIBLING RELATIONSHIPS

Four-year-old Elena was eager to have a new baby brother. Her parents told her she was the "big" sister, which impressed her. Two weeks after Jesse came home, Elena was disappointed. The new baby cried a lot, and slept even more. Worst of all, her parents spent so much time with him.

Elena's behavior changed. She cried to be held and insisted on drinking from an old two-handled cup. Elena even began to wet the bed again. "I wish you never had him," she told her mother. "I hate him."

Elena showed all the signs of jealousy, a common reaction for children her age. Children under five are still dependent on their parents. They have limited relationships and activities outside the family. Seeing parents so attentive to a new child can threaten a child's sense of security.

To help Elena adjust, what would you suggest? Some ideas that her parents could try are:

♥ Involve Elena in the baby's care. Making real contributions increases self-esteem at a time when children feel insecure. Elena could talk to Jesse while his diaper is being changed or hand a towel to the person giving Jesse a bath.

♥ Spend time alone with her. Neglecting rituals or time spent together often breeds resentment in the child. Elena's mother might say, "I know we missed your bedtime story when Jesse was hungry, and I'm proud of how patient you've been. Tomorrow, if you want, we'll play a game while Jesse takes a nap."

♥ Tolerate some babyish behaviour, while drawing attention to Elena's more mature actions.

♥ Encourage Elena to talk about her feelings toward Jesse, accepting even negative responses. She must never be allowed to hurt the baby, however.

♥ Tell her frequently how much she is loved. Remind her that she is a very special person in the family, and thank her for being a helpful big sister.

RELATIONSHIPS WITH RELATIVES

New parents often have mixed emotions about relatives. They appreciate support and attention but also want to protect the baby and their role as parents. If relatives try to take over or offer too much advice, parents can gently but firmly say that they need to make their own decisions. Using a kind, diplomatic manner helps prevent hurt feelings.

More often than not, relatives are eager to help, and parents often need that help. Taking advantage, however, isn't right. Asking for help is better than simply expecting it. A parent can say something like, "I know you have a busy schedule, but would you mind taking care of Kristen when I go to the doctor on Thursday?"

By clearly expressing their gratitude for help, new parents can preserve good relationships with relatives. As one mother explained, "When my parents watch my baby, I say thanks and have them over for dinner. They raised their own family, and I don't expect them to raise mine too."

A willing relative can be a wonderful asset for new parents. Babies and grandparents thrive on their mutual admiration. At the same time parents get a break from the child-care routine.

Managing Stress

Parenthood is full of wonderful moments. Few people adjust to parenthood, however, without some difficulties along the way. What do waiting in traffic, hosting a family dinner, and caring for an infant all have in common? All three can produce stress.

A certain degree of stress is positive and even necessary in life, pushing you to solve problems and get things done. If people overschedule their time or try to control what is not controllable, negative stress can result. Stress can cause headaches, muscle aches, and digestive problems. People under stress may be tired all the time, but unable to sleep. They may lose their appetite, yet overeat.

Tips for Managing Stress

No one can, or should, avoid stress completely. Everyone can learn to manage it. In fact, just knowing that stress is controllable can help relieve it. You can use the ideas below to help prevent or manage any negative stress in your life, now and in the future:

- ♥ Eat a nutritious diet.
- ♥ Schedule times for relaxation and exercise.
- ♥ Plan ahead and set priorities.
- ♥ Look for the humourous side of situations.

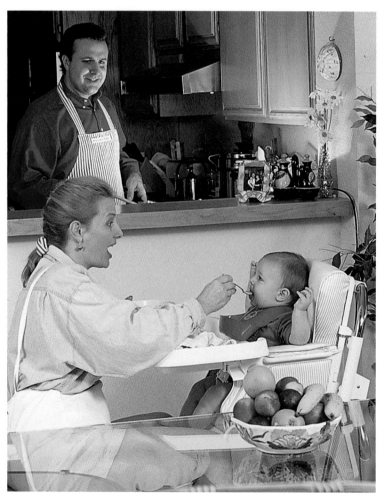

A happy partner is more fun to be around than one who is stressed.
◆ **Why would sharing parenting responsibilities make a difference?**

- ♥ Have a good cry to relieve tension.
- ♥ Let go of negative feelings.
- ♥ Maintain a close friendship.
- ♥ Avoid comparing yourself to others.
- ♥ Remember that no one is perfect.

Depression

If ignored, stress can result in serious health problems or possibly depression. **Depression** is a prolonged period of sadness marked by feelings of helplessness and an inability to enjoy life. Treating depression requires immediate professional help. A physician can recommend a mental health specialist who will help the person deal with the problem.

FINDING SUPPORT

You've probably seen winners on award shows accept their prize by thanking all the people who helped make that moment possible. If parents got awards for their "performance," they would be grateful for these sources of support, information, and encouragement: relatives; health care providers; other parents; libraries, bookstores, and even the Internet.

Seeking support is not a sign of poor parenting. Rather, it shows a person's desire to give parenthood a positive start, and a good beginning can set the stage for a bright future.

Parenting Q & A

The Internet Dilemma

Q "After our baby was born, I had some questions that needed answers, so I looked on the Internet. I couldn't believe all the web sites that contained information about my questions, but some of it was contradictory. How do I know what to believe?" *Josie*

A Unfortunately, there's no simple answer to your question. Anyone can put information on the Internet, and many are not authorities. Some even have incorrect information. As a user, you have to be cautious. Evaluate what you see to determine whether a web site seems reliable or questionable. Look at the domain section of a web site address. Those that end in *.edu* are educational institutions, a university, for example. Others are: *.gov* for government agencies, *.org* for nonprofit groups, and *.com* for commercial businesses. Many excellent sites provide useful information, but you may find some that aren't what they seem to be. If the answers you need as a parent are critical, you may want to personally consult a doctor or other professional instead.

Review

Looking Back

♥ New mothers have numerous physical and emotional adjustments to make after a baby is born.

♥ Fathers have adjustments to make too.

♥ The adjustments that couples, singles, and adoptive parents go through when they become parents are not all the same.

♥ As parents, a couple mustn't lose sight of the responsibilities they have to each other and the partnership.

♥ Parents can help their children adjust to the arrival of a new baby.

♥ New parents need to maintain good relationships with relatives after a baby is born.

♥ Parents can cope with their new responsibilities by taking steps to manage stress and by getting support from others.

Knowledge and Understanding

1. What physical changes does a woman notice after childbirth?
2. What can a new mother do to help her body recover after childbirth?
3. How might a couple's relationship be affected if the father is not aware of postpartum depression?
4. How might a new father be affected physically and emotionally? What can he do to cope?
5. How can a couple keep their relationship strong after the birth of a child?
6. Summarize the challenge single parents face in adjusting to parenthood.
7. How do the emotions of adoptive parents differ from those that birth parents feel?
8. How can a parent respond positively to a sibling's jealousy toward an infant?
9. How can assertiveness be useful to a new parent?
10. Give six suggestions for coping with stress.
11. What is the relationship between stress and depression?
12. Who can help new parents when they have questions and problems?

Review

Thinking and Inquiry

13. A single parent you know tells you, "My baby isn't going to feel deprived because she has only one parent in her life. I'm going to take care of her as well as any two parents ever could." What might result from this attitude?

14. A new father asks his supervisor at work if he can reduce his hours to part-time so he can be home with his new son when his wife returns to work. His supervisor responds by asking, "Is something wrong? Are you having any problems with your job?" What assumptions might the supervisor be making?

15. You and your spouse have a one-month-old infant. One morning, after getting up twice for night feedings, and just before leaving for work, your spouse mutters, "If I'd known babies were so much trouble, I wouldn't have had one." How do you interpret this remark? How do you respond?

16. You and your spouse have a four-week-old infant. You recently moved to a town that is far from friends and relatives, and you haven't met many people yet. You both feel the need to have a little time away from the baby, especially together, but there doesn't seem to be anyone to turn to. What could you do?

Communication

17. Using the Internet, newspapers, magazines, or journals, find a current article on managing stress. Summarize the main points of the article. Do you think the source is reliable? Is the information fact or opinion? Explain.

18. Imagine you are a Children's Aid worker in charge of interviewing prospective adoptive parents. Make a list of questions you would ask these people and develop a scoring checklist to use for your interviews.

19. Survey your friends to see if they would consider adopting a child from a different country in the future. Analyze the data by way of a graph and present your findings in a visual form of your choice.

Application

20. Create a plan that would help new parents cope with the responsibilities of parenting. Your plan should include a daily schedule, a list of parents' guidelines, a list of local resources for parents, or other ideas that you may have.

21. Suppose a mother earns $8000 a year working part-time. She pays $100 a week for child care for her two children. Discuss whether it makes financial sense for her to keep her part-time job, assuming she has a choice. What other factors might influence this decision?

22. With a partner, write about a situation in which a new parent faces a stressful situation that commonly occurs when caring for an infant. Have the parent respond in a way that does not help, and possibly worsens, the situation. Ask classmates to suggest more constructive, positive responses for your character.

Understanding Infants

CHAPTER EXPECTATIONS

While reading this chapter, you will:

▶ Demonstrate an understanding of how new parents can become capable and confident in making choices that are in the best interests of their children before and during birth, and in the first few months after birth.

▶ Explain how development from conception to three years of age affects and is crucial for development in later life.

▶ Analyze behaviours, conditions, and environments that influence positive or negative growth and development of the fetus, infant, and young child.

KEY TERMS

attachment behaviour
emotional development
fontanels
intellectual development
motor skills
object permanence
physical development
reflexes
sensorimotor period
social development
stranger anxiety
temperament

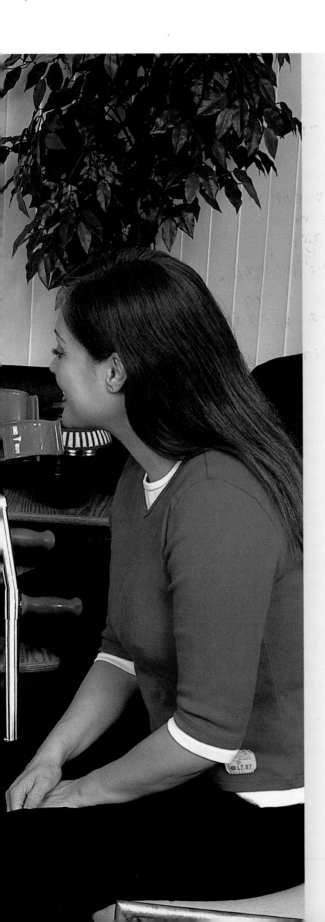

"Okay, Emily, what are you looking at?" Aaron looked down at his ten-month-old niece. Emily paused, then held out her hand. She slowly uncurled her fingers and grinned.

Aaron heard a noise behind him and saw a flash of light. As Emily gave a little cry of recognition, Aaron turned to see his sister, Crystal, enter the room. "I didn't know you were such a good babysitter," she said.

"I didn't know babies were so interesting," Aaron replied. "Last time you visited, she seemed like she was in her own little world. Now I think she's actually trying to talk to me. Taking care of her is getting to be fun."

Crystal sat on the floor beside her daughter. Emily rolled onto her knees and crawled into her lap. Crystal felt Emily's diaper and smiled at her brother. "Want to have some more fun? Let me introduce you to the joys of diapering, Uncle Aaron!"

---◆---

What do you think? Do you agree with Aaron that a ten-month-old would be more fun to care for than a younger infant? Explain your thoughts.

All babies are different, even twins.
◆ **When twins are identical, how might parents tell them apart?**

What Is Typical?

At no other time in life are growth and development so dramatic as during infancy, the period between birth and one year. *Growth* refers to an increase in size or weight. *Development* is the increase in physical, intellectual, emotional, and social skills. Moral awareness is also part of development.

By studying children around the world, researchers have identified average ages when changes are most likely to occur. Parents must remember, however, that "average" only identifies the midpoint in a range. What is "typical" or "normal" can be anything within the range.

As a guide to growth and development, parents need to know what the averages are, as well as the typical variations, in order to evaluate their child's progress. This chapter tells you how to recognize what is typical. In the next chapter, you will learn ways to help an infant grow and develop properly.

Physical Development

A ten-month-old's ability to take cereal from an adult's hand shows progress in physical development. **Physical development** is the increasing ability to control and co-ordinate body movements. This biological change occurs as the baby's muscles grow stronger.

GROWTH DURING INFANCY

When first held by her parents, Tabitha weighed 3.4 kg (7½ lbs.). To their surprise, a few days later she weighed only 3.2 kg (7 lbs.). The pediatrician assured Tabitha's parents that the loss was normal. A newborn loses fluid naturally and doesn't have much of an appetite during the first days after birth. Within a week, Tabitha had regained the lost weight and started to grow.

Tabitha continued to grow quickly during her first year. She gained about .6 kg (1½ lbs.) and 2.5 cm (1 in.) each month. By her first birthday, she weighed 10 kg (22½ lbs.) and was 76 cm (30 in.) tall.

Is this stunning growth rate typical? It is for infants. Most newborns triple their weight and grow 50 percent taller during their first year. After that, they slow down. If they didn't, Tabitha would be 1.5 m (5 ft.) tall by age three!

REFLEX BEHAVIOUR

When you hear a favourite song on the radio, do you turn your head, lean closer, and turn up the volume? Actions that come easily to you are impossible for newborns. They have very little control over their bodies. Instead, they come equipped with **reflexes**. Infants are born with these reactions to sensory experiences. For example, they react to a touch or a loud noise in ways they cannot control. Several infant reflexes are described in the chart below.

A Newborn's Reflexes at Birth

Name of Reflex	Stimulation	Behaviour	Approximate Age Reflex Ends
Rooting (sucking)	Cheek stroked with finger or nipple	Head turns; mouth opens; sucking movements begin	3-4 months
Moro (startle)	Loud noise or sudden change in baby's position	Extends legs, arms, and fingers; arches back; draws head back	4-6 months
Palmar grasp	Palm of hand stroked	Makes a very strong fist	3-5 months
Swimming	Put in water on stomach	Well-coordinated swimming movements	6 months
Tonic neck	Laid down on back	Head turns to one side; body assumes "fencer" position (arm and leg on preferred side are straightened; those on other side are bent)	4-5 months
Babinski	Sole of foot stroked	Toes fan out; foot twists in	6-24 months
Walking	Held under arms with bare feet touching flat surface	Makes step-like motions that look like well-co-ordinated walking	2 months
Placing	Back of feet drawn against flat surface	Withdraws feet	1 month

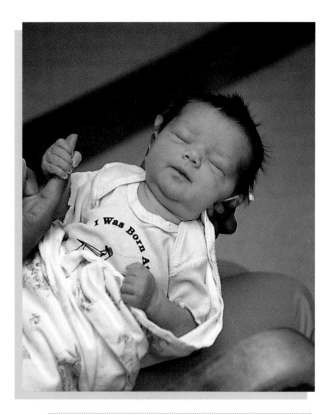

Caregivers should never rely on the grasping reflex to lift up a baby. Newborns have no control over their grasp and may let go at any time without warning.

MOTOR SKILLS

Suppose that every time you tried to smile, you waved your arms instead. A newborn baby's muscular control is like that. At first the motions of newborns are very general because they can't focus energy on selected muscles. At this age, they lack **motor skills**, abilities that depend on the use and control of muscles.

During infancy, motor skills develop quickly but unevenly as reflexes disappear. At first, infants learn simple tasks, such as learning to grasp an object. These skills form the basis of all physical abilities to come. As 11-month-old Bailey removes and replaces the lid on a plastic bowl, for example, she develops skills that may one day allow her to play the piano skillfully.

Some of the benchmark motor skills of infancy are described next. The material on pages 232–233 lists more, along with other signs of growth and development.

BODY DEVELOPMENT

Judging by adult proportions, the newborn's body may seem comical. Although the average newborn is 50 cm (20 in.) long, the head takes up 13 cm (5 in.), or one-quarter of the baby's total length. In contrast, your head is about one-eighth of your total height. The infant's arms and legs are small in comparison to the rest of the body.

A newborn's torso (excluding head, arms, and legs) looks too short for the body. As an infant grows, the torso begins to "catch up." In fact, this part of the body doubles in size several times by the time a child graduates from high school.

As the body develops, infants gain greater control of individual body parts. Each part develops in its own way, allowing the infant to master basic skills.

Head

You may have been warned not to touch the "soft spots" on a baby's head. These areas between the bone plates at the top, back, and sides of the infant's head are called **fontanels** (fahn-tuh-NELZ). These areas are surprisingly tough. Because fontanels keep the skull flexible, a baby rarely gets a serious head injury from bumps or falls. A heavy, direct blow, however, could cause serious injury.

A baby's head is very wobbly. You need to support the head and neck with your hand when picking the baby up, otherwise serious injury is possible. By about three months, most infants can hold their head up for a short time. Not until infants are six months old, however, can they fully control the head.

Vision

Imagine that you see this book in your hands clearly, but your shoes are a blur. What if the food on your plate at mealtime became an indistinct blob as you lifted it to your mouth? This gives you some idea of how a newborn sees the world.

Newborns can focus clearly on objects only between 13 and 33 cm (5–13 in.) away. This is just about the distance to a parent's face when an infant is held during feeding.

By three to four months, a baby's vision expands beyond the initial 33 cm (13 in.). Depth perception, the ability to see objects as three dimensional, starts to develop around the second month and is fully achieved by the seventh. By the end of infancy, babies can see almost as well as adults. Normally, however, vision continues to improve until the child is seven years old.

Hearing

Would you believe that babies start hearing even before birth? Research shows that babies can hear in the womb, as early as three months before they are born. This early experience probably helps them recognize their parents' voices.

The human face is one of an infant's favourite sights. At birth newborns can focus only on single features, yet within three weeks they can distinguish a parent's face from others.

The First Year of Growth and Development

Each baby grows and develops at an individual rate. Here you see how a typical baby progresses during the first year. Since few babies are completely typical, you can expect the ages to vary in real life.

TRY THIS ☛ **Observe an infant you know. Compare that baby's development with the typical accomplishments shown here. What variations do you notice?**

What can a three-month-old baby do?

At three months, a baby is alert and responding to the world. A typical three-month-old:

- ♥ Holds chest and head up for ten seconds when lying on the stomach.
- ♥ Tries to swipe at objects.
- ♥ Cries less than a newborn.
- ♥ Smiles (at six weeks).
- ♥ Turns the head toward an interesting sound and listens to voices.
- ♥ Stares at people's faces and begins to recognize family members.
- ♥ Coos and gurgles.

What can a six-month-old baby do?

At six months, a baby is developing body control. A typical six-month-old:

- ♥ Creeps by dragging the body around on the belly.
- ♥ Sits with support and perhaps sits alone for short periods.
- ♥ Rolls over from front to back and vice versa.
- ♥ Explores objects by putting them in the mouth.
- ♥ Reaches for objects with accuracy.
- ♥ Holds a bottle and switches objects from hand to hand.
- ♥ Holds out arms to be lifted up.
- ♥ Laughs out loud, babbles, calls for help, and screams when annoyed.

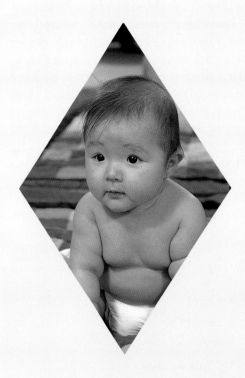

What can a nine-month-old baby do?

At nine months, a baby explores the environment. A typical nine-month-old:

♥ Sits unassisted.

♥ Crawls, pulls up to a standing position, and side-steps, holding on to furniture.

♥ Uses fingers to point, poke, and grasp small objects.

♥ Eats finger foods.

♥ Imitates simple actions and plays such games as peek-a-boo and pat-a-cake.

♥ Knows own name and responds to such simple commands as "Wave" and "Say bye-bye."

♥ Produces babbling that sounds almost like a foreign language.

What can a 12-month-old baby do?

At 12 months, a baby is striving for independence. A typical 12-month-old:

♥ Stands and perhaps walks without help.

♥ Climbs up and down stairs and out of the crib or playpen.

♥ Drops and throws toys.

♥ Prefers using one hand over the other.

♥ Fears strange people and places.

♥ Expresses affection.

♥ Remembers events and uses trial and error to solve problems.

♥ Says "mama," "dada," "hi," and "bye-bye."

Healthy babies are born with excellent hearing. As early as three days old, babies turn their head in the direction of a noise and even stop what they are doing to listen. A favourite sound is the human voice, especially the parents'.

Babies react to a surprising sound much as you do. They may become quiet and still, blink their eyes, catch their breath, or cry out. At six months, babies start to investigate sounds around them. At nine months, they listen attentively to sounds they know and search for sounds out of sight.

Such reactions are encouraging. An infant who fails to respond to sound may have a hearing problem. The child should be checked by a doctor. If necessary, even a tiny infant can be fitted with hearing aids.

Taste and Smell

Since newborns actually have more taste buds than an adult, their sense of taste is quite refined. They can tell the difference between bitter and sweet tastes, and they prefer the sweet.

Until they learn to use their hands, infants feel objects by putting them in their mouth. This is why small objects that might cause choking are hazardous around infants.

Newborns also have a good sense of smell. Even young babies can tell one aroma from another. As early as six days of age, they recognize the pleasing smell of their mother's milk.

Near a strong, unpleasant odour, however, a baby will cry and turn away.

Teeth

Only one of every 2000 babies is born with a tooth. The rest enter the world toothless. Acquiring teeth, called teething or cutting teeth, typically begins when the baby is between six and ten months old. Under the gums are tooth buds, formed during prenatal development. Eventually, the tooth buds push through the gums in a process called eruption. Gum tissue gently splits open as each tooth appears, which can take up to ten days per tooth.

Even a baby seems proud over the appearance of those first baby teeth.
◆ **Why do women need to drink plenty of milk during pregnancy?**

Teething can be difficult for child and parent. A baby may be restless and cranky while each tooth comes in. A pediatrician can recommend a teething medication or a pain reliever to reduce fever and discomfort. A cold teething ring offers temporary relief.

The first set of teeth is called the primary, or baby, teeth. Usually, the first teeth to appear are the two lower front teeth, followed by the four upper front teeth. These front teeth are called incisors (in-SEYE-zurs). By the second birthday, a child usually has a mouth full of teeth.

Baby teeth are not permanent. They fall out when the child is six or seven years old, usually in the same order they appeared.

Arms and Hands

Imagine clenching your hand in a tight fist for a month. What is difficult for you is natural for newborns. They have no real control over their hands or their arms. Moving or jerking the arms and hands is automatic.

Raising Children With

Character

Teaching Compassion

Five-year-old Isabel glared at her mother and her squalling infant brother. She put her hands over her ears dramatically. "Why won't he stop crying?" she demanded.

"He's not feeling well," her mother explained. "His teeth are coming in." She managed to quiet the baby long enough to show Isabel the tiny teeth emerging from the gums. "The new teeth are bothering him."

Isabel watched her mother try to soothe the baby by crooning to him and massaging his gums. Her expression softened, even as the baby's whimpering went on. She stroked his tiny hand hesitantly. "Don't cry, Thomas," she whispered. The baby gripped her finger and drew it to his mouth. He began gnawing vigorously on her knuckle.

Isabel looked delighted. "I made him stop!" she said with pride, as the peacefulness of new-found quiet surrounded them.

◆◆◆◆ Thinking It Over ◆◆◆◆

1. How did Isabel's attitude toward her brother change? What was responsible for this change?
2. How did Isabel's mother encourage a sense of compassion in her daughter?
3. If Isabel's mother had become upset by the crying, what might have happened?

By two months, many babies "discover" their hands. They may spend hours staring at them, sucking on them, and opening and closing them. The grasping reflex begins to fade. By three months, infants open their hands easily. They experiment with holding and releasing objects, and moving them from hand to hand and to the mouth.

Over the next year, infants refine their arm and hand movements. At first they make only broad swipes at an object and grasp whatever is within reach, a motion called raking. By seven months, most can reach for a single large object and pick it up. They can also throw a smaller one. Also at that age, babies can hold a bottle or cup with both hands. By ten months, they are able to pick up an object with the thumb and forefinger, or the "pincer grasp."

As babies gain control of their arms and hands, they tend to use both hands equally. They begin to favour the left or right hand by the end of infancy. By about 18 months of age, they establish a definite preference. Nine of ten babies become right-handed.

Legs and Feet

Infants gain control over the legs and feet last, after the head, arms, and torso. For the first few months, the legs tend to fold into the fetal position, as they were in the uterus. They gradually straighten as muscles develop. Until the legs straighten by age two or three, most infants are bowlegged.

Use of the legs begins with kicking, around three months of age. Regular progress is made as the infant moves toward walking ability. Walking is a very complex skill that requires balance, coordination, and muscular development. Children master this skill at different ages, usually around 12 to 14 months.

You may have heard of "late walkers," infants who didn't begin to walk until they were 15 or 16 months old. ◆ **Why does walking have this wide age variation?**

Internet Connects

www.mcgrawhill.ca/links/parenting
To learn everything there is to know about toys, go to the Web site above for *Parenting Rewards & Responsibilities, First Canadian Edition*, to see where to go next.

Intellectual Development

Shaping the mind of a child is the same as shaping that child's future. Without the ability to think, remember, understand, reason, and use language, people don't function well in the world. **Intellectual development** is the process of learning these skills, and parents and other caregivers have a critical role in this process.

THE DEVELOPING BRAIN

What if the growth of the infant mind were as obvious as the growth of the body? As dramatic as changes in a child's appearance are, they are minor compared to the changes going on inside the brain.

Recent research on brain development shows that a child's brain grows at an amazing rate during the first few years of life. The brain actually gains weight by becoming more complex instead of bigger. You'll read more about the fascinating process of brain development in Chapter 19.

At birth, an infant's brain performs only physical maintenance tasks. For example, the brain regulates heartbeat and controls reflexes. Areas of the brain that perform high-level thought processes don't work yet because they haven't been stimulated. That's where parents and other caregivers come in.

To develop a baby's mind, parents and caregivers need to provide new and repeated sensory experiences. These involve sight, sound, smell, taste, and touch. Right from birth, babies need plenty of warm, loving interaction with others. Without these influences, intellectual development cannot progress the way it should.

As you read about helping children develop, remember that everything you do in working with them has an impact on brain development. Look for ways to help a baby's brain grow. The mind that forms when a child is very young is the one that child will use throughout life. If you miss opportunities to shape a child's mind, you can't go back and make them up.

CLUES TO INTELLECT

As the mind develops, parents need to evaluate progress. Certain physical abilities show that mental skills have been mastered.

What baby wouldn't delight in a game played with a caring adult? Many people don't realize that this is exactly the kind of interaction that makes an infant's brain develop.

Language

How infants learn language is something of a mystery, one that has become better understood in recent years. Researchers increasingly believe that the human brain is "wired" to learn language, just as the body is designed to use calcium to build bones and teeth. As evidence, they cite the fact that babies in every culture and country acquire language in similar ways.

Like all healthy infants, listening was Aciel's first language skill. By six months, she could imitate single vowel sounds, such as "e" and "o." By nine months, she was combining vowels and consonants into syllables. She would babble "ma-ma-ma" and "boo-boo-boo." Interestingly, if Aciel had been born unable to hear, she would have soon stopped babbling.

By her first birthday, Aciel had a limited but useful vocabulary. She could speak and understand short, frequently used words, such as "no," "hi," and "bye-bye." She responded to her name. Like other one-year-olds, Aciel understood more words than she could pronounce. She responded when her parents said "Clap your hands" or "Look at the doggie!"

Imitation plays a large part in language development. So do cause and effect. When Aciel's parents rewarded her babbling with smiles, attention, and words, she continued to make the same sounds in order to produce those reactions.

Memory

The ability to remember is another sign of a growing intellect. As early as two months of age, some infants show they expect feedings at a regular time. Some six-month-olds can recognize an object after seeing just a part. Dylan, for example, grinned and squirmed with anticipation when he saw the ears of his favourite stuffed rabbit as his sister Shelly slowly raised it out of the toy chest.

It's never too early to begin reading to a child. ◆ **In what ways would reading to an infant differ from reading to an older child?**

At about nine months of age, children begin to understand the concept of **object permanence**. They discover that something exists even when totally out of sight. If Shelly hid the toy rabbit and gave six-month-old Dylan a set of plastic keys, he jingled the keys and forgot about the stuffed animal. At nine months, he might look for the rabbit. Understanding object permanence also helps Dylan realize that he exists separate from his environment.

PIAGET'S THEORY

Jean Piaget, the Swiss psychologist, spent his career studying children's intellectual, or cognitive, development. His theories about the ages and stages of development, formulated some 50 years ago, are widely accepted today.

Piaget observed that infants, children, and adults use different thought processes to learn. He determined that children advance through a series of intellectual stages that use increasingly complex thought processes. These stages occur in one fixed order and at approximately the same ages in all children. Development is gradual, so the end of one stage may overlap with the beginning of the next.

Sensorimotor Period

According to Piaget, the first major period in a child's intellectual development is the **sensorimotor period**. *Sensori* refers to the five senses; *motor* refers to movement. During this period, infants use their senses and movement to explore and learn about their surroundings. The idea that an infant learns by interacting with the environment is central to Piaget's theory.

The sensorimotor period begins at birth and ends at about age two. Included are six stages; the first four fall within the first year of life. In Chapter 19 you will read about the two stages that follow infancy. As you read about the early stages, notice how they correspond to the infant's physical development at each age.

Inspired by objects in the environment, an infant can't wait to explore. ◆ **What effect would a child's interest have on motor skill development?**

♥ ***Stage 1: Birth to one month***. The baby's reflexes are apparent. They are the infant's only means of learning about the world. Infants learn about textures through the Palmar grasp reflex, for example, but only those textures that happen to touch the hand.

♥ ***Stage 2: One to four months***. Infants begin to sort out their environment through greater use of their senses. They start to make simple but deliberate actions, rather than acting solely on reflex.

♥ ***Stage 3: Four to eight months***. Infants begin to use and manipulate objects. Combined with their use of the senses, this ability allows them to learn about cause and effect. Babies discover, for instance, that every time they shake a rattle, it makes a certain sound.

Building Parenting Skills

PARENTING WITH LOVE

Love is unconditional acceptance. Love shows in what you say and do. Parenting with love means letting children know you care about them and will support them always, regardless of their actions or accomplishments. Ideally, parents love a child at every age—simply because that child is theirs. As the parent of two children, Blake showed love when he:

▶ Cuddled his eight-month-old daughter Katie and talked to her warmly.

▶ Looked in on Katie while she was sleeping just to make sure she was all right.

▶ Stayed up at night with Katie to comfort her when she was sick.

▶ Shouted encouragement to his six-year-old son Spencer regardless of how well the boy was playing in a softball game.

▶ Said "I love you" to Spencer just so the boy could hear the words.

▶ Insisted that Spencer wear a helmet while riding his bike.

▶ Gave plenty of hugs and kisses to both of his children every day.

◆ ◆ Your Thoughts ◆ ◆

❶ How can a parent love a child unconditionally, yet still set standards and expectations?

❷ Some parents are afraid to say no for fear of losing a child's love. Why is this a problem?

❸ Can anything make up for a lack of parental love in a child's life? Why or why not?

❹ Evan grew up in a family that never expressed love through words or affection. He wants things to be different in his own family. What would you suggest?

♥ *Stage 4: Eight to 12 months.* At this time, the ability to combine actions lets infants act more purposefully. As they learn the concept of object permanence, they become more aware of the outside world. At the same time, greater motor skills promote exploration.

Emotional Development

Do babies get angry? Can they feel joy? If you've ever listened to an infant who had to wait for a meal or seen a baby's expression at a parent's return, you know the answer is yes. **Emotional development** is the process of learning to recognize and express feelings.

As with physical development, infants have very limited emotions at first. Over the course of a year, their emotions become more varied and distinct. Also like physical growth, emotions develop in a predictable sequence. Infants typically develop certain emotions at these ages, although variations do occur: *excitement*—birth; *distress*—during the first month; *delight*—two months; *anger and disgust*—four-five months; *fear*—six months; *elation*—seven-eight months; *affection*—nine-ten months.

HOW EMOTIONS DEVELOP

Although feeling emotions is inborn, infants have to learn to identify emotions and express them. Infants gain these abilities with experience and intellectual development. They link feelings with physical sensations, such as hunger, or circumstances, such as a lack of attention.

Trying to interpret a baby's emotions isn't always easy. What upsets one child may not even bother another.

As a newborn, Kyle cried at every discomfort, even boredom. At around two months of age, his cry was different when he was hungry or wet. A few months later, he showed real anger by throwing down the toy his mother substituted when he reached for the cup on the kitchen table.

Kyle's positive emotions also grew more complex. At two months, he genuinely smiled at a funny face his father made. He showed delight over a neighbour's puppy at seven months. At 11 months, he gave his mother a hug of affection and love.

Could Kyle have experienced anger at six weeks old? Anger occurs when you can't have something you want. At six weeks, Kyle's responses were still automatic. He couldn't think, "I want that," or recognize an obstacle. For this reason, emotional development parallels intellectual growth.

At about nine months, Kyle could recognize threatening situations. He began to fear unfamiliar people, called **stranger anxiety**, which occurs between six and ten months of age.

TEMPERAMENT

Suppose you showed three infants a wind-up toy and let it run on the floor beside them. One infant might smile and crawl after it. Another might watch passively. A third infant might shriek and pull away as the toy passed by. Even at this early age, these infants are showing their **temperament**, an inborn style of reacting to the environment and relating to others.

Three temperaments are often used to describe infants. Baby A is *easygoing*. This infant is interested and responsive. Baby A adapts to change, sleeps soundly, likes to play, and is easily soothed when upset. Baby B is *cautious*. This infant prefers watching to participating and withdraws from close contact. Reassurance is needed by Baby B, who may be bothered by change. Baby C is *sensitive*. This baby upsets easily, especially over change. This less predictable baby is hard to comfort and may have sleep or digestive problems.

Emotions are shaped by the experiences a baby has.
◆ **What effect might a calm, loving parent have on a baby's emotional development?**

A baby's mood doesn't always stay the same. A happy moment can become a fretful one in a matter of minutes. A baby's pattern of temperament, however, can be seen over time.

Parents may have to adapt the way they handle a child to best suit the infant's disposition. For example, a very social baby might need extra play time. Sometimes parents must manage their own temperament effectively if it is different from the child's. A very active, energetic parent, for instance, might have to slow down somewhat for a passive baby.

GOALS FOR EMOTIONAL DEVELOPMENT

Just as infants learn basic physical and intellectual skills, they also gain certain emotional "accomplishments." Basic emotional progress includes:

♥ *Forming an attachment.* Between three and six months of age, infants begin to recognize the people who take care of them the most. They become excited when those people appear and show distress when they leave.

This is called **attachment behaviour**. Attachment gives babies a secure base to reach out from and explore surroundings. Research indicates that the most confident, outgoing children are those who had a firm attachment to a caring person during infancy. Therefore, infants need at least one caring person who takes regular care of them during the first year.

♥ *Learning to give and receive affection easily.* For infants, affection is like food and warmth. Infants instinctively seek affection but learn about it only through experience. Parents who show plenty of affection are "educating" the child about giving and receiving love.

Even the simplest situation can become a social event for a baby. ◆ **What social lessons might an infant learn while meeting a new neighbour?**

♥ ***Developing a sense of self-worth.*** Children need to grow up feeling good about themselves. Such feelings give them the confidence to try new things and learn more. Armed with a sense of security and well-being, children have a better chance of growing up well-adjusted and able to get along with people. They are more likely to become successful, caring individuals who make a positive impact in the world. Infants who are hugged and cuddled and hear positive, tender words begin to conclude, "I am a lovable, worthwhile person." When parents respond to their cry, babies learn, "Someone cares about me." Babies need these lessons right from the start.

Social Development

Can a three-day-old baby be social? You might not think so, but in fact humans are born with social instincts. However, positive **social development** is not automatic. Learning to relate to other people is cultivated or stunted depending on how others treat the child.

HOW SOCIABILITY DEVELOPS

Close physical contact is a routine part of an infant's life. Throughout the day people hold and touch infants for feeding, bathing, diapering, and play. Positive interaction is an opportunity for social development.

A description of Laura's "social life" shows what happens. At six months, Laura easily recognized her foster parents by sight and sound. She smiled and wriggled with delight when she saw them. Sometimes she deliberately cried just to get their attention. When they smiled, talked to her, or picked her up, Laura smiled and made eye contact, She also enjoyed the entertainment value of others, who supplied comfort too.

Infants love contact with siblings and other children. They are fascinated by the actions of those who are closer to their own age and size than adults are.

Eventually, Laura crawled after people, even looking for them from room to room. "Chase me" was a favourite game. She practised verbal skills by babbling at her stuffed animals and her family.

As she became a little older, Laura learned that some behaviours are not acceptable. Hitting the dog and throwing toys brought gentle signals of disapproval. She learned that social interaction comes with rules.

THE FAMILY'S ROLE

Since the family is a baby's first social group, the home needs to be a place where sociability can grow. Babies become sociable if they live in a happy, stable environment. They can sense a parent's emotional state. Anger and tension can make a child fearful. People can't always be in a good mood, but they can make sure that an infant is moved to a different room or location or put in the care of someone else when situations might be upsetting.

Moral Development

Some research now suggests that infants have an inborn tendency toward moral behaviour. Studies of identical twins have shown that they are more likely than fraternal twins to respond positively to people in need. Other research shows that extremely neglected infants fail to develop that area of the brain associated with a healthy attachment to others.

These studies suggest that caring behaviour is rooted in biology before it is encouraged by a loving environment. As scientists continue to explore the role of genes and the workings of the mind, they may answer more questions about the development of morality in children.

Health & Safety

FAILURE TO THRIVE

Why would a seemingly healthy infant stop eating, be inactive, and not grow properly? The answer could be failure to thrive, a condition that is something of a mystery because the exact cause may be hard to pinpoint.

Genuine failure to thrive results from unmet social and emotional needs, as well as physical ones. In some cases, parents may be providing the basic physical necessities, without realizing the importance of holding and interacting with the baby. They may be distracted by family problems. Without stimulation, the baby loses interest in the world. Some parents become worried, but others think the baby's reaction is normal. They may even be grateful that the baby is so undemanding. The cycle continues until the child loses weight and develops health problems. Hospitalization may even be needed.

Before diagnosing failure to thrive, health-care professionals must rule out any physical cause for the condition. Sometimes a simple change to a more nutritious diet is all that is needed. Otherwise, a family counsellor can educate the parents about relating to the baby with more affection and interest.

Review

Looking Back

♥ An infant's physical growth includes changes in size, weight, and proportions. Development includes refinement of motor skills and physical senses.

♥ Newborns have a variety of reflexes with which they are born and cannot control.

♥ Studies of the brain have led to new understandings about its development.

♥ Advances in language and memory are two signs of intellectual development in infants.

♥ Jean Piaget believed that infants learn as they use their senses and developing motor skills to explore their surroundings.

♥ Emotions develop as infants learn to associate feelings with physical sensations and outer circumstances.

♥ Infants' natural sociability is reinforced through positive contact with others.

Knowledge and Understanding

1. How might references to what is "average" progress in a child's growth and development sometimes cause problems for parents?
2. Why do infants need reflexes? Name and describe two reflexes.
3. How do a baby's physical proportions compare with those of an adult?
4. Would a two-month-old baby enjoy the sights and sounds of a Canada Day celebration? Why?
5. How do motor skills develop in a typical infant's hands?
6. What changes will you see as an infant develops motor skills in the legs and feet?
7. Why are sensory experiences important to brain development?
8. What methods does an infant use for learning during the sensorimotor period?
9. Five-month-old Sierra cries when her father leaves her with the babysitter. Why is this a good sign?
10. Describe how infants learn social skills.
11. How does the most fundamental moral development show in infants?

Thinking and Inquiry

12. Jake is an infant who babbles, laughs out loud, and screams when he's angry. He can sit up by himself but he cannot yet crawl. How old would you guess Jake to be?

13. What problems might occur if a caregiver is not knowledgeable about motor skill development in infancy?

14. An acquaintance mentions that her infant son has been unusually active and high-spirited all day. "He must be excited about his first birthday party tomorrow," she says. Is this a likely reason for her son's behaviour? How would you explain his excitement?

Communication

15. Create a poster for the Public Health Department that shows the different types of reflexes found in healthy newborns.

16. Imagine that you're a parent of a seven-month-old boy. You are becoming concerned that the child cannot sit up by himself. Your spouse says that you're worrying for nothing and that you worry about too many things concerning the child. What are your feelings and thoughts in this situation? Write your ideas in a paragraph.

17. Describe a toy you enjoyed playing with as a young child. Why did you like it? What did it teach you?

Application

18. At birth, Natalie weighed 2.5 kg ($5\frac{1}{2}$ lbs.) and measured 46 cm (18 in.). What do you predict her weight and height might be near her first birthday? How did you arrive at this answer?

19. Choose a common toy for infants. Describe how an infant would interact with the toy at each of the first four stages of the sensorimotor period.

20. Suppose you are the parent of a newborn, but you have never had a course in child development. Having very little experience with children, you are concerned about caring for the baby. You want to be a good parent, but you know so little about what to expect as your baby grows. What specific efforts could you make that would help you become knowledgeable?

Parenting Infants

CHAPTER EXPECTATIONS

While reading this chapter, you will:

▶ Demonstrate an understanding of how new parents can become capable and confident in making choices that are in the best interests of their children.

▶ Explain how development from conception to three years of age affects development in later life.

▶ Analyse behaviours, conditions, and environments that influence positive or negative growth and development of the fetus, infant, and young child.

▶ Summarize the main points of information gathered from various reliable sources.

KEY TERMS

colic
cradle cap
demand feeding
immunizations
puréed
sterilization

sudden infant
death
syndrome
(SIDS)
weaning

As Melanie nestled ten-month-old Rebecca in her lap, she reached into the grocery sack nearby. The two were sitting outdoors after returning from a shopping trip.

"Do you remember the corn we bought at the farmers' market this morning, Rebecca?" she asked. "Tonight, we'll have it for dinner." Melanie took one ear out of the sack and held it up so her daughter could see it. Rebecca smiled and babbled in response.

"First, we peel away the husk. See? All the leaves are layered. Then—oh, look at the pretty silk. And what's under here?" Melanie asked as she pulled off the bottom husk. Rebecca watched, pumping her arms with excitement. "Look, Rebecca, rows and rows of golden yellow corn." Melanie let her daughter grasp the fibrous, grooved leaves and twist the strands of corn silk between her fingers. Then she probed the bumpy ridges of kernels. At each new texture, she looked up as if to say, "Amazing!"

"Corn on the cob is very good to eat," Melanie said, softly brushing the flossy strands against Rebecca's cheek. "And the silk, " she continued while Rebecca squealed with delight, "is good for tickling babies!"

◆

What do you think? What signs do you see that Melanie is a good parent?

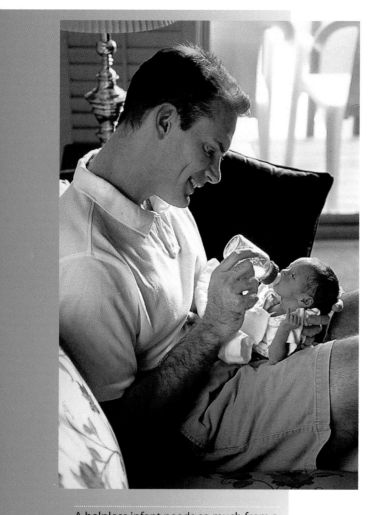

A helpless infant needs so much from a parent. This father is taking care of the baby's physical need for nourishment.
◆ **Is he doing something more?**

What Infants Need

What do infants need? Everything! Imagine having to rely on others all the time. Nourishing food, dry clothing, and a safe place to sleep—everything an infant needs has to be supplied by someone else.

When you are a parent, your child depends on you and learns from you. Your child gains trust and a sense of well-being when you are attentive. Self-confidence and curiosity about the world also develop. Strong parenting skills bring about these positive results.

Meeting Physical Needs

Meeting physical needs is understandably the first concern of people who care for infants. Parents spend many hours on these time-consuming tasks.

FEEDING AN INFANT

The familiar image of new parents rising sleepy-eyed for the baby's 2:00 a.m. feeding is accurate. A newborn's tiny stomach typically holds only about 60 mL (4 tbsp.) of milk. An infant who falls asleep full and contented will probably wake in a few hours crying with hunger. Since a newborn's feeding "clock" takes several months to become set, the feeding schedule may be irregular and unpredictable.

Most authorities recommend **demand feeding**, which means feeding the infant whenever the child is hungry rather than on a fixed schedule. Fortunately for parents, feedings soon become less frequent and more regular. By age seven months, most babies need three or four feedings a day.

Breast-Feeding

Most mothers who make the decision to breast-feed find it very satisfying. As described in Chapter 10, the health benefits alone make it worthwhile. A nursing mother should eat nutritiously and drink plenty of fluids. She should avoid chocolate, spicy foods, and strong-flavoured vegetables. Medical professionals, experienced friends, and the La Leche League, an organization that promotes breast-feeding, can offer support.

When a baby is breast-fed, some family members may wish they could feed the baby. By including everyone in the infant's care, a sense of involvement grows. Fathers and siblings can sit close during a feeding. They can also hold, play with, and care for the baby at other times.

Mothers who are experienced with breast-feeding can offer support to first-timers.
◆ **Why would one mother's advice to "take it one day at a time" be helpful?**

Bottle-Feeding

When a baby is bottle-fed, certain precautions must be taken. These relate to preparing formula and feeding techniques.

PREPARING FORMULA. A pediatrician usually recommends one or two of the many formulas available for bottle-feeding. They must be prepared exactly according to directions. Bottles and nipples, plus all equipment used, must be washed thoroughly in hot, soapy water and rinsed several times, also in hot water. Many people sterilize bottles and nipples before using them. **Sterilization** means bringing the items to a high temperature, usually by boiling, to kill germs that cause illness. A pediatrician can be consulted for guidelines on sterilization.

Prepared formula should be refrigerated before use. To warm for feeding, the bottle can be placed in a pan of hot tap water. A drop or two of formula on the inside of the wrist should feel pleasantly warm.

Experts caution against using a microwave oven, which may warm the formula unevenly. Even though the rest of the formula feels just right, "hot spots" may burn the baby's mouth and throat.

FEEDING FROM THE BOTTLE. Newborns may be given up to 90 mL (3 oz.) of formula at one feeding. To meet the infant's demands and increasing nutritional needs, the amount is gradually increased to 200 to 250 mL (6–8 oz.).

Using the bottle as a pacifier can cause problems. First, letting the baby suck on an empty bottle or fall asleep with one still in the mouth can cause tooth decay when formula (or juice) pools in the mouth. Ear infection is a second potential problem. Liquid that drips into the back of the throat and trickles into the tube that connects the nose and ears can cause infection. Thirdly, an unhealthy association between food and stress relief can lead to later eating problems.

Burping Techniques

Babies often swallow air while drinking. If not released, the air causes discomfort. Breast-fed babies should be burped about every five minutes while feeding. Bottle-fed babies need to be burped after every 50 or 60 mL (couple of ounces) of formula.

To burp a baby, hold the infant against your shoulder, face down across your lap, or in a sitting position on your lap. Place a clean towel where it can catch any expelled milk. Gently pat or rub the lower back until the air is expelled.

Caring for an infant is a time-consuming job that never ends, not even when the phone rings.
◆ **What would you say to someone who calls while you're feeding the baby?**

About Weaning

As bottle-feeding or breast-feeding is replaced with drinking from a cup, **weaning** occurs. Infants may begin to show less interest in the bottle or breast around age nine to 12 months. Experts recommend that a baby give up the bottle entirely by about twelve months.

An infant can be held in one of several positions for burping. Placing a clean towel under the baby's head protects clothing in case the baby spits up.

Parents give the child milk or juice from a cup, slowly increasing the number of offerings over a period of several weeks. First, parents hold the cup so the baby can practise sipping. Eventually, the baby wants to hold the cup alone. Special covered cups with spouts are useful until spills are less likely. The child's pediatrician can offer specific suggestions about weaning.

Introducing Solid Foods

In recalling his daughter's first experience with solid food, one father said, "Erica acted like she wanted to eat from a spoon, but she pushed the first little bit I put in her mouth right back out, and it rolled down her chin. She looked at me as if to say, 'Is this what you eat?' Eventually she swallowed some, I guess, and decided it wasn't so bad after all."

Erica's reaction to her first taste of solid food is typical. Although these foods are thinned and **puréed**—blended into a smooth consistency—their taste and texture are unfamiliar to a baby. Even the action of the tongue in swallowing solid food is a new skill for the baby.

When introducing solid foods, experts recommend several useful suggestions:

♥ *Don't rush solid foods*. Keep a baby on just breast milk or formula for the first four to six months. Both are easy to digest and nutritionally complete. By waiting to introduce solid foods until the infant is this age, food allergies are less likely to develop.

♥ *Introduce foods gradually*. Here is a typical order for starting foods: iron-fortified cereals; single-grain cereals, such as rice, oatmeal, and barley; wheat cereals (harder to digest and may cause allergies); yellow vegetables, such as sweet potatoes and carrots; simple puréed fruits (apples, bananas, peaches, and pears); green vegetables; other fruits and vegetables; strained meats; and vegetable-meat combinations. New foods should be introduced one at a time, no more than one per week. That way parents can identify any food that causes an allergic reaction, upset stomach, or other problems.

♥ ***Choose nutritious foods***. Infants need a healthy diet. The most nutritious foods are those with the fewest added ingredients. Plain pears are a better choice than sweetened, for instance. The food should taste bland by adult standards since babies have more sensitive taste buds and prefer milder flavours.

♥ ***Be patient***. Starting babies on solid food takes patience. Babies need time to adjust to the new experience. Some develop definite likes and dislikes. Others refuse a new food several times before accepting it.

When babies are old enough to sit up, they like to join family meals and may be offered tastes of certain foods from the table. Applesauce, cottage cheese, and mashed potatoes are a few of the foods they might share. By about one year of age, they can eat many of the same foods as the rest of the family. Large pieces of food, such as grapes and hot dogs, must be cut into small pieces to prevent choking.

Learning to Self-Feed

For babies, spattering food all over themselves, you, and the table, is just part of the fun of self-feeding. Self-feeding usually begins around nine months of age. The process is likely to be messy and time-consuming. Babies are still developing their motor skills and co-ordination. Also at this age, food is for exploration as much as for eating. Smashing, smearing, and spilling make self-feeding an adventure.

Finger foods are best for first attempts at self-feeding. Small pieces of fruit, cooked vegetables, cheese, soft toast, and hard-boiled egg are good starter foods. Cooked, crumbled meat can also be given.

Learning to self-feed is messy business. ◆ **What could a caregiver have done to make this cleanup a little easier?**

IMMUNIZATIONS

Children need to be protected against a number of childhood diseases through **immunizations** (i-myuh-nuh-ZAY-shuns). These are vaccines that are given in shots or taken by mouth.

Unless babies receive immunizations, they can become ill with certain diseases. Regular immunizations are given according to a schedule, as shown in the chart below.

Some babies react to immunizations. They may be unusually cranky or run a slight fever. The doctor can advise parents about what to do if a reaction occurs. Parents should keep a careful record of all the immunizations a child receives.

Recommended Immunization Schedule Through Age Six

Diseases Prevented	Immunizations Required	Birth	1 Mo.	2 Mo.	4 Mo.	6 Mo.	12 Mo.	18 Mo.	4-6 Years
Hepatitis B (Hep B vaccine)	3		✖						
				✖			✖		
Diptheria, tetanus, and pertussis (whooping cough) (DTaP or DTP vaccine)	5			✖	✖	✖		✖	✖
Meningitis, pneumonia, and certain infections (Hib vaccine)	4			✖	✖	✖	✖		
Polio (Polio-virus vaccine)	4			✖	✖			✖	✖
Measles, mumps, and rubella (MMR vaccine)	2						✖		✖
Chicken pox (Var vaccine)	1						✖		

DIAPERING NEEDS

A steady supply of clean, dry diapers is the basis for an infant's "wardrobe." Regular diaper changes help keep a baby comfortable. Regular changing also helps prevent diaper rash by keeping the diaper area clean and as dry as possible. A diaper change is needed after every bowel movement and whenever the diaper is obviously wet.

When the diaper is changed, the diaper area should be gently cleaned. Baby soap and a damp washcloth are needed after a bowel movement. Disposable, premoistened towelettes, sometimes called diaper wipes, can also be used. If the baby has a diaper rash, a medicated ointment may be applied to the diaper area. Lotions and baby powders are not needed.

Soiled cloth diapers should be rinsed in the toilet, then soaked with other diapers in a covered diaper pail with a soapy solution until they are washed. If disposable diapers are used, they should be folded over, tightly retaped, and tied in a plastic bag for disposal in a trash can.

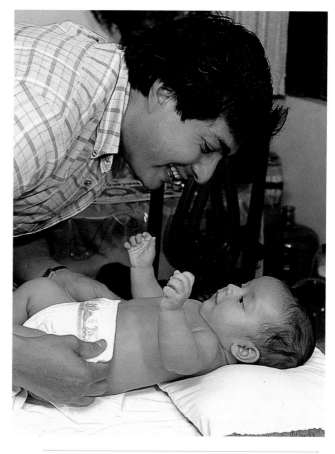

Diaper changing can be difficult if the baby squirms and kicks. ◆ **How is this father eliminating that problem?**

SLEEP PATTERNS IN INFANCY

As seven-year-old Clayton watched his baby brother sleeping peacefully, he wondered, "Why do babies sleep so much? They don't do anything all day." Actually, babies' bodies are always active—because of growth.

Infants need sleep to help fuel rapid development during the first year. Most newborns need from 14 to 20 hours of sleep a day. During the first month, $16\frac{1}{2}$ hours of sleep per day is the average. By the fifth month this number decreases to an average of $14\frac{1}{2}$ hours per day. Most babies begin to sleep through the night around three months of age. By the end of the first year, most do so regularly.

As the baby grows, nap patterns change too. At about five months, a typical infant takes three or four hour-long naps each day. In the months ahead, this pattern usually changes to one nap in the morning and one in the afternoon. Around the child's first birthday, one nap becomes typical.

Sudden Infant Death Syndrome

Occasionally, a seemingly healthy baby is put to bed and later found dead. This tragic event is called **sudden infant death syndrome (SIDS)** or crib death. Babies should be placed on their sides or back to sleep, but *not* on their stomachs. Use firm bedding with nothing soft near the baby's face to block breathing. Since pillows have been linked with SIDS, they shouldn't be used. Keep the room cool and don't allow smoking around the baby.

BATHING AN INFANT

Babies need regular baths. A sponge bath is used until the navel heals at about two weeks after birth. After that, a regular bath two or three times a week will usually do until the baby begins to crawl. In between baths, spot cleanups are needed during diaper changes and after feeding. As the infant becomes more active, daily bathing is fine as long as the skin doesn't become too dry.

Some babies need several weeks or months to learn to relax in the water. Choose a good time for bathing. A hungry or tired baby might not co-operate. A baby who has just eaten may spit up.

Shampoo a baby's scalp once or twice a week, rinsing well—without letting water splash onto the baby's face. Watch for **cradle cap**, an oily, yellowish, patchy, scalp condition. If it occurs, a little mineral oil can be massaged onto the scalp before shampooing. Since cradle cap is aggravated by sweat, keeping the head uncovered most of the time is a good idea. If cradle cap worsens or becomes infected, parents should consult a pediatrician.

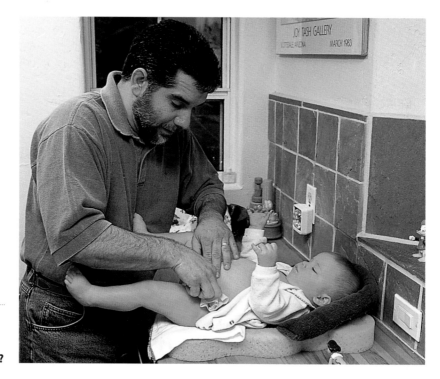

Making bath time safe helps an infant feel secure.
◆ **How is this father promoting bath time safety?**

Most babies love bath time. Soap and water, however, can make an infant slippery, and hot water is always a potential hazard. Take these precautions so bath time is safe and pleasurable:

- Choose a warm, draft-free place.
- Put all needed items—soap, baby shampoo, bath toys, washcloth, and towel—within your reach, but not the baby's.
- Fill the basin with only about 5–7 cm (two or three in.) of water and put it in a safe place that is easy to reach. A small, portable, plastic tub works well. The regular bathtub should not be used until the infant can sit up.
- Turn off the water and test the temperature with your elbow before putting the baby in. Make sure the faucet is not hot to the touch.
- Keep one arm around the infant at all times. Wrap your arm around the baby's shoulders, supporting the neck and head with your forearm and holding the baby's arm with your hand. Your other hand is free to bathe the baby. Remember that fear of baths can develop if the baby slips or feels insecure.
- Don't let the baby practise sitting without support. The child could fall over, resulting in injury or a fear of baths and water.
- Never leave the room, or even turn away. Ignore the phone and doorbell or take the baby with you. It takes only a second for the infant to slip under the water or for an older infant to turn on the hot water.
- Make sure electrical outlets and appliances are out of reach.
- Make bath time fun with reassuring words and smiles.

Promoting Motor Development

The first time Gina saw her foster daughter pull herself up in the crib, she was delighted. Gina knew this was a milestone for an eight-month-old. As Tiffany grew through her first year, Gina promoted her motor development by:

♥ *Playing infant exercise games*. "Pat-a-cake" and similar games helped Tiffany learn how to move her legs, arms, and hands in new ways.

♥ *Providing toys for motor-skill practice*. These included a crib gym that Tiffany could kick and reach for and a plush stuffed doll that encouraged stroking and squeezing. A toy keyboard played a tune when Tiffany pressed a button. Brightly coloured, rolling balls invited a chase.

♥ *Providing safe areas for exploration*. When Tiffany was crawling and pulling up to furniture, Gina moved objects that might fall and covered the sharp corners of a table.

♥ *Support-ing efforts to walk*. Even when Gina was tired, she often held Tiffany's hands so that the ten-month-old could practise "walking" down the hallway in the apartment.

Without pushing Tiffany beyond her abilities, Gina encouraged Tiffany's natural desire to try out new skills. Had Tiffany lagged behind in some area of motor ability, Gina would have told the pediatrician.

Promoting Intellectual Development

As parents like Gina play with their infants, the children develop motor skills, but they also learn early lessons about sounds and words. They begin to develop intellectually. Parents need to look for ways to promote intelligence during infancy as this is a prime time to do so.

For an infant, learning to walk is a joyous experience.
◆ **What can you do to keep the environment safe while an infant learns to walk?**

PROVIDING STIMULATION

According to the latest research, the brain's ability to make connections and absorb knowledge in the first year of life is even greater than previously believed. This ability drops markedly if not used. Brain cells that are not activated will die, resulting in a lower level of brain function throughout life.

New knowledge on how the brain functions, as described in Chapter 19, sends a strong message about what infants and young children need for intellectual development. Growing up in a sensory-rich environment sharpens an infant's intellectual skills. As you have learned, infants need to see, touch, taste, smell, and listen. To provide an environment that stimulates all the senses, parents can:

♥ *Supply toys that stimulate the senses*. A month-old baby is fascinated by colourful wall decorations and music boxes. Around four months, the child can shake rattles and squeeze soft toys. An older infant enjoys tossing balls and pounding with a rubber hammer.

♥ ***Provide new experiences***. Visits around the neighbourhood, to the supermarket and even to the laundromat bring new sights, aromas, and sounds.

♥ ***Get face-to-face with the baby***. Babies seem to prefer human faces over inanimate objects. A parent's face is probably the most important visual stimulus. A baby learns from the close, one-on-one interaction with a parent or caregiver.

♥ ***Play with the baby***. Infants need someone to play with them and talk to them about what they see. "First we put the dish in the microwave. Then we set the time. Listen; it goes 'beep'!" In short, infants need someone to help them make sense of the world. The material on pages 262–263 shows how easily this can be done.

ENCOURAGING LANGUAGE SKILLS

Even before they talk, babies are learning language skills. As they hear people speak, they absorb the sound of the human voice, the repetition of sounds and variety of tones. When spoken to, they make eye contact and notice facial expressions. All of this builds a rich store of knowledge, preparing them for their first attempts at speech.

Parents can talk to babies about anything. Infants are just as interested in hearing about the ball game on television as they are in listening to the description of a tuna casserole recipe.

Parents can name items in the room and describe pictures while looking at a magazine or picture book. Songs, rhymes, and rhythm add to the appeal of language.

Parents can encourage babies' efforts to communicate as well. Responding to an infant's babbling and gurgling shows that communication is a two-way street. Repeating the baby's "words" helps teach how language expresses ideas.

Infants even show they appreciate good conversation. They will lean forward and gaze at a person's face early in the "discussion," then lean back or turn away after a time as if to say, "Let's take a break." Parents should follow this lead and wait for the baby to show renewed interest in their "talk."

Imagine having to learn a new language just by listening to others speak it. Frequent face-to-face conversations help a baby discover what language is all about.

Promoting Emotional Development

The responsibility to promote a child's emotional development begins at birth. Parents can do much to raise children who are emotionally prepared for life.

THE POWER OF TOUCH

For years scientists have studied the impact of touch. When infant monkeys were raised in isolation, scientists discovered that they did not grow and develop normally. The monkeys became loners who later could not relate to others. Evidence is mounting to show that touch is a basic physiological need for humans as well, at all ages.

Physical contact is particularly important to an infant. Touch conveys safety and love. Infants who are frequently held, hugged, and cuddled show better development. They may even form close relationships more easily as they mature.

Some authorities suggest light massaging as a special way to insure that baby is touched. By gently stroking a baby's back and legs, the infant benefits from a soothing touch that has powerful, long-range impact.

Touch is needed by parents as well as children.

USING A POSITIVE APPROACH

What parent doesn't want a child who is happy, secure, contented, and well-adjusted? Such qualities don't just develop by chance. They happen because parents take specific actions during infancy. Here are some guidelines:

♥ **Hold the baby**. Infants need physical contact. Holding an infant is more important than getting the laundry done or washing the car. Those tasks can often wait, but an infant's emotional well-being can't.

♥ **Use loving words and expressions**. This approach makes the infant feel good and secure. Such feelings build a foundation for getting along in the world.

♥ **Smile often**. When you show approval with smiles, an infant feels loved.

♥ **Respond to needs**. Meeting a baby's needs provides a sense of security and trust. It says that someone cares.

Playing Sensory Games with an Infant

Playing games with an infant is stimulating. Little games between adult and infant can bring both pleasure and development.

TRY THIS  **Even a simple game with an infant can have many positive outcomes. In the games described here, what senses are challenged? What kinds of development are promoted? Think about the sensory games you've seen parents play with infants and describe one to your class.**

Silly Sounds

Babies laugh with delight at the sputtering, motor sound an adult makes with the lips. Clicking noises with the tongue and repetitious sounds encourage imitation.

See and Talk

Try touring the room with the baby. Stop and look at pictures on the wall. Point out colours and objects. Move the baby in front of a mirror, asking, "Where's Jacob?" A bird in a cage, a lamp that goes on and off, a telephone that rings, objects on a shelf—all are opportunities to learn.

Many Questions

A game of questions helps babies identify objects and make connections. You can ask, "Where's your nose? Your mouth?" Eventually the baby can point to head, ear, and eyes too.

Discovery

While in the car, or walking in the park, point things out to the baby. When infants see flowers, airplanes, dogs, and trucks for the first time, you will see the same objects through new eyes or in a fresh way.

Rhythms & Rhymes

Most people are familiar with the old standards, "pat-a-cake" and "this-little-piggy." Look for others or make up your own. Try waving the baby's arms to the music on the radio.

Easy Exercises

Babies love to use their muscles. They will kick and squirm while on your lap. Try moving the baby's legs in bicycle fashion or in other safe motions. Combine these actions with sounds and the baby will really get in the spirit.

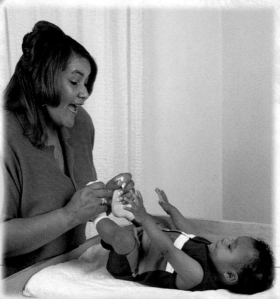

The way an infant is treated affects what that child becomes. A child learns trust and gains a sense of self-worth when raised by a loving, attentive parent.

♥ *Spend time with the baby*. Infants need attention. They especially need contact with the people who are most important in their lives. Spending plenty of time with an infant may even make the baby less demanding. Having fun with a baby need not involve expensive toys. Many parents devise their own special games that bring joy to the baby's life as well as their own.

♥ *Take out your frustrations elsewhere*. If you have problems, are tired, or feel angry, vent your feelings away from the infant. An innocent child can be frightened and hurt by an upset adult. Caring for an infant's constant needs can be overwhelming, especially when one person is responsible most of the time. Families that share caregiving prevent one person from feeling overburdened. Any adult who feels out of control should seek relief from a spouse, friend, or relative. Phone numbers for hotlines to call are often listed under social service organizations in the telephone book. Never take out frustration by yelling at the baby or resorting to rough treatment. *Never* shake an infant. Doing so can cause permanent injury or death.

♥ *Protect the child from negative influences*. Babies are sensitive to tension. Family disagreements and harsh actions and words can be disturbing. Be willing to tell others that inappropriate behaviour is harmful to the baby. If things don't change, take the infant to a calmer place.

RESPONDING TO INFANTS

Infants are precious, but they aren't always agreeable. Parents don't worry about how to handle the positive emotions of happy, contented babies, but they do wonder what to do when negative emotions take over.

Parents have to remember that babies, especially very young ones, aren't being difficult on purpose. Infants react on impulse. Knowing this helps parents cope with trying situations.

Handling Specific Emotions

What do you do when a child cries or is afraid? Parents can try these techniques:

♥ *Crying*. Meet the simplest needs first—a dry diaper, food, or comfort. Prolonged crying, often at the same time every day, may indicate **colic**, a pain in the abdomen with no definite cause. Gently rubbing the baby's stomach may help. You can also try holding the baby in your lap over a blanket-covered, hot-water bottle that has been lightly warmed.

♥ *Anger*. Punishment is never appropriate. Since infants don't understand punishment, the angry behaviour won't stop. Sometimes the best way to deal with anger is to fix whatever is bothering the baby or redirect the baby's attention.

♥ *Fear*. Loud noises, sudden actions, and rough handling can cause fear. This includes "playful" bouncing and tossing the baby in the air. Rough play can also cause head and brain injuries. Infants should be lifted slowly and gently and held securely. To manage stranger anxiety, parents should try to allow the baby to decide when to accept a new person.

Promoting Social Development

An infant learns how to relate to others more through daily living than direct teaching. How else can an infant with no knowledge and experience learn except through the examples of parents and family? These are the people who teach a baby first lessons in how people should behave toward each other.

Infants don't cry to cause trouble. They cry for a reason. Parents need to offer comfort and fix the problem.
◆ **Why might a parent have a hard time figuring out why a baby is crying?**

A typical day for ten-month-old Isaiah is filled with social experiences. His mother sings and talks to him as she feeds him and changes his diaper. His older brother plays with him before leaving for school. Isaiah pokes an inquiring finger into a neighbour's open-toed shoe and returns her smile with a grin of his own. Pushed in his stroller by his father, Isaiah sees the neighbourhood children at play and hears their loud, excited voices. Later his father bathes him and they look at a picture book together.

Internet Connects

www.mcgrawhill.ca/links/parenting
To learn about Early Years Initiatives and what the Ministry of Community and Family and Child Services offer, go to the Web site above for *Parenting Rewards & Responsibilities, First Canadian Edition,* to see where to go next.

LEARNING SOCIAL LESSONS

What does Isaiah learn throughout a day's activity? He learns that people are friendly and caring. They come in different sizes. They can be calm and quiet or boisterous and energetic. Such basic concepts are the building blocks of learning to relate to others. The more positive interaction Isaiah has with others, the more sociable he will become.

Parents promote social development in several specific ways. Providing positive examples is number one. Early lessons

---

Building Parenting Skills

PARENTING WITH ALERTNESS

Alertness means paying attention—to the child as well as to the surroundings. Alert parents learn to recognize clues that may be significant. Since parents know young children lack understanding and can't always put their thoughts and feelings into words, parents have to be watchful. As a parent of three young children, Nadia showed alertness when she:

- Talked to the pediatrician about a hearing test for three-month-old Ian, who wasn't responding to sounds the way he should.

- Noticed that two-year-old Jenna seemed unusually tired and fussy and took her temperature to see if she might be sick.

- Plugged the coffee pot into a different outlet in order to keep the cord away from Jenna's reach.

- Took five-year-old Billy's hand and crossed to the other side of the street after he cringed at the sight of a large dog on the sidewalk ahead.

- Directed her children away from some poison ivy along a path in the park.

◆ ◆ Your Thoughts ◆ ◆

❶ Does alertness become less important as children grow older? Why or why not?

❷ How is knowledge of child development related to alertness?

about manners begin in infancy when parents begin teaching children to say "hi" and "thank you" and wave "bye-bye." Contact with people outside the family helps build an interest in people of all ages and types. Parents can also provide "social" toys. Although stuffed animals and dolls don't respond, they do encourage one-sided conversation from infants.

Busy adults appreciate the time and attention an older child gives to a baby. Babies like a change and often respond more readily to a child than to an adult.

The Beginning of Moral Development

As children develop morally, they learn principles of right and wrong. Although most of such learning occurs when children are older, some early messages about right and wrong do begin in late infancy.

As an example, suppose 11-month-old Chantel repeatedly drops crackers on the floor from her high chair. In response, her mother quietly removes the bowl of crackers from the tray, saying, "These don't belong on the floor, Chantel." By repeating this response at other times when Chantel drops crackers, the mother teaches Chantel that she won't have a bowl of crackers to eat if she drops them on the floor. The "wrong" behaviour eventually stops.

Parents who begin teaching simple lessons about right and wrong behaviour set the pattern for future lessons. In addition, they help a child begin to see that the world does not revolve only around them. Although they are loved and their needs are important, every wish will not be met.

The Right Start

"Babies are such a nice way to start people." This sentiment from writer Don Herold is shared by many. Infants have an innocence and sweetness that is very appealing. Such qualities help create a desire to have an infant. Babies, however, come with many responsibilities.

Without a doubt, babies can be "nice" to have around, but people need to look beyond this attraction. They must realize that a baby is a person in the making. The kind of person that develops depends greatly on how parents and other caregivers handle the responsibilities described in this chapter, and it doesn't stop there. The next unit in this text will show you why.

Looking Back

♥ Parents are responsible for meeting all of their infant's physical needs, including food, sleep, and cleanliness.

♥ Parents need to provide opportunities for babies to develop their motor skills and recognize when development is not progressing correctly.

♥ Infants thrive intellectually in an environment that includes a variety of experiences and adults to help make those experiences understandable.

♥ Infants begin to absorb language skills even before they can talk.

♥ By responding positively to infants' emotions, parents help them feel secure and avoid some tears and anger.

♥ Spending time with infants and responding to them affectionately promote social development.

♥ The seeds of moral development are planted during infancy.

Knowledge and Understanding

1. What can be done to make breast-feeding a successful experience?
2. What precautions should parents take when bottle-feeding infants?
3. Why do children need immunizations?
4. How can a parent promote an infant's motor development?
5. What precautions can a parent take against SIDS?
6. Do parents need to provide expensive toys in order to encourage intellectual growth? Explain your thinking.
7. How do infants begin to acquire language skills?
8. What are some specific ways for parents to promote an infant's emotional development?
9. When a parent feels upset by the constant care an infant needs, what could he or she do?
10. How do infants learn social skills?
11. What moral lessons might begin during infancy?

CHAPTER 14

Review

Thinking and Inquiry

12. When Craig and Kate's four-month-old was crying, Craig said, "Leave him alone, Kate. You'll just spoil him." How would you respond if you were Kate?

13. Suppose an adult in your family is bouncing your three–month–old on his leg and then abruptly lifting the baby over his head. What is the problem with his actions? How would you react?

14. What problems might occur if Jeannine feeds her baby three new foods at one feeding? If Alex places the bottle on a pillow beside the baby's head during feeding?

Communication

15. Complete the following statement in writing. Then compare your thoughts to what others in the class have said. "The most important reason for a parent to interact with an infant in positive ways is . . ."

16. As a parent, you are worried about your two-week-old infant. He has crying spells that start around supper time and last for several hours. You have tried everything to comfort him, but nothing works. He continues to cry whether he is held or lying in his crib. He cries so hard that his face becomes red. How will you handle the problem?

17. Survey five parents and ask them how they handled a crying baby. Write your findings in a summary paragraph.

18. Design a baby's room that is intellectually stimulating. Illustrate the room on a piece of graph paper. On the back of your graph paper, summarize what makes this room intellectually stimulating. Share your room design with your classmates.

Application

19. With a partner, discuss appropriate responses to the following situation. Six-month-old Taylor is tired, hungry, and crying on the way home from a family picnic. Your spouse is yelling angrily at Taylor to be quiet.

20. Some parents use disposable diapers for their baby. Suppose a six-month-old infant needs an average of 8 diapers every day. The parent pays $7.89 for a package of diapers. Each package contains 24 diapers. What would the parent's diaper expense be for 30 days?

Cory General, Aboriginal Family Support Worker

What volunteer activities did you do as a teenager that led you to choose a career that involved working with children/people?

▶ As a teenager, once a week I tutored elementary students in my community, mostly in reading and math. I found tutoring to be a lot of fun and very rewarding.

▶ I was also on a Peer Panel for Promoting Aids Awareness to Aboriginal Students living on reserve. The panel travelled to different schools promoting information on healthy sexuality and healthy choices.

*Please describe your **specific education pathway.***

▶ I graduated with a Bachelor of Arts degree from McMaster University in 2000. My major areas of study were Canadian Children and Adolescents, Sociology of the Family, and Sociology of Gender.

Have you completed any further study to enhance your professional development?

▶ I have participated in many training sessions to increase my knowledge pertaining to the workplace and to working with families and children. During my career I have gained a tremendous amount of knowledge of the Aboriginal Peoples' traditional teachings from elders in Ontario communities. I have learned about the importance of storytelling, and of using Mother Nature as a guide and resource in teaching our children. I have learned traditional cooking and had lessons on traditional birthing practices. I recently took steps to get into teachers college. I would like to go back to school to increase my lifelong learning and to continue working with children.

*Please describe your **career pathway.***

▶ My very first job was when I was 13, peeling potatoes at a French fries stand located just outside a small rural town. It was a summer job, and I had a lot of fun.

▶ My second job was washing dishes and waiting tables on the breakfast shift at a local restaurant. I had this job throughout my high school years. It taught me a lot, especially how to interact with people.

▶ One of my most rewarding jobs was in the summer before going to university. I was a camp counsellor for the Mississauga of the New Credit First Nations. This job was tremendously rewarding and helped me realize the true potential of mentoring and being a positive role model for children. Counsellors were responsible for creating crafts, games, outings and other special events for children in the camp, who varied from ages six to 12 years.

▶ In my last year at McMaster, I decided to do some volunteer work with families and their children. Being Aboriginal, I contacted the Hamilton Regional Indian Centre. I started on a weekly basis at a Parents & Tots group. Shortly afterward, I became an assistant in the Aboriginal Family Support Worker position. From there I moved on to the Aboriginal Healthy Babies Program and now have my current job as the Aboriginal Family Support Worker.

Did you switch jobs along the way? If so, why?

▶ After my first position as an assistant, I took part in the Aboriginal Healthy Babies Program and am now the Co-ordinator and Supervisor for the Aboriginal Family Support Worker Program. I am not sure that I switched jobs, as each one involves work with children zero to six years of age and their families. As for the switch from Healthy Babies to my present position, my new role allows me to provide more programs and services to the Aboriginal community in the city of Hamilton.

*Please describe your **current position**.*

▶ I am currently the Aboriginal Family Support Worker at the Hamilton Regional Indian Centre. The goals of this program are to provide support to children zero to six years of age and their families; to provide quality programs and services that are culturally based; and to target and direct services and support to single-parent families regarding issues such as child development, infant stimulation, family dysfunction, role modelling, and discipline.

▶ My main responsibilities include providing programs that address parenting/care-taking skills, child development, and nutrition. I also ensure that the community receives up-to-date information about our services. My team and I do outreach and fundraising, and we maintain program operations through client contact, keeping statistical information, and maintaining client files. Other responsibilities include keeping a healthy work environment, working well with others, and honouring our traditions.

*What are the **rewards** of your current position?*

▶ One of the rewards is welcoming a new baby into the world. I am rewarded when parents attend groups and share their stories. Hearing children's laughter rewards me. Having a child ask if I can read and share rewards me. I am rewarded when we come together as a community to celebrate our culture, and when I see parents and children use the information they have learned.

*What are the **challenges** of your current position?*

▶ Our biggest challenge is not having enough funds and space to do everything we would like to do. Sometimes I am challenged when I hit a barrier or lack information. It is a challenge to educate professionals about our cultural heritage.

Looking back over your education and career pathways, as a young person in high school, did you ever believe you would follow the pathways you have?

▶ My mom had always told me as a child the importance of having dreams and learning from all things that are given to you. If I could go back to the 16-year-old who wasn't very good in English and tell her she would do just fine writing a paper for a university professor, I don't think she would believe me. If I told her that she would be getting up and speaking in front of a group of people, I know she would laugh. I know she would have found it hard to believe that she would be where she is today. But one true lesson in life is to take one day at a time and go where your path leads you. Along that path, stop to ask questions, have a look around, and make choices.

What other careers are related to your career?

▶ Teacher
▶ Social Worker
▶ Counsellor

UNIT 4

Child Development

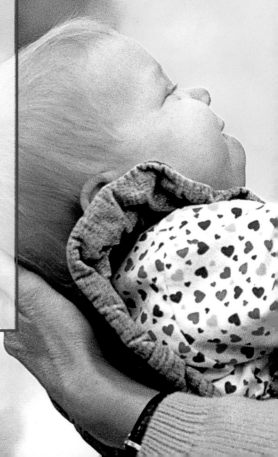

A Parent's Perspective

from Erika

"My sister's tears were what started me thinking. When her son Ethan was little, Ellen had to work full-time.

On the day that Ethan took his first steps, she called me, crying. Mrs. Klemson, the babysitter, had watched Ethan walk for the first time, and Ellen had missed it. I thought about that a lot. When my baby was born last year, I decided to stay home with her. I was lucky that I could make that choice since not everyone can. I've experienced so many firsts with Hannah, and I'm really glad. It isn't easy for our family. We've had to do without things that would have been nice to have, but they can come later. Right now the most precious thing I have is Hannah, and I'm determined to spend time with her and give her a good start in life. Hannah took her first shaky steps from a chair to me yesterday. The look on her face was something I'll never forget."

Unit Expectations

While reading this unit, you will:

* Describe factors that contribute to the healthy development of children before and during birth, and in the first few months after birth.
* Explain patterns in the social, emotional, intellectual, moral, and physical development of children.
* Evaluate your own practical experiences involving children.
* Demonstrate an understanding of the responsibility parents have for ensuring quality communication in their family.
* Describe the nature of and the responsibilities involved in parenting.
* Identify social and cultural variations in family forms and parenting approaches.
* Identify and evaluate various child-rearing practices and beliefs, and parenting techniques.
* Demonstrate an understanding of the challenges facing parents throughout the early-childhood years.
* Describe the role society plays in the lives of children and families.

Meeting Physical Needs

CHAPTER EXPECTATIONS

While reading this chapter, you will:

► Identify, through practical experiences in a classroom or community setting, the changes in social, emotional, intellectual, and physical development that take place in young children.

► Explain how development from conception to three years of age affects and is crucial for development later in life.

► Analyze behaviours, conditions, and environments that influence positive or negative growth and development of the fetus, infant, and young child.

► Identify and describe the capabilities and behaviours of young children of different ages in a variety of settings.

► Explain the differences in capabilities and behaviours observed in children in classroom and community settings.

KEY TERMS

ambidextrous
eye-hand
  co-ordination
flame retardant
growth spurts

large motor skills
manual dexterity
orthodontist
small motor skills
sphincter muscles

This is odd, David thought. It's 7 o'clock and John hasn't asked for his evening snack. Just then he heard a noise in the kitchen and went to investigate.

His four-year-old son stood on the step stool beside the counter. He had found the loaf of oatmeal bread in the bread box and was now working intently at removing the twist tie from the wrapper. He mastered the plastic tie and drew out a single slice of bread.

David watched the rest of the production from the doorway. John set the bread on the kitchen table. He opened the refrigerator door and removed a plastic container of sliced cheese. Again with great concentration, he peeled one slice from the stack and laid it deliberately on the bread. He stopped and stared at his creation. David wondered if he would try to get a knife to cut the slice in half, as his parents did. He was about to step forward when John solved the dilemma by folding the bread in half, more or less, pressing it down for good measure. He climbed onto a chair and took a triumphant first bite.

David went to the sink and got himself a glass of water. "Good sandwich, John?" he asked casually and grinned at the boy's vigorous nodding and chewing. David thought, I'll bet it tastes better than ever tonight.

What do you think? What might have happened if David had walked into the kitchen while John was making his sandwich?

275

Beyond Infancy

The first birthday is a bridge from infancy to childhood. Just the advance from crawling to walking changes a child's world remarkably. Development proceeds full steam ahead in other ways too, propelling the child toward greater independence.

Taking care of a growing child is quite different from caring for an infant. The child's personality and intellect are rapidly developing, presenting new challenges for parents and caregivers at every turn. They must learn strategies to make sure that physical needs are met. In a sense, the hard work of parenting has just begun.

The Growing Child

As a child progresses from toddler to preschooler to schoolchild, parents can expect to see some common physical developments at each stage. Among individual children, however, growth differs greatly. One toddler at 16 months may look much like some two-year-olds, while another 16-month-old looks more like a baby.

As long as children fall within the height and weight range for their age, as shown in the chart on page 301, parents probably have no reason to worry. If they do have concerns, their pediatrician can respond to them.

Allowing for variations, parents can look for the following physical changes as children grow:

♥ **Toddlers.** Growth between the first and third birthday continues at an impressive rate, though nothing like that of infancy.

The switch from infancy to toddlerhood often takes parents by surprise. "When did she become a child instead of a baby?" they ask. Although the rate of change during infancy is amazing, there is still much change ahead.

Physical proportions change dramatically with each year. The arms, legs, and lower body lengthen in comparison to the trunk. The chest becomes more prominent, the head and abdomen less so. These changes redistribute a toddler's weight, improving balance and posture.

♥ **Preschoolers.** Growth in children ages three to five years continues steadily. The body becomes straighter and slimmer. The abdomen flattens, the shoulders widen, and the neck and legs lengthen. The muscles and skeletal system become more developed. Preschoolers may become aware of their own growth and also notice how they are different from their friends. Sensitive parents help children feel proud of growth but not overly concerned with it.

♥ **School-age children.** Growth remains steady up to about age ten. Weight and height gains are similar to those of preschoolers. From age ten to 14, however, children experience **growth spurts**, periods of accelerated development. Girls go through this stage about two years before boys do. During a growth spurt, parts of the body tend to grow at different rates. The legs, arms, hands, and feet usually grow most quickly. The child may look—and often feel—gangly, awkward, and bony. The trunk then lengthens, making the child taller. Due to spurts, growth patterns vary greatly among older school-age children.

PUBERTY

Growth spurts also signal the onset of puberty. This stage of growth marks the period when a person becomes physically and sexually mature. In females, the breasts develop, body fat increases, and menstruation begins. In males, the genitals grow larger, and the muscles develop. Facial and body hair begin to grow.

Children are often embarrassed by the changes of puberty, especially if their development exceeds or lags behind their peers. Parents should be sympathetic, pointing out that everyone grows at different rates. Praising the child for qualities other than appearance also helps.

	Males		Females	
Age	**Height**	**Weight**	**Height**	**Weight**
2 yrs.	91 cm (36 in.)	14 kg (30 lb.)	89 cm (35 in.)	13 kg (28 lb.)
3 yrs.	97 cm (38 in.)	16 kg (35 lb.)	97 cm (38 in.)	15 kg (32 lb.)
4 yrs.	104 cm (41 in.)	18 kg (39 lb.)	102 cm (40 in.)	17 kg (37 lb.)
5 yrs.	112 cm (44 in.)	20 kg (44 lb.)	109 cm (43 in.)	19 kg (43 lb.)
6 yrs.	117 cm (46 in.)	22 kg (49 lb.)	114 cm (45 in.)	21 kg (47 lb.)

Average Height and Weight for Young Children

Promoting Good Nutrition

"Eat your vegetables and drink your milk so you'll grow big and strong." This bit of parental advice may sound old-fashioned, yet it's as true now as when first uttered. Proper nourishment is the surest way to promote physical development. A healthy diet provides energy for growth, for daily activity, and for resistance to disease.

The chart below shows what children need for healthy eating. Exact serving sizes, although given, are less important than a daily balance of nutrients. Also, since a child's small stomach limits the appetite, every bite should count. Filling up on empty calories leaves less space and appetite for essential nutrients.

Canada's Food Guide to Healthy Eating

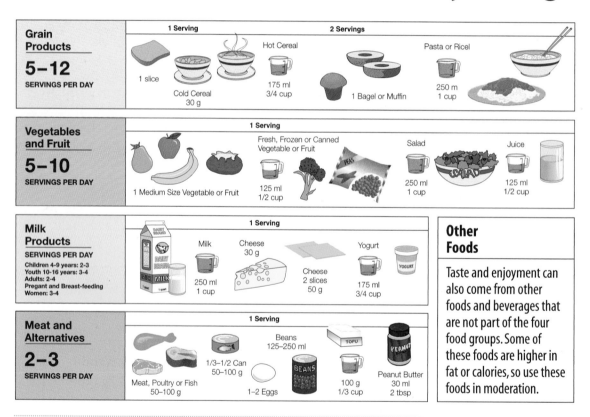

Grain Products 5–12 SERVINGS PER DAY	1 Serving	2 Servings
Vegetables and Fruit 5–10 SERVINGS PER DAY	1 Serving	
Milk Products SERVINGS PER DAY Children 4-9 years: 2-3 Youth 10-16 years: 3-4 Adults: 2-4 Pregnant and Breast-feeding Women: 3-4	1 Serving	
Meat and Alternatives 2–3 SERVINGS PER DAY	1 Serving	

Other Foods

Taste and enjoyment can also come from other foods and beverages that are not part of the four food groups. Some of these foods are higher in fat or calories, so use these foods in moderation.

Different People Need Different Amounts of Food

The amount of food you need every day from the four food groups and other foods depends on your age, body size, activity level, whether you are male or female, and whether you are pregnant or breast-feeding. That's why *Canada's Food Guide* gives a lower and higher number of servings for each food group. For example, young children can choose the lower number of servings, while male teenagers can go to the higher number. Most other people can choose servings somewhere in between.

SELF-FEEDING

"Reckless" was how Tracy described 14-month-old Brianne's attempts at self-feeding. In aiding her daughter's success, Tracy found ways to make the process easier for both of them.

At first, Tracy supplied a child-size spoon only with foods that stuck to the bowl even when turned upside down. Mashed vegetables, hot cereal, cottage cheese, and applesauce were good choices. As Brianne became more skillful, Tracy offered the spoon with all foods. Brianne ate from a sturdy plastic bowl, with a non-skid bottom and steep sides to keep food from "escaping." Her two-handled cup was also unbreakable and weighted at the bottom for stability.

Brianne learned quickly, but Tracy was prepared for spills. She placed plastic or newspaper under the high chair and dressed her daughter in a plastic feeding apron. When a spill occurred, Tracy stayed calm, knowing that Brianne was still working on control. Also, she didn't want to reward spills with attention. She kept finger foods on hand to offer when Brianne tired of using the spoon.

Some other tips that Tracy used made mealtimes easier:

♥ Setting Brianne's high chair next to the family table, away from walls and non-washable furniture.

♥ Filling Brianne's cup only one-quarter full to minimize waste and spills.

♥ Providing opportunities for Brianne to experiment with clay, water, mud, or finger paint, which reduced the child's temptation to play with her food.

♥ Planning bath time for after the meal.

By 16 months, practiced toddlers can feed themselves quite capably. Near age two, they may begin to pick up pieces of fruit, vegetables, and meat with a child-size fork.

SERVING APPROPRIATE AMOUNTS

In general, a serving of meat, vegetables, or fruit is 15 cc (1 tbsp.) per year of age. Assuming children are eating a balance of nutritious foods, however, an appropriate serving may be as much as the child wants.

Feeding Young Children

The amount toddlers eat may vary greatly from meal to meal. Children involved in a fascinating activity might break for only a few bites for lunch. Hunger catches up by dinner, when they enjoy larger servings. By noting a child's *daily* intake, parents avoid overfeeding or underfeeding.

In contrast, making children sit at the table until they clean their plate encourages them to eat more than they need. Overeating and obesity can result. Uneaten food should be taken away after 10 or 15 minutes without comment.

Remember that toddlers are exploring the power of the word "no." If you say to a two-year-old, "Do you want some carrots?" even a child who likes carrots might refuse. A better approach is: "Here are your carrots. See if your spoon can pick them up."

By age three or four, children have outgrown most eating problems of earlier years. They may still find playing and exploring more interesting than eating, however, and may need reminders to stop for a meal.

Feeding School-Age Children

By age nine, children may be more willing to try new foods. During growth spurts, a child's appetite, activity, and food needs usually increase. Parents and other caregivers can help children understand how a hearty appetite can be satisfied healthily. Since children need extra servings of calcium-rich foods, for instance, parents can offer a variety of milk products and green vegetables.

Parents should avoid excessive discussion of children's dislikes. They can be taught to try each food and, if they don't like it, to leave it quietly.

Food is okay for eating, but sometimes it is more fun to watch it fly and fall through the air. A plastic cloth under the high chair offers a good landing place for food and promises easier cleanup after an eating adventure.

INTRODUCING NEW FOODS

Three-year-old Ming eyed the small mound of green flowerets that his father Hoy spooned onto Ming's plate. "This is broccoli," Hoy said. "Try some."

Ming nibbled one piece and made a face.

"It's a new taste, isn't it?" Hoy remarked. Hoy ate his own broccoli and mentioned to the family how much he liked it. Clearing the table later, Hoy noticed that Ming had eaten a few more bites. Hoy would serve broccoli again next week.

Hoy's attempt to introduce a new food to his child is a good model. He offered Ming only a small serving, asking him only to taste it. He was patient but persistent in deciding to try again.

If Hoy had insisted that Ming finish the broccoli, Ming might have hated the experience and decided to resist all new food.

Worst of all, Ming would have learned that eating—or refusing to eat—is a source of power and control. This attitude could lead to poor nutrition habits and serious eating disorders.

Children have individual preferences, which are influenced by their cultural background. However, children are more apt to try new foods that are:

♥ Served separately, rather than combined in casseroles or salads.

♥ Mildly flavoured and seasoned only lightly.

♥ Served at room temperature.

Parents should show a spirit of adventure toward unfamiliar foods. A meal might end with a sampling of an exotic fruit that the family has not tried before.

"Can I trust you, Grandpa? That last spoonful tasted a little funny." Imagine trying something new at every meal. Who wouldn't be a little wary?
◆ **What foods do you think a toddler would like the most?**

ENCOURAGING WISE FOOD CHOICES

As children grow, they make more food choices. Television ads for sugary cereals tempt them. Vending machines packed with chips and chocolate bars are everywhere. Eventually, friends may suggest stopping at a fast-food restaurant on the way home from school. How can parents combat these influences?

In nutrition as in many areas, home is the best classroom. Providing nutritious foods from the very start helps form positive eating habits for a lifetime.

Parents teach by example as well. Suppose as a parent, you prepare a breakfast of hot cereal, wheat toast, and orange juice for your child, then grab a donut and cup of coffee as you rush off to work. What does your child learn from this example?

SNACKING

With their high energy level and small stomachs, most young children need snacks. Healthy choices include whole-grain crackers, low-fat cheese, and raw vegetables and fruit. Some children enjoy a peanut butter sandwich or yogurt. Most commercial snack foods, such as chips and cookies, are high in calories, fats, and sugar. They provide few of the nutrients needed for growth and health.

Snacks should be spaced between meals. Snacking just before mealtime dulls the appetite for the meal. Likewise, giving snacks after children refuse a meal encourages them to skip meals in favour of snacks.

Older children begin to purchase and prepare some meals and snacks on their own. Parents who are knowledgeable about nutrition can teach children facts for making wise choices. In most communities, parents can get information on food and nutrition from their public health unit, family doctor, the Internet, the Health Canada Web site, or the provincial ministry of health.

Other ways you can use to increase a child's awareness of food and nutrition include:

♥ Involve the child in helping you prepare meals.

♥ Find children's books about food in the library.

♥ Give a child's cookbook as a gift.

♥ Point out the nutritional value of foods found in recipes, on labels, and in grocery stores.

Healthy snacks provide children with needed energy.

Health & Safety

Healthy eating habits are among the most important behaviours parents can instill in children. The rewards extend well into the future. Parents can employ several strategies to guide food choices:

▶ Encourage children to explore the sensory experience of food. Let them touch, smell, and taste foods: soft, fuzzy kiwis; cool, pebbly cottage cheese; sweet, chewy raisins. Offer a variety of tastes and textures at one meal.

▶ Offer children small portions of each food. This encourages them to taste everything and include many foods in their diet.

▶ Teach children the basics of nutrition. Using simple explanations, tell children why different foods are needed for good health.

▶ Let older children help choose or grow and prepare foods. Show them the different forms in which foods are available. Teach them to read nutrition labels. Point out healthy methods for preparing meals.

▶ Model good eating habits. Order nutritious foods when eating at a restaurant. Guide children toward healthy choices too.

▶ Make mealtimes enjoyable. A relaxing, reassuring atmosphere not only aids digestion but also encourages the association of food with pleasant experiences. Meals should be positive, nurturing times.

Promoting Motor Skills

After keeping up with an energetic toddler all day, a parent might wish the child had come with an "off" switch. Parents are grateful, however, to see their children in motion. Bones, muscles, heart, and lungs—all develop better with exercise. Active children gain co-ordination, balance, and muscular strength and control. Even minor physical feats, such as jumping off a step onto the ground, are a source of pride.

The information on pages 308-309 shows how children gradually gain motor skills. Eventually they combine skills. For example, they learn to bounce a ball while walking.

Motor skill development is not automatic. Children need opportunities and a parent's support to test and gain confidence in their abilities. An involved parent is a powerful incentive to keep a child moving. Children flourish physically and emotionally when parents play with them and admire their efforts.

Physical–Motor Development Age One to Five

On these pages, you see some typical physical achievements for children at different ages. What if a child seems to be lagging behind? In most cases, "Don't worry" is the right response. Children don't all develop at the same pace. Some play "catch up" with the rest. A parent who has concerns, however, should talk to the pediatrician. Reassurance—or help—is only a phone call away. ◆ **Why would early intervention for a problem be important?**

One-Year-Old

♥ Walks haltingly.
♥ Walks up stairs with assistance.
♥ Holds objects in fist grip.
♥ Scribbles randomly.
♥ Self-feeds, using fingers.
♥ Picks up objects using pincer grip.

Two-Year-Old

♥ Walks and runs confidently.
♥ Walks up and down stairs.
♥ Scribbles in deliberate directions.
♥ Removes slip-on clothing.
♥ Self-feeds, using spoon.

Three-Year-Old

♥ Stands briefly on one foot.
♥ Tries to climb jungle gym and pump while swinging.
♥ Draws simple pictures.
♥ Builds tower with blocks.
♥ Pours from pitcher.
♥ Puts on own shoes.

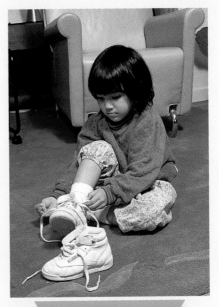

Four-Year-Old

♥ Hops and spins in place.
♥ Throws ball over head.
♥ Attempts circles and squares in drawings.
♥ Washes face and brushes teeth.
♥ Dresses and undresses with supervision.

Five-Year-Old

♥ Walks backward, heel to toe; runs on tiptoe.
♥ Imitates dance steps performed by others.
♥ Takes long walk with an adult.
♥ Prints own name.
♥ Writes numbers 1 to 5.
♥ Cuts food with knife.
♥ Dresses and undresses without help.
♥ Laces and ties shoes.

LARGE MOTOR SKILLS

Skills that use the large muscles in the arms, legs, and back are known as **large motor skills.** These include walking, climbing, and running. Healthy children begin to practise large motor skills when they kick and crawl as infants.

With her son's first wobbly steps, Laurie knew their world was about to change. As a toddler, Cody proved her right. He walked with assurance. He tried running, climbing steps, and other new activities. Laurie encouraged him by creating safe places for him to practise his newfound skills. She cleared the home and yard of potential hazards and joined a neighbourhood play group. On nice days she took the group to a well-maintained play park, where they kicked large balls and climbed low ramps.

Laurie also recognized the dangers of having a newly mobile child. She kept him close in crowded stores. She moved breakables out of his reach at home.

As a preschooler, Cody will grow in physical awareness and control. Preschoolers run with even strides and hop with both feet. They climb stairs by alternating feet, rather than leading with the same foot on every step. They move quickly yet seldom fall. Parents can provide swings and riding toys to help preschoolers develop muscle strength and co-ordination. Playing simple running games, such as tag, is fun. "Dancing" to music improves agility and co-ordination.

School-age children are ready for greater challenges. Parents might introduce them to swimming or skating. Younger school-age children often enjoy rough-and-tumble play, with chases and mock fights. Parents should watch to keep this play from turning aggressive.

Internet Connects

www.mcgrawhill.ca/links/parenting
To learn more about physical development and caring for a child's physical needs, go to the Web site above for *Parenting Rewards & Responsibilities, First Canadian Edition,* to see where to go next.

Children love to play active games. Not only do they use up energy, but they also build their large muscles and develop skill in using them. ◆ **What active games that you played as a child are still played by children today?**

Catching and Throwing

A simple game of catch is a developmental bargain. Children enjoy a parent's attention and praise while developing the large muscles in their arms.

Toddlers catch a large ball by scooping it up and trapping it in a bear hug. They keep their feet squarely planted, so a parent needs to toss the ball right into their arms. Preschoolers can throw a small ball, but probably not catch it. A seven- or eight-year-old can catch a softball in a glove. When they are nine or ten, children will be more successful in sports that require a combination of skills, such as catching a ball while running.

When a child is learning to throw a ball, a parent must be coach as well as catcher. At first, the child tosses the ball and steps off with the foot on the same side as the throwing arm. By age six, a child can be taught to step off with the foot opposite the throwing arm, which increases momentum and improves aim.

Riding Tricycles and Bicycles

At age three, many children learn to ride a tricycle. At first, they may straddle the seat and walk. With instruction and perhaps a gentle push from behind, most children quickly learn the thrill of "pedal power."

Kindergartners are often eager to move up to a bicycle. Training wheels give confidence to beginners. These two small wheels attached to the back wheel add balance. Other children reject "baby wheels," preferring a parent's steadying hand on the seat. Either way, learning to ride is faster and safer on a vehicle that fits. The child's feet should rest easily on the tricycle or bicycle pedals when the child is on the seat. A helmet must be worn.

Children learn to ride wheeled vehicles as they develop physically. Pushing children who are not ready or criticizing them for a fall can sour them on trying anything new. Coaching must be light, low-pressure, and good-humoured.

The mastery of every skill has to begin somewhere. Learning to catch and throw a ball might begin with simply reaching out for the ball and grasping it with the arms. ◆ **How would you help a young child gradually build this skill?**

SMALL MOTOR SKILLS

Small motor skills use small muscles in the fingers, wrists, and ankles. These skills proceed naturally from large motor skills. They develop as children refine their **eye-hand co-ordination**, the ability to move the hands and fingers precisely in relation to what is seen.

Parents can use certain toys to promote manual skills in young toddlers. Blocks, building sets, and large pop beads all serve this purpose. Children improve **manual dexterity**, or skilled use of the hands, by handling unbreakable household items, including containers with lids and plastic measuring spoons. Older toddlers can manipulate large crayons, small cars, and dolls.

Preschoolers love to take things apart and put them back together. Lacing kits and simple puzzles with large pieces encourage this skill. Art activities and self-dressing tasks are other good ways for preschoolers to practise small motor skills.

Many schoolchildren develop interests that use manual skills. Parents can provide a budding flute player with a quiet time to practise. They can give the young model builder room to work. Using computers also improves dexterity.

Along with other types of support, children need a parent's patience. When you see a child concentrate on buttoning a shirt or piercing green beans with a fork, remember that these tasks are more complex than any the child has yet mastered.

Hand Preference

The preference for using one hand over the other in such activities as colouring, eating, and throwing a ball begins around 18 months. By about age five, 85 percent of all children use their right hand for most activities, a trend that continues into adulthood. A few children become **ambidextrous** (am-beh-DEK-struhs), able to use both hands equally well.

Some studies indicate that hand preference is hereditary. Another theory states that parents influence preference by placing objects into one of the child's hands more than the other.

A walk through a toy store shows how many toys are designed to help children develop small motor skills. Many parents find such toys at garage sales.
◆ **What objects in the home could be safely used by a child for this purpose?**

Building Parenting Skills

PARENTING WITH ENTHUSIASM

Enthusiastic people like what they're doing and they show it. They throw themselves into an activity and give it their all. From the simple joy of chasing fireflies to the more involved task of baking cookies together, parental enthusiasm creates energy and excitement. Since children are active and vibrant by nature, they easily catch the spirit of an enthusiastic parent. To parent with enthusiasm, Larry:

▶ Helped his son build a car for a racing derby.

▶ Showed the children how to play frisbee.

▶ Volunteered to help at the school carnival and chili supper.

▶ Began a play group for his four-year-old and three friends.

▶ Woke the children early for a surprise fishing trip to a nearby lake.

▶ Helped organize a non-violence program at school.

▶ Encouraged his children to invite their friends over to play.

◆ ◆ Your Thoughts ◆ ◆

❶ How can parents maintain their excitement when raising a second or third child?

❷ Parents often show enthusiasm by participation. How might a parent participate effectively in these situations: snow play; water play; music activities; school events?

❸ Do you think a parent's enthusiasm is affected by the money and other resources the family has available for leisure activities? Explain your reasoning.

In any case, parents should avoid trying to change the preference of a left-handed child. Rather, they can show the child how to hold a pencil correctly for that hand and how to adapt to activities as needed. This encouragement fosters both motor skills and self-esteem.

Teaching Hygiene Skills

For children, learning hygiene skills is a practical and emotional milestone. Caring for personal needs is basic to healthy independence. Toileting, brushing teeth, and bathing are significant accomplishments that make a child feel competent and confident.

TOILET TRAINING

Most children want to use the toilet as soon as they are physically and emotionally ready. Readiness means the child can close and release the **sphincter muscles** (SFINK-tuhr) in the bowel and bladder regions that control elimination. This ability comes only after a child is walking well.

Children must be able to recognize the need for a toilet ahead of time, and to get to the bathroom or signal an adult for help. These factors may come together between two and three years of age. Forcing the process doesn't work.

Signs of Readiness

How can you tell when a child is ready to learn toileting skills? Akiko noticed signs of readiness in her daughter Michi just after her second birthday. Michi's diapers were dry for several hours at a time.

She complained when they were wet. Her bowel movements became predictable. One day Michi asked what the toilet was for. Akiko explained, adding, "From now on, you can use it too."

After that, when Michi showed signs of needing a toilet, Akiko announced, "You have to use the potty. Let's go." She set regular times for using the toilet, before meals and at bedtime. Michi accepted a small seat attached over the bathroom toilet. Some toddlers, afraid of falling in, prefer a child's potty chair set on the floor. Michi was bothered by the sound of flushing, so her mother flushed the toilet after Michi left the room.

Making Progress

For most children, toilet skills come slowly but surely. A child will have an occasional accident, especially with wetting, and may temporarily go back to using diapers. Most children gain full daytime control over both bladder and bowel within a year or so. Nighttime control comes later, so diapers may still be needed at bedtime and naptime. Most preschoolers stay dry day and night. They use the toilet without help, often insisting on privacy.

Internet Connects

www.mcgrawhill.ca/links/parenting
To learn more about health issues, go to the Web site above for *Parenting Rewards & Responsibilities, First Canadian Edition,* to see where to go next.

Parents have many stories to tell about toilet training. Some say their child mastered the skill by 18 months. Some say they taught the child in one day. The relaxed parent who watches for readiness and doesn't expect "miracles" is usually rewarded with success.

Throughout the process, parents must show pride as the child advances, without acting too disappointed by a lack of success. Scolding or humiliating the child is useless and hurtful. These tactics have no place in teaching any skill. If a child is very slow to learn to use the toilet, parents should consult their pediatrician.

BATHING

Most children enjoy bathing. Some parents make baths part of a relaxing evening ritual. Creating a happy experience with a few floating toys builds a positive association with good hygiene.

Hair washing can be combined with bathing. A mild children's shampoo and, if necessary, a rinse that prevents tangles makes this task easier.

Showering is an option for older children. A shower head attachment that fits over the faucet can make the experience more pleasant.

At least until they enter kindergarten, children need constant supervision while bathing but can do much for themselves. Preschoolers can wash, rinse, and dry everywhere but their back.

Around age seven, children may show less concern with hygiene. Bathing may seem like a chore. Parents can encourage children by complimenting them when they are clean and neatly dressed. By adolescence, children are more aware of their bodies, more sensitive to peer approval, and typically more careful about hygiene.

Although children love bubbles, some types of bubble bath have been found to cause urinary tract infections in little girls. ◆ **What other ideas could a parent use to make bath time fun?**

Good health practices become habits when children start young. If trained to brush their teeth daily, they learn that clean teeth feel good. Brushing can be an automatic part of the bedtime routine.

DENTAL CARE

Dental care should begin as soon as a child has teeth. Brushing and flossing help retain primary teeth, ensuring proper spacing for the permanent set.

Parents should brush the toddler's teeth, stroking gently with a soft, child-size brush. The child, meanwhile, can practise brushing with a small amount of toothpaste. Likewise, parents can floss their children's teeth, demonstrating the correct technique to older children.

Limiting sugary foods promotes good dental health. Preschoolers and older children can be taught the benefit of avoiding sweets. If the child is allowed to chew gum, only sugarless gum should be purchased.

Seeing a Dentist

Parents should schedule their child's first dental checkup around their third birthday, and regularly thereafter. Appointments may be needed to fill cavities, although these aren't common today.

Children should be checked for dental nerve damage if they receive a blow to the mouth, even if teeth are not loosened or bleeding. A tooth that is knocked out can sometimes be reset. As permanent teeth come in, a dentist can detect decay or improper alignment when these problems are easier to correct.

If teeth do not come in correctly, a child may be referred to an **orthodontist** (OR-thuh-DON-tist), a specialist in straightening and realigning teeth. Correcting the problem may mean wearing braces for two years or longer, but the result is a significant improvement in a child's health, appearance, and self-image.

Selecting Clothing

"I couldn't believe it. Just two months ago, I bought some jeans on sale for Clark. Then when I got them out for him to wear yesterday, he had already outgrown them." This parent's lament is common. Selecting clothing for active, growing children can be a challenge. Here are some things parents need to think about.

DURABILITY

Active children need clothing made of sturdy woven or knit fabrics, such as denim. Reinforced seams and knees help clothes last longer. Adjustable straps provide room for growth.

COMFORT

Garments should be cut to allow freedom of movement. Stretchy, knit fabrics don't constrict motion. Fabrics that breathe well (allow air to pass through) and absorb moisture add to comfort and don't irritate the skin. Cotton fabrics meet these requirements. Comfortable clothes are suitable for school and most events a child attends.

EASY CARE

Children's clothing should be economical and easy to wash and dry. No-iron fabrics are desirable. Most cottons launder well but can shrink and may require ironing. Cotton mixed with small amounts of synthetic fabric shrinks and wrinkles less. A cotton and polyester blend, for example, wears well. Care labels and hangtags describe a garment's fabric and recommended care.

Choosing clothing can frustrate parents and children. Mom may be looking at price tags and practicality while the child only sees something "pretty." ◆ **How might a parent handle these situations?**

Health & Safety

To choose clothing with safety in mind, parents should follow these guidelines:

▶ Choose garments made of **flame-retardant** fabrics, which resist burning quickly if accidentally ignited. Federal law requires these fabrics for children's sleepwear.

▶ Make sure pants fit well and allow a child to move freely without tripping.

▶ Select shoes with non-slip soles and Velcro™ fasteners instead of laces to prevent falls.

▶ Avoid garments with decorative trim and buttons that can be pulled off and swallowed.

▶ Avoid long strings, skirts, and scarves that can catch on play equipment.

▶ Be sure hoods aren't so large that they block a child's vision.

ECONOMY

Children's clothing can take a large chunk from a family's budget. Children outgrow clothes quickly. A name brand or cartoon character on a garment increases its cost. To dress children in attractive, serviceable clothing at reasonable expense, a parent can:

♥ Recycle clothing among relatives, friends, and neighbours.

♥ Find store sales and special discounts.

♥ Buy slightly flawed garments or clearance items at outlet stores.

♥ Shop at garage sales and resale stores. Some benefit local groups and worthy causes. Parents might also donate outgrown clothing to these places.

CHILD'S PREFERENCES

Whatever the price, clothing is no bargain if a child doesn't like it and won't wear it. A young child's preferences are based on personal likes, especially favourite colours. School-age children generally want styles similar to what their friends wear. They can be told that the family clothing budget must be stretched to meet the needs of the whole family.

EASE OF DRESSING

Children are eager to learn to dress themselves. By age three, most children can do so with little assistance. They still need help starting a zipper, tying laces, and pulling on boots.

A little inventiveness helps when teaching self-dressing. One mother places her child's snow boots in plastic bags. The child puts on each boot by pulling up the bag. Parents encourage self-dressing by choosing clothes that are easy to put on and take off. "Child-friendly" garments include:

♥ Pants with elastic waistbands, especially when children are learning toilet training.

♥ Clothes that fasten in the front with large buttons and snaps, and zippers with big tabs.

♥ Roomy shirts that slip on quickly.

♥ Shoes with Velcro™ closings or buckles.

Parental Examples

Parents should be aware that their own decisions set an example for those that children eventually make themselves. Suppose your child clamoured for the same name brands in clothing that friends coaxed their parents into buying. Would you give in to help the child fit in with peers? Or would you stick with safe, practical purchases, even if the child disliked wearing them? Either choice sends a message about the role and importance of clothing.

The same is true for many of the decisions a parent makes about a child's physical needs. Every choice you make for the child now is an example for the child's future. As children go on to make their own decisions, parental influence continues to guide their thinking.

Clothing offers new challenges for children.
◆ **What would you say to a child who had the buttons in all the wrong holes?**

Looking Back

♥ All children follow the same growth pattern, though individual growth rates vary.

♥ Teaching self-feeding skills is a first step in promoting good nutrition.

♥ Parents should encourage children to eat a wide variety, but not necessarily large amounts, of healthy foods.

♥ Parents should provide opportunities and equipment to help children develop large and small motor skills.

♥ To teach children toilet training, parents must watch for signs of readiness.

♥ With encouragement, children gradually become responsible for bathing and dental care.

♥ Clothing for children should be comfortable, safe, and easy to launder.

Knowledge and Understanding

1. In general, how do children change physically between the toddler years and school age?
2. Lisa has prepared pork chops for her family's dinner, knowing that her three-year-old doesn't like them. What might she substitute for the child's main dish?
3. Describe a place setting for a toddler who is learning self-feeding. What other items might be useful?
4. How should you introduce a new food to a child?
5. What activities would you recommend for developing a child's large motor skills?
6. What items can parents make available to encourage manual dexterity?
7. Describe a positive process for teaching toilet training.
8. How do parents promote good dental hygiene?
9. What factors make a child's garment a good buy? What would not be a wise purchase?
10. Describe a child's outfit that promotes self-dressing skills.

Review

CHAPTER 15

Thinking and Inquiry

11. How might a parent's daily life change when a toddler learns to walk? What aspects of parenting would be easier? Which would be more challenging?

12. Nick's two-year-old wants to help his father prepare dinner. What tasks might the toddler be physically able to carry out?

13. Despite her parents' pleas, four-year-old Christina refuses all foods at dinner. Later, when she asks for a sandwich, they prepare one for her. What do you think is the motive for Christina's behaviour?

Communication

14. Try using your non-dominant hand to write the alphabet or to eat soup. Compare this to a young child trying to master small motor skills. In a paragraph, describe what a child might feel while learning these skills.

15. Suppose you are the parent of a six-year-old boy. Your son enjoys physical activities but isn't very co-ordinated. He always has a new scrape or bruise from falling from his bicycle or tripping while racing his friends and seems rather proud of his injuries. You're worried about this behaviour and what it might lead to. How do you deal with this situation?

Application

16. Using a clothing or department store catalogue, calculate the cost of these items for a toddler: one pair of pants or jeans; one shirt; one pair of bib overalls; one pair of canvas shoes. How much would you pay for these items at a thrift shop, assuming the shop charges 40 cents on the dollar?

17. Using menus, select healthy choices for two children, ages three and seven. Use *Canada's Food Guide* on page 278 as a guideline. How much would their meals cost?

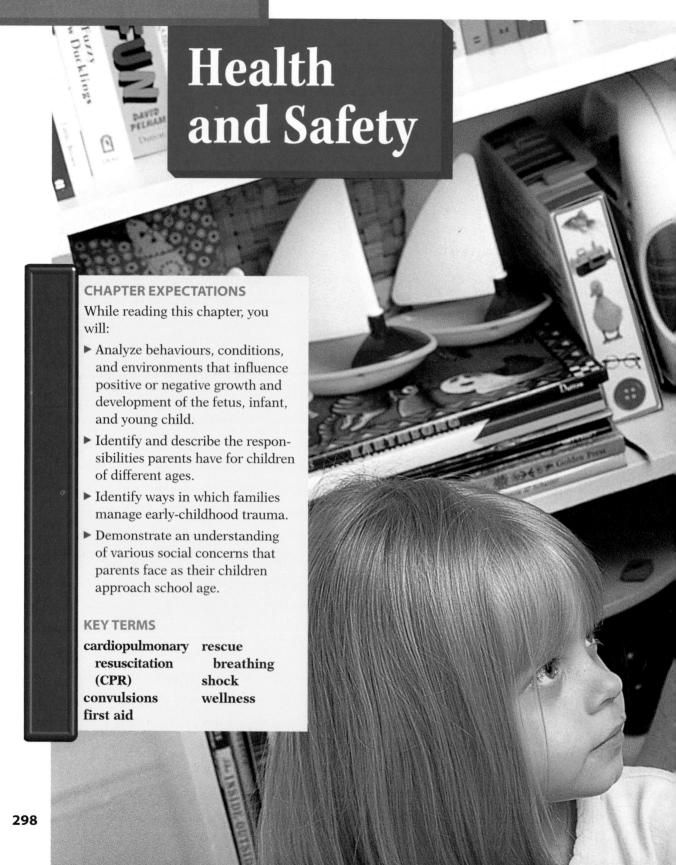

Health and Safety

CHAPTER EXPECTATIONS

While reading this chapter, you will:

▶ Analyze behaviours, conditions, and environments that influence positive or negative growth and development of the fetus, infant, and young child.

▶ Identify and describe the responsibilities parents have for children of different ages.

▶ Identify ways in which families manage early-childhood trauma.

▶ Demonstrate an understanding of various social concerns that parents face as their children approach school age.

KEY TERMS

cardiopulmonary resuscitation (CPR)
convulsions
first aid
rescue breathing
shock
wellness

From down the hall, Josephine could hear her daughter's voice. She peeked in the bedroom doorway to see four-year-old Noelle tucking a small blanket around her favourite doll, Marcella. Noelle leaned down and kissed the doll's forehead.

"Don't be scared, Marcella," she said. "Everything will be okay." She placed the prongs of a toy stethoscope in her ears, resting the other end on the doll's dress. "Hmm," she murmured. Using her finger as a needle, Noelle gave Marcella an imaginary shot. "Now don't cry, Marcella. It doesn't hurt that much. Here, Toby will sit with you. He'll make you feel better." Noelle reached for a teddy bear with worn fur and soft, loving eyes. She placed him close beside Marcella. "There. You like having Toby here, don't you?"

Josephine glanced at her watch. "We have to get going now, Noelle," she said gently. "Your appointment with Dr. Stone is in half an hour." Noelle turned to her mother, her face clouding with concern. "Would you like to take Toby along to-day?" Josephine asked. "He's never met Dr. Stone, has he?" Noelle nodded and picked up Toby, clutching him close as they headed for the door.

———— ◆ ————

What do you think? If you were Noelle's parent, how might you use Toby to soothe Noelle during the appointment?

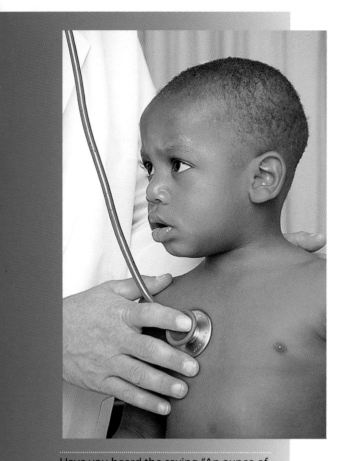

Have you heard the saying, "An ounce of prevention is worth a pound of cure"?
◆ **How does that relate to the health of a child?**

Protecting Health

If six-year-old Eric is always tired or sick, how well can he do in school? With poor health, concentrating will be hard for him. Eric may not make the progress he should. Caring about Eric, or any child, means protecting health and safety so that the child can grow and develop successfully.

Most parents are not experts in health and safety. By teaming with medical professionals and others, parents can provide a full range of appropriate care. Parents need to keep good medical records to help doctors diagnose and treat illnesses. They should keep track of symptoms and past treatments in order to give a clear picture of any health problem.

Children cannot always explain how they feel, so parents become skilled at "reading" their child to notice subtle clues about health or illness. They learn to recognize more obvious signs of trouble as well, and how to respond when those signs appear.

Practising Wellness

Unfortunately, many people pay too little attention to their health. They take their health for granted until they start to feel sick or are diagnosed with a problem. Then they change their ways by getting more rest, eating right, and improving bad health habits. They hope for a cure because it's too late for prevention.

Other people think about their health every day. They strive for **wellness**, a positive state of mental and physical health. As the term implies, one feature of *well*ness is avoiding *ill*ness. By making healthy practices a way of life, you are more likely to feel good and avoid health problems.

For parents, the commitment to a child's wellness is a gift to the whole family. Wellness behaviour helps prevent problems: disrupted work and school schedules, anxieties about illness, and the stress of coping with such difficulties.

PREVENTIVE MEDICAL CARE

Regular medical care helps children stay in good health. Parents and medical professionals can often identify medical problems before they become serious. By beginning treatments early, a potential problem may have less impact on the child.

Internet Connects

www.mcgrawhill.ca/links/parenting
To learn more about caring for children, go to the Web site above for *Parenting Rewards & Responsibilities, First Canadian Edition,* to see where to go next.

Examinations

Parents like to know that their child is making good progress. Regular physical exams give that reassurance. Toddlers should have medical checkups at 15 and 18 months of age, then every six months or so through the preschool years. Beginning with preschool, exams should include vision screening. School-age children need to see a doctor annually.

Health & Safety

A TRIP TO THE DOCTOR

"Going to the doctor" is a big fear for some children. Visits are filled with unfamiliar people performing mysterious procedures that sometimes involve real pain. If let go, such fears can create problems for parents and serious consequences for the child later in life.

Parents need to help children develop positive feelings about health-care professionals. Choosing a pediatrician or family doctor they like and trust and who has a friendly way with children is a good start. Taking the child in for regular checkups also helps. This not only safeguards the child's health but also links medical care with something other than sickness and pain.

Of course, not all families can "shop" for doctors. If families live in a community that is experiencing a shortage of doctors, parents may have to use walk-in clinics and the emergency department of the local hospital. In such cases, developing a relationship with a doctor is difficult to do. In this case, parents need to be especially supportive of their children's medical health. The simplest way is just to be there. Children take great comfort in a parent's presence.

As a parent, you can distract your child during unpleasant procedures. Lightly blowing on an infant's face, for example, often diverts the baby's attention. With older children, singing songs, playing games, or talking about happy times keeps the mind occupied.

Sometimes a procedure is particularly painful or drawn-out. Parents must remain posi-tive but honest. Explain in simple terms why the procedure is needed and what will happen. Offer reassurance that the procedure is needed to help the child feel better.

Parents should also examine their own attitudes toward health care. Do they have regular medical, dental, and eye exams? Do they only complain about the system or inconvenience of health care, without describing its benefits? Do they threaten children after misbehaviour by saying, "I'll tell the doctor to give you a shot"?

Children who are raised with positive experiences in medical care have an important advantage in life. They not only have a happier, less stressful childhood, but they may also be more likely to use medical services to be happier, healthier adults.

Young children are sometimes anxious about medical exams. Parents should be sure their doctor takes the time to establish a friendly, trusting mood. The doctor may explain a procedure or let the child handle a piece of equipment. Positive experiences create positive feelings toward medical care and caregivers. Each visit becomes easier and more productive.

A parent's attitude also makes a big difference in how a child views a medical exam. Some parents are biased by unpleasant childhood memories. They expect the exam to be an ordeal, so it is—for both child and parent. Saying "I'm afraid you have to see Dr. Cho next week" causes needless worry. A positive remark, "Dr. Cho will be impressed at how much you've grown," is more helpful.

Immunizations

As you read in Chapter 14, all children must be immunized for protection against certain diseases. The recommended schedule shown in that chapter continues vaccinations from infancy and into the toddler, preschool, and school years. Additional immunizations against hepatitis B, tetanus, and chicken pox may be recommended around ages 14–16.

In order to attend school, children must be up to date on their immunizations.

Early Detection

As children grow older, they are better able to help parents detect illness early, when easiest to treat. With their expanding vocabulary, they can tell whether a pain is dull or sharp, constant or recurring. They can point out the location.

Older children might remember when they last experienced the pain and what it was like. A child who says, "My throat feels scratchy," alerts a parent to an illness before it becomes severe.

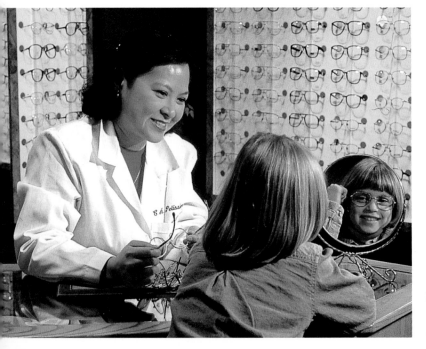

You might not notice when a young child is having vision problems. ◆ **What signs could give clues?**

Treating Common Childhood Illnesses

Illness is a fact of life, and children are especially at risk. They're sociable and affectionate and don't always practise good hygiene or preventive health measures. Parents need to learn the symptoms and treatment of common childhood ailments, as listed in the chart below.

GIVING CARE DURING ILLNESS

While a child's sickness is often difficult for parents, it's usually worse for the young patient. Physically the child may feel miserable. The child may not understand why he or she is sick. Lying still or playing quietly for days at a time can be frustrating, especially as the child begins to feel better.

Restoring the child's physical health is a parent's first concern. To aid this process for common illnesses, parents should:

♥ Feed a light diet of mild foods. Avoid forcing food if the child isn't hungry.

♥ Give children plenty of water and juices to prevent dehydration.

♥ Give any prescribed medication exactly as the physician directed and for as long as directed. Not following the directions can lead to the medication becoming ineffective later as the child's system builds a resistance to it.

Common Childhood Illnesses

Illness	Symptoms	Treatment*
Colds and Coughs	Runny nose, sneezing, coughing, possibly fever.	Give fluids; keep child warm. Moisten air in child's room with cool mist humidifier or vapourizer. Call doctor if symptoms worsen.
Ear Infections	Pulling at ear, fever, crying, irritability.	Call doctor. Antibiotics may be needed.
Sore Throat	Difficulty swallowing; sneezing; coughing; redness in throat, sometimes with white spots.	Give fluids and non-aspirin pain reliever. If symptoms persist or there are white spots, call doctor to check for strep throat.
Influenza	Fever, head or body aches, fatigue, chills, cough, sore throat, nausea, digestive disorders.	Encourage rest. Give fluids and bland diet. Call doctor if child can't retain fluids or if symptoms worsen.
Allergies	Skin rash, itching, sneezing, coughing, hives, breathing difficulty.	For mild symptoms, make an appointment with doctor. Take child to hospital immediately or call 911 for breathing difficulty.

*When in doubt about whether your child needs to see the doctor, phone the office for advice from a nurse or call your provincial health helpline.

♥ Keep children with a fever or bad cough out of school, to provide needed rest and to avoid exposing others. A child should be fever-free for 24 hours before returning to school.

♥ When giving medication, be sure the dosage is correct. Most are based on weight, which can change quickly during childhood.

♥ Avoid products that contain aspirin. They have many potential side effects, including a sometimes fatal condition called Reye (rye) syndrome.

Keeping a sick child quietly occupied can challenge a parent's creativity. Children can colour, read, or work on a puzzle if they feel well enough. Some parents allow older children to telephone friends or relatives or watch a movie or a little more television than usual.

For a parent who stays home with a sick child, perhaps the best option is spending time in shared activities: reading a story, playing a game, or just talking. A parent's caring and reassuring presence is one medicine children enjoy taking.

HOSPITALIZATION

If you've ever been hospitalized, even for a planned procedure, you know how stressful that can be. For children, the situation can be traumatic. They are among strangers, in an unfamiliar place, surrounded by odd-looking devices. They worry about what's going to happen next. Having a parent nearby is essential for a young child.

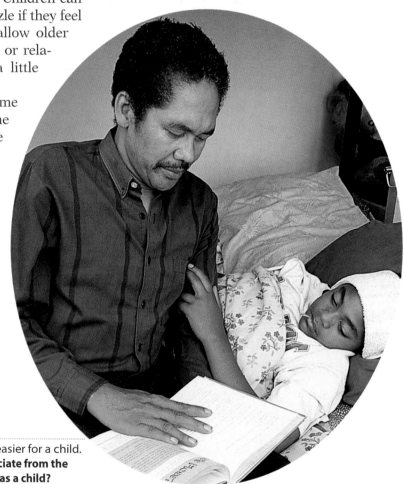

A comforting parent can make illness easier for a child.
◆ **What kind of support did you appreciate from the people around you when you were sick as a child?**

Parents can also help by answering questions simply but honestly and with reassurance. As part of the pre-admission process for young patients, a hospital tour is useful. Becoming familiar with the hospital and some of its staff members helps build trust and gives the child a sense of control.

Taking Safety Precautions

Some children treat the world as one big playroom. Every item is a potential toy. Parents know otherwise. Rather than discourage all of their child's explorations, they take precautions to prevent accident or injury.

CHILDPROOFING ROOMS

By the time her son David was six months old, Kate had childproofed their apartment for a crawling infant. Childproofing, however, is an ongoing job. David the toddler would be taller, more mobile, and more resourceful. He would be able to reach onto countertops and climb cabinets by standing in drawers.

Anticipating her son's development, Kate later re-evaluated the safety of each room. Sitting on the floor, she asked herself: What might attract David's interest here and cause him danger? She noticed any items that particularly fascinated her son and placed these out of sight as well as out of reach.

At the same time, Kate taught David to respect dangerous objects. After learning that the oven was "hot" and knives could "hurt," he avoided them.

Despite many safety precautions, children still seem to find trouble. Some have been seriously injured by standing on an oven door and toppling the range over. Curious and unpredictable toddlers always need to be supervised by alert adults.

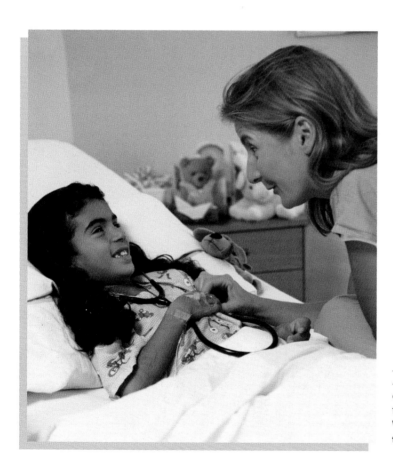

A child usually can't rely on past experience and knowledge to figure out what's going on. ◆ **What might this nurse be saying to her young patient?**

To create a safe environment for her son, Kate took many of the steps listed below. Which of these are a problem in the illustration on pages 332-333?

♥ Use a mesh gate to keep the child in safe areas.

♥ Cover electrical outlets with special caps; tape cords to floor or wall moulding.

♥ Keep fans and space heaters out of reach.

♥ Install guards over a fireplace.

♥ Keep emergency phone numbers next to the telephone.

♥ Put away the ironing board when not in use.

♥ Store dangerous household products in high, securely latched cabinets.

♥ Lower the water heater temperature to 49°C (120°F) to prevent scalding.

♥ Lock up medicines and use childproof caps.

♥ Use rubber appliqués or a non-slip mat in the bathtub.

♥ Use cribs or playpens in good condition, with bars no farther apart than 6 cm ($2\frac{3}{8}$ in.).

♥ Keep crib sides at the highest level and the mattress at the lowest level for toddlers.

♥ Buy flame-retardant sleepwear for children and follow washing instructions.

♥ Cook on rear burners when possible and turn pot handles back.

♥ Store food items and non-food items separately.

♥ Never store non-food items in such containers as beverage bottles.

♥ Keep all chemicals out of reach of children and in childproof containers.

♥ Avoid tablecloths that hang over the table edge.

♥ Fasten safety belts in vehicles, high chairs, strollers, and shopping carts.

♥ Unplug and hide cords from appliances that can be pulled over.

♥ Use unbreakable cups and keep breakables out of reach.

Dangers lurk behind cabinet doors for young children in many homes. ◆ **What are some of those dangers? How will this device help?**

♥ Shut the clothes dryer door when not in use.

♥ Lock up power tools and craft and hobby supplies.

Use of Playpens

Should parents confine infants and toddlers in a playpen to keep them from harm? Many authorities oppose this practice. Regular confinement may inhibit development by limiting exploration.

Occasionally placing young children in a playpen, however, can protect them when you must do something that could harm the child. Folding playpens can be moved from room to room as needed. When travelling, they're a safe sleeping and play space.

PROTECTION AGAINST ACCIDENTS

In the dictionary, "accident" is defined as a "chance or unexpected event," "unintended," and "non-essential." From accidents, about 600 children under age 14 die each year in Canada. This means that nearly 43 percent of all deaths of one-to-14-year-olds are injury-related and, therefore, preventable. Another 43 000 children in the same age group are hospitalized each year for injuries— injuries that, like most accidents, didn't need to happen.

Preventing Falls

Toddlers' softer, more flexible bones help them escape minor falls uninjured. Left unsupervised, unfortunately, toddlers put themselves in position to suffer major falls. They run beyond their ability to control their legs, so rooms and play areas must be free of such hazards as toys, loose rugs, and slick or sticky spills.

Climbing is a favourite way of conquering new parts of the world. Parents must enforce strict rules against climbing on furniture and cabinets. They should leave nothing near a window that might serve as a step stool for reaching it. Since a determined child will move objects to the window, parents should install safety gates over the screen or glass to prevent the child from falling through.

Stairs, another falling hazard, should be closed off with latched doors or gates. Toddlers need practise navigating stairs, but only under an adult's watchful eye. Preschoolers and school-age children may need to be reminded to take one step at a time, without rushing, and to use handrails.

Children are naturally curious.
◆ **What mistake has the caregiver made in this situation?**

Is This Home Childproof?

Nothing moves more quickly than a child in pursuit of an adventure! That may be an exaggeration, but as any parent will tell you, young children can slip out of sight and into trouble in an instant. By childproofing the home, parents reduce the risks of harm.

TRY THIS 👉 **Here's a house that spells trouble for a child. Read the childproofing tips on pages 330-331 and the other tips in the chapter. What could you do to make this home safer for the child?**

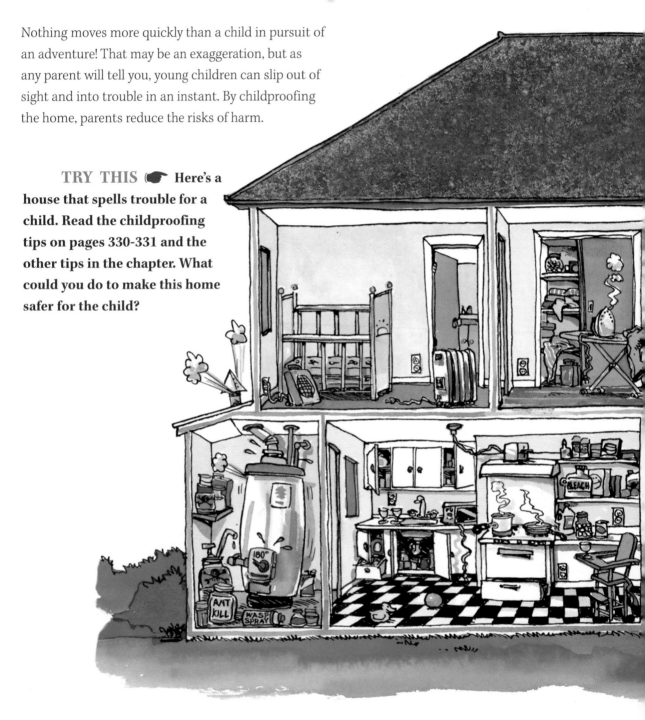

GET
DRS.
PHONE
NUMBER

Safety in Baths

Bath time is fun for most children. To keep baths safe as well, parents should follow these guidelines:

♥ Test the water temperature. Swish the water around to eliminate hot spots.

♥ Unplug and remove all electrical appliances. Children can pull these into the water and electrocute themselves.

♥ Avoid turning on the hot water with a child in the bath. If the hot water is running, warn the child that the faucet is hot.

♥ Keep the water heater at a low temperature setting.

♥ Supervise baths for children until at least age seven. If necessary, let the phone ring.

♥ Don't assume that two children bathing together can be left unattended. The older child may not recognize when the younger one is in danger, much less know how to respond.

Crib and Bed Safety

A 90-cm (3-ft.) toddler is able, and sometimes determined, to climb out of a crib. Parents can delay this feat by setting the mattress at its lowest level and removing anything that might help the adventurer scale the crib rail.

A nightlight guides a child in a darkened room, while a mesh gate across the doorway keeps the child from roaming. Some parents use a monitor to alert them when a child has awakened at night or from a nap.

Other precautions apply as children switch from a crib to a bed. A child's bed should be low and equipped with safety rails. It should be set at least 60 cm (2 ft.) from windows, heating vents, lamps, and drapery cords.

Internet Connects

www.mcgrawhill.ca/links/parenting
To learn more about safety information for adults and children, go to the Web site above for *Parenting Rewards & Responsibilities, First Canadian Edition,* to see where to go next.

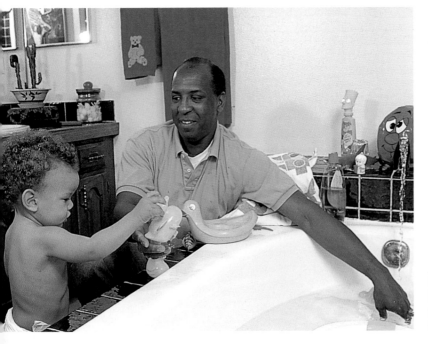

Never leave a child unattended in or near a bathtub. ◆ **Besides bath time, what other water situations require a caregiver's watchful eye?**

Health & Safety

Injuries from fire are usually preventable. Here are some ways to protect the family:

▶ Never leave an infant or young child alone in the house. You may not be able to go back if a fire starts.

▶ Keep matches and lighters out of children's reach.

▶ Place a smoke detector on every floor in the home and check batteries monthly.

▶ Practice a fire escape plan.

▶ Have the home heating system checked and serviced annually.

▶ Don't overload electrical circuits.

▶ Store flammables, such as gasoline and kerosene, in appropriate containers outside the home. Remember that a furnace pilot light could ignite fumes in the basement.

▶ Have a roll-out fire escape ladder on upper floors, and make sure children know where it is stored.

Mealtime Safety

Standing in a high chair, a toddler is on top of the world—and in danger of falling off. Children in high chairs should be supervised, and the chair's safety strap should be fastened to hold them securely. The chair should be set away from the range and any hot dishes. It should be placed away from tables or counters that children could push against, tipping themselves over.

Tablecloths are tempting to curious toddlers. One tug can bring heavy dishes, sharp knives, and scalding food down upon them. Place mats are a safer choice.

Kitchen Safety

The kitchen is a mysterious land of forbidden treasures to a young child. Here adults play with shiny, grown-up toys that whir and ring. Parents get to chop, pound, and mix foods. Satisfying dishes and tasty treats emerge from ovens and pop out of toasters. What child wouldn't be "under foot" amid such fascinating activity?

Simple changes can make kitchens safer for children. Refrigerator and cabinet doors can be equipped with locks or latches. Trash containers should be tightly covered and preferably out of sight. Removing refrigerator magnets eliminates a choking hazard. Foods can cook on a range's back burners, with pan handles turned toward the rear.

Keeping children safely occupied is helpful. Choose a lower kitchen cabinet, located away from the range, trash can, and sink. Fill it with safe, intriguing kitchen items to provide hours of rummaging and fun.

Keep a close eye on toddlers when you're visiting other people's homes. Unfortunately, everyone does not childproof his or her home. Cabinets like this one are very dangerous.

Safety Around Heaters

A source of warmth can also be a source of danger. Young children should be kept away from radiators and space heaters and warned about the risk of burns.

Gas heaters should be vented, with a valve that shuts off the gas if the pilot light goes out. Otherwise, the unburned gas can explode or cause carbon monoxide poisoning. Turning on an oven after its pilot light goes out presents the same danger. A gas oven should never be used for heat.

Health & Safety

LEAD POISONING

Even at low levels, lead can cause long-term brain and nerve damage and significantly affect intelligence. How does this happen?

Although numerous sources of lead poisoning exist, the leading offender is the lead-based paints found inside and outside many residences. Children may breathe in or swallow tiny particles of peeling and chipped paint. An affected child may: be irritable, sluggish, or hyperactive; have stomach problems; or have headaches.

To protect children from this hazard, homes built before 1992 should be checked. Call the public health unit for information. Never let children chew on woodwork and keep floors and windowsills clean. Also, wash children's hands and toys frequently. Children should have a blood test every year until age seven to make sure that lead poisoning is not threatening their life.

Parenting Q & A

Raised Safe or Raised Scared?

Q "Children seem to face so many dangers these days. How can I teach my two young sons to protect themselves and avoid trouble without making them afraid and distrustful?" *Karen*

A You'll want to take a positive approach when teaching children how to stay safe. Make sure your children know their address and phone number and how to use the 911 emergency service. Children should recognize their neighbours and be familiar with their community. Instruct them to "Always walk in a group, so someone can get help if you need it" or "If you are lost, go to someone in a uniform or to a person working at a job." You can also teach attitudes that promote safety. Children who are given choices in daily matters learn to be selective, not passive. They think before following a stranger into a dangerous situation. Children don't need to be told "horror stories" when learning about possible threats. You can simply say, "Most people are good, but a few are not. Since you don't know whether strangers are good or bad, it's safer to avoid them."

Preventing Suffocation

The warning you see on large plastic bags against using them as toys is an important message. Toddlers find plastic bags entertaining. They like the noise they make. They enjoy pulling a bag over their head, unaware that the plastic can cause suffocation within minutes.

Safety-conscious parents keep food storage bags and garbage bags out of reach. They tie knots in dry cleaner's bags and discard them immediately.

PERSONAL SAFETY

Perhaps the most frightening thought for parents is that their child may be harmed, not by accident, but deliberately by another person. Parents can protect young children from crime by keeping them close when out in public and by leaving them only with trusted adults.

As children grow, however, they take more responsibility for their own safety. Parents guide them by setting rules for safe behaviour. Parents should insist that a child get permission before going anyplace. They should meet their child's friends and acquaintances. They should remind children to never accept gifts or rides or to "help" a stranger, even if that person claims to know their parent.

Children must also be taught that certain parts of their bodies are private. They should tell a parent if anyone tries to touch them there or in any way that makes them feel uncomfortable. A teacher or family counsellor can explain how to communicate this message in an age-appropriate way.

Take time to safely secure children in safety seats. Rushing this task could lead to a fatal accident.

Motor Vehicle Safety

Motor vehicle accidents are the leading cause of childhood injuries. Parents must make auto safety a priority.

From birth, children in motor vehicles are legally required to be secured in a child safety restraint. All safety seats must meet safety standards. Always follow the manufacturer's instructions.

Infants must ride in a reclining position, facing backwards in the back seat, until they are one year old and weigh 10 kg (22 lbs.). Children weighing 10 kg (22 lbs.) or more can ride upright, facing forward. A child of 18 kg (40 lbs.) or more, or aged roughly 4½ to 8, should use a seat belt and a booster seat. Each child should have a separate seat belt. The shoulder strap should fit across the chest, not the neck, with the lap belt low and snug over the hip bones.

Many vehicles are now equipped with front-seat air bags, which can be deadly for children. If the air bag inflates, it can strike a backward-facing safety seat with enough force to injure or kill an infant. An older child in a forward-facing seat or wearing a seat belt can be suffocated. To avoid this hazard, the safest place for any child is properly secured in the back seat.

Parents should always wear seat belts themselves. They should never let children ride with a driver who has consumed alcohol or drugs.

Handling Emergencies

Even the most safety-conscious parent may have to deal with an emergency. A quick response can spell the difference between life and death. Responsible parents teach children their phone number and address at an early age.

Emergencies can be made less serious when parents use the following guidelines:

♥ Make sure all caregivers and older children know how to call for emergency help. Many communities have 911 service for all emergencies. Others have separate phone numbers for the police, fire department, poison control center, and ambulance service. These numbers are usually listed in the front of the telephone directory and should also be posted near the phone.

♥ Learn the best route to hospitals and the exact location of the emergency room.

♥ Teach children how to respond in case of fire. Practise escape routes from different rooms. Rehearse phoning for help from a neighbour's and the "stop, drop, and roll" technique for extinguishing burning hair or clothing.

♥ With older children, discuss how to handle other emergencies they may encounter, such as natural disasters. Decide how family members will contact each other if separated during a disaster.

♥ Establish a family password.

GIVING FIRST AID

First aid is immediate care given to an ill or injured person, often provided until medical help is available. Learning first aid and keeping a kit of basic medical supplies is a good idea for anyone, but especially parents.

Giving first aid may include performing **cardiopulmonary resuscitation** (car-dee-oh-PULL-muh-nair-ee reh-SUH-suh-TAY-shun), or CPR. This technique revives or keeps a person alive until advanced care arrives. A person provides oxygen by breathing into the victim's lungs and applies pressure to the chest to force the heart to pump. Because CPR can cause serious damage if done incorrectly, only certified individuals should attempt it.

First aid and CPR courses by trained instructors are offered by St. John Ambulance and the Canadian Red Cross, sometimes free of charge.

Basic steps for giving a child first aid are:

♥ Reassure the child by acting and speaking calmly and confidently.

♥ Get trained medical help quickly. Don't leave the child, however, unless you have to find help.

♥ Keep the child warm and still to prevent shock. **Shock**, a dangerous slowing of the circulation and breathing, is the body's reaction to trauma. It is fatal if not treated. Treating shock may require CPR or **rescue breathing**, which is forcing air into the lungs, either mouth-to-mouth or mouth-to-nose.

♥ Stop any bleeding as quickly as possible.

♥ Do not move an injured child unless necessary for safety reasons. Broken bones or internal injuries could be made worse.

Children seem to be accidents waiting to happen. Many injuries can be quickly handled with a bandage and a comforting word and hug.

♥ Check for breathing. If the child has an open air passage but isn't breathing, start rescue breathing at once. If a child is choking, there are different procedures to follow. The one chosen depends on the child's age, as explained below.

♥ Check the pulse. If there is no pulse, call for help immediately. If you have been trained and certified, begin CPR.

HANDLING SPECIFIC EMERGENCIES

Specific emergencies require specialized treatment. Professional medical help is always preferred but not always immediately available. Therefore, parents need to have some idea of how to respond to common health emergencies.

Rescue Manoeuvre for Choking Infants

Step 1: Turn the infant's face down over your arm.

Step 2: Using the heel of your other hand, give four quick blows between the infant's shoulder blades.

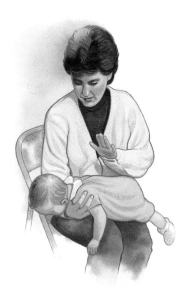

Step 3: Turn the infant over, supporting the head, neck, and back. Position your two middle fingers below the rib cage and above the navel. With your fingers in that position, give four quick thrusts toward the chest. Repeat these three steps until the object is expelled.

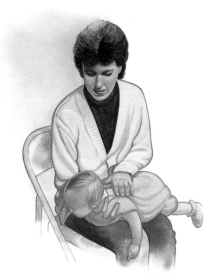

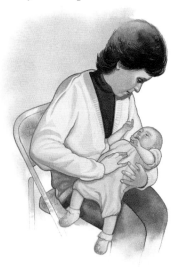

Choking

A choking child who is coughing forcefully should not be given first aid for choking. Forceful coughing will often dislodge the object in the throat. If the child starts to turn blue, however, or coughs or breathes only with great difficulty, assistance is needed. See below for instructions on the Heimlich Manoeuvre.

Bleeding

Small wounds stop bleeding naturally as air helps the blood to clot. Serious bleeding should be stopped by applying direct pressure to the wound, using sterile gauze, clean towels, sanitary napkins, or fresh diapers. Pressure should be maintained for at least ten minutes to allow the blood time to clot. If possible, the area of the wound should be raised above the heart.

Heimlich Manoeuvre for Children One Year and Older

If the victim is standing or sitting:

Step 1: Stand behind the victim. Clasp your hands with your fists just below the victim's rib cage.

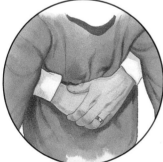

Step 2: Press your clasped hands into the victim's abdomen with a quick upward thrust. Repeat step 2 if necessary until the object is expelled.

If the victim has collapsed:

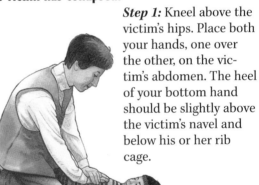

Step 1: Kneel above the victim's hips. Place both your hands, one over the other, on the victim's abdomen. The heel of your bottom hand should be slightly above the victim's navel and below his or her rib cage.

Step 2: Use the force of both hands to press with a quick upward thrust. Repeat Step 2 if necessary until the object is expelled.

Poisoning

Poisons may be swallowed, inhaled, or absorbed through the skin. Symptoms include nausea and vomiting, headaches, and burning or irritation of the eyes and skin.

A parent who suspects poisoning should contact the hospital emergency department or the Poison Information Centre immediately. In addition to the symptoms, medical personnel will need to know the child's age and weight and the source and time of the poisoning, if known. If the poison was swallowed, parents should have the container on hand to read the list of ingredients and to see how much was consumed.

Parents should induce vomiting of swallowed poison only if instructed by a physician or Poison Information Centre, even if the container's label says otherwise. Some poisons damage the mouth and esophagus as much coming up as going down. All families should have syrup of ipecac (IH-pih-kak) on hand to induce vomiting. The parent may be told to save any vomited substance in order to identify the poison.

Convulsions

Convulsions are a series of strong, involuntary muscle contractions. Head injuries, poisoning, and epilepsy are causes. Convulsions sometimes accompany high fevers and the start of a serious illness.

A child having convulsions should be protected from injury but not restrained. Guide the child to a clear space on the floor, with a pillow or folded towel to cushion the head. When the convulsions have passed, turn the child onto one side, allowing saliva to drain from the mouth, and call the physician.

Electric Shock

A child in contact with a live electrical wire could electrocute a would-be rescuer. The electric current must first be turned off, if possible. Otherwise, the child may be separated from the current with a dry stick. Wet surfaces and objects that conduct electricity must be avoided at all cost. Emergency help should be sent for immediately. CPR or rescue breathing may be needed.

TREATING INJURIES

Fortunately, most childhood injuries heal with only a gentle cleansing, a bandage, and a comforting hug. Other injuries, while not life-threatening, have the potential to cause serious pain and damage if not handled properly. The chart on page 343 describes some common injuries and how they should be treated.

Internet Connects

www.mcgrawhill.ca/links/parenting
To learn more about illnesses and other health-related information, go to the Web site above for *Parenting Rewards & Responsibilities, First Canadian Edition,* to see where to go next.

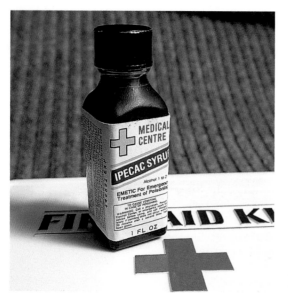

If they're lucky, parents never have to use the syrup of ipecac they keep on hand. ◆ **If a child swallows something poisonous, why must the Poison Information Centre be called before giving the child this syrup?**

Common Childhood Injuries

Injury	Treatment	Of Special Concern
Bone Fracture	Keep child still; do not move child, if possible. Place a pillow under injured limb. Call doctor.	Treat even suspected fracture as a fracture. In case of possible spinal injuries, do not let child move until trained medical help arrives.
Burns	Cool minor burns with cold water soak. Flood chemical burns with cold water; cover lightly with gauze; get medical help. Get medical help if skin is charred or destroyed; do not apply water or ice, or remove charred clothing.	If clothing is on fire, smother flames by wrapping child in heavy material, such as a rug or coat, or roll child on ground.
Insect Bites	If stinger remains, remove by scraping with knife or fingernail. Do not use tweezers, which may squeeze out more venom. Apply a paste of baking soda and water. Get medical aid if child has large number of bites or is allergic to insect bites.	Get to emergency room if child has allergic reaction: swelling of the face, tongue, or throat; difficulty breathing; or fainting. Treat for shock. May need to perform rescue breathing or CPR if trained.
Embedded Tick	Swab area with alcohol. With tweezers or fingers, grab tick near the head or as close as possible to child's skin. Pull upward gently and steadily, without squeezing tick. Cleanse the wound with mild antiseptic. Call the doctor if the tick's head does not come out.	Deer ticks carry Lyme disease. The longer the tick is attached, the greater the chance of infection. Remove tick with head as soon as possible. Save unfamiliar tick for doctor. Immediately report signs of Lyme disease: red circle around bite, flu-like symptoms.
Animal Bite	If bleeding, apply firm pressure until it stops. Then gently wash with soap and water. Call doctor. Report any redness, tenderness, swelling, drainage, or red streaks that spread out from bite.	Learn whether animal had rabies vaccine. Trap animal for rabies testing if safe, or call animal control.
Splinters	Wash area. Remove splinter with a sterilized needle or tweezers. Cleanse with antiseptic. Soak any remaining splinters in warm, soapy water. Call doctor if splinter remains after a few days or if skin reddens.	
Puncture Wound	Soak in hot, soapy water for 15 minutes. Call doctor to verify date of child's last tetanus shot.	A puncture is a hole through the skin into deeper tissue. A wound is deep, narrow, and difficult to clean and has a greater risk of infection than other types of wounds.
Nosebleed	Sit child with head tilted slightly forward. Have older child blow nose. Pinch lower half of nose between thumb and finger. Hold firmly for ten minutes. Release. If bleeding continues, apply pressure for ten more minutes. Get medical help if bleeding continues.	

Review

Looking Back

♥ The appropriate focus of health care is overall wellness, rather than illness.

♥ Preventive care, including regular medical exams and immunizations, helps maintain a child's wellness.

♥ Since young children cannot always describe their illness, parents need to recognize symptoms.

♥ At home or in the hospital, a sick or injured child needs emotional comfort as well as physical care.

♥ Parents can prevent many injuries by taking simple childproofing measures.

♥ Parents must discuss personal safety with older children.

♥ Learning general and specific first aid procedures lets a parent react positively during an emergency and possibly save a child's life.

♥ Parents need to treat lesser injuries correctly in order to prevent more serious damage.

Knowledge and Understanding

1. What are some advantages of preventive health care?
2. What might you suspect if you saw a child repeatedly tugging at the ear? How would you respond?
3. Give suggestions for helping a sick child recover.
4. How can a parent make hospitalization less frightening for a child?
5. Give three suggestions for preventing falls.
6. How can parents make mealtimes safer?
7. What steps can a parent take to keep a school-age child safe from intentional harm from others?
8. List three steps a parent can take to prepare for emergencies.
9. Should you induce vomiting if a child swallows a poison? Why or why not?
10. How would you treat a child with a bee sting?

Review

Thinking and Inquiry

11. What might be some consequences to emotional and intellectual development if a child is continually exposed to unsafe or unhealthy conditions?

12. Explain how illness might be more upsetting for a toddler than for a ten-year-old, and less so.

13. Do you think parents take children to the doctor more frequently or less so as the child gets older? Explain your answer.

Communication

14. Suppose your three-year-old doesn't like to go to the doctor. You don't look forward to the visits either. In a paragraph, describe how you might be able to improve the visits.

15. Imagine your preschooler has just returned from a play day. "Cory gave us candy," she announces, and holds out a fruit-flavoured, chewable children's vitamin. Knowing that large amounts of vitamins can be toxic, you ask how many she and the other children ate. Your daughter shrugs, "I don't know." She seems to sense she did something wrong and begins to act defensively and unco-operatively. What will you do?

16. Create a pamphlet titled "Keeping Your Toddler Safe" to distribute to parents of toddlers.

Application

17. With a classmate, demonstrate the procedure for performing the Heimlich manoeuvre. *Do not actually perform the manoeuvre.*

18. Use the Internet or recent publications to locate infant's and children's products that have been recalled by manufacturers. Focus your search on Health Canada's Product Safety Bureau.

Meeting Emotional Needs

CHAPTER EXPECTATIONS

While reading this chapter, you will:

▶ Identify the changes in social and emotional development that take place in young children.

▶ Analyze behaviours, conditions, and environments that influence positive or negative growth and development in young children.

▶ Identify and describe the capabilities and behaviours of young children of different ages in a variety of settings.

▶ Identify and describe the responsibilities parents have for children of different ages.

▶ Identify ways in which families manage early-childhood trauma.

KEY TERMS

autonomy	industry
egocentric	initiative
empathy	temper tantrum

The rip of construction paper and hail of crayons told Yoko that Micki's homemade card for her father's birthday was not going well.

"I can't draw pretty flowers!" Micki sobbed. "They're all ugly. I want them to look like Amy's!"

Yoko knelt down and touched Micki's shoulder. "Drawing can be frustrating, Micki. You have to remember that Amy is three years older than you are."

Micki sniffed. "But I want to make them pretty for Daddy."

"That's because you love him and want him to be pleased," Yoko explained. "It feels good to make someone you love happy. But you know what? The flowers don't have to be perfect. Daddy will like them because they're from you." She handed Micki a tissue for her tears. "You pick up the crayons, and if you want, I'll show you a different way to make flowers."

A little later, Micki was making flowers by gluing together brightly coloured strips of construction paper. "These flowers don't have to look like anyone else's," her mother reminded her. "You can put together whatever shapes and colours you like. Each flower can be one of a kind—just like you."

What do you think? Describe specific ways that Yoko's handling of this episode helped Micki grow emotionally.

One of the joys of parenting is sharing happy, loving moments. If a parent creates these moments with a child, the child may return the joy someday by creating them with the parent.

emotional development. Each child has a unique way of feeling, expressing, and acting on emotions. By providing positive models and guidance, parents direct a child's emotional progress in a way that benefits the child and society.

Emotional Development

Twenty-month-old Mara patted the cat energetically, grinning with delight. The cat began to grumble, then hissed and bared his fangs. Bewildered, Mara watched the cat slink away, then burst loudly into tears.

As Mara's behaviour demonstrates, young children have a range of emotions. They know basic emotions, including joy, sadness, anger, and fear. They also have more complex feelings, such as affection and jealousy. Where children are concerned, however, emotional control lags. Great and small pleasures produce equal joy. Children may rage instantly at minor frustrations, then calm to contentment very quickly.

Given a young child's intellectual development, intense feelings are natural. You might think a child is overreacting, but that isn't true. Toddlers and preschoolers are basically **egocentric**. They see things from their own point of view, understanding a situation only as it affects them. Children this age also think in the present. What's happening right now, whether fright or delight, is all-important.

Trained for Life

Have you ever noticed how grapevines grow? A young plant throws out vines that coil stubbornly around the nearest support. Gardeners provide a sturdy frame to train the plant to grow in the right direction. Otherwise, the vine will cling to whatever is available, which may or may not help it grow properly.

Parents and other caregivers have a similar responsibility in supporting a child's

By school age, children have a wider world view. They recognize other people's feelings. They can see events in perspective and respond more appropriately. Moods tend to be more even and predictable. Outbursts decrease as a child gains emotional control.

Adolescence has been called a second toddlerhood, because physical and personal changes again cause emotional swings. Like toddlers, preteens are alternately excited and frightened by new freedoms and expectations. A 12-year-old might leave for school feeling cheerful and optimistic and arrive quiet and sad.

For healthy development, children at every stage need to experience more positive than negative emotions. Parents can create an environment that builds positive emotions and teaches children to manage the negative ones.

Someone once said, "Great people never lose their child's heart." ◆ **What do you think that means? How can parents hang on to the heart of a child? Why do they need to?**

Responding to Emotions

It's natural to think that positive emotions are "good" and negative emotions are "bad." Children learn to handle emotions better, however, when parents don't pass judgment on feelings. Instead, parents acknowledge that even unpleasant emotions are legitimate. At the same time, they guide children to express emotions in acceptable ways and offer reassurance.

AFFECTION

What happens to a child who is deprived of affection? According to some studies, areas of the brain where feelings of emotional closeness originate may not develop.

Such reports confirm what many parents have always known. Children need affection, especially during the early years.

Infants thrive on parental affection. With encouragement, toddlers begin to give affection also. When T.J.'s grandfather says, "Give me a hug," T.J. gives him one and gets a smile of approval and a hug in return. T.J. learns that giving and receiving love and affection feels good.

This example illustrates something else. Parents teach a child not only *to* show affection, but also *how* to show it. T.J. and his grandfather hug. In other cultures, they might kiss. Children learn acceptable signs of affection for different situations. Parents need to show positive expressions of love: hugs, kisses, praise, and kind deeds and words.

ANGER

Everyone feels anger at times. Teaching a child how to manage this basic emotion is part of good parenting.

An infant feels anger, but seldom until age three does the child hold anyone responsible. Toddlers are most likely to feel angry when they don't get their way. Explosive outbursts are common. Anger in preschoolers is less frequent and less physical.

Don't expect toddlers and preschoolers to control their anger. Do teach them how to express anger acceptably. When Lindsay tried to kick her father, he told her calmly and firmly, "I understand why you're angry, but I won't let you hurt me. If you want to kick something, you can kick your ball in the backyard."

By school age, children try to hurt feelings more than bodies. They may threaten and call names, or pout and act sorry for themselves. Sneers and insults are typical reactions among older children. Adolescents may hide anger by pretending indifference. It isn't unusual for them to retreat inward gradually until they explode.

Older children and adolescents need more mature strategies. Sulking is useless. Denying feelings is dangerous. Instead, caregivers should encourage children to talk about why they are angry. Parents are more convincing if they handle their own anger well. They can show children how they talk through angry feelings and use up angry energy with exercise instead of by hurting others.

Temper Tantrums

Imagine you're grocery shopping when your two-year-old picks up a box of doughnuts and proudly carries it to the cart. You explain that doughnuts are not on your list and you aren't buying them. As you take

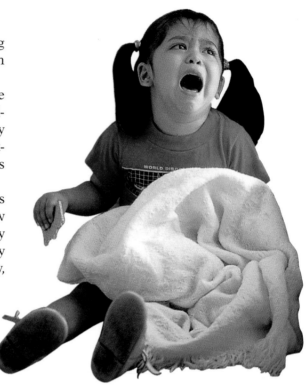

Temper tantrums are common with toddlers for many reasons. If a child takes on a parent's personal problems, tantrums may worsen. ◆ **What does the blanket mean to this little girl?**

the box, the toddler drops to the floor, arms and legs flailing, and wails miserably for all to hear. You are witnessing a **temper tantrum**, a fit of anger accompanied by crying, screaming, hitting, or kicking.

Toddlers are tantrum-prone for several reasons. They want to be independent, but that wish collides with adult authority and is undercut by a lack of physical abilities. Toddlers want to describe how they feel, but they can't. Their verbal skills are limited.

When upset, some children hold anger in and pout. A parent could ignore the actions, offer comfort, or talk calmly about the problem. ◆ **What situations might cause each approach?**

The tantrum is an easy, all-purpose form of expression. Toddlers try to get what they want by the means they know best, yelling and screaming. That's one reason why parents dread these episodes.

How do you respond to a temper tantrum? These suggestions can help:

♥ Speak softly, remaining calm and objective.

♥ Be sure children do not harm themselves, others, or possessions.

♥ At home, ignore the tantrum if there is no danger of injury. Don't plead for the child to stop. Generally, the less attention given tantrums, the less often they occur.

♥ Maintain the rules previously set. Don't reward a child for ending a tantrum.

♥ Save explanations for a calmer time. In the midst of a tantrum, a child isn't listening.

♥ Play quietly with a toy or start an interesting activity. The child may join in.

♥ If a tantrum occurs in public, take the child to a quieter place. Children learn that having an audience helps their cause. A private tantrum is seldom worth the effort.

Parents can prevent some tantrums by reducing the times "no" is used in a child's life. They might:

♥ Avoid denial situations. Put away breakable items at home. Steer clear of junk foods at the supermarket. Ask the manager to provide a checkout lane that is free of candy and toy displays.

♥ Save commands and denials for big issues. A child's life is already heavy with needed rules and limits. If Connor eats the nutritious soup his mother serves, she can ignore the cracker "rafts" he sails across the soup bowl "pond."

♥ Offer limited choices to help children feel more in control. Open-ended choices, such as "Pick out a shirt to wear today," invite unacceptable decisions. Options should be limited to two: "Do you want to wear your blue shirt or your red one?"

♥ Let children express negative emotions before tantrums erupt. Parents can teach a child to put feelings into words by saying, "I get angry too when things go wrong. You seem angry now. Tell me how you feel." Children may need to show anger harmlessly, perhaps by hitting a pillow.

Building Parenting Skills

PARENTING WITH PATIENCE

Patient people stay composed and act properly even when a situation is tiring. Caring for children often tries an adult's patience. Patient parenting means accepting and planning for a child's limitations. Patient parents give children time to practise their skills until they succeed. They are rewarded as children grow in skills and confidence. To parent with patience, Jamie:

▶ Sang the same song with two-year-old Keith over and over.

▶ Calmly wiped up the milk Keith accidentally spilled.

▶ Let five-year-old Kayla tell the whole story she wanted to relate without interrupting.

▶ Waited in the cold while the fascinated children watched a repair crew work on telephone wires.

▶ Waited while Kayla worked to start the zipper of her coat.

▶ Counted to ten when tempted to snap at the children.

◆ ◆ Your Thoughts ◆ ◆

❶ Besides counting to ten, how can a parent keep from losing patience?

❷ When a parent is routinely impatient, how might that affect a child?

❸ When might a patient approach not be possible with a child?

❹ Scott was playing catch with his six-year-old son. Despite all of Scott's coaching, the boy kept dropping the ball. Scott's frustration was growing. What would you recommend he do?

Internet Connects

http://www.mcgrawhill.ca/links/parenting
To learn more about parenting from A to Z, go to the Web site above for *Parenting Rewards & Responsibilities, First Canadian Edition,* to see where to go next.

In the midst of a full-blown tantrum, a parent can feel frustrated and helpless. Often the fury subsides if the parent doesn't overreact.

FEAR

Moving in an ever-widening world, children come across people, things, and situations that frighten them. Their reaction is both typical and healthy. Fear is a positive emotion if it drives children away from real dangers and toward a parent's protection.

Like adults, children also experience unreasonable fears. Children, however, don't know when a fear is irrational. A new experience that they don't understand can frighten them. Children need a parent's support to overcome the feeling.

Preventing Fears

Positive modelling prevents some common fears. Jay knew that many children are afraid of thunderstorms. When a storm approached, Jay and his three-year-old daughter Dani watched together out the window. "Look at the lightning," Jay said as the sky lit up. "Isn't that beautiful? Now wait for the thunder. Listen... Listen... There it is!" Dani laughed as thunder rumbled, just as Jay had predicted. As the first drops of rain hit the pane, Dani watched with excitement. With a father so confident and knowledgeable, Dani had nothing to fear.

Information helps eliminate some fears. One five-year-old cringed at the screaming sound of a fire engine. His mother explained, "The fire engine is rushing to put out a fire. That's an important job! The siren warns cars to move over and let the engine go by." She read her son a story about a fire engine and offered to help his teacher with a class visit to a fire station.

Coping with Fears

As the mind grows, children often develop imaginative fears. These fears are based on fantastic, impossible events, so a

As children overcome some fears, different ones surface. A bad experience on the school bus, for example, could cause a new fear. ◆ **What do children need at these times?**

parent can't always predict when they will happen. The active imagination of a preschooler commonly triggers fears because the child can't tell the imaginary from the real. To a preschooler, a wild animal living in the zoo could just as easily live in the basement.

Dealing with imaginative fears may take a special approach. As a child, did you ever hear this argument: "There's no such thing as monsters"? When you *know* that a monster lives under your bed, this explanation carries little weight. Instead, parents need to help children see the difference between imagination and reality. Though it may take several months, children do learn. Until then, patience helps, and so does a little indulgence. A child who is afraid of wild animals might sleep better after mom or dad sets a cardboard box "trap" in the basement.

Whatever a child's fear, your most helpful response as a parent is to show that you're in control. Comforting, reassuring leadership brings a sense of security.

JEALOUSY

Jealousy is a typical emotion for children. They appreciate only their own need for attention and don't want anything to interfere.

Toddlers may be jealous when they see a parent spending time with the other parent or a sibling instead of with them. Parents can help toddlers by using these approaches:

♥ Be reasonably tolerant. Toddlers become more secure about parental love as they become less self-focused.

♥ Use simple words to explain that you have plenty of love for the toddler as well as other family members. Parents don't need to apologize for having other interests and relationships,

♥ Don't let the toddler have control. Two parents can enjoy a quiet moment together, for example, without the toddler climbing in between to separate them and demand their attention. Although toddlers need to be at the centre sometimes, they need to learn that other people count too.

♥ Spend plenty of meaningful time with the child. A parent who is physically present for a child must be emotionally present as well.

A child who feels left out may be jealous. A child who feels included and content probably won't.

Jealousy of parents drops after age three, as a child begins to form close relationships outside the home. New rivalries may develop. Children may be jealous of peers who appear more capable, more popular, or more privileged. They may grow possessive of friendships, protesting if a friend plays with another child.

As parents help children deal with inequalities in life, jealousy is less likely. Children need to see that, while only one person can be the best student or the fastest runner, human worth is not measured by a single quality. Each person is unique and equally valuable. By showing appreciation for the talents and contributions of all people, parents promote a spirit of generosity rather than jealousy.

Raising Children With Character

The Music Lesson

Julie sat reading the newspaper on the front porch. Inside, her son Chase slowly, deliberately struck the same swirl of notes over and over on the piano. Suddenly came the discordant thunder of many keys pounded at once. Julie winced and folded up the newspaper.

She found her son scowling at the piano keys. "I want to play like you, Mom," Chase complained, "but I can't."

"Get up a minute," Julie said. She reached inside the piano bench and began sorting through sheet music until she found a well-worn booklet near the bottom. "This was my first book," she said. "Take a look."

Chase thumbed through the pages. "*You* used to play this? It's not very hard."

"That's right." Julie smiled and went on, "You have to start simple, Chase. I was just as eager as you are to play beautiful music, but learning to do something well takes time and effort. It takes the will to succeed and the drive to keep at it. Here, let me find a song in my old book. If you learn to play this, I'll bet that someday you'll be playing the way I do now—maybe even better."

◆◆◆◆◆ **Thinking It Over** ◆◆◆◆◆

1. How might Chase's attitude change by playing a song from his mother's book?
2. What does Julie hope Chase will realize from their conversation?
3. Give an example of how this lesson might serve Chase in other aspects of life.

Influencing Personality

Personalities are seen through the behaviour and emotions of children. A parent who notices that Ryan is a worrier and Anya is typically even-tempered is noticing personality.

HEREDITY AND ENVIRONMENT

Heredity provides the foundation for personality. You may see a child who has similar traits to a parent—a quiet, studious father and son, for example. These traits may have been mostly inherited.

Inherited traits can be reinforced or changed by what happens to a child in life. In other words, environment makes a difference. In one study, for example, only 20 percent of children who were shy as newborns remained so at age four. All the shy newborns had unique experiences that caused some to keep the trait and others to change.

Spotlight On
——Erikson and Personality

Psychologist Erik Erikson proposed that personality is shaped by how certain emotional challenges are handled over a lifetime. The challenges occur in eight stages. Erikson linked a favourable and unfavourable outcome with each stage. Mastering a stage leads to the favourable outcome and progress to the next stage. If a challenge isn't mastered, the unfavourable outcome creates emotional and behavioural problems that make it difficult to tackle the next challenge.

The first four stages, covering progress from infancy to school age, are described below. Of course, children encounter favourable and unfavourable outcomes every day. What counts for emotional growth is the experiences they have overall.

1. ***Trust versus mistrust (birth to about 18 months).*** Infants gain trust when needs are consistently met. They view the world as safe and themselves as worthy individuals. Infants who are neglected feel insecure about the world and their place in it.

2. ***Autonomy versus doubt (18 months to age three).*** Children strive for **autonomy**, or independence. They delight in learning self-sufficiency. Toddlers who do not feel autonomous start to doubt their abilities and themselves.

3. ***Initiative versus guilt (preschool age).*** Children begin to develop **initiative**, the readiness and ability to start a task on their own. They feel pressure to act acceptably. Guilt can stifle initiative when children believe they have acted improperly.

4. ***Industry versus inferiority (school-age).*** Children feel the pull of **industry**, the desire to be productive and make contributions. They want to master the skills their culture values. Failing to do so causes feelings of inferiority.

Although scientists continue to study how heredity and environment impact personality, no clear answer tells which one has the most influence. The important fact to remember is that environment cannot be discounted. Heredity may set the stage for what a child will be, but plenty of shaping is ahead.

PARENTAL IMPACT

What parent wouldn't want to have a child with a likeable personality? Parents may wonder if they can do something to make that happen. To some extent, personality traits are caught, not taught.

If you want a child to have a positive personality, the child has to develop positive emotions and know how to handle negative ones. A child who witnesses love and caring is able to show those qualities. A child who is curious or courageous has developed these qualities because he or she was nourished in many ways.

As one parent noted, "For me, having a thoughtful child was very important, so I decided right away to look for ways to be thoughtful myself and to draw attention to my son's considerate actions. I've been rewarded by seeing him develop a quality I really wanted him to have."

Traits of Happy People
Parents naturally want to give their children the tools for lifelong happiness. Psychologists have determined that happy people share four traits: high self-esteem; a feeling of personal control; optimism; and extroversion (an outgoing personality). Another psychology professor has developed a list of suggestions that seem to reinforce those findings. These include: be productive at meaningful activities; develop a healthy social life; value close personal relationships; get organized; focus on the present; avoid negative emotions; be yourself; and stop worrying. **What are the experiences that have made you happy?**

Promoting Self-Esteem

Six-year-old Cameron could do no wrong. All the adults who influenced him sent him that message. Relatives took pride in everything Cameron did, no matter how little he tried. They put Cameron in the centre of their world and made him feel as though he was the best all the time. The adults wanted Cameron to feel good about himself, and he did. The problem? They overdid it.

Some research now shows that people who think too highly of themselves may develop problem behaviours. For one thing, they may become aggressive when someone criticizes them. After all, if a person like Cameron thinks that everything he does should be admired, he won't be pleased when admiration doesn't come.

What does this research say about building a child's sense of self-worth? Building *self-esteem*, the way people feel about themselves, has been promoted by authorities for a long time. Has that idea changed? With a common-sense approach, building self-esteem is still worthwhile in parenting.

GOING TO EXTREMES

Even good things can be carried to an extreme. You might be someone who likes chocolate bars and potato chips. These foods taste good, but what happens if you eat them too often? They threaten your health. Likewise, cough medicine offers relief when you're sick, but taking too much can be harmful.

Something similar can happen with self-esteem. A good sense of self-esteem promotes emotional health. Building self-esteem is an essential part of parenting. However, if adults build self-esteem in a child by overdoing the message that "You're the best," high self-esteem may not bring positive results.

NECESSARY FOR SUCCESS

To be successful, people need to have positive feelings about themselves and their abilities. The poet Virgil once said, "They can because they think they can." If one child doesn't believe she can learn to skate, she might not ever try. If another child thinks he isn't good enough to draw a picture, he may never pick up a paintbrush.

Internet Connects

http://www.mcgrawhill.ca/links/parenting
To learn more about raising children, go to the Web site above for *Parenting Rewards & Responsibilities, First Canadian Edition,* to see where to go next.

Children need to believe in themselves.
◆ **How can parents raise children who feel good about themselves without becoming self-centred?**

Children need to believe they are capable in order to try. Only when they try, can they eventually succeed. Parents who help children believe in themselves raise children who can accomplish things, sometimes even great things. This purpose is why self-esteem was encouraged in the first place.

WHAT PARENTS CAN DO

Now that the alarm has been sounded about pushing self-esteem too much, parents are wondering how to draw the line between promoting self-esteem and promoting self-centredness. Might society overreact in the opposite direction? Could parents become so afraid of raising self-focused children that they neglect self-esteem completely?

Certain dangers accompany overreacting. Children who feel inferior or worthless fear making decisions and taking responsibility. They dwell on their mistakes. Some withdraw in shyness or anger. Others try to prove their worth with acts of daring or aggression. They may lack the confidence to resist pressure from others to do the wrong things.

Parents don't want these results. They need to understand that they can build self-esteem without creating a "monster."

Focus on Other Traits Too

Self-esteem must function within the framework of other important qualities. Without love, understanding, caring, compassion, humility, respect, self-control, responsibility, and other positive traits, high self-esteem can backfire.

At age ten, Eddie was confident of his abilities and was becoming a leader. He was leading his friends to be bullies and destroy property. Eddie had a high opinion of himself, but he didn't have the full range of traits needed to make him an upstanding person.

With a can-do attitude, a child eagerly tries new things. These experiences build skills and interests that may later transfer to lifelong pleasures and pursuits. What will a child become in life? By giving encouragement, parents help a child move toward success.

Some people have high regard for themselves, but they haven't learned how to be good citizens. When parents teach their children to respect all people's rights, children are more likely to balance their own needs with those of others.

Offer Praise Appropriately

When handled carefully, praise and admiration are useful. These principles should be kept in mind:

♥ ***Keep praise under control.*** Too much praise builds conceit. Notice when Sean accomplishes something special instead of drawing attention to everything he does. Praise that is overdone sounds insincere.

♥ ***Mean what you say.*** Honest statements are the best. Tell Maggie that the colour she used for the umbrella in her picture is your favourite instead of saying that her picture is great or the best you've ever seen.

Correct Misbehaviour

In thinking about a child's self-esteem, some parents wonder about discipline. "Won't I hurt Nate's self-esteem if I discipline him?" one parent asked.

Avoiding appropriate discipline techniques is a serious mistake. Parents need to learn how to guide behaviour appropriately and then do so. A child who thinks he or she is above the rules won't learn how to behave responsibly.

Looking Critically at Praise

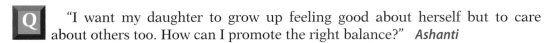

Q "I want my daughter to grow up feeling good about herself but to care about others too. How can I promote the right balance?" *Ashanti*

A You'll want to give praise sensibly, because overdoing it can backfire. If your daughter is showered with praise, she won't learn which actions are truly deserving. She may expect, but not get, the same recognition from teachers, friends, and other family members. If they don't offer as much praise, your daughter may become confused and even angry as she tries extra hard to get approval. She may focus too much on herself and too little on others. If your daughter thinks your praise isn't sincere, she may start to doubt your words. You won't want her to ignore what you say or lose faith in you, so you need to send sincere messages. Honest praise for specific actions will make your daughter feel good about herself while teaching her what kinds of behaviour people truly value.

Be Accepting

Parents can correct inappropriate behaviour and still show acceptance of the child. Parents who accept a child's personality, abilities, appearance, and gender provide a solid core for developing self-esteem. Feeling loved "as is" gives children a sense of security.

A parent must clearly communicate, "I love you no matter what, but you owe it to yourself to be your best. Not *the* best—*your* best." This message reinforces a child's sense of natural worth.

Stay Involved

Parents foster self-esteem by taking interest in the child's life and activities. As a preschooler, Lars was proud to see his "story" about Chipper the squirrel displayed on the refrigerator at home. He felt a sense of achievement when his father Klaus cheered his climb on the jungle gym.

When Klaus wanted to meet Lars' friends, Lars felt his father's caring.

Like Klaus, parents have chances everyday to get involved in a child's life. They might go to music recitals, take walks together, go on outings, or attend parent-teacher interviews. These actions show children that they are worth a parent's time, effort, and attention.

Teach Empathy

Has a one-year-old ever offered you a soggy teething biscuit? Limited by egocentric thinking, the child believes you will enjoy a half-eaten biscuit as much as he or she does. Would you grumble and toss the biscuit aside or accept it with enthusiasm and pretend to take a bite? "Sharing" this morsel shows you have **empathy**, the ability to understand another's feelings. Those who acquire this trait don't focus on themselves at the expense of others.

When parents are actively involved in their children's lives, the children know they care. ◆ **How can busy parents stay involved?**

To encourage empathy, parents need to remind young children that others have feelings like their own. Praise follows generous and supportive acts: "Abdul is happy that you gave him a turn on your tricycle. You were nice to share." A child's harmful actions should bring explanation: "You hurt Jim when you pulled his hair. Now he's crying. Remember how it hurt when Jill pulled your hair?"

Criticism must be sparing and constructive, used only to teach and not to hurt. Calling children "mean" doesn't show them how to be kind. Children learn to be empathetic when they see adults practising the trait.

They learn to believe that they are worthwhile beings, just as others are. That's what real self-esteem is all about.

Aiming for Independence

Emotionally healthy children are eager to become independent. Growing up, however, can be overwhelming at times. Children may briefly slip back into old ways, taking "breathers" on the road to maturity. Understanding parents encourage a child's efforts without pushing too fast.

STAGES OF INDEPENDENCE

The steps taken toward independence are sometimes predictable—and sometimes not. One child progresses at a different rate from others and may even seem utterly helpless one day and remarkably competent the next.

YOUNG CHILDREN. Toddlers and preschoolers waver between dependence and independence. Growing motor and intellectual skills spur them to do more for themselves. In the same way that teens look forward to driving, young children are excited by learning to walk. Both allow distancing from parents.

As children learn to do things for themselves, few qualities are as helpful to a parent as patience.
◆ **Why do you think this is true?**

Daily experiences, however, remind young children how much they still need parents. Self-doubt clouds the desire to grow up. Pierre got up early on his third birthday. After dressing himself in sweat pants and a T-shirt, he skillfully speared his waffle with a fork. The next day Pierre struggled with his shirt buttons and let his mother spread jam on his toast.

Not knowing their limits is another reason for contradictory behaviour. Shopping with her father, Gina pushed a toy cart full of groceries up and down the aisles. Tired by her activity, she cried to be carried the short walk to the bus stop.

OLDER CHILDREN. School-age children have mastered most personal care skills. Their feelings of independence come from physical feats—riding a bicycle or running races—and from success in school activities. Lack of success can lead to feelings of inferiority, especially as children in school compare their abilities to those of classmates. If parents show concern, the sense of failure deepens.

ENCOURAGING INDEPENDENCE

The drive for independence is natural, yet independence doesn't come naturally. As the material on pages 340–341 illustrates, parents promote independence by creating an environment that encourages a child to practise skills and try new things.

This process is a growth experience for parents as well. In teaching children to overcome a lifelong habit of dependence, parents themselves must overcome an equally long habit of authority. Children only learn responsibility as parents gradually let them assume it.

If children learn to make small decisions, someday they'll be better able to make big ones. Parents can guide decisions at first as children practise what they learn.

Helping Children with Stress

You might think that the life of a child is stress-free, but it's not. The simple process of growing up can be difficult for children. The years are filled with change, and change can be stressful. Learning to make friends, and sometimes losing them, is a typical, but stressful childhood experience. Such events as a move or the first day of school can create anxiety.

Leading a Child *toward* Independence

Getting "bigger" is the dream of every child. They yearn to do things on their own, to be independent. Step-by-step, parents lead children toward their dream, using ideas like the ones suggested here.

Designed for Success

A child needs an environment where success is possible. You can provide age-appropriate toys and low shelves for storage. Choose clothing and equipment that promote self-dressing and self-feeding.

I Can Do It!

Children are eager to try. Teach them the skills they need, but let them practise and learn on their own. You can say "Try holding the crayon like this" or "I'll make the front part of the "B" and you can draw the straight back."

Patience Counts

What's easy for you can be difficult for a child. Resist the urge to do things for the child. Allow time for dressing, eating, and bathing to give the child a chance for success.

What Do You Think?

Asking children for their opinion encourages them to reason and solve problems. You could say "Where does this puzzle piece go?" or "Which goes on first, your shoes or your pants?"

You Can Do It!

When you believe in children, they learn to believe in themselves. Instead of criticizing failure, slowness, or clumsiness, tell them what a good effort they made. Whether successful or not, the child can be instilled with a spirit to "try and try again."

Thinking Like a Parent

How would you advise these parents?

1. Calvin: "With my schedule, I can't wait for my three-year-old to dress herself to go somewhere."

2. Louis: "My four-year-old is afraid to try things. I often have to do things for him because he won't try."

3. Holly: "My friends say I overprotect my four-year-old. I worry about safety, and I'm just not sure what I can allow her to do."

In troubled families, children sense the difficulties. They may be stressed by divorce, financial problems, or anything that causes tension among family members.

Not all stress is harmful. Some activities produce positive stress. Excitement at learning to swim, for example, can give children extra incentive to succeed. On the other hand, uncontrolled, negative stress can cause problems. When parents recognize signs of stress in children, they should take action to ease the situation.

What Parents Can Do

Children may not understand stress, but with a parent's help, they can manage it. Knowing what a child is feeling isn't always easy. An observant parent notices when something is wrong and encourages conversation. "You seem unhappy about your day at Aunt Sheila's. What do you think of her new puppy?" What a parent hears can give clues about events and how to respond.

Children sometimes think they are responsible for family problems. Hearing parents talk about financial or other troubles can create concerns in a child. A parent should be honest about difficulties and offer reassurance. "When Daddy and I were talking last night, it wasn't about anything that you've done. We're worried about paying for a new refrigerator, but we'll work it out."

Stress can also surface when children feel too much pressure from parents. Parents need to evaluate their own approach. Are their expectations reasonable or do they expect their child to be too perfect or too skilled? Children need to be challenged but not beyond their capabilities.

Parents can teach children to manage stress. Physical activity releases tension. Listening to favourite songs or working at

Spotlight On
Signs of Stress

Since young children don't know what stress is and how to manage it, parents must watch for these warning signs in order to provide help:

- ✔ Behaviour problems, including bed-wetting, overeating, undereating, and stuttering.
- ✔ Physical complaints, including headache, stomach ache, neck pain, and asthma.
- ✔ Cruelty to pets or people.
- ✔ Self-critical remarks.
- ✔ Nervousness, fear of sudden noises, or anxiety with no apparent cause.
- ✔ Lying or stealing.
- ✔ Nervous habits, including nail-biting, thumb-sucking, teeth-grinding, and hair-twisting.
- ✔ Unusual shyness.
- ✔ Poor sleeping habits or nightmares.
- ✔ Explosive crying or screaming.

a hobby can distract children from their worries. Some children enjoy playing in a warm bath. Others feel better after expressing their feelings through drawings or in a journal. Parents can take dictation for younger children. Reading stories about a child facing a similar, stressful event can also help.

Self-confidence is a good defense against stress. Parents bolster self-confidence by finding tasks that make children successful.

Although stressed children often have trouble eating or sleeping, a nutritious diet and adequate sleep help prevent stress and reduce its symptoms.

DEALING WITH DEPRESSION IN CHILDREN

Children as young as preschool age have been diagnosed with depression. Depression in children may result from unrelieved stress or the conditions that cause stress. Physical causes are also possible.

Depressed children lack energy. They lose interest in school, grooming, friendships, and activities they once enjoyed. They have trouble making decisions and may cry or grow angry for no apparent reason. Eating or sleeping too much or too little is another sign.

Children showing these signs should be taken to a family doctor. If depression is diagnosed, the doctor can refer parents to a specialist.

While most cases of childhood depression eventually disappear by themselves, the psychological damage can be long-lasting. Parents should seek treatment for depression just as they would any other childhood illness.

Children want someone to listen to them. A child's stress may disappear, and even turn into a positive moment, when an adult values a child's concerns enough to talk about them.

Looking Back

♥ As children grow, they are capable of greater emotional control.

♥ A parent's response to a child's emotions influences emotional growth.

♥ Parents model appropriate ways to express positive emotions.

♥ To help children manage anger, parents avoid frustrating situations and give children strategies for expressing angry feelings.

♥ Children overcome fears with reassurance, explanations, and a degree of indulgence.

♥ Erikson's theory of personality development helps parents understand emotional growth.

♥ Parents guide children to gain self-esteem that is based on genuine positive qualities.

♥ A parent promotes independence by urging, and allowing, children to do more for themselves.

♥ Parents must be alert to signs of stress and depression in children and give them ways to manage their feelings.

Knowledge and Understanding

1. Briefly describe emotional development from toddlerhood to the teen years.
2. Why do children need affection?
3. Suggest ways to minimize a temper tantrum.
4. How can a parent keep fears from troubling a young child?
5. How can Erikson's theory of personality development help parents promote emotional growth?
6. How should parents try to build self-esteem in children? Explain your reasoning.
7. To praise a child appropriately, what do you need to know?
8. How are empathy and other positive traits related to self-esteem?
9. How can parents help children move toward independence?
10. How can you recognize stress in children?
11. What activities would you suggest for a child who is feeling stress?

Review

Thinking and Inquiry

12. Last week, Roland let Sudi, age three, watch a movie about an invasion by aliens from outer space. Now the preschooler is afraid of loud noises and street lights. How do you explain Sudi's fears? Why, at his age, might he easily develop such fears?

13. If the parents in your neighbourhood failed to promote good emotional development in their children, what impact might this eventually have on you?

14. If you were a parent and could choose three specific personality traits to have in your child, what would they be and why?

Communication

15. Using a foreign language dictionary, try to express a common need, such as, "I'm hungry" or "I need to use the bathroom" in that language. Compare your feelings after this exercise to a toddler's feelings at trying to express similar ideas.

16. Do you agree that the teen years are "a second toddlerhood"? Complete a Venn diagram showing the similarities and differences between the two.

17. Imagine you have a ten-year-old son who enjoys needle crafts. Recently, however, he seems to have lost interest in the hobby. When you ask about it, he says that some of his classmates make fun of him for liking "girl stuff." How do you encourage him to continue developing a talent and pursuing his interests despite peer pressure?

Application

18. In small groups, discuss fears you or someone you know experienced as a child. Suggest parental strategies for handling a similar fear.

19. With a partner, act out one of the following parenting situations: handling a toddler's tantrum; helping a toddler learn to put on shoes; discussing a fear with a preschooler; discussing a freedom or restriction with a ten-year-old. Afterward, ask classmates to comment on the "parent's" skill in responding to the "child."

Helping Children Relate to Others

CHAPTER EXPECTATIONS

While reading this chapter, you will:

▶ Identify the changes in social and emotional development that take place in young children.

▶ Analyse behaviours, conditions, and environments that influence positive or negative development.

▶ Explain the role of parents and family members in teaching children socially acceptable behaviour.

▶ Compare and contrast cultural expectations for male and female children.

▶ Identify the role of societal agents in teaching young children how to live in society.

▶ Demonstrate an understanding of various social concerns that parents face as their children approach school age.

KEY TERMS

co-operative play
parallel play
peer pressure
peers
prejudice

separation anxiety
sibling rivalry
socialization
stereotype

Andrew heard his daughter returning to her room after brushing her teeth. He quickly propped Marci's favourite doll in a chair. He'd been worried about Marci's loneliness at Elmwood Child Centre.

As she climbed into bed, Marci noticed her doll wasn't in the usual place. "Why is Carly sitting there tonight?"

"Why, I don't know." Andrew acted surprised. "She looks kind of lonely, though." Marci looked down, saying nothing.

Andrew went on. "Maybe she needs a friend." Marci raised her eyes uncertainly to her father. "Maybe."

"Well, what could she do?" Andrew asked. "Would Carly feel brave enough to talk to the other dolls if she wore a special ribbon in her hair? Or what if she showed the other dolls the picture of the giant pumpkin we grew last fall? They might like to see that."

Marci grew excited. "Or what if Carly gave some pumpkin bread to the other dolls to taste? Like a boy at school brought cider for everyone to try."

"That's a great idea." Andrew smiled. "I'll bet we can think of lots of ways for Carly to make friends." As he tucked Marci in, Andrew was pleased to see a brighter smile than he'd seen in days.

---◆---

What do you think? How else might Andrew have responded to Marci's shyness?

Parents want their children to be able to handle all kinds of social situations.
◆ **How might an airplane trip, and other kinds of travel, test a child's social skills?**

Problem Prevention

"I feel like a square peg that won't fit into a round hole." With these words, Kyle echoed a sentiment felt by many at one time or another. Feeling socially uncomfortable can be a minor problem, but for many, social discomfort is a regular experience.

Walking into a crowded room of strangers may be the most difficult social problem some people have. For others, having few or no friends or not getting along with family causes greater concerns. People who can't hold a job or who get in trouble with the law face serious consequences in society. Social difficulties are often intertwined with emotional problems; thus, solving them can be complicated.

Parents and other caregivers face the challenging task of raising children who relate well to others. They want children to become socially well-adjusted in order to live full and happy lives. Parents who understand what that takes are a real asset in society.

The Socialization Process

Have you ever been impressed by a well-mannered child in a restaurant? If so, you were noticing a child who appeared well socialized. Through **socialization,** people gain attitudes, beliefs, and behaviour patterns accepted in society. They use these to get along well with others.

Socialization begins in infancy. Infants and young children repeat social behaviours that are rewarding. If reaching out to a parent results in being cuddled, the baby wants to reach out again later. The baby learns that parents, and other people, are worth reaching out to.

Children learn socialization in other ways as well. Often they imitate. If big brother says "goodbye" to departing relatives, little sister may do the same.

Some lessons are taught directly. Reminding a toddler to "say thank you" is an example. Social lessons are also learned as parents approve or disapprove a child's actions. Parents who guide behaviour skillfully can inspire a child to do what is expected.

As children grow, they need greater social skills. If they are to get along with classmates, friends, teachers, and neighbours, they have principles of behaviour to learn. They also learn the rules that groups outside the family use, whether on a team or in an organization.

Older children begin to understand what society expects. They learn respect for the rules that protect people, property, and the environment. They learn values that govern behaviour. When taught honesty, for example, children learn not to take what doesn't belong to them. Children may need to be reminded occasionally how their behaviour affects others.

Relating to Family Members

If a child doesn't learn to get along within the family, getting along in the outside world will be difficult. As you can see, that makes early social lessons learned in the family very important.

Internet Connects

http://www.mcgrawhill.ca/links/parenting
To learn more about raising children, go to the Web site above for *Parenting Rewards & Responsibilities, First Canadian Edition,* to see where to go next.

By showing appreciation for his mother, Conrad learns to demonstrate his respect and concern for others. This social skill will be useful to him throughout his life.

PARENTS

From day one in a child's life, parents are building a relationship with the child. As a parent, the relationship you have with your child will be what you make of it. Young children are learning, not leading, as the parent-child relationship develops. You have to begin early to make that relationship strong.

As children grow, they develop minds of their own. Some even face outside influences that can turn them away from families. If parents build a solid relationship with children, however, the children will have something they value. They will want parental support and return to the comfort of family even if they stray at times.

How can parents build the kind of relationship that children want to share? Much of this text is about doing just that. Parents who follow the ideas you are studying have a good chance of relating well to their children. They have a good chance of raising children who transfer the characteristics of a strong parent-child bond to other relationships in life.

Overcoming Separation Anxiety

When children are very young, they feel closely linked to parents. Their first realization that parents have to be away from them at times can produce what is called **separation anxiety**. This is the stress an infant or toddler feels when separated from familiar people, usually parents.

Separation anxiety generally occurs around the first birthday. Children at that age have little concept of time. They don't know when the parent will return or why they must separate. Children react with crying, anger, or withdrawal. Some seem to "punish" the parent by acting indifferent when they are reunited.

Separation anxiety is a stage that passes in a few months. Meanwhile, parents can take these steps to make parting less painful:

♥ *Avoid leaving when the child is asleep or distracted.* If this is not practical, the child should be told in advance what will happen.

♥ *Discuss the separation matter-of-factly.* Even before a child can talk, a parent can say, "I know you don't want me to go. I love you and I'll be back. You'll be fine." Children don't need long explanations, just short statements.

New experiences and stress can renew a child's fears about being separated from parents. For example, going to school can be frightening. ◆ **What would you say to a worried child?**

- ♥ **Spend time together before leaving.** This reassures the child and makes parting feel less like abandonment.

- ♥ **Involve the child in an interesting activity.** Returning to the activity after the parent leaves occupies the child's mind.

- ♥ **Leave quickly, with a smile and a wave goodbye.** Lingering indicates a parent's own separation anxiety.

SIBLINGS

Through interaction with siblings, children learn many social lessons. Parents guide these lessons.

Siblings who are close in age act as a child's first **peers**, individuals of similar age or status. Siblings may teach each other as much about relating to others as parents do.

Parents should try to let siblings themselves decide the nature of their relationship. Forcing a child into a certain role may cause resentment. Siblings should be encouraged to play and work together, yet be allowed to have personal friends, interests, and possessions. Balancing togetherness with "breathing room" is vital to building healthy relationships.

Responding to Sibling Conflict

Most siblings truly care for each other, yet they do "act like children." They bicker and have disputes. Some siblings tattle on each other in order to look good by comparison in a parent's eyes. Parents should be sure to give all children enough positive attention, so they don't seek it at a sibling's expense.

Teasing is common among siblings. Some is good-humoured, but cruel teasing damages the self-esteem of its target. Telling a child, "I get upset when you tease

your sister. Explain to me why you do it," can lead the child to recognize the sibling's hurt and anger. Parents might uncover a deeper conflict.

Sometimes too much closeness is a problem. Four-year-old Meg was her six-year-old sister's biggest fan. She imitated Diana and tried to include herself in her older sister's activities. Their father explained to Meg, "Diana wants to be alone or with her friends sometimes." He reminded Diana, "Please try to include Meg sometimes." He let the girls know he enjoyed seeing them play together.

Handling Sibling Rivalry

At the park, Paul climbed to the top of the slide. His sister Ruthie then scrambled to the top of the jungle gym. They argued about who would sit in the front seat of the car. At dinner, Ruthie asked why Paul got two scoops of potatoes and she got one.

Paul and Ruthie had an intense **sibling rivalry**, the competition among brothers and sisters for parental attention. Sibling rivals are grasping for a parent's love as well as status in the family. Sibling rivalry occurs most heavily in preschoolers and younger school-age children. Typically, rivalries slowly fade as each child develops outside interests and a surer sense of identity.

A degree of sibling rivalry can be expected. However, parents may unintentionally reinforce rivalry among children. They use "friendly" competition, challenging, "Can you get ready for bed before your brother?" Some parents openly compare or label siblings, remarking, "Navjo is so graceful, but Hasan is the brains of the family." Other parents try to deny children their feelings. They might tell a jealous sibling, "You should be happy for Zach. He works hard to get good grades." What comments would be better for parents to make?

Parents may try to prevent sibling rivalry by treating each child alike. "One-size-fits-all" parenting doesn't take the special qualities of each child into account. Children are inclined to keep track of each favour and penalty.

Parents can reduce sibling rivalry by realizing that each child is an individual. A parent should treat children fairly, not equally, and be sure they understand that. "I've spent more time with Jenna this week," a parent explained. "She's having trouble at school and needs me. When you were sick, I was there for you."

Parenting Q & A

When To Step In

Q "I want my children to learn to settle their own disagreements. How do I know when to step in?" *Cameron*

A Children need to learn positive ways to settle disputes. You'll need to teach them how to express feelings and reach agreement. These lessons should begin when children are young. As children grow, they need to test their skills on their own, so when do you intervene? Before stepping in, give your children a chance to settle a problem alone. Step in only when you must. A feud that turns physical, of course, calls for preventing injury. With young children, notice when "suggestions" may be helpful. Older children should be better able to manage disputes. If you try to figure out who's "right," you may be wrong, which can lead to resentment. When you insist on using communication and conflict-resolution skills, children will discover that they don't have to turn to you every time they have a problem.

Siblings may still become rivals. A parent must then accept a child's feelings, yet affirm that those fears are unfounded: "I know it's hard to hear people say how smart Zach is, but I don't love him any more, or you any less. You're both special."

Managing Multiples

Promoting individuality is a special concern for parents of twins, triplets, and other "multiples." An action as simple as using each child's name rather than referring to them as "the twins" or "the triplets" encourages the siblings to establish their own identities. These ways to encourage uniqueness in multiples can also be applied to any siblings:

♥ **Offer children different choices for clothing and hairstyles.** If children choose to dress alike, a parent might suggest, but not insist on, different coloured socks or backpacks.

♥ **Provide separate toys and possessions for each child.** Multiples need personal items as much as other siblings do.

♥ **Encourage each child's interests.** More than other siblings, multiples may need "permission" to be different.

♥ **Spend time with each child alone.** This tells the child that he or she is valued as an individual. The child is more free to express personal feelings and pursue personal interests, as opposed to accepting the "majority opinion" of the siblings.

♥ **Try to have children assigned to separate classrooms or child care groups.** Toddlers may need the siblings' companionship, but older children can benefit from a chance to make their own friends and assert their own personality.

Multiple births present special challenges for parents—both in managing daily life and in promoting the children's individuality.

OTHER RELATIVES

Members of the extended family in a child's life can bridge the gap between immediate family and the outside world. Many more social lessons can be learned. Cousins may become as close as brothers and sisters, especially if a child has no siblings close in age. Aunts and uncles are caring, familiar faces who are authority figures, yet different from teachers and other adults children meet.

Grandparents, too, offer children a special relationship. They are a link to the past that shaped the parent's life. Hearing a grandparent tell of "the old days" when the parent was a child can deepen a child's sense of family. Some grandparents have time for leisure activities with children.

Also valuable are a grandparent's personal qualities. As parents themselves, grandparents are often patient and understanding. They may be less demanding and more accepting, inspiring a special trust in children. A child can admit fears and mistakes to a grandparent without facing parental judgment or discipline.

Spending time with aging grandparents has the added benefit of giving a realistic view of older adults. Children learn to respect an older family member's wisdom and stamina. They learn close-up what aging is like.

When extended family members live far apart, maintaining relationships takes extra effort. Parents should suggest children communicate with letters, thank-you notes, phone calls, or e-mail. They can display photos of relatives and gifts from them. A parent could ask, "Do you want to wear the shirt Grandpa gave you?"

Internet Connects

http://www.mcgrawhill.ca/links/parenting
To learn more about parenting, go to the Web site above for *Parenting Rewards & Responsibilities, First Canadian Edition,* to see where to go next.

Relating to Other Children

Children like and need the company of other children. They grow socially by interacting with peers. Parents promote development by allowing children to play together. Early childhood schools offer ready-made social experiences. Parents can also take children to playgrounds or set up informal play groups.

PATTERNS OF SOCIAL GROWTH

Like physical growth, most children follow a pattern of social growth. While allowing for individual differences, parents can expect to see certain behaviours as children learn to relate to others.

You often see toddlers in parallel play. They like having company, but they don't yet have the skills or interest needed for playing together.

Gender Identity

Around age two, children become aware of the two different genders. By preschool age, they know their own. Children learn male and female roles by watching family members.

Parents should encourage a child to develop interests and abilities regardless of gender. Both boys and girls can develop physical skills through active play. Both can learn to express emotions and give and receive love. Both can learn to compete. When parents provide toys and books that show men and women in both traditional and non-traditional professions and activities, children realize that gender can be broadly defined.

Toddlers

True to nature, toddlers are in a social transition. They enjoy being around other toddlers as they watch and imitate.

At the same time, toddlers don't interact with each other. They don't share. A toy belongs to the one who is bold enough to claim it and hold onto it. Large groups overwhelm toddlers. Two or three are enough for a play group. Even then, two toddlers may have friction because they are unable to talk things over. This lack of social skills limits toddlers to **parallel play**, playing beside, but not with, each other.

By age four, most children have the language and social skills needed for **co-operative play**, playing together at agreed-upon activities. Preschoolers might build a fort or play "house." Also, as temperament and personality become better defined, preschoolers learn to adapt to each other. When they draw pictures together, Mallory finds the whole crayons, while Britney is content to use broken stubs.

Preschoolers begin to experience friendship, although they don't fully appreciate the

Co-operative play is a good way to broaden a child's perspective of gender roles.

concept. They talk a great deal about friends. The idea of having friends is so appealing, preschoolers may even have imaginary ones.

School-Age Children

Five- and six-year-olds are outgoing and talkative. They play well in groups of four or five, and at more socially complicated games. They may play team sports, but they are not "team players." Personal success matters the most.

School-age children value peer approval. Relationships become exclusive and inclusive. Some peers are chosen as friends, and others rejected. Friendships are closer, longer-lasting, and usually between children of the same gender. A small group may organize as a club. The club may act as a micro-society, as children try out various social roles: leader, follower, peacemaker, or individualist.

LESSONS IN FRIENDSHIP

Forming and maintaining healthy friendships is a learned process. A child must be taught basic social skills in order to become a good friend to others.

Taking Turns

Waiting in the cafeteria line, you probably don't congratulate yourself on practising an important social skill. Taking turns, so basic to you, is at first incomprehensible to a toddler.

Janet helped her son learn this skill while reading to him. She turned one page, then let Tim turn the next. They took turns with puzzle pieces and picking up toys. Like most children, Tim was not consistent about taking turns until he was about three. Janet found that using a timer helped Tim wait for his turn.

Sharing

Sharing is more socially taxing than taking turns. It takes generosity, empathy, and a sense of fair play to willingly let another person enjoy something that belongs to you.

Toddlers are often confused about the concept of ownership. Three-year-old Ben sees that "his" plate is "his" only for as long as he eats from it; therefore, he may think his toys are his only for as long as he plays with them. If he lets Chantel use them, they become hers. His confusion is confirmed at child care, where materials are for all children to use.

To help Ben learn that his possessions are his permanently, his parents label his toys and clothes with his name and provide special places to store them. His toys have their own shelf. His clothes go in his closet.

Children learn to share when parents help them feel good about it. Ben's father told him, "I like the way you share your ball with Chantel." Earning adult approval made him feel proud. Children who feel secure share more easily, even voluntarily.

Sharing is easier in small groups where children know each other.

Children learn gradually to be generous. As a young child, Lauren might offer her friend a banana simply because she doesn't like bananas herself. Later, when she sees that her friend enjoys the fruit, she discovers that sharing feels good.

Raising Children With Character

A Moment of Sharing

Five-year-old Jason stared thoughtfully at his dinner plate as he listened to the adults around the table. "The house was a complete loss," his grandfather was saying. "The Sanfords lost everything. Becky said Pauline even dropped the doll she was playing with when the fire broke out."

As the conversation drifted to other subjects, Jason slipped from his chair. A few minutes later he was back. "Here." He set a small bank shaped like a baseball before his grandfather. "I want to give this to Pauline to buy a new doll."

"Well . . ." Grandpa Riley began. He noted a brief nod from Jason's mother. "Why, thank you, Jason. This will make Pauline very happy. What a fine thing to do." Grandpa Riley wrapped Jason in a loving hug. He and Jason's mother exchanged a proud smile.

◆◆◆◆◆ Thinking It Over ◆◆◆◆◆

1. How do you think Jason felt at his grandfather's response?
2. Suppose Grandpa Riley had said: "That's not enough money to help" or "That's nice, Jason, but don't worry about it." How could such an attitude affect Jason now and in the future?

Parents should allow some compromises in sharing. They might let a child decide what to share. When Ben invited Brian over, his father told him, "Brian will want to play with your toys." Ben said, "He can play with my truck, but not my robot." His father agreed. "We'll put your robot away while Brian is here."

Similarly, parents should respect a child's feelings about giving away or passing on a certain toy to a sibling. The child should decide when to give up the toy.

Popularity

As children grow aware of similarities and differences, they grow more selective about friends. They choose to play with one child and not with another.

Young children like those who are likable. A child who is often excluded may be disruptive or bossy. A shy child may be forgotten more than rejected. Parents can help these children learn to make friends. A child with esteem problems may use attention-getting behaviour. Such children need to learn to value themselves.

Some children have talents or personality traits that mark them as different. Peers may misunderstand a very creative or sensitive child. Such a child will likely find friends among peers with common interests. Some community organizations, including libraries, museums, and the YWCA, have children's groups.

Some children seem happy to be alone and make no effort at friendship. Parents should make sure the child has the social skills needed to be accepted by others. Socially competent children are comfortable in a group or by themselves.

Sometimes parents notice their own child reject another. Parents should find out why their child isn't interested in the newcomer. They can help the children find common interests that may bring them together.

Fortunately for children who have problems with popularity, childhood loyalties are very changeable. Parents should help them practise friendship skills and praise their good qualities.

Handling Peer Pressure

Although not everyone feels the pressure to "fit in" with others, most do. People typically look for an accepting friend or a circle of friends where they can belong. What do people have to do to fit in? Do common interests, attitudes, clothing, or appearance make the difference? The answer to that question is complicated.

For children, even into adolescence and beyond, **peer pressure** influences fitting in. This pressure is the strong influence that others of a similar age apply. The pressure may be subtle or obvious.

Health & Safety

BULLIES AND THE BULLIED

Although bullies have been around for years, there seem to be more of them these days, and they are more aggressive than ever. Bullies tease, threaten, and punch other children. They put their own feelings of inferiority and insecurity on display by trying to gain power over other children. They will hurt and humiliate in hopes of getting attention, even for misdeeds.

Parents need to help children who behave as bullies as well as those who are on the receiving end of a bully's aggression. An insecure child who bullies needs love, encouragement, and understanding, but must also be held accountable for mistreating others. Bullies must learn empathy in order to understand how their actions feel to others.

Usually the best advice to give a child who is being bullied is to walk away from taunts or cruel words. Given the rise in youth violence, children need instructions on how to report problems. Children should feel that parents are willing to listen to their concerns and support them. Parents can join educators and other adults to find ways to turn the bullying problem around.

Responding to peer pressure, a child follows others to avoid feeling different. Peer pressure can be positive, encouraging children to be in a school play, for instance. It can also be troublesome, as when a child begs for a brand of running shoe because "all the kids wear them." Peer pressure can lead to dangerous behaviour as well.

Parents who help children develop a secure self-identity and healthy self-esteem give them valuable tools for resisting negative peer pressure. As children grow older, parents can help them develop firm values and belief in their judgment. More about helping children resist peer pressure can be found in Chapter 23.

In many instances, peer pressure is harmless. Buying a lunch box with popular cartoon characters doesn't hurt a child. However, parents should think about the message they send by constantly giving in to peer pressure. Children need a sense of belonging, but parents must weigh children's desire to please others with the parent's desire to teach them to think for themselves.

CO-OPERATIVE AND COMPETITIVE GAMES

Around age four, children are ready for co-operative games in which players work together toward a common goal. Each child has a chance to succeed with a minimum of pressure. For example, everyone wins when a group of children keep a large balloon afloat.

The same is true of co-operative learning activities in the classroom. The group succeeds by listening, sharing, encouraging, and resolving conflict. A child needs these skills for successful relationships at home and later, on the job.

By age six, children are more competitive. They like simple activities, such as board games and running races, where they can win.

For children, the pressure to go along with friends can easily override knowledge that the action is wrong.
◆ **What challenges do parents have in such situations?**

Many people have mixed feelings about the social value of competitive activities for children. Competition does help children identify special talents. Those who try their best tend to be rewarded. Team competitions can be as effective as co-operative games at teaching teamwork and leadership skills. Children learn how to be gracious in victory and defeat alike. Also, competition is a part of adult life for which children must be prepared. Losing is not easy.

However, competition promotes division. Winning may depend as much on one child's failure as on another child's skill. Drawing attention to a lack of talent is unfair and damaging to children who are still trying to develop their abilities.

Parents might want to evaluate each competitive situation before allowing their child to participate. They might ask themselves: Is my child, at this age, ready to compete? Is the competition fair, with rewards based on actual performance?

Managing Competition

All children eventually face competition. Parents need to model a healthy attitude toward winning and losing, as part of an overall attitude toward success and failure. They can admit their own defeats, without blaming others, and point out what they learned. From this example children see that everyone fails, even parents, yet they try again. People need not be perfect to be loved.

Similarly, parents should model humility in success. They should share credit for their achievements and avoid criticizing those who didn't fare as well.

The senstive parent is also careful when observing competitive games. Shouts from the sidelines should offer positive support for all players, rather than anger or frustration over mistakes.

These children are rightly proud of their team's success. In the quest for victory, however, this familiar saying is sometimes forgotten: "It's not whether you win or lose, it's how you play the game." ◆ **What can parents do to help a child put winning in perspective?**

Dealing with Diversity

As children spend more time in activities outside the home, their relationships expand beyond the family. Eventually they meet people who do not look, speak, or hold the same beliefs as they do. If parents help children appreciate the differences they find, children will find they can get along better with all kinds of people.

APPRECIATING DIFFERENCES

Around age four or five, children use physical differences to help define themselves. Preschoolers also notice differences in abilities and personalities. Joel sees that his skin is darker than Rosa's, and Rosa's skin is darker than Anita's. Rosa is talkative, while Anita draws well. Rosa uses a hearing aid; he and Anita do not.

Children note differences outside their peer group too. In movies and in malls, they see people from a range of cultural groups and with varying physical abilities. Young children tend to accept such differences as matter of fact. They do not feel one quality is better than another—until someone tells them otherwise. To help children continue to appreciate diversity, a parent can:

♥ Introduce a child to differences from an early age. Many children's books and videos feature diverse characters. Art exhibits and ethnic neighbourhoods celebrate the richness of diversity. Parents might consider cultural diversity when choosing child care or forming a play group.

Young children easily accept the differences in people.
◆ **Why does that sometimes change as they grow older?**

♥ Discuss and answer a child's questions about differences, giving facts as requested. People use a wheelchair because their legs don't work. They may have hurt their legs in an accident. Explanations should be free of judgment. A person who has Down syndrome doesn't necessarily suffer from it.

♥ Discuss ways that people with differences are also alike. All people feel the same emotions. They all eat, whether it is beans and rice or bread and borscht. They observe holidays and holy days, some with similar meanings though different dates. They tell jokes in different languages, but all laugh at humour.

Avoiding Stereotypes

A **stereotype** is a standardized mental picture of a group of people. Stereotypes are unfair. They presume that all individuals who share one characteristic are the same in other ways. Even positive stereotypes may be a problem, since they encourage people to make generalizations about others before they get to know them.

Parents must teach a child to reject stereotypes by stressing that each person is unique. You cannot know someone based on one quality. Parents can remind children how people they know defy a stereotype: "Some people say older people are grouchy. Grandma Clark is older, and you have a lot of fun together."

Combating Prejudice

"I never even tried sour cream until I was an adult. It just sounded like something I wouldn't want to eat. Now I love it on a baked potato." With these words, Tyrone talked about **prejudice**, a negative opinion or feeling formed beforehand and without knowledge. The word prejudice comes from the word "prejudge," to pass judgment before learning all the facts.

Getting to know people as individuals helps prevent prejudice. Two children who like each other because of what they are on the inside don't even care about the outside.

People form prejudices against others, often because they believe negative stereotypes about them. Prejudice thrives where diversity is feared. Prejudice is unfair. Judgments should be based on facts. Sometimes you have to look very carefully to discover what the facts really are.

Sadly, children learn to hate as surely as they learn to love. Prejudice seeded in toddlerhood may be firmly rooted in a five-year-old and flourishing by age nine.

Parents need to take a vocal stand against prejudice, starting with their own attitudes and behaviours. Do they treat all people fairly and with respect? Do they ask friends and family to avoid promoting stereotypes around their child?

Many countries, such as Canada, are increasingly multicultural. Children need to accept classmates of various racial, ethnic, and religious backgrounds as social equals. Parents should encourage a child to examine all the evidence before judging a person or cultural practice.

Learning Other Social Skills

Jake recalled: "When my son Adam got into fights, I thought, 'Kids will be kids. I was the same way at his age.' But the world is different now. You have to raise kids to be kind. I'm teaching that to Adam."

Like Jake, many parents see the value in teaching children more than basic social skills. Some parents hope to reverse the trend toward youthful crime. Others want to cultivate their child's sense of caring. To these parents, letting children learn social skills by trial-and-error is like giving them books and hoping they learn to read. Building positive relationships is too important to be left to chance.

CONFLICT RESOLUTION

A single swing remained in the play yard. Shannon reached it first, but Seth hopped aboard and shoved his classmate aside. Shannon shrieked and pushed Seth off. The fight was on.

Children don't know how to settle disputes. You can help them learn by staying calm yourself and providing guidance. ◆ **What is this mother doing to help her communicate better with the two small children?**

Conflicts like this one occur every day, but a fight is not inevitable. Seth's mother, Pam, helped the children use the conflict-resolution process to settle their disagreement. As she coached them, Pam spoke calmly and respectfully, listening to each child. She let them take the lead when possible. Pam's goal was to give Shannon and Seth experience in resolving conflicts by having them:

1. *Identify the problem.* Amid their shouts and accusations, Pam helped Shannon and Seth focus objectively and agree on the reason for the conflict: "So you both want to use the swing. Is that right?"

2. *Suggest possible solutions.* Pam listened to every answer, from "You can ask Jeremy to let you use his swing" to "I want to fight. I was winning."

3. *Evaluate each suggestion.* She tried to help the children see the outcome of each alternative. "You could keep fighting," she agreed, "but then neither of you would get to swing."

4. *Choose the best solution.* Pam guided Shannon and Seth to agree to one of the acceptable suggestions. They decided to swing for five minutes each, with Pam timing them.

5. *Check if the solution was working.* Later, Pam asked the children, "Did you like the way you shared the swing? Do you want to try something else if this happens again?"

6. *Avoid a fight.* Pam told the children that they might not always come to an agreement. "It's better to walk away than to fight," she said. "Someday you might work it out."

TEACHING MANNERS

Consideration for others is the heart of good manners, or etiquette. All people feel more at ease when they know the right things to do. Teaching children good manners is a favour to them and to those around them. When teaching a child etiquette, parents should remember to:

♥ *Explain the reason for a rule of etiquette.* Knowing how an action shows respect for others' feelings helps children appreciate positive social behaviour.

Using good manners shows that you care about others. Children learn about courtesy through relatives—in several ways. ◆ **How will a parent's treatment of relatives affect the child's actions and attitude?**

♥ *Set age-appropriate expectations.* Being polite is enough for a young child. Preschoolers can't manage several utensils at one meal; they *can* manage chewing with their mouths closed. A seven-year-old should learn to make introductions and later learn the proper order for making them.

♥ *Let a child master one skill before introducing another.* Children might first learn when to say "please" and "thank you." Later they can learn when to say "excuse me" and "I'm sorry."

♥ *Practise in real life and in make believe.* If you want a child to learn to use a salad fork, you serve a salad and provide the utensil. Making a phone call can easily be part of pretend play with children.

♥ *Acknowledge a child's efforts.* Parents should notice and thank a child for showing kindness. Children lose heart at constant corrections and reminders.

♥ *Set a good example.* Parents should treat their child with courtesy, and let the child see them using good manners themselves.

KINDNESS TO ANIMALS

Teaching kindness toward animals is more than a safety precaution. Pets are often social "starter kits." Children who learn respect and empathy for animals transfer those feelings to people. A child who learns to take care of a pet can learn responsibility and love for other living things.

Cruelty to people in adult life often begins as cruelty to animals as a child. Parents need to take such behaviour very seriously. Children who abuse animals may need counselling in order to solve problems that might worsen.

Children learn many lessons through pets. Becca learns about responsibility as she feeds her puppy every day. She also learns to be gentle and kind when taught to hold the puppy properly and never to tease him.

Looking Back

♥ Society relies on parents to socialize children.

♥ Socialization skills are learned in various ways.

♥ Interacting with siblings can teach a child how to get along with others.

♥ Relatives offer children a bridge to a larger social world.

♥ Children need opportunities to play with peers in order to learn friendship skills.

♥ Parents must guide children in dealing with competition.

♥ With a parent's example, children learn to appreciate diversity in society.

♥ Children need experience in resolving conflicts peacefully.

♥ Children grow socially by showing good manners to others and kindness to animals.

Knowledge and Understanding

1. What happens during the socialization process in childhood?
2. How should a parent respond to sibling rivalry?
3. What can a relationship with grandparents offer a child?
4. Contrast a toddler's social skills with a preschooler's.
5. What might you do to help a child who has trouble making friends?
6. How can you help a child manage competition?
7. Suggest ways to help a child appreciate diversity.
8. Briefly describe a process that parents can use to teach conflict resolution to children.
9. Describe the parent's role in helping children resolve conflicts.
10. If Sondra wants to teach her young daughter manners, what suggestions would help her?
11. How does teaching kindness toward animals help a child grow socially?

Review

Thinking and Inquiry

12. Some parents reject a classic work of children's literature if it contains stereotypes or reflects a prejudice. Do you support this practice? Why or why not?

13. While in the toy department, a young boy chooses a toy that his father thinks is too violent. "But all the kids have it," the boy whines. What should the father do?

Communication

14. In a paragraph, describe your earliest memory of noticing differences among people or different treatment based on different qualities. How did you feel about that? How did your parents guide you?

15. Describe your views on competition. Is it generally beneficial or harmful? At what age should children begin to compete? Do they need to compete to feel successful? Do they learn to be passive if they don't compete? Will children find ways to compete regardless of what parents do?

16. Imagine that you have a five-year-old son who will soon be starting kindergarten. You know that some of the values you have taught him are noticeably different from those he may find among some classmates. How do you prepare your son—and yourself—to handle the questions, teasing, and pressure he is likely to experience? Write a one-page summary of your strategies.

17. Describe the actions of two parents leaving a child at a child-care centre. One handles separation anxiety well, and the other doesn't. Write a case study to show the differences.

Application

18. Alone or in pairs, identify one way that you would like to improve society. List ways that you would socialize children in order to realize this improvement. What social skills would children need to learn? How would these skills be taught? Share your ideas with your classmates. Do your ideas complement theirs? Do they conflict?

19. In small groups, list as many ways as you can to identify that you are socialized, that your beliefs or actions reflect the dominant beliefs and actions of society—for example, wearing blue jeans or eating cereal for breakfast. As a group or individually, write five sentences describing the impact of socialization on a person's life. Why is socialization a major concern for parents?

20. Describe your relationship with a member of your extended family. How has that relationship influenced who you are today?

CHAPTER 19

Helping Children Learn

CHAPTER EXPECTATIONS

While reading this chapter, you will:

▶ Identify the intellectual development that takes place in young children.

▶ Analyse behaviours, conditions, and environments that influence positive or negative growth and development of the young child.

▶ Explain the differences in capabilities and behaviours observed in children in classroom and community settings.

▶ Describe the advantages and disadvantages of parenting techniques advocated by current authorities on parenting.

KEY TERMS

bilingual   intelligence
centration   neurons
classification   reason
concept   seriation
conservation

Five-year-old Brant sagged against the shopping cart as his mother Helen sorted her grocery coupons. It seemed to Brant that they had been shopping for hours. "Are we *done* yet?" he whined.

"We just need a few more things," Helen replied. She handed him one of her coupons. "Can you find the box of cereal that looks like this one?"

Brant studied the coupon with interest and scanned the aisle. After two passes down the long row of cereal, he pointed to a box. "Here it is."

"Right," Helen encouraged him. "Now, can you bring me the *bigger* box?"

Brant stared at the smaller box, then the larger one. Finally he grasped the taller of the two and carried it triumphantly to his mother. "Good job, Brant!" Helen placed the cereal in her cart. She folded the coupon and zipped it up in her son's coat pocket. "You'll be our official coupon keeper. You hold onto these until we check out. Then you give them to the cashier."

Brant seemed reenergized. "What else?"

Helen p
shopping l
edly. "Can
likes? Do y
the box?"

Wha
tal skill

ca
has
velop
If you g
child will be
Having lived i

Children are born with curiosity. Teaching them a love of learning is one of the best lessons a caregiver can instill.

Making a Difference

Imagine two four-year-old children, one who receives good nutrition and medical care and one who does not. The first child many opportunities to play and de- motor skills. The other has very few. them each a tricycle, which more willing and able to ride? a supportive environment,

the first child is probably better equipped for the challenge.

Environment makes a difference in how children develop, not just physically but in all areas. Recent research on the brain reveals how powerful the impact of environment is on intellectual development. If you want to raise a child who has a strong mind, you need to harness that power.

Developing the Child's Brain

Even before birth, the brain is developing. As the fetus grows, the brain becomes ready to receive information. This process sets the stage for the incredible period of brain development ahead.

After birth, the baby hears the sound of a voice, which causes a nerve cell in the brain, called a **neuron** (NOO-ron), to connect with another. The baby sees a loving face, and neurons connect. The scent of the mother's milk or a loving touch from the father triggers more neurons to connect and be reinforced. The baby's brain develops with every bit of input offered.

In the weeks and months ahead, the baby's brain density increases. Every experience contributes to the brain's growth. See pages 372–373 for a quick overview of what happens.

PEAK TIMES FOR DEVELOPMENT

Research reveals that the brain is better able to gain certain skills and abilities at specific times. Parents and other caregivers can take advantage of these peak opportunities.

For example, the best time for learning basic motor skills is from birth to about age five. Fine motor skills are acquired between the ages of two and ten years. The area of the brain that easily learns the rules of language remains open to stimulus until around age six. The area for learning vocabulary stays open a lifetime but is most receptive in early childhood.

Does this mean you could raise a concert pianist by starting a child on music lessons at age three, when fine motor skills are most easily learned? The process is not so simple. Heredity and other influences are also at work.

Internet Connects

http://www.mcgrawhill.ca/links/parenting
To learn more about children and youth issues, go to the Web site above for *Parenting Rewards & Responsibilities, First Canadian Edition*, to see where to go next.

Every Action Counts

As you think about developing a child's brain, stimulation is the objective. Connections can form and be reinforced through hundreds of simple interactions between family members and child. What the child sees, hears, and feels is important. You can change a diaper and not say a word, or you can make diaper changing an enjoyable event, with changing facial expressions and loving touches. As you pack a young child's daily routine with pleasant sensory experiences, just imagine all those connections developing the baby's brain power.

You don't have to be a scientist to understand one thing about brain development: activity with children develops their brains. Here a father plays chess with his daughter. ◆ **How else could he help her develop intellectually?**

Wiring the Brain

Within a few years, a helpless infant becomes a person who can perform thousands of skills. What makes that development possible? If you could see what's going on inside the brain, you'd be amazed.

Sounds

Sights

Feelings

Smells

Touches

Tastes

1 Billions of Neurons

Before birth, the brain forms cells called neurons—billions of them. Just how many neurons will a child's brain have and how will they be arranged? That depends on the number of connections made among the neurons.

2 Connecting the Neurons

The brain can't work unless neurons connect and communicate, by sending and receiving impulses. Each neuron ends with fibres that reach out to other neurons. Although the fibres don't touch, gaps called synapses (sih-NAP-seez) allow impulses to jump across. As the "wiring" grows, each neuron links to not one, but thousands of others. Trillions of connections are made, causing the brain to double its weight by age two.

3 Wired for Results

With ample circuitry, the brain works well. The child learns language and builds understanding. Among many other skills, the child learns to reason and solve problems. Creativity develops. The stronger the circuitry, the better the brain works.

Understanding
Creativity
Associations
Language Skills
Reasoning
Problem-Solving

4 The Power of the Parent

Research on the brain shows that it takes positive childhood experiences to build and reinforce connections between neurons. When parents stimulate a child's senses—sight, hearing, smell, taste, and touch—the brain wires for thinking. Even the simplest actions count. People who talk to the child, play games, and give affection help the child's mind grow. Although the first two or three years of life are absolutely critical, the windows of opportunity for strengthening brain circuitry continue throughout childhood. Limiting a child's experiences limits the capabilities of the brain.

Internet Connects

http://www.mcgrawhill.ca/links/parenting
To learn out more about early learning and child development, go to the Web site above for *Parenting Rewards & Responsibilities, First Canadian Edition,* to see where to go next.

Parenting Q & A

Playing Computer Games

Q "My six-year-old daughter loves to play games on the computer, but I heard that's a poor use of time. Should I discourage her from playing computer games?" *Gerard*

A Not necessarily. Computer games can be a great learning tool. New studies show that computer games help develop spatial skills, the ability to see and rotate objects mentally. This basic skill is used in advanced thought processes. With these games, your daughter can learn skills and technology for tomorrow's workplace. Moving three-dimensional figures on a screen, for instance, is how engineers and city planners design machines and communities. Some software lets children write their own programs. You should be aware that some games reward violence and show killing too realistically. Children need activities that promote social skills and physical development. You'll need to monitor how your daughter uses the computer.

Multiple Intelligences

Studies of the brain are changing the way parents think about **intelligence**, the ability to acquire and use knowledge. Many people have measured intelligence by success in school, where IQ tests have typically measured strength in language and logical-mathematical abilities. Recent research by Harvard Professor Howard Gardner suggests that the brain has eight areas of intelligence. These are linguistic, logical-mathematical, spatial, bodily-kinesthetic, musical, interpersonal, intrapersonal, and naturalist.

The theory of multiple intelligences suggests that all people have the same areas of intelligence, but with different degrees of strength or weakness. One child might have musical strength but be weaker in the language area. Parents should be open to valuing the strengths of each child. They should help the child develop and put these strengths to meaningful use.

Evaluating Influences

The findings on brain development also influence parental decisions about infant and child care. Since the first few years of brain development are so critical, parents need to be sure that those who care for the child provide the love and stimulation a child needs.

Parents who use organized child care need to be confident of a high-quality setting. Stay-at-home parents must make sure they are attentive to the child's mental growth.

Social Implications

Brain research has broader implications as well. For example, educators are changing some teaching methods in light of this new knowledge. Should business and government change their policies on families and child care? Parents must stay informed and involved if society is to be influenced by brain research.

Piaget's Theory

In Chapter 13 you were introduced to Jean Piaget's theory of intellectual development. Here you will see how his theory continues beyond infancy.

SENSORIMOTOR PERIOD

As you read earlier, the sensorimotor period (ages birth to two) includes six stages. The first four occur during infancy. The last two take place between the first and second birthdays.

Piaget called Stage 5 the "little scientist" stage because of the way young toddlers explore. Children may repeatedly turn a lamp off and on and poke fingers in every food on the plate. Their growing intellect gains more and more from each experience.

In Stage 6, symbolic thought, or imagination, begins. Children solve simple problems. Twenty-two-month-old Safa used a low stool to reach the bathroom sink. When she wanted a cookie from a plate on the kitchen counter, she looked for the stool. Experience told her the stool helped her reach the sink, so with symbolic thought, she reasoned it would help her reach the cookies.

Not finding the stool, Safa used a chair instead. With symbolic thought, she imagined a chair as a stool. Safa accepted an object for what it was and for what it served as. This skill, which Piaget termed "mental combination," forms the basis for understanding language and math. Children recognize words and numbers as symbols for objects and ideas.

Music is one of possibly eight areas of intelligence. According to some studies, learning music may help children understand math more easily. ◆ **What do you think about the elimination of music education in many schools?**

Piaget's Theory of Intellectual Development

Sensorimotor Period Ages 0-2	Preoperational Period Ages 2-7	Concrete Operations Period Ages 7-11	Formal Operations Period Ages 11-Adult
✖ Use of senses to learn about world ✖ Control of body ✖ Egocentric thinking ✖ Object permanence ✖ Beginning of symbolic thought	✖ Egocentric thinking ✖ Classification based on one characteristic ✖ Seriation ✖ Centration ✖ Language skills ✖ Symbolic thinking	✖ Some logical thinking ✖ Classification based on several characteristics ✖ Conservation ✖ More socialized thinking; less egocentric ✖ More refined symbolic thinking	✖ Abstract thinking ✖ More complex logical thinking ✖ Hypothetical thinking ✖ Predicting consequences ✖ Use of reasoning and creativity to solve problems

PREOPERATIONAL PERIOD

The preoperational period lasts from about ages two to seven. Children organize information from the senses to form concepts. A **concept** is a general mental category of objects or ideas formed from other information.

In conceptual thinking, children group objects according to some quality. They see relationships between objects. They use **classification** to group objects by common traits and **seriation** to order objects by size or number. At age six, Anthony could pick all the blue balls from a box of red and blue balls, then line them up from largest to smallest.

However, Anthony couldn't pick out only blue balls from a box of red and blue balls and blocks. His classification skills were limited by **centration**, the ability to focus on only one quality at a time. He couldn't focus on both colour and shape at the same time.

Also in this period, children grow skilled in symbolic thinking. They see what an object is and what it stands for. Mommy's coat, for example, symbolizes "going out." Through symbolic, or dramatic, play, they assume different roles, create characters, and act out stories.

PERIOD OF CONCRETE OPERATIONS

Children between the ages of seven and 11 are in the period of concrete operations. Like birds learning to fly, they take short "hops" into complex thinking but are not quite capable of long flight. They tie their thought processes to concrete objects. An eight-year-old may understand the idea of adding numbers yet work through a problem by counting on fingers.

Children take significant leaps in logical thinking in this period. They grasp the principle of **conservation**, understanding that an object's physical properties stay the same even when the appearance changes. Ten crackers have the same weight, density, and volume whether stacked on a plate or laid out on a table.

Also, children realize that other people experience things differently than they do. At age four, Joey picked up a pear and asked his mother, sitting in another room, "Can I have one?" A few years later, he knew that she couldn't see what he saw. This awareness is the beginning of empathy.

PERIOD OF FORMAL OPERATIONS

This last period begins around age 11. As formal operational thinkers, adolescents can think logically and abstractly. They can form hypotheses and predict consequences, two important decision-making skills. They can solve problems through reason and creative thinking. Not all children develop these skills equally. Piaget believed that some people never develop them at all.

As children move into toddlerhood, they have more physical ability to explore. A frustrated parent might wish the adventurous toddler would slow down a little. ◆ **What would you tell that parent?**

Helping Children Learn Concepts

Piaget believed that each experience a child has teaches lessons that lead to higher levels of thinking. Rushing a child through a stage is like building a house before the foundation has set. A young child needs to learn many basic concepts as a broad foundation for later understanding. As the chart on page 378 shows, parents can use many ways to make concepts real to children.

Promoting Basic Concepts

Developmental Concept	Activities for Children
Classification Children under seven can classify items by one characteristic only. Older children can perform more complex tasks.	✖ Sort socks on laundry day. ✖ Group canned goods on shelves after grocery shopping. ✖ Dry forks, then spoons, returning each type of utensil to its proper place. ✖ Help clean house by stacking magazines and newspapers in separate piles. ✖ Find items belonging to one broad category, such as yellow things, on walks. ✖ Make a family tree (for school-age children).
Shape Activities that encourage comparing or experimenting with shapes help children notice similarity and difference, an important skill for reading.	✖ Help cut or roll cookies into various shapes. ✖ Fold square slices of cheese diagonally into triangles and place them on round crackers for a snack. ✖ Create designs and patterns from colourful paper cut into different shapes. ✖ Make pictures by combining shapes to form different objects. (A house, for example, might be a rectangular building with square windows and a triangular roof.) ✖ Respond to requests indicating shape, such as, "Please bring me the scarf with the big red diamonds."
Size and Space Grasping concepts of size and space paves the way for the mental skills of seriation and conservation.	✖ Help to prepare meals by setting out measuring cups and spoons. ✖ Track their growth on a height chart. ✖ Sort their own laundry in a laundry basket. ✖ Respond to requests involving space relationships, such as, "Put the spoon next to the plate. Put the napkin on top of the plate." ✖ Draw and send a map to an out-of-town relative, showing how to get to their home (for school-age children).
Number and Quantity Children don't understand the purpose of numbers until about age seven. They must understand that a written numeral stands for a specific amount; that numerals in sequence stand for progressively larger amounts; and that each item in a group is counted only once.	✖ Find recipes in a cookbook by page number. ✖ Change television stations using a remote control. ✖ Change the family page-a-day calendar, tearing off one page each day to reveal the next number. ✖ Help set the table for meals, counting each plate and utensil while setting it out. ✖ Help parents count individual pieces of fruit or vegetables bought in the supermarket.
Time Until about age five, children link the passage of time only to their own needs and to immediate, familiar events. By school age, most children can tell time using a digital clock and recite the days of the week in order.	✖ Respond to commands that refer to sequences of events, such as, "Wash your hands; then sit down to eat." ✖ Grow plants from seeds. ✖ Help prepare for special events, such as a family celebration. ✖ Help organize a family photo album, dating and discussing pictures that record growth and past events.

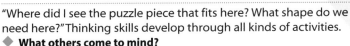

"Where did I see the puzzle piece that fits here? What shape do we need here?" Thinking skills develop through all kinds of activities.
◆ **What others come to mind?**

Promoting Thinking Skills

Intellectual growth is a building process. The more experiences children have, the more they use thinking skills. The more they "practise" thinking, the more they understand new experiences. As an athlete builds certain muscles through exercise, parents can help strengthen thinking skills by giving children opportunities for practice.

MEMORY

Memory strengthens as children link words and concepts to experiences. When parents supply background information before an event, the images are remembered more clearly afterwards. Experiences that are appealing and understandable are also better remembered.

Francine used these principles when she took five-year-old Mark to a petting zoo. First they looked at pictures of the animals they would see. Francine named them: llama, lamb, peacock. When they saw the billy goat at the zoo, Francine said, "Look, Mark. He has a beard, just like Uncle Carl." When Uncle Carl visited a few days later, what do you suppose were Mark's first words to him?

Parents can help older children develop strategies for improving memory. Clustering, for instance, helps children recall items based on a common quality, such as the same colour or beginning sound.

CURIOSITY

Curiosity motivates a child to learn about the world. To arouse an active sense of curiosity, a parent can:

♥ **Encourage questions.** A patient response to "why?" encourages a child to be curious. Saying, "I don't know, but I'll try to find out," leaves the door open for more exploration.

♥ **Model curiosity.** Children need to see that an inquisitive spirit should last a lifetime.

♥ **Show children how to find and use resources.** When you use the dictionary to look up a word, the child learns to do the same.

♥ **Be positive, even when results are unpleasant.** Pulling up flowers, for instance, may be against the rules, but a child who just wanted to see how they grow deserves understanding.

IMAGINATION AND CREATIVITY

Imagination takes a child beyond reality. A child who produces or invents something new uses imagination to be creative. These skills flourish when parents are sensitive about the child's feelings. Criticism quickly puts an end to a child's enthusiasm.

Spotlight On
——Learning with Computers

With software that is designed just for children, the computer can be a valuable resource for learning. Programs feature bright colours, appealing characters, and action. By stressing the fun and satisfaction of learning, they challenge children with more advanced activities. Some types of programs available are:

✔ **Games that teach basic concepts and vocabulary to toddlers.** Some respond when a child taps a key or speaks into a microphone.

✔ **Time travel games.** A character guides children through historic eras. Each "stop" includes problems to be solved and opportunities to learn about the time period.

✔ **Learning "adventures" featuring favourite literary characters.** Figures from children's literature are used to help teach basic reading and math skills.

✔ **Map-making programs.** Children create and drive through neighbourhoods, including streets, homes, businesses, and traffic signals.

✔ **"Living" encyclopedias.** Topics come to life when presented in a "real" environment, from a city to a rain forest.

✔ **Graphic design programs.** Older children can choose design elements to create labels, bookmarks, signs, and cards.

Building Parenting Skills

PARENTING WITH CREATIVITY

Creativity in parenting means taking a fresh approach to everyday situations. Fueled by imagination, creative parents make simple events interesting and even exciting. They see new solutions to problems and unexpected uses for available resources. As the parent of two young children, Megan used creativity when she:

▶ Took her children "treasure hunting" in the supermarket to look for each tasty treasure on their list.

▶ Used pita bread and tortillas to make sandwiches.

▶ Let her children "feed" dirty clothing to the "hungry" washing machine.

▶ Pretended she and her daughter were duck and duckling when giving the child a bath.

▶ Misted her son's bedroom with "monster repellent"—water in a spray bottle—to help him get to sleep.

◆ ◆ Your Thoughts ◆ ◆

❶ Must a parent be "artistic" to be creative?

❷ How might creativity in a parent prevent misbehaviour in a child?

❸ Suggest some creative ways to make the following situations appealing to a child: reading a story to a child; a child's birthday celebration; a walk in the woods; cooking at home; trying a new food.

A creative parent promotes creativity in many ways. You might point out how you change a recipe to fit your own tastes or ask a child to look at a situation in a different way. Asking "What can you do with this empty box?" helps a child think of new possibilities. You can provide art activities without any pressure to copy someone else's ideas. When young children make up stories for fun, you can listen and accept that this is imagination, not lying.

Older children often show creativity and individuality through unusual clothing and food choices. Parents should tolerate these decisions, as long as they are not harmful or offensive to the parent's values.

REASONING

The ability to **reason**, to think logically, rationally, and analytically, is limited in young children. Like other skills, it grows with practice, guidance, and maturity.

Parents can help children use reason to make sense of experiences. Hiro and his young daughter Tama noticed their parakeet Sunny had not touched the bird seed in her feeder all day. "Why isn't Sunny eating?" Hiro wondered. "What do you think, Tama?"

"Maybe she's not hungry," Tama suggested. "Maybe she's sick. Maybe she ate lunch at school today." Not all of Tama's ideas were reasonable, but they made sense to her.

Later, Hiro and Tama found empty seed hulls all around the feeder. "Tama, look. I think you were right when you said Sunny wasn't hungry before." As Tama looked at the evidence (the seed hulls), she saw support for one of her theories. Distinguishing supported ideas from unsupported ones is another reasoning skill.

Giving children choices also promotes reasoning. Children soon learn the value of making good decisions by weighing evidence and drawing conclusions. As children grow intellectually and face bigger decisions, parents can coach them through the steps of the decision-making process.

Encouraging Language Skills

Of all intellectual skills, is anything more impressive than acquiring language? Children go from speechless infants to enthusiastic talkers in just a few years. They advance from sounding out single words in picture books, to reading traffic signs and grocery ads with great pride.

ENCOURAGING SPEECH

Child development experts say children need about two years of listening to others in order to speak understandably. During this time, children absorb not only words, but also subtle rules about how phrases and sentences are formed. Children pattern language after those around them. Parents must choose and pronounce words carefully. Using "baby talk" doesn't help infants learn language.

Building Vocabulary

Teaching a child to talk is like opening a floodgate. The 20-month-old toddler who speaks perhaps 50 words will know about 300 words by age three. One year later, the figure may triple to 1500. The average kindergartner speaks about 2200 words.

This explosion does not occur by chance. Many new words are learned when parents:

♥ Speak to children and name objects, starting in infancy.

♥ Listen as children describe experiences, asking questions to draw out details. Parents should expand on a child's comments with remarks of their own.

♥ Use visual aids and demonstrations. As Evan's son helped with chores, Evan explained, "I'm vacuuming under the chair. Can you help me dust the end table?"

♥ Teach children concepts. Learning about shape, for example, a child learns the meaning of *big*, *small*, *round*, and *square*.

♥ Point out the fun of language. Rhyme, rhythm, and repetition appeal to children. They like silly-sounding words. Six-year-olds appreciate wordplay, such as simple puns. They enjoy using homonyms (words that sound alike but have different spellings and meanings) to create the image of a hoarse horse or a bare bear. Songs and finger plays also make language fun.

Improving Listening

When listening is fun, mastering language is easier. Songs and rhymes teach children to anticipate sounds and tell them apart. Identical containers filled with rice, beans, or other materials make simple sound-matching toys. The child shakes each container and tries to identify the contents. A parent can make pairs of containers with the same material and ask the child to match the two that sound alike.

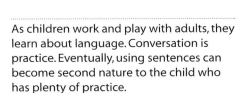

As children work and play with adults, they learn about language. Conversation is practice. Eventually, using sentences can become second nature to the child who has plenty of practice.

Promoting Bilingual Skills

Would you believe a three-year-old child can learn a second language more quickly than you can? Brain research suggests this is so.

In your brain, the neurons responsible for learning language have already connected. The best time for learning has passed. With practice, however, you can use existing connections in the brain to learn a new language. Therefore, your French teacher probably won't believe you failed a test because your brain is too old.

People who are **bilingual** are able to speak two languages. At one time, teaching children a second language was thought to hamper language skills. Parents who were bilingual were encouraged to speak only one language to their children.

Newer research suggests that speaking two languages improves abstract thinking skills (the type used in higher thought processes) and actually aids language skills. Parents who speak two languages should encourage children to learn them both. Knowing the language of another culture is a definite advantage in today's global society.

Responding to Language Errors

Any time you learn a new skill, mistakes happen. With its odd collection of pronunciations and grammar, the English language is particularly tricky. For instance, children may be temporarily confused by irregular plurals, such as *foot* and *feet*. A child may talk about two foots until the rule is clearer.

The best way to correct a child's language mistakes is to model proper usage, restating the child's remark without pointing out the error. When a child says, "Kitty runned away," a parent might reply, "Yes, Kitty ran away from that dog."

Children raised in a bilingual family can become bilingual if parents make an effort to speak both languages. Children who learn when they are young can become fluent as they grow older.

Health & Safety

As children learn to speak, they often mispronounce words, drop syllables, and leave entire words out of sentences. Depending on the age, parents might suspect a speech impairment.

Environment causes some speech difficulties. Parents who rarely talk with their child may delay the child's language development. Other causes are physical, such as an ear infection that damages hearing.

Most mysterious are problems caused by a dysfunction in the brain's language processing centres. Using language is a complex skill. Your brain must distinguish between similar sounds, decide what meaning is intended, apply the correct rule of grammar, and perform many other mental tasks. A breakdown can literally leave you speechless.

One obstacle to identifying speech problems is that children develop language skills at different rates. A serious problem may first appear as a simple lag. Also, parents may grow used to a child's problem over time. A teacher or family friend may point it out.

A pediatrician can refer parents to other professionals who treat speech disorders. An audiologist is a specialist in hearing disorders. A speech therapist or speech-language pathologist can treat people with speech, language, or voice disorders. A psychologist may be called in to determine a child's overall intellectual abilities. Neurologists identify physical brain abnormalities using tests and brain scans.

ENCOURAGING READING

Reading is intellectual calisthenics. When children read, they strengthen the mind by using memory, symbolic thought, and imagination. Reading also provides information, spurring greater intellectual growth. Older children discover new ideas and entire worlds that come to them through books.

The ability to read is critical for a child's future. Success in school and on many jobs depends on reading. Functioning well in society does too. From simple tasks like reading letters and product labels to more difficult ones like filling out income tax forms, reading is part of everyday life. People feel good about themselves when they can read.

Parents and teachers share the responsibility for helping children become readers. When parents set the stage for reading during the early years of life, children are better prepared to learn the reading skills taught in school. A child who misses the early preparation may struggle.

Some children grow into adults who can't read. This is how Jim described what happened to him: "At 30, I'm finally learning to read down at the community centre, but it's hard. When I was a little kid, nobody at home cared about reading. By the time I got to school, I was already behind, and it just got worse. I used to try to hide that I couldn't read. Somehow I got through school, but I didn't learn much. Last night I read a story to my son for the first time, and that felt really good."

As a parent, how could you prevent this kind of experience from happening to a child? From the time a child is born, you can build literacy. Talk to infants. Raise an interest in words as toddlers and preschoolers see you writing letters and reading newspapers, magazines, and books. Share greeting cards and cartoons. Point out how you write a shopping list. Above all, provide books and read to children. Get them hooked on books by taking them to the library as toddlers. Few if any gifts to a child can be greater than preparing him or her to read.

Choosing Books for Children

When you choose books for children, make sure they have enjoyable stories. Allowing for the child's age, parents should look for literature with a simple, understandable plot. Stories should have an appropriate theme, likable characters, and familiar situations. The story should be respectful of diverse cultures and beliefs. Language should be basic, but descriptive. Pleasing rhythms and rhymes help children remember words, and strong illustrations capture attention and help explain the words.

Books should also be well constructed to stand up to a child's sometimes clumsy treatment. Sturdy cloth or cardboard books with large pages are best for toddlers.

Reading to Children

Research has shown that reading to children is the single most important factor in their success as readers themselves. Other research also shows that good reading skills lead to better success later in life.

The best way to promote a child's intellect is also easy and great fun—reading. Children's books today are filled with humour and sentiments that children and adults can appreciate. ◆ **Can you name some specific ones?**

No child is too young to read with a parent. Snuggling together to listen to a story adds to the magic of books. A tale comes to life when you read with emotion and enthusiasm, speaking loudly or softly and giving each character a different voice. Take time to comment on the pictures and point out words. Ask questions that encourage children to share their feelings about a character or situation. An older child can follow a longer story over several days. To strengthen memory and sequential thinking, ask the child, "Where did we stop last night?"

PREPARING FOR WRITING

The idea of telling stories and expressing themselves excites children, even before they can write. Scribbling (which children often "read" for parents) shows they understand the function of writing and helps refine small motor skills. Parents can provide pens and pencils, crayons and scratch paper, and envelopes with colourful stickers for stamps. A child can dictate a story to a parent, then illustrate it with drawings or magazine pictures. Parents can write a child's dictated thank-you letter to a relative or record a collection of the child's favourite jokes.

As children begin to write words, parents can trust them to make shopping lists, fill in gift tags, and make place cards for a special dinner. Some dramatic play themes, such as school and restaurant, also encourage budding writing and reading—all-important literacy skills.

You might think that colouring is just play for children. Well, it is, but at the same time it prepares them for writing. ◆ **Why is this true?**

Looking Back

♥ New research on brain development reveals that parents and other caregivers can make a huge difference in building a child's brain power.

♥ Creating a rich learning environment during the first three years of life helps the child's brain grow.

♥ Piaget theorized that children move through four periods of intellectual development, grasping new concepts at each level.

♥ Exposing young children to a variety of ideas, information, and experiences prepares them for learning throughout life.

♥ To promote thinking skills, a parent can help children use their memory, satisfy their curiosity, and express creativity and imagination.

♥ Helping children solve simple problems improves their reasoning skills.

♥ Children gain skill in speaking when parents help them build their vocabulary and appreciate sounds.

♥ Reading to children helps prepare them to read for themselves.

Knowledge and Understanding

1. Describe how the brain develops and what makes that growth occur.
2. What do recent findings on brain development mean for parents of young children?
3. Briefly describe the four periods of intellectual development according to Piaget.
4. What is symbolic thought? Why is it so important to intellectual growth?
5. How should you respond to a child's "why" questions?
6. What could you do to help a child learn new words?
7. How could you prepare a four-year-old to learn reading skills?
8. List qualities that make a book appropriate for a young child.
9. What can parents do to encourage a child's interest in writing?

Thinking and Inquiry

10. Explain which of the following statements is more effective for strengthening a child's concept of time: "Dinner will be ready in twenty minutes" or "After you take your bath, we'll eat dinner."

11. Six months after her birthday, four-year-old Chelsea still remembers the date. However, she regularly forgets her hat and gloves at school. How do you explain this occurrence?

12. Until Sam was four years old, he said *went* for the past tense of *go* and *ate* for the past tense of *eat*. About that time, he began using *goed* and *eated*. What do you think caused this change?

13. Lynne likes to watch soap operas on television. She leaves her two young children in the crib or playpen for many hours every day. In relation to the chapter, what do you think about this situation?

14. Some people learn better by watching, and others by doing. That's why parents need to provide both hands-on activities and verbal explanations. Describe which method of learning suits you best.

Communication

15. With a partner, suggest five questions or comments a parent might make to a child to encourage conversation in one of these situations: the child returns from a kindergarten trip to a conservation area; the child helps the parent wash the family car.

16. Nursery rhymes and fairy tales are favourites in children's literature. Many of these stories, however, include stereotypes and violent images. With a partner, choose one classic work and identify the elements that you think would offend many people today. How would you change the story to give a more balanced, realistic treatment? What would the story gain or lose by these changes?

17. Create a poster for parents titled "How to Support Your Child's Learning."

Application

18. List three simple, everyday "problems" children could help solve that would strengthen their reasoning skills. Share your list with the class.

19. Imagine you are a parent on a tight budget. Your four-year-old daughter seems to have an active mind. Recently she has become fascinated with animals and plants. How can you provide inexpensive, enriching experiences to stimulate your child's interest and intelligence?

Robert J. Blunsdon, Jr., Primary Junior Information Technology/ Music Teacher

What volunteer activities did you do as a teenager that led you to choose a career that involved working with children/people?

▶ I began my volunteer career at age 11 at the Ottawa Street Community YWCA. I had completed all of my swimming levels but was not old enough to begin my Bronze Medallion, so one night a week and Saturday mornings, I volunteered to help the Aqua Tots and Yellow-levelled swimmers.

▶ I loved volunteering and kept it up through the summer. At age 12 I became involved with the Recreation Department at the YWCA as well, helping to run a drop-in program for the children in the community. Within a few weeks I was given the privilege of planning the program. This turned into my first paying job at the YWCA's Day Camp the summer I turned 13. However, I kept volunteering there all through high school. By the time I started university, I had volunteered in every department at the YWCA.

▶ At university I volunteered as a reading program leader at the Hamilton Public Library, did youth work with the United Church, and ran extra-curricular activities at the local school. Music clubs and after-school programs hooked me on the school environment and I decided to become an "official" teacher.

Please describe your specific education pathway.

▶ In 1997 I received a BA in Music from McMaster University. Then I became Recreation Director at the Ottawa Street YWCA. During my two years there, I attended several seminars on leadership, which led me to a Teachers Education Program. In 2000 I graduated from York University with a BEd from its Teacher Education Program.

Have you completed any further study to enhance your professional development?

▶ I am currently working on a Computers in the Classroom Specialist course at Queen's University.

Please describe your career pathway.

My first job was a paper route. At 13 I had my first summer job at the YWCA as a camp counsellor in charge of a group of ten children. Throughout high school I worked for the YWCA as a lifeguard, program instructor, and department head. When I started university, I became the Recreation Director at Ottawa Street Community YWCA. There my responsibilities included:

▶ Hiring, training, and supervising 50 program instructors and volunteers throughout the department.

▶ Providing a wide range of programs/initiatives within the YWCA and surrounding community.

▶ Providing instruction for 250 children between the ages of six months and 16 years each week in a variety of programs.

▶ YWCA Camp Director.

▶ Promoting the YWCA at various schools and community organizations in the Hamilton-Wentworth region.

For two years I was a Grade 2 teacher at Memorial Elementary School (City). Since 2002 I have taught Information Technology and Music at Bennetto Elementary School, both in the Hamilton-Wentworth District School Board.

Did you switch jobs along the way? If so, why?

Yes. After my first degree I worked full time as Recreation Director for the Hamilton YWCA. It was a great job and I loved the work, but when you get into any career in recreation with children, you work when they are available. With the exception of preschoolers this means you work after school, weekends, and all summer. This was all right at the time, but I knew it did not fit in with the rest of my goals.

I love learning and teaching, so I volunteered at the local school. It was great promotion for my programs at the "Y". I made many friends and it gave me something to do in my downtime between programs.

The school environment was for me, so a teacher education program was my next step. My first teaching job was at the school I volunteered at (Memorial City)!

*Please describe your **current position**.*

▶ I am an Information Technology/Music Teacher at Bennetto School with the Hamilton-Wentworth District School Board. I teach 500 eager students every week.

▶ In my current position I am responsible for teaching the Ontario curriculum through the integration of technology. My lessons range from Science and Math to Language and Art. I organize and implement many extra-curricular activities throughout the school. If you are a creative person and love working with children, you can organize any club you are interested in at school.

*What are the **rewards** of your current position?*

▶ Teaching and learning with children every day.
▶ Seeing 500 smiling faces every week.
▶ Trying to give each and every student the knowledge and confidence to succeed.
▶ Challenging my leadership skills.
▶ Having a job that allows me to play music.
▶ Never watching the clock, because the day flies by.
▶ Feeling proud of the work I do at the end of a day.
▶ Knowing I have made a positive difference in the life of a child is the greatest reward going!

*What are the **challenges** of your current position?*

▶ Overcoming issues in education, such as inclusion, funding, and encouraging teacher support of extra-curricular initiatives, are my biggest challenges. Making sure all children feel included in my school community is my number one priority. The next is ensuring I have the funding to keep all the extra-curricular activities running in the school.

Looking back over your education and career pathways, as a young person in high school did you ever believe you would follow the pathways you have?

▶ I realize now that my path was always to become a teacher. I wouldn't trade any of my work or volunteer experiences for anything. These experiences have developed and shaped my leadership style and given me the ability, imagination, and confidence to be the best teacher I can possibly be.

Do you have any comments for young people who might be considering their own educational/career pathway?

I have worked with children for 18 years. Here are a few pieces of advice I can offer:

▶ Proper preparation prevents poor performance.
▶ A person with integrity, intensity, intelligence, and a sense of inclusion produces students who are engaged, enriched, educated, and excited to learn.
▶ A positive mental attitude will take you far in life.
▶ When life gives you lemons, make lemonade.
▶ If you can dream it, you can do it!

What other careers are related to your career?

▶ Day-care Worker
▶ Children's Recreation Director
▶ Educational Assistant
▶ Principal

CHAPTER 20

Child-Care Options

CHAPTER EXPECTATIONS

While reading this chapter, you will:

► Identify and describe the capabilities and behaviours of young children of different ages in a variety of settings.

► Demonstrate an understanding of what is involved in planning, organizing, and carrying out age-appropriate activities for preschoolers in classroom or community settings.

► Describe the legal and social responsibilities of parents and guardians.

► Demonstrate an understanding of various social concerns that parents face as their children approach school age.

► Identify the laws that regulate children and parents in society.

KEY TERMS

au pair
day-care centre
licensed

nanny
self-care
sliding scale

Ingrid stared at the chess pieces on the board and turned toward the infant in the high chair. "Any ideas, Lydia?" Lydia stretched a hand toward the board and gurgled brightly.

From across the table, Kate exclaimed, "No fair! She's coaching!" Both women laughed. "Won't you miss her if you go back to work?" Kate asked her friend.

Ingrid sighed. "Sure, but I feel like I'm getting out of touch with the job."

Kate nodded. "I know the feeling, but taking care of Lydia is an important job too."

"*Very* important!" Ingrid echoed, "and I'm not sure about turning it over to someone else. I hear the good places have waiting lists. And then there's the money," she went on. "Right now, we'd pay almost as much for child care as I'd bring home each week. On the other hand, I should be able to move up to something that pays better. Raising this little one is only going to get more expensive. I don't think we can afford for me to stay home." Ingrid gazed tenderly at Lydia. "She's so precious. We don't want to make the wrong choice. How did you decide when your kids were young, Kate?"

Kate smiled. "We asked the same questions you are. The choice we made was right for our family. Now it's your turn. You and Jim will have to make this move for yourselves."

What do you think? What concerns, besides finances, might Ingrid consider when making her decision?

393

When you entrust your child to the care of others, you have one primary concern in mind. You want quality care.
◆ **How do you think a parent identifies quality care?**

A Need for Care

People tend to think of supplemental child care as something new. Actually, this regular supervision of young children by someone other than the parents has been going on for a long time. What's new is the widespread demand for child care. Parents in recent decades have relied much more on outside care for their children than earlier generations did.

Many parents struggle to decide whether to use supplemental care or stay home with a child. No evidence points clearly to one answer. Parents must decide for themselves, based on their values, finances, and their commitments to work, community, and family.

Types of Child Care

At one time, turning to grandmother for child care was common when both parents worked. Prosperous families could hire a children's maid or governess.

Today, extended family and live-in caregivers still take care of children. As families have changed, however, other child-care options have been added.

HOME-BASED CHILD CARE

As the name implies, home-based care takes place in either the family's or the caregiver's home. This situation is usually the least structured and demanding, and most like being home with a parent. Is that an advantage or a drawback? That depends on your philosophy and the situation.

Relatives and Neighbours

When Tamara's babysitter moved away, her great-aunt Eileen offered to care for her. Peter, Tamara's father, liked the idea. Aunt Eileen wouldn't charge a high fee, and Tamara would be with someone familiar.

Problems eventually arose, however. Eileen let Tamara watch too much television, which bothered Peter. He noticed that keeping up with an energetic toddler left Eileen drained. Neither adult wanted to hurt the other by complaining, but they weren't happy with how things were going.

Peter's story illustrates both sides of care by a relative or friend. A parent's convenience and savings must be weighed against any concerns about how the arrangement might work. For some families all goes well. In others, the relationship can suffer. If they are comfortable with the formality, the two parties can agree in writing on such basic issues as meals, discipline, and activities.

Nannies and Au Pairs

A **nanny** is a trained professional who cares for a child in the family's home. Nannies generally receive room, board, and a salary as payment. An **au pair** (oh PARE) is a young person from another country who lives with a family and cares for the children. Au pairs also receive room and board, plus the chance to learn about life in a different country.

Some people adapt their homes to care for a small number of children. How will you know if they are skilled and reliable? By talking to other parents, you can learn a great deal about a child-care service.

Not only are nannies and au pairs professionals, but they also give personal attention. Except for days off, they are available at all times. Of course, feeding and housing another person plus paying wages can be expensive. A family may also have trouble adjusting to a new person in their home.

Parents must carefully interview and check references of a potential live-in caregiver. They should use only a reputable employment agency, especially if they hire an au pair, since they may not be able to get personal records from a foreign country.

An au pair must have needed working papers and other documentation. All parties should sign a contract, making sure they understand its language about duties and benefits, such as insurance and vacation. Make sure that you clearly understand immigration, labour, and tax laws when hiring someone to care for your children.

Family Child-Care Homes

In family child care, the caregiver's home is adapted for the care of children. Family child care can provide a home-like setting where children enjoy personal attention in small groups. Infants and toddlers might be served well in such situations.

Raising Children With Character

An Honest Mistake

Four-year-old Rebecca raced up to her father Eli when he met her at the family child-care home. She chatted excitedly about her day as they walked home.

After a few blocks, Eli noticed a stuffed blue rabbit in her knapsack. He knew it wasn't hers. He pulled the toy out of the bag. "This is a pretty bunny, Becky. I don't remember seeing it before. Where did you get it?"

Rebecca fixed her eyes on the toy. "Ms. McCoy said I could have him," she replied quietly.

"I see," said Eli. "I think Ms. McCoy meant that you could have him to play with, not to take him home. He has to stay there, so the other children can play with him too."

Rebecca was silent. She didn't look up.

"Let's take him back," Eli suggested, gently turning her around, "and you can explain to Ms. McCoy what happened. I know she'll understand."

◆◆◆◆◆ **Thinking It Over** ◆◆◆◆◆

1. Do you think Rebecca knew it was wrong to take the rabbit? What tells you this may be so?
2. Why did Eli avoid accusing Rebecca of stealing?
3. Why was it important that Rebecca herself return the toy and tell Ms. McCoy?

Some family child-care homes may not be what parents want. Parents may be concerned about a lack of structured, enriching activities, inconsistent discipline, and poor supervision. Meals may be based more on the caregiver's convenience than the child's nutritional needs. As with any child-care situation, parents must evaluate a home carefully, using the guidelines described later in the chapter.

Play Groups/Co-operative Child Care

Sometimes friends or neighbours set up informal play groups that meet for a few hours once or twice a week. Parents take turns watching the children on assigned days. This way, all the parents get some time to themselves, knowing their child has playmates and supervision. As with relatives or neighbours, however, one parent may disagree with another parent's methods.

Community and religious organizations sometimes sponsor formal play groups. Fees, if any, go mostly to pay the caregiver.

CENTRE-BASED CARE

Many parents who need child care choose a **day-care centre**. These facilities provide supervised group care and socializing experiences by a trained staff. Large centres often separate children by age group, helping to create an appropriate environment for each.

Because of their larger size, child-care centres may offer some advantages over home-based care. Parents like them for their convenient hours and reliability. A centre may provide third-shift hours, for example, and still be able to operate when employees call in sick. Typically, the staff provides planned learning activities.

Parents should also weigh the drawbacks of centre-based care with their needs. Contact with so many other children increases the chance of illness. A shy child may feel lost in group care. Also, good programs can be expensive and have long waiting lists. Day-care centres are licensed and inspected by provincial authorities.

In a day-care program, a larger staff is needed for younger children.
◆ **Why would that be true?**

Sponsorship of Centres

Day-care centres are sponsored in several ways. Fees vary depending on the handling. Subsidized spaces may be available based on needs in many different types of centres.

♥ **Non-profit Centres.** Some day-care centres are run by religious organizations, the Y, and other non-profit groups. They are partly supported by donations and volunteers, so fees are more affordable. Church-affiliated centres may provide religious instruction.

♥ **Government-Sponsored Centres.** Some centres are mostly or entirely funded by the local or provincial government. These non-profit programs are often available only to families whose income falls below a certain level. Fees may be set on a **sliding scale**, varying according to a family's ability to pay.

♥ **Employer-Sponsored Centres.** Some companies and governmental bodies offer child care to their employees. The facility may be on-site or located nearby. Fees are low because the employer pays most of the operating costs. Some companies don't maintain a centre on-site, but they help the family pay the cost of outside care. For many businesses, money used for child care is well spent. Their efforts build employee goodwill and loyalty. Workers can focus on their jobs and worry less about children.

Emergency care is getting greater attention these days. Finding someone to care for a sick child on short notice is especially difficult for employed parents. As one father said: "We have a great family child-care home where Lewis goes. When he was sick, however, we didn't have a place to take him. Either my wife or I had to stay home, or we had to call around looking for a friend or relative to help out at the last minute. Now my company provides emergency care. That has really made our lives easier."

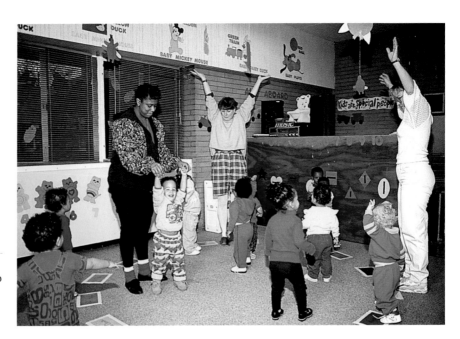

Parents who are looking for child care may find help in many places. This Y centre is typical of many non-profit programs.

♥ **School-Sponsored Centres.** At school-sponsored centres, future child-care workers get hands-on learning while parents continue their education. In secondary school, teen parents attend regular classes and learn parenting skills from teachers in the school nursery. At the university level, child-development students observe and interact with young children as part of their education. If qualified, parents who are also students may get a tuition break by working at the centre.

♥ **Privately Owned Centres.** Some centres are both owned and operated by individuals. They may be run by people with prior experience in child care or teaching. These programs often try to be flexible regarding parents' needs and beliefs. A centre might stay open later, for instance, if enough parents have a need. Fees at franchised and privately owned centres are usually higher, since they must cover all operating costs and provide an income for the owners.

Internet Connects

http://www.mcgrawhill.ca/links/parenting
To learn more about child and youth issues, go to the Web site above for *Parenting Rewards & Responsibilities, First Canadian Edition,* to see where to go next.

Health & Safety

HOME ALONE

"But I'm old enough to stay by myself!" Sometime during their school-age years, many children who are old enough are trusted at home alone for an hour or two. As a parent, you and your child can feel more confident if you have prepared with the following safety tips:

▶ **Telephone check-in.** Have the child call you at work or a family friend or neighbour on arriving home. You can call home at certain times.

▶ **Using the telephone.** Teach the child to call 911 and provide a name, address, and description of various emergencies. An answering machine, with a taped message from the parent, can handle incoming calls. Alternatively, the child can tell strangers, "My mom can't come to the phone now. Can you leave a number?"

▶ **Emergency numbers.** Keep numbers for the Poison Information Centre, doctor, parents at work, and a reliable neighbour or friend beside the phone.

▶ **Rules about visitors.** Tell children not to answer the door or allow friends to visit. Friends often do together what they would never try alone.

▶ **Rules about activities.** Reduce the risk of trouble by having a child do homework or household tasks. Make sure they know what they can and cannot do.

▶ **Tools and appliances.** Let children use only those items that they need and can use safely.

▶ **Meals and snacks.** Stock the kitchen with healthy foods. Make sure that children are capable of preparing foods left for them to eat. Do not expect a young child to use a stove or a microwave.

▶ **Special situations.** Make sure your child knows what to do if the house key is lost, a pet gets loose, the electricity goes out, the weather turns severe, the smoke alarm sounds, you don't return home when expected, and in various emergencies.

SPECIAL NEEDS PROGRAMS

Many day-care centres offer spaces for children with special needs. The integration of children with special needs into day-care centres allows for all the children to learn from one another. The ratio of caregiver to children is adjusted when a special-needs child is cared for in the same classroom.

Respite-care programs offer parents of special-needs children time to do things that are difficult to do with their child. Depending on the special need of the child, the care can be so demanding that parents do not have the ability to do something as simple as shopping. Knowing that their child is cared for by a qualified caregiver allows the parents to leave the child with the confidence that the child's needs will be met.

SCHOOL-AGE CHILD CARE

What time do children in your community get out of school? What time do their parents typically get off work? Unless parents can find other options, **self-care** may be the only answer. They leave the child for a few hours regularly without adult supervision. In Canada, by law, children under 12 cannot be left alone to look after themselves.

Of course, leaving young children on their own is far from ideal. Recognizing this fact, some schools, churches, and community agencies have before- and after-school programs where a child can enjoy stories, crafts, sports, or science projects. A quiet place for doing homework may be provided. Parents pick up their children after work or have them ride the school bus to their usual stop.

As with care for younger children, however, school-age child care is in short supply. Publicly funded groups may not have the budget for these programs. Private programs can be expensive and inconveniently located.

Evaluating Day-Care Services

Who would you trust to take care of your child? Unless you know caregivers personally, choosing a facility isn't easy. What goes on when you're not there? You can't drop by every day to check. You can, however, look for signs that tell you, "This is a quality program."

Child-care professionals need specific qualities to be effective. First, they should have a love and respect for children. They also need to be patient and energetic. In fact, all the qualities that a parent needs are the same ones to look for in a caregiver.

SIGNS OF QUALITY

Quality may be hard to describe, but "you know it when you see it." In child care, quality is revealed in several ways.

Directors and Staff

Employees are the heart of any program. Directors shape a program to their child-care philosophy and pick a caring, effective staff. Caregivers, who supervise and guide children hour by hour, often spend as much time with children as parents do.

Parents should learn as much about staff members as possible. What are their qualifications and background? What are their beliefs about children and guidance? How do they interact with children? Other parents who are familiar with the program might offer helpful opinions.

Parents should also ask about the staff turnover rate. A low turnover rate, where employees stay with the program a long time, indicates stability and reliability.

Licensed day-care facilities are subject to ratios of caregiver to child. This is regulated by provincial governments. In Ontario, for example, the ratios of staff to children in a day nursery are as follows: for children under 18 months of age—3 : 10; 18 months to 30 months of age—1 : 5; 30 months to 5 years of age—1 : 8; 5 to 6 years of age—1 : 12; 6 to 12 years of age—1 : 15. The regulations also set ratios for day nurseries for handicapped children and the maximum number of children in a group.

Licensing and Accreditation

When minimum standards for health, safety, and staff are met, a child-care facility is **licensed** by the province. For example, it must have a certain amount of space for each child. Various staff positions need specific qualifications. Most day-care centres are licensed. Larger family child-care homes are also licensed. Provincial ministries can give parents information about these minimum standards.

When you check out a day-care program, notice the toys and equipment. Everything should be safe for children's play and use.

Child-Care Evaluation Checklist

Caregivers

✖ Children are constantly supervised.

✖ Groups are supervised by at least two staff members at all times.

✖ An acceptable staff-to-child ratio exists.

✖ The director and caregivers are experienced and educated in child development.

✖ The centre has an up-to-date license.

Development

✖ The program provides enough time for active play.

✖ Caregivers show children affection and encourage it in return.

✖ Language skills are promoted through conversation and picture books.

✖ Creativity is promoted through art, music, and problem-solving activities.

✖ Caregivers model and encourage consideration and co-operation.

✖ Equipment is developmentally appropriate and safe.

Safety

✖ Storage space is tidy and organized.

✖ Children have a place for belongings.

✖ Floors are free of clutter.

✖ Fire exits are well marked and unobstructed. Smoke detectors work.

✖ Emergency procedures are posted.

✖ Emergency numbers are posted by all telephones.

✖ The centre is childproof.

✖ Visitors cannot enter unnoticed.

✖ Adults other than parents must have authorization and identification to pick up children.

✖ Program vehicles are maintained and serviced regularly.

✖ Transportation is organized for safety.

Health

✖ Children and caregivers appear healthy.

✖ Children are required to have all immunizations.

✖ Parents are notified and a rest area is available when children become ill.

✖ Caregivers wash their hands after diapering.

✖ Caregivers and children wash their hands after using the toilet, coughing, and sneezing.

✖ Playrooms are cleaned daily and bathrooms are sanitized.

✖ Sanitation procedures are followed when handling food.

✖ Meals and snacks are nutritious.

✖ Food areas are separate from diapering and washroom areas.

Parents

✖ Parents may visit without notice.

✖ Parents are encouraged to meet and socialize with each other.

✖ Activities are planned to help parents get involved.

Provincial family and child-welfare agencies regulate and license child-care facilities. They determine what qualifications, if any, are necessary for those who operate child-care centres. While Canada does not have a national child-care accreditation program, the Council on Accreditation in the United States accredits some Canadian child-care facilities, and the province of Alberta has started an accreditation program.

Equipment and Activities

Safe play is a high priority for children in group care. Programs need plenty of carefully chosen toys and equipment to avoid conflicts over sharing. Large equipment should be well-spaced, giving children enough room to swing and slide without hurting themselves or others.

Activities should be well-planned, age appropriate, and well-supervised. Group activities need to be balanced with small-group fun and playing alone. Caregivers should be relaxed but involved and in control while leading activities. They should guide children patiently to learn skills while having fun.

Communication with Parents

With regular communication, parents and caregivers build trust and co-operation. For instance, Jeff told Franklin's teacher that the two-year-old had developed a fear of dogs. "I don't get it," he said. "He always loved our neighbour's old St. Bernard. Yesterday I wanted him to pet her, but he started screaming." Ms. Buchanan told Jeff that it might be a phase. Meanwhile, she advised against pushing Franklin to pet any dog. She offered suggestions for helping the boy cope with his fear.

Later that week a volunteer from the animal shelter brought a puppy to visit the class. Ms. Buchanan showed Franklin how soft and friendly the puppy was. When Franklin excitedly described the puppy to his father, Jeff felt relieved. He was grateful to Ms. Buchanan for remembering their conversation. What might have happened if Jeff and Ms. Buchanan had not communicated?

Taking time to find the right child-care setting for your child is time well spent. You'll feel much more comfortable when your child is in good spirits at drop-off and pick-up times.

Caregivers and parents share other information also. Parents need to know about changed hours, an outbreak of chicken pox, or just how their child is doing. Likewise, they need to tell caregivers about events at home that may affect the child, or if the family will be out of town.

Communication takes many forms. Jeff and Ms. Buchanan talked at a regularly scheduled conference. Caregivers and parents can send notes or talk on the phone. Brief messages may be exchanged when the child is dropped off or picked up. Programs often pass on general news, announcements, and parenting tips in a newsletter.

CHOOSING A CHILD-CARE PROVIDER

Looking for child care may take a systematic search. Starting several months in advance is a good idea. The decision can't be rushed. In some communities, a shortage of quality programs means a lengthy wait for an opening.

Telling children early about plans for child care helps prepare them for the change. Parents who stay positive and enthusiastic throughout the process encourage the same attitude in the child.

To make a good choice, here's an organized approach that works:

♥ *Explore the options.* List child-care needs. For instance, when is care needed? What can you afford? Provincial agencies and area schools may have information about local licensed programs. Upon request, the Canadian Child Care Federation will send a brochure on choosing child care, along with a list of accredited programs in the area. Calling each program to learn needed information can narrow the search. Talk to other parents in your community as well.

♥ *Compare facilities.* Visit services that sound promising. Call ahead to schedule an appointment. Going without the child makes it easier to focus on details. A reputable facility encourages parents to meet and observe the caregivers with the children and even to take notes. Pay attention to the overall mood. Does the place feel friendly and caring? Do you sense a love of children? The checklist on page 402 gives other signs to look for.

Spotlight On ──Goodbyes

When a child is in child care, the hardest part of the day may be the moment the parent leaves. These tips can help parents make saying good-bye easier:

✔ *Announce you are leaving.* Slipping away while the child is distracted can be frightening. A child who is already "clingy" will become more so.

✔ *Be swift and sure.* Say good-bye and leave. Don't linger for "just one more minute."

✔ *Be cheerful.* Make comments such as,"You get to feed the rabbit today. That sounds like fun." Avoid saying, "Don't miss me" or "I wish I could stay."

✔ *Be reliable.* Children leave parents more easily when they are confident of the reunion. Make sure the child is picked up as expected. Show trustworthiness in all situations.

♥ **Choose a facility.** Ideally, several options will seem suitable. List the advantages and disadvantages of each, weighing them carefully. Try to take the child to visit your top choices before enrolling, preferably when other children aren't present. Watching the child's reaction to the caregivers, the equipment, and the layout can help you evaluate the match.

Issues in Child Care

The use of child care raises many questions for society. Some, including those below, aren't easily answered. What do you think?

♥ **What is the impact on children?** Many children in child-care programs have become happy, productive adults. The same is true of many who received full-time care from a parent. On the other hand, some children from both situations have not thrived. Quality of care and the amount of time spent there certainly have an impact, but those vary with each child.

♥ **What is the effect on the family?** Parents want to be the centre of a child's life. Many worry that family closeness will suffer if other adults take over parental roles and responsibilities.

♥ **How should standards and licensing be handled?** Currently, each province sets its own licensing regulations. Agreeing on national standards could be difficult, however, and takes away local control.

♥ **What role should government have in child care?** Many people believe that finding child care is a family's duty. Others argue that the government must step in if quality programs aren't there for parents who must have child care in order to hold a job. Universal day care, which is publicly supported, is desired by many Canadians. Many studies, such as The Early Years Report in Ontario, list the quality of early care and early learning as indicators of future learning.

These issues may seem complex and distant. They are worth thinking about, however, because decisions about child care are among the most important you will make as a parent.

Internet Connects

http://www.mcgrawhill.ca/links/parenting
To learn more about Early Childhood Education and care in Canada, go to the Web site above for *Parenting Rewards & Responsibilities, First Canadian Edition,* to see where to go next.

Cross-Curricular Social Studies CONNECTIONS

No Place Like Home

What is the effect on a child when both parents work? In Canada today, about 60 percent of mothers with children under the age of three work outside the home. But this does not necessarily have a bad effect on their children's development. What is important is not how much time parents spend with the child, but the quality of the time spent. Working Canadian parents are much more aware of the importance of early childhood development, and they are spending more quality time with their children aged five and under.

Research also shows that making use of good quality child care does not harm the parent-child relationship. Parental behaviour and attitudes are most important in childhood development, but good child care can also enhance that development. What are some activities parents can do with their children to strengthen family closeness?

Looking Back

♥ Different types of child-care providers exist to meet different parenting needs.

♥ The environment in family child-care homes can range from safe and stimulating to unsafe and disorganized.

♥ Day-care centres offer the benefits of professional organization and trained caregivers.

♥ The fee a day-care centre charges is influenced by who sponsors the centre.

♥ A quality program is safe and inviting; is licensed; and has a caring, knowledgeable staff.

♥ Parents who choose to use child care are responsible for carefully exploring their options to find one about which they feel good.

♥ When deciding whether to use child care, parents should consider larger, related issues that affect them, their children, and all of society.

Knowledge and Understanding

1. What advantages and disadvantages does care by a relative and family child-care homes share?
2. What is the difference between a nanny and an au pair?
3. What features of day-care centres are appreciated by parents?
4. Why would the fee charged by a privately owned centre likely be higher than that charged by an employer's program for workers?
5. What might a parent conclude when visiting a day-care facility where children are loud, screaming, and running all over?
6. How is accreditation related to quality?
7. Why is communication between parents and caregivers important?
8. Your neighbour is going to visit a day-care facility that he is thinking of using. What tips would you give him?
9. Does good child care make up for a home where a child's development is neglected?

Thinking and Inquiry

10. Decide which of the child-care options discussed in the chapter would be the best for each of these children, giving reasons for your choice: six-month-old Ethan is easily upset by new situations and changes in his routine; three-year-old Inez is being raised by a single mother who works part-time as a sales clerk and attends community college two nights a week.

11. Many of today's parents were in child care themselves. Do you think this makes them more or less likely to use child care for their own children? Explain your reasoning.

12. Find out the name of the provincial ministry that regulates day care. What criteria do they use? What ratios are in place?

Communication

13. You have been asked to contribute ideas for making an after-school program interesting to children and useful to parents. Write five guidelines for making this venture a success. Share your ideas with your classmates.

14. Write an article for your local newspaper explaining to parents what to look for in child care.

15. Imagine that you are a working parent with a three-year-old daughter in a day-care program. You notice that the child's behaviour is changing. She seems unhappy when you pick her up and is more aggressive at home. Make a list of questions to ask caregivers to try to find out what is bothering your daughter.

Application

16. Working with a partner, choose one of the child-care issues mentioned in the chapter. Debate opposing views on the topic. Begin with each partner arguing his or her position. Gradually find common ground and reach some kind of agreement.

17. Obtain a copy of your province's day-care licensing laws. Are they adequate? How might they be improved? If you were a parent, would you feel confident placing your child in a facility that meets these standards?

18. Suppose your friend is a single father of a 14-month-old. His supervisor at work just informed him that he has been reassigned to the night shift, from 10:00 p.m. to 6:00 a.m. "Who's going to look after my son?" he asks. "I don't have any family in town. I can't impose on my friends, and there are no all-night day-care centres." What suggestions can you offer?

Diane Bajus-Harrison, Early Childhood Educator—Supervisor

What volunteer activities did you do as a teenager that led you to choose a career that involved working with children/people?

▶ Any childcare/babysitting that was available since I was 12 years of age.
▶ Sunday school teacher for four years.
▶ Camp counsellor (age 16–18) and administrator (age 20–22).

*Please describe your **specific education pathway**.*

▶ Early Childhood Education diploma, a two-year program at Mohawk College in Hamilton, ON.
▶ Educational Assistant Certificate, a one-year program at Mohawk College.

Have you completed any further study to enhance your professional development?

▶ Continued attendance at conferences and seminars.
▶ Took First Aid course every two years.

*Please describe your **career pathway**.*

▶ 1989—High school co-operative placements in a day care-elementary school (JK) as a teacher's assistant.
▶ 1990–1998—College placements (four in total) and implementation of skills taught in the Early Childhood Education program.
▶ 1992—First job at Holy Spirit Elementary School as a heritage language teacher for the JKs; followed the complete Catholic School Board curriculum. Began to teach JK in the Ukranian language in the afternoon (still working at the school).
▶ In 1999 began employment at Delta Honey Bears Co-op Preschool—a morning program for children ages 2–5 years of age. As supervisor/teacher I plan and implement activities that provide physical, intellectual, social, and emotional development of children in my care.

*Please describe your **current position**.*

▶ 8 am–12 noon—Delta Honey Bears Co-operative Preschool supervisor/teacher.
▶ 12:30–3:20 pm—Holy Spirit Elementary School supervisor/teacher.

I provide a program that gives children the opportunity to play and learn with their peers. Through play and the learning process, children can build their knowledge of themselves and their world, acquire many new skills, have opportunities to self-express, gain self-confidence and self-esteem.

*What are the **rewards** of your current position?*

▶ The accomplishment of knowing that a child has reached his or her level of growth, and that it was done socially, emotionally, and intellectually. Smiles and hugs from children. Being remembered as a student's first teacher on his or her graduation day from Grade 5. Parents continually thank me for the work that I've done with their children.

*What are the **challenges** of your current position?*

► Meeting the needs of every child can be somewhat of a challenge because most children are developing at different levels and some have special needs.

► The different personalities of the parents may also cause challenges, because I also work with the parent volunteers at the preschool.

Looking back over your education and career pathways, as a young person in high school did you ever believe you would follow the pathways you have?

► Yes, I have always wanted to make a positive impact on children in this age group.

► I believe that the period of most crucial development in children are the years before the age of five,"and the years before age five last the rest of their lives."

► This is the most rewarding job a person can have.

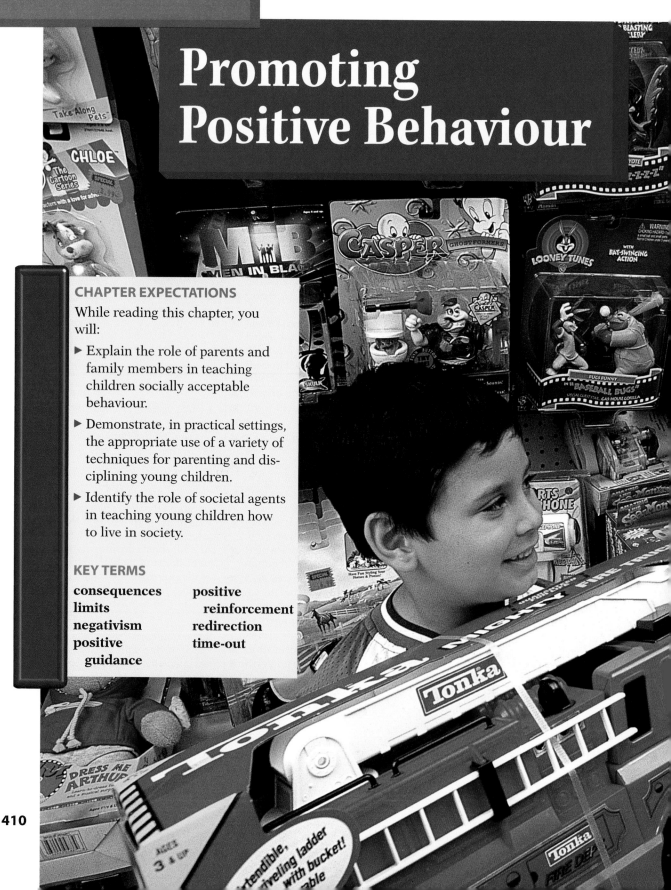

Promoting Positive Behaviour

CHAPTER EXPECTATIONS

While reading this chapter, you will:

▶ Explain the role of parents and family members in teaching children socially acceptable behaviour.

▶ Demonstrate, in practical settings, the appropriate use of a variety of techniques for parenting and disciplining young children.

▶ Identify the role of societal agents in teaching young children how to live in society.

KEY TERMS

consequences
limits
negativism
positive
  guidance
positive
  reinforcement
redirection
time-out

"Put that back right now!" the woman yelled at the little girl beside her. "We're not buying that stuff." The girl set the box back on the shelf with the other toys. "Now get over here. Why can't you be good just once?" As the woman grabbed the child's arm, a look of sorrow, then hostility, appeared on the girl's face.

Mark reached out for his son's hand, leading him from the troubling scene. "Look, Daddy, a fire engine with real ladders and a hose!" the boy exclaimed.

Mark stopped for a moment with his son. "That's quite a fire engine, Nate. I can see why that would catch your eye."

"Can we get it, Daddy? I'd play with it a lot."

"I know you would, Nathan, but we're not here to buy toys. We have to spend our money on other things today," Mark responded firmly but calmly. Nathan looked disappointed. "I'll tell you what. When we get home, let's read that story about a fire engine. Then you can make a pretend fire engine with two chairs. Maybe Jason can come over and be a firefighter with you." As Nathan's face brightened, the father and son moved on to the hardware department discussing how to equip an imaginary fire engine.

◆

What do you think? Compare the approaches of the two adults. Why does Mark's work, while the woman's is a sign of serious trouble?

Even a trip to a ball game can turn into an ordeal if a child misbehaves.
◆ **What do these parents do to prevent a problem?**

in the rain." She's talking about *punishing* her son. Many parenting experts and this text believe there is much more to shaping a child's behaviour than simply punishment. Brandon needs to learn not to take the phone outside in the first place. He should also learn to put objects back where they belong. Parents who know other ways to direct behaviour use punishment less often.

Rather than "punishment," people often talk about "consequences" instead. **Consequences** are the results of inappropriate behaviour. As you will see, some consequences happen naturally and some are decided by parents.

What Is Positive Guidance?

You often hear people talk about discipline, but the term **positive guidance** is preferred by many. Through positive guidance, adults direct children toward acceptable behaviour. They teach children the beginnings of self-control and the difference between right and wrong. Children feel reassured knowing parents are in charge and have set limits. As children gradually learn to respect other people, they become less self-centred. Satisfaction in adulthood is more likely when you consider the needs of others.

Suppose a mother says, "Brandon needs to be *disciplined* for leaving the phone out

Starting Young

A shared sense of humour is what first attracted Cheryl and Matt to each other. As their young son grew, they enjoyed his antics. Both liked to tell stories about how ornery he was. They figured he would straighten out when he entered kindergarten the next year.

One Saturday in a busy grocery store parking lot, the couple was forced to re-examine their parenting approach. Refusing to leave a grassy island in the lot, Justin ran toward the traffic every time they tried to approach him. His tantrum scared them, not to mention some motorists. The dangerous situation made Matt and Cheryl finally realize who had control—Justin.

Parents who begin to shape their children's behaviour at a young age are likely to face fewer problems and frustrations later. Like Cheryl and Matt, parents who don't guide their children when they are very young have little or no control later. Regaining control can be difficult.

The Confident Parent

In their role as Justin's parents, Cheryl and Matt lacked confidence. They never made it clear that they were in charge. Instead they wanted to be his friends. In neglecting to guide Justin's behaviour from the time he was a toddler, they blindly assumed good behaviour would just fall into place naturally. Picking up on his parents' indecision, Justin manipulated and controlled situations.

How does a parent gain confidence? The first step is learning as much as possible about child development and parenting. That's exactly what you are doing now by reading this book.

Depending on which expert you follow, you'll find that advice on raising children isn't all the same. Some authorities prefer rigid rules, yet others are much more permissive. The contradictions confuse many parents. The key is to decide which approach, or combination of approaches, seems right and is most sensible for your family and your value system.

Parenting Q & A

Discipline Dilemma

Q "My mother thinks I let my daughter, Kelly, get away with too much. Sometimes Kelly does get me to change my mind. How can I discipline her without making her resent me?" *Chris*

A "It's good to be liked; it's better to be respected." You may need to remember this saying. Kelly may be unhappy when you say "no" or enforce rules, but don't confuse that with thinking she doesn't like you. Giving in to her pleading teaches that she can get what she wants. Children may be happy at first to escape negative consequences, but eventually they lose respect for the parent. When making decisions, they ask themselves, "What can I get away with?" rather than, "What's the right thing to do?" Parents who want what is best for their child may have to accept being unpopular for a while. If a child is frequently or extremely angry, however, parents should do some thinking. Their methods of discipline might be too strict, or something else in the child's life might be causing the anger.

Choosing an approach becomes easier as parents get to know their children. Over time parents start to figure out children's personalities and how they think. Confident parents realize that what seems to be working in a neighbour's family might not be right for their own.

You can't be a confident parent without one more vital quality. A parent has to be willing and energetic enough to follow through on guiding the child. Often parents who are immature and burdened with problems of their own find it difficult to parent with confidence.

Relating Development to Behaviour

Have you ever heard someone say "You need to act your age"? Often that statement has some merit. For instance, no one wants to listen to an eight-year-old talk baby talk. Other times, expectations can be misguided. Children who are large for their age can be criticized for acting babyish when their behaviour is actually quite reasonable.

Before parents can promote positive behaviour, they have to know the basics of child development. When parents aren't sure what abilities and limits are typical at a given stage, they may expect too much from children. Planning that a two-year-old will sit still through a long wedding ceremony, for example, is wishful thinking.

DEVELOPMENTAL IMPACT

All types of development—physical, intellectual, emotional, social, and moral—affect the behaviour that parents can reasonably expect. Physically, most 18-month-olds feed themselves, but should you trust them to hold a fragile object? Probably not, because they're likely to drop it. Children this age probably get up earlier on weekend mornings than their parents would like. Forcing them to stay in bed for hours would be inappropriate guidance.

"We don't throw balls in the house. That's the rule." Confident parents who set boundaries increase the odds of having well-adjusted children.
◆ **Do you know a family without any set rules? How do the children behave?**

Most young children want to be Mom's or Dad's special helper. They love to be praised for their efforts. ◆ **Would you expect a toddler to do a task as well as a five-year-old?**

Parents enjoy watching their children socialize with other children. A mother of a two-year-old should know that toddlers play along side each other but not with each other. If she doesn't realize this, she might frustrate herself and the toddlers by coaxing them to interact.

A couple who leaves their tearful 12-month-old with a babysitter for an evening is reassured to know that separation anxiety is common at that age. They don't have to worry that the baby might be getting sick or is unstable emotionally.

Morally, a mother might wish that her child in kindergarten would volunteer to send some toys to children who lost theirs in a flood. Five- and six-year-olds are in the preconventional level of moral development, so they're not likely to think in terms of helping someone they've never met.

Learning as much as possible about child development arms parents with knowledge they need to guide their children effectively.

ANALYZING BEHAVIOUR

Most children enjoy attention. At times, many will try to get it any way they can. If good behaviour doesn't bring them attention, they may misbehave. Evaluating misbehaviour helps parents decide what to do. Parents should ask themselves these questions:

♥ *How old is the child?* A 14-month-old may hit or bite another child without understanding the action is wrong. The parent can say "no" and direct the offender to another activity. If a four-year-old sibling did the same thing to a playmate, the parent would choose a different response.

♥ *Was the behaviour intentional or unintentional?* Having to wait for food at a restaurant may make a hungry two-year-old cry. That's unintentional behaviour that can probably be solved with a few crackers. A bored five-year-old who decides to throw sugar packets is a different story.

♥ *Does the child know right from wrong?* Children must learn the difference between acceptable and unacceptable behaviour. Two- and three-year-olds routinely need these lessons. Mistakes are part of their rapid development.

When three-year-old Amanda used her crayons on the back of some important documents, her mother was angry. Then she realized the papers had been left on the same desk where Amanda's drawing paper was stored. Amanda didn't know they were off limits for artwork.

Internet Connects

http://www.mcgrawhill.ca/links/parenting
To learn more about individual and family well-being, go to the Web site above for *Parenting Rewards & Responsibilities, First Canadian Edition,* to see where to go next.

Accidents do happen, but some actions are deliberate. Confident parents take a moment to analyze children's behaviour.
◆ **Why do caregivers need to think about whether a child's actions were intentional?**

Guidance Techniques

Through positive guidance, parents teach children how to deal with their feelings in acceptable ways. Children learn the skills needed to get along with other people. They learn what is right and wrong. Most important is that children develop self-control and become self-directed. In other words, the goal is for them to make correct decisions about behaviour even when adults aren't there to instruct them.

Parents can use a number of positive guidance techniques to encourage, direct, and reinforce behaviour. Parents who skillfully use the techniques described in the rest of this chapter are usually rewarded with well-behaved, well-adjusted children. The reward is worth the effort.

PREVENTING PROBLEMS

Certain parenting strategies prevent problems before they occur. They include keeping children busy, offering choices occasionally, and using positive reinforcement. These techniques take time, and parents must be alert to use them.

Keeping Children Busy

Boredom can lead to misbehaviour for children of all ages. Providing fancy toys isn't necessary, but parents should try to have toys, books, and activities suited to the age of their children. Boredom can be minimized by rotating toys and play materials from time to time, putting some away for a while.

When Jordan's family attended a children's play in the city, his mother packed a bag of quiet toys and activities for the train ride and the wait in the auditorium. They chatted about what they saw from the train window too.

Chasing after a troublesome child can be time-consuming and wearing. Why not involve the child in something interesting to do? That approach is easier on both parent and child. List some activities that would help keep a preschooler occupied.

A word of caution about keeping children busy: Don't appoint yourself full-time activity director. You don't always have to make sure there's a video or DVD to watch or something fun to do. Invite the child to "help" with what you're doing. Include the child as you work on household duties.

Children shouldn't expect to be entertained at all times, but they do need interesting activities to fill their time.

Offering Choices

Like adults, children sometimes resist direct commands. At times children respond better when they feel they have some control over a situation. Parents can go overboard offering choices, but occasionally allowing children to choose between alternatives is a good idea. The result may be positive behaviour, raised self-esteem, and improved decision-making skills.

Choices should be offered with care. Parents need to follow through with the child's choice. Timmy's stepfather had learned not to offer him a choice when the child really had none. He didn't ask, "Do you want to put a coat on?" because Timmy was likely to say no. Instead he would say, "Do you want to wear this jacket or your new sweatshirt?"

Using Positive Reinforcement

Good behaviour should be acknowleged with **positive reinforcement**. Such attention and sincere praise encourage a particular behaviour. Children learn that parents are proud of them and approve of their actions. After their day trip, Jordan's mother said, "We had a fun day, didn't we? The play was long, but you really paid attention." Positive reinforcement isn't always verbal. Timmy's stepdad gave him a thumbs-up signal from the side of the ice arena when the boy was learning to skate backwards.

When you observe children behaving well and treating others with kindness, mention it to them. Acknowledging desirable behaviour can reduce misbehaviour significantly.

SETTING LIMITS

Limits are rules and boundaries that children must follow. Limits teach children what is safe and acceptable for them to do.

Children may act as though they want to run the show, but actually they crave limits. Having too much power is frightening. Obviously, they lack the experience and maturity to make decisions that are in their best interests. As they mature, children are able to put some limits on themselves.

Clear and Consistent

Parents have to be clear when stating limits. They need to watch what they assume. What if a mother told her daughter to come home at dinnertime? That request is somewhat vague. The child might be unsure whether the mother meant their family's usual supper hour or the time when her friend's family sits down to eat. Telling her to be home at 5 p.m. is simple and clear.

Consistency makes limits enforceable. Bedtime shouldn't be 8 p.m. for a couple of nights and then whenever the child gets tired the next few nights. Infrequent exceptions can be made for special occasions, but keeping rules consistent helps children know what to expect. It makes family life run more smoothly—for children and their parents.

Having all caregivers in agreement about limits is necessary for consistency. Whether Bobby is at home, Grandma's, or his father's for the weekend, knowing the same rules apply is comforting.

Reasonable and Age Appropriate

Children are most co-operative when they have limits, but not too many. They need to know that some of the rules will change as they get older and more mature. When Bobby started school, Mrs. Gerace extended his bedtime by half an hour. She also let him cross the street to his buddy's house while she watched from the porch. The day will come when he can cross the street on his own. Then his mother will change the rule. If she doesn't, Bobby won't make progress.

Building Parenting Skills

PARENTING WITH CONSISTENCY

With consistency, things stay the same. Parents stick to a clear set of simple rules from day to day. They demonstrate the same behaviour that they expect from children. Parenting with consistency gives children a sense of security and trust. Children aren't confused or frightened by parental action that constantly surprises them. Dan has two children who live with their mother. To parent with consistency, he:

▶ Established a bath and story routine at the same time before bed each evening that they stayed with him.

▶ Limited his daughters' TV viewing to one hour, following the same rule they had at home.

▶ Tried to use time-out consistently, not getting upset over misbehaviour one day and then ignoring it the next.

▶ Picked up his children and their friends on time when it was his turn to drive the carpool.

▶ Didn't give his daughter a cookie because he knew that her grandma had already said no.

▶ Made only those promises he knew he could keep.

◆ ◆ Your Thoughts ◆ ◆

1 Why do you think it might be hard for parents to be consistent all the time?

2 Some children manipulate their parents. Why would this happen more easily when parents are inconsistent?

3 Paul yelled at his four-year-old son when the boy walked into the house with muddy shoes. The child had done the same thing earlier in the day with no response from Paul. What would you suggest to Paul?

Parents need to keep in mind that what one child may be ready to do at age five, another may not be mature enough to do until age seven. Children's desire for more freedom can't override the parents' responsibility for their safety. Never allow a child to do something risky just because "everyone else does it."

IGNORING CERTAIN BEHAVIOUR

If you believe a child is deliberately misbehaving to get attention, try ignoring the behaviour. Seeing that no attention is forthcoming, the child may stop. If that doesn't happen, you'll need a different approach.

This tactic should be used sparingly. It doesn't work with certain personality types. Don't ignore behaviour that might be bothering other people. A child yelling at home and a child yelling at the mall's food court are entirely different.

REDIRECTION

Sometimes a child can be distracted from an activity to avoid a problem. This technique is called **redirection**.

As a baby crawls toward the family cat with an open hand and a determined look, you might point out a toy to examine. Thrashing to escape a high chair, the same child may stare in wonder as you show how the rind curls away when you peel an orange. If the running footsteps of several preschool visitors may be disturbing the neighbours downstairs, you could seat them around the kitchen table for a snack or a session of drawing.

GIVING REMINDERS

Parents who expect their young children to get it right the first time every time are being unrealistic. Effective guidance takes many reminders about limits. Friendly reminders shouldn't be confused with lectures. "How many times have I told you..."

isn't a positive way to remind children. Written reminders often work well when children are old enough to read.

APPLYING CONSEQUENCES

Breaking the rules doesn't seem like a big deal when there's no penalty. Without consequences, limits aren't very effective. Children learn that parents don't mean what they say when parents fail to enforce rules.

A consequence should be something the child notices and cares about, without being unnecessarily severe. In other words, the punishment should fit the crime. Generally, taking away a privilege is most effective if related to the misbehaviour.

After five-year-old Caleb ate little of the unfamiliar food he ordered at a restaurant, his father told him, "You know that we don't waste food. Now you won't be going to the water park with Uncle Norm tomorrow." Do you think his dad was being fair?

Distracting children often prevents problem behaviour from occurring.
◆ **Why do you suppose so many doctors' waiting rooms have aquariums?**

Raising Children With Character

Whose Job?

As Darcy walked by the back door, she glanced down at Fluffy's bowl. It was empty. "He got away again without feeding Fluffy," she said to herself, shaking her head in dismay. "Something has got to change—now."

That evening, seven-year-old Max came rushing in the door after his Cub Scout meeting. "What are we having?" he called to Darcy. "I'm starving."

"Are you? It *is* time for dinner, isn't it. I seem to have 'forgotten' about it. Oh well, we can eat tomorrow." Darcy responded.

Max turned a startled look upon his mother. He looked around the kitchen, where no dinner preparations were apparent. "But I'm hungry now."

"Fluffy was hungry this morning too—until *I* fed her. You know that's your job."

Max looked dismayed. "I'll do it tomorrow," he said. "I promise."

"And every morning," Darcy said firmly. "Now, since I've 'forgotten' about dinner tonight, you'll have to fix a sandwich for yourself. Maybe I'll 'remember' to fix spaghetti tomorrow night."

◆◆◆◆◆ Thinking It Over ◆◆◆◆◆

1. What is Darcy trying to teach Max in this situation?
2. If Darcy were to take over feeding Fluffy, what would Max learn?
3. Why didn't Darcy go ahead and fix Max's dinner?
4. If Max forgets to feed Fluffy tomorrow and you were Darcy, what would you do?

Another father informed his five-year-old that his bike was put away in the garage for two days because it had been left on the driveway behind the car again. What do you think of that consequence? Do you see how it fits the offense better than the previous example?

Natural Consequences

Sometimes consequences come naturally from sources other than parents. No one creates them. They just happen. Tanya's dawdling made her late to day camp the morning her group was going to the zoo. She had to stay behind with the youngest group of campers.

When school started, Tanya was unhappy that the librarian wouldn't let her check out books. Why? She had neglected to return two books the previous spring.

Inappropriate Consequences

Some consequences should never be used by parents. Likewise, there are situations when children should not be punished. Comments like the ones below are harmful:

♥ Don't punish for toilet-training accidents: "You must still be a little baby. We're buying you diapers again."

♥ Don't punish for showing emotions: "Big boys don't cry. You're going to have to be tough to make it in this world."

♥ Don't make idle threats: "I'm going to give all your toys away to needy children if you don't pick them up this minute."

♥ Don't use shame tactics: "I thought you were a nice girl. I can't believe you did that."

♥ Don't inflict physical harm: "That's it! Get the belt."

♥ Don't withhold love as a punishment: "No, I'm not giving you a kiss goodnight. Get to bed now."

CHOOSING WORDS WITH CARE

Words can be weapons, as you can see from the inappropriate statements above. It's not easy to take back angry words once they're spoken. Counting to ten before speaking in anger is an old technique that's worth remembering.

Watch your tone when speaking to children. Try to be encouraging and reassuring. Using a loud voice or belittling tone may get attention, but it isn't an effective way to guide. An exception is when no has to be used emphatically for safety reasons. Another word to watch is "bad." Use it to describe a behaviour, not a child.

Internet Connects

http://www.mcgrawhill.ca/links/parenting
To learn more about programs that help build a child's character, go to the Web site above for *Parenting Rewards & Responsibilities, First Canadian Edition,* to see where to go next.

Negativism

Toddlers often delight in saying "no" in order to exercise their new sense of control. Around the age of 18 months, they enter a stage of **negativism**, a tendency to resist suggestions and commands.

Children's feelings are just as important as adults'. Children should be spoken to with respect, even when dealing with misbehaviour.

Guiding a young child who is fighting to be independent is challenging. Parents of toddlers can find themselves also being negative, saying "no" more than ever before. Remember that there must be some "yes" responses to balance those very necessary "no" responses. Using some of the other guidance techniques, such as redirection and keeping children busy, can eliminate the need for some of the "no" responses.

One solution to "arguing" with a toddler is to take the child's decision seriously. Tell the two-year-old who refuses to eat lunch: "Okay, but playing at the park will make you too hungry. We'll just stay home this afternoon."

However parents choose to deal with negativity, they shouldn't give in or bribe children. If toddlers discover that being disruptive gets them what they want, you can guess the result. Misbehaviour becomes routine.

Negativism isn't always a phase. Depression, illness, and lack of confidence can be causes. Older children may rebel when parents expect too much. Parents can search for events in their lives that might explain too much negativity.

MAKING MISTAKES

Children make mistakes. Parents make mistakes. That's part of being human.

What's not all right is continuing to make the same mistakes with little or no effort to change. Likewise, it isn't okay to cover up a mistake, act like it never happened, or find someone else to blame.

Parents can let their children know that parents aren't perfect. They can apologize when warranted. "I'm sorry I yelled at you when you spilled your milk again, Brian. I know you didn't do it on purpose," apologized his mother Brook. Another time she

Spotlight On
Time-Out

Many child-rearing experts recommend using **time-out**, a method of removing children from a problem situation to give them time to calm down. Older children can use the time to think about their behaviour. Time-out also gives the *parent* time to regroup, possibly preventing an angry outburst.

Time-out helps teach self-control. The child sits quietly in a time-out chair in a designated spot where there are no distractions—no television or toys. A timer is set, often for one minute for every year of the child's age. Disruptive behaviour like yelling or arguing results in the timer being reset. Experts recommend using time-out as early as eighteen months.

When used calmly and in a positive way, children can learn to use the time-out principle for self-control throughout their lives.

said, "Mommies need time-out sometimes too. I'm going to read the newspaper in the kitchen now while you put away your cars."

CONTROLLING ANGER

Raising children can be stressful and frustrating at times, yet parents need to remain in control. Brook decided to take her own time-out when she felt her anger rising.

Alone in the next room, Brook realized her mood had stemmed from an argument with a friend and had little to do with her son's behaviour. She was able to regain her composure and be a positive model for Brian at the same time. He wasn't conscious of the impression his mother's actions were making, but he stored away the effective way she handled her angry emotions.

There are several effective ways to manage anger:

♥ Walk away from the situation briefly.

♥ Take a deep breath before speaking or acting on impulse.

♥ Count to 10, or even 100.

♥ Take a walk or a warm bath if someone is there to watch the child.

♥ Call a friend who is willing to listen as you vent your frustrations for a few minutes.

♥ Pause to imagine how your child will feel hearing your angry outburst.

Thinking About Reactions

Analyzing how a situation could have been handled differently or avoided entirely can prevent a replay.

Driving home from a disastrous after-work trip to the mall, Melissa was furious. Her daughter Hannah had climbed out of the stroller and run from Melissa, hiding herself inside a round rack of clothes. As they passed the bakery on their way out, Hannah kept screaming that she needed cookies.

Melissa's anger and embarrassment subsided as she considered her own role in Hannah's behaviour. She knew that Hannah didn't adapt well to changes in routine. After Melissa picked Hannah up at the babysitter's house, they usually went home and ate an early supper. Shopping for clothes when they were both tired and hungry had not been a good idea. Melissa would plan better next time.

Everybody wins when families try to handle problems effectively.
◆ **What do children learn from the way their parents react in stressful situations?**

Melissa's first impulse had been to give Hannah a swat on the bottom, but she changed her mind. As she thought about why the trip had been such a failure, Melissa was glad that she hadn't spanked Hannah. She would have been venting her own anger, and it probably wouldn't have improved Hannah's behaviour. Simply leaving the mall had been a good move.

Many people disagree with spanking for any reason. Instead, they rely on other techniques to shape behaviour. They believe that spanking teaches children to control others by hitting. In addition, they fear that spanking produces problem behaviour in children and can lead to abuse.

Other people believe that spanking isn't harmful, but only if the adult is in control and never acting out of anger. They define spanking as using an open hand to strike a child's bottom without causing physical injury. When a child repeatedly does something unsafe or doesn't respond to other discipline techniques, they might spank, using two guidelines—*not too hard and not too often*. With adolescents and children under age two, experts agree that spanking is never appropriate.

Research can be found to support the differing views on spanking, which can be confusing. Parents need to read what authorities say and talk about the issue while their child is a baby.

Cross-Curricular Psychology CONNECTIONS

Can Children Be Too Good?

Most parents would be thrilled if their children always obeyed and gave their best effort in everything they did. However, psychologists have discovered that other, less desirable traits are often found in extremely obedient children. Some are afraid of taking risks. They feel secure doing only what their parents ask. Others identify too closely with adults. They don't see themselves as "one of the gang" of other children, and are often rejected in return. Still other children are perfectionists. They try to carry out their parents' wishes flawlessly. Unhealthy attitudes such as these deny children some of the adventure and learning opportunities of childhood. They may become socially isolated and frustrated. How would you encourage your child to take chances and enjoy being a child?

Looking Back

♥ With positive guidance, parents teach children to be self-directed.

♥ Parents need to have the confidence to let children know that parents are in charge.

♥ Knowing what behaviour is typical at a certain age helps parents decide how to guide their child.

♥ Preventing problems before they occur and using other positive guidance techniques lessen the need for punishment.

♥ Threatening and withholding love are inappropriate responses to a child's negative behaviour.

♥ People make mistakes, but parents must work to avoid repeating the same mistakes.

♥ Parents must control anger to avoid hurting their child physically or emotionally.

Knowledge and Understanding

1. How is positive guidance different from what people typically mean when they talk about discipline?
2. Why is confidence needed for parenting?
3. What might happen if parents let their daughter do whatever she pleases until she turns five?
4. Why should parents analyze why a child is misbehaving?
5. What techniques might help a parent prevent misbehaviour from happening in the first place?
6. To offer a choice, what might you say instead of "Should we have vegetables with dinner tonight?" Why is your suggestion better?
7. Why do children want limits, even if they act as though they don't?
8. If a six-year-old watches a movie that he was told not to by his parent, what would an appropriate consequence be?
9. How could time-out be handled away from home and the usual time-out place?
10. What are four ways that parents can help control their anger?

Review

Thinking and Inquiry

11. Your friend's child played very poorly during a soccer match. Knowing the importance of positive reinforcement, your friend said to the child, "Great game, honey." What do you think about this comment?

12. As a parent who wants to limit how often a child hears the word "no," what might you do or say instead?

Communication

13. Your mother has given your three-year-old daughter a porcelain doll. You find the fragile doll in the toy box with its fingers broken off. What would you say to your daughter and to your mother?

14. Everyone gets angry at times, and young children can be very frustrating. To get in touch with your feelings and thoughts, complete the following two sentences in writing: "Caring for a young child who is having one tantrum after another would make me feel . . . If this ever happens to me as a parent, I will do the right thing by . . ."

15. For each of the inappropriate consequences listed on page 422, suggest a better response. Write what you would say or do instead.

16. Suppose a friend asks for your advice on being a good parent. She seems concerned about making sure her toddler likes her. Write your response.

Application

17. Make a list of positive reinforcements for a toddler, a preschooler, and a school-age child.

18. Suppose you are a parent of a three-year-old. He has started acting up and being defiant every time you take him somewhere. You want to punish him immediately when this happens. Your husband doesn't want to make a scene in public. How might you reach an agreement?

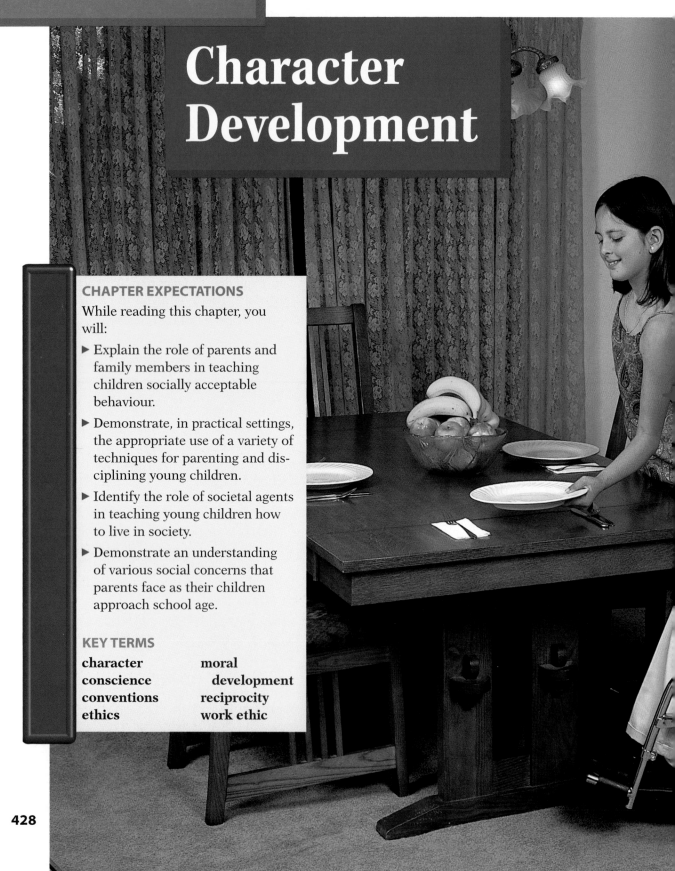

Character Development

CHAPTER EXPECTATIONS

While reading this chapter, you will:

▶ Explain the role of parents and family members in teaching children socially acceptable behaviour.

▶ Demonstrate, in practical settings, the appropriate use of a variety of techniques for parenting and disciplining young children.

▶ Identify the role of societal agents in teaching young children how to live in society.

▶ Demonstrate an understanding of various social concerns that parents face as their children approach school age.

KEY TERMS

character	moral
conscience	development
conventions	reciprocity
ethics	work ethic

"I'm glad we could all get together before school starts," Zoe said to her dad. They were setting the table for dinner.

"Where is Ethan?" Zoe asked. Zoe glanced around the room but didn't see Ethan.

"I have a feeling he's in the other room—where the refreshments are," her dad replied, excusing himself to go and check. As Zoe's dad reached the doorway, he saw Ethan by the counter holding a paper plate in his hands. He placed two cookies on the plate and hesitated.

I wonder if he's going to take another, Zoe thought as she stood behind her dad and watched. Ethan knew that two cookies was the limit. To Zoe's disappointment, Ethan reached out, took two more cookies, and turned toward the door.

As Zoe moved toward him, she thought about what she would say. She was disappointed that as soon as Ethan was on his own, he lost sight of the rules.

Seeing Zoe, Ethan's face brightened. "Look," he said happily. "They have my favourite cookie. I got two for me and two for you."

---◆---

What do you think? If you were Zoe, what would your thoughts be after hearing Ethan's words?

429

It takes civilized people to make a civilized world. Parents are responsible for raising civilized children. ◆ **What does it mean to be civilized? How does civility relate to character?**

What is Character?

Even when no one is watching, many people do the right thing. Those who have that kind of moral strength are said to have **character**. When Ethan followed his mother's two-cookie rule, he showed character in its early stages.

Developing character is a gradual process that spans a lifetime. If you spend much time with young children, you may have noticed that their sense of right and wrong differs from yours. They are just beginning to develop morally.

Character is shaped by ideas of what is right and wrong. As children learn these standards, **moral development** takes place. Parents are responsible for helping children gradually develop a sense of morality to guide them through life.

Kohlberg's Theory of Moral Development

Researcher Lawrence Kohlberg developed a theory on how people develop morally. He described three levels of moral development: preconventional, conventional, and post-conventional. According to Kohlberg, people move through these levels in order. Some never reach the highest point of moral development.

THE PRECONVENTIONAL LEVEL

Most children's moral reasoning is at the preconventional level from the time they are toddlers through the early school years. Kohlberg calls this level preconventional because children don't understand the **conventions**, or accepted standards, of behaviour.

As this level begins, moral behaviour is related to obedience. A young child like Ethan decides, "I won't do this because I'll get in trouble. Mommy will be mad." Children don't consider the point of view of others. They have no clear sense of right and wrong. Their main concern is avoiding punishment. Toddlers know they must do certain things, but often they don't understand why.

The word no is the easiest way to let toddlers know they must control their impulses. However, toddlers lack the self-discipline to do that all the time. For example, 18-month-old Maura had been told to stay away from the large plant in the hall. She often repeated the rule aloud to herself: "No touch." At other times, she would just smile and dig into the dirt. Her behaviour is typical for her age.

As children become older, they learn to follow rules based on reward and punishment. Their thinking is to help people who help them and hurt people who hurt them. They still evaluate actions in terms of the consequences. They believe that what their parents say or do is right.

These children tend to measure right and wrong in terms of the size of the misdeed. It doesn't matter if the act was accidental or intentional. Most preschoolers would think that a child who accidentally breaks several glasses deserves greater punishment than the child who intentionally breaks just one.

THE CONVENTIONAL LEVEL

Usually between the ages of nine and 15, Kohlberg theorized that people reach the conventional level of morality. They understand the conventions of society. In the early years at this level, there is a great deal of conformity. Children are sensitive to what other people want and think.

A sense of **reciprocity** (res-uh-PRAHS-uht-ee), or giving to someone and getting in return, emerges. Children do the right thing not only to satisfy their own needs but also to satisfy the needs of others.

By about age ten, most children begin to change their attitudes about rules. They no longer see rules simply as laws laid down by adults. For example, rules can be changed during a game as long as all the players agree. They grasp the concept of justice and equal treatment under the rules. They are beginning to think beyond the notion of adult authority.

When children realize that other people have a point of view, they begin to understand fairness. Playing by the rules becomes easier. Winning and losing graciously does too. ◆ **At what age might a child be willing and able to play by the rules of a game?**

At about 11 or 12 years of age, many children become aware of individual motives and circumstances. They begin to see another person's point of view. Graeme told his buddies, "We shouldn't make fun of Mrs. Naidu's clothes. Where she comes from, that's the way women dress."

Eventually, children adopt a law-and-order kind of thinking. They realize that living by the rules wins approval from others. Children begin to see more than one side of a situation. They no longer identify exclusively with their parents. Kohlberg viewed this ability to see another's perspective as the real beginning of morality.

THE POST-CONVENTIONAL LEVEL

Kohlberg believed that the post-conventional level was reached at about age 16. By this time, people have progressed beyond just following the rules. They grasp the concept of human rights. People at this stage are capable of thinking abstractly.

Some adults move to the highest point in this level. Those who make this progress develop universal ethical principles based on reciprocity and human equality. The development of a true conscience lets them value behaviour that respects the dignity of all other people, as well as their own dignity. Such an individual might say, "I won't perform this action because it's morally wrong."

Developing a Conscience

As emotionally healthy children grow, they develop a **conscience** (KAHN-shens). This inner sense of what is right and wrong prompts good behaviour and makes the person feel guilty for wrong or bad behaviour. To develop a conscience, people must have empathy for others. They must have the desire to understand how another person might be feeling.

Experts believe that the conscience develops between ages five and seven, often when children are exposed to larger groups of their peers in school. At that age, youngsters have a real interest in determining right and wrong.

When their behaviour is wrong, children need to know why. A brief explanation helps them learn empathy. An appropriate consequence teaches them responsibility for what they did.

Younger children are also learning right from wrong. The ground work for developing a conscience is laid as parents teach them to pet animals gently, not to be selfish with toys, and to understand what no means. They start to feel remorse when they know they've misbehaved.

Some parents worry about making children feel guilty at times. Without such feelings, however, children don't learn to do right by others. They care only about themselves. To live successfully in society, people need to feel some degree of guilt over not treating people the way they want to be treated themselves.

SAYING NO

Setting limits for children and being able to say no to them is an important part of developing their conscience. Parents shouldn't deny everything a child requests, but they shouldn't cater to every whim either. Just as it is wrong for parents to shame children, they shouldn't shield them from feeling bad when appropriate.

According to Harvard professor Dr. Robert Coles, children need to learn that the world doesn't revolve around them. He stresses that parents must teach children self-control instead of letting them act on any impulse.

Michelle had been raised under the watchful eye of a very critical adult. She wanted her twins' childhood to be more fun. Her mistake was planning child-oriented activities almost non-stop. No amount of catering to her daughter and son was enough. When Michelle did say no, the children skillfully made her change her mind. The twins, Terry and Tina, were demanding and disrespectful toward Michelle, their father, and others. They hadn't learned the moral lesson of respect for others.

Often something is missing in the people who commit violent crimes—empathy. As children, they never learned to understand and respect the feelings of others. ◆ **What might the children in this photo learn as they volunteer with adults in a soup kitchen for homeless people?**

Internet Connects

http://www.mcgrawhill.ca/links/parenting
To learn more about parenting from A to Z, go to the Web site above for *Parenting Rewards & Responsibilities, First Canadian Edition*, to see where to go next.

THE ROLE OF EMPATHY

Because Michelle's twins were raised to think the family revolved around them, they had little empathy for other people. They fought with each other constantly. They expected to be entertained. At the movie theatre, Terry made the rest of the family late for the movie by demanding popcorn and then running to talk to a school friend. Tina took Terry's drink when she didn't like her own. The resulting argument disturbed everyone in the theatre.

What could their parents have done differently? From the time the children were very young, they could have discouraged behaviour that hurt or inconvenienced other people. Going to movies without the children would have shown that parents have a right to their own interests. As for the incident at the theatre, the parents could have refused to buy snacks and allowed Terry to talk for only a moment on their way in.

To learn empathy, children need positive examples to model. Kissing a bruised elbow can make the injury feel better and let the child know the parent cares. Having children help select and carry cans to a food drive helps them participate in sharing with people who are less fortunate. Can you think of other ways children can be exposed to empathy in action?

Teaching Values to Children

People believe strongly in their values. Some core values are universal to society. They include such traits as honesty, trust, and respect. Other values depend on the individual. The list of possibilities is very long, but includes ideas about religion, health, family togetherness, education, volunteerism, protecting the environment, and a sense of humour.

When children are young, parents can begin to convey family values. Values influence how parents guide children and spend their time and money. Parents should discuss their personal values with their children. Allowing children to form values with no parental input is unwise.

SETTING AN EXAMPLE

You can probably think of people you've known who said one thing and did another. No person is perfect, but parents need to strive to set a good example. Preschool children are very impressionable. They need large doses of positive modelling because they believe that what their parents do is right.

Parish Car Wash

FEED THE HUNGRY

Internet Connects

http://www.mcgrawhill.ca/links/parenting
To learn more about raising children, go to the Web site above for *Parenting Rewards & Responsibilities, First Canadian Edition,* to see where to go next.

Examples teach better than lectures. Many parents involve children in character-building activities, such as having a car wash to raise money for charity.
◆ **What similar activities could include children?**

Some opportunities are obvious. You don't want your children using drugs or bad language, so you don't expose them to either. You treat other people with respect so children will model your behaviour. You don't spend so much money on yourself that there isn't enough for the family's needs.

Honesty is a value that can be hard to display at all times. Experts recommend that parents avoid telling "white lies" in front of children. Often, there is a way to avoid them. Instead of fibbing by saying "Your tuna casserole is great, Ellie," a guest could say, "It was so nice of you to have us over." If a phone call comes at an inconvenient time, truthfully saying, "He can't come to the phone right now" is much better than saying, "He's not home."

Raising Children With Character

I'm Sorry

Kelly balanced the overloaded grocery bag as she climbed the front steps and fumbled for her key. What a day, she thought, relieved to be home. She set the heavy bag on the coffee table and heard a strange crunch.

As eight-year-old Joe came into the room, his welcoming smile turned to a horrified stare. "My model!" he cried.

Kelly moved the grocery bag. A model airplane lay broken on the table. She felt a rush of anger. "What was that doing there?" she demanded.

"Dad and I put it there to dry," he said, blinking away tears.

"Well, that's not the place for it!" Kelly sputtered, and took the groceries into the kitchen.

A minute later she returned. Joe knelt by the table, holding pieces of his model in both hands. Kelly sat beside him. "I'm sorry I broke your model. I was the one who was careless. It wasn't your fault at all, and I'm sorry I yelled at you."

Joe sniffled. "It's okay." He held up the model and fit the broken wing back in place. "Look, we can glue it again."

Kelly ruffled Joe's hair. "I'm glad one of us is acting grown-up today."

◆◆◆◆◆ **Thinking It Over** ◆◆◆◆◆

1. Why did Kelly yell at Joe if she knew it wasn't his fault?
2. What are the two most important words in this scene?
3. What did Kelly teach Joe by apologizing?

DIRECT TEACHING

Setting a good example is the first step in teaching values. The second is talking to children about the importance of **ethics**, a system of moral values and obligations.

With a little practice, teaching values can be a natural part of daily living. For instance, on an afternoon walk Mrs. Molinari bent down to pick up some food wrappers. "We want our city to be a nice place to live, so we don't want litter on the ground," she said. Later, she pointed out the high school. "That's where you two will go to school when you're older. You'll learn all about people in different countries and maybe even how to speak another language."

Books and stories can also be used to teach ethics. As you read, ask your children how they feel about each character's behaviour and how they think it makes the other characters feel. Then tell them what you think. More information on how to raise ethical children can be found on pages 438–439.

Encouraging Responsible Behaviour

As children grow and mature, following a set of positive values should result in responsible behaviour. Parents have to be clear about how they expect their children to behave, appropriate to their age. They need to make sure children understand why certain things have to be done. In turn, behaving responsibly builds a sense of self-worth in children.

For instance, when Cody accidentally kicked the dog's bowl, his stepmother could have just told him to wipe up the water. Instead she handed him a paper towel and explained, "You need to wipe that up right away. We don't want Grandma to slip in it. If she fell, that could really hurt her, couldn't it?"

She also tried not to make it convenient for Cody to lie. Knowing that no one else had been downstairs, she didn't ask, "Did you get Dad's tools out?" Instead, she reminded him, "Dad doesn't want you using the tools unless he's there with you. Put them back where you found them."

The towels may not be folded perfectly, but who cares when you're teaching a child responsibility? By showing gratitude for a young child's effort, you just might have a willing towel-folder for many years ahead.

PERSONAL RESPONSIBILITY

Children can be taught at a young age that they are responsible for their actions. They shouldn't be allowed to blame others for their mistakes and problems. Many of today's social problems can be traced to people who shift blame for their shortcomings to others. When parents make mistakes, children need to see them taking steps to correct them.

Kyle's father had a long talk with him after the five-year-old said, "It wasn't my fault. All the other kids were throwing rocks at that old van, and Austin said I was chicken if I didn't do it." What would you have said if you were his parent?

Parents are responsible for the health and safety of their children. Children need to be taught their own role in staying safe and healthy too. Schools often do a good job with these lessons, but reinforcement is needed at home.

Spotlight On
Managing Money Responsibly

No matter what a family's income, children need to learn how to handle money. An allowance can teach this responsibility. Some allowances are tied to helping out at home, but some parents believe that money shouldn't be an incentive for pitching in. Linking an allowance to good behaviour can be a problem if children can't count on having a consistent amount to manage.

Even preschool children may receive a small allowance. They can plan ahead for a purchase, such as buying a small toy when they go shopping. Children shouldn't expect to get something every time they enter a store, however.

Preschoolers have limited understanding about what money can buy. A small handful of change doesn't go far when looking at the toy shelves in a store. One mother devised her own "Saturday store" in a shoebox, where she placed inexpensive trinkets for her children to select. To help their budding concept of money, she marked each with a price they could afford.

As children become older, their understanding grows. When Sam and his mother were shopping for shoes, the $50 she had budgeted wasn't enough for the brand he wanted. She gave the third-grader a choice. "I'll buy one of these two pairs, but if you want the basketball shoes, you'll have to pay the extra money yourself. That's $22, Sam."

Sam asked if she would use her convenience or credit card. His mother said no and briefly explained about convenience and credit cards. Sam had to decide for himself whether the expensive shoes were worth more to him than the video game he also wanted.

Most experts agree that children should be free to spend their allowance as they wish. If they waste it occasionally, that's their choice. Otherwise, the money isn't really theirs and the allowance isn't a teaching tool. Children learn from making poor choices as well as good ones.

Raising an Ethical Child

Doing what is right doesn't come naturally. Parents begin to teach children the difference between right and wrong at a very early age. When parents teach these lessons well, children become ethical adults who do what is morally correct. They become the doctors, lawyers, salespeople, and auto mechanics people can count on.

RESPONSIBILITY

Responsible people have a sense of duty. When your child picks up toys, encourage that to happen again by admiring the good job.

RESPECT

Teaching courtesy teaches respect for others. Use simple lessons at first, such as saying "please" and "thank you."

CONCERN

To teach concern for others, show a child how to be helpful and thoughtful. Let your child be the one to take a gift to someone special.

TRUSTWORTHINESS

Being trusted is a good feeling. A child learns about trust when you keep your own promises. Don't say, "I'll take you to the park," unless you know you can follow through.

FAIRNESS

Through sharing, children learn about fairness. Teach a child to consider another person's rights and feelings by sharing a snack.

CITIZENSHIP

Children won't respect authority and rules in society unless they first respect them at home. Explain that wearing a seatbelt in the car is a rule. Then make sure your child is always buckled in.

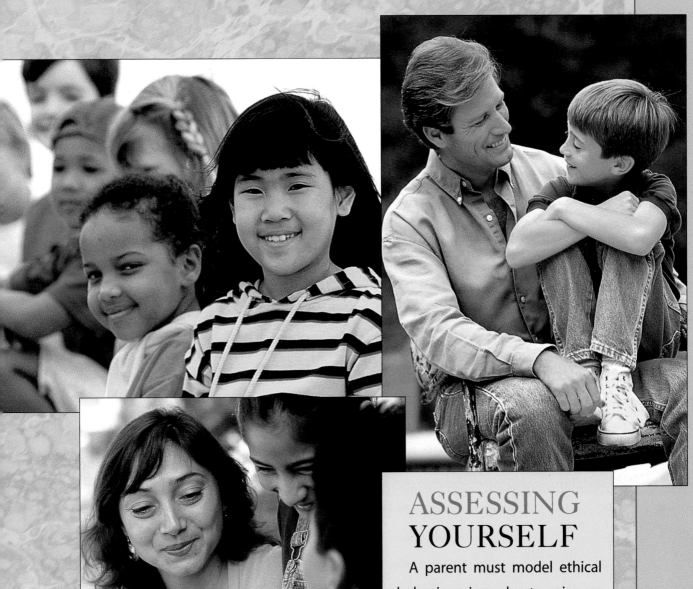

ASSESSING YOURSELF

A parent must model ethical behaviour in order to raise an ethical child. What kind of role model would you be as a parent? For each of the qualities described, complete the following sentence in your own words: "Some of the ways I show (fill in the quality) are…"

439

RESPONSIBILITY AT HOME

Children don't always do a perfect job when they help out at home. They might miss spots while dusting and leave a chalky film of cleanser on the sink. To have a job done perfectly, some parents simply find it quicker and easier to do it themselves. That's a mistake. Children need to be involved.

Very young children often love to help because they feel grown-up. While they're enthusiastic, recruit them as special helpers. If Alex likes to play in water, teach him step-by-step how to clean the sink. If Robin changes her outfit repeatedly, show her how to fold towels and sort laundry.

Good judgment must be used in doling out jobs, however. A preschooler shouldn't be drying slippery china plates or dusting a shelf of fragile figurines.

After demonstrating how to do a job, a child may modify the procedure somewhat. Unless there's some risk to the new method, let the child proceed.

Express appreciation for children's efforts, but make your expectations clear. If you want Timmy to make his bed everyday, don't let him off the hook for a week. That will teach him to put things off.

Promoting a Work Ethic

Children who are raised thinking life is all play and no work have a rude awakening ahead. Giving children duties at home helps instill a **work ethic**. This is a knowledge of the value of work and its ability to strengthen a person's character. Doing a good job makes children's confidence and self-esteem grow.

Parents must examine their own behaviour. Is their attitude positive? Grumbling about the drudgery of housework and going to work can rub off on a child.

RESPONSIBILITY IN THE COMMUNITY

Being a good neighbour and citizen is something most young children are eager to do. Children as young as age two can help in family recycling efforts.

Some children resist doing chores at home, but parents need to take a strong stand. Children should begin young with simple duties and continue to help as they grow up. The work ethic they learn will help them work responsibly in a career someday.

Essential skills such as co-operation and teamwork can be developed both in and out of school.

Witnessing a parent being a good citizen is a powerful teacher. Children can accompany their parent into the booth on Election Day. They can go along to visit older neighbours or help rake their yard. With a parent, they can look for a neighbour's missing pet. They can help collect donations door-to-door for a worthwhile charity. While performing good deeds, parents should explain why neighbours need to pull together.

RESPONSIBILITY AT SCHOOL

Once children begin school, it becomes a major life influence. The lessons learned at home must be applied in a new setting.

School requires children to acquire the responsibility and discipline needed for learning. At each successive grade, students are expected to assume more independence in their learning. Parents play a vital role in this process. Their words and actions convey the importance they place on education. Is completing homework more important than watching the ball game? Do parents support teachers? Do they help their children learn critical skills, such as time management, that are needed to succeed?

Parents often wonder how much help they should give children with their homework. There's no one right answer. In general, parents should provide help when it's needed but not do the homework or a project for the child. Often giving specific suggestions or helping develop a plan for how to complete a project helps improve the child's own skills.

The desire to be accepted by peers starts early. Children try out the behaviours they see in others, though these may be inappropriate. Parents need to keep lines of communication open so children share their thoughts and feelings. Talking about how to handle difficult situations can help children learn to adapt what they've learned about right and wrong to new situations. When parents establish a good relationship with teachers, they also receive a clearer understanding of how their children are handling the social aspects of school.

Dealing with Outside Influences

As much as parents want their children to remain innocent, living in a fast-paced society exposes them to a great deal.

Building Parenting Skills

PARENTING WITH GOOD JUDGMENT

Parenting with good judgment means accurately sizing up a situation and choosing a wise response. You know children's abilities and limitations, as well as your own. You recognize problems before they arise and act to avert them. To parent with good judgment, Terry, a parent of three:

▶ Makes sure the two youngest children have eaten lunch and taken naps before an outing.

▶ Watches them closely when visiting a friend with a swimming pool.

▶ Maintains the family car to ensure everyone's safety.

▶ Accompanies four-year-old Eli to the store to return a candy bar after discovering he took it.

▶ Makes a rule that Stephanie, a Grade five student, can't ride her bike from 4:30 to 6 p.m. when traffic is heavy in their neighbourhood.

▶ Reduces the children's fevers with medication, but keeps them home for 24 hours after the fever breaks.

◆ ◆ Your Thoughts ◆ ◆

❶ What thinking skills are needed for good judgment?

❷ Why must you know your own strengths and weaknesses in order to use good judgment?

❸ How would you use good judgment as a parent in the following situations: a child pleads with a busy, tired parent to go camping next weekend; the ice on a lake appears thick enough to allow children to skate.

As a parent, you can encourage your child to talk when the time seems right.
◆ **How do you think a parent might know that the time is right?**

Parents of preschoolers can tell you that life is never the same after a child leaves the controlled environment of home to be with new peers. Children pick up on things the parent may have hoped to shield them from for a long time.

Fortunately there are ways parents can counteract negative messages. Helping children recognize the values behind various options can help them stay true to their own morals. This, in turn, reinforces and deepens their character.

PEER INFLUENCE

Most people agree that life can be affected by who your friends are. Children need to be taught that the way friends behave and treat people, not their popularity or how much money their family has, is what's important.

Once children enter grade school, helping them select friends is difficult. For younger children, focusing on friends with traits you want your child to display is possible. In Logan's neighbourhood, two other boys about the same age lived across the street. One was very active, but he obeyed his parents. The other had been caught playing with lighters and other serious mischief.

Logan's mother made a point of inviting the first boy over to play. She also joined a babysitting co-op where Logan could interact with other children his age. Without labelling the troubled neighbour child as a bad boy, Logan's parents discussed the risks of his negative behaviour. Their discussion led to talk about not going along with behaviour you know is wrong.

When a playmate becomes a serious threat to a child's well-being, parents may need to step in and end the friendship. The degree of danger and risk to the child is the key. Hearing the friend using bad language, a parent can say "We don't use words like that at our house." Then they can monitor the situation.

If a friend encourages a child to steal or cheat, however, it's time for a serious talk with the child. A parent may have no choice but to discourage the friendship and create opportunities for the child to spend time with others.

MEDIA INFLUENCES

Do you know any families who would invite strangers into their homes, knowing they would promote negative values to the children? Many people believe that unsupervised television viewing does just that,

Some parents use the television as a babysitter for children. ◆ **Why does that happen? What are the dangers?**

Watching television as a family ensures the content is appropriate and enjoyed by everyone.

shown that over a period of time, children become desensitized to what they watch.

Television programming often undermines family values. Besides questionable content in the programs, the 400 commercials the average child sees every day fuel their desire to acquire many "things."

By encouraging passivity, television watching has also been linked to unhealthy snacking and childhood obesity. Watching television is a passive experience. Children are better off being actively engaged in learning and other activities. Even educational shows cannot provide personal attention. A child doesn't have the chance to ask questions or explore an idea further. Television moves at its own pace, not the child's.

Since few families want to get rid of their television set, they need to set rules about what children may watch. They might follow these guidelines:

♥ Limit television watching to an hour a day or to certain times. Schoolwork and household jobs must be done. Some shows may be off limits.

♥ Teach children to monitor their own viewing. Children don't have to go along with popular opinion or accept what doesn't meet their standards.

♥ Check ratings but watch programming themselves. Their family's values may not coincide with someone else's ratings. Turn off the set or switch channels when necessary.

♥ Eliminate programs that will trouble children. Consider blocking questionable channels.

♥ Make sure children know the house rules and follow them when parents aren't around.

and the influences don't stop with television. Many movies, magazines, lyrics, and Web sites contain inappropriate content for children.

Psychologist Mary Pipher fears there is too little distinction between adults and children in today's society. Adults have less information to share with children because they watch the same shows. Monitoring children's interests and activities is time consuming, but it's part of being a parent.

Television

Many parents agree that television has much to offer. Documentaries show children the wonders of nature and how people live half a world away. Some network programming is enjoyable and motivating.

Other shows, however, are unsuitable for children. Some are violent or contain sexually explicit material. Research has

POOR ROLE MODELS

Mrs. Grieves had forgotten to tell a new babysitter about their TV rules. Six-year-old Whitney was quick to fill her in. "We're not allowed to watch this show. We can't use the computer when Mom's gone either."

Whitney's babysitter said, "I'll make you a deal. This is my favourite show. It's really funny. You can have chocolate milk and stay up late if you don't tell your parents we watched it. They'll never know the difference."

Not surprisingly, this sitter was not asked to watch Whitney again. Her actions made her a poor role model. Sometimes it isn't easy to keep children away from people who set a poor example. Whether a babysitter, a family member, or family friend, children are bound to observe poor role models. The key is for the parent to set a positive example that will override the negative ones.

Celebrities

Unfortunately, popular personalities in the media frequently end up to be negative role models for children. They may be athletes, movie stars, or entertainers who live in ways that conflict with family values, provoking some interesting discussions between parents and children. Such conversations help children become aware of different social and cultural pressures beyond the family.

Parents can help children decide what is right or wrong, just or unjust, true or false, significant or insignificant. They can lead children to explore, question, and discuss their ideas and feelings. Children will not always agree with parents, but they need a clear understanding of what parents believe. With that kind of standard in life, children always have something to guide them and to return to when they face tough decisions.

Internet Connects

http://www.mcgrawhill.ca/links/parenting
To learn more about family issues, go to the Web site above for *Parenting Rewards & Responsibilities, First Canadian Edition,* to see where to go next.

Children need positive role models as they grow up. In busy families, relatives can help parents demonstrate and teach the values that help children build character.

Looking Back

♥ Character is having moral strength to act the way you believe is right.

♥ Kohlberg's levels of moral development are preconventional, conventional, and post-conventional.

♥ Caring about other people's feelings helps children develop a conscience.

♥ Values influence how people live.

♥ Parents can teach children to be responsible by setting a good example and talking to them about values.

♥ Children's TV viewing needs to be monitored by parents.

♥ Outside influences can be counteracted by parents to lessen the harm they might do.

Knowledge and Understanding

1. How is character related to moral development?
2. What are two characteristics of toddlers' moral development?
3. What is reciprocity? When does it become apparent that children have a sense of it?
4. What does reaching the highest level of moral development mean?
5. Can children begin to develop a conscience before age five? Explain your answer.
6. Don doesn't want to hurt his son's feelings by making the boy feel guilty. What would you say to Don?
7. Can children develop a conscience if they don't have empathy? Explain your answer.
8. How might parents set an example showing that they value education?
9. When children blame other people or things for their own mistakes, what should parents do?
10. Why is it important for parents to be positive about their own work and household duties?
11. How can parents monitor what their children see on television?

Review

Thinking and Inquiry

12. Two 16-year-old cousins have grown up next door to each other, attending the same schools. Why might they have entirely different thoughts about character?

13. Lawrence Kohlberg (1927–1987) used only boys in his research. Based on children you know, how might that have affected his theory on moral development?

14. Evidence exists that it takes increasing amounts and levels of violence in movies to cause emotional reactions in people. How does this principle relate to people's attitude toward real-life violence?

Communication

15. Suppose a family spends Thanksgiving with relatives who drink too much. On the way home, the parent wants to explain the situation to children, ages six and eight. Write a dialogue of how you would discuss this with your children.

16. Kohlberg based his theory in part on Piaget's work. Reread the section on Piaget's theory of intellectual development in Chapter 19. Write a few paragraphs explaining how intellectual development and moral development are linked.

17. Suppose you are the parent of a two-year-old girl. While you are watching a detective show on television, a noisy scene with shooting and yelling comes on. You notice that your daughter stops playing and stares at the television. Then she lifts her beloved teddy bear in the air, and slams him to the floor. What has happened and how will you respond?

Application

18. Write an evaluation of a TV show or movie you watched recently that involved a child's or teen's struggle with a moral issue. Did the person end up exhibiting strong character?

19. With a partner, make a list of chores a three-year-old could handle at home. Then list what a seven-year-old could do. What reasoning did you use for assigning the chores to each age?

Communicating with Children

Adam peered into his stepson's bedroom. Ben sat on his bed reading.

"Are you feeling better, Ben?" Adam asked.

Ben nodded and quickly dropped his gaze.

"Good." Adam sat down on the edge of the bed. "But I'm worried about these stomach aches. I wish I knew what caused them so I could help you get better. It's no fun being sick, is it?"

Ben shook his head without looking up. "Sometimes it feels tight inside, and I think I'm going to throw up."

Adam winced. "That's pretty bad. And I'll bet you miss everyone at school when you're absent. That reminds me. How is Mrs. Parnelli doing?"

Ben sighed as if exasperated. "She's not there anymore," he exclaimed. "She left to have her baby two weeks ago. Now we have Ms. Grissom. Everyone calls her 'Ms. Gruesome.' She's mean."

"Oh, yes, now I remember," Adam said. "She started—well, just about the time your stomach aches did." Adam leaned forward. "Tell me more about this gruesome Ms. Grissom."

---◆---

What do you think? How will communication help Adam and his father?

Talking to a child about behaviour at Aunt Jo's and choosing milk over a soft drink is fairly simple. As children grow older, however, more difficult topics arise, such as friends, cheating, and drugs. ◆ **How do simple conversations pave the way for tougher ones?**

Communication Counts

Fortunately, the days when "children should be seen and not heard" are long gone. Good communication between parents and children is an ideal that every healthy family desires. **Communication**—the process of sharing information, thoughts, and feelings—starts early, long before children learn to talk. Developing and maintaining good communication

with very young children helps ensure a better relationship when they are older. The entire family is strengthened.

When parents listen to their daughters and sons express their ideas, they make the children feel important, that their thoughts have merit. This is a natural, sincere way to build self-esteem. In contrast, children feel rejected when their attempts to communicate are ignored or denied.

"Have you ever gone for a whole day without talking to anyone?" 12-year-old Wesley asked his mother. "There's a seventh-grader at school who says he does. He lives with his aunt and sometimes she has to work out of town on Saturdays. She leaves real early and then gets home late at night. She lets him order pizza and rent videos, but still he says he doesn't like being by himself all day. I was thinking about asking him over this weekend."

Non-verbal actions give clues to what a person is really thinking, even when the actual words don't.
◆ **What verbal and non-verbal communication is going on between this mother and daughter?**

Internet Connects

http://www.mcgrawhill.ca/links/parenting
To learn more about communicating with children, go to the Web site above for *Parenting Rewards & Responsibilities, First Canadian Edition,* to see where to go next.

Verbal and Non-verbal Messages

Some people think that talking and communicating are the same thing. It's true that most people use verbal communication throughout the day. Besides the words they speak, a verbal message includes the tone that's used. Consider the phrase "That's quite a sight." Try saying it in different tones of voice. How does the meaning change?

Communication goes beyond words and tone, however. **Non-verbal communication** involves facial expressions, eye contact, posture, and body movements that convey a message without words. Non-verbal messages are also referred to as body language. Often, people aren't aware of the non-verbal messages they're sending. Communication can be especially confusing when verbal and non-verbal messages don't match.

Danny and Kate's mother called a family meeting when she began working overtime and needed to ask for more help at home. Uncle Patrick, their mother's brother who lived with them, slumped in his chair and looked out the window during the discussion. At one point with eyes closed, he spoke: "What do you want me to do?" Which do you think had more impact at the meeting: Patrick's words or his non-verbal communication?

Wesley's mother agreed that his idea was a good one. To her, it sounded like the boy's physical needs were being met, but maybe not his emotional needs. "I'm sure your friend gets lonely. You know, people actually have a need to interact with other people."

Whether they live with one parent, both parents, or another caregiver, children need to feel that someone is there who cares. Through words and gestures, adults can communicate love, as well as limits. Wesley and his mother heard some good news a few weeks later. His new friend's aunt had started a job that didn't require travel.

Strategies for Communicating

Some people seem to have a knack for saying just the right thing at the right time. For many others, effective communication is a skill that takes practice. By developing good communication skills, parents can keep the lines of communication open.

Keep in mind that what works in one family may not be appropriate for another. The family members' unique personalities and situations have to be taken into account. For instance, at breakfast Mrs. Li chats with her preschoolers about their busy day ahead. Her neighbour, Mr. Barnett, is just happy to get his son to the day-care centre on time. Since the four-year-old resists getting up so early, the Barnetts communicate much better later in the day.

BEGIN EARLY

One recent study linked the number of words that babies and toddlers hear with the way they scored on aptitude tests taken at ages three and nine. Babies living in "talkative" homes where as many as 2100 words were heard per hour scored remarkably higher than babies in households where only 600 words were spoken per hour. The researchers noted that voices from television or radio didn't have the same effect.

What should parents talk to a baby about? Just about anything. The weather, what you're fixing for lunch, the pretty flowers and vegetables at the supermarket, and the neighbour's dog might all be topics of conversation. Talking, making eye contact, and smiling at babies, combined with patting and holding them, are essential to giving them a warm feeling about the world in general. As you speak to infants, pause to allow a response occasionally. Watch for cues they might give indicating that they're tired or don't want to "talk" anymore.

USE THE RIGHT TONE

High-pitched baby talk and silly words may sound funny to casual listeners, but it is enjoyed by most babies. Don't worry about what other people think if your pitch raises somewhat when interacting with a baby. This form of talking is called parentese and it occurs around the world.

Cross-Curricular — Technology CONNECTIONS

Computers and Speech Problems

Children who have trouble understanding spoken words may overcome the disability by playing special computer games. The games are based on the findings of two American university researchers. Their studies suggest that some of these children can't process certain sounds, such as "ba" and "da," as quickly as people speak them. The computer games slow these sounds from 400 to 800 times their natural length, and award the children points for recognizing them. The sounds are gradually speeded up, and the time between them is shortened. In a four-week trial, the children who played these games gained one to two years' worth of language development. When they were retested six weeks later, much of that improvement remained. **What skills might children improve by playing certain computer games?**

Babies love it when someone imitates their own sounds. If they coo playfully and you coo back, they'll be delighted. Singing is also a wonderful way to communicate. Infants don't mind if you can't carry a tune.

As babies grow into toddlers, use your natural voice to speak to them. You want them to pick up proper grammar and language from your example. Don't try to correct their grammar and choice of words, however.

All children need to be spoken to with respect. Avoid yelling and speaking with a belittling tone. Of course, children are much younger and smaller than adults, but they should never be regarded as inferior.

THINK ABOUT TIMING

Would you approach your mother for a favour when she is having a serious conversation on the phone? Probably not. The results might not be what you wanted.

Parents also need to take timing into account when dealing with their children. Children should not be expected to be talkative just because the parent has time and is in the mood to talk. A meaningful conversation isn't likely to occur when children are concentrating on another activity they're enjoying. Children and adults, alike, are not at their best when they're hungry or tired. Most conversations can wait until the family members have eaten or rested.

Choosing a Place

Bedtime is often a time when children like to talk. The hustle and bustle of the day is over, and the children have the parent to themselves. Asking "What good things happened today?" or "What did you like about today?" are ways to communicate and to build optimism in a young child.

Riding in the car can also be an ideal time for conversation. Eye contact with the driver may not be possible, but distractions like household jobs and a ringing phone and doorbell are missing.

Some of the best conversations can take place while playing catch or a simple card game, taking a walk, cooking something together, or stopping for ice cream. Why do you think sitting together in front of the television is not a very good place to communicate?

Infants want to converse, even if they don't understand the words. Plant the seeds of communication by responding to what the infant says, even if you don't understand the sounds.

Sometimes it's necessary to "schedule" a talk. When a child wants to talk and the parent is truly busy doing something else or simply doesn't have time to listen, it's a good idea to set a specific time to continue the conversation. Saying "I have to get to the dentist. Let's talk about that after your nap," or "Be sure to tell me more while I'm fixing dinner tonight" lets children know you value what they have to say.

Respecting Others

Children learn to respect other people when they realize that their activities and feelings are important too. It's all right to say "You know how you like to play when a friend comes over. Mrs. Murphy is my friend and she's here to talk to me" or "Wait until Marie finishes her homework to ask her to play the game." Making them realize that it's unacceptable to interrupt people helps children develop empathy.

ASK QUESTIONS

"Where's the kitty, Michael?" Carolyn asked. He pointed to the top of the page. After the story, her 18-month-old ran to the kitchen. She figured he wanted a snack but couldn't make out his words.

Instead of handing him any snack, Carolyn asked, "Do you want a banana or a cracker?"

"Mean-ah," he responded with his word for banana.

"See the little spots on this pretty yellow banana, Michael? That means it will taste extra sweet," Carolyn explained. She didn't expect her son to understand every word she said, but his brain was storing her message.

Asking questions is a vital part of communicating for people of any age. Parents involve children in storybooks by asking an occasional question as they read. They also use questions as a conversation starter.

Internet Connects

http://www.mcgrawhill.ca/links/parenting
To learn more about advice for talking with children, go to the Web site above for *Parenting Rewards & Responsibilities, First Canadian Edition,* to see where to go next.

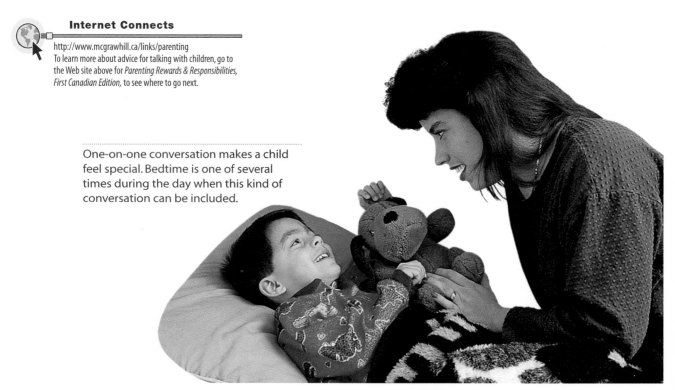

One-on-one conversation makes a child feel special. Bedtime is one of several times during the day when this kind of conversation can be included.

Phrase Questions Well

The way parents phrase questions can affect the success of a conversation. Make a practice of asking open-ended questions, instead of those that can be answered with a yes or no. When asked about their day, what do most children respond? "Fine." A conversation is more likely to result if you ask "What did you have for a snack this morning?" or "What story did Miss Kim read today?"

Becoming familiar with school or child-care activities and meeting a child's playmates shows children that their parents are interested in their life. It also gives everyone more to talk about. Get in the habit of asking to see art projects and schoolwork that children have brought home. Ask them to check backpacks in case they forgot to share their papers. Use a positive tone. "Tell me about your picture" is a better way to initiate conversation than "What's this supposed to be?"

Good social etiquette is learned easily by children whose parents model polite conservation during social activities, such as board games or meals.

POLITE CONVERSATION

Part of a parent's job is teaching children to interact with other people respectfully. Children will learn by following their parents' example, but they need to be taught some basics too. Sometimes it's possible to make a game of teaching manners. To communicate in social situations, here are some basics to teach children:

♥ While someone is speaking, wait to have your say.

♥ When it's your turn to talk, speak briefly. Let others have a chance too.

♥ Talk in a voice that others can hear, but not too loudly.

♥ Call the person by name. "Hi, Mr. Stallings" and "Thank you, Aunt Trudy" are appropriate.

♥ Leave private matters out of conversations. That includes secrets you've overheard or very personal things about yourself.

♥ Avoid personal questions, such as "How much did that cost?" or "How much money does your spouse make?"

♥ Avoid topics that might upset somebody or hurt his or her feelings. "My friend says your brother is in jail" and "Your house looks haunted" are examples of this.

♥ Never laugh at or make fun of the way a person speaks, whether with an accent or bad grammar.

♥ Teach children the way you want them to answer the phone and take messages.

Once you ask a question, pay attention to the child's answer. If you don't, the child may soon learn that responding to your questions is pointless.

USE ACTIVE LISTENING

Letting the other person do the talking is a technique used by psychologists and counsellors. **Active listening** is a useful skill for parents too. It often requires accepting the way the son or daughter feels without judging or making them feel "bad" for having such feelings. Active listening means more than hearing the speaker's exact words. It involves sensing the person's message and how he or she feels about it.

Casey complained to her mother: "I hate Jimmy. He came in my room and got into my stuff again. I'm sick of him." Mrs. Williams could have said, "Don't say mean things about your little brother. You don't hate him. You love him." Instead she responded with empathy, "You don't want anyone using your new art supplies, do you Casey?" That was a green light for Casey to continue talking about her feelings. Because she had been allowed to express herself, Casey felt better after only a moment. If Mrs. Williams had instead instructed her to love Jimmy more, Casey might have felt guilty and probably even angrier.

Active listening involves "inviting" the person to say more. Parents can use such words and phrases as these: "Really?" "How about that." "Oh." "You did, huh?" and "You're kidding!" Such phrases are a way to keep the child talking without appearing to judge the situation. This technique can be much more effective than interrupting with a question or giving unwanted advice.

Building Parenting Skills

PARENTING WITH A SENSE OF HUMOUR

Research indicates that laughter contributes to good health. Parents need to know that laughing *at* themselves and *with* children is okay. Laughing *at* children is not. Humour adds joy to daily tasks. Some serious situations can be lightened with humour, if done with sensitivity. Humour can even be an effective guidance tool, catching children off guard and causing them to stop their misbehaviour. To parent their children and stepchildren with a sense of humour, Raj and Anis:

▶ Stop the children's bickering in the car by mimicking their favourite cartoon character's voice.

▶ Demonstrate how to make faces on burgers with mustard and ketchup.

▶ Instead of acting irritated, chuckle and say, "Oh, no. We got all the way here and forgot the library books we were going to return!"

▶ Let everyone have a night to tell a joke or riddle at the supper table.

▶ Make a talking hand puppet out of a washcloth to clean the five-year-old's scraped elbow.

▶ Leave an official looking note on the twins' bedroom door: "The M.O.M. Health Department will inspect these premises on Tuesday."

▶ Tell about the first goal Raj ever scored in hockey—for the opposing team—when their son's soccer team gets shut out.

◆ ◆ Your Thoughts ◆ ◆

❶ How is using humour a sign of self-confidence in parenting?

❷ How do children benefit when they see parents laughing at themselves?

❸ What are two instances when a parent shouldn't try to use humour?

PAY ATTENTION

Make a point of paying attention as children speak. Don't turn away when they begin talking. Make eye contact and relax as you listen. Stop occasionally and try to put yourself in their place. Do you remember how it feels to be little and to be dealing with people who are much larger?

Avoid cutting off or finishing sentences for children, even when it is difficult for them to get the words out. This is especially true when a child stutters. As many as 90 percent of children between the ages of one-and-a-half and five experience some stuttering.

Choosing the Best Words

Young children have limited understanding and often fragile feelings. Remember that what you say may have unintended effects, so choose your words carefully.

USE "I" MESSAGES An **"I" message** explains without attacking. These messages preserve self-esteem and expect responsible reactions. Simply putting "I" before a statement may not work. Some very hurtful messages begin this way. "I" messages can be used to show positive feelings. You might say, "I was proud of the way you thanked Grandma so nicely for the present." By modelling "I" messages, children may be less likely to criticize others and resort to name-calling.

Say This . . .	Instead of This . . .
"I'd like you to put the toys away now. When they're all over the floor, the house looks messy."	"Your toys are still all over the floor. You're always making a mess."
"I'm upset to see my favourite flower pot broken. I want you to use your allowance to buy another one."	"Look what you've done! You know you're not supposed to play ball in the front yard."

SEND CLEAR MESSAGES Do you understand the next sentence? "The magniloquence of his amplitude was supererogatory." Imagine a young child's frustration with unknown words. Use simple words and short sentences with a child, especially when giving directions. Speak clearly and distinctly. At other times, of course, you can build vocabulary with more difficult words.

Say This . . .	Instead of This . . .
"Please put on your sweater."	"Put on your sweater, find your raincoat, and bring me the note to sign."
"Please wear your boots outdoors."	"If it's really rainy outside, you probably better wear boots. I don't want mud on the floor."

BE POSITIVE Trying to control behaviour with too many "don'ts" doesn't work well. More positive expressions make the child feel that not everything is either forbidden or wrong. Of course, an exception is when a child is in immediate danger. Adding "please" and "thank you" to messages teaches children how to be polite.

Say This . . .	Instead of This . . .
"Finish your milk so you can have dessert."	"You can't have dessert if you don't finish your milk."
"Plants are pretty to look at, but they're not for touching."	"Don't touch Aunt Jenna's roses."
"Go outdoors, please, to play loud games."	"Shut up!"

AVOID JUDGMENTS When you make judgments, children think, "I'm not okay." Comparing children to yourself at their age or to others is unfair.

Say This . . .	Instead of This . . .
"Would you like to invite Tracy over to play?"	"You need to be friendlier to the other kids. You're too shy."
(nothing.)	"Grandma says Daddy was a wild little boy too. I think that's why you act the way you do."
"If you put less in the bowl, it won't spill."	"Can't you do anything right today?"

MAKE MESSAGES TIMELY A child's attention span isn't as long as yours. Distractions occur easily. Give a direction at the time you want it carried out, rather than expecting a child to remember.

Say This . . .	Instead of This . . .
"Put the crayons away now that you've finished colouring."	"After you finish colouring, put the crayons away."

> **TRY THIS** ☛ **Can you choose the best words?**
> **Write three messages to a child that are inappropriately**
> **stated. Then trade with a partner to improve the wording.**

Some children love to talk, but others have little to say. ◆ **If your child seemed troubled and reluctant to talk, what could you say that might help him open up?**

USE POSITIVE WORDS

Speaking impulsively can hurt children's feelings, just as it can adults. Parents are wise to consider the impact of their words before speaking. Examples of clear and positive messages to convey to children are on pages 458–459.

Most of the techniques involve common sense, but busy parents might have to remind themselves to use them. For instance, parents need to give directions at the time they want their young child to do something, not far in advance.

Children often model a parent's communication style. That's a powerful incentive for parents to work on improving their own habits. When family members say "please" and "thank you," children also model that example. Parents should use these words with children, not just other adults.

COMMUNICATE ACCEPTANCE

Genuine acceptance can be communicated by what you don't say sometimes. That's why occasionally it can be better to watch a child play than to get involved yourself.

When you connect with a child, conversation stays on track. Maintaining eye contact, holding a child's hand, and touching the head or shoulder all convey love and respect.

Think about a preschooler building a structure of blocks. Suppose an adult consistently prods the child by saying, "Why don't you build a castle?" or "You could turn that into a two-story house if you added these." The implication is that what the child is doing isn't correct or good enough.

Providing Encouragement

All children need **encouragement**. This is a message of confidence in another's ability. Providing encouragement is vital for children at all stages of development. Children gain a sense of hope and develop confidence in their abilities. They feel worthy. Encouragement is one of the most positive ways that parents and caregivers can help children develop into healthy and happy individuals.

Brittany and her father were at the playground in the park. She loved the swings. As she swang back and forth, she watched the other children on the slide. As her swing slowed to a stop, Brittany jumped off. She walked to the slide and stood at the bottom. It looked very high.

Brittany's father noticed her hesitation. He went near her but waited to see what she would do. She looked at him, then back at the slide. "I'll stand right here," he assured her. He moved closer to the slide so he could reach her if necessary.

Her father continued, "You can hold on tight as you climb the steps. I know you can do it, and then you can slide down." He let her think about the situation for a while. A few children passed her and climbed the steps.

At last Brittany made her decision. She climbed the stairs. In a nervous, but excited voice, she called down from the top, "Look Daddy! See how high I am." She slid down and immediately ran to the steps for another try. Her father had given her just the right amount of encouragement.

Some of the best communication comes when parent and child share an activity together. Have you ever become closer to an adult who taught you a particular skill? ◆ **Why do these situations build communication?**

INSTILLING MOTIVATION

Encouragement is especially important when children face new tasks. Trying new skills is more comfortable when children feel that others have faith and confidence in their abilities. They want to do their best. Encouragement leads to **motivation**, an inner desire to act or behave in a certain way. This driving force makes people work toward a particular goal. A high level of motivation makes children learn and achieve more. In turn, they feel better about themselves.

Raising Children With Character

The Club

Four young boys huddled together in their makeshift clubhouse. "Okay," Jesse said, "we all promise not to let anyone else join, right? This club's just for us." Three heads nodded in agreement.

The conversation continued as they settled on the rules for their club. "No girls allowed inside," one boy said. "We'll have secret meetings on Saturdays," another proclaimed. Scott joined in the excitement of planning until it was time to disband for the day.

That evening at dinner, Scott talked about the club he and his friends had started. He firmly pointed out to his sister and younger brother that no one else was allowed to join.

"You know, I remember a club in my neighbourhood when I was about your age, Scott," Mr. Cassidy said.

"What was it like, Dad? Was it fun?" Scott asked.

"Oh, it sure was. The guys fished together at the pond. There were biking trips to the McCalister place to hunt for fossils. There was even a treehouse for holding meetings. That club lasted for about two years."

"I'll bet you really liked it, didn't you, Dad?" Scott asked enthusiastically.

After a long pause, Mr. Cassidy responded, "No, Scott, I didn't. They never let me join."

◆◆◆◆◆ Thinking It Over ◆◆◆◆◆

1. What thoughts do you think Scott had after his father's last response?
2. What lessons might Mr. Cassidy have had in mind for Scott?

Chelsea was proud and excited when she was selected to be an angel in *The Nutcracker Suite*. Last year as a four-year-old, she had witnessed the fun her older sister had in the ballet. The costumes were so pretty. Chelsea had asked their mother if she could take ballet lessons too. During every class, she watched the teacher closely. At home, Chelsea's family encouraged her. She and her sister practised together. Her desire to be in the ballet with her sister was Chelsea's motivation. It prompted the actions she took to achieve her goal.

Children who feel loved are better able to develop positive attitudes and behaviours toward others. They learn from their parents' example to be kind and loving.

"My family was never good at expressing positive emotions. I've really worked hard at changing that with my own children," said Marcie. "I make a point of hugging them and telling them I love them, but it's more than that. We spend lots of time together and they know I'm always here for them—even when they get into trouble. It makes me feel good about myself, too."

The Most Important Message

No family has perfect communication. Even the experts have times when conversations with family members are less than satisfactory, but there is one thing that parents must communicate to their children.

Children need to feel that they are loved unconditionally—that their parents are there for them even when they misbehave. Children who feel loved are better able to face life's challenges. They can handle the inevitable disappointments that come their way. It is easier to overcome stress and crises when people know there is a loving, caring family to be supportive.

Parents have many messages to convey to their children, but none is more important than love.

Looking Back

♥ Good communication helps strengthen families.

♥ Communication is confusing when verbal and non-verbal messages don't match.

♥ Communication strategies include using the right tone, timing, asking questions, active listening, and paying attention.

♥ "I" messages, sending clear messages, and avoiding judgments are techniques that parents can use in communicating positively with their children.

♥ Encouragement leads to motivation, the desire to act or behave a certain way.

♥ Parents should communicate unconditional love to their young children.

Knowledge and Understanding

1. Why is positive communication from a parent so important to a child's well-being?
2. What non-verbal message do you think a frown sends? Tapping fingers on a counter? Looking past the person to whom you're speaking?
3. Do non-verbal messages help or hinder communication? Explain your answer.
4. Apply this saying to communicating with infants: "It's not what you say; it's what you don't say."
5. What is parentese?
6. When are some of the best times for a conversation with children? What are some of the worst times?
7. Why should parents avoid asking questions that can be answered with yes or no?
8. What is active listening?
9. How could you restate this sentence to be more positive? "You won't grow up to be strong if you don't drink your milk."
10. Why should parents use a mix of simple and more complex words when conversing with their young children?
11. How are encouragement, motivation, and goals related?
12. What is unconditional love? Give an example.

Thinking and Inquiry

13. Can a child succeed without encouragement? On the other hand, could a parent possibly offer too much praise and encouragement? Explain your reasoning.

14. Which of the communication strategies do you feel would be the most difficult for a parent to use on a daily basis? Why?

15. Do you know a "perfect family" where every interaction seems to go smoothly? Does such a family exist? Explain your answer.

16. How do good communication strategies and poor communication strategies influence parent-child relationships?

Communication

17. Respond to the "Dear Anne" letter below:

> Dear Anne:
>
> My co-worker has a two-month-old son. She seems to enjoy motherhood, but you've noticed that she speaks to the baby very little. She talks about how much more fun the baby will be when he's older. What advice should I give her?
>
> *Concerned in Woodstock*

18. Make a poster to show "Tips for Positive Communication."

19. a) Write a case study to show poor communication.
    b) Rewrite your case study to show good communication.

Application

20. Think of three sentences that are critical "you" statements disguised as "I" messages. For example, "I feel sad when you act so bratty at the store." Rewrite them in an improved format.

21. With a partner, exchange memories of parent-child exchanges you've heard in supermarkets or department stores. Were they gentle or nasty? What will the effect be on the children?

22. Suppose you're a parent who earns a little extra money by working a second shift. That means you're at work all evening, leaving before your two daughters get off the school bus. Your spouse handles the situation well, but you miss the family time. What can you do to make the most of your weekends? How do communication strategies count? Do you see another solution to the problem?

23. Give an example of age-appropriate communication strategies for each of the following:
    a) Infants
    b) Toddlers
    c) Preschoolers
    d) School-age children
    e) Teens

UNIT **5**

Challenges for Families

A Parent's Perspective

from Perry

"One day a few weeks ago, my five-year-old came home from school all excited and told me what had happened.

She had found a quarter on the playground. When she took it to the office, the secretary explained to her that if no one claimed the quarter within two days, it would be hers to keep. What a wondrous thought that was for Jessica. Two days later, of course, she took possession of the coveted quarter and happily showed it to me that night. 'A quarter!' Jessica's older brother Connor laughed, 'but that's …' '…the first step toward buying something special,' I finished for him, looking him straight in the eye. Then Connor smiled at me. At that moment he understood that the coin was not much different from a lost wallet or a gold bracelet found in the hallway at his junior high school. We both realized that practising honesty in this small way would help set a pattern of honesty for Jessica throughout her life."

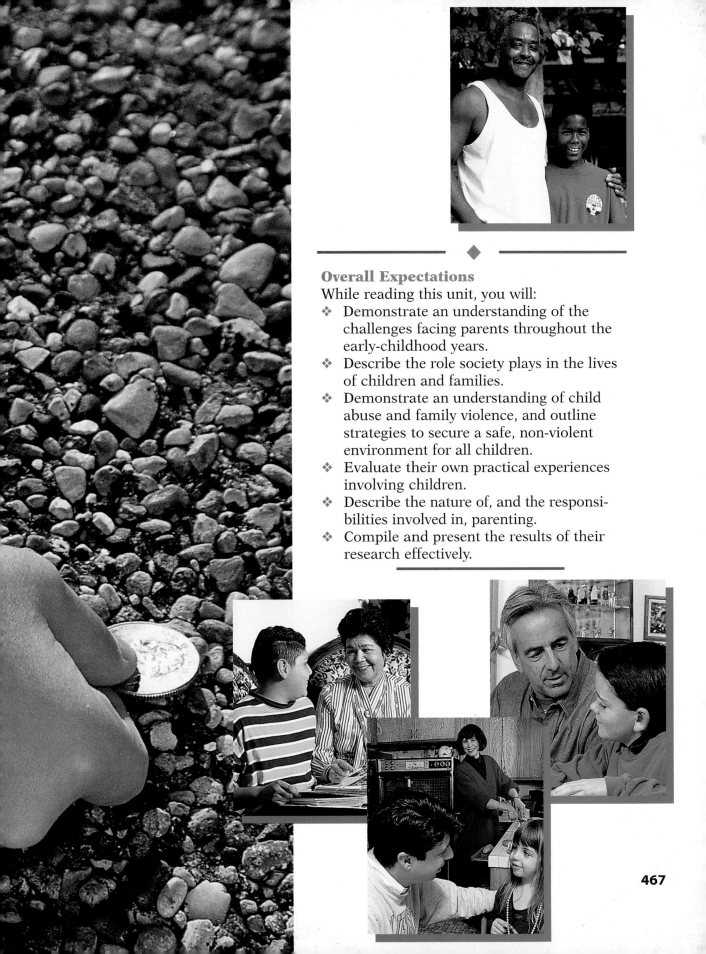

Overall Expectations

While reading this unit, you will:

❖ Demonstrate an understanding of the challenges facing parents throughout the early-childhood years.

❖ Describe the role society plays in the lives of children and families.

❖ Demonstrate an understanding of child abuse and family violence, and outline strategies to secure a safe, non-violent environment for all children.

❖ Evaluate their own practical experiences involving children.

❖ Describe the nature of, and the responsibilities involved in, parenting.

❖ Compile and present the results of their research effectively.

The Value of Play

CHAPTER EXPECTATIONS

While reading this chapter, you will:

▶ Identify and describe the capabilities and behaviours of young children of different ages in a variety of settings.

▶ Demonstrate an understanding of what is involved in planning, organizing, and carrying out age-appropriate activities for preschoolers in classroom or community settings.

▶ Effectively communicate the results of your inquiries, using a variety of methods and forms.

▶ Demonstrate an understanding of the universal belief in the importance of play in the lives of children.

KEY TERMS

active play
dramatic play
exploratory
  play
facilitating
  play
quiet play

Vance and Lina watched their daughter Gretchen play "house" on the porch.

"What are you drawing?" Lina asked.

"Windows," Gretchen said.

Curious, Lina peered over Gretchen's shoulder. Gretchen continued to add curtains to her windows. "This window has pretty curtains because it is my bedroom window," she explained. "How pretty," replied Lina. Gretchen continued to colour.

Vance smiled at his daughter's dedication to her cardboard house. He hugged Lina and whispered, "She is quite an interior decorator." Lina smiled and leaned against Vance's shoulder. "I'm proud she is interested in the things I've done to improve our home. Perhaps Gretchen will enjoy turning a house into a home someday," reflected Lina.

——————◆——————

What do you think? How did Gretchen show imagination in her play?

————————

469

Play is the spontaneous activity of children. To a child, crumbling dry leaves is as much play as pushing a toy truck. Child's play has the added dimension of learning. Children are constantly absorbing knowledge, but during play they are actively exploring. It's the difference between watching snow fall and sinking knee-deep into a snowdrift.

Benefits of Play

Children can easily spend most of their time playing. Chances are that sometime through the day, they will grow in each area of development:

♥ *Physical*. Large muscle groups are exercised by walking, chasing balls, and riding tricycles. The heart, lungs, and immune system strengthen. Weight is controlled and stress reduced through activity. Co-ordination and perceptual motor skills improve also. Small motor skills are refined when children put puzzles together, turn knobs on toys, and even twist off jar lids.

♥ *Intellectual*. Through **exploratory play**, children use their senses to find out how things look, smell, sound, taste, and feel. They expand language skills. Play also stimulates creativity and abstract thinking. When children pretend, toy teapots pour real tea, and rocks turn into rolls. In older children, games of strategy sharpen their ability to think logically and in sequence. They solve problems and practise reasoning skills. To win as a team, they make decisions and set goals.

♥ *Emotional*. Play allows children to feel "big." They gain a sense of control, which is needed for emotional health.

Maybe there's a good reason why children have so much energy. Activity is what helps them develop physically. ◆ **What might happen to an inactive child?**

What Is Play?

Child's play. The phrase describes a simple task, requiring little effort. For children, however, child's play is a complex business. It's the work to which children are born.

Play can raise self-esteem by providing opportunities for real and imagined success. Children can choose activities in which they excel. Play also provides a way to explore and express feelings. Children learn to manage difficult emotions. A fear of starting school, for example, can be explored in the safety of make-believe.

Raising Children With Character

Small Steps Forward

Hanging onto her grandfather's hand, eight-year-old Tracy leaned around the line of people in front of her. Halfway up the block, the cashier was still selling tickets to the movie that Tracy had been waiting all week to see.

"This line is too *long*, Grandpa," she sighed. Suddenly she began tugging at his arm. "Look, there's Lisa O'Brien." She pointed far up the line. "I'll bet we could get in line with her."

Grandpa Zarley stood firm. "We didn't come with Lisa's family," he reminded her gently. "We have to wait our turn."

Just then two new arrivals walked past. They stopped beside another couple in line ahead of Tracy and her grandfather. "Here," the man in line said, "you can get behind us."

Tracy turned to her grandfather. "*They* did it, Grandpa. Why can't we?"

"Well, we could," Grandpa Zarley said thoughtfully, "but think about it, Tracy. If everyone who got here after us managed to get in line ahead of us, where would we be?"

Tracy furrowed her brow. Finally she replied, with surprise, "Always at the end."

Her grandfather nodded. "That's right. So isn't it a good thing everyone doesn't act like that? That's why we make rules—to make things fair for everyone. People who break the rules only care about themselves. Say, let's play the alphabet game. It'll help pass the time. What do you see that begins with the letter "A?""

◆◆◆◆◆ **Thinking It Over** ◆◆◆◆◆

1. What difficulty with teaching children about rules and fairness does this story illustrate?
2. How did Grandpa Zarley help Tracy follow the rule? Why were his techniques especially effective for teaching a young child?
3. What qualities might this episode help Tracy develop? How will these traits help her in the future?

♥ *Social*. Children practise social skills through play. Stuffed animals are good "playmates" as children learn how to treat others. Playing with parents gives them models for polite, respectful behaviour. In group play, children learn communication, co-operation, conflict resolution, and following rules.

♥ *Moral*. Children learn principles of right and wrong through play. They show respect for children from diverse backgrounds. Fairness means sharing equipment and taking turns. Make-believe play lets children demonstrate the values they absorb from their family.

The Parent's Role in Play

Amanda watched her six-year-old play with her dollhouse. "Daphne was using the markers from the Bingo game as dishes for her dolls," she recalled. "I wanted to warn her that she would lose the markers, and then she couldn't play Bingo. However, I was impressed by her creativity, and I told her so. With that imagination, she'll easily find something else to use to play Bingo."

Amanda was right to take her role in Daphne's play seriously. By responding appropriately, a parent and other caregivers can help a child get the most from play.

FACILITATING PLAY

Imagine a child exploring a large cardboard box. A parent says, "You could make a boat with that. I'll get an old blanket for a sail, and my old fishing pole. You can pretend you're fishing at sea." When the first parent leaves, the other parent comes by. "I'll bet you could have fun with that big box," the second parent says. "Do you have any ideas what you could do with it?"

You can buy expensive toys for children—or you can give them a cardboard box. Here the caregiver has provided an opportunity for play, including toy cell phones, and then the children took over.

The difference between the first and second parent is the difference between directing a child's play and **facilitating** it. Facilitating helps play happen without control.

When parents facilitate play, children learn by doing most of the work. If you were the second parent, for instance, you might suggest ideas for using the box: as a clubhouse, a train, or a cave. You might provide skills and materials needed to help create whatever the child has chosen. You might prime the child's imagination with comments or questions: "Where is this train going?" You would offer only the help that is really needed.

Creating a Play Environment

Providing space at home is a basic way to facilitate play. Children don't need a special area. However, whatever arrangements a parent makes should feature:

♥ *Well-defined boundaries.* Children should know exactly where and when an activity is permitted. A parent might say, "Keep your paint and pictures on the table," or "You may play your drums only until Hayley's nap. Then it's quiet time."

♥ *Accessibility.* For the child's safety, play space should be easily reached from the rest of the home.

♥ *Inviting furnishings.* A comfortable chair and lamp encourage quieter activities. A small table and chairs make the space truly the child's own.

♥ *Carpeting.* Children play more readily on a warm, comfortable floor.

Health & Safety

SAFETY IN THE SUN

Exposure to the sun has been linked to skin cancer, making it a concern for everyone. Children tend to play outdoors more than adults. Overexposure to the sun at an early age increases the chances of health problems later on. Teaching young children safe habits for playing in the sun will help them avoid the dangers. This information can guide your approach:

▶ Playing in the shade or taking breaks in the shade lessens sun exposure.

▶ Damaging ultraviolet rays are strongest between 10:00 a.m. and 2:00 p.m.

▶ A wide-brimmed hat shields the eyes as well as the face, shoulders, and back.

▶ Sunscreens are rated by an SPF (sun protection factor) number from 2 to 60, which indicates how well they screen out ultraviolet rays. Choose a sunscreen made for children, with an SPF of at least 15. Fragrance-free varieties are best, since a child's skin may be sensitive to additives found in adult products. Reapply the sunscreen at least every two hours.

▶ Sand, water, and snow intensify ultraviolet rays by reflecting them off their surface. Remember that most ultraviolet rays can penetrate clouds, fog, and haze.

▶ A stroller with a hood or awning offers sun protection.

Parents can also support a child's play by providing playmates, which children most need after age two. They might arrange play dates, host play groups, or coach a shy child in starting a friendship. Showing young children that their friends are welcome in their home begins a good habit for the future.

A parent's attitude is also part of the play environment. A parent should encourage a child to use play to grow. Camille and her five-year-old son Andrew were visiting her mother and her mother's foster child Brianne. As Andrew began plunking at his grandmother's piano, Camille said, "Andrew, please stop. You're making too much noise." Andrew started to rock Brianne's doll in his arms. Camille suggested, "Andrew, why don't you play with the truck you brought instead?" In what ways were these experiences discouraging to Andrew's development?

Participating in Play

Under certain conditions, a parent's participation can add to a child's play. As an infant's first playmate, parents teach language and social skills. They promote growth by encouraging children to new feats. Time spent playing with children can be relaxing and rewarding for the parent as well.

Playing with a child can have other benefits too. Children reveal interests and abilities during play, which parents can guide and encourage. Play can also be a good gauge of development. Suppose you were working a picture puzzle with your child. You noticed the child squinted at each piece while picking it up and leaned close to the puzzle to place it. What problem might you suspect?

As children get older, parents must be more selective about joining their play. Children may not depend on a parent's involvement once they develop friendships. Play can be a way to take a break from adult authority.

A wise parent follows the child's lead. Children sometimes indirectly say, "Play with me." A child might hold up an empty plate and announce, "Look at all these cookies I just baked." How would you respond?

Internet Connects

http://www.mcgrawhill.ca/links/parenting
To learn more practical information on the formative years of a child's life, go to the Web site above for *Parenting Rewards & Responsibilities, First Canadian Edition,* to see where to go next.

Toys don't replace parents. Children love to have a parent participate in the fun. ◆ **Could a parent participate too much?**

ENCOURAGING RESPONSIBILITY

Play can be an occasion for learning responsible behaviour. Making play dates with others shows the importance of keeping commitments and planning time. Having children put away toys teaches them to take care of belongings and to clean up after themselves.

Cleaning up can become part of the play itself. Parents should provide storage space that is convenient, then remind the child when it's time to drive the toy cars back to the "garage" and herd the stuffed animals into the "barn."

Choosing Toys

Many parents have told the story of a child who ignored a new, expensive, popular toy only to play with the box in which it came. This anecdote makes a good point: toys should be chosen carefully with the specific child in mind.

When buying toys, parents should remember the principle, "less is more." Children with fewer toys tend to get more use from each one. They are motivated to be inventive. If parents find their child is accumulating too many playthings, they might try rotating toys. Toys seem new and fresh after they've been kept on the shelf a while. Unused toys in good shape might be given to charity.

AGE-APPROPRIATE TOYS

Children benefit most when toys challenge their skills without frustrating them. Toys should be neither too simple nor too advanced. The age recommendation found on toy packages is a good guide, but parents should go by the child's level of development to make the final decision. Parents should be realistic about their child's abilities.

The chart below suggests games and toys that are appropriate for children of different ages.

Age-Appropriate Games and Toys	
Age Group	Toy Ideas
Infants	Mobiles, mirrors, shaker toys, squeeze toys, plush toys, plastic blocks
Toddlers	Push toys, pull toys, riding toys, building blocks, child's tape player, spools to string, containers and items with which to fill them
Preschoolers	Water-play toys, dolls and accessories, beads to string, hand and finger puppets, alphabet blocks, magnetic letters and numbers
School-Age Children	Board games, chess and checker sets, dominoes, child's chemistry sets, beginner needle craft sets

TOY SAFETY

At best, inappropriate toys are useless. At worst, they are dangerous. Imagine a toddler trying to ride a bicycle or a preschooler using a wood-burning kit.

Age is one factor to consider when judging toy safety. Parents should also look at:

♥ *Size.* Infants naturally put toys in their mouths, and young children like to take them apart. Small toys, or those with decals, small batteries, and removable parts, put a child at risk of choking. A general rule is that play items should be larger than the child's fist. Parents can buy "choke tubes" to determine whether a toy is a safe size. Any item that fits inside the tube is a choking hazard.

♥ *Durability.* Toys should stand up to more than normal wear and tear, since young children do not always handle them carefully. They should be shatter-proof to avoid the danger of jagged edges and broken pieces that could be swallowed. Any broken or worn toy is a potential danger that should be either repaired or discarded.

♥ *Composition.* Except for electrical parts, materials used in toys should be non-toxic, especially paints and finishes. This information should be stated on the label.

Parents should note certain features that make a toy unsafe. Strings or chords longer than 15 cm (6 in.) can strangle a child. Snaps, gears, and hinges can trap fingers and hair. Sound effects louder than 100 decibels can damage a child's hearing.

Some toys are hazards in themselves. Darts, archery sets, and high-powered water shooters can cause eye injuries. Broken or uninflated latex balloons can be easily swallowed and stick in the throat. Even the Heimlich manoeuvre may not dislodge one. Sponge toys are tempting to teething babies, who might bite off and swallow a piece.

Thanks to monitoring by private groups and government agencies, most toys and play equipment are

Making sure that toys are safe is part of responsible parenting. ◆ **Why is this a safe toy for a child?**

safe when used as intended by children of the recommended age. If parents feel a toy is dangerous, they should take it out of use. If they have questions about a toy's safety, they can contact Health Canada's Public Safety Department through the Internet or on its toll-free number. This federal agency investigates complaints about product safety.

Internet Connects

http://www.mcgrawhill.ca/links/parenting
To learn more about toy safety, go to the Web site above for *Parenting Rewards & Responsibilities, First Canadian Edition*, to see where to go next.

Guiding Play Activities

No one type of play is best for a child, but many different kinds of activities are needed. For balanced development, children need both books and bicycles, drum kits and dress-up clothes. Variety in children's play is as important as variety in their diet.

ACTIVE PLAY

Healthy children are naturally active, and **active play**, activities that are primarily physical, helps them stay healthy. Recent studies have shown that children today are in poorer shape physically than in the past. As with adults, many leisure activities compete for children's time. Parents must make sure that active play stays part of a child's life.

Spotlight On
—Toy Selection

Toys must be safe, but they should also fit other requirements as well. To find toys that are fun for children and acceptable to adults, parents should consider:

✔ *Sensory appeal.* Bright colours, contrasting textures, and lively sounds hold a child's interest and stimulate learning.

✔ *Versatility.* The more ways a child can use a toy, the better. Simple toys are often best. A mound of play dough may be a work of art one day and a plate of meatballs the next.

✔ *Care and maintenance.* Toys should be washable to prevent the spread of germs. Parents should realize that any special maintenance, such as recharging or replacing parts, will fall to them.

✔ *Learning potential.* A toy should spur children to use their minds and bodies. Building blocks, for example, let a child create structures while developing small motor skills. Does a wind-up toy promote this kind of involvement?

✔ *Values.* Toys can send messages about behaviour and relationships. Does the toy promote violent play or co-operation? What ideas about age, gender, ethnicity, or beauty does it reinforce?

✔ *Economy.* A toy may be worth greater expense if it lasts a long time and several children can use it.

Facilitating Active Play

Resourceful parents can facilitate active play without spending a great deal of money. Toddlers enjoy rolling and chasing a large ball. Older children can throw and catch smaller ones. Balls are fairly inexpensive and can last for years.

To keep active play fresh, parents can build low balance beams (about 10 cm [4 in.] off the ground) from scrap lumber. Large appliance boxes can be arranged and rearranged into twisting, turning tunnels.

School-age children develop balance and muscle strength using bicycles and in-line skates. These and other costly items may be bought used from want ads and garage sales. A group of parents might form a toy co-op, buying toys together and rotating them among their children.

Games such as tag and hide-and-seek cost nothing but do require space. Most communities have public parks. More neighbourhoods are developing "green spaces" for residents' use.

Most parents are justifiably concerned about injuries from active play. Seeing toddlers trip on their own feet or preschoolers collide while chasing a ball, some parents try to limit play. However, skills improve only with practice. Children are built to withstand the normal tumbles and falls of "basic training." With adequate supervision and safety precautions, most children avoid serious injury.

Parenting Q & A

Getting Dirty

Q "My four-year-old son gets covered with dirt after he's outdoors for only a few minutes. What can I do?" *Claire*

A To a child, a mud puddle may mean splashing fun. To an adult, the puddle may mean ruined shoes and footprints on the carpet. Parents have to accept that children need to play. You can make your son's link with dirt a little easier on you by trying these ideas. Set some limits. Tell him when he must stay clean but allow plenty of free time for messy play. Provide play clothes that can get dirty. Teach your son how to use mats by doorways. You might limit him to one entrance and provide a place to leave muddy shoes. A pair of clean shoes or slippers near the door could be a reminder. Remember that getting dirty is simply a by-product of the play needed for development.

QUIET PLAY

Frank found his five-year-old daughter Amy sitting on the back stoop, sorting a wagon full of brightly coloured autumn leaves. All her toys, he thought, and this is what she plays with. "Amy," he called, "What would you like to do?"

"I *am* doing something," Amy declared impatiently, and returned to her task.

Frank mistook **quiet play**, play that involves primarily thinking and small motor skills, as a pleasant but unproductive pastime. He forgot that quiet play, though it may seem useless, can be a learning experience. Handling the leaves, Amy noticed shape and size, similarity and difference. She discovered that red and yellow blend into orange, and that dry leaves make a different sound than supple ones. She also admired the beauty of nature. Like much quiet play, hers was also exploratory.

Encouraging Quiet Play

Parents can inspire exploration with many quiet but stimulating activities. Giving a toddler a collection of clean, empty food containers and lids invites stacking, nesting, and tower building. Parents can show children how to make shadows on the wall, using different objects and lighting. Experimenting with magnets and a home full of ordinary items, perhaps with paper and pencil to write down results, is also worthwhile. For school-age children, models, puzzles, and card games are challenging yet relaxing.

When quiet play is spontaneous and child-initiated, parents need to show patience and support. A toddler in the bathtub might pour water from one container to another, comparing the amount each one holds. The tolerant parent not only waits until the child's curiosity is satisfied, but even provides another container for an additional round of "tests."

Children love to dig in dirt and sand, making roads for toy trucks and filling containers. This type of play might be followed by more quiet play in a bathtub of water.

Computer and Electronic Games

Computer and electronic games also provide quiet fun and learning. High-quality graphics and constant feedback appeal to children. Interactive programs let children control the images or the sequence of events to create stories. Some programs can help a child with a physical or learning challenge where other means fail.

However, electronic games that can be played by one child at a time lack a social element. Young children learn best through direct experience. Playing with blocks has more meaning to them than manipulating blocks on a screen. Parents should choose carefully when providing children with electronic games.

DRAMATIC PLAY

"It sounds odd," one parent noted, "but I think kids like make-believe because it lets them be themselves." There is truth in those words. Through **dramatic play**, when children assume different identities and take part in make-believe events, they can work out what's going on in their real lives.

Pretend play is valuable because it *is* pretend. Children can try on different identities. They can express difficult emotions and behaviour, such as sibling rivalry. In role playing, children explore relationships, such as husband and wife or boss and employee. They gain empathy by learning to look at a situation from different points of view. Dramatic play can also uncover talents and interests.

Supporting Dramatic Play

Children rarely need urging for dramatic play. As with eating, they satisfy their appetite for make-believe as the need arises. They might be inspired by a story or movie, or intrigued by a real-life event, such as a wedding. Children do appreciate parents' support, especially in the form of props. To make "playing house" more realistic, parents can supply old clothes, jewellery, and household items. Paper, pencils, and old books help recreate a classroom for "school." Parents can inspire imagination as they create props from other items. An old blanket draped over a few chairs can be a mountain cave or a submarine.

Parents can offer guidance with the props. Reuben noticed his son and friends pretending to eat at a restaurant. He found a menu and chopsticks he had saved from a Japanese meal. Reuben showed them how to use the chopsticks, explaining that Japanese people traditionally eat seated on floor cushions, after removing their shoes. How do you think this added to the children's social development?

Sites for dramatic play are wherever children gather, from a playground to a garage. Parents who can provide a sandbox or wading pool open the door to more play themes.

As with other types of play, parents should involve themselves only minimally. They should supervise for safety, of course. They can redirect play that seems to be growing violent or hurtful, or that reinforces negative attitudes. Resolving conflicts and solving problems should be left to the children, as much as possible. This is part of their learning.

Imaginary Friends

Some children invent imaginary friends, complete with names, personalities, and histories. They react to these unseen playmates as they do real ones, and expect parents to also. They may insist on setting a place for the "friend" at meals, and act as go-betweens to make the friend's wishes known. This behaviour is most common among young, bright children who are the oldest child or the only child in a family.

Parents may worry that imaginary friends are an unhealthy blurring of fantasy and reality. Generally, though, children outgrow such companions as they make friends at school, or when a sibling is born. Unless the "friend" interferes with a child's functioning in the real world, parents should indulge the "presence" calmly and matter-of-factly.

ART ACTIVITIES

Art teachers say "process, not product" is what makes art activity valuable for young children. What do you think that means? They mean that the creative process, and what children learn from it, is more important than any product they make. Parents should take the same approach and remember that successful art activities generate learning and enthusiasm. Children gain more when they are urged to create art to please themselves.

Even when very young, children want to become bigger. They can become imaginatively bigger, for a little while anyway, through dress-up play.
◆ **Where could you find dress-up clothes that children would enjoy?**

Encouraging Art Activities

Since children are often more enthusiastic than careful, the creative process can be a messy one—which may be part of the attraction. An art area should be protected with newspaper, plastic, or drop cloths. Children should be protected too, if necessary, in smocks, aprons, or old clothes.

Children progress from simpler activities, such as drawing, to those requiring more muscle control and patience, such as making a collage. When planning an art project, a parent should be sure it matches the child's skills. Some common activities are described in the chart below.

Responding positively to children's art also encourages their efforts. A child's drawing may be hard to identify, but asking "What is it?" is apt to disappoint a child who has laboured long over a creation. An enthusiastic response like this is better: "What a beautiful picture! I love the way you used those bright colours. Tell me about this picture." Children see that you are interested in their work, and they can practise language skills as they describe their drawing.

Parents must also resist "improving" a child's artwork. Learning technical skill is not the aim of art activities. If a child thinks a creation is beautiful, who is to say otherwise?

Choosing Art Activities

Activity	Suggested Supplies	Tips for Success
Drawing	Crayons, washable felt markers, chalk, drawing paper, brown wrapping paper, computer paper	Encourage children to create their own drawings, rather than using colouring books.
Painting	Tempera paint, large paint brushes, sponges, yarn pompoms, unused flyswatters, newsprint, computer paper, paper sacks	Supply a separate painting tool for each colour.
Finger Painting	Commercial finger paints, soap flake paste with tempera colouring	Let the child paint in the bathtub. Both are easily cleaned up afterward.
Collage Making	Magazines, greeting cards, gift wrap, fabric scraps, twigs, leaves, pine cones	Use sturdy backing material, such as cardboard, and white glue thinned with water.
Modelling and Shaping	Commercial and homemade play doughs and clays, cookie cutters, coins, buttons, shells	Make homemade play doughs from recipes in parenting books or magazines.

MUSIC ACTIVITIES

Children at every age enjoy music. Infants often become quiet in order to listen to a song. Toddlers take an active interest in music, marching, dancing, and clapping to the beat. Preschoolers enjoy singing, often making up songs to go along with their play.

Promoting Music Activities

A parent doesn't need musical talent to provide musical experiences. Infants love a parent's voice, regardless of technical quality. They are delighted by sound-making toys.

Young children begin to learn rhythm and beat. They develop physical agility by moving to music. Parents can encourage them by singing and playing recorded music. Some recordings by children's artists are made for singing along. Why not increase the pleasure by providing rhythm instruments in the form of pots, pans, and other non-breakable household items? For older children, joining a school band or a choir is a pleasant way to explore a musical interest.

Internet Connects

http://www.mcgrawhill.ca/links/parenting
To learn more about strengthening family bonds, go to the Web site above for *Parenting Rewards & Responsibilities, First Canadian Edition,* to see where to go next.

The concert pianist of tomorrow begins in simple ways today. In fact, parents inspire many careers and lifelong hobbies by providing toys and activities that encourage children to develop their interests.

Making Play a Priority

Too often, parents think of play as strictly "kid's stuff." While they are right to avoid intruding on their child's play, parents should be willing to invite children and playfulness into their own lives. Suppose you were raking leaves with your child. Why not dive into a pile of leaves together before stuffing them into recycling bags? Could you turn a family picnic into a "pioneer family" adventure?

With the busy lives families lead today, making time for play could be a way to bring children and parents closer. Parents who are used to telling children "Go play" might say "Come and play" a little more often instead.

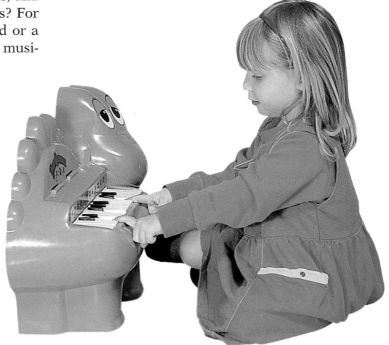

Review

Looking Back

- ♥ Through play, children develop physically, intellectually, emotionally, socially, and morally.

- ♥ A parent should facilitate play for children, but not intrude on it.

- ♥ Toys for children should be safe, age-appropriate, and versatile.

- ♥ Children need time, space, and proper equipment for active play.

- ♥ Children often strengthen intellectual skills during quiet play.

- ♥ Parents can support dramatic play by providing props and ideas for themes.

- ♥ Parents should encourage a child's appreciation of art and music, regardless of technical ability.

Knowledge and Understanding

1. How can play strengthen intellectual skills?
2. How can play aid emotional growth?
3. Explain how you, as a parent, might involve yourself in your child's play.
4. When her daughter finished playing, Inez always picked up the toys and put them away. What do you think about this practice?
5. At age four, Wayne stayed with his aunt and her two-year-old son, Jay, during the day. Wayne usually played with Jay's toys since no others were available. What may be the consequences of this situation?
6. How would you decide if a toy is safe for a child?
7. Besides safety, what qualities make a toy a good choice?
8. How could you inexpensively provide an active play environment?
9. Which is more important, active or quiet play, and why?
10. How might you encourage a child's dramatic play?
11. Describe an atmosphere that encourages children to try art activities.
12. If a parent has no musical talent, can he or she promote music with children? Explain your answer.

Review

Thinking and Inquiry

13. Can an activity be "play" at some times and not at others? Explain.

14. A parent sees a child overturn on a tricycle and scrape a knee. The parent rushes to the child and says, "Poor baby! Does it hurt? Let's put a bandaid on your knee. Then I want you to stay in the house and play instead." How might this response affect the child's attitude toward physical play? To life in general?

15. Why do you think children create imaginary friends? How might this be a strategy for coping?

Communication

16. Create an electronic newsletter for parents titled *The Value of Play*. Be sure to use correct spelling, grammar, and appropriate illustrations. Post your newsletter for the class.

17. You are the parent of a five-year-old girl. For the past few months, your daughter has had an imaginary friend, Janey. Whenever she does something that displeases you, your daughter insists that "Janey did it" or "Janey made me do it." You are concerned that she isn't developing a proper sense of responsibility. How do you handle the situation?

18. Assemble in a group of four students. Using the Internet, each person selects one age group of child (ages 0–2 years, 3-year-old, 4-year-old, or 5-year-old). Each person identifies and describes the capabilities and behaviours found in his or her specific age group. Put your information together (all four age groups) in an informative way. Be prepared to present your information to the class.

Application

19. With a partner, create two ways that a parent could make a game of cleaning up a play area.

20. Devise a toy made from items found at home or obtained by parents at little or no cost. With sketches and descriptions, explain how the game or toy would be made and how a child would use it.

21. With a partner, suggest items you might find around the home or at garage sales that could be used as props for the following dramatic play themes: life on a farm; a sea adventure.

Diane Trembley-Griffin, Storyteller

What volunteer activities did you do as a teenager that led you to choose a career that involved working with children/people?
► Working with children in church groups.
► Volunteering to look after children of friends and relatives.
► Babysitting.

*Please describe your **specific education pathway**.*
► 1969 Elementary Teaching Certificate, Hamilton Teacher's College
► 1982 Bachelor of Arts Degree, Sociology and Religion, McMaster University

Have you completed any further study to enhance your professional development?
► 1990–95 Team Mentorship, Speech and Language Pathologists
► 1987 Instructor at Brock University Primary Methods Course, Mathematics
► 1985 Learning Styles, Continuing Education Credit, Dunn and Dunn Model, York University
► 1985 Primary Specialist Certificate
► 1983–85 Mohawk College, Fine Arts courses
► 1974 Human Growth and Development Certificate
► 1974 Integrated Studies Certificate
► 1973 Language Arts Certificate
► 1972 Elementary Mathematics Certificate

*Please describe your **career pathway**.*
► Cashier at Loblaws Groceteria.
► Clerk at Fabric Store.
► Teacher at Hamilton Wentworth District School Board, JK–Grade 6 (all subject areas).
► Professional storyteller. I travel to different schools and groups to present one-hour programs focused on storytelling.

Did you switch jobs along the way? If so, why?
Teaching students of different ages across different subject areas gave me the chance to work as a consultant helping principals, teachers, parents, and students to carry out Ministry curriculum objectives. I switched positions within the profession to improve my knowledge and skills so I could do the best for the students.

*Please describe your **current position**.*
Professional storyteller with the The Original Griffin Storytelling Thyme. I travel to different schools, and to groups of children and adults, to tell stories based on themes or the needs of the group.

*What are the **rewards** of your current position?*
Students enjoy hearing the stories and seeing the wide variety of props that are used. They also enjoy becoming involved in the drama activities that precede or follow a story. Teachers can observe new techniques to try out with their classes. Adult listeners are entertained when I share humorous, poignant, or inspirational stories. I just love telling the stories, and a bonus is that I am paid to do it.

*What are the **challenges** of your current position?*
Organizing and running an independent business can be a challenge. Responsibility rests solely on me to acquire clients and choose stories that adults will enjoy and stories from which students will learn. It is extremely important that I stay healthy, as I cannot work if my voice is hoarse due to a cold or laryngitis. Storytelling is much like performing in a play. I tell the story without using the book, so all my stories must be in my head.

Looking back over your education and career pathways, as a young person in high school did you ever believe you would follow the pathways you have?

I recall wanting to be a teacher when I was in elementary school. In high school, I looked at other career opportunities, but I kept coming back to teaching. Having the other jobs helped me to know that they were not the kind of jobs I wanted for my entire working career.

Do you have any comments for young people who might be considering their own educational/career pathway?

If you are truly passionate about a particular career path, follow that passion. There is nothing more rewarding than having a job that you love to go to each day. You get up each morning looking forward to the challenges, and life is too short not to enjoy each moment.

What other careers are related to your career?

Teacher:
► Leader of Scouts, Girl Guides
► Coach
► Educational assistant

Storyteller:
► Actor
► Children's programmer for radio or TV
► Public speaker

CHAPTER 25

Responsibilities of Parents

CHAPTER EXPECTATIONS

While reading this chapter, you will:

▶ Identify the role of societal agents in teaching young children how to live in society.

▶ Demonstrate an understanding of various social concerns that parents face as their children approach school age.

▶ Identify the laws that regulate children and parents in society.

▶ Identify and describe the responsibilities parents have for children of different ages.

▶ Explain the role of parents and family members in teaching children socially acceptable behaviour.

KEY TERMS

bullying	social values
child labour	societal agent
dovetailing	street-proofing
materialism	time
prioritize	management

Gina ran her finger across the dust on the table. Didn't I dust Tuesday? she thought. Eight-month-old Garrett was nearly asleep on her shoulder.

In the kitchen, the ring of the timer told Gina the pasta was done. Bill and three-year-old Amanda were due 20 minutes ago.

A few minutes later, her husband and daughter came rushing in. "We stopped to pick up the prescription so I won't have to go back out. Do I have time to toss my work clothes in the washer before we eat?" Bill asked.

Just then Amanda let out a wail. "Oh, she's hungry, Bill. We'll do laundry later. Besides, dinner is more than ready."

Bill had just settled Amanda in her booster seat when the phone rang. Bill answered. After a brief conversation he reported, "I forgot—Dad's bringing the lawn mower over in a few minutes. He thinks he's got it fixed. I don't suppose you made any extra..." Gina's weary expression answered his question. Bill smiled weakly. "Should I even ask how work went today?"

Gina returned an identical smile. "I think we need to make some changes in the way we do things around here. I feel like I'm going nuts."

Bill nodded. "Things do get hectic, don't they? What do you say we talk it over—after a movie on Saturday night?"

───────── ◆ ─────────

What do you think? How typical is this family scene?

─────────

Finding a balance in life means figuring out how to blend work, family, and personal life. Employed parents need time with children and time for relaxation.
◆ **What could happen if one area of life gets overemphasized at the expense of the others?**

The Time Crunch

Do you ever have days when you feel that you just can't get everything done? Classes at school, a paper due, a part-time job, duties at home, plans with friends—all of these can fill a schedule very quickly.

If a high school student feels pressure, just think what parents with young children must feel. For them the time crunch can be even worse.

Work, Family, and Personal Life

In general, people devote time to three major areas of life. Work, family, and personal life are crowded into typically busy schedules.

Work life is time spent on the job. Since school prepares young people for the working years ahead, attending classes and studying are a student's work.

The time you spend with family members, or doing things for them, makes up family life. Caring interaction among family members has personal and practical rewards. They share trying times as well as happy ones.

Personal life is time set aside just for you. Hobbies and interests, friends, relaxation, and spiritual fulfillment are all part of personal time.

A BALANCING ACT

According to psychologists, all three areas of life are needed for good physical and mental health. Balancing your life means including all three areas in a way that works for you.

What happens when one area gets too much or too little attention? Problems and regrets can result, as some parents discover. Ben didn't realize until his children were grown that he wished he had worked less and spent more time with them. Kris developed health problems because she was so busy tending to everyone else that she didn't do healthy things for herself.

Whether or not you become a parent, you must strike a balance between work, family, *and* personal time. This may be harder as you become busier.

Balance Versus Equality

When thinking about how to spend your time, remember that balanced doesn't always mean equal. Imagine dividing your day equally between work, family, and personal life. Do you need to spend five hours every day with friends? On the other hand, school may require more than that.

What may happen, though, if a teen spends too much time working and studying, and forgets the family? If neglected, family relationships weaken. Once weakened, they can be hard to repair.

The balanced life includes all areas on a regular basis. On any given day, one area may get more attention than another, but none is forgotten for days at a time. A balanced life is like a balanced diet. As long as you get the right amount of nutrients overall, you can tolerate the occasional, less nutritious meal.

FEELING THE EFFECTS

Suppose you work late one night at your part-time job. You come home too tired to study for a math test. The next day, angry at having to struggle through the test, you ignore a friend after class. What has happened? Your work life has affected your personal life. Stress from problems in one area carried over into another area.

With a busy schedule, this mother meets a work deadline by taking advantage of commuting time on the train. Tomorrow she might use the trip to talk with her son. ◆ **How could these conversations help both mother and son?**

The same situation can occur between all areas of life. For instance, when Thea's three-year-old son was sick, she couldn't concentrate at work. Sometimes she couldn't even get to work. When Kevin was given added duties at work, he came home late, tired, and irritable. His family learned to avoid him. What "carry over" effect do each of these examples illustrate?

By solving problems in one area of life, you improve the quality in others. In contrast, ignoring problems in one area leads to trouble elsewhere. Whether you have to talk with an employer, change jobs, hold a family meeting, or make time to exercise, problems can be met with thoughtful solutions.

EVALUATING CHOICES

How do you make room in your life for what's important? When society offers so many choices, demands on your time can pile up. The ability to say yes and no when you need to increases your control over life.

Why is saying no so often difficult? People want to be liked. They don't want to let others down. Overcommitment leads to frustration and stress, therefore, at times people have to say no. An already rushed parent might say no to working overtime, ironing a spouse's clothes, chairing a committee, or driving on a field trip. When necessary, you don't have to feel guilty about saying, kindly but firmly, "Sorry, I can't." A polite response is better received by others.

Saying no when necessary makes it easier to say yes with enthusiasm. People who choose their commitments feel more dedicated to them. Your contribution is needed in the world, so saying yes is vital. An employee works a double shift when a co-worker is sick. A person looks in on an older neighbour. A teen raises money for a group that helps people who have an illness. Saying yes to others brings a sense of accomplishment and fulfillment. Saying yes to what you truly want to do brings even greater satisfaction.

Internet Connects

http://www.mcgrawhill.ca/links/parenting
To learn more about individual and family well-being related to work, go to the Web site above for *Parenting Rewards & Responsibilities, First Canadian Edition,* to see where to go next.

What can a busy parent say to requests from others? A little common sense helps. For example, the parent could agree to buy cookies for a school party instead of baking them or to work a shift at the church chili supper instead of leading a committee. Putting yes and no in balance also helps.

Managing Work Life

When asked why he worked so hard at his craft, a professional comedian replied, "I like to eat." Most people could say the same thing. Work, one of the three basic areas of life, is necessary for survival. The belief that work is valuable and beneficial in its own right is called the work ethic. A solid work ethic helps support a strong society.

People who value work gain personal rewards too. Earning money honestly through hard work is satisfying. People are rightfully proud of contributing to their community by doing their job well, whether they brighten a customer's day with a pleasant smile or help cure a sick child.

Unfortunately, all may not be rosy on the work front. Settling workplace problems when they arise can make other parts of life more enjoyable.

EVALUATING WORK HOURS

Why would someone spend every spare moment at work? Some people feel pressured by an employer and fearful of losing their job if they don't. Some want to earn more and to get ahead. Others need extra money to make ends meet.

Working long hours, when neccessary, may not interfere with life and can even be rewarding. For many people, however, overwork creates problems.

Problems from Overworking

Overwork can be a health hazard. People who work long hours may not take time to eat properly, exercise, or relax. They feel stressed and tired, yet won't take time off. These poor health habits leave them more vulnerable to ailments, from headache to heart disease.

Many parents look back at their child-rearing years and wonder where they went. Those who didn't allow their career to overshadow family life usually have fewer regrets.

Long hours are also a problem when relationships are neglected. Family members feel hurt and angry. Friends give up on someone who is never available.

People who discover that overwork is causing problems in their life need to make changes. They may need to find a different job or just learn how to enjoy other areas of life. Work *is* important, but most careers can be reasonably paced. To enjoy family, friends, and good health, now and in the future, you must decide to take care of them all along the way.

Thinking About Income

What does the good life cost? For many parents, the answer is, "More than I earn." In more than 60 percent of all two-parent families in Canada, both partners are employed. In many others, one parent works more than the standard 40 hours a week.

Many parents need every dollar they earn. Even a moderate income may barely cover basic costs of food, clothing, housing, and routine expenses. Added income gives parents a financial cushion or savings for the future.

Spotlight On
——Simpler Lifestyles

In good weather, Kevin rides his bike to and from work. Otherwise, he takes a city bus. He brings lunch from home in a brown paper bag, which he reuses during the week.

Kevin and his wife, Amy, plan their family's meals around economical buys in fresh produce and meats. They buy foods in bulk and save plastic bags to line garbage cans. Much of what they throw out goes in a recycling bin or compost pile. They mix the compost into their garden every spring to grow the flowers that decorate their home.

Today, an increasing number of people are scaling back their lifestyle to a more basic level. What are their reasons? Some are moved by the global situation. With so many people living at or near poverty level, they feel that living with too much luxury isn't right. Many donate money to groups that work to help poorer families become self-sufficient.

Similarly, some people worry about the environmental impact of the typical lifestyle. Manufacturing goods usually produces some type of pollution. Throwing them away adds to the problem. Buying fewer items and making them last longer helps the environment on both accounts.

People who follow a simple lifestyle often say they feel liberated. With home-made items and home-grown food, they are less reliant on others. They also feel freed from the stress of trying to acquire more things. As Kevin explained, "When you make the decision to live simply, you stop asking yourself, 'Can we afford that?' You lose the habit of wanting things. When you do want something, it's more likely to be something of real value."

Living more simply is a goal that any family can have to some extent or another. Some start in small ways and then move on if the lifestyle works for them.

Some parents, however, wonder how much income they really need. Could they get by on one income so one parent could be home with the children? Should they take lower-paying jobs that leave them more family and personal time? Would better money management help them get by with less? These adjustments are working for many families.

Another approach is to take a second look at what is truly needed. Today's consumer in Canada has more buying choices than ever. In addition, manufacturers spend vast amounts of money to convince you that whatever they produce, you need. These pressures encourage **materialism**, the belief that money and possessions bring happiness. Experience, of course, shows that happiness cannot be bought.

To avoid materialism, parents must look closely at what they give up in order to buy more. Which is more important, an hour on the job or an hour spent with a child? Few would argue that what children need most from parents is time and attention. Possessions can't make up for what is lost when time and attention from parents are missing.

SOLVING WORK PROBLEMS

Jobs can be very demanding. An employer's expectations, getting along with co-workers, updating job skills—all of these forces can cause stress.

Solving problems at work is the best way to keep stress from harming other areas of life, and vice versa. Some employers, especially larger ones, have programs that help employees solve workplace problems. They may offer workers options to help them manage personal and family obliga-

tions. Job seekers often look as closely at a company's family-related policies as they do at the job itself.

Employers are finding that a family-oriented approach benefits them as well as the employee. Workers with satisfying lives at home can focus better on their job. They may be more loyal to the company. Those who are anxious about personal matters are often unproductive at work. If they leave the job due to personal problems, the company must spend money to hire and train replacements.

Cross-Curricular Technology CONNECTIONS

From Home to Office

For parents whose family management includes working at home, technology is a valuable servant. The modem, for instance, allows a computer at home to "talk" to one at the workplace. A computer stores each bit of information as a series of numbers, called digital data. The modem at the transmitting end converts this number code into microwaves. This is called *modulation.* As microwaves, the data can be transmitted over telephone lines. A modem at the receiving end translates the microwaves back into digital data, so it can be understood by the other computer. This is called *demodulation.* The word *modem* is derived from these two terms. The same technology is at work in a fax machine, which is essentially a printer with a modem. To fax a document requires the additional step of converting the words or images on the page into digital data before they are converted into microwaves. What other types of technology are often used in homes or offices?

Work Schedule Options

Traditionally, workers have tailored their lives around the nine-to-five, five-day-a-week schedule. To meet family needs, however, parents have pushed for more options. Alternative work schedules are now offered, including:

♥ **Flex time.** Parents adjust their hours to fit the family situation. Working from 7:00 a.m. to 3:00 p.m., for example, lets them be home with children after school.

♥ **Job sharing.** Two workers share the duties and hours of one job. They might work on alternate days or split the job into a morning and afternoon shift.

♥ **Compressed work week.** By working four 10-hour days instead of five 8-hour days each week, parents have an extra day for family matters.

♥ **Rotating shifts.** In workplaces that have several shifts, employees regularly alternate between them. This gives all workers some time to spend with family.

♥ **Working from home.** Some work today is done on computer. Parents can e-mail, fax, or mail work they have completed at home.

Family-Friendly Policies

Companies have found family-friendly policies in greater demand, especially when employees themselves help design the benefits. A few examples are:

♥ On-site child-care facilities or assistance in paying for outside care.

♥ Wellness programs for employees' families.

♥ Personal time to be used as needed, including illness of children.

Many businesses provide parental leave for special circumstances. Some are required to. Since 2001, the *Canada Labour Code* has given workers in Canada up to 52 weeks unpaid leave for the birth or adoption of a child. The law, and eligibility requirements, varies among federal and provincial or territorial jurisdictions.

Many fathers have been reluctant to use parental leave, but that picture is changing. According to several surveys, most men want to be more involved in their children's lives. The value of the family is gradually overriding concerns about what an employer might think of men who take time off for parental duties.

Cross-Curricular Social Studies CONNECTIONS

Parental Leave

Many countries have a national policy on parental leave. Parents in Sweden are entitled to paid parental leave for one year after the baby's birth. Their jobs are guaranteed when they return. Employers in France must offer 12 weeks paid maternity leave, also with job protection. In the United States, the Family and Medical Leave Act assures workers of 12 weeks unpaid leave for the birth or adoption of a child, or for serious health problems in the family. They must be given their original job or a similar one upon return. In Canada, provinces vary in their provisions, but workers have up to 52 weeks unpaid leave. **What factors do you think contribute to the differences in parental leave laws?**

Managing Family Life

As a teacher, Lynn organized her classroom and lessons for efficient learning. At home, meanwhile, bills were mislaid and forgotten. She and her daughter often couldn't find clothes to wear when the laundry didn't get done. "I can manage 22 students for six hours a day," Lynn sighed. "Why can't I manage my home?"

Many parents echo Lynn's frustration. Managing family life can seem much harder than managing a career. At home live several people with individual schedules and demands. A parent takes on duties at home that occupy more than one person at work, supervising, accounting, and maintenance, to name a few.

Parents don't need to run their homes like factories, but they do need to realize that good management techniques can be applied to any situation. When they do, family life becomes more satisfying and less stressful. In return, a parent's personal and work life shows a positive impact.

USING THE MANAGEMENT PROCESS

Professional managers know that using a set order or process helps them run their operation smoothly. A parent-manager can do the same at home. The process outlined below uses basic management principles in a logical order:

♥ *Plan.* Size up the situation. Identify the jobs to be done and the resources needed to do them.

♥ *Organize.* Prepare to act. Assign jobs, gather resources, and make a schedule.

♥ *Implement.* Carry out your plan, checking its progress regularly.

♥ *Evaluate.* Decide whether the plan worked as expected. Could you have carried it out more effectively?

Busy parents shouldn't have to do everything themselves. Children can help. ◆ **What tasks would you expect children to do?**

This process is so simple for small tasks, such as dusting, that you hardly know you're using it. Some steps may not be needed. For larger projects the process may be used several times. Suppose you were planning a family vacation. For what separate tasks would this process prove valuable?

SIMPLIFYING TASKS

When making yeast bread, kneading the dough and waiting for it to rise is part of the fun. To make sandwiches every day, however, you're grateful to open the bag holding a store-bought loaf and pull out two slices.

The same is true of family tasks. For routine jobs, you look for a simple but effective method. Simplifying tasks can simplify home management.

Some tasks are easier when done frequently. Sorting through mail as it arrives is less tiring than tackling a pile of letters at the end of the week. Washing dishes after each meal takes less energy than scrubbing off dried food and stains.

Some tasks can be broken down for convenience. You might put a load of laundry in the washing machine when you get home from work, then dry it on the line or in the dryer after dinner. You could sort and fold clothes the next day.

SHARING TASKS

Have you heard that "many hands make light work"? That saying points out one advantage of dividing household tasks among family members. Contributing to running a home also promotes growth in children and feelings of real self-worth in everyone.

No one system for sharing tasks fits every family. Parents might decide who does what based on these principles:

♥ *Family members.* Those who live in the home are its work force. Their age, abilities, and preferences help determine which jobs they can do best.

♥ *Schedules.* Outside commitments and activities might make a task more convenient for one person than for another. An early riser might pour juice and set out cereal for the rest of the family. Someone who regularly travels past a supermarket could be assigned grocery shopping.

Mathew feels good about his job—feeding Goldy.
◆ **Why would a parent need to supervise the responsibilities given to a child as young as Mathew?**

♥ *Fairness.* Without "keeping score," family members should give equal time and effort to running the home.

♥ *The task itself.* Difficulty and frequency of a task also influence how it's assigned and completed. Some families work as a team on larger, less frequent tasks, such as house cleaning. They rotate smaller, daily tasks.

MANAGING TECHNOLOGY

Probably ever since people learned to draw on cave walls with charcoal, parents have tried to manage the effects of technology on family life. No one denies that scientific advancements simplify and improve life on many fronts. Thanks to technology:

♥ Families can have nutritious meals at almost a moment's notice, by freezing foods and cooking them in a microwave oven.

♥ People can research countless topics and contact others from around the world through the Internet.

♥ Children can use interactive computer programs to make learning more meaningful.

♥ Parents can provide children with education and entertainment using selected videotapes and a VCR, or DVDs and a DVD player.

For every advantage of technology, however, there seems to be a disadvantage. Note that:

♥ Using a microwave oven, people can eat meals when it suits their schedule. Family meals may not seem necessary.

♥ Negative as well as positive influences can reach children over the Internet.

♥ Many families and schools cannot afford computer learning programs, perhaps putting some children at a disadvantage.

♥ Passively viewing videos or DVDs can hinder development.

Technology has changed the way many families operate. Molly's father uses a computer for farm management, but his father didn't even own a computer. ◆ **If Molly manages the family farm someday, will her approach be different from her father's?**

Parents must lead families as they use technology. Is an item needed? Do its advantages outweigh its disadvantages? Staying current on new developments lets a parent make decisions confidently. By setting rules and talking with children, parents guide the family to use technology positively.

Parents can also influence what happens with technology. One parent wrote to an appliance maker, asking for more energy-saving features on its products. Another called a politician to voice support for a measure concerning information children could find on the Internet.

IDENTIFYING RESOURCES FOR FAMILIES

Combining parenting and a career is common today, as is the frantic feeling this juggling act can produce. Wise parents look for resources to help them cope.

As you have read, employers may be a resource if they have family-friendly policies. Many companies employ human resource workers who help parents identify company programs that can serve their family.

Child care is a resource of some working parents. Finding safe, enriching, quality care lets them focus on their job, while meeting many of a child's needs.

Community resources are another help. Health clinics provide affordable medical care at convenient hours. Provincial mental health departments offer counselling and guidance. Community social services inform families on a variety of home management topics, from making a budget to cleaning a home in an environmentally safe way. Libraries provide all kinds of information useful to parents, including lists of other community resources.

In many families grandparents help with child care, but not all families have this option. Many grandparents are employed and have busy lives of their own. Having raised their own families, they may not wish to start again.

Building Parenting Skills

PARENTING WITH RESOURCEFULNESS

"What do I need in order to parent successfully?" Parents who ask this question are looking for resources. When they figure out how to get and use what they need, they are being resourceful. Resourceful parents notice people and things that can help them. Through creativity, they use items in multiple ways and think of substitutions. As a parent, Alex showed resourcefulness when he:

▶ Asked his grandmother about past family traditions that he could start with his own children.

▶ Traded babysitting hours with his sister, who also has a child.

▶ Taught his son, Jason, colours while making a fruit salad together.

▶ Went to the county health department to get Jason immunized.

▶ Used the Internet at the public library to find information on good places for a family vacation.

▶ Helped his daughter Chelsea make a drum set from empty coffee cans.

◆ ◆ Your Thoughts ◆ ◆

❶ When money is limited, how might a resourceful parent entertain a child?

❷ How can a newspaper and a calendar be resources for parents?

❸ Describe examples of resourcefulness that you have seen parents use.

❹ Gloria's six-year-old son loves art projects, but she can't afford expensive supplies. What can she do?

Family and friends can be a special source of help. Patti's sister, for example, is always ready to watch Patti's children, and her sister's husband often helps with home maintenance. Patti is careful to protect the relationship, though. "I don't turn to them all the time," she explained. "They're more a last resort, not a first call. And I always try to repay the favours. That keeps us all on good terms."

Managing Personal Life

Looking through a family album, Emmy came across some sketches her father had done years before. "These are good," she told him. "Why don't you draw anymore?"

Her father shrugged. "I got too busy, I guess—between the job and the family and the house. It was only a hobby anyway."

Like Emmy's father, some parents find themselves giving up personal interests after their children are born. Demands at home and at work take so much time and energy. Parents often vow to take time for themselves after everyone else's needs are met. Instead, they find that everyone else's needs are never met for long.

Giving up all personal time is seldom a solution. Leisure time is play for adults, and adults need to play as much as children do. Whether through sewing or karate, parents need the chance for self-expression and accomplishment. They enjoy spending time with their peers.

Leisure time can be a safety valve for releasing pressures of everyday life. Without it, a person can become tense, irritable, and stressed. Physical and mental health suffer. It's hard to be a good parent in this state, and easier to be a poor one.

Finally, parents set a good example by keeping up personal interests. They show children that life can and should include some recreation. They can pass on special skills or knowledge. Remember, too, that children naturally view themselves as the centre of their parents' life. Seeing a parent involved in something other than themselves reminds children that parents have a personal life too. Children gain a more mature view of the parent-child relationship.

FINDING PERSONAL TIME

You can easily adapt some personal interests to the parenting lifestyle by treating them as any other task. Break them down into parts. Simplify them with technology. Ask family members for help. If reading is your hobby, you can probably set aside some quiet time each day to enjoy a new magazine or a few chapters of a novel.

Time and expense make some pursuits harder to maintain. Creativity is needed to fit them in around other obligations. Sydney liked making and decorating specialty cakes. As the demands of family and career grew, she found shortcuts to her hobby. Boxed cake mixes were fast, easy, and just as delicious as homemade. Rather than buy costly cake pans, Sydney created and cut out her own patterns.

How do you feel when you have to spend all your spare time working on a term paper or studying for finals? You probably look forward to a break. It's the same with parents. They need regular time for relaxation too in order to stay physically and mentally healthy.

To frost cakes, she snipped one corner from a sturdy plastic bag and forced frosting through. Different cuts produced different effects.

Sydney found that making this effort helped her better understand why she enjoyed her pastime. For her, experimenting and resourcefulness were a big part of the attraction. Practising these skills in her hobby built her confidence to try new things and look for creative solutions, at work and at home.

TIME MANAGEMENT

Time management means using time effectively to achieve goals. It's a valuable tool for anyone who wants to get the most from each day. It is invaluable for working parents who need time for themselves.

Time management offers mental as well as practical benefits. Using time well helps you complete needed tasks. You also feel a sense of accomplishment and control. You feel less stressed and more capable.

Like sharing tasks, each parent develops individual techniques for managing time. Every good time-management system, however, recognizes the importance of planning, prioritizing, and organizing. Try these time-management tips:

♥ Write it down. Making a list of your tasks for the day helps you stay focused. Crossing off items as you complete them gives a feeling of satisfaction.

♥ Make a schedule. Write down your schedule and commitments as soon as you learn of them. This helps you plan time and prioritize tasks. A calendar is a handy scheduling tool. A bulletin board is another place to post events.

Dovetailing tasks such as the laundry and paying bills can help you manage time.

♥ Use scraps of time. With a few spare minutes, you can complete small tasks or make progress on larger ones. You might empty the dishwasher or set out a pen and stationery for a letter you need to write.

♥ Double up on tasks. When you can do so safely, work on two tasks at once. Fold laundry while helping a child study for a test. Combining tasks in this way is called **dovetailing**.

♥ Identify and eliminate time-wasters. Avoid situations where you tend to dawdle, or save them for when you have time. If you get sidetracked by browsing through catalogues, use it in the evening as relaxation before bed.

Even when schedules are busy, children shouldn't be overlooked. Here, Taylor does her "work" at the same time that Daddy does his. The extra effort made to include Taylor has benefits. ◆ **Can you name two?**

Planning

One key to managing time is deciding in advance how to spend it. With a plan, you arrange tasks and events for efficiency and convenience. You save time by knowing what to do next.

One key to planning is flexibility. Things don't always go as expected. What indoor activities can the family do if it rains on your picnic? What foods on hand can be quickly prepared if you're running late at mealtime? Preparing several "game plans" helps you meet an unexpected turn of events.

Prioritizing

Suppose you plan more for one day than you can do. Rushing through tasks is unwise and may be dangerous, especially with a child around. A sensible alternative is to **prioritize** tasks, to rank them in order of importance, and complete them in order. Tasks not done today might get higher priority tomorrow.

Decisions about prioritizing are sometimes obvious. Taking a sick child to the doctor is more pressing than taking a car to the car wash. Other times, importance depends more on circumstances and values. If you were a parent, would you finish a report for work or go to your child's music recital? If it were the child's first performance and the other parent couldn't go, you might give the recital higher priority. What if your boss needed your report the next day in order to close a large business deal? How might you choose then?

Organizing

Planning and prioritizing are two examples of organizing your time for better use. Organizing your physical surroundings can be equally helpful. If you've ever stayed up late to rewrite a lost assignment, only to find it the next day in a pile of old papers, you know this is true.

Often the organization principles you see in the workplace can be used at home. Each workplace has a system of organizing space for efficiency and productivity. You can apply these same principles to living space. For instance, one basic rule of organization is to store things where they are used. As a restaurant chef, John appreciated having pot holders hanging beside the oven and the can opener beside the shelves of canned goods. At home, he naturally kept the laundry soap on a shelf near the washing machine, and the telephone directory in a drawer next to the phone.

Another rule of organization is to keep things in the same place. John knew he could find vegetables above the meat and below the ice cream in the restaurant freezer. Arriving home, he always hung the car keys on the hook beside the door and set the day's mail in the rack on the desk.

Good organization can help you get control of life. Applying management skills to all areas of life—work, family, and personal—helps give you a balance that works now and in the future.

The Role of Societal Agents in Teaching Young Children

Children interact with people individually, in informal groups, and in organized groups. These **societal agents** help children develop thinking skills, teach them how to behave in different situations, and provide emotional support. Societal agents include family, caregivers, school, peers,

Doing two things at once is a handy skill for busy people. This mother sets up the carpool schedule on the phone and takes care of the laundry at the same time. ◆ **How else can families dovetail tasks?**

community groups, the media, religion, and culture. Each societal agent has different rules and standards for acceptable behaviour, as well as different ways to promote **social values**. For example, the rules and expected behaviours in school or in church may be more formal than those that children experience in the home.

Some societal agents have more influence at certain times in a child's life. For school age children, the peer group becomes more and more important. Behaviours that are valued by the peer group, such as "success in a game," are often different from those valued by adults, for example "playing fair."

Social Concerns Faced by Parents

In 2002, there were 66 532 reports of missing children in Canada, and 35 of these children were abducted by strangers. As school age children become more independent, they spend more time away from family and caregivers. A main social concern for parents is the risk relating to the child's interactions with other people.

Parents can teach their children how to act in suspicious situations and where they can get help. Some communities have Block Parent homes, where children can go when they feel threatened. Stay Alert . . . Stay Safe is a **street-proofing** program to teach school-aged children skills for becoming aware of potential dangers and how to handle them.

Canada's Stay Alert ... Stay Safe program alerts adults and children to potential dangers. It also helps give children the awareness and confidence to deal with such situations.

Bullying

The problem of **bullying**, intentionally intimidating or forcing another person into doing something, is of great concern for many parents and schools. Bullying can take many forms, including physical violence, name-calling, teasing, and sexual harassment.

Children who become bullies often have emotional difficulties, poor social skills, and/or negative attitudes. Bullying may be learned in the home by observing conflict between parents. At school, bullying occurs more frequently when children have little supervision or when less emphasis is placed on children's individual strengths and weaknesses. Efforts to reduce bullying involve good communication between parents and schools, talks with both victims and bullies, and clear consequences for unacceptable behaviour.

STAY ALERT...STAY SAFE

Laws Regulating Parents and Children in Society

Federal and provincial governments have a critical role in providing a safe, healthy, and secure environment in which children can grow up. Canada's Criminal Code states that parents are required to provide "the necessities of life" for children up to age 16. It is illegal to abandon or expose a child younger than ten to life-threatening danger. A child's rights are protected by the Canadian Charter of Rights and Freedoms, which also specifies the child's right to education in either English or French. Provincial laws, such as Ontario's Family Law Act, say that parents are obligated to support children younger than 19. Federal and provincial statutes also regulate schools, **child labour**, child protection, young offenders, Children's Aid Societies, adoptions, and rights for Aboriginal People's children.

Responsible parents work to ensure that their children are safe and protected from possible dangers around them.

Responsibilities Parents Have for Children of Different Ages

Children depend on their parents to meet their basic needs for food, shelter, and medical care, as well as to support their social, emotional, and cognitive development. Parental responsibilities include providing for basic needs, keeping children safe, teaching skills, and guiding behaviour. Parents decide what values and beliefs are important in the family, and reinforce behaviours that are consistent with family values.

It is important for parents to have reasonable expectations about what children need to learn about at each age level. While four-year-old Michael may need help learning to get dressed, his nine-year-old sister Nadia may need help with social issues such as lying or being rejected by the group. Parents are the child's first role models for learning about relationships, social interactions, and communication. By valuing the child's opinions and encouraging independence, parents help the child build self-esteem and learn to respect others.

Internet Connects

http://www.mcgrawhill.ca/links/parenting
To learn more about the Early Years Initiatives and what is available from the Ministry of Community and Family and Child Services, go to the Web site above for *Parenting Rewards & Responsibilities, First Canadian Edition,* to see where to go next.

Looking Back

♥ Parents need to devote a satisfying amount of time to work, family, and personal life.

♥ All aspects of life are interrelated. Experiences in one area can affect your effectiveness in another.

♥ People must balance their need and desire to work with the value of good health and caring relationships.

♥ Employers offer workers options to help them meet parenting duties, thus balancing work with family life.

♥ Basic management principles, such as sharing tasks, can help family life run more smoothly.

♥ Technology and other resources that help parents meet family needs also help them balance home life with other areas.

♥ Good time management helps parents schedule time to enjoy personal interests.

Knowledge and Understanding

1. What does it mean to balance work, family, and personal life?
2. Explain why having a job you dislike can hurt your personal life.
3. How is materialism an obstacle to balancing work life with family and personal life?
4. Why should an employer be concerned about a worker meeting family obligations?
5. Describe some alternative work schedules. Why do employers offer workers these options?
6. Briefly describe the management process.
7. Robert needs to decide which of his sons should be assigned the task of washing windows. What factors should he consider?
8. Describe a helpful approach to managing technology in the family.
9. Can a parent include personal time in his or her life without neglecting the family? Explain your answer.
10. Summarize the key components of a good time management system.

Thinking and Inquiry

11. A friend who is a new parent comments, "It's strange. Everyone expects you to have children. Yet when you do, people act surprised that you want to spend time raising them." How do you respond to this observation?

12. What problems might people without a strong work ethic have? What rewards come to those who have a strong work ethic?

13. If you were part of a team working on a school assignment, how would you feel if the others expected you to do all the work? If you were managing a household, how would you feel if others expected you to do all the work? Compare these two situations.

Communication

14. Choose one of the families described here. List the daily and weekly tasks each needs to accomplish. Then draw up a task-sharing plan for that family.
    a) *Celia, Ryan, and their four-year-old Cara.* Celia works full-time days; Ryan works three evenings a week. Cara attends preschool each afternoon.
    b) *Jessie and his two children, seven-year-old Marta and nine-year-old Chris.* Jessie works full-time days; the children stay with their next-door neighbour after school.

15. Compose a job advertisement that would appeal to a single parent. Be sure to use the terms found in the text under the Work Schedule Options on page 496.

Application

16. With one or more partners, write a company policy that would help workers balance work and family roles. Include details about scheduling, benefits, and other workplace practices.

17. You are a single parent of two children, ages two and four. Although you work full-time, you are proud that you make time for your family every day. Recently, your employer offered to pay you for a job training course that will prepare you for a better position in the company. If you don't update your job skills, you may not have a job in the future. However, the training and the new job will take away time with your family. What will you do?

18. Using Internet research, how has compulsory education/attendance changed since the 1800s in Canada?

Children with Special Needs

While reading this chapter, you will:

▶ Describe the legal and social responsibilities of parents and guardians.

▶ Demonstrate an understanding of the challenges faced by parents of young children in today's rapidly changing society.

▶ Identify ways in which families manage early-childhood trauma.

▶ Identify effective methods for collecting information from a variety of sources.

▶ Effectively communicate the results of your inquiries, using a variety of methods and forms.

KEY TERMS

allergen
attention deficit
    disorder (ADD)
autism
dyslexia
inclusion
learning
    disability

mentally
    challenged
prostheses
special needs
syndrome

"Mom, what's di-al-y-sis?" Nine-year-old Tyler sounded out the word carefully. Gwen turned from chopping vegetables to look at her son, doing homework at the kitchen table. She was surprised but answered, "That's when a person is hooked up to a machine that cleans the blood. It's for people whose kidneys don't work right. Why do you ask?"

"There's a new girl at school—Sondra. She said she has to sit for three hours for dialysis three times a week. That sounds pretty boring to me. I thought I'd loan her some of my animal magazines to read. She likes lizards, the same as me."

"That's a great idea, Ty. I think she'll like that. You can pile them on the hall table, so you remember to take them. Now I need you to clear off your stuff and help set the table."

Tyler gathered his books in his lap. Stuck in the same place for hours, over and over, he thought with a sigh. Then Tyler spun his wheelchair around and rolled down the hall to put his books in his room.

◆

What do you think? How would you describe Tyler's attitude toward his own health condition? How might his parents have shaped his attitude?

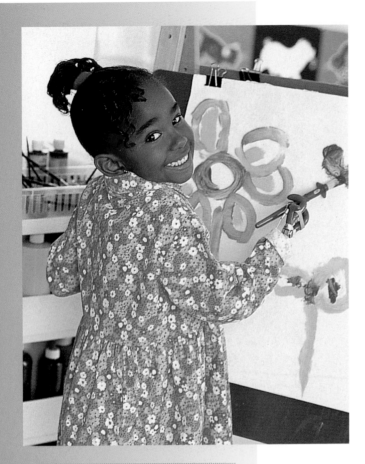

A child who has a disability will see herself through her family's attitude. A child's positive, can-do spirit follows that same spirit in family members.
◈ **How would you describe Danielle's spirit?**

A Range of Needs

What is your image of a child with special needs? Is it someone like Tyler, who has a physical challenge? Does it include a child who learns more slowly than others, but also one with remarkable musical talent? All of these children have **special needs**, circumstances caused when development differs significantly from the average.

Special needs vary in degree as well as area of development. Asthma may limit a child's physical activities during certain weather conditions, while blindness presents quite different challenges.

Raising a child with special needs can present a challenge for parents. They face many situations and emotions that other parents don't experience. They often need added skills and knowledge to help their children live up to their potential.

Parenting Children with Health Conditions

"I hate the word disability!" Victor exclaimed. "It's such a label. When I look at my son Alex, I don't see a mentally challenged boy. I see a happy, active three-year-old who likes fire engines, hates to get his hair washed, and has a condition that limits him in certain ways. But don't we all, to some extent?"

Victor made a valid point. Some people see a person's disability and focus only on that quality. In reality, a disability is only part of a person. Health conditions affect more than 180 000 children in Canada. Is it fair or reasonable to make broad generalizations about so many people?

As you read about the following conditions, remember that these are only the most common of several thousand recognized disorders. You can find more about these conditions and their treatment through the Internet and other resouces.

ALLERGIES AND ASTHMA

An allergy is the body's overreaction to a triggering substance, called an **allergen**. The immune system mistakes the allergen as a threat and takes defensive measures. Depending on how contact is made, symptoms may include sneezing, a congested nose, watering eyes, vomiting or digestive problems, and itching welts called hives. Most reactions are only annoying, but a few can be fatal. Common allergens include dust, mould, pet hair, and pollen. A child may be allergic to a certain food or plant.

A parent who suspects a child has an allergy should consult with a physician. Many allergies are outgrown; however, a child with untreated allergies could develop asthma and other disorders.

With asthma, the muscles around the windpipe tighten, and its lining becomes inflamed and congested. Wheezing, coughing, and shortness of breath result. Attacks may be severe or mild. They may occur daily, monthly, or less often. An attack may be triggered by allergens or by impurities in the air. Exercise, stress, and a change in the weather are also contributing factors. Frequent attacks can lead to lung infections, including pneumonia.

Asthma is not always linked to allergies, but the treatment is similar. Avoiding the trigger is the simplest and surest response. Medication can lessen and sometimes prevent reactions. When symptoms do occur, a parent must remain calm and reassuring. Anxiety only makes the situation worse.

HEARING AND VISUAL IMPAIRMENTS

Problems with hearing and sight range from slight to severe. Parents can take an active role in managing both conditions.

Besides getting children regular medical exams, parents should note possible warning signs. Delayed speech may result from the inability to hear words clearly. An accident-prone child may have trouble seeing objects well enough to avoid them. Squinting may indicate a vision problem.

Asthma is common and is increasing. Although wheezing and shortness of breath are usually associated with asthma, some children may have only a chronic cough. Most children with asthma can function normally with proper care.

Many corrective measures are available for both conditions. Hearing aids and eyeglasses can improve physical abilities. Children with impaired hearing can communicate through lip reading, American Sign Language, and cued speech, which combines speaking and gestures. Visually impaired children can learn to read and write using the Braille alphabet, which represents letters as patterns of raised dots.

Parents should discuss their options with a specialist. As they learn how to make the home safe, children gain independence. With strong parental support, most children with hearing and sight impairments can become confident, successful adults.

DIABETES

In some people, the body fails to produce enough insulin, a chemical needed to turn food sugars into energy. This condition is called diabetes. Sugar levels build, which can damage the eyes, kidneys, and nervous system.

With doctors' help, most parents can manage their child's diabetes. Giving regular injections of synthetic insulin makes up for what the body lacks. Feeding a nutritious, individualized diet helps stabilize blood sugar levels. Parents can time the child's exercise to help the body use sugars effectively without the levels dropping dangerously. Home monitoring kits help keep track of blood sugars. Therapy today helps school-age and older children manage their own diabetes.

EPILEPSY

With epilepsy, the brain "short circuits," sending an unusual electrical charge through the nervous system. The result is a seizure, which ranges from a brief loss of

Spotlight On Technology

Every day new advances in technology make life easier for those with disabilities. Have you heard of these?

✔ Computerized hearing aids. These amplify speech while muting background noise.

✔ Devices that stimulate the inner ear using a tiny transmitter behind the ear and a receiver implanted within the skull. Sound quality is poor, but children hear again.

✔ Customized artificial limbs, or **prostheses** (pross-THEE-sees). Newer models are made of durable, lightweight materials to allow a freer, more natural range of movement. Some can even be used for participation in sports activities. One experimental prosthesis has a computer chip in the knee that can be programmed to match the wearer's unique pace and stride.

✔ Computer programs with a voice synthesizer that converts words typed on a keyboard into speech.

✔ Computers with power pads that respond to a nod of the head or the wiggle of a toe. These are used by children with paralysis or poor motor skills.

awareness to convulsions of the entire body. Epilepsy often results from a brain injury, before or after birth, but half of all cases have no known cause.

Medication is an effective control in about 80 percent of children with the disorder. Parents don't need to restrict them in any way unless their doctor recommends it. Since a seizure can occur while bathing or swimming, a child must be supervised at these times. Parents should learn how to respond to seizures. Children can learn to anticipate a seizure and inform others.

CYSTIC FIBROSIS

Children with cystic fibrosis have trouble breathing due to lung congestion, and they can't draw nutrients from food efficiently. They may look starved, though they eat more than is normal.

Cystic fibrosis has no known cure, but promising therapies are being developed. Children can live productively into adulthood in many cases. Parental involvement is essential. Parents perform procedures to rid the lungs of mucus and give dietary supplements and medicine. Keeping the home cool, dry, and smoke-free eases breathing.

CEREBRAL PALSY

Cerebral palsy is a type of paralysis usually caused by brain damage before, during, or after birth. Children with this condition have poor or rigid muscle tone, which interferes with motor skills. Some children have varying degrees of mental limitation. Many are quite intelligent.

Depending on their mental abilities, children with cerebral palsy can learn self-sufficiency. They may need speech or physical therapy, with special training to master self-help skills. Parents need to reinforce and support these efforts. They may need to provide modified utensils and furnishings and a wheelchair, crutches, or braces.

DOWN SYNDROME

Down syndrome is a genetic disorder resulting from an extra chromosome. It is usually detected during pregnancy or shortly after birth. Testing reveals the type and degree of impairment. A **syndrome** is a group of symptoms that characterize a certain condition. In Down syndrome these usually, but not always, include both physical and intellectual difficulties.

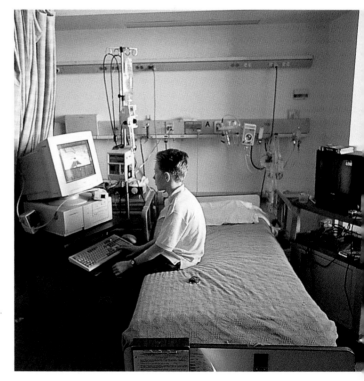

Technology helps children with more than just treatment. Here, Shawn keeps in touch with friends via computer while getting hospital care for cystic fibrosis.

Parents need to learn the exact nature of their child's condition. They can then create the home environment and get the support needed to help the child reach his or her potential. Children with Down syndrome are typically cheerful and affectionate. Most can learn at least basic skills. Many hold jobs and live in sheltered homes with light supervision.

MENTAL CHALLENGES

Mental challenges are characterized in varying degrees by low intelligence, abnormal ability to learn, and impaired social adaptation. Mental challenges can be part of other conditions, such as Down syndrome.

Children with mental challenges have trouble mastering physical, emotional, and social skills, but most *can* learn. Many learn well enough to work and live independently. Guided by professionals, parents can use techniques for teaching children many of the same skills they expect of others. A child with mild or moderate challenges can perform self-care and household tasks when given short, simple directions and repeated demonstrations.

AUTISM

Autism is a complex condition marked by a severe detachment from reality and from others. Autistic children live "in their own little world." They don't communicate or respond to most stimulation. They often engage in repetitive or self-destructive behaviour, such as continually rocking back and forth or banging the head. The cause of this condition remains a mystery.

Dealing with an autistic child can be frustrating. Treatment often requires a team of developmental specialists. Small signs of progress must be noticed and rewarded. Some children take an interest in a certain object or activity that can be used to draw them out of their isolation. A few can eventually function in society.

Internet Connects

http://www.mcgrawhill.ca/links/parenting
To learn more about the health and welfare of children, go to the Web site above for *Parenting Rewards & Responsibilities, First Canadian Edition,* to see where to go next.

With early and appropriate treatment and education, children with Down syndrome can function very well. Some have only mild limitation or challenge and some have a normal IQ.

The earlier a child with a learning disability gets help, the better. Suppose Jerome's learning disability wasn't diagnosed and he received no help. ◆ **What might happen as he moved through grade school?**

LEARNING DISABILITIES

A **learning disability** is a difficulty in processing information, especially math or language concepts. True learning disabilities are not related to low intelligence, but are often mistaken for it. They're not behaviour problems, but problem behaviour may arise from the frustration and misunderstanding they cause.

One such disability is **dyslexia** (dis-LEK-see-uh). Children with dyslexia have trouble making sense of written symbols and associating letters with sounds. Letters and numbers may appear backwards or jumbled. Other disabilities leave children unable to count objects or recognize shapes. Children with an auditory (hearing) processing disability have trouble understanding spoken words.

A learning disability often goes undetected until a child begins school. Parents might notice signs before then, however.

"Late talkers" and children with vocabulary or pronunciation problems may have a language disorder. Difficulty remembering sequences, such as the days of the week, can indicate a math disability. Other signs include difficulty with routines and directions, unusual restlessness, and poor motor and social skills.

Overcoming a learning disability takes great effort. With the help of learning specialists, children must adapt to new ways of organizing and using information. They may need counselling in order to deal with behavioural problems. Those who persevere, however, can go on to be successful.

Attention Disorders

Attention disorders are not learning disorders, but the two often occur together. Children with attention disorders have trouble focusing their mind or body on a single task. Those with the condition called **attention deficit disorder** (ADD) are easily distracted.

Chapter 26 Children with Special Needs • *MHR* **517**

Children who have ADHD function well when their attention is focused toward a single topic.

They are often labelled "daydreamers." Children with attention deficit hyperactivity disorder (ADHD) are intensely active, impatient, and impulsive. They are constantly moving and talking, often with no apparent purpose.

Attention disorders are sometimes treated with drugs. However, some children who are merely energetic or poorly disciplined can be misdiagnosed and given unnecessary medication. Parents should try less extreme measures, such as better guidance techniques, before accepting a medical solution. Parents often spend much time seeking the right help.

Other Health Conditions

Some health conditions arise from no known cause. Other causes are beyond a parent's control. Down syndrome and cystic fibrosis, for example, result from genetic defects. Some conditions, however, are related to parents' health and safety habits.

Exposure to drugs, alcohol, or sexually transmitted diseases during pregnancy can cause a number of problems, including blindness, deafness, and mental limitation. Very low birth weight (under 1.5 kg [3.5 lbs.]) and extremely low birth weight (under 1 kg [2.2 lbs.]) are a particular danger. They are often responsible for both mental and physical developmental delays. The tiniest children are at highest risk. They may begin life with breathing and muscular difficulties, impaired hearing and vision, or learning disabilities.

Childhood illness and injury can also produce health conditions. A fall, blow to the head, and high fever can cause brain damage, which, in turn, may cause mental and physical challenges. Accidents can also result in the loss of a limb.

Many of these circumstances are preventable. With good health practices before, during, and after pregnancy, many parents can save themselves and their children much pain and difficulty.

Guidelines for Parents

As with other children, parenting those with health conditions is more than meeting physical and intellectual needs. The experience is literally life-changing, yet it isn't always the burden some parents imagine. As one father of a child with a health condition said, "Raising a child with a special need is a lot like raising any other child. You get hugs and smiles and spilled glasses of milk. You deal with the special need as part of the child. And every time we overcome a problem, the rewards are sweet."

ACTING ON THE DIAGNOSIS

"I felt something was wrong with Lianne as a baby," Patty recalled. "She responded more slowly than other babies. She didn't startle or react to my voice the way I thought she should. I had her tested, and she was diagnosed as hearing impaired."

Patty was wise to have her daughter tested. Some parents don't act because they're afraid of what they might learn. Early diagnosis, however, is critical to managing a health condition successfully. A delay can have a long-term negative impact on the child.

Upon learning her child had a special need, Patty reacted as many parents do. "At first, I gave up all my hopes for her. I was depressed, then worried. Being a parent was already a challenge. Could I cope with the added demands? I felt angry at my husband, the doctors—even at Lianne. I was angry with myself, too, because I thought I'd done something wrong."

As the shock subsided, Patty decided to meet the situation head-on. "I started to see the hearing problem as a bully that we had to stand up to. That seemed to give me the strength I needed."

The stages that Patty went through as she dealt with Lianne's diagnosis are similar to the grief process people commonly go through when faced with any serious loss, whether a death, a severe illness, or destruction of their home in a fire.

BECOMING INFORMED

Many parents lack knowledge about their child's condition, which fuels their fears. Becoming informed lets them direct their energies toward helping the child.

The child's pediatrician, often first to recognize a problem, is a parent's initial source of information. The doctor usually refers the parents to a specialist, who may enlist several others, if necessary. Parents should listen carefully to each expert opinion. They should take notes and ask questions.

For some children with a hearing impairment, cochlear (COH-klee-ur) implants can often restore limited hearing. For any impairment, parents need to seek help and learn what the possibilities are as soon as they suspect a problem.

Other sources of information may also be helpful. Many libraries have good medical reference books to round out a parent's understanding. Parents of other children with the condition can offer insights about what to expect.

While a parent's main concern is usually helping the child cope, learning the cause of the condition might prevent it from recurring in the family.

FINDING SUPPORT

All parents need support in their role, especially those who have children with health conditions. Parents need specialized help and information, in addition to a support system.

National Organizations

Many national associations inform parents and others on a variety of topics, including new research and proposed laws, that will affect them. They may raise funds to educate the public, lobby legislators, and find a cure. Well-known groups include the Canadian Cystic Fibrosis Foundation, the Muscular Dystrophy Association of Canada, and the United Cerebral Palsy Association of Canada. Doctors can supply the names of helpful organizations.

In addition to groups for specific conditions, parents should use the resources of other national agencies. The local office of Human Resources Development Canada can help them learn whether their child is eligible for benefits.

Parenting Q & A

When Helping Hurts

Q "Our daughter has cerebral palsy. She needs our help more than other children do. My husband calls me overprotective, but I'm just trying to be realistic. Who's right?" *Marina*

A When a child has a health condition, a parent may exaggerate the physical and emotional dangers to save the child from failure. Like all children, your daughter will learn through challenges. Of course, this carries the risk of failure. Your family will never know how much your daughter can do unless she is encouraged to try. Helping children deal with disabilities sometimes means letting them struggle with things that come more easily to others. Children gain pride and self-esteem through accomplishment. Many children learn to manage well because a parent, as much as possible, acted as though they didn't have a disability.

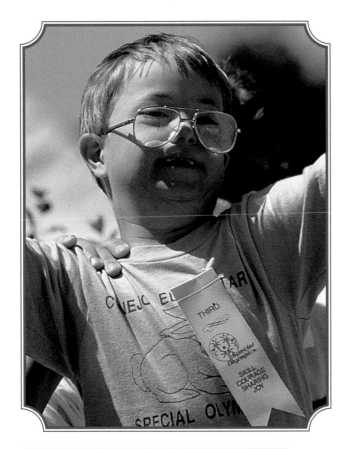

Many organizations, such as the Special Olympics, support families and children with disabilities.
◆ **Do you know of any in your area?**

Internet Connects

http://www.mcgrawhill.ca/links/parenting
To learn more about the health, well-being, and rights of children and youth through monitoring, education, and advocacy, go to the Web site above for *Parenting Rewards & Responsibilities, First Canadian Edition,* to see where to go next.

Community Resources

The provinces offer a network of services for families of special needs children. When Greg's daughter Alisa was diagnosed with cerebral palsy, Greg contacted the Special Needs Education project. Helpers there put him in touch with other groups that could help. The school district, for example, offered special education classes. A class at the hospital helped the family deal with practical and emotional challenges. A volunteer group drove Alisa to appointments in a wheelchair-accessible van. The caseworker even located students at a technical school who built a ramp over the family's front porch steps as a class project.

Support Groups

Parents of children with special needs have problems and emotions that other parents may not understand. Support groups allow them to express feelings, including negative ones, that might otherwise be taken out on family members. Within these groups, people share advice and listen to speakers. They organize outings, with child care provided.

Family and Friends

What family and friends lack in expertise, they often make up for in loyalty and concern. They may be able to help in many ways that parents really appreciate. A neighbour might offer to watch the home if the family must travel to a distant treatment centre, or watch the child to give the parents a few hours alone. To parents, just knowing someone cares can be as valuable as the practical help they offer.

Spouses may need added support from each other too. They should share the responsibility of meeting with doctors, caring for the child, and finding extra help. They can bolster each other's spirits against the physical and emotional demands.

SUPPORTING THE CHILD

Have you ever been sick the night you were invited to a party? Have you been baffled by a lesson that all your classmates understood? Then you have some understanding of what a child with a health condition is exposed to daily. Even a toddler can feel left out, different, or inferior. Parents must actively send the opposite message to a child with a special need.

Through their words, actions, and attitude, parents show love, respect, and acceptance. To demonstrate support, parents can:

♥ *Explain the condition, using terms the child understands.* Some parents try to preserve their child's spirits by "sugar coating" the truth. Instead, the child feels betrayed and disappointed when the facts are learned. Parents must show faith in their child's ability to cope. Coming to terms with the condition, the child gains inner strength.

♥ *Choose furnishings that promote growth and independence.* To encourage intellectual growth, parents can place a touch-control lamp on a wheelchair-accessible desk. Headphones allow a hearing impaired child to appreciate music without disturbing others. Handrails and grab bars let children with motor impairments move independently.

♥ *Choose clothing that emphasizes self-care.* Large buttons, zippers, pull tabs, and Velcro™ fasteners all make self-dressing easier. Markers sewn inside garments, such as an odd-shaped button, make them identifiable to visually impaired children.

Caring for a child with a physical challenge can be demanding, especially when the family has other children too. Through support groups, parents can share experiences and ways of coping with those who understand.

♥ *Give the child the chance to do tasks.* Out of compassion, families may be inclined to do too much for the child. Children need to try, even when trying is difficult.

♥ *Set limits for behaviour, according to the child's abilities.* Expecting appropriate behaviour emphasizes the child's capabilities. It recognizes ways that the child is like any other.

♥ *Recognize achievements.* Progress usually comes in small steps. Rewarding it with a smile, a hug, or a compliment boosts the child's feelings of pride and encourages independence.

♥ *Point out the child's unique qualities.* Everyone likes recognition for doing well. Children with health conditions especially may need to hear praise for their particular contribution, whether it is a fine singing voice or the desire to help others.

♥ *Encourage the child to enjoy life.* Experiences that enrich life, such as smelling flowers, take the child's focus off the condition and onto the world outside.

SUPPORTING SIBLINGS

"My sister gets all the attention," grumbled seven-year-old Ian, "because she can't walk. Mom and Dad are always taking her to the doctor, or giving her a bath, or something. She even needs help using the bathroom. Once I had a really bad stomachache, but Mom just said, 'Oh, you'll be better tomorrow.' Sometimes I wish I'd break my leg so they'd spend more time with me."

Health & Safety

FRIENDLY ENVIRONMENTS

Like any child, one with a health condition needs a secure home environment that promotes success. To create these surroundings, parents can:

▶ Arrange furniture to provide clear traffic lanes through rooms, to benefit children with limited vision and mobility.

▶ Remove throw rugs and area rugs, or secure them to the floor.

▶ Use contrasting colours to mark cabinet edges and changes in floor surfaces and levels. This alerts children with visual impairments.

▶ Replace door knobs with lever handles, which are easier to turn for children with poorly developed motor skills.

▶ Make sure children with intellectual impairments understand health and safety rules. Unlike other children, their ability to learn may not increase with age and experience.

If Ian were your child, how would you respond to his complaint? His feelings are natural for his age, but how might they affect his relationship with you and his sister if they weren't addressed?

Siblings of children with special needs deserve careful handling. Young siblings are especially prone to fear and jealousy. To keep a health condition from dividing brothers and sisters and causing a lifetime of resentment, parents should:

♥ Explain the condition to the healthy child in simple terms, stressing that it's not contagious and not the sibling's fault.

♥ Keep demands reasonable. A sibling shouldn't be a caregiver but could help or entertain the child at times to give parents a break.

♥ Show acceptance of a sibling's negative feelings, but not harmful actions, toward a child with special needs.

♥ Avoid having higher expectations for the sibling in order to "make up" for the child with the condition.

♥ Make time for the healthy child. At times, *every* child needs a parent's undivided attention.

Many adults who grew up with siblings with special needs say the experience brought the family closer. They learned patience, empathy, and the rewards of feeling needed.

PROVIDING EDUCATIONAL OPPORTUNITIES

Parents everywhere want their children to discover and develop their talents to the fullest. As more children with special needs grow to adulthood, their parents want them to have the training needed for satisfying, productive lives. Responding to this strong demand, society is helping parents provide these children with appropriate educational opportunities.

Inclusion

In Mrs. Sandoval's first-grade classroom, Caleb watched her demonstrate a math concept using pine cones. Because Caleb was hearing impaired, an interpreter signed to him. Caleb had grown skilled at reading gestures and other non-verbal cues, and followed the lesson without help. Seated ahead of him, his friend Daniel remembered to sit to one side so Caleb could see Mrs. Sandoval better. Later, a speech therapist would come in to help Caleb improve his pronunciation.

Caleb's situation is an example of **inclusion**, educating children with special needs in a regular classroom. In Canada, provincial policies specify the educational provisions made for children with special needs or health conditions. In the same way, provinces and territories determine the extent to which public facilities are physically accessible to people of all abilities, though access is guaranteed under Section 15 of the *Canadian Charter of Rights and Freedoms*.

By being able to act like a typical six-year-old, Caleb benefitted from inclusion. Going to school and making friends nurtured his intellectual, emotional, and social growth. He learned to live by the same rules as the rest of the world, reinforcing his parents' efforts at home.

Caleb's peers gained too. They saw that, with a few accommodations, people with health conditions can be just as capable as others. Educators may profit also, by learning more creative teaching techniques. Mrs. Sandoval, for instance, used more demonstrations and hands-on experiences, which helped her entire class.

Finally, inclusion benefits society, by encouraging all its members to develop and use their abilities. An educated, socialized individual contributes more and makes fewer demands on society's resources.

Not everyone supports inclusion as the best option, particularly in certain cases. Some teachers aren't trained to work with special needs children, especially in a regular classroom. Children with serious conditions need a more specialized environment. Parents should consult their child's doctor and educators to learn whether the child would benefit.

Many children with disabilities go to school in regular classrooms.
◆ **What efforts should be made to ensure that the arrangement works well for everyone?**

MAINTAINING A POSITIVE SPIRIT

Conveying a spirit of optimism and reassurance is perhaps the most important thing parents do for a special needs child, siblings, and themselves. They don't offer children false hope or hold unrealistic expectations for improvement. Rather, they use a cheerful approach to make the best of the situation. As one parent explained, "I won't let this difficulty be a cloud that darkens our family's day. There's plenty of sun out there if you are patient and make the effort to look up."

Parenting Gifted Children

Six-year-old Emma was fascinated by numbers. Playing with blocks, she taught herself addition and subtraction. Her classmate Jay was a natural storyteller. He developed complex plots for his toy figures that sometimes took days to play out.

Both Emma and Jay were gifted, showing exceptional talent in one or more areas. Parenting such children is a mirror image of parenting those with an impairment. The concerns are the same but are approached from opposite perspectives.

UNDERSTANDING GIFTEDNESS

How do you identify a gifted child? The term is a vague one. Every child has special skills and strengths. Tests can measure some abilities, such as Emma's math skills, but how could you test Jay's imagination?

Children considered gifted tend to show other, general traits. They develop skills earlier and grasp concepts more easily than their peers. They have excellent memories, longer attention spans, and great concentration. They often prefer the company of older children and show an advanced sense of humour.

A gifted child who feels "different" as a child may feel the same way as an adult. Many parents encourage children to explore interests without pushing them into adulthood.
◆ **How will the nature of the child affect a parent's approach?**

Some gifted children take part in special programs within a regular classroom. Others are placed together in special classrooms or schools.
◆ **What pros and cons go with each approach?**

Finally, remember that gifted children benefit from the same childhood experiences that others enjoy. They need time to ride bicycles, read adventure stories, and play with friends. Some children are so attuned to adult concerns that they feel guilty about having fun. Parents should encourage balanced development.

SUPPORTING GIFTED CHILDREN

Like all children, those who are gifted thrive in a loving, disciplined, stimulating environment. They benefit from a parent's attention and conversation, and from new experiences. A parent can also provide enriching activities, where a child can explore a range of interests. Parents might arrange to have older children spend time with an adult who shares their talent and can help cultivate it.

As with other special conditions, parents should remember that the child's talent is only one part of personality. A child who is gifted in one area may be no more advanced than peers in other ways. Since Emma was at the same emotional and social level of other six-year-olds, her parents had to remind her that anger wouldn't help her solve a problem.

Likewise, parents must avoid pushing a child to develop a skill. Many gifted children are already self-motivated. Excessive pressure from parents can cause stress and resentment. The child may abandon the talent to escape the anxiety.

Gifted children, especially very sensitive ones, may need added emotional support as well. They may have trouble fitting in with peers, yet they don't fully belong with an older group. This can lead to loneliness. Parents might find a club or activity that lets a child share interests and make friends. They can also teach children how to relate to others who are different from themselves and how to appreciate time spent alone.

Older gifted children often show concern for society's problems. With a parent's guidance, they can put their skills to good use. A budding author can write letters to elected officials voicing concern about endangered species or homelessness. A child who is talented with computers might create greeting cards for classmates to sign and send to nursing home residents.

RECYCLE

PAPER

• White Bond
• White Stationery
• White Xerox Paper
• White Fax Paper
• White Envelopes
(remove plastic windows if present)
• Staples are O.K.

Do NOT Include:
• Cardboard
• Newspaper
• Glossy Paper
• Carbon Paper
• Index Cards
Thank You For Your Cooperation

For Information
Call EXT. 5307+

Gifted children are often willing and eager to take on special projects. Simply giving them more of the same work to do isn't necessarily the answer.

EDUCATING GIFTED CHILDREN

Public schools must accommodate gifted children, like those with health conditions, according to provincial education policy. These arrangements may take several forms, including:

♥ *Accelerated programs.* A child moves through grades at an accelerated (faster) rate, or skips grades entirely. This promotes intellectual growth but can cause social and emotional problems by separating a child from peers.

♥ *Enrichment programs.* Students take regular course work but expand their learning through additional assignments. They may work on selected projects, guided by a specially trained education consultant. Some schools offer advanced courses in various subjects. A college may sponsor advanced summer classes, which are held on campus and use the school's facilities.

♥ *Extracurricular activities and clubs.* Groups such as a school band, chess club, or literary magazine let gifted children develop their talents and socialize with other students.

♥ *Tutoring.* Older gifted students often enjoy using their skills to help others.

RESOURCES FOR PARENTS

Many outside sources can aid a parent's efforts at encouraging their gifted child. Educators can suggest at-home activities. Museums and nature parks often sponsor events for children, such as specialized art classes. Some communities have a children's symphony or theater company.

Some organizations exist to provide enriching experiences for children. For example, Aboriginal theatre groups introduce them to the culture and traditions of the Aboriginal Peoples of Canada. These events often include histories, storytelling, pow-wows, and dances.

Special Parenting

Does it take a special parent to raise a child with special needs? The answer may be both yes and no. Certainly these parents need great reserves of love and patience. They need the support of family, friends, educators, and the community. A strong, committed relationship and financial resources are valuable also.

Does that list sound familiar? Those are the qualities every parent needs, as you have discussed and examined throughout this text. One parent speaks for many others when she says, "Parenting a special needs child is just parenting, only more so. It really teaches you what being a parent is all about."

You can accelerate gifted children's education by moving them ahead faster with a subject, or you can enrich education by providing new experiences. ◆ **Which might music lessons be?**

Review

Looking Back

♥ A special health need may affect physical, intellectual, emotional, or social growth.

♥ When a child is diagnosed with a special need, parents should act quickly to learn the best way to manage it.

♥ Support for families comes from medical experts, national groups, community resources, family, and friends.

♥ Parents can modify the home environment to help a child with a health condition succeed.

♥ Parents must avoid neglecting or overburdening the sibling of a child with a special need.

♥ Inclusion and technology can help parents educate and improve life for a child with a health condition.

♥ Parents should look for enriching activities, at home and at school, for children who are gifted.

♥ Whatever their condition, special needs children need the same love, support, and guidance as other children.

Knowledge and Understanding

1. Why should a parent be concerned about treating an allergy?
2. How might you support a child who is hearing impaired?
3. What signs might indicate a child has a learning disability?
4. What positive steps can a parent take upon learning that a child has a health condition?
5. Suggest ways that you could encourage growth and independence in a child with a health condition.
6. How could you help a child who has a sibling with a special need?
7. What benefits are linked to inclusion?
8. What technological products can improve life for a child with a health condition?
9. How might you support a gifted child's talents?
10. What educational opportunities can benefit a gifted child?

Thinking and Inquiry

11. Might a child who earns poor grades in school be gifted? Explain your answer.

12. Some children acquire a health condition later in childhood, from accident or illness. Do you think it's easier or more difficult for parents to cope with this situation? What advantages or added challenges do they and their children face?

13. The parents of a three-year-old with Down syndrome excuse the child's poor behaviour and give in to his tantrums because "he can't help himself." What might be the consequences of their handling of the situation?

Communication

14. You and your spouse have a four-year-old daughter with cystic fibrosis. Except for a few evenings out, the two of you have cared for her almost single-handedly since she was diagnosed two years earlier. Now you both feel you need some time away together. You feel guilty about leaving her, however, even if you could find a qualified, affordable caregiver. How do you resolve this situation?

15. Research a "special needs condition" involving children. Such a condition could be Down syndrome, spina bifida, muscular dystrophy, cystic fibrosis, or a special needs condition of your choice. Create a poster describing the special needs situation and outline what parents might expect of their special needs child.

16. Using the library, book stores, or other sources, suggest five "how-to" books that you feel would be appropriate for parents with special needs children. Write up an annotated "bestseller list" of your five books. State why you believe they would be helpful to parents.

Application

17. Use the Internet to find more information about the health conditions that children and their families face. Report your findings to the class.

18. People are sometimes tactless when encountering a child with a health condition. With a partner, list five careless remarks parents may hear, such as "What's wrong with that child?" and "Isn't he talking yet?" For each remark, develop a polite and helpful response.

19. Parenting a child with a special need can be expensive. In small groups, discuss the financial aspect of special needs. What added costs might parents face? What resources can help them meet expenses? What is the cost to society if a special need is not properly managed?

Handling Common Parenting Problems

CHAPTER EXPECTATIONS

While reading this chapter, you will:

▶ Describe the legal and social responsibilities of parents and guardians.

▶ Demonstrate an understanding of various social concerns that parents face as their children approach school age.

▶ Demonstrate an understanding of the challenges faced by parents of young children in today's rapidly changing society.

KEY TERMS

aggression	enuresis
assertive	meek

Andrea tossed her coat and purse into her locker, flustered. "This is the second time this week I've been late," she told Al, her co-worker. "I just can't seem to get Mandy going in the morning."

"Maybe she's tired," Al said. "When is her bedtime?"

Andrea sighed. "Nine o'clock, supposedly."

Al smiled understandingly. "Can I make a few suggestions?"

That night at 8:30, Andrea hoisted her four-year-old daughter onto her hip. "We're starting something new tonight," she announced, heading for the bedroom. "It's called cuddle time. We're going to snuggle up with Winny Bear and Little Rabbit and read them a story. Then you're going to bed. Now, would they rather hear about Peanuts the pony or the little lost kitten?"

When she woke Mandy the next morning, Andrea placed a timer, set for ten minutes, on her dresser. "This timer wants to race." she said. "If you can wash up and get dressed before the bell rings, we'll have time for waffles."

"Waffles?" Mandy bounded out of bed. They were her favourite.

Andrea smiled as Mandy dashed to the bathroom. She had forgotten how much fun parenting could be.

◆

What do you think? Can you think of other ideas Andrea might use to motivate Mandy in the mornings?

It's not unusual to find children with very different personalities in the same family. ◆ **What challenges do you think the parents encounter?**

A Daily Challenge

The scenes are familiar to parents and caregivers everywhere. A parent looks up to see her pajama-clad four-year-old peering out from the bedroom door for the fifth time after being put to bed. A parent stares in astonishment when his three-year-old utters a phrase that most adults don't even say. A parent walks into the room where his preschooler and a friend are clobbering each other with a set of toy golf clubs. "Now what do I do?" each parent wonders.

The challenges of parenting are ongoing. Just when you pat yourself on the back for having solved one dilemma, a new one may surface.

PREPARING FOR CHALLENGES

As children grow, challenges change. Handling a stubborn three-year-old is far different from handling a head-strong adolescent. The quantity and variety of challenges typically decrease as children grow older. On the other hand, even one serious problem, such as experimenting with drugs, can overshadow all the challenges a parent may have previously faced.

Learning to solve challenges appropriately when children are young helps in several ways. Parents learn what works for them and their children. With increased skills and resources, parents may face fewer problems later on. If problems are solved when they happen, they are less likely to contribute to new ones.

So what does a parent do when challenges arise? Parents often talk to other parents, reaching out for ideas that will help them.

PARENTING WITH RESPECT

Parenting with respect means you recognize the dignity and value of each child. You treat children with the same consideration you give others. Even when you discipline children, you do nothing to humiliate them or make them feel unloved. To parent with respect, Max:

► Disciplined his five-year-old daughter for current misbehaviour, not for what she did last week.

► Praised his seven-year-old son's energy and enthusiasm in the school play, not mentioning that the child forgot his lines.

► Told his children the truth when the family's dog died, in a way they could understand.

► Chose not to say that his daughter had "the brains in the family," thinking of both children's feelings.

► Let his son cry when he was angry.

◆ ◆ Your Thoughts ◆ ◆

❶ How do children learn to respect their parents?

❷ How can people show respect for others even while disagreeing with them?

❸ How can a parent show disapproval in a respectful way?

❹ Amber was rude to a store clerk while shopping with her son. When her son spoke to her in the same tone, Amber disciplined him. What is your analysis of the situation?

They listen to relatives and read books and magazines. They watch authorities on television and scan the Internet. They follow positive principles learned about guiding and nurturing children. These approaches are all better than ignoring a problem or doing the wrong things out of frustration and anger.

Thinking ahead about common problems that parents face is an excellent idea. That way you can be prepared. You have some ideas ready to use at the moment you need them.

Problems Getting Along with Others

When children don't do well socially, both children and parents suffer. A child knows very quickly when he or she isn't accepted by others. Behaviour that causes others to withdraw or be unfriendly hurts the child. The child may not understand what is going wrong. Parents want to be able to take their children out in public without being embarrassed or hurt by their behaviour.

They want children to be liked by others. When parents make an effort to help children solve social problems, fewer problems are likely to result.

SUSPICION OF STRANGERS

Two-year-old Avery clung to his father and hid behind him when an unfamiliar adult drew near, even a relative. "It's kind of embarrassing," his father Tim admitted, "but it must be scary. He's so little and everyone else is so big."

Tim's assessment was right. "Stranger suspicion" is a natural reaction as a toddler becomes aware of the outside world. Parents shouldn't worry too much, nor force children to be friendly. Rather, they should show support while helping the child adjust. For example, Tim held Avery and explained to people, "Avery likes to get to know people before getting close." At the same time, he took Avery to the park and to shopping malls, non-threatening settings where they met adults. Tim's patience was rewarded as Avery grew into a typically curious and sociable preschooler.

Should Tim have preferred that Avery be outgoing and friendly to everyone? Trusting strangers can be dangerous, but "stranger danger" should be a parent's concern, not a toddler's. At that age, telling a child, "You must ask me before talking to anyone" helps ensure safe behaviour. School-age children can handle a more specific, but carefully worded, warning to avoid strangers. Keeping a close eye on children at *all* times is basic to keeping them safe.

SHYNESS

Like stranger suspicion, periods of shyness are an expected but difficult part of emotional and social growth. Parents should encourage, not force, children to overcome shy feelings.

Shy or not, children are more confident about social situations when they feel prepared. Explaining or rehearsing upcoming events helps. By arriving early, the child can get comfortable in the surroundings and meet later arrivals one by one.

Outgoing parents are sometimes bothered by a child's shyness, but showing acceptance is very important. ◆ **Why do you think a parent shouldn't say "Oh, she's just shy"?**

Parents can also teach children techniques for starting conversations. One mother had her son carry pictures of his pets in his knapsack. Pets were a topic he and other children could share. She suggested helpful questions and comments, such as, "I like your shoes" and "Do you want to play on the swings?"

Sometimes a parent can encourage friendships that bring out a child's social side. Some children blossom with the admiration of a younger friend. Others feel more comfortable with an older one to take the lead.

Shyness that persists into preschool or grade school can seriously hamper a child's happiness and success. If a child has few friends or withdraws at social events, a teacher or school counsellor might be consulted.

However they handle shyness, parents should always show acceptance and support. Shy behaviour is not misbehaviour. In fact, most experts believe it is partly genetic. Children who feel positive about themselves and others gain confidence for satisfying social interaction. As adults, they will feel comfortable whether choosing to have many close relationships or a few.

MEEKNESS

Like shy children, **meek** children are passive and quiet. Carin was such a child. She let other children take toys that she was playing with and interrupt her when she spoke. Her father, Stephen, taught Carin to be **assertive**, to express herself firmly and positively. At first, he spoke up for her: "Martin, Carin was looking at that book. Please give it back to her. Thank you." Carin saw this was an effective way to stand up for her rights.

Spotlight On
Moving

Moving is a common experience for many children. That doesn't make it easy, however. Changing homes can be exciting but difficult, especially when children are moved to completely new surroundings. Young children understand little about what is happening. School-age children see that they are leaving their home, friends, and school—the most important things in their lives.

A parent's optimism and enthusiasm can help make moving a lesson in dealing with change. To ease the transition, parents can:

✔ Talk honestly about their own and the child's concerns.

✔ Show the child pictures of the new home, neighbourhood, and neighbours.

✔ Help the child choose small items to keep from the old home.

✔ Write down names, addresses, and phone numbers of the child's friends.

✔ Help the child pack a small suitcase of clothes and favourite belongings.

✔ Pack the child's room last and unpack it first at the new home.

✔ Make an adventure of exploring the new neighbourhood.

✔ Resume a familiar routine as soon as possible.

Stephen knew that not every child would respond to this calm approach. He instructed, "If someone really angers you or hurts you, tell your teacher. Don't hit or kick or bite. Some people haven't learned to be as polite as you are."

INAPPROPRIATE LANGUAGE

Young children are just learning to use language. Like a new driver in an expensive sports car, they are not entirely in control of a powerful vehicle. Verbal "accidents" occur.

Responding to unacceptable language means taking a middle course. You want to show your disapproval, but very strong reaction may feed the habit.

Foul Language

Most young children try out foul language. Sometimes they are just repeating a new word, not realizing its impact. The parent ignores the child, and the child forgets.

Other times a child obviously wants a reaction. A parent might say firmly, "We don't use that word. Don't say it again, please." If the child continues, the parent might reply, "If you want to use that word, go to your room. Then you can say it all you like, and no one else will hear you." With no audience, the word loses its appeal. Meanwhile, the child can be given acceptable substitute words.

Name Calling

Young friends in a name-calling contest delight in thinking up crude or silly names. They soon learn that names, especially racial and ethnic slurs, can be used to isolate and hurt others.

Parents must express disapproval for name calling in any form, from a friend talking about a neighbour, to political rivals in a debate. They should also watch their own speech. Do they call a child "slow-poke"? Do they discuss only the negative qualities associated with certain professions? By talking about and treating others with respect, parents demonstrate the unfairness of name calling.

Internet Connects

http://www.mcgrawhill.ca/links/parenting
To learn more about social inclusion and cultural diversity regarding children's behaviour, go to the Web site above for *Parenting Rewards & Responsibilities, First Canadian Edition*, to see where to go next.

"I don't care if they say it on TV. We don't talk like that in this family." ◆ **Why is it necessary for family members to watch their language too?**

AGGRESSIVENESS

Few behaviour problems alarm parents as does **aggression**, physically violent or threatening behaviour, and with good reason. If ignored or mishandled, violence can become a way of life.

Young children may resort to aggressive behaviour, such as hitting, biting, and hair pulling. Children have only basic language and social skills. When they are angry, frustrated, hungry, or tired, aggression is a quick and definite way to make a point.

Raising Children With Character

Not Like the Rest

Jana watched Seth trek home from the bus stop, lurching with the weight of an armload of books. She turned and set out for her own house. Everyone at school is right, she thought. He does look weird. Still, Jana felt uneasy recalling how her best friend Jackson had imitated his odd accent at lunch. They'd all laughed—Jana included.

"No one likes Seth," she told her father that night as they washed dishes.

"Why do you think they feel that way?" Mr. Norquist asked.

"Well…," Jana struggled for an answer, "he's kind of different."

Her father chuckled. "Aren't we all? I mean, can you imagine a world full of people like me?" He paused. "Now, maybe that wouldn't be so bad."

Jana raised a quick smile, then turned earnest. "Why do they do that to Seth, Dad?"

Mr. Norquist soaped a plate thoughtfully. "I wonder about that myself, Jana. Sometimes people are afraid of what they don't know or understand. It's easier to push someone away than to try to find the good in him. People forget one thing that everyone has in common: everyone hurts at being rejected."

Jana stared silently at her fistful of silverware. She started to smile, imagining everyone at school afraid of Seth—herself included.

Mr. Norquist spoke. "I saw Seth's dad clearing out for a garden today. I think I'll see if he needs help. Do you want to come, Jana, or are you going to Jackson's tonight?"

"Well…no, I'll come," Jana decided, "and I'll take some fossils from my collection. I want to show them to Seth."

◆◆◆◆◆ **Thinking It Over** ◆◆◆◆◆

1. Why do you think Jana discusses Seth's situation with her father?
2. How does Mr. Norquist make an impression on Jana's feelings and actions toward Seth?
3. How would you explain to a child why people mistreat each other?

They may not realize that a punch or kick hurts others just as it hurts them. Even when they know this, they often cannot control their actions.

Sometimes a child's motives are less serious. Teething toddlers may bite to relieve the discomfort. When Emily was three, she hit her brother with her toy shovel for no real reason.

Preventing Aggression

When parents see aggression as a natural response for a young child, they can take the following steps to prevent it:

♥ *Identify and act at signs of strain.* Parents can avoid an outburst by learning how their child signals stress, then removing the source. One father noted, "When Reese starts to whine, I know he's getting tired. We cut short what we're doing so he can rest."

♥ *Balance control with freedom*. For managing aggression, too much restriction is as harmful as too little. Giving a child a limited say in decisions helps prevent a build-up of frustration.

♥ *Provide a positive outlet for negative feelings.* Children need to know that negative feelings are acceptable, but expressing them violently is not. Instead, they can punch a pillow or kick a ball. Children age two and older can be given words to make their feelings known.

♥ *Set a good example.* Children learn more from experience than words. Parents who use violence, yet speak against it, may cause the child to doubt them in other matters also.

Responding to Aggression

The first rule when a child acts aggressively is: don't return the aggression. This response increases anger and frustration. Some parents inflict pain to show how the victim feels, but young children don't make the connection.

Which sister started the fight? Some parents defend the youngest child without getting the facts. ◆ **How does it feel to be blamed for something you didn't do?**

Anna dealt with this problem more effectively. Her three-year-old son Cory grabbed a toy truck from his playmate Rick. When Rick tried to take it back, Cory bit him until he let go. Rick began to wail. Anna acted quickly in these ways:

♥ **She comforted Rick and made sure he was all right.**

♥ **She showed Cory the consequences of his actions.** "You hurt Rick by biting him. If you can't play nicely, Rick will have to go home. I won't let you hurt him again."

♥ **She offered an acceptable alternative.** "If someone has something that you want, ask if you can have it. Don't just take it."

♥ **She shifted the focus away from the source of the problem.** "You and Rick have been playing trucks for a while. Which crayon colours would you like to use to draw some new pictures for the refrigerator?"

Notice that Anna didn't lecture or yell at Cory, but didn't defend him either. Had Cory hurt Rick again, she would have acted on her warning and taken Rick home.

Usually, aggressive behaviour decreases as parents teach children verbal and social skills and help them develop self-control. A child who remains aggressive into preschool and grade school may have deep-seated anger. Parents may ask help from a teacher, school counsellor, pediatrician, or other child behaviour experts.

LYING

Duane was upset. "My son Ryan ate a big hole in the pie I made for a bake sale, then told me the dog did it. When did my three-year-old learn to lie?"

Ryan had not learned to lie. A child his age is too intellectually immature and inexperienced to be deliberately dishonest. Ryan may not have understood that the pie was to be saved. He might have forgotten that he ate it. Perhaps he saw a dog eat a cake on a television show, and he was confused. His story certainly was entertaining, and unlike the actual events, it would save him from punishment.

Realizing these facts, Duane told his son, "That pie must have looked very good, but next time, remember to ask when you want something to eat. Now you can help me bake another pie." To be safe, Duane kept that pie out of sight.

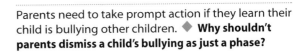

Parents need to take prompt action if they learn their child is bullying other children. ◆ **Why shouldn't parents dismiss a child's bullying as just a phase?**

Removing temptation is one way to instill a habit of truthfulness. Other ways include:

♥ **Model honesty.** Without "blowing their own horn," parents should let children see honesty in action. Admitting mistakes is a common, honest act.

♥ **Help children tell the whole story.** A child may forget details or fail to realize their importance. If a child has a stomach ache, asking, "When did it start?" or "What did you eat?" teaches the child to recognize relevant facts.

♥ **Lead children to truthful responses.** Giving children the facts gives them the chance to tell the truth. A parent might say, "This tablecloth has marker stains. I know you were drawing at the table this afternoon." Asking, "Did you get this tablecloth dirty?" leaves an opening for a lie.

♥ **Respond appropriately to misbehaviour.** A child may lie to cover up mistakes from fear of punishment. Understanding parents who administer reasonable, constructive discipline make it easier to be honest.

Children's facial expressions and body language often signal to the parent that they're lying. ◆ **What do people who are lying often do with their eyes?**

♥ **Praise truthfulness, especially when the news is bad.** Telling children, "I'm proud of you for telling the truth" encourages them to trust parents in difficult situations, even when they know their honesty will bring unpleasant results.

STEALING

The idea of property rights confuses young children. Why can they collect leaves on the sidewalk, but not flowers in someone's garden? Why can they eat an apple at home, but not in the store? They need help to see the difference. For a toddler, just saying "You may not touch things in the store" is enough. Letting preschoolers buy small items with their allowance teaches them that they must exchange money for goods.

Reinforcing the idea of ownership at home is helpful, especially if a child has siblings. A parent can say "That toy is your brother's. Ask him if you can play with it" or "These are Daddy's books. Let's find your books in your toy box."

Occasionally a young child takes something from a store or a friend's house. Parents shouldn't accuse the child of stealing but should make sure he or she knows that taking things without asking is wrong. They should have the child return the item and explain, "I took this, and I shouldn't have."

CHEATING

To a toddler, cheating doesn't exist. All ways of reaching a goal are equal. Preschoolers may understand that cheating means breaking a rule, but since they obey rules only to please parents and avoid punishment, cheating may not bother them. Still, this desire to please is a foundation for honest behaviour. Parents can set rules that encourage children to treat others fairly.

By age seven, children are more aware of right and wrong. They may feel more pressure to cheat. Winning games and getting good grades are important now.

Parents must be careful to send the right message about achievement. While encouraging a child to do well, they must stress that it's more important to do what's right. One father, learning why his daughter failed a math test, said, "I'm sorry you copied your friend's answers, but not because you got a zero. I'm sorry because you cheated. Copying answers is unfair. Next time, ask your teacher or me for help if you don't understand something. I'm proud of you when you try your best, even if you get some answers wrong."

Problems with Routines

Earlier you read about Mandy, whose irregular bedtime left her unco-operative in the morning. As a result, her mother Andrea was late for work. How do you think this situation affected the rest of Andrea's day? Of Mandy's?

The story illustrates the value of a smooth routine. Problems in one area can upset a family's schedule and emotions all day.

Games are more fun when parents don't emphasize the importance of winning. Family members will want to play games together when everyone has learned to play fairly. ◆ **How does learning fairness transfer to other situations, such as school and friendships?**

When establishing a routine, parents can expect some resistance. New problems may arise if the routine is not revised to keep up with the child.

FINICKY EATING

Jess served Brett's meals on a divided tray saved from a frozen dinner. This satisfied the three-year-old's latest mealtime quirk: different foods must not touch. Jess's solution was a creative response to a common childhood problem. His matter-of-fact approach kept Brett's phase in perspective.

Young children may have other eating habits that make feeding them nutritiously a challenge. Toddlers tend to lose interest in a meal before they've eaten what parents think they should. Preschoolers go on food jags, eating one particular food every day. Some parents go to great lengths to keep children eating.

Spotlight On
Travelling with Children

Travelling with children can be hectic. Planning ahead for their needs makes a trip go more smoothly. Here are some ways to prepare for successful travel with children:

✔ *Make getting there part of the fun.* To combat boredom on long trips, pack crayons and pads of paper, a deck of children's cards, and other small toys. Simple games, such as listing the different cars on the highway, help pass time. Hungry children are not happy travellers. Healthy, easy-to-eat snacks should be on hand. Allowing time for extra rest stops helps keep everyone relaxed. Sharing facts from a tourist's guide adds to a child's interest and appreciation of the world. An older child can act as "navigator" if parents highlight their route on a map.

✔ *Pack an emergency kit.* Besides a first aid kit, parents should carry items for minor mishaps, such as extra clothes and a plastic bag for toilet-training accidents.

✔ *Help children feel at home.* Travel can be disrupting for children. Bringing a few special decorations from their room can help them feel settled. Keeping the same mealtime and bedtime smooths the transition too. Parents should make sure a crib is available, if needed. They might bring small items for childproofing, such as electric outlet covers.

✔ *Plan activities with the child in mind.* Constant going and doing tries a child's endurance—and disposition. An ideal schedule is flexible and includes activities that parent and child both enjoy, when the child can enjoy them. Visiting relatives all day might bore a four-year-old. A trip to the park, after lunch and before an afternoon nap, can be a refreshing family outing.

Children who help prepare meals may be more interested in eating them. ◆ **What other benefits come from involving children in preparing meals?**

There is a happy medium. Parents can get children to eat without sacrificing nutrition or convenience. Helpful measures include:

♥ *Set a positive mood.* Mealtime should be quiet, enjoyable, and free of distractions. The television should be turned off and toys and books put away. Conversation should be pleasant and polite.

♥ *Be flexible about mealtimes.* Routines are meant to teach children to act as part of a group. Sometimes, however, rules can be stretched to satisfy a child's changing appetite. A child who is hungry a half-hour before dinner might have a roll or salad, then eat the rest of the meal with the family.

♥ *Mix up menus.* The novelty of eating waffles at 6:00 p.m. or spaghetti for breakfast appeals to children—and sometimes to adults. A healthy food is equally nutritious whenever it is served.

♥ *When possible, let the child help prepare meals.* Children usually take more interest in dishes they helped create.

♥ *Disguise unpopular foods.* A parent may need to sneak nutritious foods into a child's diet. A five-year-old who decides that vegetables are "icky" may like spice muffins made with shredded carrot and zucchini, and spaghetti sauce made of puréed tomatoes.

♥ *Serve liquids later in the meal.* Children eat better when they're hungry. Drinking fluids right before or early in a meal dulls the appetite.

RESISTANCE TO BEDTIME

Young children are so active, you might think they would be eager for bedtime. Instead, some find the energy for one more story, then one more question, then one more kiss good-night.

Why do children delay bedtime? Some like the attention. For a four-year-old, staying up late is proof of independence. A child overstimulated by activity or excitement may have trouble quieting down. Stress can keep a child awake.

Whatever the cause, resistance at bedtime requires patience and firmness. For three-year-old Adrian, for example, Kevin set a relaxing routine of a bath, one story, and "dream food," a pleasant memory or image to think about while falling asleep. Then Kevin declared, "Now you're set, so I want you to go to sleep" and closed the bedroom door.

If Adrian got out of bed, Kevin calmly led him back. If Adrian whimpered, Kevin said, "I know you want me to stay, but you need to sleep. You can keep crying, but I'm not coming back. I'll see you in the morning." Adrian learned that he gets attention during their bedtime rituals and not after.

At times, Kevin was tempted to give in to Adrian's stalling. Other times he wanted to be harsh. Like most bedtime problems, this one came when Kevin felt tired himself and least able to deal with it. He had to guard against being too severe or too lenient just to settle the problem quickly.

Internet Connects

http://www.mcgrawhill.ca/links/parenting
To learn more about family issues, parenting tips, and child development, go to the Web site above for *Parenting Rewards & Responsibilities, First Canadian Edition,* to see where to go next.

FEAR OF THE DARK

For some children, a darkened bedroom is full of frightening possibilities. This fear is normal. Imagination develops more quickly than reason, especially when fed by real-life or television violence or suspenseful stories. Parents cannot force a child to be unafraid, and shouldn't try. Rather, they should accept the fear as real and support the child in mastering it.

For some children, having a light in the bedroom helps them manage fear of the dark. Others take comfort in the sound of family members moving about. Sleeping with a stuffed toy or family pet can also be reassuring.

Other times, parents may need some imagination of their own. One parent did a "monster sweep" to clear scary creatures from out of the closet and under the bed. Another had a large, stuffed dog standing guard outside his child's door. A third parent gave her child a cardboard tube from a roll of paper towels, decorated with stickers, ribbons, and small bells. The device was guaranteed to scare off any cowardly creature that lurked in the dark.

In some families bedtime becomes a serious power struggle between parent and child. If a parent wavers, the child may try to make the rules. ◆ **How does a loving bedtime ritual, along with a firm, consistent approach, help a parent manage bedtimes?**

Parents can also encourage a child to associate the dark with positive images. In the darkness created by closing their eyes, children can recall pleasant times and imagine great adventures. Snuggling in an unlit room adds magic to telling stories or watching a snowfall. A beautiful starry sky is seen only after dark.

Most important is to show respect for a child's feelings, even unreasonable ones. Children who know that it's okay to be afraid express fears more readily, allowing parents to help them cope.

Nightmares

When children wake from a nightmare, the frightening images are still real. Children need comforting. Parents must assure them that the events did not happen and show them that no terrible creature lurks in their room. Objects that look menacing in the dark, such as clothes draped over a chair, should be rearranged. Talking about the dream, especially in the security of morning, makes it less mysterious and less frightening.

Nightmares are a part of life, but some can be avoided. A soothing bedtime routine promotes calm sleep. Resolving conflict and addressing a child's real-life concerns relieves the stress that can cause bad dreams.

BED-WETTING

Most preschoolers are toilet-trained. Occasional **enuresis** (en-yoo-REE-sis), the inability to control the bladder, is a common problem at night. Recognizing and responding to a full bladder is harder for a sleeping child.

Parents can take precautions to help children stay dry at night. Fluids should be limited in the evening. Making sure the child urinates shortly before bedtime reduces the need to do so afterward. Adequate lighting encourages a child to get up at night to use the bathroom. A very sound sleeper may need to be awakened and taken to the washroom.

A child who feels safe during the day is more likely to have fewer nightmares. Avoid scary games before bed. This is not the time to play "chase" or read a story about monsters. If a child does wake during the night, offer reassurances but don't overreact.

About 90 percent of all children outgrow bed-wetting by age six. No amount of teasing, bribery, or punishment can hurry the process. In fact, such tactics can seriously damage a child's sense of self-worth. Enuresis that continues beyond this age may need medical treatment.

Enuresis can embarrass and isolate a child. A parent's understanding and patience are especially needed. A parent's words and actions must say, "I know this is hard, but we'll get through it together. It doesn't change my love for you. We won't let it make us miserable."

DAWDLING

Do you remember the fable about a race between a tortoise and a hare? The hare sprints off, while the tortoise plods steadily on. The hare lets the tortoise catch up, then bounds away again.

When activities include a young child, parents sometimes feel they are playing the hare to the child's tortoise. Like the tortoise, however, children may not be dawdling. They are just moving at their natural pace. Children need more time to finish tasks. With their short attention span, they are easily distracted. Children are present-oriented. Until about age five, their concept of time and the future is sketchy at best.

To help children move at an adult's pace, you must work within the child's limits. Successful techniques include:

♥ *Plan to take longer.* Knowing that children need more time, parents can plan accordingly. Waking ten minutes earlier gives a child that much longer to get ready in the morning. Parents should allow more time for outings with children.

♥ *Give notice.* Children need time to make the mental and physical shift between activities. Announcements are most effective when phrased in concrete terms. Saying "We can play this game once more, but then it's time for bed" tells a child more than "Bedtime is in ten minutes."

Picking out clothes the night before saves valuable time in the morning. ◆ **What would you do if the shirt and pants your preschooler chose didn't match?**

♥ *Make the transition inviting.* The transition itself can be an enjoyable event. Promising "We'll pick flowers in the field and take them home to Grandpa" can hurry a child on a walk.

♥ *Make the goal appealing.* Parents can usually find something attractive in the next event. To persuade a child to leave child care, they might say, "If we hurry home, we can play with the doggie before dinner."

♥ *Use good management.* Teaching basic management skills, such as organizing space and doing tasks in advance, saves time and stress. Children learn efficiency by storing toys in one place. Making lunch the night before leaves more time for getting dressed the next morning.

Parents who can't get a child on their timetable might rethink their priorities. No parent should be too busy to listen to a child describe a dream or to join a child kicking through fallen autumn leaves.

The Relaxed Parent

The challenges you have just read about are only a few that parents may encounter. Because there are no truly simple answers to every situation, one piece of good advice for parents remains. Relax. An uptight parent might not think clearly or react appropriately. By contrast, a parent who responds with patience, self-control, humour, and flexibility will get through most challenges with sanity preserved.

Giving Children Reasons

Q "I'd like my child to understand why I expect certain things, but sometimes I just don't feel like getting into it. Do you have to give children reasons every time they ask?" *Carmen*

A Giving your child reasons for your decisions can be helpful. Explanation is part of parent-child communication and a sign of respect. Knowing a reason may teach children a lesson or give valuable information. Identifying reasons can also help parents think about their motives and their understanding of a situation.

Parents are not obliged to explain everything, however. A parent is justified in saying "I'll tell you when we have more time" or "I'm your mother and I expect you to do this." Likewise, a child who demands "Why?" in hopes of wearing you down may be told, "I think it's best for you. This discussion is ended." Parents should not apologize or ask permission for their decision, even an unpopular one. Children appreciate the confidence of parents who act on what they believe is right.

Looking Back

♥ Parents can show children appropriate ways to overcome a natural shyness toward strangers.

♥ Parents discourage offensive language in children by treating and speaking respectfully of others.

♥ Children typically respond to frustration with aggression. As they mature, parents teach them more acceptable, non-violent behaviour.

♥ Parents encourage honest behaviour by modelling honesty and by responding positively to a child's mistakes.

♥ Parents must be understanding but consistent when helping children follow routines.

♥ Travelling with children is more successful when a parent considers the child's interests and physical and emotional limits.

♥ Moving is easier when children feel involved and parents show optimism.

Knowledge and Understanding

1. In general, what can parents do when they face challenges with children?
2. How can parents help a child overcome shyness around other children?
3. How might a parent respond when a child uses inappropriate language?
4. What are positive and negative ways that parents respond to a child's aggression?
5. How can you encourage honest behaviour in a child?
6. Why do some children want to put off bedtime?
7. How can parents help a child who wets the bed?
8. How can you help a child cope with your schedule?
9. How can a parent help a child enjoy travelling?
10. How might you help a child feel more at home after moving?

Review

Thinking and Inquiry

11. Trying to help her daughter Sara overcome her shyness, the mother and daughter planned a birthday party and invited five children. How do you think Sara will react at the party?

12. Would you let a child eat a blueberry bagel with peanut butter for lunch every day for two weeks? Why or why not?

13. Brian's parents recently began letting him stay up until after the evening news. Brian has had nightmares several times since then. His parents think he is stressed from lack of sleep. What do you think?

Communication

14. Describe one or more ways that you have seen parents use to deal with problems. Were these methods effective and positive? Why or why not? If you would have handled the situation differently, explain how.

15. Describe what you would say to a child who swore at you. Why would you say this?

16. Research and plan a day trip that a child would enjoy (for example, going to the Toronto Zoo, the Calgary Stampede, Anne of Green Gables' house, etc.). Write a flyer advertising the activity, the cost, the time it runs or is open, etc. Be sure to include information that would be valuable to parents. On the back of the flyer, state what a child might learn and/or enjoy about this activity.

17. Whenever you notice your three-year-old daughter and her playmate start pushing or grabbing a toy, you stop the play, explain that hitting isn't allowed, and direct them to another activity. Your spouse, however, prefers not to step in unless injury is likely, saying this approach helps them learn to settle their differences. How do you resolve this clash of parenting techniques?

Application

18. With a partner, write and perform a skit in which a parent gently hurries a child through a task or activity, such as cleaning up a room or getting dressed.

19. Locate quotations that apply to dealing with parenting problems, for example, "A stitch in time saves nine." Select one or two that make good rules to remember. Use the computer to make a poster for parents.

20. Imagine you and your young child are visiting relatives in another province for a few days. With a group, work out a schedule and plan that would make the trip enjoyable to you, your child, and other family members.

Finding Solutions to Family Problems

CHAPTER EXPECTATIONS

While reading this chapter, you will:

▶ Explain how parents of very young children can support them during the grief process.

▶ Describe the indicators of child abuse.

▶ Explain the strategies and support needed for a child to survive abuse, neglect, or family violence.

▶ Describe the skills and attitudes that can be developed to secure a safe and peaceful family, community, and social environment.

▶ Identify community programs and agencies that provide family support and identify some of the barriers parents face in accessing that support.

KEY TERMS

alcoholism
child abuse
child neglect
co-dependency
custody

grieving
resilient
Shaken Baby
   Syndrome

"Why, you're full of surprises," Mitch remarked as his seven-year-old stepbrother, Adam, settled quietly beside him on the sofa, book in hand. "Since when do you want *me* to read you a story? Doesn't Mom usually do that? What's the deal?"

"Mom told me...," Adam said, hesitating.

"About going to the hospital?" Mitch finished for him.

"Yeah," Adam responded, looking at Mitch's face for a sign of what he might be feeling.

Mitch sighed. "It'll be okay, Adam. I'm counting on that." A flash of concern slipped into Mitch's eyes as he gave his stepbrother a half-hearted smile. Here was the kid who could drive him crazy at times showing concern for him. It gave Mitch a feeling of warmth that he needed.

"Mitch, I can help Joe with your paper route while you're in the hospital. And I'll take your turn at feeding Shep. Do you think they'll let me come up and see you?"

"I hope so, Adam. I'd like that, you know. I really would. And thanks for your help. Now, what is this story you want to read? Is this the one about that monkey who gets into all kinds of silly situations? Now there's a fellow who can cheer me up—just like you do."

◆

What do you think? How is a difficult situation bringing Adam and Mitch closer?

In the midst of a family problem, imagination may lead a child to false conclusions. A parent's attention and reassurance are comforting.

Facing Changes in the Family

Imagine driving late at night through an unfamiliar part of town, realizing you are quite lost. You cruise up one street and down the next, fighting off a rising tide of panic.

At last you recognize one building, then another. Soon you have your bearings. You feel relieved—and safe.

To a child, experiencing a major change feels like being lost. Even more than adults, children draw security from familiar habits and places. When these things fall away, children tend to fear the worst. More than ever, they need a parent's strength and reassurance.

UNEMPLOYMENT

Losing a job affects a parent's confidence and self-respect, as well as the ability to care for the family. If the job also provided the family's health benefits, parents worry that one major illness could put them in financial trouble.

During this time, parents must reassure children with a calm and confident manner. Concerns about money and other anxieties can be shared with other adults. Not working for a long stretch of time can cause frustration and anger. Parents must learn to recognize these feelings and handle them appropriately. If the strain becomes too great, they should talk to a counsellor.

Most parents who lose their job do find another one. Until then, taking practical action can help the family cope.

Economizing

If they are not doing so already, parents should try to save money. They can:

♥ Put off large purchases. Repair items rather than buy new ones.

♥ Get value when shopping. Use coupons, sales, bulk buying, and thrift shops.

♥ Eat at home more and fix lunches to carry.

♥ Find inexpensive entertainment, such as board games, free videos or DVDs checked out from the library, and community parks.

♥ Conserve energy. Set the thermostat in the home at 20°C (68°F) in cooler weather and 26°C (78°F) when it's hot. Dry laundry on a clothesline when possible. Adults and older children can take short showers instead of baths.

♥ Learn money-saving skills. Simple clothing and home repairs can extend the life of older items for a fraction of the price of new ones.

Even when cutting costs, parents should try to remain upbeat. They can make saving money a game to children and show pride in resourcefulness. Allowing occasional small luxuries may reassure a child that the situation is not desperate.

Staying Positive

When not actively on the job hunt, unemployed parents set a positive example by using time well. Taking job-training courses can make them more employable. Volunteer work is a valuable service that can teach new skills and lead to contacts that result in job offers. Giving time and help to others also helps ward off self-pity and hopelessness, which benefits parent and child alike.

Children may be teased by their peers when a parent is unemployed. Parents can take this chance to break down some stereotypes and negative societal messages. A parent might explain, "A lot of people want to work, but can't find a job," or point out, "People are more than their jobs. Everyone has something to offer, even if you don't get paid for it."

If a family's income decreases for some reason, they may need to economize. With sewing ability, for example, a parent could make items rather than buy them. ◆ **How else could a family save money?**

Divorce is very difficult for children. Sleep problems are common. The child may fear that a parent will be gone upon waking. Patience, understanding, and extra love at bedtime can help the child.

SEPARATION AND DIVORCE

Separation and divorce are painful enough when only the couple is involved. The wrenching effects are multiplied many times over when children are present. Even when parents remain civil toward each other, marital break-up causes emotional upheaval. When income drops as a result, the toll is greater still.

Parents can't eliminate a child's anger and sorrow at separation and divorce. By acting with maturity, however, they can avoid adding to the distress.

Children's Reactions

When his parents divorced, five-year-old Jason displayed a range of difficult behaviours, including aggression, clinging, and crying easily. His 18-month-old sister acted confused for a few months, but otherwise seemed to cope well.

Both responses were typical for the ages of the children. Younger children tend to be more **resilient** than older ones. This means they typically recover more easily. Sensitive children have more trouble adjusting than do their easygoing peers.

Otherwise, most young children have a similar response to divorce. One of the first is confusion. Young children, you recall, cannot think abstractly. They can't imagine not having both parents at home. Instead, they deny the situation. Their level of understanding says: if I've never experienced it and can't understand it, it's not possible. They grow very upset if pressed to deal with the reality.

Guilt is another common reaction. Children are naturally egocentric, believing that the family centres around them. If parents are unhappy, children think they did something wrong. This idea is reinforced if child-rearing is one thing parents argue over, as is often the case.

By the same reasoning, children may believe they can save the marriage by being "extra good." They try to please their parents in all things, and are intensely disappointed when their efforts fail.

As children see what a break-up means for them, they fear abandonment. They worry: if Daddy left me, will Mommy leave too? Even worse is the fear: if Daddy stopped loving Mommy, will he stop loving me? Children with such fears demand more of a parent's attention. For a month after her father moved out, four-year-old Caitlin acted very insecure. She insisted on being held and was suspicious if her mother left the room for more than a few minutes. She woke in the middle of the night to make sure her mother was still there.

Along with negative reactions, children may also feel relief. Often they sense the tension and unhappiness in the home. They are frightened by the fighting. If either parent is abusive, divorce is an escape from the violence.

Helping Children Cope

Divorce is never easy on children, but parents can act to make the ordeal more bearable. They must separate their anger at each other from their love for their child. After deciding to seek a divorce, they have to move forward. Dwelling on guilt and doubt prevents them from showing the leadership children need. Avoiding hostility also lessens the strain on the child.

When Marshall and Anita filed for divorce, the well-being of their four-year-old son, Brent, was foremost in their mind. To help Brent cope, they:

♥ *Gave an explanation he understood.* They said clearly, "This is a problem between Dad and Mom. We fight too much and make each other unhappy. We've decided that we can't live together anymore." They stressed that Brent was not to blame for their problem, and he couldn't solve it.

♥ *Told the truth.* Even before separating, Anita and Marshall told Brent they would not get back together again.

♥ *Respected Brent's loyalties.* Neither parent used their son to pass messages or "spy" on the other. They didn't criticize the former spouse in his presence. They avoided situations that would force him to choose between them.

In a divorce situation, parents have to control their own emotions and think of the children. They should never "use" children to hurt or spy on each other. Counselling can help children deal with their feelings. Early counselling by the couple may even help them prevent divorce.

♥ **Set the same expectations for Brent in both parents' homes.** Consistent rules offered a measure of stability.

♥ **Treated each other with respect.** Throughout the process, both parents tried to remain polite and reasonable. They worked for a fair divorce settlement and honoured their agreement.

Marshall and Anita also agreed to a custody arrangement to benefit their son. **Custody** is the legal right and responsibility to make decisions affecting children and to care for them physically. They chose joint custody, sharing parental rights and responsibilities equally. Brent lived with his mother but spent weekends with his father.

Raising Children With

Character

The Gift

As usual, Terrence found his six-year-old daughter waiting alone outside the front door. It had been six months since the divorce. He picked up Shawna almost every weekend, yet his former wife rarely met him and she never invited him in.

Now, even as he pulled away from the house, Shawna said, "Mama wants me to ask you something."

Terrence sighed. "What does Mama want you to ask me?"

"She wants to know," Shawna recited carefully, "if I can spend next weekend with her and not you. It's her birthday."

"Yes, I know," Terrence said. "Do you want to spend next weekend with her?"

Shawna nodded vigorously. "She said we can go shopping, and go to lunch, and see a movie, and make pizza!"

"Hmm." Terrence grinned at his daughter. "If it's her birthday, why is she taking you to lunch, and to a movie, and shopping?"

Shawna giggled and shrugged emphatically. "I don't know."

"Tell Mama it's okay with me," Terrence said. "It sounds like her birthday present is going to be something very special—you."

◆◆◆◆◆ **Thinking It Over** ◆◆◆◆◆

1. How do you think Terrence feels about his former wife's coolness toward him?
2. Why doesn't Terrence insist that Shawna spend next weekend with him?
3. What does Shawna learn about relating to others in this situation?

Brent's parents felt joint custody would let him build a close relationship with both of them. They wanted to reinforce that they loved him as before. They were no longer husband and wife, but they would always be his father and mother.

REMARRIAGE

The remarriage of a parent can be as great a challenge as the divorce, for all family members. Disagreements are likely as stepparents and stepchildren learn to get along. This is true even when children don't live with the parent who is getting remarried.

Parents need to be sensitive to all of the adjustments this change brings about. They should have reasonable expectations for new relationships, their own as well as their child's, giving each relationship time to develop in its own way.

Supporting Children

Many children develop loving relationships within a blended family. A stepparent becomes a trusted and respected authority figure. Acquired siblings grow as close as biological ones. Nonetheless, parents should be aware of some built-in challenges.

Remarriage forces a child to give up any hope that parents will reconcile. It might also mean sharing a parent with a whole new family, whom the child may not care for, at least initially.

Joining a blended family means adjusting to new roles. The only boy may now be one of several. A child who was the youngest may be expected to help with a baby.

Children may feel their customs and routines are being questioned. The simple remark, "We always buy whole wheat bread," can sound like criticism to a child who eats white bread. Moving into a stepparent's home can deepen feelings of insecurity.

Adjustment in a blended family can take as much as three to five years. The family unit strengthens when members share activities they enjoy. Spending time alone with each child, including stepchildren, strengthens individual relationships.

Parents need to tell their children that these feelings are natural and will pass. They can find ways to remind the child, "You will always be special to me."

At the same time, parents must guard against showing favouritism to biological children. Their words and example should encourage all children to get along. Siblings should be guided to settle conflicts and solve problems themselves.

Likewise, parents should teach their children to respect a stepparent's authority as equal to the birth parents'. They shouldn't take their child's side in disputes or make excuses if the child misbehaves. In short, parents should demonstrate the same qualities in the new family that strengthen any family.

Relating to Stepchildren

If you've ever had a substitute teacher, you know what problems can occur. The substitute may know the subject, but doesn't know what to expect from your class. Less interested students sometimes test the teacher by acting disruptive, frustrating the ones who want to learn. In desperation, the substitute becomes either very strict to gain control of the class or very lenient to try to win them over. Very little learning goes on.

Stepparents may feel like the substitute teacher. As caring and skilled as they may be, stepparents can't just pick up where the birth parent left off. They don't have the shared experiences that bond children and birth parents in a unique way. Even if stepparents and their new family were already close, their relationship will be different after the marriage.

Also, gaining stepparents can be emotionally confusing for a child. When eight-year-old David's father remarried, David felt disloyal to his mother for liking his stepmother, Kristina. David tried to prove his loyalty by acting cool to his stepmother but knew he disappointed his father by hurting Kristina's feelings. For David, who was still learning to identify and express emotions, the situation was very stressful.

Parents should take the lead in forging relationships with stepchildren. Maturity helps a parent understand what children are going through. ◆ **Do you think younger or older children adjust more quickly in blended families?**

Given these circumstances, trying to force a relationship with a stepchild is unwise. Kristina dealt with the problem by telling David, "I'm not going to try to be your mother, because you already have one. I'd like us to be friends, because I want us all to be happy."

Internet Connects

http://www.mcgrawhill.ca/links/parenting
To learn more about statistics on family issues, go to the Web site above for *Parenting Rewards & Responsibilities, First Canadian Edition,* to see where to go next.

Dealing with Family Crises

"Life is very fair," says a French proverb. "Sooner or later, it breaks everyone's heart."

If you have trouble accepting that bleak outlook, you're not alone. Pain and crisis are easier to ignore than to accept—at first. You know, however, that this approach only makes a bad situation worse. A responsible parent recognizes and acts in a family crisis, rather than pretending "it can't happen to us."

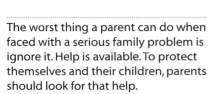

The worst thing a parent can do when faced with a serious family problem is ignore it. Help is available. To protect themselves and their children, parents should look for that help.

SUBSTANCE ABUSE

"I was a 'social drinker,'" Carol recalled. "Then I started to drink to calm my nerves. When they started tightening up the deadlines at work, I drank to cope with the frustration and pressure. Then I drank to escape my husband's nagging about my drinking. Pretty soon, I just drank."

Carol's downward spiral is typical of people whose use of alcohol turns into **alcoholism**, the physical and psychological dependence on alcohol. People who abuse other drugs experience the same decline.

As Carol's family learned, substance abuse harms an entire family, children in particular. When a parent's need for the addictive substance competes with a child's need for love and guidance, the child frequently loses. No one can be responsible and attentive under the influence of drugs or alcohol.

Carol's husband's response was also typical. "I denied it," Kevin admitted. "I couldn't believe the woman I married was an alcoholic. I thought she could stop if she used a little willpower—she told me she could."

Realizing his family's welfare was at stake, Kevin forced himself to overcome these mental obstacles. Taking positive steps to cope with the problem, he:

♥ *Confided in one person he trusted.* Kevin finally realized that he couldn't handle this problem alone. He reached out to a friend who was also a clergy member. A trained counsellor or family doctor were other possibilities.

♥ *Attended a support group.* Kevin benefitted from Al-Anon, a partner group of Alcoholics Anonymous that supports friends and family members of alcoholics.

♥ *Stopped "nagging."* Criticism only deepened Carol's guilt and her desire to escape through alcohol. Overcoming her addiction had to be her own choice.

♥ *Made sure the children's needs were met.* When possible, Kevin kept Carol's drinking from hurting them. When their mother's drinking interfered with a family outing, Kevin went ahead with their plans without his wife.

♥ *Took care of his own health.* Eating right and trying to get enough sleep gave Kevin the physical strength for parenting. Support from friends and Al-Anon members helped him cope with the emotional stress.

Kevin's actions show how a parent can keep a family intact without abandoning a spouse who is a substance abuser, whether alcohol or other drugs. When Carol's employer intervened, she decided to enter a recovery program at a nearby hospital. She began attending Alcoholics Anonymous meetings daily.

A parent who abuses alcohol or other drugs may not recognize the problem, although the rest of the family sees it very clearly. The abuser's spouse should make sure that children get needed support through counselling and organizations like Alateen.

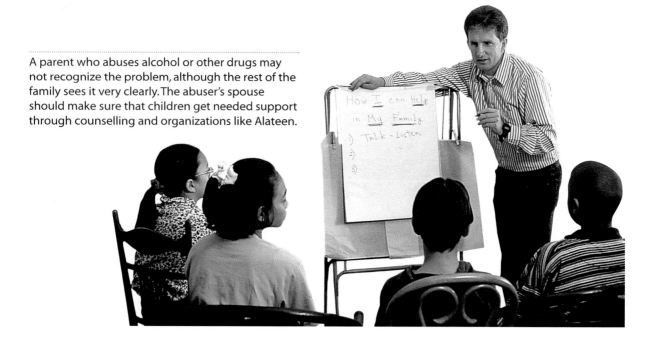

"The first step was the hardest," Carol said. "I'm a parent. *I'm* the caregiver and problem solver. To admit that *I* needed help—that felt like defeat. It was actually my first victory. I'm fighting to stay sober and to be a good parent."

FAMILY VIOLENCE

Every parent has "one of those days." You can imagine what it's like. Working all day leaves you tired and tense. Your toddler is in a defiant mood. Dirty dishes are stacked in the sink. You need paper plates to serve dinner, which you don't feel like fixing. Parenting, you think, is more trouble than it's worth.

Then you set a steaming plate of macaroni and cheese before your child. He thrusts an eager spoonful into his mouth and immediately spits it out again, shrieking with pain. "It's hot!" he wails, and begins to cry.

Stunned, you comfort your son and pour him cold milk with shaking hands. Through carelessness and frustration, you have hurt your child. How could you do that to someone you love?

Most parents have this type of experience at least once. Most are dismayed at their actions and never repeat them.

Health & Safety

CO-DEPENDENCY

The effects of substance abuse on the troubled parent are obvious enough. The damage done to other family members may be less apparent, even to them.

The first response to signs of abuse is often to deny the seriousness of the problem. Parents may point to outside factors, such as trouble at work. "As soon as that passes," they say, "things will get better." Eventually, they may urge their partner to seek help. The more they beg or threaten, the more they are shut out.

Parents may then choose another approach, often without realizing it. They make themselves responsible for protecting the family from the consequences of the problem. They "cover" for the abuser with lies and excuses. They rearrange their lives and ignore their own needs to keep peace in the family. This behaviour, often called **co-dependency**, is seen in children as well as parents. Children cannot understand the complexity of the problem. They think they could solve it easily by being more obedient or doing better in school.

Co-dependency is no solution either. Shielded from the harm he or she causes, the troubled partner has no reason to change. Meanwhile, the co-dependent feels increasingly angry, guilty, and mentally and physically exhausted.

To solve serious family challenges takes outside help. Support groups offer information on problems and options for treatment. They help the family confront the troubled individual and urge him or her to get help. Even if the person refuses, family members still benefit by learning how to keep their own lives intact. Seeing that others are no longer "held hostage" by the behaviour sometimes leads a person to seek help.

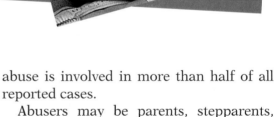

All children have an occasional bad day. ◆ **How does this mother's knowledge of child development benefit both her and her daughter?**

Abuse or Neglect

A tragic fact of life is that some parents abuse and neglect their children. **Child abuse** refers to physical, emotional, or sexual injury to children.

By contrast, **child neglect** is failure to meet a child's physical and emotional needs. Parents who leave young children alone or don't provide adequate food are guilty of neglect. Some children suffer from both abuse and neglect.

As many as 33 000 children under the age of 18 are *reported* victims of child abuse each year in Canada. The actual number of victims is much higher. Abuse and neglect occur in families from all income levels, racial and ethnic groups, and religions. Unless help is sought, both abuse and neglect tend to occur repeatedly, increasing in frequency and severity.

CAUSES OF ABUSE

Why would someone injure a child? In some cases, parents or caregivers may incorrectly think they are actually helping to guide the child. Beatings may have been used in their own upbringing, making them seem "appropriate." That's no excuse for such child abuse, however.

Anger and frustration are often involved in child abuse cases. Adults who lose control can inflict serious, even life-threatening, injuries on infants and children. The abuser may know little about child development and expect too much of a child. Some research indicates than substance

abuse is involved in more than half of all reported cases.

Abusers may be parents, stepparents, older siblings, relatives, or non-related adults living in the household or nearby. Tragically, the rate of infants and young children injured or killed by their mother's boyfriend has risen sharply.

SIGNS OF ABUSE

Physical signs of child abuse are unexplained cuts, bruises, burns, or broken bones. **Shaken Baby Syndrome** occurs when a baby is shaken, often resulting in a serious or fatal injury to the brain or eyes.

No child should ever be shaken for any reason. For a child two years old and younger, shaking is especially dangerous.

Possible symptoms of sexual abuse include irritation of the genitals or rectum, sudden interest and knowledge of sexual terms, acting out with other children, depression or mood changes, nightmares or clinginess, and fear of a caregiver or another person. Parents shouldn't jump to conclusions when one symptom exists, but they do need to pay attention. Investigate when a child makes a questionable remark, even if it sounds outlandish.

Emotional abuse occurs when unreasonable demands are placed on children to act beyond their level of development. Withholding love and affection from a child is also emotional abuse. Verbal abuse, such as routine teasing, insulting, or belittling, is often involved. As a result of feeling humiliated, unworthy, and unloved, such children suffer from low self-esteem.

GETTING HELP

As a parent, if you ever suspect your child has been physically or sexually abused, a doctor should be consulted. The doctor can help confirm suspicions or calm fears.

To help prevent abuse, never leave a child with someone who becomes easily angered or is bothered by a baby's cries. Make your feelings about spanking known to caregivers.

If anger is a problem for you, do yourself and your child a tremendous favour and seek professional help. A toll free 24-hour anonymous phone line, where parents can get support, referrals, and information, is available to all parents in Canada. The Parent Help Line is also accessible on the Internet. Your telephone book also has local emergency numbers listed that you can call for help. Local Children's Aid Societies and social service agencies in most communities have self-help groups that support parents through regular meetings.

GETTING INVOLVED

People who believe in minding their own business may be reluctant to get involved when they suspect child abuse or neglect. They must remember that child abuse is illegal and that young children can't speak for themselves.

All types of abuse and neglect leave lasting impressions on children. Some children avoid interacting with others. Others become offenders themselves. The longer abuse continues, the more serious the problem becomes.

Child abuse should never be hidden. Abused children need help. Trained professionals use special techniques to help them open up.

General information about child abuse and its prevention can be obtained from organizations such as Health Canada, the Centre of Excellence for Child Welfare, and other community agencies that work with children and families.

Reporting Child Abuse in Canada

In most Canadian provinces, anyone who thinks a child is being abused must tell child protection authorities. For example, in Ontario, the Child and Family Services Act says that any person who reasonably suspects a child is being abused must report his or her suspicions to a Children's Aid Society. This includes the general public as well as people who work closely with children. People who work with children have more knowledge about the signs of child abuse and neglect. If they notice these signs while they are working and don't report them, they can be fined up to $1000 if convicted. These professionals include teachers, principals, health-care workers, dentists, clergy, and youth workers who are not volunteers.

You do not need to have proof of abuse or neglect to make a report. As long as you have good reason to suspect that a child is being abused or neglected, you must contact a Children's Aid Society. The Children's Aid Society will investigate further and decide whether the evidence indicates child abuse or not. Suspicions based on good reasons that turn out not to be child abuse are not the same as false reports. Occasionally, an individual will intentionally make a report of child abuse without any evidence. This is illegal, and the individual may be charged with an offence.

To report child abuse or neglect, call a child and family services agency. If you cannot find the phone number of your province's children's services agency in the directory, call directory assistance. In an emergency, call the police, a hospital, or another community agency that works with families.

Education can help children recognize what constitutes child abuse, and it can give them vital information about how and where to find help if they find themselves in an abusive situation.

It is important to handle anger appropriately. Anger can easily turn into violence and abuse.

A few parents, male and female, harm others regularly. They buckle beneath the pressures of daily life and repeatedly lash out with violence against those closest to them. This, of course, is never justified. It is, in fact, a crime.

Avoiding Violent Relationships

Children aren't the only ones subjected to abuse. Some adults abuse their partners. Some abuse both children and a partner.

Many potential abusers give early clues to their nature. Since violent relationships are hard to leave once they start, you need to notice things about a person before you become too involved. That way you can avoid being with someone who may end up hurting you and your children. These clues can help you identify people who are likely to use violence as a release for anger and stress:

♥ *Unrealistic expectations.* They expect a partner to know and meet all of their needs. They make demands of a child that are beyond the child's ability.

♥ *Poor problem-solving skills.* They are easily frustrated when things don't go right. They choose the quick and simple "solution" of violence.

♥ *Refusal to accept responsibility.* A hard-to-please boss "gets" them fired. A child "makes" them angry.

♥ *Extreme sensitivity.* They take personal offense when a reasonable person wouldn't, such as getting cut off in traffic by another driver.

♥ *Cruelty to animals.* They handle pets roughly or discipline them severely.

♥ *Drug or alcohol abuse.* This is another sign of the inability to handle problems well. It also lessens self-control, making abuse more likely.

- ♥ **Verbal abuse.** They criticize and belittle partners and children, wearing down their self-esteem. People with low self-esteem are more likely to accept the violence.

- ♥ **Threats of violence.** Many people use violent figures of speech. The abuser means them.

- ♥ **A background of abuse.** Children who grew up in an abusive environment learn it as a normal way of relating to others.

- ♥ **A history of violence.** Violent behaviour is a habit. It is a dangerous "coping skill" that some people use to deal with frustration.

Additional traits to those just listed can be seen in men who are likely to batter female partners. They tend to hold very traditional views on male-female relationships. They are often intensely jealous, trying to isolate partners from friends, family, and even work relationships.

These men also demonstrate a need for control. They demand detailed reports of where their partner is going and with whom. If they control the money in the relationship, they use it to restrict their partner's behaviour.

Escaping the Violence

No one should stay with a violent partner. No one deserves the abuse.

Unfortunately, people who endure abuse have little sense of self-worth. If they had the self-confidence to leave, they wouldn't have begun the relationship in the first place. A woman, the more likely target of violence between partners, often fears for her physical safety, even her life. If she is financially dependent on her abuser, she may worry about providing for herself and her child. She does not want to break up the family.

Like the substance abuser, the abused woman must make the decision and act on it. She will get no support from her partner, but she can find it from others. Resources for a woman in this situation are described on page 570.

When a partner abuses a child also, taking action is even more urgent. A parent

A violent parent can cause physical as well as emotional harm to a spouse and children. An abused woman should contact the closest centre for abused women. There, she and her children can learn what to do and get help.

Parenting Q & A

Children and Violence

Q "My children and I live in a neighbourhood where violence is common. I worry about how that will affect them. What can I do?"

A Living with violence is serious for children. They may become fearful and unable to move forward with their development. By holding back feelings, they may not develop empathy for others. Often they feel helpless, losing hope for the future. As a result, they may be unwilling to learn. Some children become aggressive, even violent themselves, and can't get along with others. As a parent, you have to take steps to counteract these possibilities. Keep your children indoors if necessary. Make sure home is a safe and wholesome place. Keep people out if they don't support your efforts. Avoid increasing fear by reacting too fearfully yourself. Be a calm role model and focus on positive activities. Listen to children's concerns and give support. If you are a strong, nurturing parent, your children will be better able to withstand the forces outside the family.

who sees a child being abused—by a partner, a caregiver, or the other parent—must act. In addition to the resources listed on page 570, a parent can contact Children's Aid Society. Social workers will investigate and decide how to ensure the child's well-being. That may mean separating family members, but often requires only counselling. The agency checks the family's progress periodically.

STRATEGIES AND SUPPORT TO SURVIVE ABUSE, NEGLECT, AND FAMILY VIOLENCE

There are many programs aimed at helping people deal with abuse, neglect, and violence. Some offer intensive help for families at high risk. Parenting education can help parents understand how children develop at different ages, and how to discipline children without hurting them. Other programs are aimed at educating children in schools. Children can be taught how to recognize abuse, as well as strategies for saying no or getting help. Places to turn for help include the Children's Aid Societies, women's shelters, police, family and friends, children's shelters, and parent support groups. Children in need of support can call the Kids Help Phone, available 24 hours a day across Canada.

> **KIDS HELP PHONE**
> **1 800 668 6868**
> w w w . k i d s h e l p p h o n e . c a

Spotlight On
Resources for Battered Women

A battered woman need not face her ordeal alone. She can turn to:

✔ *Family and friends.* Those closest to the woman often see the problem before she does.

✔ *Hotlines and shelters.* Hotlines can calm a frightened woman and tell her where to get help. Shelters offer emergency housing and the support of others facing the same dilemma. Counsellors help women identify their options and other resources. Shelters' locations are not publicized in order to protect their clients.

✔ *Housing and financial aid programs.* If a woman chooses to leave her abuser, she and her children may qualify for public assistance. Provincial welfare programs may help with transitional housing or shelters. The Canadian Health Network lists a wide range of federal, provincial, and territorial resources available to battered women. Private groups, including the YWCA, provide similar support.

✔ *Legal aid.* A battered woman has recourse in the law. She can get a legal restraining order to bar her abuser from contacting her or their children. A lawyer can explain support and custody laws if she seeks a divorce. The province's or territory's legal aid office provides some services to women who cannot afford a private lawyer. A few women choose to press criminal charges against their partner. The threat of prosecution, and pressure from police or the court, may persuade the abuser to seek counselling.

Safe, Peaceful, and Healthy Families

To break the cycle of violence, government, communities, and individuals need to work together. Campaign 2000 is a program in which national, provincial, and community groups work together on child and family issues, such as child poverty, one of the risk factors associated with abuse. By increasing awareness and support, they work to strengthen families. In a healthy family, children feel safe.

According to author Dolores Curran, healthy families communicate well, praise and support family members, respect others, trust one another, and have a sense of fun and playfulness. They share responsibilities, teach about right and wrong, and have a strong sense of family with traditions and rituals. Canadian researcher Ben Schlesinger agrees. He also points out that families today cope with many daily stresses within their unique family structures.

Families don't all need to be the same. They can draw on their own unique strengths to meet all the needs of children.

COMMUNITY AND SOCIAL PROGRAMS THAT PROVIDE FAMILY SUPPORT

When families face difficult times, there are places they can turn to for support. Many community programs work toward strengthening families. Participants develop skills and confidence by working toward common goals that benefit everyone involved. These groups include:

♥ *YMCA/YWCA Canada*—This organization encourages a sense of belonging to society and works to improve the well-being of individuals and families. It has many community programs, including child-care facilities, finding employment, helping newcomers, outreach programs for youth who need shelter and support, and health and fitness services.

♥ *Big Brothers and Big Sisters*—These Canada-wide programs provide adult role models for children and youth by matching adult volunteers with children who need support.

♥ *Scouts Canada*—Scouts give boys and girls from ages 5 to 26 the chance to develop independence and responsibility by being involved in group and community activities.

Good communication is central to the development of strong families.

♥ *Girl Guides of Canada*—This group is particularly concerned with helping girls and young women ages 5 and up to develop leadership skills, independence, and self-confidence, in the company of other women and girls.

♥ *LifeSpin*—This organization in London, Ontario, provides information and resources for low-income families. Their

Families with non-English-speaking members may sometimes find it hard to seek necessary support. They might need encouragement to find what assistance is available to them as well as help to learn where to find it.

resources include support groups, a place to exchange goods such as clothing and household items for free, and help with obtaining nutritious food and finding places to live.

♥ ***Community recreational programs***—By participating in sports or other recreational activities, people become connected to the community. Children and youth benefit by mastering skills and strengthening their sense of self.

BARRIERS FACING PARENTS WHEN ACCESSING FAMILY SUPPORT PROGRAMS

Although there are many programs available to provide support for families, some families who could benefit from them do not make use of them. Low-income families may not be able to afford programs that have user fees, or may feel uncomfortable about identifying themselves as being in financial need. Parents who do not speak English or French fluently may feel awkward about participating. They may worry that their values or culture won't be understood by other members of the group.

Families who have never used community programs before may be reluctant to do so, or may be unaware of the benefits. Often, even when some parents see the value of a program, they have trouble making time to take their children. Children and youths who rely on buses may not be able to get to a program location if it is far away from their school. They also might feel pressured by friends who say the activities aren't "cool."

Serious Illness and Accidents

Few things are as frightening, for child or adult, as watching a family member struggle with prolonged illness or life-threatening injury. Life is thrown into disarray. The emotional and financial impact can test a family's strength.

John and Jody learned this when their son Andrew was badly hurt in a bicycle accident. They explained to the younger son, four-year-old Simon, "Andrew got hurt and went to the hospital. We need to be with him until he gets better. Later on you can come too."

To calm Simon's fears in the stressful days that followed, they:

♥ Explained Andrew's condition in simple terms.

♥ Involved Simon by having him draw pictures to brighten Andrew's hospital room.

♥ Took turns at the hospital in order to spend time with Simon too.

♥ Brought Simon to visit Andrew as the older boy recovered.

♥ Arranged for Simon to have a tour of the children's ward.

As stressful as this ordeal was for Simon, think how it affected his parents. They absorbed the shock of Andrew's accident. They shouldered the mental and physical strain, juggling work, hospital visits, and meetings with doctors. They worried about caring for both boys.

To cope with this stress, Jody and John turned to each other for support and to family and friends for help. Their religious beliefs offered comfort and direction.

Internet Connects

http://www.mcgrawhill.ca/links/parenting
To learn more about family wellness and strengthening its links, go to the Web site above for *Parenting Rewards & Responsibilities, First Canadian Edition,* to see where to go next.

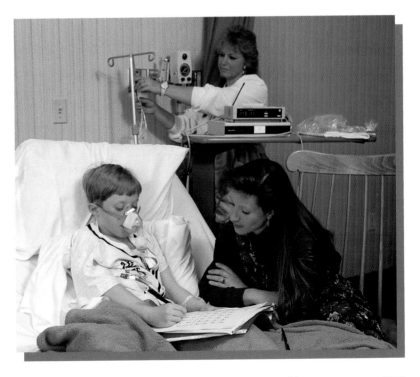

Serious illnesses can have a high impact on a family. ◆ **What are some of the problems that could occur?**

DEATH

Death is hard to accept and hard to explain, even for adults. Losing a loved one can leave parents stunned and directionless, yet they are expected to deal with their child's sorrow and confusion as well as their own. Providing leadership can be a challenge.

Parents don't need to have all the answers to help a child deal with death. They should tailor their words and actions carefully, however, to suit a child's level of understanding.

How Children Understand Death

Until about age five, death is literally unreal to children. They don't think about it unless someone they know dies. Even then, they can't comprehend that death is permanent and inevitable. They may think the dead person is living elsewhere, and ask when he or she is coming back.

Children feel the loss, however, and see it in others. The heightened emotions and disruption in the home upset them. They may wonder if they caused the death by misbehaving. Due to stress, children may act unusually sensitive, aggressive, or fearful. Some revert to more immature behaviour.

By age nine, most children have experienced death directly, through the loss of a pet, a grandparent, or a senior neighbour. They see that death is final, and start to realize that it will someday happen to them. Many children demand detailed answers about how and why people die. In part, they want reassurance that they, and their parents, will not die soon. They may also try to relieve any guilt they feel, especially if they and the deceased parted on bad terms or if they wished the person harm.

Parents need to provide reassurance and understanding to help children deal with the complex emotions they may feel after the death of a family member or friend.

Older children still have many questions about death. However, they know that death comes to everyone, themselves included. This awareness can be very troubling. Children need to accept the reality of death without becoming obsessed with it. Some become curious about the physical process of dying and the customs and rituals of funerals and burial. They show concern about how a death affects the living. If a friend's father dies, they might ask, "What will Jenny's family do? Will they have to move away?"

Helping Children Cope with Death

Because the death of a loved one evokes such pain and confusion, parents may have trouble sending the desired message to children. On the other hand, answering a child's questions can remind parents of their own comforting beliefs.

These suggestions can guide parents in helping a child cope with death.

♥ *Be gentle but honest.* Children eventually find out when someone dies. Breaking the news kindly spares the child unnecessary pain. Trying to hide the truth could damage the child's sense of trust, doing more harm than the death itself. A child may reason that death is too terrible to even talk about.

♥ *Use clear, simple language.* Adults often try to soften the blow by using vague terms, such as "passed on" or "was called away." A real explanation that is suited to a child's understanding might be: "When people die, their body stops working and won't start again. They can't think or feel happy or sad. They don't hurt or get hungry."

Children—and adults—react to death in different ways. One person may hold emotions in, and another may let them show freely. Caregivers should help children talk about their feelings in both situations.

♥ **Encourage children to accept and express their feelings**. Children may feel frightened by death and sad at their loss. They may feel angry at the person for dying, then guilty for feeling angry. They need to know that these reactions are normal and nothing to hide. They also need to know it's okay to start feeling happy again.

♥ **Make sure you understand each other.** Parents should be sure to give the facts the child asks for. Rephrasing a child's question and adding, "Is that what you mean?" can help clear things up. A parent might ask, "What do you think?" The response shows whether the child understands the explanation.

♥ **Take the child to the funeral.** Children accept and understand death better when they "say good-bye." If you think a funeral would be too upsetting, you could hold a quiet ceremony of your own or put flowers on the loved one's grave.

♥ **Watch and listen.** Children may not be aware that they have questions about death. Their actions and conversations reveal their concerns, however. A child who resists going to bed after hearing that someone "died in his sleep" needs to have that misunderstanding explained. A child who plays "funeral" may benefit by talking about his or her feelings.

A child under age four doesn't understand death. Including the child in the rituals of a funeral isn't necessary. After that age, children need to be included in some appropriate way so they can face the death and cope with their loss.

When helping a child deal with death, parents must remember that affirmation is as important as information. They should take children seriously and respect their intellect as well as their emotions.

The Grieving Process

Grieving, the experience of great sorrow, is a normal reaction to loss. Grieving is to the mind what the immune system is to the body. It is a response to a serious blow, an emotional defense and recovery.

Parents should be aware that children, like adults, grieve in their own way, in their own time. There is no one correct way to express grief, no timetable for coming to terms with death. A child may take two years to recover from the death of someone very close.

At the same time, parents should be alert for signs that the child is denying the death. Continued fearfulness and anger, and refusing to talk about the death, are two signs that the grieving process has stalled. A professional counsellor's help may be needed.

Although experts differ on the names and number of stages, the grief process consists of these basic reactions below. People move through the grief process at different rates, depending on the severity of the blow. Making steady progress is the main goal.

♥ **Shock**. People are numbed by the news. They hear the words but the situation doesn't seem real.

♥ **Denial**. People do not accept the news. They busy themselves, sometimes with insignificant tasks. They refuse to discuss the situation and talk as though no problem exists.

♥ **Despair**. People are overwhelmed by feelings of helplessness, anger, and depression.

♥ **Recovery**. People accept the situation and take steps to deal with the problem. They adapt their lives to their new situation.

Spotlight On
—Anger—

Frustration caused by family problems can quickly turn to anger. To avoid angry feelings or release them constructively, parents can:

✔ *Avoid piling up stress.* Trying tasks should be saved for when a parent has the patience to deal with them.

✔ *Think soothing thoughts.* A happy memory or favourite song or poem might help.

✔ *Put themselves in time-out.* Children aren't the only ones who benefit from a quiet spot to calm down and think things over.

✔ *Hit something that can't feel pain.* Pillows are good for punching. However, actions that might increase fear or anger, such as slamming doors, should be avoided.

✔ *Get out of the home.* Parents may want to get some distance from family members until their anger passes, but only if another adult can watch the child.

✔ *Get active.* Washing dishes, vacuuming, and jogging release energy. Getting a job done removes a possible source of aggravation.

Looking Back

♥ A child needs a parent's model of confidence and optimism to survive difficult times.

♥ To deal with unemployment, parents need to take money-saving measures and stay positive.

♥ Parents help children cope with marital break-up by remaining civil and reassuring children of their love for them.

♥ Parents must be patient and supportive to help children adjust to life in a blended family.

♥ When one parent is a substance abuser, the other must meet the family's needs while supporting a partner who is taking steps to overcome the addiction.

♥ Canadian law requires that anyone who believes child abuse is taking place must report it. Numerous programs exist to protect children and strengthen families in such circumstances.

♥ Parents must recognize when physical abuse is a danger. They must leave an abusive relationship or seek help if they feel they may become abusive.

♥ It is not unusual for families to need support in hard times. While many agencies are available to help, it is sometimes necessary to help families overcome their embarrassment at needing such assistance.

♥ When a family member is seriously ill or injured, letting children feel involved and useful helps manage their fears.

♥ Children need honest but appropriate explanations when a death occurs. They need time to grieve.

Knowledge and Understanding

1. What positive steps can a parent take to help the family cope with unemployment?
2. What does a child typically experience when parents divorce?
3. How can parents help children cope with divorce?
4. How can parents help children and stepchildren adjust to becoming a blended family?
5. How can a parent help the family survive when the other parent is a substance abuser?
6. Tami has decided to leave her abusive spouse. Describe the types of help available to her.
7. What might you do to reassure your child if your spouse were seriously ill?
8. Describe a child's growing understanding of death.
9. Explain whether you should urge a child to "get over" someone's death.

Review

Thinking and Inquiry

10. Why does loss of employment often affect a parent's self-esteem?

11. Should parents who want a divorce ever stay together "for the children?" Explain your answer.

12. The wife of an alcoholic was very careful not to upset him. She kept the house especially neat and made an effort to keep the children out of his way. How would you explain her behaviour?

13. In times of crisis, some families become stronger and closer, while others are driven apart. Why do you think this happens? How can parents make the difference in how a family responds to crisis?

Communication

14. Devise a radio announcement targeting the resources in your community for children who have been abused.

15. Research the poem "Children Learn What They Live," by Dorothy Law Nolte, and write a paragraph stating why the advice in the poem is very wise.

16. Watch a television show depicting family life. Were there any incidents of child neglect, abuse, or family violence? Did anything bother you about the show? Would you allow a seven-year-old to watch this show? Why or why not?

Application

17. Complete the following sentence in writing: "During a divorce, the worst thing that can happen to a child is...." Compare your thoughts with the class.

18. Make a list of simple activities a parent in a blended family might try in order to give a biological child extra time and attention and to strengthen bonds with a stepchild.

19. Working in pairs, write three questions a child might ask about the death of a loved one. Develop an appropriate response to each question.

UNIT **6**

Topics in Parenting

A Parent's Perspective

from Corina

"Now that I'm a parent, I'm also building a family.

When that thought started churning around in my mind, I wondered how I could make my family the best that we can be. I started remembering things my mother did when I was growing up. I guess you'd call them traditions or rituals. Like the way she always tucked us in at night and said the same silly rhyme as she slipped out of the room. Or the Sunday evening 'snack suppers' when we partied on apple slices, mini-pizzas, popcorn, carrot sticks, and anything else that was easy to fix. Or the way she read out loud from classics like Winnie the Pooh and Tom Sawyer while my brother and I washed the dishes. You know, I think I was 12 before I realized that washing dishes was supposed to be work. Now I realize how good my mother was at building a family. I hope my own children will say that about me someday."

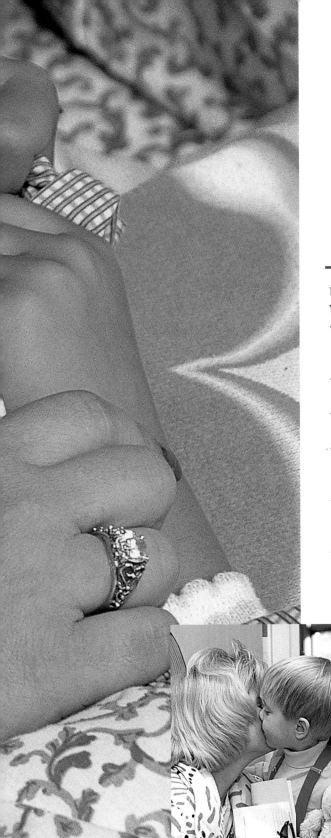

Unit Expectations

While reading this unit, you will:

❖ Explain patterns in the social, emotional, intellectual, moral, and physical development of children.

❖ Describe the nature of and the responsibilities involved in parenting.

❖ Identify social and cultural variations in family forms and parenting approaches.

❖ Demonstrate an understanding of the common experiences of young children across cultures.

❖ Demonstrate an understanding of the challenges facing parents throughout the early-childhood years.

❖ Demonstrate an understanding of child abuse and family violence, and outline strategies to secure a safe, non-violent environment for all children.

581

Strengthening Families

While reading this chapter, you will:

▶ Identify and describe the responsibilities parents have for children of different ages.

▶ Compare the changing roles of parents and children as both grow older.

▶ Describe how fathers, mothers, and grandparents transmit their cultural and religious heritage to infants, toddlers, and preschoolers.

▶ Describe the legal and social responsibilities of parents and guardians.

▶ Demonstrate an understanding of the challenges faced by parents of young children in today's rapidly changing society.

▶ Identify community programs and agencies that provide family support.

KEY TERMS

accommodation   consensus
compromise   negotiation

If ever Angie wanted her baby to be on her best behaviour, it was now. This was only their second visit to Marcel's parents since their wedding, their first since Taylor's birth. Angie had never met Marcel's two sisters, and she wanted everything to go well.

Six-month-old Taylor had no such concerns. She began to fuss and whimper during dinner, and Angie's efforts didn't stop the crying. "I'm sorry," she sighed as she hoisted Taylor from the infant seat, "excuse us, please..."

"Let me try." Marcel's father reached for the baby. "You sit down and enjoy your meal. That chicken gumbo is an old family recipe. We don't make it for just anybody." He rocked the baby and spoke to her softly. "What's wrong, little girl? All these strange people have you upset? It's okay if you want to cry—that's what babies do." Taylor seemed fascinated by the soothing, rolling tone of his voice. Mr. Doucet sang a lullaby, half English and half French, that charmed her to sleep. He smiled at Angie's wondering eyes. "That's an old family favourite too."

"I can see why," Angie agreed. "I hope you'll teach it to me. That's a tradition I'd like to help pass on."

— ◆ —

What do you think? What signs do you see that Angie and her father-in-law are on the way to building a strong relationship?

583

Growing up in a secure and happy family is what children need. Parents who live their commitment to family every day are rewarded in many ways.
◆ **Can you name some of those rewards?**

Family Fitness

Imagine that a man is walking to a store on a warm morning. It's not far and the exercise feels good to him. Winding through the large supermarket, he starts feeling tired. After the walk home, he's exhausted from the heat and carrying the heavy groceries. He realizes that if he were in better shape, the trip might have been fun. Instead, it turned out to be an ordeal.

Families are a little like the man and his trip to the store. Strong families are able to carry out daily tasks when they are "fit" enough to meet the challenges. Otherwise, a challenge, especially a serious one, can be threatening.

Family strength is built in small ways every day. Parents need to recognize and take advantage of these opportunities. In strong families, parents take charge of situations, giving children confidence. The children are less likely to look outside the family for direction.

What Are Families For?

Many of the parenting skills you're learning help a family operate well. The family can do what it's supposed to in taking care of all members. These basic functions include:

♥ **Creating a home.** Everyone needs a place to live, a safe shelter.

♥ **Child-rearing.** This includes all parenting duties: meeting physical needs, educating the child, providing guidance, and teaching skills for socialization.

♥ **Meeting economic needs.** When one or more people in the family are employed, they provide what the family must have for survival.

♥ **Providing emotional support.** Families show love, trust, acceptance, comfort, and encouragement.

♥ **Transmitting culture.** The family is the earliest setting for passing on a culture's values, customs, religious beliefs, and other traditions. This is how a society, as well as a family, preserves those things they find important.

What Makes Families Strong?

People talk about the value of "strong families," but what does that phrase mean? In what ways are families strong? Some very important ones are described here.

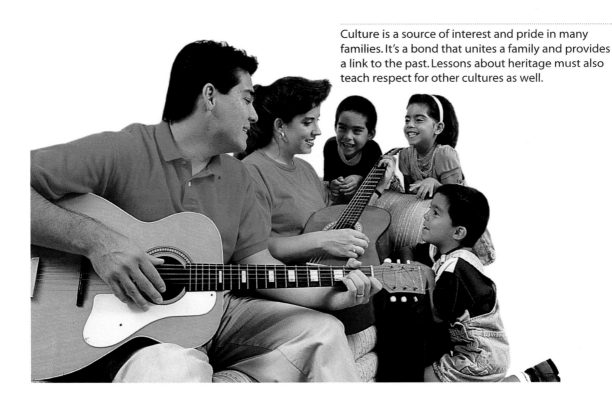

Culture is a source of interest and pride in many families. It's a bond that unites a family and provides a link to the past. Lessons about heritage must also teach respect for other cultures as well.

What better way to discover what's on your little girl's mind than over a cup of tea? And when she has your total attention, she feels especially loved and appreciated.

EXPRESSING LOVE AND ACCEPTANCE

Think about the words used for relationships. You "make" friends, "earn" respect, and "win" approval. These images reflect the work needed to maintain good relations.

In contrast, children in healthy families don't need to work for a parent's love. Unlike other relationships, parental love is unconditional, accepting a child "as is." Knowing they are loved unconditionally gives children the self-confidence to cope with life. When they need help, they know to turn to family first. Emotional well-being can flourish within a loving family.

In strong families, parents communicate messages of love and acceptance every day—to all members. When they sing to an infant during a diaper change or snuggle with a preschooler on the sofa, they're saying, "I'm happy that you're mine." Older children need to hear this message too, as they begin to form relationships outside the family. A funny note in a lunch box, a favourite food at dinner, or a hug reminds children of their value.

SPENDING TIME TOGETHER

Spending time together is basic to building any strong relationship. In families with busy schedules, parents must *make* time for children. Children don't need special events or activities, only an involved parent. Reading a story or talking about the day lets a parent focus on the child. Children thrive on the attention, and parents and children get to know each other. Sharing jobs at home can build closeness too.

Some people wonder if "quality time" can make up for limits on the amount of time people spend together. Opinions vary. Think about your relationship with your parents and your friends. Think of examples when parents and children spend quality time together or quantity time together. Consider the good relationships and the poor relationships. What factors affect the good relationships? What factors affect the poor relationships?

The most important aspect of parent-child relationships is caring. Children need to know that their parents care for them and will be there for them when needed.

SHOWING RESPECT

Respect is vital for healthy relationships. Parents teach respect by showing it—to spouse, children, and others. Parents model self-respect by caring for their own health and by acting on their values. They expect to be treated with the same respect they show others.

Raising Children With Character

Family Character

As Georgia wrote on the family calendar, she announced, "The family reunion is on the eighth."

Nine-year-old Will frowned. "Will Aunt Mae be there?"

"I hope so," Georgia said. "You don't sound too pleased."

"She's, well, ... kind of weird," Will complained. "Remember last year, when she wore that big skirt and showed us that dance?"

"That big skirt was Grandma's. She learned that dance as a girl in Poland," Georgia explained. "Mae thought we should know that. Do you remember your seventh birthday, when Mae bought you the baseball glove you wanted so much? I said it was too expensive, but Mae said, 'A great athlete needs the best equipment. Our family is full of greatness.' Wasn't that the glove you wore when your team won the league trophy?"

Will sighed. "I forgot about that."

Georgia gently tapped his chin. "Mae is a lady well worth knowing," she declared. "She's also part of our family. Don't forget that."

◆◆◆◆◆ **Thinking It Over** ◆◆◆◆◆

1. What was Will's attitude toward Mae? Why do you think he felt as he did?
2. What was Georgia trying to make Will understand?
3. Do you think Will's attitude will change with time? If so, how?

Children learn respect from parents in several ways. Parents set a good example by speaking politely to and about others. They listen as well as honour the opinions and confidences of others. They pay attention to others and treat them courteously. Respect also shows when parents allow family members emotional and physical privacy and treat personal and family possessions with care.

BUILDING TRUST

Children learn trust when parents take good care of them and keep promises. Consistency in parenting also inspires a child's confidence. Like respect, trust is a two-way street. People trust more readily when they're trusted in return. An older child might be asked to take a letter to the corner mailbox. A younger child might deliver cookies next door.

Ideally, parents show they trust their partner's abilities. Before making a decision, a parent might say, "Let's see what Mom thinks about this." Having faith in parents helps keep children close as they grow older and face difficult choices.

ESTABLISHING TRADITIONS

Traditions help strengthen families. They are "points of reference," experiences all family members share and look forward to repeating. Many traditions are related to holidays and other special events.

To personalize a celebration, a family might allow a family member to pick the dinner menu on his or her birthday. They could attend a religious service together.

Others examples are having a grandparent or child read a holiday poem or story and displaying decorations that are used only at that event or time of year.

Common routines can also become traditions. When Brett and Mandy's children were young, he worked as a pizza chef. Before work on Saturdays, Brett would ask what toppings the children wanted. Sharing "Daddy's pizza" was something they all looked forward to. "I haven't worked there since I got my degree," Brett said, "but we still order or make pizza together most Saturday nights."

Cross-Curricular — Art CONNECTIONS

Family Totem Poles

A sense of family identity is one sign of family strength. Family identity for some Aboriginal Peoples was symbolized by the totem pole. This is a tall post carved and painted with a series of animal-like figures. Each figure represents one aspect of a family or the family's heritage. A totem pole was also a status symbol. A very old and influential family might need several poles to illustrate its history and identity fully. Considering that a totem pole took a group of men up to one year to carve, the effort alone showed the community the family's high position. **What objects in today's society serve a similar purpose as the totem pole?**

COMMUNICATING

Parents are the models for communication in a family. When parents talk to children and listen attentively, children are more likely to become communicators too. If good communication practices begin when children are small, the benefits can be felt as children grow into adolescence and adulthood. Communication becomes a valuable tool that the family uses for many purposes.

When parents talk to children, they provide information and guidance that helps children develop as they should. Not many lessons can be learned with silence.

When family members discuss problems, they work toward reasonable solutions. Anger and physical force intensify problems, but good communication solves them.

People want to be heard. They like to know that their point of view is noticed and respected by others. When family members, including the extended family, share their feelings and opinions in positive ways, they understand each other better. They typically become closer.

SETTLING CONFLICTS

True or false: successful families never have conflicts. That statement, of course, is false. All families have conflicts, but problems can be settled. One goal of parents should be that family members continue to love and respect each other despite their disagreements.

Talking It Over

During a conflict, discussion can help whether a parent has already made a decision or is still thinking about what to do. Sometimes a cooling-off period is needed to avoid doing or saying something harmful.

Communication between parent and child changes as the child grows older. ◆ **Why is skillful listening important at any age?**

Generally by age five, children have the intellectual and emotional skills to benefit from talking over a problem. Letting each person involved share ideas can shed some light on the conflict. Parents can weigh the good points of each argument and make as fair a judgment as possible. The parent can guide the discussion by:

♥ **Staying calm.** Speaking quietly and taking a deep breath can help maintain self-control. If a child can't avoid being angry, a parent should suggest, "This isn't helping. Let's wait a bit until we're ready to talk."

♥ **Staying focused.** Children may have trouble keeping to the point. Parents should mention that if they jump from issue to issue, they'll never settle anything.

♥ **Recognizing all valid points.** Acknowledging any strengths of a child's case demonstrates respect. This is crucial to conflict resolution. Although parents make the final decision, children will feel that their wishes were fairly considered.

Reaching a Consensus

With older children and adolescents, a parent may choose to resolve a conflict by **consensus**, looking for a decision that is acceptable to everyone. In showing how to reach consensus, a parent may use some of the following strategies:

♥ **Negotiation** is the process of discussing an issue to reach a mutual agreement.

Not in Front of the Children

Q "Whenever my husband and I argue, I try to avoid letting our son hear us. My husband says disagreements are part of life and nothing to hide. Does it hurt children to see their parents fight?" *Lucy*

A The answer to your question is both yes and no. Showing children "the real world" doesn't have to be a negative experience. A disagreement can be a chance to show children how people settle disputes rationally and for their mutual good. As long as your emotions are under control and you work toward a peaceful resolution, little harm is likely. On the other hand, angry arguments are harmful, especially if they are frequent and they resort to yelling, name-calling, or physical actions. Children may lose their sense of security. Can you learn skills that will help you avoid arguing and allow you to settle more issues without an argument? If so, your family will be better off.

♥ Through **compromise**, parents and children each give up something in order to reach an agreement that satisfies them both. Compromise works when all parties feel the deal gives them something they wanted.

♥ **Accommodation** occurs when a family member decides to adapt his or her behaviour or expectations in order to resolve a conflict. One father was tired of his son's messy bedroom. Finally he decided to simply close the door. As he explained, "I decided this issue wasn't worth all the arguing. If he doesn't mind the mess, why should it bother me?" Accommodation may be necessary from time to time. It's part of the give-and-take of family living. It becomes a problem, however, if the same person is always the one to be accommodating.

Limits on Consensus

Not every conflict in a family can or should be solved by consensus. Parents must often settle issues in ways they believe are best for the family. They may have to take a strong stand at times.

Most parents look for a balance between the issues that have to be settled by them alone and those that allow input from all family members. They want the family to feel secure in their leadership, but they also want children to feel valued and to learn how co-operation works. As Linda put it, "I usually find myself stopping to think for a minute. Is this something the kids should have a say in, or does the solution have only one answer? Then I go from there."

Some conflicts can be settled with compromise, but some can't. ◆ **How does a parent decide when to consider what the child has to say and when to lay down the law?**

SOLVING PROBLEMS

Parents encourage their children to be independent, but sometimes they need help solving their problems. In Chapter 5 you learned a process for making decisions. A similar process exists for solving more complex problems. A problem can usually be broken down into manageable parts. If you can outline a problem as a series of questions to answer and decisions to make, you have a better chance of using your reasoning skills to solve it. The information on pages 592–593 illustrates one way to do that.

THE PROBLEM-SOLVING PROCESS

When building a tree house, extra hands make the job easier. Similarly, families that work together solve problems more effectively. Using the six-step problem-solving process can guide a family to success.

1 Identify the Problem.
Some family members may not see that a problem exists or may have different opinions about the problem. As leaders, parents make sure everyone understands and agrees on the starting point.

2 Gather and Analyze Information.
Once a problem is identified, the family needs information. When and why did the problem start? What should the solution accomplish? Reviewing and sifting through information may suggest what to do.

3 Compare Possible Solutions.
Next, the family writes and evaluates possible solutions, using values as a guide. What are the pros and cons of each? What are the consequences? What resources can be used?

4 Choose the Best Solution.

At this point, the family selects the best option. The solution needs to be manageable for each family member.

5 Create a Plan of Action.

Still working together, the family decides what needs to be done by each person and when. An imaginative approach helps identify resources.

6 Evaluate the Results.

Periodically, the family checks to see if the solution is working as expected. If not, they make corrections. The skills and knowledge they gain can help them solve future family problems—as well as personal ones.

You Solve It

When the Butlers married, Adam moved in with Leann and her children, Heidi and Blake. Two years later, Adam's 11-year-old daughter, Ashley, came to live with them after her mother died. Gradually, Ashley became outspoken, showing contempt for the children and Leann. Heidi, age six, resented having to share her room, and Blake, age 12, didn't like the way Ashley intruded in their lives. Adam felt sorry for Ashley. Leann tried to keep the peace, but was hurt by the changes in their family and Ashley's hostility. *Working with a group from your class, take the Butler family through the problem-solving process in search of a solution.*

593

Locating Resources

When pioneer families ventured west in the early 1800s, they had little to rely on except themselves. The nearest neighbour might be far away. If parents encountered a problem, such as illness or a lack of food, they had to solve it themselves.

Today, no parent has to "go it alone." Parents have a variety of helpful resources.

COMMUNITY RESOURCES

Nearly every community has organizations that support parents' efforts to create a strong family. Some offer their services for free. Others charge a fee, sometimes based on the ability to pay.

Internet Connects

http://www.mcgrawhill.ca/links/parenting
To find out more about services offered to families by the provincial and national governments, go to the Web site above for *Parenting Rewards & Responsibilities, First Canadian Edition*, to see where to go next.

Educational Services

To succeed in society, children need education. Parents typically look to others to help fill this need for knowledge.

♥ *Elementary and secondary schools.* Both public and private schools continue parents' efforts in helping children learn. They also help socialize children and often offer nutritious meals.

♥ *Libraries, museums, and art galleries.* Education and enrichment come from these sources. Many libraries offer special children's services and programs, such as puppet shows and story hours. Some museum exhibits feature interactive displays that fascinate children while teaching. Art galleries often have art programs for children.

♥ *Continuing education programs.* These help parents who decide they need more education in order to care for their family better. Career training can help them increase earnings. Parenting classes can show how to relate to their children more effectively.

All families need support at times. The money you pay in taxes funds many programs that help families. Here a young boy with a hearing disability practices sign language in a special educational program.

♥ ***Social and health services.*** There are a wide variety of services offered to families through local, provincial, and federal government agencies. These agencies offer services and support for the social, emotional, and physical needs of families.

Legal Services

Sometimes parents need legal recourse to help them create or maintain a strong family. When Annette and Frank married, they agreed he should legally adopt her two daughters. They consulted an attorney who specialized in family law.

Parents can also contact politicians about legislation that affects children and families.

Health and Human Services

Canada's publicly funded health-care system provides needed support for all Canadian families. Access to prenatal care, support services for new parents, and doctor's care for young children is an important part of the Canadian social fabric.

Canadian families have access to other forms of support. The Early Years Centres in Ontario are an excellent example of how the provincial government is supporting families. With the increased understanding of the importance of early learning, Early Years Centres focus on supporting the early learning experiences of Ontario's children.

Internet Connects

http://www.mcgrawhill.ca/links/parenting
To find out more about how parents can promote growth, go to the Web site above for *Parenting Rewards & Responsibilities, First Canadian Edition,* to see where to go next.

Other programs that are funded by different levels of government are: Children's Aid Societies, which deal with child protection, counselling, foster care, and adoption; child and youth wellness agencies, which provide counselling and other support to children and their families; public health units, which provide health and nutrition information through public health nurses and nutritionists.

Families that need help may wonder where to go. Does the phone directory in your area have Blue Pages? Look for the directory in the front of those pages. Check under these listings to see what's available: social services; health; education.

Emergency Services

Imagine your family lost your home to a flood or a fire, or because you couldn't pay the rent. How would you cope?

Emergency shelters help parents keep a family together in times of crisis. Shelters provide food, clothes, and a place to stay. Some locate counselling to help parents get their families back on their feet financially and emotionally. Mothers and children who are fleeing domestic violence can find safety in women's shelters. These shelters offer immediate protection from the abusive partner and put the woman in contact with counselling and other services.

Some crises are less dramatic, but still potentially damaging. Irene became seriously depressed after having her second child. It affected her ability to care for her family and herself. She called a toll-free number sponsored by a national mental health organization. A volunteer listened and told Irene where to go for help. Other hotlines assist parents whose families are threatened by substance abuse, suicide, or accidental poisoning.

Recreation Services

Many communities offer recreational services that enrich family life. A community recreation department may offer art classes and nature walks just for children. In some communities, various groups help children explore dance, music, science, and the environment. Families can bicycle, swim, take walks, and play baseball or soccer at local parks.

Religious Organizations

Many religious groups sponsor family-oriented programs that are open to the public. They might have a family film night, a day-care centre or preschool, or a counselling centre. Some sponsor clothing drives, food banks, or even open their doors to homeless families.

Family emergencies come in many forms. After a flood, community volunteers collected food, clothing, and bedding for families affected by it. ◆ **What other disaster relief plans have you heard of?**

FINDING ASSISTANCE

As a parent with a problem, how would you find the help you need? The search could start with the phone book. Directories list the names, phone numbers, and sometimes addresses of most public and private groups. Government agencies are listed separately in the Blue Pages. Directories are available at most libraries, and librarians are often available to help. Many offer Internet access.

Child-care professionals can provide leads for parents who need help. A doctor might tell a parent about a clinic that cleans children's teeth. A teacher might recommend a summer library program for a struggling young reader. Other parents may have advice on locating needed services too.

PERSONAL SUPPORT GROUPS

Sometimes help is closer than a parent realizes. Extended family members and friends are often willing to help when they realize there's a need.

Some parents can benefit from organized support groups. These include Parents Without Partners, Al-Anon, Parents Anonymous, and local parent support groups. School Councils at school can be a source of general advice and information.

Parents can help solve each other's problems, since they share many concerns. Leo found support when a new job made it impossible for him to pick up his son, Drew, at school. In a conversation Leo had with the mother of Drew's friend, she offered to pick up Drew and watch him for an hour. In exchange, Leo agreed to take both boys to school. That meant the mother didn't have to wake her toddler on school mornings.

Leo discovered something else. Families helping other families is sometimes the simplest, most effective solution. When parents work together to build strong families, all families—and an entire community—share the benefits.

Families should never ignore the need for support. There is no shame in seeking help for problems. Finding solutions can mean many happier, stronger years of family life in the future.

Review

Looking Back

♥ Parents must take responsibility for building family strength.

♥ All the parenting skills people learn help them fulfill the functions of a family.

♥ Parents encourage family love by modelling unconditional acceptance.

♥ Parents need to find ways for all family members to spend quality time together.

♥ Treating others with trust and respect is one way parents promote those feelings among family members.

♥ Family traditions and personal communication provide a sense of shared identity and closeness.

♥ Unity and respect grow in families that practise open and fair conflict resolution.

♥ A problem-solving process gives families a tool for resolving difficulties for themselves.

♥ Parents can call on many resources to help them create strong families.

Knowledge and Understanding

1. What functions do families serve?
2. How do expressions of love help a family?
3. What impact does the amount and quality of time spent together have on families?
4. How can parents teach respect?
5. What makes a child trust a parent?
6. Must family traditions be involved and expensive to bring people together? Explain.
7. What purposes does communication serve in a family?
8. To guide a family discussion well, what should a parent do?
9. Should consensus be used to solve all family disagreements? Explain your answer.
10. Briefly describe a process parents can use to help their family solve problems.
11. Give three examples of community resources that help parents educate their children.

Thinking and Inquiry

12. Rachel often works late, but gets home in time to read to five-year-old Joel, share a snack, and put him to bed. Recently, Joel has started calling for Rachel in the middle of the night, saying he has a nightmare or a stomach ache. What might be causing this behaviour?

13. What problems might arise when family members are not encouraged to share their feelings with each other?

14. You've read what makes a family strong. Looking at the opposite side, what makes a family weak?

Communication

15. Imagine you are the parent of a 12-year-old. You and your child have always enjoyed a close relationship, but your recent conversations have been one-sided. Explain your concerns and your desire for more conversation with your child. Write a dialogue of that conversation.

16. Diane works part-time but is home most days to care for her daughter, age six. A six-year-old neighbour girl, whose parents are seldom home, often comes over to play. The child shows up all the time, even at mealtimes, and stays for hours. What should Diane do? What should she say to the other child's parents?

Application

17. With a partner, identify a problem that families commonly face. Using the problem-solving model in the chapter, think of some possible solutions and choose one to carry out. Write a summary or make a chart showing how you used the process and explaining why the solution you chose seems best.

18. Make a list of family traditions that are familiar to you. Share these with the class and discuss why the traditions are useful. Thinking creatively together, see if you can add original ideas to the list.

19. With a partner, use the telephone directory to find five or more resources mentioned in the chapter. Compare lists with the class. Are some resources unavailable in your community? If so, how could you find the help needed?

Ray Swinarchin, Supervisor of a Today's Family Centre

What volunteer activities did you do as a teenager that led you to choose a career that involved working with children/people?

▶ I began to volunteer while in university. I considered teaching but also explored other options. A friend of mine told me that she worked with children in a day-care centre. I volunteered at the centre once a week to find out more about her career as an Early Childhood Educator. I also began to volunteer at our church's Sunday school, where I was responsible for setting up the curriculum for ten children. I also began to teach children Ukrainian dance, choreographing dances, planning annual concerts, and supervising children on community outings.

*Please describe your **specific education pathway**.*

▶ After receiving a BA in History from McMaster University, I applied to Mohawk College for the two-year Early Childhood Education Program. The major areas of study included child development and curriculum planning. Another major component of the program was four field placements, which allowed me to work with different age groups.

Have you completed any further study to enhance your professional development?

▶ In the Hamilton area, I attended workshops that dealt with every-day situations, such as behaviour management strategies for children and new curriculum ideas for the classroom. I went on to attend workshops on conflict resolution, recruitment of staff, running effective meetings, and presenting workshops to adults.

▶ I also attend night school and have enrolled in Human Resources courses, including employment law, recruitment and retention of staff, and organizational behaviour. These courses have helped me better understand my administrative responsibilities.

*Please describe your **career pathway**.*

▶ My first full time position as an Early Childhood educator was with Child's Play. My role was to plan a curriculum for the children and to offer a safe and nurturing environment. After leaving Child's Play, I was a supply teacher at various children's centres, including McMaster Children's Centre, Waterdown District Children's Centre, and Chedoke Children's Centre.

▶ I was hired by Today's Family as a school age teacher at the Dundas location. Here my role was to offer a program to children before and after school. At the end of the school year, I worked in the camp program for children between the ages of six and 12. Then I returned to my job as school age teacher, but I was given other opportunities in the classroom, as well as supervising a program giving non-custodial parents a chance to visit with their children. In 1997, I was part of a pilot project that took our camp off site on a daily basis and became the program's supervisor. In September 1997, I transferred to Today's Family's new children's centre in Saltfleet High School. In the next few years my role developed, first as assistant supervisor in Dundas and Hamilton, then in our accounting department.

All these experiences led me to my current role as supervisor at Today's Family in Hamilton.

Did you switch jobs along the way? If so, why?

▶ When I took my first job, I was looking to gain experience. Once I had some experience, I wanted to find a place where I would be proud to work. I wanted to find an organization that would allow me to grow within the profession and that would compensate me adequately. I did change jobs within the field so that I could find out what was out there. Once I joined Today's Family, each change within the organization was a new challenge and gave me a chance to grow.

*Please describe your **current position**.*

▶ I am currently a supervisor at Today's Family—Caring For Your Child at our Burlington location, in CH Norton Elementary School. The program offers child care to children from two-and-a-half to 12 years. We have 32 children enrolled on a daily basis and an additional 60 children in our after-school program. I am also responsible for a staff of eight teachers. My responsibilities include communicating with parents on a daily basis, mentoring and motivating staff, and a number of administrative duties.

*What are the **rewards** of your current position?*

▶ Flexible work schedule—I can often start earlier or later depending on my schedule for the day.
▶ Motivating Staff—I have worked with many people who have given me a lot of their knowledge. I would like to do the same for those that I work with.
▶ Professional Development—I always have the opportunity to go to workshops related to my profession.
▶ Community involvement—As a supervisor I have the opportunity to be involved with a great many people from within the community.
▶ A final reward is the ability to have a direct influence on the centre's progress.

*What are the **challenges** of your current position?*

▶ The biggest challenge I have is finding supply staff. Most people want a full-time position. I often explain that if they take on supply work and excel at it, they will get the long-term position they are looking for.
▶ Another challenge is time management. It is important to schedule the day and yet be flexible enough to deal with any concerns from parents and staff at the same time.

Looking back over your education and career pathways, as a young person in high school did you ever believe you would follow the pathways you have?

▶ My plan was very simple. I would attend university and obtain my degree, then apply to teacher's college. Once I graduated, however, I felt I did not have the experience or the grades to attend teacher's college and, thus, had to change what I wanted to do.

Do you have any comments for young people who might be considering their own educational/career pathway?

▶ It is very difficult to know today what you want to do with the rest of your life. Set goals for yourself so you know what and where you want to be. Be open to new ideas and experiences. If you find that you do not like the direction you have taken, you can always re-evaluate your goals and decide where you want to go to next. Always leave yourself with as many options as possible until you figure out what it is you want to do. Any experience you gain will come in handy, wherever you end up.

What other careers are related to your career?

▶ Resource Teacher—Work with special needs children
▶ Support Facilitator—Work one-on-one with special needs children
▶ Home Child Care—Take children into your own home
▶ Summer Camp Leader
▶ School Age Teacher
▶ Respite Care Worker
▶ College Professor
▶ Placement Supervisor—Observe students on placements
▶ Professional Development Facilitator—Present workshops

Early Childhood Education

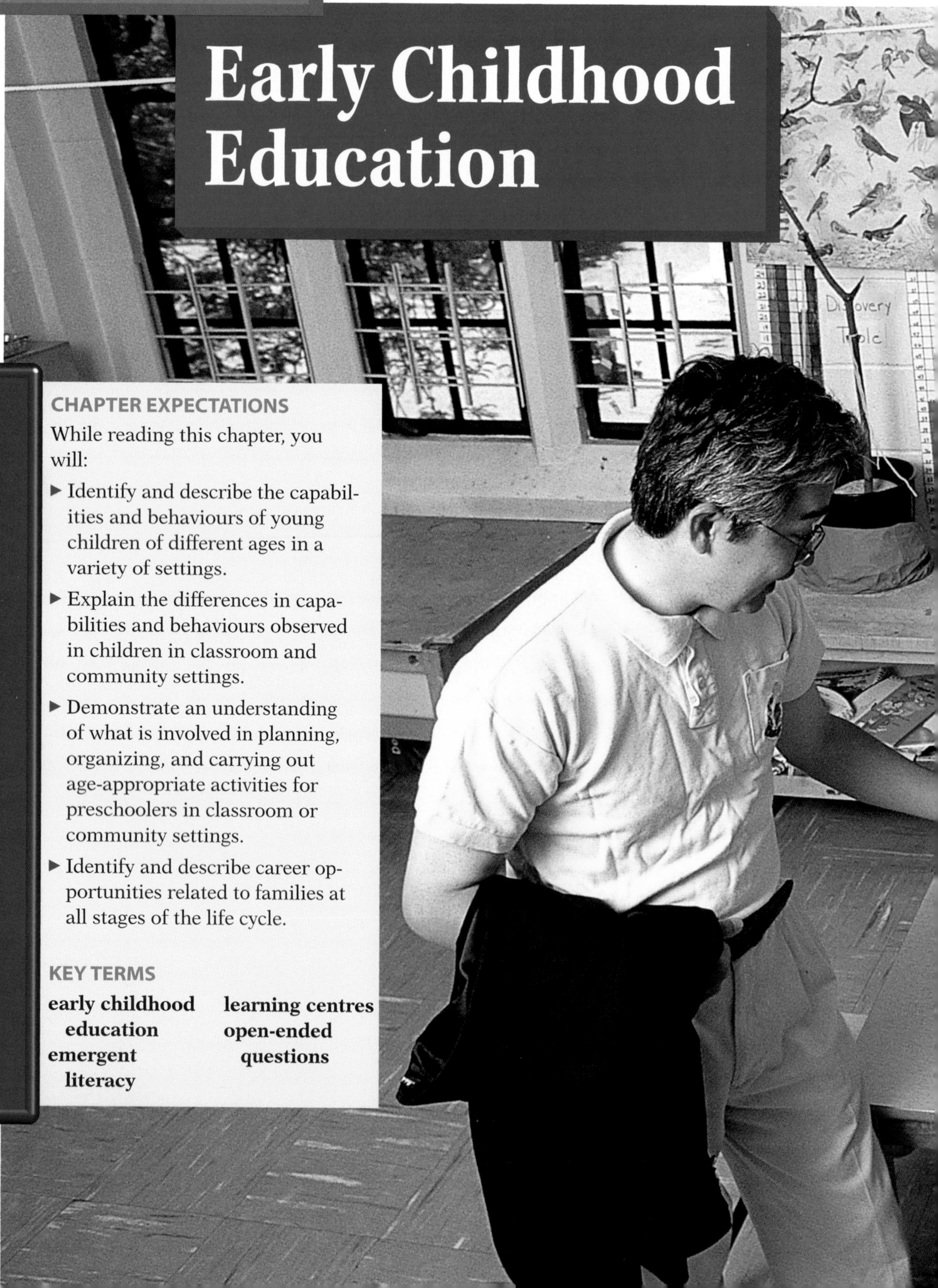

CHAPTER EXPECTATIONS

While reading this chapter, you will:

▶ Identify and describe the capabilities and behaviours of young children of different ages in a variety of settings.

▶ Explain the differences in capabilities and behaviours observed in children in classroom and community settings.

▶ Demonstrate an understanding of what is involved in planning, organizing, and carrying out age-appropriate activities for preschoolers in classroom or community settings.

▶ Identify and describe career opportunities related to families at all stages of the life cycle.

KEY TERMS

early childhood education

emergent literacy

learning centres

open-ended questions

Ken hurried through the doors and down the hall to the early childhood classroom. There his daughter Kumi and her teacher were organizing shelves in the library centre. "I'm sorry I'm late," he said. "Thanks for waiting with Kumi."

"Thank you for letting us know," Miss LeBlanc replied with a smile. "We had a good time together, didn't we, Kumi? Tell your father what we saw on our walk."

"Geese!" exclaimed Kumi. "They were wa-a-ay up in the sky. And I could hear them." Kumi spread her arms and flapped them like wings.

"Really?" Ken knelt to face his daughter. "We'll have to look for more on the way home. Could you count how many there were?"

Kumi shook her head, sounding regretful. "They went fast."

"What else did we see?" Miss LeBlanc prompted.

"Mr. Andrews was fixing a light in the parking lot," Kumi said.

"That's pretty high up, too, isn't it?" Ken remarked.

"Uh-huh," Kumi explained seriously, "Mr. Andrews was up in the sky, too, but he didn't need any wings."

———————◆———————

What do you think? How did Miss LeBlanc use the delay to promote Kumi's development?

In Chapter 19 the latest thinking about brain development was emphasized.

◆ **What implications might that information have on the need for early childhood education?**

What Is Early Childhood Education?

Early childhood education programs promote development with formal teaching and learning experiences for young children. Planned activities help children explore basic concepts in language, math, science, and social studies. Children are supervised as they learn self-help and hygiene skills. Children practise the thinking and social skills they will need to succeed in grade school and in daily living.

For some children, early childhood education gives them experiences they could not get at home. Early childhood education has proven especially valuable for children of lower-income families, whose parents cannot provide all the enriching experiences needed. For them, these programs can be critical for success. The early years are a key part of future learning.

Early childhood education is incorporated in many types of programs. Sometimes you will hear the programs called preschools or day cares. The programs may be either for-profit or nonprofit. Programs are staffed by qualified teachers and possibly teacher aides and parents.

Early childhood education is also part of many child-care programs. A separate early childhood education program, however, may not replace the need for child-care. Some early childhood education progams run on limited schedules. They may last only during the school year or for a few weeks during school vacation. Parents who need child care at other times must arrange for that care too.

Types of Early Childhood Education

"**I**f I wanted to," commented the parent of a month-old infant, "I could enroll my son in some sort of class from now until grade school. Do children really need all of this?"

Of course, children need to be continuously involved in learning, either at home or in organized groups. Families often look for programs that will help them supplement what they are able to do at home. Some families need more than others. Parents must decide which of the programs available are right for them.

INFANT-PARENT CLASSES

Infant-parent classes educate parents on interacting with their baby. They let parents share experiences and ideas. Some classes focus on a single activity, such as exercise. Others resemble parenting classes, teaching infant care, nutrition, and budgeting.

The Y, Early Years Centres, and Health Units often sponsor infant-parent classes, as do recreation centres, religious organizations, and schools.

PRESCHOOLS AND DAY CARES

Preschools and day cares offer learning experiences before the start of formal education. Children are two to four or five years old. Program hours vary considerably.

Parent Co-operatives

Forming a co-operative gives parents unique responsibilities. They actually become part-owners and administrators. They hire teachers, choose the curriculum, and set program goals. They also become part of the staff, since each parent volunteers several hours a month at the school. A parent might assist teachers, clean classrooms, repair equipment, or do clerical work. Some sit on fund-raising or storybook review committees.

Parenting Q & A

Starting School

Q "My friend is sending her two-year-old to day care next year. Should I send my son, too, or would it be better to wait?" *Anne-Marie*

A The answer to your question could go either way. Remember that even without the special training of a preschool teacher, you can make home life stimulating for your child. Your son learns as much by matching socks at home as by matching playing cards at day care. Shopping for groceries with you can be more of a learning experience than playing "supermarket" with other children. Parents and researchers alike are rethinking the argument that "quality time" makes up for a lack of time with your child. Spending time with a parent may be more important to proper development than many people have thought. On the other hand, for employed parents and those who want to extend a nurturing home life and social experiences, preschool can be a wise choice.

Parents who join co-operatives like being involved in how the school is run. They can discuss education and child development and work with teachers to educate children as they believe is best. They can also spend more time with their child.

Parent co-operatives may be organized by parents or sponsored by community or religious groups. Tuition is usually lower than at other private preschools because parents do much of the work.

Early Years Centres

Ontario makes a special effort to give parents information and guidance on the first six years so vital in preparing children for later learning and development. More than 100 Early Years Centres in the province offer a variety of free services and programs to parents of children up to the age of six. The centres are also open to caregivers of young children. Program topics include pregnancy and parenting, early learning and literacy, and early child development. Early Years Centres also provide

Raising Children With Character

Pitching In

"What a nice surprise!" Malcolm took off his work gloves to hug his wife Lisa and son Nick. He was cleaning up the grounds of Nick's preschool with other parents in the co-operative.

"We were coming back from the store," Lisa said. "I thought we should see how you were doing."

Nick recoiled and wrinkled his nose. "You're all dirty, Daddy."

Malcolm grinned. "Yes, I am. I'm raking all the leaves and sticks that blew under these bushes all winter. That will keep mice and bugs from building nests here, so they won't bother you while you play."

Nick was unimpressed. "That doesn't look like much fun."

Malcolm shrugged. "It needs to be done. And you can help." He hoisted Nick atop one full bag. Holding him at the waist, he instructed, "Now stomp down on those leaves so I can fit in some more. That's right, mash them down. Pack them in! Good job!" He swung his giggling son down to the ground. "Now you can tell everyone how you helped clean up your school."

◆◆◆◆◆ **Thinking It Over** ◆◆◆◆◆

1. Why do you think Lisa wanted Nick to see the parents working?
2. What did Nick seem to think about his father's efforts? What did Malcolm stress about the job?
3. How might this experience shape Nick's view of volunteer work?

information about community programs, health and social services, and other resources to help parents.

At Early Years Centres, parents can meet professionals and volunteers who can advise about childhood development and related matters. These staff, trained by Ontario's Ministry of Children and Youth Services, can also refer parents and caregivers to other useful sources of information.

Ontario also provides all new parents a Newborn Literacy Kit, consisting of materials designed to engage parents in reading to their children from the very beginning. Usually provided by a Healthy Babies Healthy Children nurse, they are sometimes obtainable from an Early Years Centre.

Junior Kindergarten

Provinces have differing requirements for when children should start kindergarten. Ontario emphasizes early learning by providing funds to school boards that wish to offer early learning programs such as Junior Kindergarten. This is a half-day program for four-year-olds, intended to promote children's learning and

Internet Connects

http://www.mcgrawhill.ca/links/parenting
To find out where Early Years Centres are located near you, go to the Web site above for *Parenting Rewards & Responsibilities, First Canadian Edition,* to see where to go next.

A child who falls behind in learning early in life may never catch up with other youngsters. In fact, the child may get further behind every year. Early Years' programs aim to improve early learning experiences for all children.

development and to give children a successful start in school.

Laboratory Schools

Like laboratory child-care centres, these schools are affiliated with high schools, colleges, and universities. They are staffed by child development students and their instructors. Because a lab school's purpose is to train teachers of the future and to test new child development theories, children have the advantage of advanced thought.

Laboratory schools are open to the children of student-parents, school employees, and the general community. Thus, different teaching methods can be tried with a variety of children.

Montessori Schools

Montessori schools carry on the teaching methods of Maria Montessori, the influential Italian educator. In a sensory-rich environment, children compare textures of cloth swatches, explore sounds with musical instruments, and distinguish odours in smelling jars. Students are given housekeeping tasks, including sweeping classroom floors and tending plants. They develop the motor skills and the sense of competence needed to explore their world.

These schools are noted for educational materials, designed by Montessori herself, and for the less involved role of the teacher. The instructor determines which materials best help a particular child learn a certain concept. After demonstrating how to use the materials, the teacher lets the student work independently. Materials are **self-correcting**. They give immediate feedback to tell children whether they have performed the task correctly. Children work at their own pace, moving on to more complex tasks.

The Preschool Program

Ask a child, "What do you do in preschool?" and you might hear what sounds like a day's worth of activity: singing, feeding pets, listening to stories, and playing outdoors. Preschool activities are short and varied, to accommodate a young child's limited attention span and need for balanced development. Play is supervised, but direction is minimal to encourage creativity.

Preschool classrooms are divided into **learning centres**, areas clearly defined and equipped for specific activities. However, preschoolers tend to think of their day as things they do, rather than things they learn. Preschool lets them do things to learn skills in different areas, including:

♥ *Literacy.* Literacy means speaking, reading, writing, and understanding or comprehending language. Preschoolers learn language as they speak and listen to stories, songs, and rhymes. To encourage children to express themselves verbally, teachers ask **open-ended questions**, which require more than a yes or no answer. In the language arts centre are paper, pencils, and envelopes for "writing" letters. Books on tape let a child "read" along with a favourite story.

♥ *Science.* Science activities are chosen to stimulate a child's curiosity and to point out the wonders of nature. In the science centre children can handle different types of seeds, shells, and rocks. They watch plants grow and care for a classroom pet.

Cross-Curricular History CONNECTIONS

Maria Montessori

As a teen in 1880s Italy, Maria Montessori studied engineering at a boys' technical school. She became Italy's first female physician. While working with children in a psychiatric centre, she came to believe that many so-called mentally delayed children could be better helped through education than by medicine. Many of the children under her guidance scored as well as average children on national exams. Montessori opened her first preschool in Rome in 1906 for children of poor working parents. Montessori believed that a truly appropriate education included spiritual as well as intellectual growth, and could ultimately transform society. How do researchers compare public schools to Montessori schools?

♥ **Math.** Playing in the math centre strengthens thinking or numeracy skills. A game of shape bingo teaches children to recognize similarities and differences. Putting together a puzzle takes logic and problem solving. Teachers also point out simple math concepts in daily routines. Getting dressed, for example, includes putting on one left shoe and one right shoe, for a total of two shoes.

♥ **Physical growth.** Preschoolers delight in practising new physical skills. Programs include time and equipment to develop muscle strength and co-ordination in a safe, supervised environment.

♥ **Social skills.** In a group setting, away from home and family, children learn to share, take turns, and get along with others. Teachers guide them in resolving conflicts.

♥ **Self-care.** Children practise independent tasks, including dressing, eating, and going to the washroom. They learn the importance of hand washing and personal safety.

Health & Safety

CONTAGIOUS INFECTIONS

Good hygiene is stressed in preschool and kindergarten. Caregivers help children remember to wash their hands after going to the washroom. Otherwise, children who rub their eyes and noses, then share toys, may spread contagious infections. The most serious of these are prevented by immunization. However, other communicable conditions, less threatening but very uncomfortable, lurk in group settings. These include:

▶ **Pink eye.** This inflammation of the eye is caused by a virus or bacterium. The infected eye itches, burns, tears, and turns red. A light discharge of pus may form a crust overnight. Fortunately, pink eye is easily cured. A doctor-prescribed antibiotic usually clears up the condition in a few days. Until then, parents and child can contain the disease by washing their hands after touching the eye and by using separate washcloths.

▶ **Impetigo.** This common skin infection usually appears around the mouth but can be spread to any part of the body. The tiny red spots quickly develop into small blisters that break. The moist skin beneath is soon covered with a large brown crust. Home treatment includes gentle cleaning, twice daily, with soap and water. As with pink eye, the infected child should use a separate towel and washcloth. A physician usually prescribes an antibiotic and an ointment, which clear up the condition in about ten days.

▶ **Head lice.** Lice are actually insects that live in hair and feed on blood. Their bite causes itching and scratching. The nits (eggs) resemble dandruff but cling stubbornly to hair. Red pimples may develop, which carry the slight chance of infection if broken. Lice travel rapidly in group settings, especially where clothing (such as dress-up clothes) and personal items are shared. Infested items must be destroyed. Several applications of a prescribed, medicated shampoo or lotion are needed to kill both nits and lice.

SENIOR KINDERGARTEN

Traditional kindergartens meet for half a day. In some rural areas, children attend all day every other day. A recent trend has been toward all-day sessions. This is partly in response to a larger number of working parents. It also reflects a growing concern of parents and educators that children need to be ready to learn when they start first grade. Kindergarten primes their thinking skills.

The Kindergarten Program

Kindergartners continue refining the same skills begun in preschool. They have more choice about which learning centre to play in, and whether to play with others or alone. A teacher may guide a child toward certain activities for more balanced development. Longer and more demanding activities reflect children's growing skills in:

♥ *Literacy.* Teachers encourage **emergent literacy**, the gradual process of learning to read and write. They write children's names on charts, artwork, and belongings. They relate the words to the pictures in storybooks. Art activities that use different shapes and sizes help children use these qualities to distinguish letters of the alphabet.

♥ *Science.* Kindergarten science emphasizes processes and cause-and-effect. A teacher might lead a class in baking muffins, showing them the effects of mixing ingredients and subjecting them to heat. Tending plants, children see how water, soil, and sunlight produce flowers and vegetables.

♥ *Math.* Five-year-olds begin to absorb a basic knowledge of how numbers work. Such activities as passing out snacks (one cracker for one student) and measuring objects with building blocks reinforce counting skills and math concepts.

♥ *Physical growth.* A child's improved balance and eye-hand coordination are tested in games of hopscotch and bean bag toss. Children enjoy simple, cooperative team games.

Senior kindergarten children are typically five years old.

♥ *Personal responsibility.* The idea of self-care is applied to more difficult situations. Kindergartners learn how and when to use the 911 emergency service. They take part in fire drills. With increased awareness of child abuse, some programs now stress personal protection, even in kindergarten. Children are urged to report anyone who tries to hurt them, or touch or pressure them into acts that violate this privacy.

♥ *Community awareness.* Field trips and special visitors teach kindergartners about communities and the people who live and work there. The seeds of social responsibility are planted. Community awareness also aids personal safety. To a lost child, knowing the area and recognizing a police officer or postal worker are valuable skills.

♥ *Self-understanding.* By age five, children realize they are separate and different from each other. Kindergarten programs strive to channel that awareness into appreciation for personal and cultural differences.

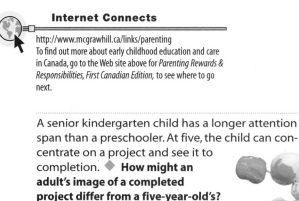

Internet Connects

http://www.mcgrawhill.ca/links/parenting
To find out more about early childhood education and care in Canada, go to the Web site above for *Parenting Rewards & Responsibilities, First Canadian Edition,* to see where to go next.

A senior kindergarten child has a longer attention span than a preschooler. At five, the child can concentrate on a project and see it to completion. ◆ **How might an adult's image of a completed project differ from a five-year-old's?**

Enrichment Activities

Denise cheered as her five-year-old son Tyler swatted the whiffle ball off the tee and scampered toward first base. "Way to go, Ty! Good job!" To herself she added: so it took him three tries to get a hit; he's an all-star in my book.

Denise was glad the recreation centre had organized the T-ball league last year. Tyler had been spending afternoons at the home of a friend, whose grandmother watched them both. Denise worried, though, about Tyler having productive activities to fill his time. In T-ball, he learned the pride of succeeding personally while contributing to a team effort. He felt the joy of physical play.

A child doesn't need talent to explore an activity. With art, for example, young children aren't likely to judge the work. They are simply proud to have created something on their own, and they learn and grow in the process.

Like Tyler, many children benefit from organized enrichment activities. In most communities, children can pursue interests like these:

♥ **Swimming.** Swimming is good physical exercise that doesn't overstress immature bones and joints. Swimming ability can also be a lifesaver. Recreation departments, the Red Cross, and the Y are reliable sources for safe swimming lessons given by trained instructors.

♥ **Sports.** Many parents have reservations about preschoolers and elementary school children playing competitive sports. When sportsmanship and learning skills are stressed over winning, however, organized sports can foster emotional, social, and physical growth in young children. Rules and equipment are often modified for safety and success. Businesses, churches, and schools may sponsor teams in a sports league.

♥ **The arts.** Many young children enjoy both the physical and creative experiences of dance and gymnastics, painting, sculpting, and playing music. Those who show particular interest can take part in activities. Music appreciation can begin early. Young dancers are encouraged to participate as their physical ability allows.

The Parent's Role

Children get more from a learning experience when parents take an active part. A quality early education program welcomes a parent's participation. Some rely on it.

GIVING SUPPORT

Suppose you got a perfect score on a school project you'd laboured over for months. Proudly you announced the news to your family. "That's nice," they said, then went back to what they were doing. What would that do to your sense of accomplishment?

Children feel the same way. They need the support of adults, and especially parents, to feel worthwhile about their achievements.

Listening is a simple but sincere way to show support. Children are usually eager to share their school experiences. All they need is a parent's interested ear. A child's memory and perception may be sketchy, however, making early attempts at "reporting" hard to follow. A spirited "Then what happened?" encourages children. With practice and maturity, they become skilled storytellers. Also, a detail to you can be a major event to a child. The ride on the school bus can be as memorable as the field trip. Let the child decide what's important.

A more reluctant child may need to be coaxed with open-ended questions that draw out details. For example, what might you ask a child whose teacher had carved a pumpkin in class that day?

Giving support also means sharing special occasions. Taking time for a Little League game or school play shows that a child's interests and achievements matter. A parent's approval enhances a proud moment. A parent's consolation softens a disappointing one.

Parents must avoid crossing the line from support to pressure, however. As one soccer coach noted, "The kids just want to have fun, run, and kick the ball. The parents sometimes forget that. They try to coach the kids, pointing out their mistakes. Then the game isn't a game anymore. It's work." How do you think such expectations affect a child's self-esteem?

Getting Involved

Sometimes parents are asked to show support by giving their time and talent—as playground supervisors, children's museum guides, and in other ways. Their volunteer labour also makes the program available to more families by helping keep costs down. Parental involvement also reassures parents that the program is safe and appropriate.

Parents have busy schedules, but having children means making time for them. Children love it when a parent visits or helps at preschool. Visits also allow the parent to see the program and child in action.

Special projects may need a parent's special skill, as when the Young Writers Club "published" a book of their poems. One parent laid out the pages on his computer. Another printed the book in her print shop. All the parents bought a copy to make the project a success.

Some programs allow parental involvement at a more basic level. Sandeep and several other parents are non-voting members of the Early Bird Preschool's board of directors. They listen to the board discuss school business and policy and offer their point of view. The board wants to hear parents' opinions, although it is not bound by them, because board members know they and the parents must work together.

Staying involved is easier when parents stay current, and vice versa. At parent-teacher conferences, parents are brought up to date on their child's progress. At parent workshops, teachers show parents what materials their children use and how children learn by using them. Some programs have a parents' room, featuring a lending library of helpful publications, where parent support groups may meet.

PREVENTING OVERSCHEDULING

You probably have a fair idea of what you'll be doing at any given time this week. On Wednesday at 10:00 a.m., you might be in history class. Next Thursday at 5:30 p.m., you might be at work. As a young adult, you need and appreciate this detailed schedule.

Children, in contrast, need large amounts of unstructured time. To them, trailing ants through the grass or sculpting fantastic structures in a sand box can be time well spent.

Sometimes Josh would just rather be a pirate than do anything else. All children need time for their own pursuits. They learn to manage their time, entertain themselves, and be creative.
◆ **How else might the child and family benefit?**

Pushing too many activities on a child can teach a habit of overcommitment. Eager to please a parent, a child may feel pressured to succeed at everything. The stress that results can cause headaches or stomach aches, irritability, or fatigue. If these signs appear, a parent might look at the child's schedule and ask, "Does my child really enjoy these activities, or are they done to please me? Do I show my child unconditional love?"

EASING TRANSITIONS

In their lives as students, children make several transitions between schools: from preschool to kindergarten, on to grade school, and finally to high school. Stressing to a young child that change means opportunity can set a positive pattern for the future.

Parents can begin to help children make a transition several months before the event. Complimenting children on how they've grown—"You can read all your books by yourself. I think you're ready for kindergarten"—raises their confidence. In contrast, warning "You'll have to read better than that in first grade" only causes useless worry.

Most programs have visiting or exploration days for incoming classes. Parents and children can tour the facility and meet the instructors. Parents and teachers can compare goals and expectations for the upcoming year.

FINDING TEACHABLE MOMENTS

When children enroll in an early education program, some parents bow out of the learning process and let "the professionals" take over. Remember, though, that all of life, and especially early childhood, is a learning experience.

Teachable moments, those unexpected opportunities for discovery that arise from daily life, are always around. A spider spinning its web and farmers selling produce at a roadside market both offer teachable moments. When parents share in the learning—by finding a book on spiders or asking a farmer about an unusual vegetable—they teach yet another lesson. They teach children that learning can last a lifetime.

Internet Connects

http://www.mcgrawhill.ca/links/parenting
To find out more about issues relating to children and youth, go to the Web site above for *Parenting Rewards & Responsibilities, First Canadian Edition,* to see where to go next.

Early childhood education is so important, but it can't take the place of parents. The learning experiences shared with a parent are critical in getting a child off to a good start in life.

CHAPTER 30

Review

Looking Back

♥ Early childhood education is part of many programs designed for young children.

♥ Preschools and day cares offer learning experiences for two- to five-year-olds.

♥ Some preschools are aimed at children who are at risk of academic failure. Montessori preschools follow the principles of Maria Montessori.

♥ Preschool activities expose children to words, numbers, and the natural world. They promote social skills and self-care.

♥ Kindergarten programs introduce children to basic concepts in literacy, math, and science. They encourage greater awareness of self and community.

♥ Enrichment activities let children pursue other interests, including sports and the arts.

♥ Parents help children benefit from activities by showing support and getting involved.

♥ Parents should continue to take an active part in their child's learning.

Knowledge and Understanding

1. What is the value of early childhood education?
2. Describe an Early Years program.
3. How do preschool and kindergarten programs promote literacy?
4. How are preschoolers taught to take care of themselves?
5. What concerns would you answer before allowing a young school-age child to play on a sports team?
6. Explain whether this statement is true or false: A parent's role in education ends when a child enters an early education program.

Review

Thinking and Inquiry

7. Your four-year-old is misbehaving. Your spouse tells the child, "If you keep that up, they won't take you in kindergarten." Is this an effective way to handle the situation? What would you have said or done instead?

8. Junior kindergarten attendance is not mandatory in some provinces. Do you think it should be? Why or why not?

9. Your kindergartner's latest art project is cutting and gluing a variety of colourful shapes into different patterns. How is this activity helpful?

10. Give tips for supporting a child's early education activities.

11. In addition to attending morning kindergarten, your six-year-old son enjoys karate class and singing in the children's choir at your church. Now he asks to take a computer course. You're pleased that he has many interests. You worry, however, that between attending classes and practising, he doesn't have enough free time for spur-of-the-moment activities. What would you do?

Communication

12. Recall your own experience in preschool or kindergarten. Describe how it shaped your attitude toward learning and education. What was most helpful or positive? How do you wish those experiences had been different?

13. Write a story based on the following beginning: "After only a week of junior kindergarten, four-year-old Patrick didn't want to go anymore. As Cindy led him to the door, he pulled back firmly on her hand and frowned. He was near tears."

14. As a class or in small groups, debate the following statement: "Children should not take part in enrichment activities until they are at least school-age."

Application

15. Imagine you are the parent of five-year-old Geneva. She is an inquisitive child who conducts her own experiments, such as trying to dissolve different substances in water. She likes to play with other children, though she sometimes seems bored with their games. Would you enroll her in an early education program, and, if so, which type? Give reasons for your decision.

16. With a partner, plan a literacy, science, or math activity for a kindergartner. Include the materials and procedure you would use and explain how the activity is appropriate for a five-year-old.

Bobbie-Jo Gramigna, Supervisor of a Children's Centre

What volunteer activities did you do as a teenager that led you to choose a career that involved working with children/people?

▶ In high school I participated in two co-op placements. My first was with a Grade 1 class at a local public school. My second placement was at a full-day child-care centre.

*Please describe your **specific education pathway**.*

▶ I received a diploma in Early Childhood Education after completing a two-year program at Mohawk College in Hamilton, Ontario. The major areas of study included Child Development; Parent, Teacher, and Child Relations; and Curriculum and Program Planning.

Have you completed any further study to enhance your professional development?

▶ I believe in life-long learning and attend and facilitate professional development in the community.

*Please describe your **career pathway**.*

▶ In college I received a student contract to work summers at the Kiwanis Preschool, where I had completed my co-op placement. After receiving my diploma, I was hired full time at Kiwanis as an Early Childhood educator.

▶ I later accepted a full-time ECE position with the Hamilton Public Library Workplace Child-Care Centre, where I gained experience as a program leader and assistant supervisor. I became a member of the Association of Early Childhood Education, Ontario (AECEO), and completed the certification process a year later. I served as an executive member of the AECEO for four years, facilitated a Toddler Network group for fellow ECEs, and was among the first ECEs to explore the Reggio Emilia Approach in Hamilton.

▶ I was the project co-ordinator for the Artists at the Centre project while on maternity leave, then worked as supervisor for a child-care centre with the YMCA. Next, I accepted a position with the Umbrella Family and Child Centres of Hamilton, where I am currently the supervisor at Umbrella Family's Templemead Children's Centre.

Did you switch jobs along the way? If so, why?

▶ Throughout my career, I have pursued new skills and experiences. These, in turn, have brought new opportunities. For example, being a member of the AECEO provided me with opportunities to network with colleagues in the same field. These networking opportunities included meetings where educators could discuss schools in Reggio Emilia. The result was a project called "Artists at the Centre," which led to three exhibits of the children's work and growing interest from colleagues. This, in turn, led to my participation in the 2004 Study Tour of the schools of Reggio Emilia.

*Please describe your **current position***

▶ Currently, I am the Supervisor with the Umbrella Family and Child Centres of Hamilton at Templemead Children's Centre. Templemead is a non-profit centre licensed for 76 children ages two-and-a-half to 12 years of age. I oversee a team of seven teachers, as well as the day-to-day operation of the centre.

*What are the **rewards** of your current position?*

▶ I find my position very rewarding! I believe that the child's early years are an extremely important time of development. Whether I am enrolling a child in our program, providing resources to a parent, or mentoring for a team member, every day the work I do affects all the families and educators in my workplace.

*What are the **challenges** of your current position?*

▶ Being responsible for so many things and to so many people can have its challenges! It can be difficult to meet everyone's needs when you are being pulled in different directions. The ability to prioritize, multi-task, and laugh at situations beyond my control are skills that I consistently rely on.

Looking back over your education and career pathways, as a young person in high school did you ever believe you would follow the pathways you have?

▶ In high school my outlook was more short term. But even then it was my goal to be an ECE for a full-day child-care program. I wanted to be a supervisor one day and felt confident that I would. I knew what I needed to do to become an ECE and put my energy into becoming that. Once I had my ECE, I knew that I wanted to become certified and, again, focused my energies. Setting goals and working toward them is a quality that has remained with me from high school.

Do you have any comments for young people who might be considering their own educational/career pathway?

▶ Ask yourself, "What do I enjoy doing?" Then ask yourself, "Can I have a career doing what I enjoy doing?" I have always enjoyed interacting with children and been interested in the way children think. I enjoyed working with children when I was in Grade 11 and continue to enjoy my work 18 years later!

What other careers are related to your career?

▶ Resource Teacher
▶ College Faculty (field related)
▶ Support Facilitator
▶ Program Co-ordinator
▶ Resource Lending Library
▶ ECE Professional Development

Glossary

A

abstinence (AB-stuh-nuns). Refraining from sexual intercourse. (5)

accommodation. When one or more family members adjust or adapt so a problem can be resolved. (29)

active listening. Giving full attention to what the speaker is saying, and listening to the feelings behind the words. (23)

active play. Play activities that are primarily physical. (24)

adoptive family. A family that includes children who have become a permanent part of the family through legal processes. (4)

adoptive parents. Adults who legally acquire the rights and responsibilities of parenthood for a child who is not biologically their own. (6)

aggression. An act marked by an attack on someone or something. (27)

alcoholism. The physical and psychological dependence on alcohol. (28)

allergen. A substance that triggers an allergic reaction, which is an overreaction in the body that produces such symptoms as sneezing, hives, or a congested nose. (26)

ambidextrous (am-beh-DEK-struhs). Ability to use both hands equally well. (15)

amniocentesis (am-nee-oh-sen-TEE-sis). A technique that enables doctors to check for fetal abnormalities that might cause birth defects. (8)

amniotic sac (am-nee-OTT-ik). The fluid-filled sac that encloses the embryo and fetus. (8)

anemia. A low blood count, or too few red blood cells. (8)

anesthetic (an-ehs-THET-ik). A medication used to eliminate pain. (11)

assertive. To express oneself firmly and positively. (27)

attachment behaviour. When an infant becomes excited when caregivers appear and shows distress when they leave. (13)

Attention Deficit Disorder (ADD). A condition in which children have trouble focusing their mind or body on a single task and are easily distracted. (26)

au pair (oh PARE). A young person from another country who lives with a family and takes care of the children. (20)

authoritarian. Parenting style in which parents are strong leaders who make most decisions concerning children and expect children to accept their judgment. (3)

authoritative. Parenting style characterized by warmth, support, acceptance, and indirect positive control and guidance of children's behaviour. (3)

autism. A severe disorder characterized by lack of communication, extreme concern with oneself, and detachment from reality. (26)

autonomy. Independence. (17)

B

backbone. Parenting style identified by Barbara Coloroso as a positive, constructive, and supportive approach that encourages children to develop fully. (3)

bilingual. Being able to speak two languages. (19)

biological parents. Two people who conceive a child; also called birth parents. (7)

birthing room. Specially designed labour and delivery room located in a hospital, or an alternative birth centre with many of the comforts of home. (10)

blended family. Consists of two parents, one or both of whom have children from a previous relationship. (4)

bonding. The creation of a loving link between a parent and child. (11)

breech delivery. When a baby is born with the feet or buttocks appearing first. (11)

brick wall. Parenting style identified by Barbara Coloroso as a rigid, competitive, and highly controlled approach that tends to make children easily manipulated. (3)

bullying. Physical violence, name-calling, teasing, sexual harassment, or other intentional intimidation of another person. (25)

C

Canada's Food Guide to Healthy Eating. Tells how many servings a person should eat from each of the four main food groups. (9)

cardiopulmonary resuscitation (CPR). A technique for reviving a person or keeping that person alive by blowing air into the victim's lungs and applying pressure to the victim's chest until an emergency team can take over. (16)

caregiver. Someone whose role is to love, care for, and guide a child. (2)

centration. The ability to focus on one quality at a time. (19)

caesarean section (si-ZAIR-ee-uhn). An operation to deliver the baby through an opening cut in the mother's abdominal wall and uterus. (11)

character. A person's moral qualities. (22)

child abuse. Physical, emotional, or sexual violence against children. (28)

child labour. The employment of children under the age of 18 in exploitative, unsafe, or undignified conditions. (25)

child neglect. Failure to meet a child's physical or emotional needs. (28)

chorionic villus sampling (CVS) (KOR-ee-ahn-ik). The first test for birth defects that may be performed during pregnancy. (8)

chromosomes. Long, threadlike particles in the reproductive cell nucleus. (7)

circumcision (sur-kuhm-SIH-zhun). A procedure in which the foreskin is cut away from the head of the penis. (11)

classification. The result of sorting or arranging items by common qualities or traits. (19)

co-dependency. When someone covers for the abuser with lies and excuses, rearranging their lives and ignoring their own needs to keep peace in the family. (28)

colic. A pain in the abdomen with no definite cause. (14)

colostrum (kuh-LAHS-trum). Fluid present in the breasts after birth and before breast milk becomes available. (11)

communication. Process of sharing information, thoughts, and feelings. (23)

compromise (KAHM-pruh-myz). Reached when each person gives up something in order to come to an agreement that satisfies everyone. (29)

concept. General category of objects and ideas formed by mentally combining their characteristics. (19)

conception. The moment when the male and female reproductive cells unite; also called fertilization. (7)

conscience. (KAHN-shens). An inner sense of what is right. (22)

consensus (Kahn-SEN-suhs). Coming to an agreement after talking things over. (29)

consequences. In child guidance, results of inappropriate behaviour; can be natural or determined by parent. (21)

conservation. When properties of objects remain the same, even though other characteristics may change. (19)

contractions. Rhythmic tightening and relaxing motions of the muscles of the uterus. (11)

conventions. Accepted standards. (22)

convulsion. A series of strong, involuntary contractions of muscles. (16)

co-operative play. Type of play in which children do things together. (18)

cradle cap. An oily, yellowish, patchy, scalp condition. (14)

custody. The legal right and responsibility to make decisions affecting children and to care for them physically. (28)

D

day-care centre. A child-care facility outside the home, supervised by trained staff, providing group care and socializing experiences for children. (20)

decision-making process. A step-by-step system of evaluating information in order to reach a reasonable conclusion. (5)

delivery. The process of birth. (10)

demand feeding. Feeding an infant whenever the child is hungry rather than on a fixed schedule. (14)

depression. Prolonged period of sadness marked by feelings of helplessness and an inability to enjoy life. (12)

diplomacy. (duh-PLOH-muh-see) Using tact and skill when dealing with others. (4)

dovetailing. Combining two tasks to save time. (25)

dramatic play. Imaginative, unrehearsed play in which children pretend to be other people or animals as they take part in make-believe events. (24)

dysfunctional (dis-FUNK-shuh-nul). A family situation in which parents do not fulfill their role as parents, causing problems for themselves and their children. (6)

dyslexia (dis-LEK-see-uh). A learning disability in which the child has trouble making sense of written symbols and associating letters and sounds. Also letters and numbers may appear backwards or jumbled. (26)

E

early childhood education. Programs that promote development with formal teaching and learning experiences for young children. (30)

egocentric. Very self-centered. (17)

embryo. The ball of rapidly multiplying cells that develops during the second stage of prenatal development, which lasts from the end of the second week of pregnancy through the eighth week. (8)

emergent literacy. The gradual process of learning to read or write. (30)

emotional development. The process of learning to recognize and express feelings. (13)

empathy. The ability to understand and share another person's feelings. (17)

encouragement. A message of confidence and faith in another's ability. (23)

enuresis (en-you-REE-sis). Bedwetting or lack of bladder control. (27)

episiotomy (ih-pee-zee-OTT-uh-mee). A small incision made at the back of the woman's vagina to prevent tearing of the vaginal opening during birth. (11)

ethics. A system of moral values and obligations. (22)

exploratory play. Type of play in which children use all five senses to find out how things look, taste, smell, hear, and feel. (24)

extended family. Name for family unit consisting of all the immediate relatives in a family, such as grandparents, aunts, uncles, and cousins. (4)

eye-hand co-ordination. Co-ordinating vision with small motor skills. (15)

F

facilitating play. Helping play happen without controlling it. (24)

family violence. A situation in which a parent physically or mentally abuses a child, or a spouse. (28)

fetal alcohol syndrome (FAS). Serious birth defect possible when a female consumes four or more alcoholic drinks a day during pregnancy. (9)

fetal monitor. A device that records contractions and fetal heartbeat. (11)

fetus (FEE-tus). Name for the unborn child during the third and final stage of prenatal development. (8)

first aid. Emergency treatment given to a person who is injured or ill. (16)

flame retardant. Not easily set on fire and does not burn quickly. (15)

fontanels (fahn-tuh-NELZ). Soft spots between the bone plates at the top, back, and sides of an infant's head. (13)

formula. A commercially prepared mixture of milk or milk substitute, water, and added nutrients. (10)

foster family. A family that includes children who cannot live with their own parents, and who are cared for on a temporary basis. (4)

G

gene. A hereditary unit that determines a particular physical or mental trait. (7)

gestational diabetes (jess-TAY-shun-ull dy-ah-BEET-is). A type of diabetes that affects about three percent of expectant women and usually disappears shortly after the pregnancy. (9)

goal. A conscious aim that requires planning and effort to reach. (3)

grieving. The experience of great sorrow, a normal reaction to loss. (28)

growth spurt. A period of accelerated development, often when parts of the body grow at different rates. (15)

H

heredity. The transfer of traits from parent to child. (7)

I

"I message". A message that explains a person's point of view without attacking in order to preserve feelings and get appropriate reactions. (23)

immunizations (i-myuh-nuh-ZAY-shuns). Vaccines given in shots or taken by mouth to protect children from childhood diseases. (14)

inclusion. The process of educating children with a disability in classrooms with children who are not disabled; also called integration or mainstreaming. (26)

industry. State of being productive and making contributions. (17)

infertility. The inability to conceive a child. (7)

initiative. The readiness and ability to start something on one's own. (17)

intellectual development. The process of learning to think, remember, understand, reason, and use language. (13)

intelligence. The ability to acquire and use knowledge. (19)

J-K

jellyfish. Parenting style identified by Barbara Coloroso as an emotional, inconsistent, and unstructured approach that tends to make children easily led. (3)

joint custody. Sharing parental rights and responsibilities. (28)

L

labour. Contractions of the uterine muscles that gradually push the baby out of the mother's body. (10)

large motor skills. Those skills involving the control and use of large muscles, especially those in the arms and legs. (15)

layette (lay-ETT). A collection of baby clothing and equipment usually assembled for a new baby. (10)

learning centres. Areas in classrooms that are clearly defined according to a theme or purpose and equipped for special activities. (30)

learning disability. A difficulty in processing information, especially math or language concepts. (26)

licensing. Approval based on certain standards of quality. (20)

limits. Guidelines and boundaries to which children must adhere. (21)

lochia (LO-kee-a). The normal discharge of blood, tissue, and mucus from the vagina after birth. (12)

low birth weight. Weight of less than 2500 g ($5\frac{1}{2}$ lbs.) at birth. (6)

M

manual dexterity. Skilled use of the hands. (15)

materialism. The belief that money and possessions bring happiness. (25)

meek. Being passive or quiet. (27)

mental challenges. Varying degrees of low intelligence, abnormal ability to learn, and impaired social adaptation. (26)

moral development. Process of learning standards of right and wrong. (22)

motivation. An inner desire to act or behave in a certain way. (23)

motor skills. The use and control of muscles. (13)

N

nanny. A trained professional who cares for a child in the family's home, often with room and board provided. (20)

negativism. A tendency to resist suggestions and commands. (21)

negotiation. The process of discussing an issue to reach a mutual agreement. (29)

neonate (NEE-oh-nate). Name for a newborn baby in the first month of life. (11)

neuron (NYOO-ron). A nerve cell in the brain. (19)

non-verbal communication. Communication that conveys a message without words, using facial expressions, eye contact, posture, and body movements. (23)

nuclear family. Consists of a mother, a father, and one or more biological or adopted children. (4)

nurture. To support and encourage growth and development. (1)

nutrient density. The relationship between the amount and types of nutrients a food has and the number of calories it contains. (9)

O

objective. Viewing without using judgment or interpretation. (2)

object permanence. The existence of something totally out of sight. (13)

obstetrician (OB-stuh-TRISH-un). Doctor who specializes in delivering babies. (8)

open adoption. An adoption situation in which birth and adoptive parents share information about themselves and the child. (6)

open-ended questions. Questions that require more than a yes or no answer. (30)

orthodontist (OR-thuh-DON-tist). A specialist in straightening and realigning teeth. (15)

ovaries (OH-vuh-reez). The female reproductive glands. (7)

P

parallel play. Type of play in which children play side by side. (18)

parental leave. Paid or unpaid time off work given to a parent after the birth or adoption of a child. (10)

parenting. Providing care, support, and love in a way that leads to a child's total development. (1)

parenting readiness. Personal qualities and life circumstances that enable individuals to be successful parents. (5)

parenting style. The particular way that a parent consistently behaves toward children. (3)

paternity. Biological fatherhood. (6)

pediatrician (PEE-dee-uh-TRISH-un). A doctor who treats infants, children, and adolescents. (10)

peer pressure. The strong influence of friends or others of the same age to make someone behave a certain way. (18)

peers. Individuals of similar age or status. (18)

permissive. Parenting style in which parents generally give children all the decision-making responsibility they can handle, offering guidance and protection as needed and relying on natural consequences rather than imposing them. (3)

personality. The sum total of a person's emotional, social, and intellectual characteristics. (3)

physical development. The increasing ability to control and co-ordinate body movements. (13)

physical maturity. Level of physical growth and development. (5)

placenta. Tissue that connects the umbilical cord of an embryo or fetus to the uterine wall. (8)

play. Any activity that individuals choose to do; activity that is fun and self-motivated. (24)

positive guidance. A process of adults directing children toward acceptable behaviour. (21)

positive reinforcement. Action that encourages a particular behaviour, such as rewarding good behaviour with a comment of approval. (21)

postnatal. After childbirth. (12)

postpartum depression. Moodiness, anxiety, depression, or anger sometimes felt by a woman after giving birth. (12)

potential. What a person is capable of becoming. (1)

preeclampsia (PREE-eh-CLAMP-see-ah). A type of high blood pressure occurring in 5–10 percent of all pregnancies. (9)

prejudice. An opinion or feeling formed without accurate knowledge about someone or something. (18)

premature. A baby that is born before development is complete. (6)

premature birth. The birth of an infant three or four weeks before its due date. (11)

prenatal care. Medical support and attention given throughout pregnancy. (6)

prepared childbirth. When expectant parents learn about pregnancy and birth and take an active role in the birthing process. (10)

prioritize. To rank in the order of importance. (25)

prostheses. (pross-THEE-sees). Customized artificial limbs. (26)

psychological maturity. Development of the mind and emotions. (5)

puberty. The stage of development when young people are physically able to reproduce. (6)

puréed. Strained into a smooth consistency. (14)

Q

quiet play. Play that involves primarily thinking and small motor skills. (24)

R

reason. The ability to think logically, rationally, and analytically. (19)

reciprocity (res-uh-PRAHS-uht-ee). The act of giving to someone and getting in return. (22)

redirection. A guidance technique used to distract a child from an inappropriate activity. (24)

reflexes. Involuntary reactions to sensory experiences. (13)

registered midwife. Person trained to care for women with low-risk pregnancies and to deliver their babies. (8)

rescue breathing. Forcing air into lungs either by mouth-to-mouth or mouth-to-nose procedure. (16)

resilient. The ability to recover easily after difficulties. (28) ˴

resource. Something that individuals or families can use to accomplish a goal. (2)

Rh factor. A condition in which a substance present in the blood can cause problems with pregnancy. (8)

role. A part one plays when interacting with others. (4)

role model. A person whose behaviour and attitudes are imitated by others. (2)

rubella (roo-BELL-uh). A disease, commonly known as German measles, which can cause mental and physical disabilities in a fetus during the first trimester of pregnancy. (9)

S

self-care. Leaving a child alone for a few hours regularly, without adult supervision. (20)

sensorimotor period. The first period of intellectual development when infants use their senses and movement to learn about their surroundings. (13)

separation anxiety. The fear of being away from familiar people or a familiar environment. (18)

seriation. Arranging items in order according to size, number, or date. (19)

sexual abuse. The use of a child by an adult or adolescent for sexual purposes. (28)

sexually transmitted diseases (STDs). Diseases that are transmitted by sexual contact. (9)

Shaken Baby Syndrome. Serious or fatal injury to the brain or eyes caused when a baby is shaken. (28)

shock. Dangerous slowing of the circulation and breathing resulting from trauma. (16)

sibling. A brother or sister. (10)

sibling rivalry. Competition among brothers and sisters for parents' attention; a form of jealousy. (18)

single-parent family. Consists of only one parent and one or more children. (4)

sliding scale. A system of charging varied fees, as for child care, based on ability to pay. (20)

small motor skills. Abilities that rely on the control and use of small muscles, especially those in the fingers and hands. (15)

social development. Learning to relate to other people. (13)

social values. The differing rules and expected behaviours of the various groups in the community or society at large. (25)

socialization. The process by which people acquire the attitudes, beliefs, and behaviour patterns of a society. (18)

societal agent. The individuals and groups that help children develop thinking skills, teach behaviours, and provide emotional support. (25)

special needs. Specific requirements of children whose development differs significantly from the average. (26)

sperm. The male reproductive cells. (7)

sphincter muscles (SFINK-tuhr). Muscles in the bowel and bladder regions that control elimination. (15)

stepparent. A person whose spouse has children from an earlier relationship. (4)

stereotype. A standardized, and typically inaccurate, image attributed to a person or group. (18)

sterilization. A process that destroys germs that cause illness. (14)

stranger anxiety. Fear of unfamiliar people. (13)

street-proofing. Teaching children the skills for becoming aware of potential dangers and how to handle them. (25)

stress. Physical and emotional tension caused by pressures, change, and important events. (9)

Sudden Infant Death Syndrome (SIDS). Crib death, or the death of a seemingly healthy infant after it has been put to bed.

syndrome. A group of symptoms that characterize a certain condition. (26)

T

temperament. An inborn style of reacting to the environment and relating to others. (13)

temper tantrum. A fit of anger that may be expressed through screaming, hitting, and kicking. (17)

teratogens (tuh-RAT-uh-juhns). Substances and exposures that can cause birth defects. (9)

testes (TES-teez). The male reproductive glands. (7)

time management. Using time effectively to achieve goals. (25)

time-out. A method of removing children from a problem situation to give them time to calm down. (21)

toxoplasmosis (tocks-oh-plaz-MOH-sis). A disease that may be contracted from eating undercooked meat or from contact with cat feces; can cause the eyes and brain of a fetus to be damaged. (9)

trimester. One of three stages of pregnancy, each with unique emotional and physical characteristics. (8)

U

ultrasound. High frequency sound waves that are bounced off the developing fetus to produce a video image, or sonogram. (8)

umbilical cord (uhm-BILL-ih-kuhl). Cord that attaches the embryo to the placenta. (8)

uterus (YOO-teh-russ). The pear-shaped organ where the embryo and fetus develop; also called womb. (7)

V

values. Ideas about what is important. (1)

vernix (VUR-niks). Flecks of blood and a greasy, white material; keeps a newborn's skin from getting waterlogged by amniotic fluid. (11)

W

weaning. When an infant no longer bottle-feeds or breast-feeds and drinks from a cup. (14)

wellness. Achieving and maintaining a state of good health. (16)

work ethic. Understanding the value and importance of work and its ability to strengthen one's character. (25)

X, Y, Z

zygote (ZY-goht). New cell formed after sperm and ovum unite. (8)

Credits

Interior Design: Design Office

Cover Photo: FPG, Arthur Tilley
Back Cover Photo: Stock Market, Ronnie Kaufman

Infographic Design: Peter Getz, Circle Design

Design Photos (Realia): Arnold & Brown, Ann Garvin, Linda Henson, Ted Mishima, Duane R. Zehr

Archive Photos, Popperfoto, 44–45
Arnold & Brown, 158, 161, 173, 272, 273
Roger B. Bean, 91, 177, 214, 230, 337, 375, 394, 397, 398, 401, 403, 432, 516, 522, 581
Keith Bery, 83, 140
Pete Christie, 292
Carol Spengel, Circle Design, 14, 109, 134, 135, 136, 137, 184, 185
Corbis
    Annie Griffiths Belt, 351
    Laura Dwight, 333
    Ronnie Kaufman, 121
    Raoul Minsart, 41
    Ariel Skelley, 507
Corbis/Firstlight.ca
    James Marshall, 431
    Tom & Dee Ann McCarthy, 412
    Gabe Palmer, 190
Luis Delgado, 234, 248–249, 262, 263
Digital Vision, 472
Dinodia, 25, 79, 238, 384
Firstlight Associated Photographers, Inc., 190
David R. Frazier Photolibrary, Inc.
    David R. Frazier, 377
    Aaron Haupt, 415
Tim Fuller, 90
Ann Garvin, 120, 481, 395, 400
Getty Images, 177
    Photodisc, 130
Grand Illusions, 500
Steve Greiner, 217, 379, 498, 614
David Grossman, Stony Creek Studio, 316–317
Linda Henson, 239, 284, 285, 349, 416
Tony Hertz, 189
International Stock
    Scott Thode, 526
    Camille Tokerud, xvi–1
LaLeche League, David Arendt, 251
Ken Lax, 2–3, 14, 36–37, 52–53, 70–71, 88–89, 106–107, 126–127, 129, 146–147, 164–165, 178, 186–187, 206–207, 274–275, 298–299, 322–323, 346–347, 368–369, 392–393, 410–411,

448–449, 510–511, 532–533, 552–553, 582–583, 602–603
Joe Mallon Photography, 11, 23, 30, 47, 138, 139, 156, 157, 174, 196, 215, 226–227, 261, 282, 294, 311, 314, 355, 428–429, 443, 455, 503, 518, 568
Masterfile,
    Peter Griffith, 420
    Michael Mihavlich, 216
Kevin May Photography, 145
Jon Mcintosh, 308–309
Ted Mishima, 32, 78, 151, 231, 237, 272–273, 370, 386, 460, 540
Christin Nestor, 460
North Wind Picture Archives, 4
Photo Researchers, 133
    Joseph Nettis, 192
PhotoEdit, 491, 515
    Robert Brenner, 343, 538
    Michelle Bridwell, 581, 589
    Rudi von Briel, 210
    Jose Carillo, 460
    Myrleen Ferguson Cate, xiii, 124–125, 325, 328, 339, 424, 434, 461, 463, 474, 536, 545, 554
    Cleo Photography, 581, 607
    Paul Conklin, 143
    David Kelly Crow, 565, 597
    Mary Kate Denny, 113, 119, 562
    Laura Dwight, 28, 103, 257, 290, 330, 451, 497, 542
    Amy Etra, 338
    Tony Freeman, xvi, 318, 327, 359, 371, 430, 440, 436, 454, 467, 559, 585
    Spencer Grant, 64, 65, 315, 591, 595
    Richard Hutchings, 525
    Bonnie Kamin, 561
    Felicia Martinez, 307
    Stephen McBrady, 305
    Tom McCarthy, 312
    Tom & Dee Ann McCarthy, 412
    Michael Newman, 1, 8, 62, 149, 250, 252, 304, 335, 433, 453, 519, 554, 555, 556, 569, 596
    Jonathan Nourok, 424, 541,
    Novastock, 72, 584
    Robin L. Sachs, 574
    Nancy Sheehan, 172
    David Young-Wolff, 1, 27, 40, 67, 167, 260, 326, 490, 528, 557, 575, 576, 586, 594, 599
PictureQuest
    Keith Brofsky, 305
    Michael Goldman, 208
Liz Purcell, 316, 317
Stewart Cohen Index Stock Imagery, 101, 116
Stock Market
    Paul Barton, 46, 221, 295
    Peter Beck, 218, 305, 499, 581
    Ed Bock, 242, 243,
    C/B Productions, 60

Donna Disario, xiii, 15
George Disario, 259, 276
John Feingersh, 1, 6, 85
Charles Gupton, 54, 302, 527
Elizabeth Hathon, 244
John Henley, xiv, 49
Ted Horowitz, 362
Ronnie Kaufman, 31, 66, 439
Michael Keller, 58
Rob Lewine, 29, 39, 59, 74, 179, 235, 331, 357, 396, 421, 435, 439, 462, 471, 502, 539, 558, 587, 606
Don Mason, 125, 175
Tom & Dee Ann McCarthy, 33, 57, 241, 300, 593
Roy Morsch, 513
Mug Shots, 505
Nancy Ney, 373
Jose Luis Palaez, Inc., 13, 38, 43, 48, 166, 281, 324, 341, 492
Javier Pierini, 205, 211
David Pollack, 265
R.B. Studio, 439
Pete Saloutos, 198
Chuck Savage, 61, 272, 365
Norbert Schaefer, 273, 279
John Scheiber, 97
George Schiavone, 348
Ariel Skelley, 1, 9, 12, 108, 114, 329, 512
Peter Steiner, 220
Tom Stewart, 10, 201
Strauss/Curtis, 125, 171
Jon P. Yeager, 529
Jeff Stoecker, 63, 115
Erica Stone, 197
Tim Tucker, 76
Vote Photography, 22, 213, 466–467, 580–581
Dana White, 73, 75, 80, 90, 92, 95, 96, 102, 103, 111,117, 125, 128, 142, 148, 155, 160, 169, 180, 188, 205, 209, 210, 219, 222, 232, 233, 234, 236, 253, 256, 264, 267, 273, 280, 284, 285, 286, 287, 288, 291, 293, 310, 334, 350, 356, 361, 363, 364, 387, 414, 417, 418, 420, 422, 431, 441, 443, 445, 450, 456, 472, 476, 479, 483, 517, 467, 543, 546, 547, 548, 604, 610, 611, 612, 613, 615
Gloria Williams, 306
Duane R. Zehr, 493, 534, 560

Acknowledgments: Greater Peoria Family YMCA Childcare Centre, Health Canada: Office of Nutrition Policy and Promotion, Kids Help Phone, PALS Preschool and Kindergarten, Friendship House, A Child's World, Stay Safe . . . Stay Alert

Models and fictional names have been used to portray characters in stories and examples in this text.

Index

F

Failure to thrive, 249
Fallopian tubes, 109, 110, 134
Falls, preventing, 307
Families
    blended, 559–561
    characteristics of strong, 585–593
    communication in, 589
    culture in, 585
    dealing with crises in, 561–577
    facing changes in, 554–561
    identifying resources for, 500–501
    influences on parenting, 40–41
    problems of getting along with others, 535–539
    problem solving in, 591–593
    problems with routines, 543–549
    purposes of, 585
    relating to members of, 349–354
    role with infant, 245
    as source of child care, 395
    as source of support for pregnant teen, 102
    strengthening, 582–597
Family child-care homes, 396–397
Family identity, 588
Family life
    impact on parenting, 490–492
    managing, 497–501
Family members, relating to, 349–354
Family planning, 106–121
    decision making in, 108
Family problems, finding solutions to, 553–573
Family support worker, 270
Family violence, 563–570
Fathers, 211, 214, 215

Fats, 149
Fear, 328–329
    coping with, 329–330
    of the dark, 546–547
    handling, in infants, 265
    preventing, 328
Feeding. *See also* Nutrition
    choosing method for, 172–174
    of infant, 250–254
Female condom, 112
Female reproductive system, 109
Fertility, problems of, 113
Fertilization, 110, 115
Fetal alcohol effects (FAE), 158
Fetal alcohol syndrome (FAS), 158
Fetal monitor, 191, 196
Fetus, 135
    dangers to, 156–158
Financial considerations, 82–83, 130
    and teen pregnancy, 95
Finger painting, 482
Finicky eating, 544–545
Fire safety, 311
First aid, giving, 315–316
First stage of labour, 189–192
First trimester, 132, 134
Flame-retardant fabrics, 294
Flex time, 496
Fluids in postnatal period, 210
Folic acid, 151
Fontanels, 230
Food Guide to Healthy Eating, Canada's, 149, 150
Foods. *See also* Nutrition
    encouraging wise choices in, 282, 283
    introducing new, 281
    introducing solid, 253–254
Forceps, 195
Formal operations, period of, 377

Formula, 174, 251–252
Foster parent, 121
Fractures, 319
Franchise operations, 399
Fraternal twins, 116
Freud, Sigmund, 45
Friends, imaginary, 481
Friendship
    and handling peer pressure, 358–359
    lessons in, 356–359
    and popularity, 357–358
    and sharing, 356–357
    taking turns in, 356

G

Gardner, Howard, 374
Gender, determination of, in baby, 115
Genes, 113–114
    dominant, 114
    and gender determination, 115
    recessive, 114
Genetic counselling, 119–120
Genetic diseases, 117–119
    cystic fibrosis, 117
    Down syndrome, 117
    muscular dystrophy, 117
    phenylketonuria (PKU), 119
    sickle-cell anemia, 118
    Tay-Sachs disease, 118
Genetics, 116
Genital herpes, 159
George, Anne, 608
Gestational diabetes, 160
Gifted children
    educating, 528
    parenting, 326–329
    resources for parents with, 529
Goals, 81–82
    parenting, 40
Gonorrhea, 159
Goodbye, saying, 404
Government-sponsored child-care centres, 398
Grandparents, 354
Great Expectations (Dickens), 48